Integrated Injection Logic

KV-435-074

OTHER IEEE PRESS BOOKS

Sensory Aids for the Hearing Impaired, *Edited by H. Levitt, J. M. Pickett, and R. A. Houde*

Data Conversion Integrated Circuits, *Edited by Daniel J. Dooley*

Semiconductor Injection Lasers, *Edited by J. K. Butler*

Satellite Communications, *Edited by H. L. Van Trees*

Frequency-Response Methods in Control Systems, *Edited by A.G.J. MacFarlane*

Programs for Digital Signal Processing, *Edited by the Digital Signal Processing Committee*

Automatic Speech & Speaker Recognition, *Edited by N. R. Dixon and T. B. Martin*

Speech Analysis, *Edited by R. W. Schafer and J. D. Markel*

The Engineer in Transition to Management, *I. Gray*

Multidimensional Systems: Theory & Applications, *Edited by N. K. Bose*

Analog Integrated Circuits, *Edited by A. B. Grebene*

Integrated-Circuit Operational Amplifiers, *Edited by R. G. Meyer*

Modern Spectrum Analysis, *Edited by D. G. Childers*

Digital Image Processing for Remote Sensing, *Edited by R. Bernstein*

Reflector Antennas, *Edited by A. W. Love*

Phase-Locked Loops & Their Application, *Edited by W. C. Lindsey and M. K. Simon*

Digital Signal Computers and Processors, *Edited by A. C. Salazar*

Systems Engineering: Methodology and Applications, *Edited by A. P. Sage*

Modern Crystal and Mechanical Filters, *Edited by D. F. Sheahan and R. A. Johnson*

Electrical Noise: Fundamentals and Sources, *Edited by M. S. Gupta*

Computer Methods in Image Analysis, *Edited by J. K. Aggarwal, R. O. Duda, and A. Rosenfeld*

Microprocessors: Fundamentals and Applications, *Edited by W. C. Lin*

Machine Recognition of Patterns, *Edited by A. K. Agrawala*

Turning Points in American Electrical History, *Edited by J. E. Brittain*

Charge-Coupled Devices: Technology and Applications, *Edited by R. Melen and D. Buss*

Spread Spectrum Techniques, *Edited by R. C. Dixon*

Electronic Switching: Central Office Systems of the World, *Edited by A. E. Joel, Jr.*

Electromagnetic Horn Antennas, *Edited by A. W. Love*

Waveform Quantization and Coding, *Edited by N. S. Jayant*

Communication Satellite Systems: An Overview of the Technology, *Edited by R. G. Gould and Y. F. Lum*

Literature Survey of Communication Satellite Systems and Technology, *Edited by J. H. W. Unger*

Solar Cells, *Edited by C. E. Backus*

Computer Networking, *Edited by R. P. Blanc and I. W. Cotton*

Communications Channels: Characterization and Behavior, *Edited by B. Goldberg*

Large-Scale Networks: Theory and Design, *Edited by F. T. Boesch*

Optical Fiber Technology, *Edited by D. Gloge*

Selected Papers in Digital Signal Processing, II, *Edited by the Digital Signal Processing Committee*

A Guide for Better Technical Presentations, *Edited by R. M. Woelfle*

Career Management: A Guide to Combating Obsolescence, *Edited by H. G. Kaufman*

Energy and Man: Technical and Social Aspects of Energy, *Edited by M. G. Morgan*

Magnetic Bubble Technology: Integrated-Circuit Magnetics for Digital Storage and Processing, *Edited by H. Chang*

Frequency Synthesis: Techniques and Applications, *Edited by J. Gorski-Popiel*

Literature in Digital Processing: Author and Permuted Title Index (Revised and Expanded Edition), *Edited by H. D. Helms, J. F. Kaiser, and L. R. Rabiner*

Data Communications via Fading Channels, *Edited by K. Brayer*

Nonlinear Networks: Theory and Analysis, *Edited by A. N. Willson, Jr.*

Computer Communications, *Edited by P. E. Green, Jr. and R. W. Lucky*

Stability of Large Electric Power Systems, *Edited by R. T. Byerly and E. W. Kimbark*

Automatic Test Equipment: Hardware, Software, and Management, *Edited by F. Liguori*

Key Papers in the Development of Coding Theory, *Edited by E. R. Berkekamp*

Technology and Social Institutions, *Edited by K. Chen*

Key Papers in the Development of Information Theory, *Edited by D. Slepian*

Computer-Aided Filter Design, *Edited by G. Szentirmai*

Integrated Optics, *Edited by D. Marcuse*

Digital Signal Processing, *Edited by L. R. Rabiner and C. M. Rader*

Minicomputers: Hardware, Software, and Applications, *Edited by J. D. Schoeffler and R. H. Temple*

Semiconductor Memories, *Edited by D. A. Hodges*

Power Semiconductor Applications, Volume I: General Considerations, *Edited by J. D. Harnden, Jr. and F. B. Golden*

Y4Y4Y
3481

STRATHCLYDE UNIVERSITY LIBRARY

30125 00069500 6

8·20
52

Integrated Injection Logic

Edited by

James E. Smith

Staff Engineer and Manager,
Device Physics,
Modeling and Characterization
Microcomponents Organization
Burroughs Corporation

A volume in the IEEE PRESS Selected Reprint Series,
prepared under the sponsorship of the IEEE Circuits
and Systems Society.

The Institute of Electrical and Electronics Engineers, Inc. New York

IEEE PRESS

1980 Editorial Board

S. B. Weinstein, *Chairman*

George Abraham	E. W. Herold
Clarence Baldwin	Thomas Kailath
Walter Beam	J. F. Kaiser
P. H. Enslow, Jr.	Dietrich Marcuse
M. S. Ghausi	Irving Reingold
R. C. Hansen	P. M. Russo
R. K. Hellmann	Desmond Sheahan
	J. B. Singleton

W. R. Crone, *Managing Editor*

Isabel Narea, *Production Manager*

Joseph Morsicato, *Supervisor, Special Publications*

Copyright © 1980 by
THE INSTITUTE OF ELECTRICAL AND ELECTRONICS ENGINEERS, INC.
345 East 47 Street, New York, NY 10017
All rights reserved.

PRINTED IN THE UNITED STATES OF AMERICA

Sole Worldwide Distributor (Exclusive of IEEE):

JOHN WILEY & SONS, INC.
605 Third Ave.
New York, NY 10016

Wiley Order Numbers: Clothbound: 0-471-08675-4
Paperbound: 0-471-08676-2

IEEE Order Numbers: Clothbound: PC01305
Paperbound: PP01313

Library of Congress Catalog Card Number 80-18841

International Standard Book Numbers: Clothbound 0-87942-137-1
Paperbound 0-87942-138-X

621.3817'3
INT

Contents

The state of the art and the future of digital integrated circuits in the early 1970's was thought to be well defined. The bipolar logic techniques such as RTL, DTL, CTL, TTL, and ECL had all been produced in volume as logic-family parts (typically single gates or of equivalent complexity) which were appropriately labeled small-scale integration (SSI). The TTL and ECL logic families were the obvious choices for the future with TTL aimed at medium-scale integration (MSI) and possibly large-scale integration (LSI). ECL was reserved for very high speed applications and largely limited to SSI, with some custom MSI for computer mainframes where the attendant expense and power consumption could be tolerated.

The younger but rapidly developing MOSFET technologies had leap-frogged the logic-family level of integration and had already demonstrated their capabilities for implementing large, custom, digital circuits. It is worth noting that (with the exception of CMOS) there has never been an MOS logic family. The p-channel, metal-gate processes were yielding to the newer n-channel polysilicon gate process, and the future of LSI was clearly in the domain of NMOS.

In 1971 at the International Solid-State Circuits Conference (ISSCC) two elegantly simple ideas were presented by S. K. Wiedmann and H. H. Berger in their landmark paper entitled "Small-Size Low-Power Bipolar Memory Cell" (paper [IX-1] of the Bibliography). These authors demonstrated the following.

1. Digital circuit operation could be achieved with bipolar npn transistors operated in the inverse (or upward) mode. In this configuration the transistors were self-isolating and no isolation diffusion was necessary.
2. The loads for the upward-operated npn's could be formed with pnp transistors which permitted low power operation and small size.

In an early 1972 publication (paper IX-3), Wiedmann and Berger demonstrated that the upward npn's and the load pnp's of their memory cell could be merged into a compact structure with no isolation diffusion separating the two devices. At the 1972 ISSCC Berger and Wiedmann (from the IBM laboratories in Germany) demonstrated their Merged transistor logic (MTL), which was a direct outgrowth of their earlier memory cell design efforts. At the same conference, a second paper presented by C. M. Hart and A. Slob (from the Philips laboratories in the Netherlands) described an identical structure which they had independently developed and which they labeled Integrated injection logic or (I^2L). The name I^2L has subsequently become the convention by way of popular usage.

The new I^2L/MTL bipolar digital technique boasted high packing density, low power-delay-product, a wide dynamic range of operating power level, bipolar current-drive capability, compatibility with existing analog and digital IC processes (except gold-doped TTL), and held the promise of high speed operation while retaining all of these features. Thus I^2L had arrived (albeit a latecomer) on the LSI scene. The reactions of the IC industry were mixed. Many bipolar technology supporters heralded I^2L as the LSI of the future. The MOS supporters simultaneously denounced I^2L, reiterated their commitment to MOS and initiated projects to develop or investigate I^2L in their own laboratories.

In a typical situation I^2L was rushed into design using an existing, standard process, which was not optimized for any particular performance characteristic of I^2L, with the attitude "let's see what we get." Consequently, the resulting performance achieved was not outstanding, and in many cases the I^2L efforts were dropped. The result was that I^2L often received a poor rating because of the lack of a rigorous effort to understand, and make adjustments for, the process and the structure-related dependencies of I^2L's speed-power performance. The complaints were always directed at the intrinsic speed limit of I^2L, whereas the packing density and low power operation capabilities typically were not questioned.

In a few exceptional cases I^2L was properly recognized at an early stage as an immediate means of 1) drastically reducing the TTL parts count in high reliability systems where bipolar technology was required, and 2) adding a digital logic capability to an analog process by way of a mask-programmable gate array. In such applications, I^2L has enjoyed significant (although unpublicized) success which began soon after its introduction.

During the ensuing years, I^2L has received much attention from the IC industry, academic institutions, and in-house IC operations of vertically integrated systems and instrumentation houses. As is the case when any new, important concept presents itself upon the semiconductor IC technological scene, the appearance of I^2L provided the opportunity for researchers in both industry and academia to carry out justifiable research projects and consequently, publish technical papers which explored all aspects of the new concept. I^2L was such an obvious boon to the waning bipolar digital IC community that there was a great rush to implement I^2L research projects and the resulting flurry of publications produced confusing, opposing, and sometimes quite controversial explanations for the process or structurally related physical mechanisms which dominate I^2L performance. The major process or structurally related limitations of I^2L were identified many times over in many independent research programs and almost every one of these produced a different solution to the problem, as if each laboratory felt it necessary to propose and support its own approach to an improved I^2L technology. However, in almost every case, the proposed improved approach exhibited some advantages and some disadvantages relative to the competing proposals.

The result of the total I^2L activity during the past decade is a vast accumulation of literature covering a wide range of topics from basic device physics to sophisticated applications and extending to the radiation hardness properties of various I^2L techniques. To the newcomer to I^2L, the volume of the literature would be overwhelming, and the isolation of the important contributions would represent a challenging task. It is the purpose of this IEEE Press reprint book to serve as a filter of and a guide through the I^2L literature. The principle objective has been to place in proper perspective the true position of I^2L in the world of digital IC technology.

It is now clear that I^2L will not displace the NMOS LSI technologies. Nor will I^2L fall by the wayside in deference to NMOS. I^2L and NMOS, each with its own special set of structural and performance characteristics, are both well suited to many digital IC applications, and the challenge is to properly match the technique to the application. There are now well-definable applications areas where I^2L offers distinct advantages. The most notable of these applications areas are as follows.

1) Analog-compatible digital logic: Here I^2L presents the opportunity to include SSI, MSI, and perhaps LSI logic on-chip with bipolar analog circuits. Thus such combinations can take immediate advantage of the highly developed state of the art in precision analog circuit techniques.

2) High-reliability and radiation-tolerant digital logic: I^2L has demonstrated high reliability and holds the distinction of being the single commercial LSI technique which may meet the radiation tolerance demands of space and military applications, thereby removing the need for expensive custom technologies for these applications (paper X-4).

3) Large, high-speed memory arrays: The classical ECL static memory cell design has resisted significant reductions in cell size and power dissipation even though the speeds have improved to the sub-10 ns range. The I^2L technique offers the opportunity to improve upon the cell size and power dissipation in very large memory arrays while maintaining acceptable speed performance. It is notable that, although I^2L evolved from a memory cell design, since that time I^2L memory techniques have been largely neglected in favor of digital logic techniques. Consequently, I^2L memory may offer the most fruitful area for future I^2L development efforts.

4) Low power, high-current-drive: In applications such as the digital time-piece, I^2L has already demonstrated its outstanding success.

In summary, I^2L has been established as a member of the LSI digital logic techniques. The SBP9900A microprocessor (with its −55 to 125° C operating temperature) from Texas Instruments serves as a direct confirmation of this statement. The extension to very large scale integration (VLSI) looks promising.

The remainder of this book proposes to elucidate those crucial aspects of I^2L which will permit the identification of those I^2L process techniques, device structures, and applications areas which can be best mated in order to arrive at optimum solutions to the needs of the digital IC consumer community.

The reprinted papers have been segregated into ten distinct topical categories which form the ten parts of this book. The papers selected in each category are intended to provide the insight necessary for the reader to gain a thorough understanding of each topic. Many of the papers overlap in their presentations and some present opposing or conflicting view-points. The introductory comments to each part are intended to clarify the issues of opposition or disagreement and provide explanatory discussions of the positive attributes or limitations of each publication. A comprehensive Bibliography, through December 1979, also segregated by topical categories, has been prepared and is included after Part X.

The order of presentation of the reprinted papers is intended to present I^2L in a building-block fashion but does not necessarily follow a tutorial sequence. The newcomer to I^2L would benefit by adopting the following reading sequence: 1) Part I, where the basic I^2L concept is described; 2) papers IV 1-3 where the foundations of the device physics are laid, especially IV-3, in which Berger and Wiedmann establish the widely adopted terminology of up and down device operation. The remainder of the book could then be approached in any order desired.

Part I
Conventional I²L

Although I²L grew out of bipolar memory cell design efforts, the memory techniques are deferred to Part IX of this book where they are described in detail. The first three papers reprinted here (Part I) represent the original complete presentations of the concepts of I²L/MTL for digital logic as conceived by Hart and Slob from Philips in the Netherlands and Berger and Wiedmann from IBM in Germany. These papers present the state of development of I²L as of 1972. One additional paper, from Texas Instruments, is included in order to indicate the state of development and application in a commercial environment, as of 1975, of conventional I²L as it was originally conceived. The papers of Hart, Slob, Berger, and Wiedmann are quite complete when taken as a whole and constitute a rather detailed introduction to I²L. The highlights of each paper are discussed briefly as follows.

The Philips papers are unique in that they demonstrate that I²L can be powered by a light source which generates electron-hole pairs in the n-type epitaxial regions near the emitter-base p-n junctions of the I²L cells. This feature of I²L has been applied in light detection circuits for use in camera exposure meters (paper VIII-2). Hart and Slob correctly point out the dependence of the I²L gate's npn up-beta and pnp forward-alpha upon the epitaxial doping. These authors also present an analysis of the dependence of I²L's noise margin upon the up-beta and point to the need for the use of larger devices and higher current levels in the input and output interface circuits in order to achieve greater noise margins. Perhaps the most impressive accomplishment presented in the first Philips paper is that, at the time of publication, six large digital logic circuits had already been implemented in I²L. The importance of the low (1 V) I²L power supply voltage in contributing to the reliability of I²L devices is mentioned in this early publication. The shortcomings of the Philips paper are that the up-beta is not well defined, nor is the measurement technique explained. The power-delay product information presented is not very quantitative and the explanations given for the high-current effects upon the propagation delay are poor. However, the prediction of lower minimum propagation delay with the use of smaller dimensions and advanced technology has subsequently been demonstrated. The second Philips paper is valuable in that it provides the first example of an I²L gate transfer characteristic and the conversion of a logic diagram into an actual I²L gate layout.

The Berger and Wiedmann paper, in addition to explaining the basic I²L structure and operation, contains several excellent contributions. The experimental technique for including the effects of the injector when measuring the up-beta of the I²L gate's npn is correctly explained. However, the reader is cautioned here that the technique as presented does not permit the effects of base series resistance nor base contact

position upon up-beta to be accounted for as it occurs in actual circuit operation. In actual operation, the drive current to the gate physically enters the p-type base region of the up-npn at the end nearest the injector. This situation results in the injector end of the base being at the highest potential whenever the drive current is high enough such that the series base resistance causes a nonconstant potential distribution in the base. Therefore, the base contact must be located at the injector end of the up-npn's base when terminal measurements are to be made as suggested by Berger and Wiedmann. Even this precaution will not account for the parasitic series resistance between the edge of the p-type base and the base contact. Therefore, highly accurate characterization (at high current levels) can only be performed by supplying the current from the injector pnp. Consequently, the injector pnp would require a separate characterization in order to obtain a complete "terminal" characterization of the up-npn portion of the I²L gate. These authors define the important concept of a recollection factor to describe the current returned to the injector. The fact that the injector is a near-equipotential is pointed out. The consequence of this situation is that the power supply parameter which is common to all I²L gates on a chip is the injector voltage, not the injector current as is often assumed. The neglect of this fact has caused problems with I²L implementations on multiple occasions. The reader is referred to my comments on paper IV-2 for a more detailed discussion of this situation.

A very important aspect of I²L, that of current-hogging immunity, is explained by Berger and Wiedmann as resulting from the high inverse beta (or down-beta) of the I²L gate. Their paper presents an analysis which shows the nature of current hogging between an npn pair as a function of up-beta and down-beta. Their analysis, which yields

$$\frac{I_{c1}}{\beta_n I_B} = \frac{\left(\dfrac{I_{c2}}{\beta_n I_B}\right) + \left(\dfrac{\beta_i + 1}{\beta_n}\right)}{1 + \left(\dfrac{\beta_i}{\beta_n + 1}\right)}$$

is in error. A correct analysis yields

$$\frac{I_{c1}}{\beta_n I_B} = \frac{\left(\dfrac{I_{c2}}{\beta_n I_B}\right) + 2\left(\dfrac{\beta_i + 1}{\beta_n}\right)}{1 + 2\left(\dfrac{\beta_i + 1}{\beta_n}\right)}.$$

However, the differences are small and their conclusions are correct.

Finally, I note that Berger and Wiedmann suggest the use of the substrate as the emitter of a vertical pnp injector device. This approach was subsequently adopted and exploited by

Blatt and co-workers at Plessey in England in their "Substrate Fed Logic" (paper III-6).

The final paper in this section by Horton *et al.* was the first publication of a commercial LSI product fabricated in I^2L: a 4-bit-slice microprocessor from Texas Instruments. Perhaps the most notable performance parameter of the circuit is its ability to meet the military −55 to 125°C temperature requirements. Note that in this paper, a propagation delay of 50 ns is considered to be representative of a fast logic gate, while in other laboratories such a speed performance was considered to be slow. An important feature of this paper is the side-by-side scale-drawing comparison of the cell sizes of I^2L, TTL, and MOS logic gates as of 1975. Finally, I note that Fig. 7 is in error. The upper output of the logic circuit should be

$$\overline{A} \cdot \overline{B}.$$

These four papers taken together completely outline the important features of conventional I^2L:

1) a simple process and therefore potential capability of high yield in established bipolar fabrication lines,
2) high density,
3) low power and low power-delay product,
4) analog circuit compatibility,
5) high reliability.

The remaining nine parts of this book investigate the exploitation of these features for building large digital logic circuits.

Integrated Injection Logic: A New Approach to LSI

KEES HART AND ARIE SLOB

Abstract—Logic gates suitable for large-scale integration (LSI) should satisfy three important requirements. Processing has to be simple and under good control to obtain an acceptable yield of reliable IC's containing about 1000 gates. The basic gate must be as simple and compact as possible to avoid extreme chip dimensions. Finally, the power-delay time product must be so high that operation at a resonable speed does not cause excessive chip dissipation.

Multicollector transistors fed by carrier injection proved to be a novel and attractive solution. A simplified (five masks) standard bipolar process is used resulting in a packing density of 400 gates/mm² with interconnection widths and spacings of 5 μm. The power-delay time product is 0.4 pJ per gate. An additional advantage is a very low supply voltage (less than 1 V). This, combined with the possibility of choosing the current level within several decades enables use in very low-power applications. With a normal seven-mask technology, analog circuitry has been combined with integrated injection logic (I²L).

Manuscript received May 1, 1972; revised June 12, 1972.
The authors are with the Philips Research Laboratories, Eindhoven, the Netherlands.

INTRODUCTION

LOGIC gates suitable for large-scale integration (LSI) must satisfy three important requirements.

1) The processing has to be simple and under good control in order to obtain an acceptable yield of reliable IC's containing about 1000 gates.

2) The basic gate must be as simple and compact as possible to avoid extreme chip dimensions.

3) The power-delay time product must be such that operation at a reasonable speed does not cause excessive dissipation on the chip.

Multicollector transistors fed by carrier injection proved to be a novel and attractive solution that fulfills the previous three requirements [1]–[3]. Two ways of injection will be discussed, viz., injection by light and injection with a p-n diode. A number of realized LSI circuits will be mentioned.

Reprinted from *IEEE J. Solid-State Circuits*, vol. SC-7, pp. 346–351, Oct. 1972.

INJECTION BY LIGHT

A junction diode, which is irradiated with light of a suitable wavelength, will act as a diode with a current source in parallel (see Fig. 1) tending to forward bias the junction. The effect is due to an increase in concentration of the minority carriers in the neighborhood of the junction, resulting from the hole–electron pairs created by light absorption.

The question is whether such a current source could be used in integrated circuits as distributed supply sources, occurring wherever they are needed.

In a transistor irradiated with light, two current sources occur, however, in the configuration of a conventional n-p-n planar transistor (Fig. 2) the current source across the normal collector–base junction (junction 2–3) is much stronger than that across the emitter–base junction (junction 1–2). There are four reasons.

1) Region 3 is much larger than region 1.

2) The lifetime of the minority carriers in region 3 is much longer than in region 1.

3) Region 1 is screened by the aluminum connections.

4) Carriers generated in region 2 will drift to region 3 owing to the built in electrical field and contribute to the photocurrent of junction 2–3. In practice it means that the photocurrent across junction 1–2 can be neglected.

When the transistor is used inversely, the result is a transistor with a forward-biasing current source between base and emitter (Fig. 3). With the base not connected externally, the collector can draw a current, which is the base current multiplied by the current gain. This collector current can be used to short circuit base–emitter photocurrents of other transistors of which the collector current is zero.

Logic circuits may now be built with the light-activated transistor: the transistor acting as an inverter, while the logic function is obtained from the way collectors are connected (wired AND). In this case, circuits are best taken together into standard arrangements in the manner shown by the dashed line in Fig. 4, i.e., bases and emitters each are connected into common regions whereas the collectors are laid out as multicollectors. Compare this with direct coupled transistor logic (DCTL) where collectors are combined and there are multiple base contacts and separate emitters. In both cases, the transistors act as inverters and the logical functions are obtained by wiring the collectors. However, since both the DCTL bases as well as the emitters must be provided with separate connections, the number of contact holes in a chip is much larger than in the corresponding circuit for light-activated logic.

Fig. 5 gives a cross section of a multicollector transistor. An n⁺ substrate has been chosen together with n⁺ isolations between the bases in order to improve the current gain and diminish parasitic lateral p-n-p action. Only four masks are required, since the homogeneous p diffusion is overdoped by the n⁺ isolation to make separate bases. Fig. 6 is a microphotograph of a digital voltmeter chip in which the power supply is derived from absorbed light. Therefore, the aluminum pattern only contains logical wiring.

p-n INJECTOR

The function of the absorbed light was to generate holes (minority carriers) in the n layer. This function also can be accomplished by a forward-biased p-n junction, called the injector.

Fig. 1. Circuit diagram of a p-n junction irradiated with light consists of a diode in parallel with a current source.

Fig. 2. Double diffused transistor irradiated with light. Current source across junction 2–3 is much stronger that that across junction 1–2, which can be neglected.

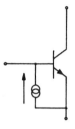

Fig. 3. Circuit diagram of an inversely used transistor irradiated with light. Current source tends to forward bias the emitter-base junction.

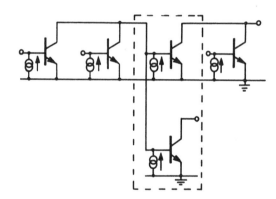

Fig. 4. Logic function is obtained by connecting collectors (wired AND). Between the dashed lines a multicollector transistor occurs, which is the standard arrangement.

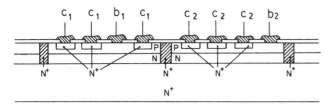

Fig. 5. Cross section of two multicollector transistors. p diffusion does not need a mask, thus, only four masks are needed.

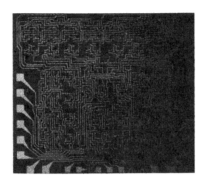

Fig. 6. Microphotograph of a digital voltmeter chip. Aluminum interconnection pattern is the logical wiring only as the power is derived from absorbed light. Chip size—2.2 × 2.4 mm².

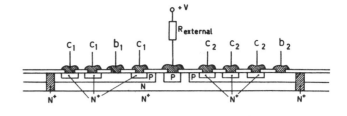

(a)

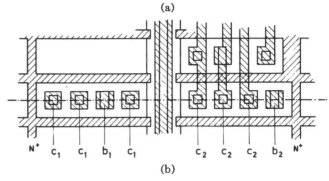

(b)

Fig. 7. (a) Cross section of multicollector transistors on both sides of the injector. Five masks are needed. (b) Layout.

Fig. 7(a) gives a cross section and Fig. 7(b) a layout of the multicollector transistors fed by a p-n injector. An additional mask for the p diffusion is necessary now.

CIRCUIT PARAMETERS AND TECHNOLOGY

Each collector of a multicollector transistor must be able to short circuit one base current. This means that the current gain β per collector has to be ≥ 1, (if all base currents are assumed equal). The hole efficiency of the injector α determines the amount of base current.

To fulfill reliability and yield requirements, the choice has been made to use one of the available factory processes.

A first set of measurements showed that both the current gain β and the hole efficiency α improved with the application of an n⁺ substrate and deep n⁺ isolations.

To find the influence of the resistivity of the epitaxial layer and of the geometries on the current gain β and on the hole efficiency α, a second set of measurements have been carried out. The results given in Fig. 8 have been obtained under the following conditions.

1) Process Description: Epilayer thickness—5 μm with a variable resistivity; base diffusion depth—2.7 μm, resistivity $\rho_\square = 200 \ \Omega/\square$.

2) Geometries: Collector area—20 × 20 μm², spaced on 10 μm; emitter area—width 40 μm, length dependent on number of collectors; aluminum—10-μm width and 10-μm spacings.

From these measurements the decision has been taken to limit the number of collectors per base area to four, which means a maximum fan-out of four. The maximum fan-in is not limited.

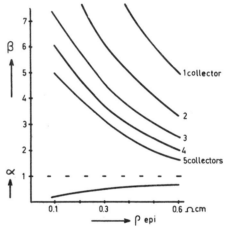

Fig. 8. Minimum current gain β and hole efficiency α as a function of epilayer resistivity and number of collectors.

NOISE MARGIN

Since there are no resistors in the circuit, the absolute current levels are not fixed and the user can choose a certain current level for the injector, which distributes the current into equal portions over the transistors. Therefore, it is impossible to give absolute noise margins. The relative noise margins, however, can be calculated easily in the form of maximum noise currents, which can be translated into maximum noise voltages.

Fig. 9(a) shows a situation in which a noise current I_{s0} tends to switch transistor T_1 in ON. The critical point is reached if in the base of T_1 a current of Ic/β is flowing. It is easily derived that

$$\beta_0 I_0 = I_{s0} + I_1 - (I_c/\beta)$$

so

$$I_{s0} = \beta_0 I_0 - I_1 + (I_c/\beta).$$

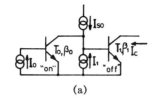

(a)

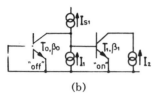

(b)

Fig. 9. Definition of noise current sources. (a) Low logical level. (b) High logical level.

The corresponding noise voltage V_{s0} is somewhat less than the forward base–emitter voltage V_j.

Fig. 9(b) shows a situation in which a noise current I_{s1} tends to switch transistors T_1 in OFF. Here the critical point is reached if in the base of transistor T_1 the base current becomes less than I_2/β. From the circuit diagram it is derived that

$$I_1 = (I_2/\beta) + I_{s1}$$

so

$$I_{S1} = I_1 - (I_2/\beta).$$

For T_1 the maximum (undisturbed) base current is I_1 and the minimum allowable base current is I_2/β, so the noise voltage will be $V_{S1} = (kT/q)\ln(\beta I_1/I_2)$.

Now two cases have to be distinguished, viz., the noise margin on the chip and the noise margin between the chips.

In the case of the noise margin on the chip, the noise production is very low and all the current sources are chosen equal for reasons of easy design. This results in

$$I_{S0} = I[\beta - 1 + (1/\beta)], \qquad V_{S0} \approx V_j.$$

and

$$I_{S1} = I[1 - (1/\beta)], \qquad V_{S1} = (kT/q)\ln\beta.$$

In the case of noise margin between the chips the noise production can be expected to be higher. To obtain correspondingly larger absolute noise margins, the first transistor on the chip and the last one on the previous chip are given a larger absolute current and a higher value of the current gain β. This can be achieved by choosing suitable geometries.

PROPAGATION DELAY TIME VERSUS POWER

The propagation delay time is determined by the amount of current supplied to the logic gates. Three current levels are to be distinguished, viz., low, medium, and high.

At low current levels the propagation delay time is determined by junction and parasitic capacitances. This

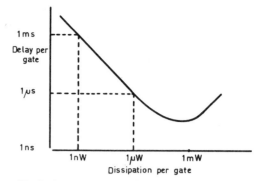

Fig. 10. Typical propagation delay time versus power. Diagram measured on a ring of five inverters.

propagation delay time τ will be proportional to the time t needed to charge or discharge the capacitances. As $Q = CV$ and $t = Q/I$, τ will be proportional to CV/I. The dissipation D will be $D = VI$, in which V is the voltage over a forward-biased junction. From this it follows that the power-delay time product $D\tau$ is proportional to CV^2, which is constant.

At medium current levels the main influence on the propagation delay time comes from the active charge in the transistors. This charge is proportional to the current and, therefore, the propagation delay time is independent of the dissipation.

At high current levels there are two phenomena that cause a worse propagation delay, first, the series resistances of the bases prevent fast charging or discharging of the active charges, and, second, these active charges increase more than linearly with increasing currents.

In Fig. 10 a measured curve of the propagation delay time versus power is shown. The measured value of the power–delay time product is $D\tau = 1$ pJ for a dissipation below 1 μW/gate. This product has been measured in a ring of five inverters that will oscillate at a period of ten times the average stage delay and consume five times the gate dissipation. In this case the fan-in and fan-out are equal to one. A more realistic value of the $D\tau$ product was measured on a chip containing a 108-bit shift register in which case the average fan-in and fan-out were 2.5 per gate. Two versions of this shift register have been made, viz., one with 10- and one with 5-μm clearances. In the version with the 10-μm clearances a $D\tau$ product of 1.75 pJ has been measured whereas for the version with the 5-μm clearance 0.4 pJ has been obtained.

It is clear that both the $D\tau$ product and the minimum propagation delay time can be improved by the use of smaller dimensions and a more sophisticated technology.

INTERFACE CIRCUITS

In the five-mask technology described in the preceding paragraphs several interface circuits are possible (see Table I). Normally, the collectors of an integrated injection logic (I²L) gate are fed by a current source, i.e., the current source between the base and the emitter of one of the other I²L gates.

TABLE I

SURVEY OF THE DIFFERENT POSSIBILITIES OF INTERFACE CIRCUITS

Type of Interface	Maximum Logic Levels (V)	Maximum Output Current in ON State
Standard output [Fig. 11(a)]	0/+5	medium
Emitter follower [Fig. 11(b)]	0/−0.7	high
Lateral p-n-p followed by emitter follower [Fig. 11(c)]	0/−20	high
Lateral p-n-p followed by inverter [Fig. 11(d)]	0/+5	medium
Lateral p-n-p [Fig. 11(e)]	0/−40	low

TABLE II

LIST OF LSI CIRCUITS REALIZED WITH THE I²L TECHNIQUE

Function	Number of Gates	Chip Dimensions (mm²)
Electronic organ tone generator	180	1.2 × 1.5
Liquid crystal display driver (Fig. 12)	200	2.2 × 2.4
Counter for digital voltmeter (Fig. 6)	325	2.2 × 2.4
108-bit shift register	820	2.96 × 2.85
1536-bit read only memory	about 1000	3 × 4
Control logic	980	4 × 4

With the latter three circuits a small calculator has been made, which works on a 1.5-V battery.

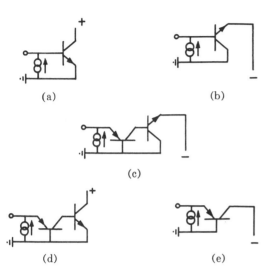

Fig. 11. Several types of interface circuits. Layouts of (a)–(d) are equal.

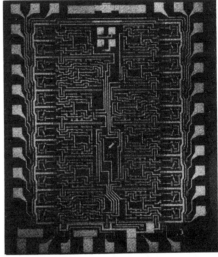

Fig. 12. Microphotograph of an ac liquid crystal driver chip. At the boundaries normally isolated transistors have been used. Middle part of the chip contains the I²L circuits.

In a first type of interface, this collector might be connected via a resistor to a positive supply voltage [Fig. 11(a)]. However, if the resistor is connected to a negative supply voltage, the n^+ area will act as an emitter and the transistor will now behave as an emitter follower. In this case the much higher current gain of a noninverse transistor determines the output impedance [Fig. 11(b)].

By applying a p-n-p transistor between the injector and the output transistor [Fig. 11(c)], the difference in logic levels can be increased because the base of the n-p-n transistor is now driven by a current instead of a voltage. When a positive supply voltage is now used [Fig. 11(d)] this interface gets the same properties as the standard I²L inverter of Fig. 11(a).

Finally in the last type of interface circuit the highest difference in logic levels can be obtained with a lateral p-n-p because of the high collector breakdown voltage [Fig. 11(e)].

APPLICATION TO ANALOG CIRCUITRY

The manufacturing process described is started from an n^+ substrate. When a p substrate is used with a n^+ buried layer for the common emitters together with the normal p isolations, linear or analog circuitry can be combined with the I²L digital circuitry on the same chip.

All types of interface circuits are possible then. In Fig. 12 a microphotograph of an ac liquid crystal driver is shown. At the boundaries of the chip, normally isolated transistors are used to deliver the ac voltage to the liquid crystal, whereas the middle of the chip contains the I²L digital circuits.

RESULTS

To prove that I²L is a realistic LSI approach, several circuits have been produced with complexities ranging from 180 to about 1000 gates as listed in Table II.

CONCLUSIONS

I²L has shown that it can fulfill the following demands for LSI: 1) simple technology (five masks); 2) high packing density, 400 gates/mm² if 5-μm clearances are applied; 3) power-delay time product is 1.75 pJ in the system where 10-μm clearances are applied, which can be improved to 0.4 pJ if 5-μm clearances are applied. The average fan-in and fan-out in the system are equal to 2.5.

An extension to a seven-mask standard bipolar technology gives the freedom of using analog and digital circuitry on the same chip. The low power supply voltage of less than 1 V contributes to a high reliability.

ACKNOWLEDGMENT

The authors wish to thank A. Schmitz for many helpful discussions and for the fabrication of the slices.

REFERENCES

[1] S. K. Wiedman and H. H. Berger, "Super integrated bipolar memory devices," presented at the IEEE Int. Electron Devices Conf., Oct. 11–13, 1971.
[2] H. H. Berger and S. K. Wiedman, "Merged transistor logic," presented at the 1972 ISSCC, Feb. 16–17, 1972.
[3] C. M. Hart and A. Slob, "Integrated injection logic—A new approach to LSI," presented at the 1972 ISSCC, Feb. 16–17, 1972.

Integrated Injection Logic (I²L)

C. M. Hart and A. Slob

In the large-scale integration of logic circuits the basic building blocks must combine great simplicity and compactness with very low dissipation. These requirements are met by the elegant combination of an inversely operated N-P-N transistor with a simple P-N junction for the power supply. In this way 'integrated injection logic' can lead to 'bipolar' integrated circuits whose performance can match that of MOST devices in many respects.

Introduction

The continuous improvement in the manufacture of integrated logic circuits was initially directed at the achievement of shorter delay times. In about 1970, however, the extent to which speeds could be increased reached a practical limit, and the trend is now towards circuits with an increasing number of gates per chip.

For applications where it is desirable to manufacture multi-gate circuits as single units, this large-scale integration (LSI) will constitute an improvement. If LSI is to be a practical proposition, the logic circuits must meet three important requirements. In the first place the basic 'building blocks' must be simple and compact to allow as many of them as possible to be accommodated on a single chip. Secondly, the circuits must be designed in such a way that a reasonable speed does not entail excessive dissipation on the chip. This means that the product τD of the delay time τ and the dissipation per gate D, which is the determining factor here, must be sufficiently low. Thirdly, the fabrication process must be simple and easily controllable and capable of producing a good yield of reliable LSI circuits with as many as a thousand gates. The circuits now in use do not always meet these requirements entirely satisfactorily, and therefore to obtain sufficiently large numbers of gates per chip a new family of logic circuits is necessary.

The circuits that will be described here represent an attractive and novel approach, which meets the requirements [1]. They are in fact multi-collector transistors, i.e. transistors with more than one collector in common base and emitter regions, which are supplied with power by injecting minority carriers into these regions. The injection can take place in two ways: by irradiation with light or by means of a P-N diode.

The first method, which could be of interest in space applications, has the advantage that it requires no external power supply and therefore no supply leads, since small light-actuated current sources are distributed over the whole circuit at the exact places where they are needed. Relatively high levels of illumination are needed, however, if high switching speeds are required.

In the second method the injection is effected by means of a forward-biased P-N diode. This does require an external power supply, but it can be connected into the circuit by a very simple pattern of central power supply rails on the chip. The switching speed can be varied over a wide range by varying the current level. The supply voltage which the circuits require is low (< 1 V). Typically the packing density is 200 gates per mm² and the τD value is 0.7 pJ per gate (the smallest detail in each mask being 7 μm).

The production technique for integrated injection logic circuits ('I²L' circuits) involves only five masking steps. This is rather simpler than the present bipolar production process. Reverting to the normal seven-mask technique, however, it is possible to combine I²L circuits with ordinary integrated circuits (e.g. with analog circuits), thus greatly widening the field of applications.

Injection by light; the photodiode

A P-N junction illuminated with light of a suitable wavelength behaves like a diode with a current source connected to it in parallel (*fig. 1*). Light quanta pene-

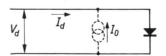

Fig. 1. Illuminated photodiode, symbolically represented by a current source I_0 in parallel with a diode. I_d diode current, V_d diode voltage.

C. M. Hart and A. Slob are with Philips Research Laboratories, Eindhoven.

Reprinted with permission from *Philips Tech. Rev.*, vol. 33, pp. 76–85, Mar. 1973.

trating into the diode release electrons and holes, increasing the concentration of both kinds of carrier. The concentration of the minority carriers is increased relatively much more than that of the majority carriers. The extra carriers formed in the neighbourhood of the P-N junction are separated by the internal field, giving the effect of a current source [2].

The current I_0 from this source depends on the illumination; its effect on the behaviour of the diode is to displace the normal diode characteristic (curve 1 in fig. 2) through a vertical distance I_0 (curve 2).

In a short-circuited diode ($V_d = 0$) a current $-I_0$ is found in the short-circuit, and in an open-circuited diode ($I_d = 0$) the voltage across the diode is equal to the voltage V_j that is normally required for a current I_0.

The idea is to use such current sources in integrated circuits as distributed supply sources, located at the exact places where they are needed. To make this clear we must first consider the situation found in illuminated transistors.

by the deposited-aluminium connections, which are opaque. Fourthly, owing to the doping gradient, there is usually a 'built-in' electric field in region 2, causing the minority carriers formed there to drift into region 3, so that they contribute to the photocurrent of junction 2-3.

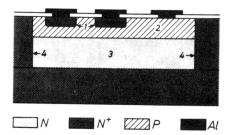

$$\square \, N \qquad \blacksquare \, N^+ \qquad \diagonalbox \, P \qquad \blacksquare \, Al$$

Fig. 3. Schematic cross-section of a phototransistor for integrated injection logic (I²L). On illumination both the junctions 1-2 and the junction 2-3 act as current sources, but the junctions 1-2 only play a subsidiary part since they are largely screened by the aluminium wiring pattern. In the light-activated injection logic described, regions 1 are used as collector and region 3 as emitter. The regions 4 isolate the transistor from its neighbours.

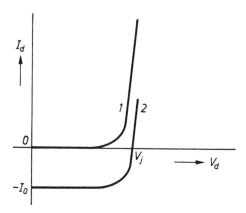

Fig. 2. Characteristics of a non-illuminated diode (curve 1) and an illuminated one (curve 2); cf. fig. 1. V_j is the value of V_d at which the current begins to increase steeply.

The illuminated transistor

Fig. 3 illustrates the structure of a phototransistor like those used in our circuits. In principle there are two current sources in this phototransistor: one across the junctions 1-2 and one across the junction 2-3. In a phototransistor of this type the current source across junction 2-3 gives a much larger current than the one across junctions 1-2. There are four reasons for this. In the first place, region 3 is much larger than the regions 1, and consequently the number of carriers generated there is greater. Secondly, the life of the minority carriers before they disappear by recombination is much longer in region 3 than in the regions 1. Thirdly, the regions 1 are normally completely screened

In practice this means that the photocurrent in parallel with the junctions 1-2 can be neglected. To produce transistor action the base-emitter junction must be forward-biased; for the photocurrent to act as the only supply source, the junction 2-3 must be taken as a base-emitter junction, with region 3 as the emitter and the regions 1 as the collector. If we compare this with a conventional planar N-P-N transistor, we see that the light-activated transistor is operated 'upside down', for in the conventional version region 1 is the emitter and region 3 the collector. If in these conditions we leave the base unconnected, this region will then become positively charged and a collector, given sufficient voltage, will be capable of drawing a current I_c, where I_c will depend on the surface area of the collector. The base current I_0, as we have seen, depends on the total area of the emitter-base junction. For each collector we can now define a current gain β:

$$\beta = I_c/I_0.$$

In the transistor shown in fig. 3 two collector regions can be seen; more could have been shown since it is a *multi-collector transistor*. The collector regions are of the same size, and since the voltage is the same everywhere in the base region, *each* collector will be capable

[1] See C. M. Hart and A. Slob, IEEE J. **SC-7**, 346, 1972 (No. 5), and C. M. Hart and A. Slob, 1972 IEEE Int. Solid-State Circuits Conf. Digest tech. Papers, p. 92.
[2] See for example: L. Heyne, Physical principles of photoconductivity, III. Inhomogeneity effects, Philips tech. Rev. **29**, 221-234, 1968.

of drawing a current βI_0. In the application of such an arrangement, the individual collector currents will usually also be approximately equal to I_0. If $\beta > 1$, the collector voltage will then be very low.

This may be explained as follows. Let us consider two identical phototransistors T_1 and T_2; see *fig. 4*. For simplicity, we assume that each of the phototransistors has only one collector and that $I_1 = I_2 = I_0$. The collector of T_1 is connected to the base of T_2, and is used as a switch for short-circuiting or open-circuiting the base of T_2. In such conditions we can construct operating points P and Q in *fig. 5* by intersecting the transistor characteristics with the photodiode characteristic of fig. 2. In this case we have taken the photodiode characteristic upside down, since the positive current direction is reversed. When the base of T_1 is earthed, the current I_0 which the current source supplies to the base of T_1 will leak away through this short-circuit and the base current I_b of T_1 will be zero. Intersection with the photodiode characteristic then gives the operating point Q. When the base of T_1 is open-circuited, however, then I_b is equal to I_0 and the collector of T_1 would then be able to draw a current βI_0. However, this collector current must be supplied by

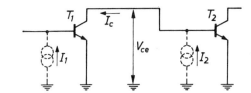

Fig. 4. Standard arrangement for injection logic, in which each collector draws only one base current.

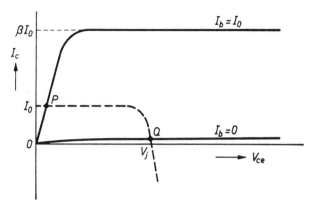

Fig. 5. V_{ce}-I_c diagram for the transistor T_1 from fig. 4 when $I_1 = I_0$. P and Q are possible operating points when the collector is connected to the base of a similar transistor. The point P applies to the case in which the base of T_1 is open-circuited ($I_b = I_0$), and the point Q to the case in which the base is earthed ($I_b = 0$).

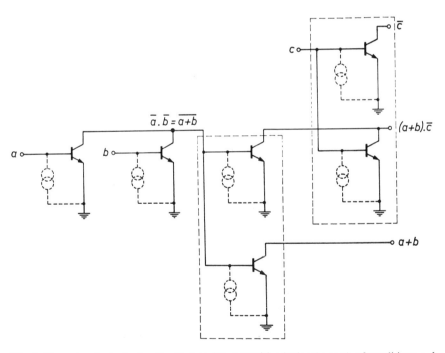

Fig. 6. Example of a logic circuit with transistors (positive logic: the truth of conditions a, b and c corresponds to a high voltage). The dashed lines indicate how the transistors can be combined to form multi-collector transistors.

the current source at the base of T_2, and can therefore be no greater than I_0. This situation then gives the operating point P. In this case V_{ce} of T_1 is very small, which means that the base of T_2 is short-circuited.

Logic circuits with phototransistors

The phototransistors discussed here are very suitable for use in logic circuits. In a circuit like the one of *fig. 6* the transistors produce the logic inversion of the base signal, while the interconnection of collectors causes the collector signals to perform a 'wired-AND' function. The result is that transistors with interconnected collectors may also be regarded as NOR gates (described in positive logic). As fig. 3 shows, our circuits can easily be given the form of a multi-collector transistor, and mainly because it is desirable to have each collector connected to only one base, the transistors within the dashed lines in fig. 6 can be lumped together to form a circuit as shown in *fig. 7*.

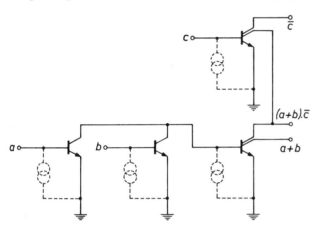

Fig. 7. Injection logic circuit corresponding to the circuit of fig. 6.

Technology

To fabricate a light-injection circuit of the type shown in fig. 3, four masks are required. The process begins with a slice of N^+ material on which a layer of N-type material is grown epitaxially; this corresponds to the layers 2 and 3 in the figure. The first mask is used to make a deep N^+ diffusion 4 in this layer to form the demarcations for the transistors. This diffusion encloses the N-type regions. In the next stage the complete slice is subjected to a P-type diffusion. In this way the bases 2 of the transistors are introduced, and no mask is required because the P concentration is lower than that of the deep N^+ regions. The second mask is now used for introducing the shallow N^+ regions 1, producing the collectors. The third mask is required for generating contact holes in the isolating oxide layer, and the fourth mask produces the final aluminium wiring pattern.

Hole injection by means of a *P-N* junction

In the circuits so far discussed, light was necessary for generating holes in the N-type material of the emitter to produce a current source I_0. This would make the circuits eminently suitable for space applications in which sunlight would be the only source of energy. In the case of illumination by artificial light,

however, the difficulty is that relatively high levels of illumination are required, which are then utilized at relatively low efficiency. This makes it a more economic proposition to inject holes into the emitter region by means of a forward-biased P-N junction. This results in the configuration shown in *fig. 8*. The only difference compared with the circuit in fig. 3 is the extra injector rail 5 now required on the chip. With this power supply system it is easy to select and vary the current level at which the circuits operate.

The fabrication of these circuits requires only one additional masking step, which is the step for generating the separate P-type regions. In some circumstances it is possible to omit the deep N^+ diffusion; *four* masking steps are then sufficient.

Circuit and layout considerations

As can be seen in fig. 8, a multi-collector transistor has the shape of a long rectangle. A suitable and convenient layout for a number of these multi-collector transistors on the chip is to arrange them in linear strips on each side of, and perpendicular to, the injector strip that provides the power supply. This is illustrated in *fig. 9*, which shows two D-type flip-flops and some separate gates. A short injector strip supplies power to three multi-collector transistors and one long rail supplies power to two sets of nine transistors each. Since the relative location of base and collector con-

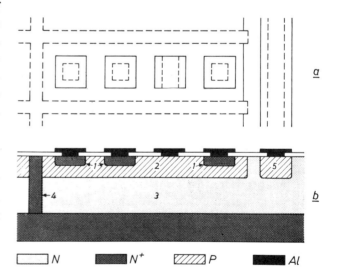

Fig. 8. Schematic cross-section and layout of multi-collector transistors with injection from a forward-biased P-N junction. The figures have the same significance as in fig. 3. Region 5 is an extra P region that with 3 forms the P-N junction for the injection of charge carriers into region 3. The multi-collector transistors are rectangular regions enclosed by the isolating regions 4 (shown dashed in the plan view); they are located in rows perpendicular to the injection rail (region 5), which extends as straight tracks over the whole chip. Compared with the circuit in fig. 3, this configuration requires only one extra masking step for applying the P regions.

tacts is not subject to any fundamental restrictions, they can be laid out in the way most convenient for the wiring pattern required. Space can also be left between collectors where connections can pass a multi-collector transistor without making contact with it, if crossovers are necessary in the wiring pattern. All this is possible provided the multi-collector transistors are not too long.

At high current levels a limit is imposed by the resistance of the base region. This resistance causes a voltage drop across the base, and if this voltage drop is too high the collector currents will not be uniform. Voltage drop across the injector, which would give rise to non-uniform injection, is prevented by applying an aluminium contact rail over the whole length of the injector region. The requirement that the collector

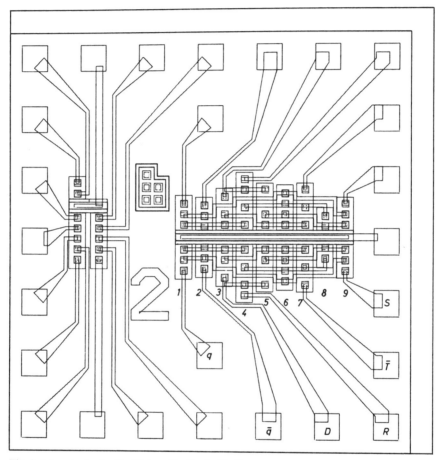

Fig. 9. Layout of a double 'D-type flip-flop' with direct set-and-reset inputs (2×9 transistors), and a few separate gates (3 transistors).

It follows from the geometry that the injected minority carriers are distributed uniformly over each multi-collector transistor. This does not however imply any fixed current level, which the user can in fact select within a wide range.

At low currents a limit is set by the current gain β becoming too small. This situation only arises, however, with currents of the order of nanoamperes. We have already seen that each collector must be capable of drawing one base current. To obtain a suitable operating point (P in fig. 5) this means that the current gain β must be greater than unity. A value of β close to unity is not advisable because of low speed and sensitivity to interference (noise), as we shall see later.

current for the worst-fed transistors should remain greater than the highest values found elsewhere for the base current can be met in a carefully designed circuit at current levels of up to a few tens of milliamperes per chip. This gives the user a freedom of choice of current level over several decades. *Fig. 10* shows a 108-bit shift register consisting of 820 gates, operated at currents ranging from 8 μA to 100 mA. At the low current (about 10 nA per gate) the maximum frequency is 300 Hz, at high currents it is about 800 kHz.

As we saw above, the current level can be selected by the user. This implies that it can be changed during operation. For example, the shift register of fig. 10 has been used in an experimental pocket calculator that can be given a very low current level during stand-by, i.e. while no operations are in progress and the machine is waiting for a new instruction. This current is automatically switched to a much higher level as soon as the calculator is given an instruction for further operations by pressing one of the buttons. This automatic switch-over makes it possible to keep the average power consumption very low.

A is closed (see fig. 12*b*). From what has just been said it will then be clear that the base of T_2 is open and T_2 forms a short-circuit for the base of T_3. Transistor T_2 is now 'on' and biased to the operating point P. We now apply at point S a noise voltage V_{S1}, which we represent in fig. 12*b* by the noise current I_{S1}.

Since T_2 short-circuits the current source I_3, a minimum base current of I_3/β_2 is necessary to maintain this

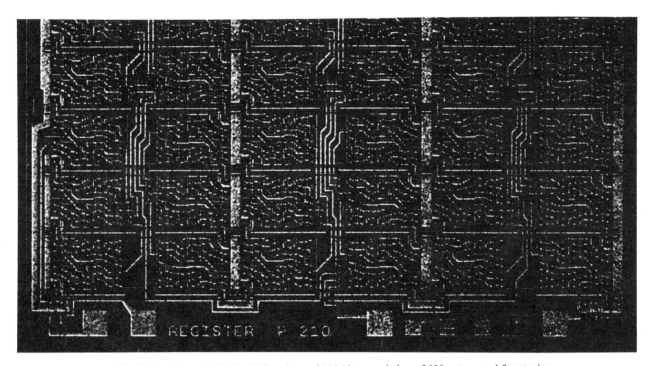

Fig. 10. Part (about half) of a shift register of 108 bits, consisting of 820 gates, used for storing three 9-decimal numbers in an experimental pocket calculator.

Noise sensitivity

The relation between the input voltage V_i and the output voltage V_{ce} of a transistor in the circuit given in fig. 4 can be found with the aid of figs. 2 and 5, or by direct measurement. This relation is shown in *fig. 11*. It can be seen that at the operating point P a relatively small negative noise voltage V_{S1} on the base is sufficient to switch off the collector current, whereas at the operating point Q a relatively large (and positive) noise voltage V_{S0} is permissible before the transistor switches from 'off' to 'on'. The noise margins are perhaps better expressed as current sources.

Let us therefore consider the noise sensitivity at point S in *fig. 12a* for two cases: switch A open and switch A closed. Transistors T_1, T_2 and T_3 do not necessarily have to be identical; there may be differences in geometry, and this is why we have given the transistors different current sources I_1, I_2 and I_3. Furthermore, the current gains β_1, β_2 and β_3 may be different.

We shall first consider the situation in which switch

current in the collector of T_2. Since I_2 is available and T_2 draws no current, the maximum value which the noise source may have is

$$I_{S1} = I_2 - I_3/\beta_2,$$

if the transistor is not to switch from the operating

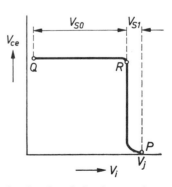

Fig. 11. Curve showing the relation between input voltage V_i and output voltage V_{ce}, e.g. for transistor T_1 in fig. 4. V_{S0} and V_{S1} are the extreme values of noise voltages that are acceptable at the operating points Q and P (see fig. 5) if the logic level is to be correctly reproduced.

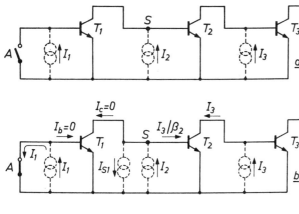

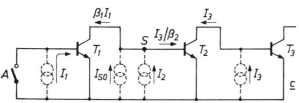

Fig. 12. *a*) Configuration of three transistors $T_{1,2,3}$ with the resultant current sources $I_{1,2,3}$, for calculating the noise sensitivity of an I²L circuit. The noise is assumed to enter at point S. *b*) Configuration for calculating the maximum permissible noise I_{S1} for the case where the base voltage of T_1 is zero (switch A closed). T_2 is then at the operating point P of fig. 5. *c*) The same as (*b*), but for the operating point Q (A open).

point P to point Q. The corresponding noise voltage is then given by

$$V_{S1} = \frac{kT}{q} \ln\left(\frac{I_3}{\beta_2 I_2}\right).$$

(k is Boltzmann's constant, T the absolute temperature and q the electronic charge.)

We now consider the situation in which switch A is open (fig. 12*c*). Transistor T_1 is now biased to point P and short-circuits T_2. Consequently T_2 draws no collector current from T_3, which is 'on'. For a noise source I_{S0} to be able to switch T_2 to 'on', T_2 must first draw the collector current I_3, for which a base current I_3/β_2 is required. In addition, T_1 can draw a current $\beta_1 I_1$ before any substantial increase in its collector voltage appears. It follows that a noise source I_{S0} is acceptable if

$$I_{S0} = \beta_1 I_1 + I_3/\beta_2 - I_2 .$$

This corresponds to a noise voltage

$$V_{S0} \approx V_{\mathrm{j}}.$$

For the situation $I_1 = I_2 = I_3 = I_0$ and $\beta_1 = \beta_2 = \beta_3 = \beta$, we find:

$$I_{S1} = I_0 \left(1 - 1/\beta\right); \quad V_{S1} = \left(- kT/q\right) \ln \beta$$

and

$$I_{S0} = I_0 \left(\beta - 1 + 1/\beta\right); \quad V_{S0} \approx V.$$

In practice there is not likely to be much noise produced on a chip. In our equations, which we obtained by assuming all values of β and all current sources to be equal, a current gain $\beta = 2$ will be quite sufficient. The noise produced in the connections between the chips is expected to be higher, and therefore the first transistor on the chip and the last one on the previous chip are given a larger β and a higher current level. This can be achieved with a suitable geometry.

Switching speeds

When considering the switching speeds of integrated injection logic a distinction must be made between situations of low and high current level. In the first situation only stray capacitances have to be charged and discharged; in the second, charge accumulation in the transistors becomes important, which means that the cut-off frequency is of significance.

At low current levels the propagation delay time per gate (τ) is determined only by junction capacitances and stray capacitances. This delay time will be proportional to the time t needed to charge or discharge these capacitances. The time t is proportional to $Q/I = CV/I$, and the dissipation D is equal to VI, where V is the voltage across a forward-biased junction. From this it follows that τD is proportional to CV^2, which is constant.

At high current levels the accumulated charges in the transistors become more important than the charges in the junction capacitance plus the wiring. In this region the transit times are independent of the current level used, since inside the transistor the charges are proportional to I_0/f_t, i.e. proportional to the current divided by the cut-off frequency. The time taken to build up these charges is proportional to the charge divided by the current I_0; the delay time τ is therefore proportional to $1/f_t$ and independent of the current level.

This reasoning explains the measured τD curves. Since the voltage of the injector rail depends only slightly on the current, the dissipation is proportional to I_0. At low currents the product τD is therefore constant, irrespective of I_0. In our circuits it amounts to about 10^{-12} joules, as can be seen from *fig. 13*. At high currents, τ is constant and dependent on the cut-off frequency, which can however, in an inversely operated transistor, as here, be about 20 times lower than with a normally operated one.

Conversion of a logical design into I²L

As we noted earlier, when our circuits are described in positive logic, they represent a negation followed by a 'wired-AND', which corresponds to a logical NOR.

In general, however, it may be more advantageous to base the design of an I²L circuit not on NORs, but on NANDs. To explain this there are three points that we should consider. First, every collector in our multi-collector transistors represents in effect the negation

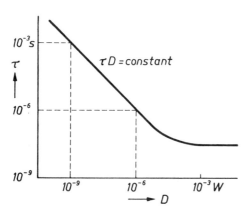

Fig. 13. Relation between delay time τ and dissipation D for a single gate (the τD curve). At low current levels (low dissipation) the product τD is constant; at high currents (high dissipation) τ is independent of the current level.

of the base signal. Secondly, a branching of the signal takes place between base and collectors. Thirdly, each collector or set of interconnected collectors in our circuits can only draw current from one base. It is perhaps more obvious to regard a transistor base, together with the preceding 'wired-AND', as an entity and to think in terms of NANDs when drawing up the design. How this works out in practice will be illustrated by reference to the circuit in *fig. 14*, a D-type flip-flop with direct set and reset inputs.

If for simplicity the symbols of *fig. 15* are introduced for a 'wired-AND' connection and for a multi-collector transistor, the circuit of fig. 14 can be redrawn as shown in *fig. 16*. The six NANDs from fig. 14 directly give the transistors 8, 6, 3, 5, 1 and 2. The double input $\bar{S}$ required is derived from the additional transistor 9, fed by S, and the inputs $\bar{R}$ are derived from transistor 4. The double clock input $\bar{T}$ comes from transistor 7, which now, however, has to be fed by T. The input D, which goes direct to a 'wired-AND', is regarded as having its associated transistor outside the circuit. The circuit thus requires nine transistors; it is in fact one half of the circuit whose layout is given in fig. 9. The rules for designing a layout of this type will not be dealt with here.

Combination of I²L with other circuits

The circuits described above are made with a five-mask technology starting with an N^+ substrate. This

means that the transistors must always have the emitter connected to the substrate. Transistors used in some other way would also be possible in this technology, but in all cases either the emitter or the collector in N-P-N transistors, or the bases in P-N-P transistor, are connected to the substrate. This design limitation can be removed by starting from a P substrate (see

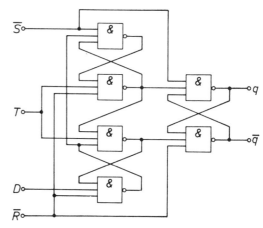

Fig. 14. Logic scheme (in NANDs) of the D-type flip-flop with direct set and reset inputs from fig. 9.

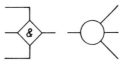

Fig. 15. Symbols for a 'wired-AND' connection and a multi-collector transistor (with three collectors), with which the diagram in fig. 14 can be converted into I²L.

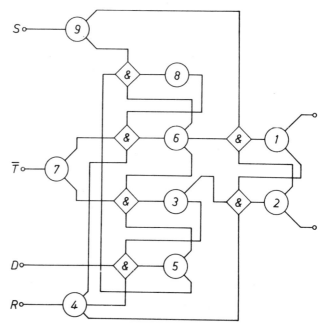

Fig. 16. Conversion of the basic diagram in fig. 14 into a form with multi-collector transistors and 'wired-AND' collector, directly suitable for translation into the layout of fig. 9.

fig. 17), using a buried N^+ layer as auxiliary substrate for the integrated injection logic, and P^+ diffusions for isolating the N-type regions from each other.

In this way, by introducing two additional masking steps (for the buried layer and isolating diffusion) it becomes possible to work with fully isolated transistors, as commonly used in conventional IC technology. Interface circuits of all types can then be produced, and analog circuits can be combined with I²L digital cir-

cuits on the same chip. An example can be seen in *fig. 18*, which shows a 24-bit shift register combined at each of the 24 outputs with a circuit of isolated transistors capable of switching a high a.c. voltage.

Conclusion and results

A convincing proof that I²L is a realistic approach to the LSI problem is our achievement of a packing

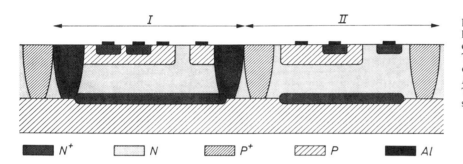

Fig. 17. Combination of injection logic with 'conventional' transistor circuits in a seven-mask technology. The region *I* enclosed by N^+ regions comprises the injection logic. Region *II* shows a 'conventional' transistor. The P^+ regions are isolation diffusions.

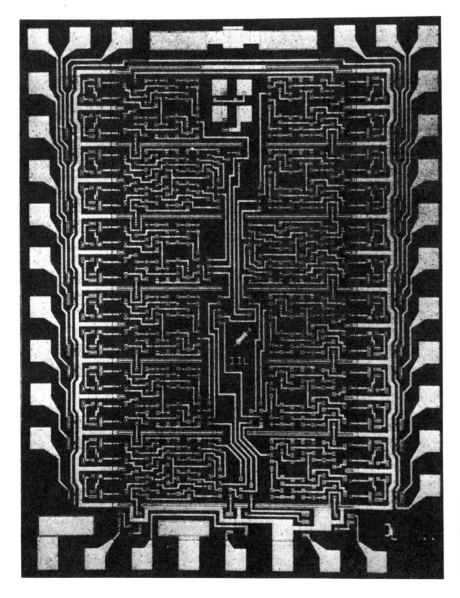

Fig. 18. Example of injection logic combined with analog circuits, showing a 24-bit shift register in which each of the 24 outputs is provided with a circuit of isolated transistors for switching a high a.c. voltage.

Table I. Data for a number of circuits made in I²L. The chip sizes given are overall dimensions, i.e. they include the area taken up by bonding pads and scribing lines. (These were not included in the calculation of the packing density.)

Type of circuit	No. of gates	Chip size (mm)
Tone generator for electronic organ	180	1.2 ×1.5
Liquid-crystal display driver	200	2.2 ×2.4
Counter for digital voltmeter	325	2.2 ×2.4
108-bit shift register	820	2.96×2.85
1536-bit read-only memory	~ 1000	3 ×4
Control-logic calculator	980	4 ×4

density of 200 gates per mm². The minimum detail was 7 μm, there were five masking steps, and established technology was used throughout. Circuits with up to 1000 gates per chip have been made and put into practical application, e.g. in an experimental pocket calculator.

With a seven-mask technology, normal integrated circuit can be combined with I²L, enabling analog and digital circuits to be produced on the same chip. A wide variety of interface circuits between all kinds of logic can also be achieved. The range of potential applications is therefore very wide. *Table I* gives data for a number of circuits made with the I²L technique (the smallest details were 10 μm). The τD product was between 1 and 2×10^{-12} J.

Summary. Large-scale integration (LSI) requires building blocks that combine great simplicity and compactness with a low dissipation per gate (D), without the speed (delay per gate τ) being too greatly affected. Integrated injection logic (I²L) meets these requirements. I²L circuits consist in practice of multi-collector transistors that are supplied with power by the injection of minority carriers, either by illumination of the base-emitter regions — no external power supply is then required — or from an injector rail that forms a *P-N* junction with the emitter region. The current level of the circuits can be varied in a wide range. I²L circuits with illumination injection can be made with four masks, the others with five. If seven masks are used integrated circuits can be made that consist partly of I²L circuits and partly of isolated conventional transistors. With a minimum detail of 7 μm packing densities of 200 gates/mm² and a τD product of 0.7×10^{-12} J have been achieved. Circuits with 1000 gates per chip have been found to be a practical possibility, e.g. in an experimental pocket calculator.

Merged-Transistor Logic (MTL)—A Low-Cost Bipolar Logic Concept

HORST H. BERGER AND SIEGFRIED K. WIEDMANN

Abstract—This paper describes a novel bipolar logic featuring a direct injection of minority carriers into the switching transistor. Since this concept utilizes merged complementary transistors, it has been named merged-transistor logic (MTL). The fabrication process is as simple as that of single transistors, requiring only four mask steps through metalization. MTL is based on inverters having decoupled multicollector outputs for the logical combinations. The devices are self-isolated and no ohmic load resistors are required. This is a key to monolithic logic chips of very high functional density and low power dissipation. On experimental chips an excellent power-delay product of 0.35 pJ has been measured. These experiments show that a density of 100 gates/mm² can be achieved with present manufacturing tolerances (minimum dimensions: 0.3-mil metal line width, 0.15-mil spacing, 0.2×0.2-mil² contact holes). Level compatibility with transistor-transistor logic (T²L) logic, good driving capability, and high noise immunity are further advantages over present FET approaches.

Manuscript received February 17, 1972; revised June 5, 1972.
The authors are with the IBM Laboratories, Boeblingen, Germany.

Reprinted from *IEEE J. Solid-State Circuits*, vol. SC-7, pp. 340–346, Oct. 1972.

I. INTRODUCTION

IN ORDER to exploit the bipolar potential for low-cost logic, new concepts are needed that allow higher functional densities but require fewer process steps [1], [2] than presently used. This paper describes a novel bipolar logic featuring a direct injection of minority carriers into the switching transistor. Since this concept utilizes merged complementary transistors, it has been named merged-transistor logic (MTL).

With MTL, the device isolation problem is totally eliminated. The process becomes as simple as that of single transistors, requiring only four mask steps through metalization. The device's self-isolation and the complete omission of ohmic resistors are the key for the high functional density. From our experimental chips we can project a density of about 100 gates/mm² with present manufacturing tolerances. Despite the simple technology, an excellent power-delay product of 0.35 pJ has been measured.

After explaining the basic logic structure and operation some pertinent device parameters are discussed based on theoretical investigations and measured data. Experimental results obtained from small logic blocks are presented to verify the improvements in power × delay product, density, and process simplicity.

II. BASIC MTL STRUCTURE AND OPERATION

MTL can be plainly derived from the principal circuit schematic shown in Fig. 1. It shows an implementation of the logic NOR function which, as is well known, can be used for realizing any kind of complex logic. This circuit resembles dc–transistor logic (DCTL) or resistor–transistor logic (RTL) [3], but fundamentally differs in the current supply mode. Each switching transistor in Fig. 1 is provided with an individual current supply at the base terminal, whereas in a DCTL gate the supply element is associated with the collectors. As in DCTL, the gate consists of inverter transistors that are dotted at their outputs to logically combine the input signals A and B. The output delivering the function $\overline{A + B}$ is connected to several succeeding inverter inputs. The logic levels are about the same as in DCTL.

Since the emitters of all n-p-n transistors are tied to a common reference potential (which is normally ground), they should be implemented in a common n plane to achieve a high density. In terms of a standard bipolar structure, it means to employ common-collector n-p-n transistors and to operate them upside down, so that the former collector region becomes the emitter. This has been done in MTL and, therefore, we shall refer to this operation mode as the normal mode here.

The current source I_B in Fig. 1 provides the drive current for the transistor switch and the charge current for the circuit capacitances. An obvious but not attractive realization of the current source would be an ohmic re-

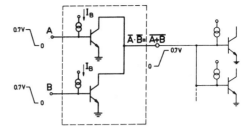

Fig. 1. NOR circuit.

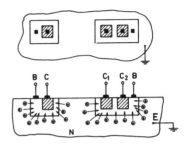

Fig. 2. Base current by minority carrier collection.

sistor tied to a positive voltage supply. However, the required current supply to the base of the n-p-n transistor can also be attained through a collection of excess minority carriers generated in the vicinity of the emitter-base junction as illustrated in Fig. 2. These excess minority carriers can be generated, e.g., by a hole injection from a p emitter in the common n-emitter region [4], [5].

A practical solution in a readily available technology is shown in Fig. 3, together with the equivalent circuit. The p_1 emitter provides the minority carrier injection into the n_1 region, where most of them are collected by the adjacent p_2 regions. Hence, the p_1-n_1-p_2 structure forms a lateral grounded-base p-n-p transistor, which is here represented in the equivalent circuit. Instead of the lateral p-n-p configuration, a vertical structure may be used as well, for instance by choosing a p substrate for the carrier injection. The p-n-p transistor has now replaced the current source in the equivalent circuit of Fig. 1. The n-p-n transistor with emitter n_1, base p_2, and collector n_2 is operated upside down as explained earlier. Since the n_1 and p_2 regions are commonly used by both transistors, we end up with a merged transistor structure having very few metal interconnections. This is a key for the high functional density of MTL.

Because of the excellent tracking of the emitter–base voltages on a chip,[1] the p-emitter regions p_1 are fed in parallel. As shown in Fig. 4(a), the p emitters may be connected directly to a chip pad and supplied by an external current source I_0, resulting in a chip voltage of about 0.8 V. However, a common series resistor R_V con-

[1] First measurements on parallel p-n-p transistors on the same chip have shown a collector current variation of less than ±15 percent.

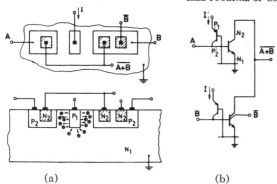

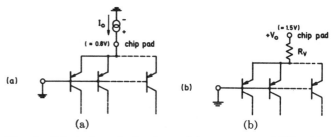

Fig. 3. (a) Principal MTL structure. (b) Equivalent circuit.

Fig. 4. Principal methods of supplying power to MTL chip.
(a) External current supply. (b) External voltage supply.

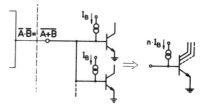

Fig. 5. MTL multicollector inverter as logic element.

nected to an external voltage supply V_0 can be used as well [cf. Fig. 4(b)]. This resistor can be implemented by the n-diffusion used for the n-p-n collectors. The currents of the MTL gates can be adjusted by the sizes of the p-n-p and n-p-n transistors in order to obtain different delay times or driving capabilities on the same chip.

After having discussed the MTL principle more from a circuit and device point of view, we will briefly characterize MTL from a logic systems aspect. This may better illustrate the differences to presently known logic.

Looking back to Fig. 1, one recognizes that an MTL gate output, the bases of the succeeding inverters are tied together. This leads to a multicollector structure as shown in Fig. 5. Thus, MTL basically consists of inverters with one input (base terminal) and several outputs (multicollectors). Of course, two or more inverters can be connected in parallel if the number of collectors is not sufficient. By dotting the collector outputs of different inverters, the NOR function is realized. Compared to standard NOR logic, the number of collectors of one dot corresponds to fan-in and the number of collector outputs of one inverter to fan-out. Hence, the logic flexibility of MTL is comparable with that of other bipolar logic circuits.

In addition, it should be pointed out that MTL fits well into an economical array layout scheme as proposed by Weinberger [6]. Fig. 6(a) shows as an example the principal layout of a three-address decoder. A similar layout configuration would result for an MTL read-only memory. If necessary, the series resistance of long p stripes can be effectively reduced by shunting low-ohmic n^+ stripes as illustrated in Fig. 6(b).

III. INTERFACING

So far, the advantages of MTL have been shown for realizing logic systems on chip level. But MTL can also cope economically with the system environment as shall be discussed below.

Main problems are noise at the input and driving capabilities at the outputs having loads by orders of magnitude larger than the circuits inside the chip.

The noise immunity of a logic circuit is not only determined by the voltage thresholds but also by the energy

necessary for switching the gate. This energy is rather high, since all nodes are at low impedance level. The more noise-endangered input stages can be operated at a higher power level in order to further increase their energy threshold. As already mentioned previously, this can be achieved by properly adjusting the MTL device size for a higher injection current and thus making it noise insensitive.

The problem of driving heavy output loads can be solved the same way; if necessary, two or more stages may be put in series for scaling up the power in steps. Furthermore, the output voltage swings can be made larger than the swing of about 0.7 V inside the chip by choosing a proper load supply. In this context, MTL has similar characteristics as T²L since both circuits use a grounded-emitter output transistor having good driving capability, the swing can be adjusted by choosing the appropriate output voltage supply and load resistors. From these common features with T²L it also becomes evident that the MTL logic levels are compatible with those of T²L-type logic circuits being widely used in present low-cost systems. Thus usually no level converters would be required.

IV. PERTINENT MTL DEVICE CHARACTERISTICS

In the foregoing section the basic structure and operation of MTL have been discussed without going into details on the device characteristics. Concluding from experience with conventional monolithic logic circuits, three basic questions would arise with MTL.

1) What factors determine the current gain in an n-p-n transistor operated upside down?

2) What is the influence of the "partially saturated" grounded-base p-n-p transistors on the supply current distribution?

3) Are there current hogging effects [7] in the parallel

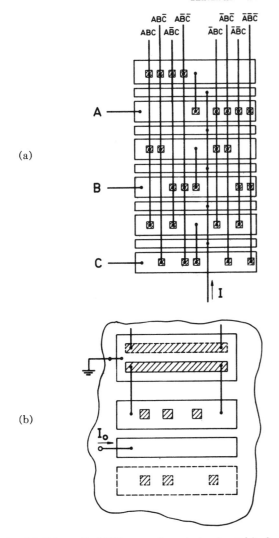

Fig. 6. (a) Schematic MTL array layout showing 3-bit decoder. (b) Example of low-ohmic bypass resistor.

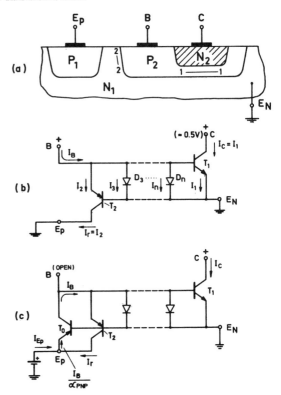

Fig. 7. (a) Cross section showing injection regions for equivalent circuit. (b) Equivalent circuit of n-p-n transistor operated upside down. (c) Equivalent circuit of MTL device.

grounded-emitter n-p-n transistors (equivalent to multicollector transistors) owing to saturation?

In the discussion on the n-p-n transistor current gain β_n, it will be shown that the question of the supply current sharing in partially saturated p-n-p transistors becomes irrelevant owing to a suitable definition of β_n. The current hogging of the parallel n-p-n transistors will be demonstrated to be insignificant because of the inherently high inverse current gain of the upside-down-operated transistors.

When the emitter–base junction n_1-p_2 of the n-p-n transistor in the MTL device [Fig. 7(a)] is forward biased, electrons are injected into the p_2 region, holes into the n_1 region. These injections may be portioned and then be represented by adequate diodes as indicated in Fig. 7(b). Specifically, the electron injection into section 1–1 has been symbolized by the emitter–base diode of an ideal n-p-n transistor T_1, assuming a total collection of the electrons by region n_2. Similarly the hole injection into section 2–2 has been represented by an ideal p-n-p transistor T_2.

The current gain $\beta_n \doteq I_c/I_B$ of the extrinsic n-p-n transistor (terminals E_N, B, C) shall be measured with E_p grounded. Obviously, to obtain a large current gain β_n, the parasitic diode currents $I_2 \cdots I_n$ must be kept small compared to current I_1 of the intrinsic transistor T_1. This ratio

$$\beta_n = I_1 \Big/ \sum_{\nu=2}^{n} I_\nu \qquad (1)$$

not only depends on the individual doping and area ratios (which are usually adverse for such a structure), but on the ratio of effective diffusion lengths of the minority carriers as well. This explains why even with the standard buried layer structure, current gains $\beta > 10$ are observed. Furthermore, it should be mentioned that an n^+ collar around the base helps to reduce the parasitic diode current.

Defining the current gain β as above with E_p grounded [Fig. 7(b)], the problem of current sharing in the p-n-p transistors supplied in parallel becomes more transparent for circuit calculation. One may assume that on an MTL chip having many gates, the number of ON and OFF n-p-n transistors is always about equal. Therefore, the common emitter–base voltage V_{EB} is constant for a given supply current. Fig. 7(c) illustrates this condition of constant V_{EB} on a single MTL device. The lateral p-n-p transistor is represented by the superposition of an active forward-

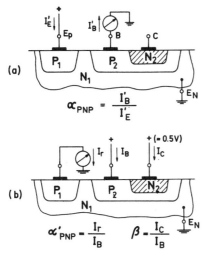

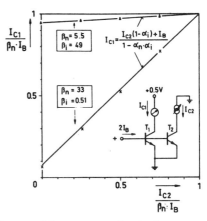

Fig. 8. (a) Definition and measurement of common-base current gain $\alpha_{\text{p-n-p}}$ of p-n-p current source transistor. (b) Definition and measurement of common-emitter current gain β_n of n-p-n transistor and of recollection factor $\alpha'_{\text{p-n-p}}$.

Fig. 9. Influence of inverse current gain β_i on current hogging.

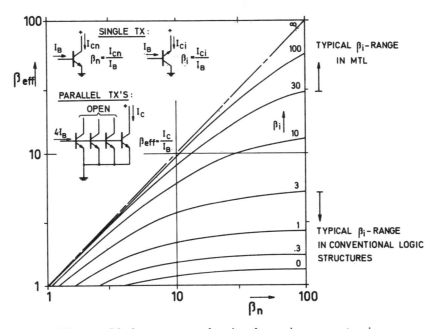

Fig. 10. Maximum current hogging for various current gains.

operated transistor T_0 and the active inversely operated transistor T_2 of Fig. 7(b).[2]

Thus, the external emitter current I_{EP} of one p-n-p transistor is

$$I_{EP} = I_B[(1/\alpha_{\text{p-n-p}}) - \alpha'_{\text{p-n-p}}] \qquad (2)$$

when the corresponding n-p-n transistor is ON and

$$I_{EP} = I_B \cdot (1/\alpha_{\text{p-n-p}})$$

when this transistor is OFF. $\alpha_{\text{p-n-p}}$ and $\alpha'_{\text{p-n-p}}$ have been defined in Fig. 8. Hence, for the total supply current I_0 of n parallel p-n-p transistors on the logic chip one obtains

$$I_0 = (n \cdot I_B/\alpha_{\text{p-n-p}})(1 - \tfrac{1}{2}\alpha'_{\text{p-n-p}} \cdot \alpha_{\text{p-n-p}}). \qquad (3)$$

All considerations may be applied to multicollector p-n-p or multicollector n-p-n structures as well by dividing them into single transistors connected in parallel.

The influence of the inverse current gain β_i on the current hogging of parallel-connected grounded emitter transistors is illustrated by the interdependence of collector currents measured on different matched transistor pairs and theoretically verified (Fig. 9). In case of the large inverse current gain of $\beta_i \approx 50$, which is typical for MTL, the collector current of the nonsaturated transistor T_1 is almost independent to the degree of saturation in transistor T_2. However, in the case of $\beta_i \approx 0,5$, which is

---

[2] This representation is justified by the Ebers-Moll equations.

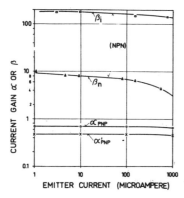

Fig. 11. Common base current gain α_{p-n-p} and recollection factor α'_{p-n-p} of current source p-n-p transistor, common-emitter gains β_n and β_i of n-p-n transistor versus emitter current.

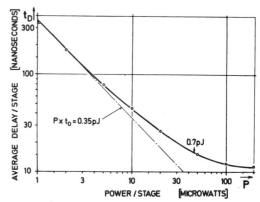

Fig. 13. Propagation delay versus power dissipation of seven-stage closed-loop MTL inverter chain.

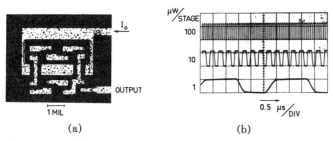

Fig. 12. (a) Chip photomicrograph and (b) output signal oscillograms of seven-stage closed-loop MTL inverter chain.

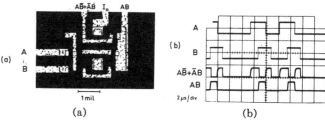

Fig. 14 (a) Chip photomicrograph (11 mils²). (b) Input and output signals of MTL half-adder.

typical for conventional gold-doped structures, both currents are closely coupled. This indicates a strong base-current hogging by the saturated transistor.

In practice, one would calculate the effective current gain of one active transistor in parallel with $(m-1)$ saturated transistors being supplied by m times I_B, when the saturated transistors carry no collector current at all (worst case). This effective current gain is

$$\beta_{eff} = \frac{\alpha_n}{1 - \alpha_n\left[\dfrac{1 + (m-1)\alpha_i}{m}\right]} \quad (4)$$

For $m = 1$ (single transistor) one gets $\beta_{eff} = \beta_n$ as expected, whereas for $m \gg 1$, (4) yields

$$\beta_{eff} = \alpha_n/(1 - \alpha_n \cdot \alpha_i). \quad (5)$$

In Fig. 10 a typical example $(m = 4)$ again confirms that with MTL the current hogging is insignificant in contrast to conventional structures.

V. EXPERIMENTAL RESULTS

Test chips have been fabricated containing single devices and small logic blocks using the simplest structure according to Fig. 3. That is, two diffusions into a blanket n wafer (0.1 Ω cm, no epitaxy). All devices have a n⁺ collar implemented with the n⁺ collector diffusion. Fig. 11 shows the grounded base current gain α_{p-n-p} and the recollection factor α'_{p-n-p} of the lateral p-n-p transistor ac-

cording to Fig. 8. This diagram says that even at very low currents a satisfactory power efficiency is achieved.

The common emitter gain of the n-p-n transistor in the normal and inverse operation modes have also been plotted in Fig. 11 as a function of the emitter current. Despite the simple structure, reasonable forward current gain values have been obtained allowing a fan-out of five which is usually adequate for the logic design. The inverse current gain β_i is sufficiently large to make current hogging negligible.

To test the propagation delay of MTL, a seven-stage closed-loop inverter chain has been built. Fig. 12 shows the chip microphotograph of this circuit and its output signal for three power levels differing by factors of 10. This oscillogram demonstrates an outstanding feature of MTL, namely that the same MTL logic chip can be operated at hugely different power levels to select the performance suitable for a given application. In Fig. 13 the measured delay has been plotted versus power dissipation over several orders of magnitude. The minimum delay time of ≈10 ns corresponds to a common base switching time constant $\tau \approx 3$ ns for the n-p-n transistor. At low power, where this switching time constant has a negligible effect compared to the charging times of the depletion layer capacitances, a constant power-delay product results as low as 0.35 pJ.

The high functional density of MTL is illustrated by the photomicrograph [Fig. 14(a)] of a half-adder, implemented on an area of only 11 mils², with 0.3-mil-wide metal lines and 0.15-mil spacing. The oscillogram Fig. 14(b), shows the input and output signals of this circuit.

VI. Summary and Conclusions

MTL as a novel bipolar logic concept has been discussed and experimentally verified. It is based on inverters having decoupled multicollector outputs for the logical combinations. These inverters are powered by a direct injection of minority carriers into their common n-emitter plane. MTL is a self-isolated structure requiring no ohmic load resistors. This simple structure offers considerable advantages of which the most significant ones are

1) high noise immunity and good driving capabilities (TTL compatible);
2) fabrication substantially simplified (only four mask steps through metalization);
3) extremely high functional density (about 1000 gates on 130×130-mils^2 chip with present manufacturing tolerances, such as 0.3-mil metal lines, 0.15-mil spacing, and 0.2×0.2-mil contact holes);
4) excellent power-delay product (0.35 pJ above 100-ns delay, 0.7 pJ in the 15–20-ns range, and power speed externally alterable).

These results have been obtained on a very simple structure implemented by using readily available processing facilities. By taking advantage of modern technological accomplishments, improvements can be expected without increasing the processing complexity.

VII. Acknowledgment

The authors are indebted to D. Young[3] and his department for the test chip artwork and to H. Rupprecht[3] and his department for test chip fabrication. Special thanks are due to C. S. Chang[3] for valuable contributions.

References

[1] B. L. Murphy, V. J. Glinski, P. A. Gary, and R. A. Pedersen, "Collector diffusion isolated integrated circuits," *Proc. IEEE,* vol. 57, pp. 1523–1527, Sept. 1969.
[2] V. J. Glinski, "A three-mask bipolar integrated circuit structure," presented at the IEEE Int. Electron Devices Meeting, Washington, D. C., Oct. 29, 1969.
[3] D. K. Lynn, C. S. Meyer, and D. J. Hamilton, *Analysis and Design of Integrated Circuits.* New York: McGraw-Hill, 1967, p. 200.
[4] S. K. Wiedmann and H. H. Berger, "Super-integrated bipolar memory device," presented at the IEEE Int. Electron Devices Conf., Oct. 11–13, 1971.
[5] ——, "Super-integrated bipolar memory device," *Electronics,* vol. 45, Feb. 1972.
[6] A. Weinberger, "Large scale integration of MOS complex logic: A layout method," *IEEE J. Solid-State Circuits,* vol. SC-2, pp. 182–190, Dec. 1967.
[7] D. K. Lynn, C. S. Meyer, and D. J. Hamilton, *Analysis and Design of Integrated Circuits.* New York: McGraw-Hill, 1967, p. 222.

[3] IBM Components Division, East Fishkill, N. Y.

I²L takes bipolar integration a significant step forward

Extraordinary compactness is achieved in new microprocessor
while speed is increased up to five-fold over n-channel devices;
4-bit controllers to 16-bit minicomputers can be simulated

by Richard L. Horton, Jesse Englade, and Gerald McGee, *Texas Instruments, Dallas, Texas*

☐ For specialty applications such as watch circuits and linear control elements, integrated injection-logic circuits are already in production. But only with the development of purely digital techniques can system designers realize the full impact of this new bipolar structure. To this end, an extremely compact I²L gate has been devised that does not require isolation between elements within the gate—in contrast to I²L linear types that rely on conventional, space-consuming pn junctions to separate their devices. In the new, non-isolated I²L form, gates shrink to the size of a single transistor, so that, together with their low power capabilities, digital I²L structures may contain thousands of gates on a single high-performing bipolar chip.

With these non-isolated gate structures, a 4-bit bipolar microprocessor chip (Fig. 1) has been built that operates up to five times faster than today's n-channel devices. At the same time, this I²L processor element, which is directly compatible with existing bipolar interface circuits, provides greater instruction capability than n-channel designs. And because the 4-bit device is expandable to larger systems with simple interconnections, this circuit element can handle a wide range of computer functions—from simple 4-bit controller jobs to full 16-bit minicomputer process control functions.

True, the processor speeds achievable with these first-generation I²L gates—propagation delays of 20 to 50 nanoseconds—are not as fast as with today's TTL technologies. But techniques to boost I²L speeds toward the TTL level while still maintaining a compact low-power LSI format are

known to be on the way. These integrated-injection logic chips will, for the first time, provide process control and computer system designers with the full benefit of highly efficient bipolar LSI circuits.

Part 1: Fundamental structure.

All the size and low-power advantages of integrated injection logic come directly from shrinking the old direct-coupled transistor logic (DCTL) into a single complementary transistor equivalent. In this scheme (Fig. 2) the resistor in the DCTL gate is replaced by an active current source; the emitter-grounded output transistor pair is replaced by a single multicollector transistor, and a simple pnp transistor is added to serve as the current injector source.

Thus the six transistors of a three-input DCTL gate are reduced to a single I²L transistor pair. The vertical npn transistor Q_1, with the multiple collectors C_1 and C_2, operates as an inverter, and the lateral pnp transistor Q_2 serves as both the current source and active load. No large ohmic resistors are required for either the source or load function. What is perhaps most ingenious, the base of the multi-collector npn transistor is made common with the collector of the lateral pnp current source, while the base of the current source is made common with the emitter of the multi-collector npn. Because of the elements in common (see panel p. 85), the entire I²L gate, when it is configured on silicon, only takes up the room of a single multi-emitter transistor.

Again, the basic I²L

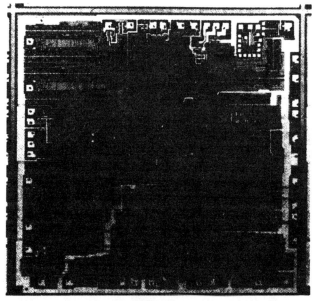

1. The first. Entering the picture is the industries first standard-product microprocessor built with the integrated injection logic bipolar technique. This 4-bit-slice device, SBP0400, bridges performance gap between today's n-channel and Schottky devices.

Reprinted with permission from *Electronics*, February 6, 1975, pp. 83–90. Copyright © McGraw-Hill, Inc. 1975. All rights reserved.

2. Structure. Digital form of I²L has vertical npn transistor Q_1 with multiple collectors C_1 and C_2 operating as inverter; and lateral pnp transistor Q_2 as current-source and load

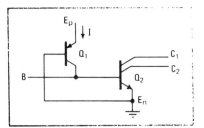

structure can take two forms: isolated or non-isolated. The isolated form, which so far has received more public attention [*Electronics*, Oct. 3, 1974, p. 111-118], makes use of a conventional reverse-biased pn junction for component isolation. Since this form of isolation completely separates adjacent devices, it is the isolated I²L structures that are used in circuits containing mixed-component functions.

Fabricated with a 6-mask bipolar process, isolated I²L allows all other standard bipolar and MOS design techniques (Schottky TTL, ECL gates and memories, and n-channel MOS devices, including linear functions) to be combined directly with the I²L gates. This means that along with I²L digital sections, a single low cost monolithic chip can hold such linear and special buffer functions as LED drivers, memory decoders, current regulators, op amps, comparators, oscillators, and very-fast digital TTL or ECL logic.

Indeed, the I²L watch, entertainment and other commercial LSI circuits already in production are made with this technique. This isolated form of I²L can also be combined with Schottky and ECL memory structure to provide fast low-cost bipolar memory designs. Here the I²L-type gates would form the internal array of the memory, while the TTL or ECL transistors would form the peripheral interface elements. RAMs with I²L-type arrays (74S209) have already been built, pointing to a new low-cost bipolar approach to medium-performance (100 ns) memories.

The boss LSI technology

Even as isolated forms of I²L have endless possibilities for combining linear and digital functions into heretofore-unattainable degrees of circuit integration, it is non-isolated I²L that results in the most dense and efficient form of bipolar logic yet devised for the fabrica-

tion of very complex digital ICs. Utilizing the single transistor switch with the common ground planes shown in Fig. 2, this logic form capitalizes on the high carrier mobility inherent in bulk silicon structures. It need not be isolated, nor does it require ground metalization, because in this single-transistor gate the output of one gate serves as the input of the next.

Nevertheless, these I²L gates are capable of operating at nanosecond speeds and microwatt power dissipation (Table 1), with a component density 10 times that of conventional bipolar circuits, and twice that of p-MOS. Furthermore, non-isolated I²L circuits can be built with a 4-mask, two-diffusion bipolar process, at high yields—an essential requirement of any LSI process where thousands of gates per circuit must be fabricated on a wafer of complex circuits.

The advantages of the I²L process are shown in Fig. 3, which compares the process complexity and gate-size relationships of the various digital technologies in use today. In process complexity, I²L is simpler than all other techniques except low-performing p-MOS, which requires the same number of mask steps but needs one less diffusion step. And, compared to I²L, the newly-evolved depletion-load MOS technology, being relied on so heavily in today's n-channel memories and microprocessors, requires an additional mask step. It also requires two ion implementation steps as opposed to none for I²L although depletion-load MOS does use one less diffusion. In any case, compared to TTL's 7 masks and 4 diffusions, and C-MOS's 6 masks and 3 diffusions, the I²L process is simplicity itself.

Even so, this process results in the smallest component size of any technology in operation—as Fig. 3 shows, the product is less than one tenth the area of either a conventional TTL or C-MOS gate. Even the newest LSI forms of TTL occupy four times as much space.

Speed-power comparisons (Fig. 4) show still another advantage of I²L gates; they have the lowest speed power product of any technology in use today, approaching a theoretical limit of 0.001 picojoule. Even non-optimized I²L test bars have operated with 100 ns propagation delays while dissipating 100nW of power per gate—surpassing today's best C-MOS circuits.

Constant speed-power

Yet, unlike C-MOS, whose power dissipation rises dramatically at higher speeds, I²L gates can be pushed to speeds of 10 to 20 ns while maintaining a virtually constant speed-power product. Indeed, an I²L gate optimized around a high-speed 50-ns format is the one used in the current 4-bit microprocessor circuit design.

Finally, Fig. 5 shows where I²L processor circuits fit into the spectrum of computer applications. I²L microprocessors can potentially handle all the jobs now being performed by today's MOS systems—from non-real time processing, to calculator jobs requiring millisecond add times, to the 50-ns real-time processing of some mainframe controller systems. Second and third generation I²L designs are expected to significantly extend this capability into higher performance applications (Fig. 6).

Taking the simplest case, one in which a single npn grounded-emitter transistor forms the basic I²L gate,

TABLE 1: COMPARISON OF I²L AND TTL PROPERTIES		
Parameter	I²L	TTL
Packing density (7-μm mask details)	120 − 200 gates/mm²	20 gates/mm²
Speed-power product	4 − 0.2 pJ/gate	100 pJ/gate
Gate delay	25 − 250 ns	10 ns
Power dissipation	6 nW − 70 μW	10 mW
Supply voltage	1 − 15 V	3 − 73 V
Logic voltage swing	0.6 V	5 V
Current range (per gate)	1 nA − 1 mA	2 mA
Interconnect	Single-level	Double-level

How it's built

Designers at Texas Instruments are evaluating a number of I²L fabrication techniques. The one used to build their first microprocessor was chosen for its compatibility with existing TTL production facilities.

An I²L circuit's high packing density is due mainly to the simplicity of designing with a single transistor gate. In the accompanying illustration, for example—working from the bottom up in the cross-section of an I²L gate—the n+ substrate serves not only as the structural base for fabrication, but also as a common ground plane to interconnect all the grounded-emitter transistor gates. This eliminates the need for any surface metallization for ground interconnections. Likewise, the thick n-type epitaxial layer, grown on top of the n+ substrate, serves not only as the grounded-emitter region of the vertical npn switch, but also as the grounded-base region of the lateral pnp injector.

Continuing upward in the cross-section, the first of the two diffusions serves as the p-base region of the vertical npn, and also as the p-collector region of the lateral pnp injector. The second diffusion completes the I²L gate by providing the multiple-collector n+ regions of the vertical npn.

Metallization is then deposited and etched to provide interconnection between various I²L transistor gates. Note that the lateral pnp is integrated into the vertical npn structure and therefore does not exist as a discrete component. Furthermore, a single lateral pnp can be utilized as a current injector for multiple npn gages as long as symmetry in the layout is maintained to avoid current-hogging. Density is enhanced by the simplicity of a single-transistor gate requiring no component isolation.

The similarity existing between I²L and TTL circuits is worth noting. This, essentially, is in the similarity between the basic multi-collector I²L transistor and the common multi-emitter TTL transistor. The I²L multi-collector regions correspond to TTL's multi-emitters, the I²L and TTL bases occupy similar regions, while the I²L emitter and TTL collector reside in the deepest n regions. An I²L multicollector transistor is, in essence, a TTL multi-emitter transistor operated upside down. Transistor logic in I²L structures is implemented by controlling inverse beta, while in TTL structures the forward beta is controlled.

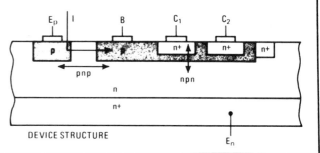

DEVICE STRUCTURE

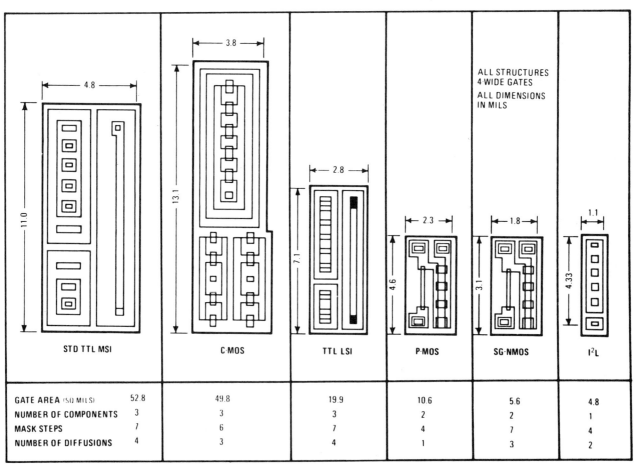

	STD TTL MSI	C-MOS	TTL LSI	P-MOS	SG-NMOS	I²L
GATE AREA (SQ MILS)	52.8	49.8	19.9	10.6	5.6	4.8
NUMBER OF COMPONENTS	3	3	3	2	2	1
MASK STEPS	7	6	7	4	7	4
NUMBER OF DIFFUSIONS	4	3	4	1	3	2

3. Shaping up. An I²L gate fabricated with non-isolated elements saves space and is simple to build, compared to other techniques. It's simpler than all but p-MOS gates and its 5 square mil area makes it the smallest. All structures shown are 4-wide gates.

Electronics/February 6, 1975

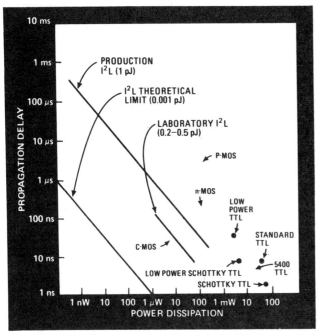

4. Speed/power. The beauty of an I²L gate is its ability to operate at very low power levels while running at respectably fast gate speeds. The same is not true, generally, of today's C-MOS circuits, whose low power properties are sacrificed at high frequencies.

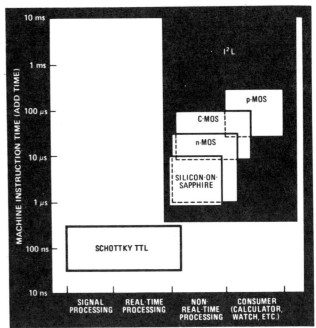

5. Tomorrow. An I²L microprocessor potentially can take over all jobs now being done by MOS units. This includes non-real-time and consumer-type applications. What's more, I²L does overlap into real-time—processing jobs now being handled by TTL products.

positive NAND logic is implemented through the use of a multiple-collector npn switch functioning as an inverter. Here the logical isolation required to perform NAND logic is accomplished by utilizing the multiple-collector outputs to function as isolated ANDing inputs to the stages that follow. Positive NOR logic can also be readily implemented by wire-ORing the I²L gate outputs (Fig. 7). Now, when the I²L npn transistor is normally biased on

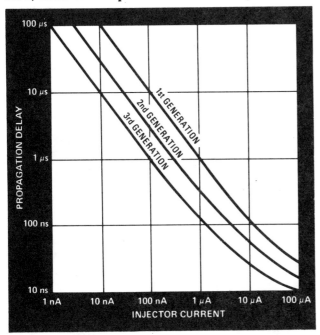

6. Only starting. Impressive as today's production I²L devices are, faster ones are coming. This year's second generation devices and next year's third generation will show steady improvements. Ten-microsecond to 20-nanosecond devices are forseeable.

(low output) by a lateral pnp current-injector transistor, which is connected between the base of the npn and an external current source, switching action is accomplished by the steering of this injector current.

This is done by adjusting the base-to-emitter gate input voltage V_{BE}. A low input voltage of less than one V_{BE} (750 mV) pulls injector current out of the input through the on (low) output of the driving gate. Robbed of its base drive in this manner, an I²L transistor gate will turn off with its open-collector output rising to a high logic level.

Steering the current

This voltage level, as with any open-collector logic, is determined by the load circuit, or pull-up, utilized. In a typical I²L circuit design this is simply the clamp level at the input of the next stage—one V^{BE} (750 mV) above ground.

A high input logic level is achieved, essentially by default, when a low-impedance path of less than one V_{BE} potential is absent from the input. Deprived of a ground path of less than one V_{BE} potential, the injector current will forward bias the I²L transistor gate into the on state and produce an output low-logic level equal to one V_{sat} above ground, or typically 50 mV. It is therefore possible to achieve, by simple steering of the injector current on the npn switch, typical I²L internal logic swings of 700 mV—this from a V_{sat} of +50 mV to a V_{BE} of +750 mV.

Figure 8 shows how I²L transistor gates are interconnected to perform a basic logic function. The NAND gate logic is that of a common TTL D-type flip-flop. The schematic directly below it shows the same D-type flip-flop in I²L NAND/NOR logic at a component count of one transistor per gate. Directly below the I²L schematic is a

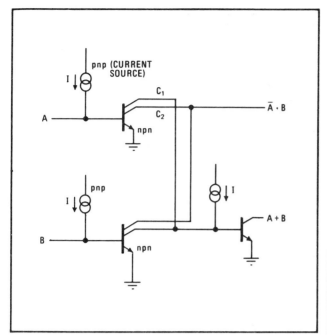

7. Sound logic. NAND functions use the multiple-collector npn switch as an inverter, where logical isolation is obtained by making the collector outputs function as isolated ANDing inputs of the next stages. NOR logic results from WIRE-ORing gate outputs.

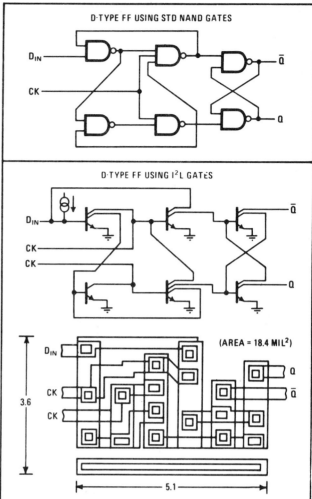

8. Easy fit. Basic to the high packing density of I²L digital circuits is its one-transistor-gate structure. Here a standard D-type flip-flop built with I²L gates takes up less than 20 square mills; it is so small it could fit under a single bonding pad.

scaled topographical drawing of the I²L D-flop. The p-injector used to power the flop is indicated along the drawing's horizontal axis. Note that an entire I²L static flip flop, which would require six 4 by 4 mil bonding pads interfaced to the outside world, would virtually fit under one of those bonding pads. It is this compact geometry that accounts for the high component density of the I²L LSI processor designs currently in production.

All told, practical I²L gates can handle a range of 6 magnitudes or more of injector current—from picoamps to microamps—at speeds ranging from hundreds of microseconds to tens of nanoseconds. They can be powered up for maximum speed, then powered down by a magnitude of 100 to 10,000 without losing functions or data (if they're memories). They do not display increased power dissipation with frequency nor produce the switching noise transients common in standard push-pull logic built with C-MOS or TTL. They require neither gold doping nor Schottky clamping, as does conventional logic in which transistors are easily saturated.

I²L logic is fully static, requiring no multiphase clocks, and temperature stability is superior, with circuits capable of military temperature range operation from –55°C to 125°C.

Designing I²L digital circuits

With the basic gate layouts of Figs. 7 and 8, a designer can use a variety of input/output circuits (Fig. 9). In the I²L microprocessor chip described in this article, input/output characteristics were selected with one objective in mind: full TTL compatibility. The input circuit, shown in Fig. 9(a), is actually an RTL configuration modified for TTL compatibility. An input threshold of nominally +1.5 volts is achieved with two 10-kilohm

resistors functioning as a voltage divider, which boosts the one V_{BE} threshold of the input transistor to 1.5 V.

The input electrical characteristics, plotted in Fig. 10(a) as input current vs. input voltage, show the 10 kilohm load line and the threshold knee at +1.5 V. These high-impedance, high-threshold characteristics were chosen to reduce input loading and to increase the input noise margin over a standard TTL input, yet they retain full compatability with all 5-v logic families. The I²L inputs also utilize an input-clamping diode to limit negative excursions, or ringing, on the receiving end of a transmission line.

The output schematic and its characteristics, as shown in Figs. 9(b) and 10(b), are virtually identical to TTL or DTL open collector outputs. When turned on, an I²L open collector output will rapidly fall towards ground potential, producing a low logic level.

Standard design practice for I²L is again patterned after TTL in that I²L outputs are generally over-designed by 100%. While a typical I²L output will sink 40 mA without pulling out of saturation, the outputs of I²L logic circuits are guaranteed to sink 20 mA (10 Schottky TTL loads) at 400 mV maximum under worst-case condi-

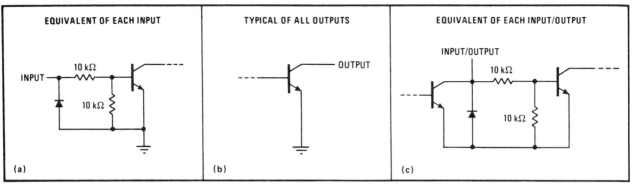

| EQUIVALENT OF EACH INPUT | TYPICAL OF ALL OUTPUTS | EQUIVALENT OF EACH INPUT/OUTPUT |

(a)   (b)   (c)

9. Compatible. These input and output sketches show how easy I²L gates can be made compatible with TTL gates. The input in (a) is actually a modified RTL structure, while outputs (b) and (c) are virtually identical with TTL or DTL open-collector outputs.

tions. The high-logic output level, output rise times, and input-noise immunity are determined by a discrete pull-up resistor.

Common I/O configurations, as in Fig. 9(c), can also be utilized for improved functional performance and higher packing densities. This schematic is recognizable as an integration of the separate I/O schematics and electrical characteristics already described.

Powering an I²L circuit

I²L gates, which are current-injected-logic when placed across a curve tracer, resemble a silicon switching diode, a fact that enables a designer to use any voltage or current source capable of supplying the desired current at a voltage of 850 mV or greater. No tricky impedance matching or feedback is required. Perfectly acceptable would be a dry-cell battery, a 5-V TTL supply, a programable current supply for power-up and power-down operation—practically whatever power source is convenient.

If a 5-V TTL power supply were to be used, for example, a series dropping resistor would be connected between the 5-V supply and the injector pins of a typical I²L microprocessor device for selecting the desired operating current. The resistor value in this case would be:

$$R = E/I, \text{ or } R_{drop} = V_{supply} - 0.85 \text{ V})/150 \text{ mA}$$
$$R = (5.0 \text{ V} - 0.85 \text{ V})/0.15 \text{ A} = 28 \text{ ohms}$$

Part II: The I²L microprocessor

The first LSI digital circuit built with non-isolated I²L logic is a microprocessor chip slice designated SBP 0400, which stands for "semiconductor bipolar processor," 400 series. It is a 40-pin, 4-bit microprogramable binary processor element containing more than 1,450 gates—easily the most complex standard product bipolar logic chip built to date.

Containing all the functions required for 4-bit parallel processing (except for sequencing controls), the features of the SBP0400, as shown in the block diagram of Fig. 11, could only be duplicated by using 30 to 40 small and medium-scale TTL integrated circuits.

The chip contains:
■ A 16-function symmetrical arithmetic logic unit (ALU) that has full-carry look-ahead logic.

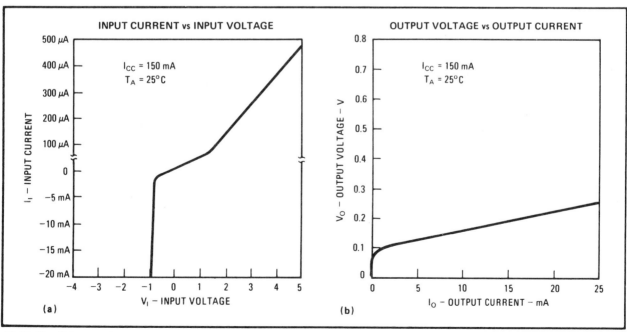

(a)   (b)

10. Plotting It. Input and output current-voltage characteristics makes designing with I²L a pleasure. The input shows a 10 kilohm load line.

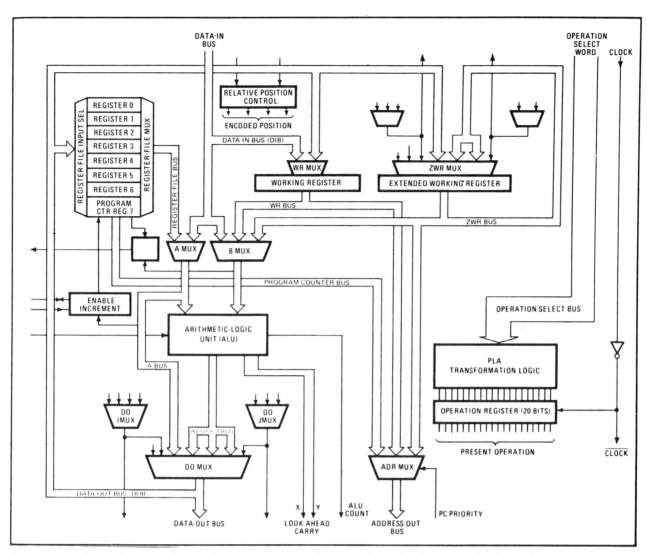

11. Organized. Among the principal blocks of the SPB0400 chip are the 16-function arithmetic logic unit (ALU), and the factory programable logic array (PLA), which provides 512 standard one-clock operations.

■ An 8-word general register file that includes a program counter and incrementor.

■ Two 4-bit working registers that can handle both single- and double-length operations.

■ Scaled-shifting multiplexers enabling the chip to handle a wide variety of interface conditions.

■ Finally—and perhaps the most innovative feature—a factory programable logic array (PLA) instead of the usual fixed-size control ROM. The 512 standard operations programed into this on-chip logic array provides a greater degree of instruction capability than is achievable by any other standard bipolar or MOS LSI processor.

This basic 4-bit I²L processor slice is directly expandable in 4 bit multiples—Fig. 12 shows the configuration for a 16-bit system. Like the single 4-bit chip, larger multichip systems provide full-carry look-ahead logic and parallel access to all control, data, and address I/O functions. It is this parallel access, together with the high bipolar speeds (typical propagation time of 110 to 530 ns at power dissipation of 128 mW), that's responsible for the device's short cycle time capability.

Thanks to the program flexibility offered by the PLA

and standard micro-programing techniques, this single 4-bit slice offers a designer a repertoire of 512 one-clock operations, from which a wide range of instruction can be implemented. This compares with a fixed instruction capability of less than 80 for today's second generation n-channel microprocessors, and less than 125 basic operations today's TTL bit-slice systems. This large one-clock operation capability means that a wide range of existing designs can be emulated without loss of software compatibility or increased software investment.

Indeed, virtually any set of instructions is available. In a single one-microsecond clock cycle, for example, any one of 459 non-redundant operations can be selected, including such complicated tasks as transferring data from the processor's register to the external memory, or from memory to register, or from register to register; modifications of the operand or combinations of modifications by means of the 8 arithmetic or 8 boolean functions residing in the ALU; single or double precision arithmetic shifts, with protection of single- or double-signed binary words; single or double precision logical shifts, and so on.

Again, the key to the processor's high flexibility is the

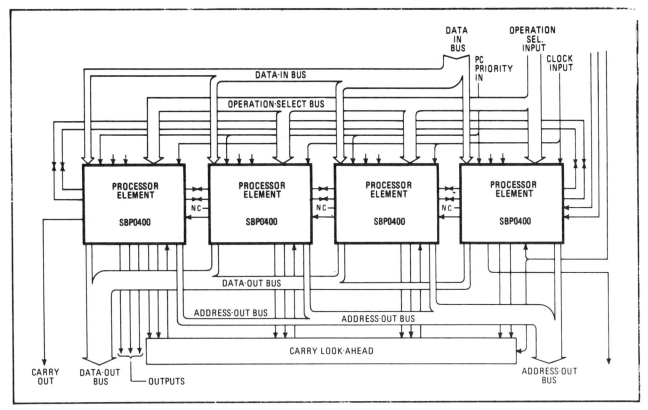

12. Expanded. Four SBP 0400 chips form the heart of a 16-bit parallel machine that has full-carry look-ahead operation. This system can efficiently emulate many low-end minicomputer applications.

programable logic array. As a factory-programable block of combinational logic that forms the operation transformation control center, the PLA decodes the 9-bit operation-select word input lines and generates a 20-bit internal control word. This control word is stored in the operations register and contains the appropriate logical operation—functional-block, bus-enable, and/or bus-select, for execution of the decoded instruction.

Using the processor

The operations register is composed of 20 D-type edge-triggered flip-flops. Upon each positive transition at the clock terminal, the operation register loads the preset PLA output. Loaded, the operations register continuously enables the various functional blocks for execution of the ongoing operation, while the PLA can be receiving the instructions for the next operation.

The 4-bit, parallel, symetrical binary arithmetic logic unit (ALU) meanwhile provides the arithmetic/boolean, operand combination/modification mechanism. The ALU, as directed by the operations register, performs one of eight arithmetic operations, or one of eight boolean operations, on either or both of two operands. The two operands are bused, one to the A input port of the ALU (Fig. 11) via the A bus, and one to the B input port of the ALU via the B bus. The A input port has access to the register-file bus and data-in bus. The B input port has access to the data-in, working-register and extend-working-register buses.

The SBP0400 has accommodations for ALU ripple carry-in and ALU ripple carry-out. To facilitate look-ahead generation across larger word sizes (over 8-bit

lengths) each SBP0400 has output accommodations for both ALU carry-generate (Y) and ALU carry-propagate (X) which are compatible for use with a standard TTL look-ahead generator.

Register file

This 8-word, 4-bit set of D-type general registers is controlled by the operations register. The registers can be used as temporary storage for source data needed in existing processor routines.

An additional register file (location seven) has the added capability of performing as a program counter. Accessed in the same manner as the other files, RF7 is not only presettable but it can also be controlled externally for incrementation by one or two on the next clock transition. This capability is available at the program-counter-carry-in input and the increment-by-one-or-two input.

In addition to the integral operation (pipelining) register, implementation of overlapping instruction fetch and execute commands is further simplified as the content of the program counter is directly available at the address-out bus (AOB). Regardless of the conditions established by the present instruction, a PC priority input overrides and routes the PC data on the AOB input terminal.

For cascading purposes, the most significant output bit at intermediate and least significant package positions is available at the PCCOUT terminal. Depending on the significance of the SBP0400's relative position, these functions are under the control of the POSO and PSOI inputs.   □

The concept of injection coupling, that is, the coupling (by direct injection of minority carriers) of a chain of side-by-side diffused islands which form successive lateral pnp (or npn) bipolar transistors was introduced by Wiedmann in 1973. His paper entitled "Injection-Coupled Memory: A High-Density Static Bipolar Memory," (paper IX-5) demonstrated the bilateral use of injection coupling between three successive p-type diffusions in order to accomplish the read-write operations in a static bipolar memory cell.

The principle of injection coupling was subsequently incorporated into digital logic techniques either as an addition to conventional I^2L (papers II-2 and -4) or as a wholly injection-coupled logic structure called "current hogging logic" (CHL) (papers II-1 and -3). These logic techniques represent direct extensions of or off-shoots from I^2L, and the study of their implementations is relevant to the development and application of the more general injection logic concept.

In paper II-1 Lehning introduces the technique of using injection coupling for the implementation of logic gates in CHL. The output current driver for a CHL gate is a normally operated, isolated npn. Thus the high current drive of the npn permits multiple fan-out while multiple fan-in is also available as in conventional I^2L. Consequently, the requirement for an isolated npn means that CHL cannot be fabricated in a simple four-mask (n⁺-substrate) process as can I^2L but must be implemented in a fully isolated buried-collector process. However, the fact that up-npn's are not used may well be the single greatest advantage of CHL. CHL represents a means of implementing digital logic along with analog circuits in a standard, high-voltage, analog process without the need for any process alterations aimed at improving the up-npn beta. The claims made for CHL are good noise immunity and high functional density. The good dynamic noise immunity arises from the high power-delay product (on the order of 100 pJ, as compared to 1 pJ or less for I^2L). This performance is mainly due to CHL's very long delay times which are the result of the switching of the lateral pnp's. The logic circuit and layout of Lehning's Fig. 6 are offered as evidence of high functional density for CHL. However, it should be noted that each of the four input currents I_1, I_2, I_4, and I_5 must be supplied by npn devices which are isolated and therefore consume a large area. Additionally, the three input currents I_3, I_6, and I_7 must be supplied by isolated npn's which may also be required to incorporate "isolation" pnp's and, consequently, consume an even greater area. Thus the claim for high functional density must not be judged merely upon an "out-of-context" portion of a complete integrated circuit. Lehning has pointed out that the transfer function for CHL (without the output npn) is strictly linear. This is a quite obvious result, since the gate merely performs an algebraic summation of currents.

In summary, because of CHL's very poor speed performance, it is not likely that CHL will be adopted as a general-purpose digital logic technique. However, since it can be implemented in a high voltage analog process without process alterations, it may find application in slow-speed, analog-process compatible digital logic, especially in circuits intended for high noise environments with only modest speed requirements.

The second paper, by Müller, presents a form of I^2L with its injector coupled to the base of the up-npn by way of an intermediate p-type collector–injector as was used in Wiedmann's original injection coupled memory cell. The basic operation of the injection coupled I^2L injector and (npn) base is the same as the CHL logic operation. Müller shows that CHIL results in an area savings of approximately 17 percent, while increasing the power-delay product by 25 percent when compared to conventional I^2L. The increase in the power-delay product is again (as in CHL) due to the increased delay incurred in the switching of the lateral coupling pnp. It should be noted that an I^2L npn which is injection-coupled to its injector receives a lower equivalent base current drive than a directly injected npn. Thus either the up-npn's in CHIL must have higher up-betas or the CHIL/I^2L gates must be scaled in order to permit the CHIL gates to be able to drive conventional I^2L gates in the same circuit. Thus CHIL (like CHL), because of its speed limitations, will not be widely adopted but may offer advantages under special circumstances.

The third paper (II-3) on computer-aided device modeling for CHL is valuable in that it offers insight into the physical operation of the injection-coupling of the lateral pnp portions of CHL and CHIL. In particular, the operation of the "floating" collector–injector is established quantitatively. The two-dimensional simulations of the CHL structure yield three-dimensional plots of carrier concentrations and potential distributions which permit the visualization of the physical mechanisms which govern the device operation. A direct consequence of the insight gained is that the correct approach to a simplified analytic model is clearly indicated. The material presented in Fig. 7 is worthy of careful study, since it offers not only insight into CHL (and CHIL) but is also useful for the understanding of I^2L in general. The major result of this paper is its equation (2), which permits the calculation of the current transfer of a gate or logic function. Note that the only example of a current transfer calculation is shown in Fig. 9c. Finally, it should be pointed out that only the lateral pnp portions of the CHL gate deserve two-dimensional numerical simulation since the down-npn output-current-drive device can be treated adequately by conventional techniques.

The final paper (II-4) presents a variation upon I^2L which provides a function similar to that provided by CHIL as described by Müller in paper II-2. Here again, a coupling pnp is used to alter the operation of an I^2L gate. However, in injection coupled synchronous logic (ISL), the coupling pnp is not intended to be capable of completely turning off the up-npn. Instead, it is used to control the time delay involved in the turn-on of the I^2L gate. Note here that the coupling pnp can only slow down the I^2L gate and cannot increase the speed beyond that which would be achieved with an I^2L gate alone. The ISL technique permits higher functional density at the expense of slower speed by incorporating the effects of the switching speed of the lateral coupling pnp. The major limitations of the paper are as follows. 1) No mention is made of the effects of the extra control pnp upon the terminal up-beta of the I^2L npn. The extra pnp collector alongside the npn's base will result in a large effective recollection factor for the I^2L gate. Consequently, either lower up-beta will result or the process and/or structure will need modification in order to maintain an adequate up-beta for the npn's. 2) The comparison of maximum toggle frequency for ISL and I^2L flip-flops is not completely fair. A better comparison would have considered the absolute maximum toggle frequencies for ISL and I^2L. Additionally, the comparison should have also included flip-flops which use the technique introduced by Tucci and Russell in paper VIII-1, whereby an asymmetry is introduced in the pnp injectors in order to reduce the number of I^2L gates needed for a divide-by-two circuit. In summary, the ISL approach offers a novel application of injection coupling which may be advantageous in special situations but probably will not receive wide acceptance. Indeed, a similar statement applies to the injection coupling principle in general when it is applied in logic operations. The technique offers advantages in special situations, but as a result of its speed disadvantage relative to I^2L, it will not be widely accepted and applied.

Current Hogging Logic (CHL)—A New Bipolar Logic for LSI

HEINZ LEHNING

Abstract—Logic functions of current hogging logic (CHL) are established by switching the lateral injection current in intermediate collector p-n-p structures. High functional density is achieved, since NOR, NAND, and complex gates can readily be realized and all logic elements can be placed within a common isolation region. CHL is fabricated with a standard buried collector process, and hence is compatible with linear bipolar circuits and other bipolar logic families. Current levels are employed as the logical variables, and the transfer characteristics of an AND-NOR gate are discussed. CHL offers high static and dynamic noise immunity. The paper demonstrates a static frequency divider as an example of an CHL circuit.

INTRODUCTION

RECENTLY, much research has been carried out in the field of bipolar logic circuits especially in regard to high functional density and low power consumption [5]–[7]. Most of the new circuit concepts make use of closely combined n-p-n and p-n-p structures in which the p-n-p sections mainly act as current sources. Moreover, lateral intermediate collector p-n-p transistors have been used as switchable current sources [1], [2]; however, these structures have not yet been employed to perform logic functions. The new logic concept, which is described in this paper, is called "current hogging logic" (CHL) [3]. It uses special intermediate collector p-n-p transistors, which may have several collectors, to realize complex logic functions in a single structure. CHL was designed for fabrication with a standard buried collector process. All results described below have been obtained with 2 $\Omega \cdot$ cm epitaxial material of 10-μm thickness and 2.5-μm base diffusion depth.

BASIC GATES

To explain the mode of operation we first consider a lateral p-n-p transistor, as it is used in standard bipolar technology (Fig. 1). Let the transistor first operate in its active region. Then the base-emitter diode is forward biased, whereas substrate and collector are biased negatively with respect to the emitter. Measurements of the collector current and the substrate current show that in this case the substrate current is more than 100 times smaller than the collector current. This relationship holds for more than four decades of collector current (about

Manuscript received March 29, 1974; revised June 5, 1974. This paper was presented at the International Solid-State Circuits Conference, Philadelphia, Pa.; February 1974.

The author is with the Institut für Theoretische Elektrotechnik, Technische Hochschule Aachen, Aachen, W. Germany.

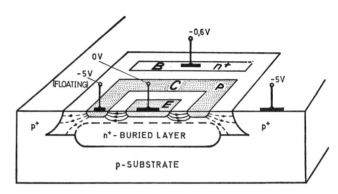

Fig. 1. Lateral p-n-p transistor. Injection current of the emitter is collected with biased collector (current distribution solid), whereas with floating collector additional reinjection appears at the outer collector edge (dashed flow lines).

10 nA through 100 μA for a p-n-p with 17.5 $\times$ 17.5 μm emitter area, 7.5-μm collector width, and 10-μm base width on mask). Hence the buried layer almost ideally screens the substrate from holes, which are injected vertically by the emitter. This results in the boundary condition, that the hole current flows laterally at the surface of the buried layer [4]. Furthermore, hardly any carriers can pass between collector and buried layer. Fig. 1 gives the appropriate current distribution in the base region (solid flow lines).

However, the substrate current with the collector floating becomes very large, about half the size of the collector current in biased condition. Now the collector is nearly at emitter potential. Thus, all the carriers collected from the emitter on the inner edge of the collector are injected into the isolation diffusion and into the substrate on the outer edge of the collector. In this case the collector acts as an emitter in relation to the isolation diffusion (dashed flow lines in Fig. 1).

By placing an additional p-diffused zone between collector and isolation diffusion, the basic logical element of CHL is realized (see Fig. 2(a), isolation diffusion not shown). The additional p-diffused zone, which now collects the injection current of the floating collector, is called the output collector C_o. The collector C_1 is called the control collector. The current of the output collector can be switched off or on by biasing the control collector or letting it float, respectively.

Two other p-diffused zones C', the so called decoupling collectors, are necessary to avoid carrier diffusion to the output collector around the control collector since the

Reprinted from *IEEE J. Solid-State Circuits*, vol. SC-9, pp. 228–233, Oct. 1974.

39

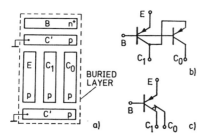

Fig. 2. Basic CHL element, logic structure of inverter: (a) geometry, (b) equivalent circuit, and (c) symbol.

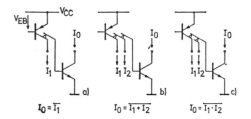

Fig. 4. Basic gates of CHL: (a) inverter, (b) NOR gate, and (c) NAND gate.

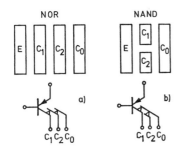

Fig. 3. Geometry and symbols of the logic structures of basic gates: (a) NOR structure and (b) NAND structure.

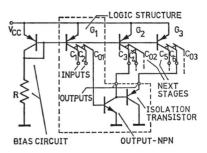

Fig. 5. A basic gate (dashed box) complete with p-n-p logic structure, n-p-n output transistor and vertical p-n-p isolation transistor.

element consists of stripes in this case. The decoupling collectors have to be negatively biased with respect to the emitter, and therefore they are usually connected to the substrate or the base.

The logic gates of CHL basically consist of two parts, the so-called logic structure, which is shown in Fig. 2 in its simplest form, and an n-p-n transistor, which is the so-called output n-p-n (Fig. 4).

Fig. 3 shows how the logic structures of the basic gates are established by placing two control collectors C_1 and C_2 between emitter and output collector. The structure in Fig. 3(a) is the realization of the NOR function. It is evident that the current of the output collector can be switched off by either biasing the control collector C_1 or the control collector C_2. The other structure [Fig. 3(b)] represents the NAND function, since the output current only disappears if C_1 and C_2 are biased simultaneously, supposing no carriers can pass the gap between the control collectors. To achieve this, the gap should not be larger than roughly 10 μm (on mask).

Currents are chosen as the logical variables. Current flow is defined as the logical ONE and no current as the logical ZERO. Applying this definition, Fig. 4 shows the basic gates of CHL.

COMPLETE CHL CIRCUITRY

The dashed box of Fig. 5 contains a CHL NOR gate. It drives two following stages. Decoupling of the inputs of these following stages is provided by isolating those control collectors with diodes, which are not adjacent to their emitters. These isolation diodes are implemented as vertical p-n-p transistors, placed within the isolation region

of the output n-p-n transistor of the previous stage (cf. Fig. 12). Some care has to be taken to avoid parasitic thyristor action.

Gate G_3 in Fig. 5 would not work properly without the isolation transistor. Suppose the base-emitter diode of the isolation transistor is shorted and the control collector C_5 is biased. Then the output current of C_{03} has to disappear since G_3 is a NOR gate. But now C_6 is connected directly to C_3. C_3, however, is placed adjacent to the emitter of G_2 and hence always gets injection current. If the output n-p-n is switched off, a significant amount of this injection reaches the control collector C_6 and is reinjected towards C_5 and C_{03}, thus delivering output current at gate G_3 though its logic output state should be ZERO. Insertion of the isolation transistor eliminates this parasitic injection.

It is evident that the control collectors, which are in the first row adjacent to the appropriate emitters, do not have to be isolated, because they are always supplied with injection current by their own emitters [for example C_1 in Fig. 3(a), and C_1, C_2 in Fig. 3(b)]. Hence, isolation transistors are not necessary if an output n-p-n drives only control collectors which are placed in the first row adjacent to the appropriate emitters.

An additional advantage of the isolation p-n-p's is the possibility to increase the fan-out, since only the p-n-p base current contributes to the collector current of the output n-p-n.

Biasing of all logic structures can be realized as in usual current source configurations, for example with a p-n-p reference transistor and a resistor. Obviously, all logic p-n-p structures of a chip can be placed within a

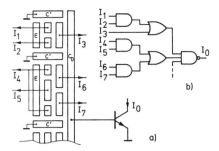

Fig. 6. A complex CHL gate: (a) geometry and (b) equivalent gate circuit.

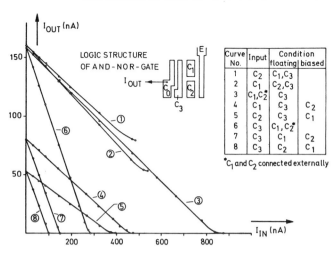

Fig. 7. Transfer characteristics of an AND-NOR structure.

common isolation region. In addition one isolation region is necessary for each gate output, containing the n-p-n output transistor and the isolation p-n-p's.

Complex Gates

An important feature of CHL is that, in addition to NOR and NAND, complex logic functions may be realized within one p-n-p logic structure. This results in the high functional density of more than 200 AND, OR, and NAND gates per mm², even with rather rough geometries. Fig. 6 shows an example of a three-level gate circuit. The two portions between the three decoupling collectors C' correspond to the two AND-OR combinations of Fig. 6(b). By summing up the output current of all gate portions with a common output collector C_o, the NAND gate of the third gate level is realized. The OR gates of the second gate level are established by placing two or more rows of control collectors in series between emitter and output collector, and the AND gates of the first gate level result from suitable subdivision of the control collectors within each row. The fan-out of such complex gates is determined by that portion which delivers the smallest output current in the logical ONE state. With the geometry chosen here, the output currents of both gate portions are equal and the fan-out of the complete gate is about ten. The exact value depends also on the current gain of the output n-p-n transistor. The high fan-in of the structure is obvious. The number of inputs at each of the single gates can still be increased.

Transfer Characteristics of a Logic Structure

As already stated, currents are the logical variables in CHL. To describe the static behavior of logic circuits, the transfer characteristics from input to output currents have to be known. The output current of gates is the collector current of the output n-p-n transistor. The current transfer characteristic of this transistor considered by itself is equal to its dc current gain β. The current transfer characteristic of the p-n-p logic structures has still to be investigated.

Measurements of the current transfer characteristics of the logic structure of an AND-NOR gate are shown in Fig. 7. A scale drawing of mask dimensions of the AND-NOR gate is Fig. 12, where the appropriate output n-p-n transistor is shown, too.

The independent variable in Fig. 7 is the input current of the respective control collector. The transfer curves for each control collector have been measured for all possible logical states of the other control collectors. The output current I_{OUT} is the current of the output collector C_0. All measurements have been made at constant emitter-base voltage ($U_{EB} = 558$ mV). Biased collectors have been connected to the base.

The transfer curves as shown in Fig. 7 completely describe the static behavior of a logic CHL structure. It was found that the injection efficiency of the control collectors and recombination do not influence the current distribution over a large range of current levels. The emitter efficiency is not of importance anyway, since the logic structures are operated with constant emitter-base voltage. Furthermore, almost no current is lost through the buried layer as measurements on circular shaped p-n-p transistors have shown. Hence, the current distribution in a CHL structure is mainly determined by geometry and the bias conditions of the control collectors.

The shape of all transfer curves in Fig. 7 remains unchanged if the emitter-base voltage of the structure is altered. In this case only the scaling in both axes has to be multiplied with a constant factor. All transfer curves are strictly linear functions except for a very small region at the maximum input current. Here the control collectors are leaving the saturation region. Two basically different slopes can be distinguished in Fig. 7. Curves 6–8 are rather steep whereas the others are significantly flatter. The table in Fig. 7 shows that for the three steep curves the control collector C_3 has been used as input, while for the other curves C_1 and C_2 were the inputs.

Curves 3 and 6 can be considered as the transfer curves of a NOR structure which is obtained when C_1 and C_2 are connected. If I_{IN} equals zero, both curves start at the same point on the I_{OUT}-axis ($I_{OUT} \simeq 160$ nA), but the input currents, for which I_{OUT} is zero, are very different (280 nA, 875 nA, respectively). These are the maximum input currents (called I_S in Fig. 8) which can be drawn from the control collectors on the edge of saturation.

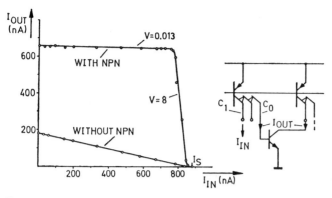

Fig. 8. Current transfer curve of a NOR structure (lower curve) and transfer curve of the complete NOR gate (current source at the output included). V is the slope.

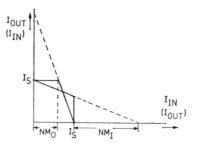

Fig. 9. Definition of the noise margins.

Naturally, the maximum input current of collector C_3 is smaller than the maximum input current of the control collectors C_1 and C_2, since C_3 has a larger effective base width (in relation to the emitter). In addition, the current which is injected by the front sides of the floating collectors C_1 and C_2 does not reach the control collector C_3. For the same reason the maximum output current ($I_{IN} = 0$) of a logic structure is always smaller than the maximum input current ($I_{OUT} = 0$) of the appropriate control collector and therefore the slope of the transfer curves of logic CHL structures is always smaller than one.

Usually one would expect the transfer curves 1 and 2, 4 and 5, and 7 and 8 to be identical. However, the gate measured in Fig. 7 has an unsymmetrical emitter in relation to C_1 and C_2. Thus, C_1 gets additional injection from the emitter head.

Transfer Characteristic of a Complete Gate

Fig. 8 shows the measured interdependence of the input and output currents using a NOR gate as an example. We see two measured current transfer curves. The input current I_{IN} in both cases is the current of the control collector C_1. If the current of the output collector C_0 is considered to be the output current of the gate, the transfer curve of the logic structure is obtained.

If now the collector current of the output n-p-n transistor is considered to be the output current, measurement yields the transfer curve of the complete gate. Now a large range of input current is obtained where the output current is nearly constant, and where the output n-p-n transistor is in saturation because of the current limiting behavior of the following stage. In the small region with high gain the output n-p-n is active and at larger current values than I_s the control collector C_1 also leaves the saturation region. Further increase of the input current is only possible due to the limited input impedance of the collector C_1. Note that the shape of the transfer curve does not only depend on the respective gate itself, but also on the input characteristic of the following stage. This results in optimum adaptation of gates which are connected in series.

Noise Immunity

To explain the static behavior of CHL logic circuits we consider a long chain of identical gates. The transfer curves are shown in Fig. 9. It is an advantage of CHL that the transfer curves of interconnected gates are adapted to each other automatically, since the maximum output current of a gate is determined by the maximum input current I_s of the next stage, provided the output n-p-n transistor is in saturation.

Leakage currents may be neglected in this consideration and so the noise margins can be defined as shown in Fig. 9. NM_0 is the ZERO noise margin. It corresponds to the current which can be drawn from the gate input without affecting the output state. The ONE noise margin NM_I is equal to the current which may additionally be fed into the input terminal of the gate (logical ONE at input) without affecting the output state. This shows that circuits with good static noise immunity can be realized in CHL.

Since currents are the logical variables, gates which are all operated from different supply and substrate potentials may be connected in series, provided all gate inputs are driven through decoupling p-n-p's or diodes. In this case voltage drops on the supply lines do not affect the circuit operation.

The dynamic noise immunity investigated by capacitive coupling in square noise voltages between two logic gates has been found to be very high. This is due to the rather large power-delay product of CHL, which is in the range of 100 pJ for 1 V supply voltage. Furthermore, the power-delay product can be significantly increased by increasing the supply voltage, since the maximum supply voltage of CHL is the V_{CEO} of the n-p-n transistor.

A CHL Static Frequency Divider

A two stage frequency divider was fabricated in CHL. Fig. 10 shows the circuit diagram of one stage. It is a master–slave flip-flop built up of four combined AND-NOR gates. Each of these gates has two rows of control collectors, equivalent to a NOR gate with two inputs. One of the NOR collectors is split into two halves yielding an additional AND gate on the one OR gate input. To each output collector an output n-p-n with a vertical isolation transistor is connected. Biasing of all gates is realized by the external resistor (common to all stages) and a reference transistor. The outputs of each stage are suited

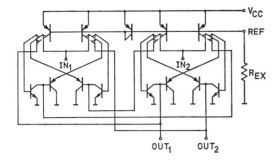

Fig. 10.   Circuit diagram of a frequency divider stage.

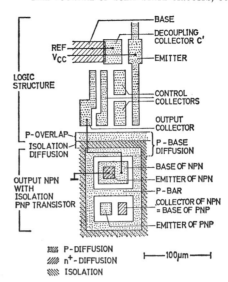

Fig. 12.   Geometry of an AND-NOR gate of the frequency divider (mask dimensions).

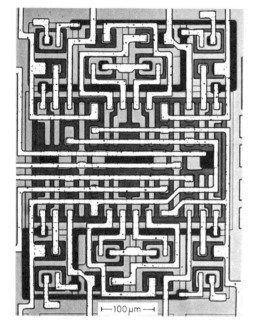

Fig. 11.   Photomicrograph of the two-stage frequency divider.

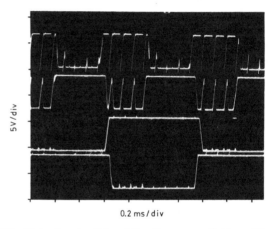

Fig. 13.   Output potentials of the frequency divider with noise.

for driving the next stage inputs. Fig. 11 is a photomicrograph of the complete two stage frequency divider and Fig. 12 shows the geometry of an AND-NOR gate of the divider.

The size of one divider stage is 0.105 mm². The aluminum width is 12.5 μm on the mask with 10-μm clearance, the smallest contact windows are 7.5 × 7.5 μm, and the smallest p-diffusions of the logic structures have a width of 10 μm.

All logic elements share a common isolation region (middle section of Fig. 11) which has a buried layer. Eight additional isolation regions (upper and lower section of Fig. 11) contain the output n-p-n transistors and the isolation p-n-p's. The p-base diffusion is also carried out in the isolation region and overlaps the n-epi islands. This p-diffusion now is used to form a p-bar between the base portion of the output n-p-n transistors and the emitter portion of the respective decoupling p-n-p transistors in order to prevent parasitic thyristor action.

An overlap of the p-diffusion is used as decoupling collector at one edge of the p-n-p logic structure (lower edge of the logic structure in Fig. 12). The same function is achieved on the other edge by an additional p-diffused collector C', which is connected to the base. The emitter facing edge of this collector serves as the reference collector.

Fig. 13 shows the output potentials of the two stage divider including noise, which is created by coupling capacitively a square noise voltage to one output of the first stage (upper trace). Noise at the second stage output is already negligible as long as the voltage spikes are shorter than the flip-flop rise times.

The maximum input frequency of the divider is some hundred kHz at high current and low supply voltage (see Fig. 14). The speed–power product for a combined AND-NOR gate is about 150 pJ for 1.25 V supply voltage. For 10-V supply voltage and 10-μA stage current most elements worked within an ambient temperature range of −30 to +150 °C.

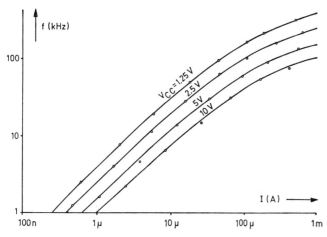

Fig. 14. Maximum input frequency of the divider versus total current of one stage.

CONCLUSION

CHL is a new logic concept which can be fabricated with a standard bipolar process, and is therefore compatible with linear bipolar circuits and other bipolar logic families. The circuitry contains lateral and vertical p-n-p structures and n-p-n transistors, but does not depend on inverse n-p-n current gain. CHL has a large supply voltage range (0.7 V to the V_{CEO} of the n-p-n transistor) and a large supply current range and can be operated over a wide range of ambient temperatures. Since it also offers good static and dynamic noise immunity and high functional density, it is best suited for large-scale integrated (LSI) circuitry which has to be operated in a very noisy environment, for example in automotive systems.

REFERENCES

[1] H. H. Berger, "Integrated separately switchable current sources," *IBM Tech. Disclosure Bulletin*, vol. 14, pp. 1422–1423, Oct. 1971.
[2] S. K. Wiedmann, "Injection-coupled memory: a high-density static bipolar memory," *IEEE J. Solid-State Circuits (Special Issue on Semiconductor Memory and Logic)*, vol. SC-8, pp. 332–337, Oct. 1973.
[3] H. Lehning, "Current hogging logic—a new logic for LSI with noise immunity," in *1974 IEEE Int. Solid-State Circuits Conf., Dig. Tech. Papers*, pp. 18–19.
[4] S. Chou, "An investigation of lateral transistors-DC characteristics," *Solid-State Electron.*, vol. 14, pp. 811–826, Sept. 1971.
[5] K. Hart and A. Slob, "Integrated injection logic: a new approach to LSI," *IEEE J. Solid-State Circuits (Special Issue on Semiconductor Memories and Digital Circuits)*, Vol. SC-7, pp. 347–351, Oct. 1972.
[6] H. H. Berger and S. K. Wiedmann, "Merged transistor logic (MTL)—a low-cost bipolar logic concept," *IEEE J. Solid-State Circuits (Special Issue on Semiconductor Memories and Digital Circuits)*, vol. SC-7, pp. 340–346, Oct. 1972.
[7] H. W. Rüegg and W. Thommen, "Bipolar micropower circuits for crystal-controlled time pieces," *IEEE J. Solid-State Circuits (Special Issue on Micropower Electronics)*, vol. SC-7, pp. 105–111, Apr. 1972.

Current Hogging Injection Logic—A New Logic with High Functional Density

RÜDIGER MÜLLER

Abstract—A new design concept for bipolar integrated circuits with high functional density will be presented. The basic current hogging injection logic (CHIL) gate consists of a lateral intermediate collector structure, where the last collector simultaneously forms the base region of an inversely operated vertical output transistor. Thus a CHIL gate can be looked at as a CHL gate with a functionally integrated output transistor, or as an integrated injection logic (I^2L) inverter with controlled injection. Dc and pulse measurements will be discussed and calculated results with a simple model suitable for computer-aided design (CAD) will be presented. The static noise immunity of CHIL circuits will be compared to CHL and I^2L. CHIL circuits are well suited for large-scale integration (LSI) and are technologically compatible to all circuits fabricated in a standard buried collector (SBC) process.

INTRODUCTION

SINCE the great impact which integrated injection logic (I^2L)/merged transistor logic (MTL) [1], [2] had on bipolar integrated circuits, much research has been done in the field of logic circuits with still higher functional density. Recently, quite a few approaches to this problem were made using double-epitaxial layers [3], two-type-barrier Schottky

Manuscript received March 31, 1975; revised May 30, 1975. This work was supported by the Technical Program of the Federal Department of Research and Technology of the Federal Republic of Germany. This paper was presented at the International Solid-State Circuits Conference, Philadelphia, Pa., February 1975.
The author is with the Research Laboratories, Siemens AG, Munich, Germany.

diodes [4], [5], and Schottky diodes on p-type silicon [3]. For the realization of these circuits, highly advanced technologies are needed, and the arising yield problems will probably limit the application to cases where some of the outstanding characteristics, e.g., low power-delay product, high speed, or good radiation resistivity are really necessary. On the other hand, a new logic concept, called current hogging logic (CHL) [6] was introduced last year. It uses intermediate collector p-n-p transistors for the implementation of logic functions and is fabricated in a standard buried collector (SBC) process. As a drawback, however, this logic has a rather high power-delay product and relatively large area consumption. The following paper will describe a new logic, called current hogging injection logic (CHIL). With this logic multiinput–multioutput gates combine the input flexibility of CHL with the performance and packing density of I^2L. It is fully compatible with I^2L circuits, electrically as well as technologically, but offers a higher degree of flexibility to the circuit designer, which leads to less area consumption for a logic circuit, due to a reduction of the number of gates and a better utilization of the wiring area.

BASIC CHIL STRUCTURE

The fundamental properties of the current hogging effect with a lateral intermediate collector p-n-p structure [6] are briefly recalled in Fig. 1. This structure is realized by three (or more) strip-shaped p-regions located in an n-type

Reprinted from *IEEE J. Solid-State Circuits*, vol. SC-10, pp. 348–352, Oct. 1975.

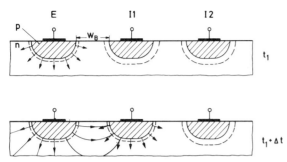

Fig. 1. "Current hogging effect" with a lateral intermediate collector p-n-p structure. The flow lines indicate minority carrier injection, collection and reinjection for floating $I1$.

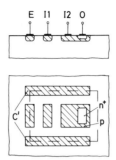

Fig. 2. Schematic cross section and layout of a two-input CHIL gate.

epitaxial layer. The injecting emitter E is fed with a constant current, and thus starts injecting holes into the epi-layer at the time t_1. If the diffusion length of the minority carriers is considerably larger than the spacing w_B, most of the injected holes are collected via the field of the space-charge layer of the adjacent p-region $I1$. If this control collector is disconnected, it will charge up, and after a time interval Δt, start reinjecting holes into the epitaxial layer. Now the same procedure is repeated for the injecting region $I1$ and the collector $I2$. Thus a continuous current flow from the emitter E to collector $I2$ (or IN) will occur. Equation (1) gives an approximate expression for the detectable current I_{IN} at collector IN, where $\alpha_{p\text{-}n\text{-}p}$ is the common base current gain of the lateral p-n-p transistor. Saturation effects can be taken into account by the use of an effective current gain $\alpha'_{p\text{-}n\text{-}p} = I_E/I_C$.

$$I_{IN} = \alpha_{p\text{-}n\text{-}p}^N \cdot I_E. \tag{1}$$

If, on the other hand, the control collector $I1$ is connected to the potential of the epitaxial layer, it will "hog" all the current. This means that only leakage currents can be detected at collector $I2$ (and all collectors located to the right of $I2$).

The current switching effect via an intermediate collector p-n-p transistor can be used for the implementation of logic functions. For a logic gate, however, it is necessary to add an output stage to invert the current direction and to compensate for the different magnitudes of detectable input currents. With CHL [6], a normally operated n-p-n transistor located in an isolation well is used for this purpose.

In contrast to this approach, CHIL uses a functionally integrated output n-p-n transistor, as can be seen in Fig. 2. The upper part shows a schematic cross section of a two-input CHIL gate, and the lower part the corresponding layout. The enlarged control collector $I2$ simultaneously forms the base region of the inversely operated output n-p-n transistor. For a CHIL circuit, the input collectors $I1$ and $I2$ are directly connected to the output transistors of the corresponding previous stage. If these transistors are both switched off, $I1$ and $I2$ are in a more or less floating condition. The injected minority carriers of the emitter E are then collected by input $I1$, and $I1$ will charge up and re-inject holes into the epitaxial layer. These are now collected by input $I2$ and supply the base current that is necessary for turning on the output n-p-n transistor.

If, on the other hand, input $I1$ is pulled down to a low-level voltage of less than approximately 400 mV, it will hog all the current, and the output transistor will be turned off. In the same way, pulling down $I2$ avoids base current flow and cuts off the output transistor. The additional collectors C' are kept at the potential of the epi-layer to avoid parasitic current flow from the emitter E to input $I2$ when $I1$ is pulled down. They can be omitted for an oxide-isolated process.

Thus the function of a CHIL gate can either be explained as a CHL gate with a *functionally integrated* output transistor, or as an I^2L inverter with *controlled injection*. This further step in functional integration results in an area reduction of up to 70 percent compared with CHL. Considering I^2L, CHIL offers the possibility of realizing complex multifunction gates with a single-output n-p-n transistor. It should be noted that this advantage leads to an increased packing density for a complete circuit, since the number of output transistors can be reduced significantly and the wiring area is utilized more efficiently. As far as multioutput gates are concerned, CHIL has the same advantage as I^2L since it uses inversely operated output transistors with multiple collectors.

Fig. 3(a) shows a photomicrograph and the schematic cross section of a two-input–two-output basic NAND gate realized in a SBC process. From left to right the additional collectors C', the emitter E, and the two control collector inputs $I1$ and $I2$ can be seen as p-type diffused regions. Within the largest p-region $I2$, the two n^+-type output collectors are located. The metallization of the additional collector bars can be omitted, as long as a series resistance does not effect the collecting properties of C'. For example, series resistances of up to 100 kΩ are tolerable for stray currents of 5 μA. The following measurements and calculations apply to structures of this type. The corresponding Karnaugh diagram for either output $O1$ or $O2$ is given in Fig. 3(b). The output voltage is low only for high-voltage levels at both inputs $I1$ and $I2$. For positive logic this is equivalent to a NAND function.

CIRCUIT MODELS

In Fig. 4(a) the equivalent circuit for the two-input–two-output CHIL gate of Fig. 3(a) is given. It uses the basic CHL symbol, proposed in [6], for the intermediate collector p-n-p structure, and the well-known multicollector symbol for the inversely operated n-p-n transistor. For positive logic, this equivalent circuit implements the logical NAND. If, on

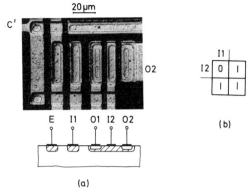

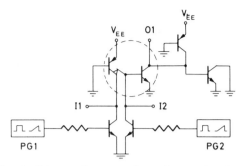

Fig. 3. Two-input–two-output CHIL NAND gate. (a) Photomicrograph and schematic cross section. (b) Karnaugh diagram for output $O1$ or $O2$.

Fig. 5. Circuit diagram of an experimental setup for dc and pulse measurements. Dashed circle indicates basic CHIL gate.

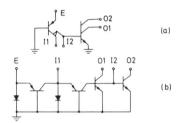

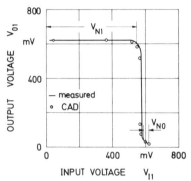

Fig. 4. Two-input–two-output CHIL NAND gate. (a) Equivalent circuit. (b) CAD lumped circuit model.

Fig. 6. Measured transfer characteristic: output voltage V_{O1} versus input voltage V_{I1}. Calculated CAD data are indicated.

the other hand, currents are defined as logic variables, as for example with CHL, the same equivalent circuit corresponds to a logical NOR [6].

Fig. 4(b) shows a simple lumped circuit model of the same gate, suitable for computer-aided design (CAD). It includes p-n diodes corresponding to the vertical hole injection into the epi-layer, and p-n-p and n-p-n transistors for the simulation of the lateral intermediate collector p-n-p and the inversely operated n-p-n transistor, respectively. All components can be weighed with different area factors. Parasitic passive elements like capacitances and ohmic series resistances can be included. Thus, this lumped circuit model is sufficiently adaptable to the layout and technological parameters of the fabricated samples. The following calculations were made with a network analysis program [7]. For the sake of simplicity, an Ebers–Moll model was used to simulate the inherent intrinsic transistors.

TRANSFER CHARACTERISTIC

The circuit diagram of an experimental setup for dc and pulse measurements is shown in Fig. 5. The CHIL NAND gate is indicated by a dashed circle. The two inputs $I1, I2$ are decoupled from the pulse generators by the output transistor of I^2L inverters, and the output is connected to an I^2L input. Accordingly, the voltage waveforms can be monitored at $I1$, $I2$, and $O1$. For dc measurements, a slow ramp function is applied via the pulse generators 1 or 2, respectively.

The measured transfer characteristic of the output voltage V_{O1} versus input voltage V_{I1} is given in Fig. 6. Calculated data of a computer-aided circuit analysis with the model shown in Fig. 4(b) are indicated. They agree quite well with

the measurements. Due to the pronounced threshold voltage of a p-n junction, the transfer curves show a switching characteristic with a very steep gradient. By the same reason, the transfer characteristic is highly unsymmetric. For input voltages below approximately 500 mV, the output transistor remains turned off. For higher input voltages, $I1$ starts injecting holes which supply the base current for turning on the output transistor. For a high enough current gain, the output transistor is driven into the saturation mode. The necessary minimum current gain per collector depends on the geometry and the current gain of the lateral p-n-p structure. Equation (2) gives an approximate lower limit for a NAND gate with N inputs.

$$\beta_{\text{n-p-n}} \gtrsim \alpha_{\text{p-n-p}}^{-(N-1)}. \tag{2}$$

DYNAMIC BEHAVIOR

Fig. 7 demonstrates an example of pulse blanking with a CHIL NAND gate. The upper two traces correspond to the input voltages V_{I1} and V_{I2}, respectively, and the lower trace gives the voltage waveform of the output signal V_{O1}. The circuit diagram of the experimental setup is the same as in Fig. 5.

As long as input I_2 is kept floating, i.e., pulse generator $PG2$ is in the "LO" state, the output signal V_{O1} is the inverse of input signal V_{I1}. The rise and fall times are increased by a factor of approximately 1.3. This is caused by charge-storing and transit-time effects in the lateral p-n-p transistor of input $I1$. The "HI" voltage level of the floating input $I2$ is modulated by current switching at input $I1$. The p-region of $I2$ is discharged via the lateral transistor between $I1$-$I2$ and charged via the lateral transistors E-$I1$ and $I1$-$I2$, respectively.

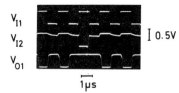

Fig. 7. CHIL NAND gate: measured voltage waveforms at input $I1$, $I2$ and output $O1$.

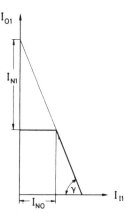

Fig. 8. Current transfer characteristic: output current I_{O1} versus input current I_{I1} with indicated noise margins.

When $I2$ is pulled down to a "LO" level voltage, the output transistor is turned off. The inherent rise and fall times of the output signal correspond to those of an I^2L inverter, since $I2$ is equivalent to an I^2L input.

Compared to I^2L, the power-delay product of a CHIL gate is increased by a factor of approximately 1.3. For a whole circuit, the slightly higher power-delay product per gate can, however, be more than compensated for by a reduction in the number of stages due to the possibility of realizing complex gate functions with a single-output transistor. Compared to CHIL, the power-delay product per stage can be improved by up to two orders in magnitude according to [6].

NOISE IMMUNITY

Since CHIL is a logic with a relatively small logic swing of approximately 600 mV, it is important to consider noise immunity of the whole circuit. In the transfer characteristic of Fig. 5 the static voltage noise margins V_{N0} and V_{N1} are indicated. Despite a very small voltage noise margin V_{N0}, noise immunity is rather high, since the CHIL output and input impedances of switched-on, saturated transistors are on the order of 100 Ω or even less. To understand this, it is necessary to look at the schematic example of a calculated CHIL current transfer curve in Fig. 8.

Two different states must be considered. In the first case, the output state should be low (logic "0") and a noise signal is applied to input $I1$. The current noise margin I_{N0} then corresponds to the excess current which can be drawn from input $I1$ without turning off the saturated output transistor. Fig. 9(a), (b) gives the simplified equivalent circuit for this state, including the schematic output characteristic of the n-p-n transistor. The difference between actual base current I_B and base current I_B' which, at minimum, is necessary for sinking the current source I_E, is equivalent to the noise margin I_{N0} multiplied by the common base current gain α_{p-n-p}' of the saturated p-n-p transistor.

If, on the other hand, the output is high (logic "1"), the current noise margin I_{N1} corresponds to the surplus current, which can be fed into $I1$ without turning on the switched-off output transistor. For a chain of identical gates, this means that with the equivalent circuit of Fig. 9 the noise signal is now fed into the output $O1$ of the n-p-n transistor. The corresponding noise margin I_{N1} is indicated in Figs. 8 and 9.

It can be seen that both noise margins depend on the slope $\tan \gamma$ of the current transfer characteristic, which is equivalent to the product of the inverse common-emitter current gain β_{n-p-n} with the saturated common base current gain α_{p-n-p}'. A higher inverse current gain β_{n-p-n} results in higher noise margins I_{N0}, I_{N1}, even though the relation is not linear,

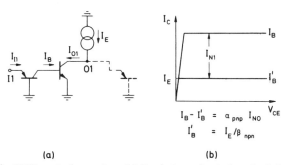

Fig. 9. CHIL noise immunity. (a) Equivalent circuit for a loaded gate. (b) Schematic output characteristic.

since the saturated α_{p-n-p}' is affected by the value of β_{n-p-n}. Comparing the static noise immunity, CHL should have a higher noise margin [6] than CHIL, since it uses normally operated n-p-n transistors with a high current gain. With an advanced technology, however, it seems to be possible to fabricate transistors with an inverse current gain well over 50. Compared to I^2L, the noise margin of CHIL should be in the same range [8]. Considering dynamic noise immunity, CHL has the advantage of having a rather large response time and thus is not affected by short pulses [6].

CONCLUSIONS

Table I, as a summary, gives a final comparison of I^2L, CHL, and CHIL, derived from I^2L, CHL publications [8], [6], and from a comparison of input $I1$ and $I2$ of a CHIL NAND gate, which correspond to a typical CHIL and I^2L input, respectively. The relative data for area consumption, power-delay product, and delay time apply to a gate with two electrically independent inputs, fabricated in an SBC process. The slightly increased power-delay product of a CHIL gate compared to I^2L can be more than compensated for by a significant reduction in the number of stages due to multi-input gates with the possibility of realizing complex gate functions. Considering area consumption, one must keep in mind that both the reduction of the number of stages and the better utilization of the wiring lead to an area reduction for a complete logic circuit.

CHIL is a logic with optimal design flexibility, which is on one hand well suitable for large-scale integration (LSI) and on

TABLE I
RELATIVE COMPARISON BETWEEN I²L, CHL, AND CHIL (TWO-INPUT GATE, SBC PROCESS)

	I^2L	CHL	CHIL
AREA	1.2	3	1
POWER-DELAY PRODUCT	0.8	100	1
DELAY TIME	0.8	100	1
MULTI-INPUT GATES	-	•	•
COMPLEX GATE FUNCTIONS	-	•	•
NO ISOLATION	•	-	•
NOISE IMMUNITY	o	•	o

the other hand technologically compatible to all circuits fabricated in a SBC process. Thus, combinations of analog and digital circuitry on a single chip are also feasible.

ACKNOWLEDGMENT

The author wishes to thank H.-H. Arndt for the technological support and the fabrication of the samples, and K. Goser and K.-U. Stein for helpful discussions.

REFERENCES

[1] K. Hart and A. Slob, "Integrated injection logic: A new approach to LSI," *IEEE J. Solid-State Circuits (Special Issue on Semiconductor Memories and Digital Circuits)*, vol. SC-7, pp. 346–351, Oct. 1972.

[2] H. H. Berger and S. K. Wiedmann, "Merged-transistor logic—a low-cost bipolar logic concept," *IEEE J. Solid-State Circuits (Special Issue on Semiconductor Memories and Digital Circuits)*, vol. SC-7, pp. 340–346, Oct. 1972.

[3] V. Blatt, L. W. Kennedy, P. S. Walsh, and R. C. A. Ashford, "Substrate fed logic—an improved form of injection logic," presented at the Int. Electron Devices Meeting, Washington, D.C., Dec. 1974.

[4] H. H. Berger and S. K. Wiedmann, "Schottky transistor logic," presented at the Int. Solid-State Circuits Conf., Philadelphia, Pa., Feb. 1975.

[5] A. W. Peltier, "A new approach to bipolar LSI: C^3L," presented at the Int. Solid-State Circuits Conf., Philadelphia, Pa., Feb. 1975.

[6] H. Lehning, "Current hogging logic (CHL)—a new bipolar logic for LSI," *IEEE J. Solid-State Circuits (Special Issue on Semiconductor Memory and Logic)*, vol. SC-9, pp. 228–233, Oct. 1974.

[7] *SINAP (Siemens Netzwerk Analyse Programm Paket)*, Siemens AG, Munich, Germany.

[8] N. C. de Troye, "Integrated injection logic—present and future," *IEEE J. Solid-State Circuits (Special Issue on Semiconductor Memory and Logic)*, vol. SC-9, pp. 206–211, Oct. 1974.

Computer-Aided Device Modeling and Design Procedure for Current Hogging Logic (CHL)

ARMIN W. WIEDER, WALTER L. ENGL, SENIOR MEMBER, IEEE, AND HEINZ LEHNING

Abstract—Modeling of functional devices requires computer simulation of lateral and vertical device structure due to geometrical complexity. It not only must meet the requirements of network analysis programs, but also has to enable quantitative design. For the basic element of current hogging logic (CHL), the computer simulation of the two-dimensional situation has resulted in and given justification for a simple model approximating the injection performance and enabling quantitative design of even complex CHL circuits.

INTRODUCTION

MUCH research has been carried out in the field of bipolar transistor modeling. Analytical [1], [2] as well as numerical [3]-[6] methods were developed resulting in a library of transistor models, offering a range from simple to highly sophisticated device models. These models describing transistor performance are mostly to be implemented in network analysis programs. Since bipolar functional devices cannot be broken down in separated decoupled transistor structures, a first attempt has been made towards modeling a functional device from lateral layout dimensions and vertical impurity profiles directly. If a given

Manuscript received April 23, 1975; revised June 9, 1975. This work was supported by the Bundesministerium für Forschung und Technologie.

The authors are with the Institut für Theoretische Elektrotechnik, Technische Hochschule Aachen, Aachen, Germany.

Reprinted from *IEEE J. Solid-State Circuits*, vol. SC-10, pp. 352–359, Oct. 1975.

50

functional device is to find a widespread application in designing electronic systems, a proper understanding of its device behavior for all injection conditions and a procedure for laying out its lateral mask geometries is mandatory.

The basic concept of most new functional circuits is the use of closely combined n-p-n and p-n-p transistors in order to achieve high functional density [8]–[11]. Modeling of these highly interactive devices with geometrically complex structures requires computer simulation of lateral and vertical device geometries. This nonregional modeling approach becomes feasible by numerical methods. The simulation results in terminal characteristics of the device, which can be compared with electrical measurements, and in the interior of distributions of potential, electron, and hole densities. Computer calculations require input data which must be measured. The calculations, which are valid for all injection levels, must be considered as a tool to get a better understanding of complex device performance as well as to get insight into the internal device mechanism. As a consequence of that and by useful assumptions and simplifications, which one can justify by numeric results, analytical device modeling for network analysis and design is enabled even for complex devices.

This modeling philosophy will be illustrated using the current hogging logic (CHL) as an example. Two-dimensional computer modeling of the basic CHL element leads to carrier concentrations and potential distributions in the device which have been used to derive a simple model approximating the dc current-voltage transfer functions of CHL. These approximations including doping levels, mask geometries, and high-level injection effects have been found to be accurate over a reasonable range of operating currents and have been found to be useful for quantitative design of CHL structures [7].

CHL

To explain the mode of operation we first consider the basic CHL element (Fig. 1). It consists of a lateral p-n-p transistor with buried layer, as used in standard bipolar technology with an additional collector, the control collector C_1 between emitter E and output collector C_o. In case of a forward biased base–emitter diode and reverse biased collectors and substrate, the control collector hogs the carriers injected by the emitter and only leakage current remains at the output collector. Under floating conditions the control collector is being charged up and hence acts as an emitter injecting holes, which are collected at the output collector. The current at the output collector can be switched off and on by biasing the control collector or letting it float, respectively. Measurements show that over a range larger than four decades of lateral collector current the vertical substrate current is more than one hundred times smaller than the collector current. Hence the buried layer suppresses vertical substrate transistor action. For the other p-diffused zones, C', the so-called guard collectors are necessary to avoid carrier diffusion towards the output collector around the control collector. These collectors must be negatively biased with respect to the emitter.

For CHL, currents are defined to be the logic variables. The NOR function is achieved by placing two control collectors in series between emitter and output collector C_o [Fig. 2(b)].

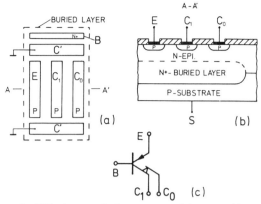

Fig. 1. Basic CHL element, logic structure of inverter: (a) geometry, (b) cross section, (c) symbol.

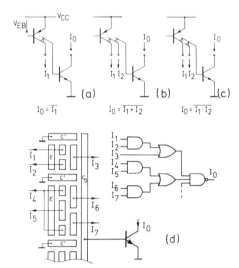

Fig. 2. CHL gates: (a) inverter, (b) NOR gate, (c) NAND gate, (d) complex gate.

NAND function results from splitting one control collector into two halves [Fig. 2(c)]. The logic gates of CHL consist of two parts, the logic structure discussed in Fig. 1 in a simple form and the output n-p-n transistor. It restores the current level and inverts the polarity of the output current, thus enabling subsequent gates to be driven (Fig. 2). The important feature of CHL is that complex logic functions may be accomplished within one isolation region yielding high functional density. High functional density is achieved by placing between emitter and output collector up to three rows of control collectors, each of which can be split into separate control collectors. Fig. 2(d) shows an example of a three-level gate circuit [10].

The current of the common output collector has to bias the output n-p-n transistor, which in turn drives the next stages. This current depends on the logical conditions of the control collectors and especially on the geometry and layout of the logic structure. The layout must be designed such that for the logical condition giving the smallest output current [i.e., in Fig. 2(d), all control collectors biased except C_1 and C_3 ($I_1 = 0$, $I_3 = 0$)], the output n-p-n has still enough base drive in order to properly feed the control collectors of the following

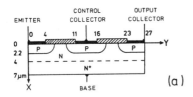

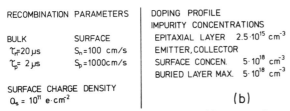

Fig. 3. Input data for the basic CHL element: (a) cross section under consideration, (b) physical input data.

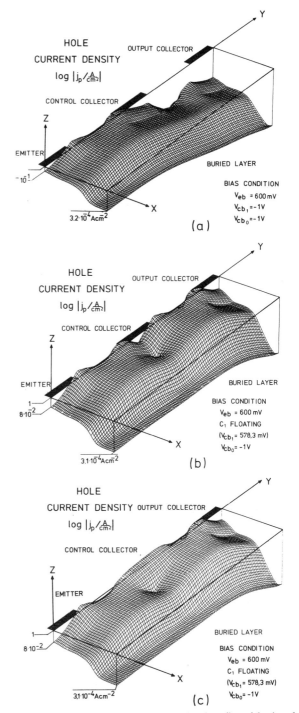

Fig. 4. Absolute value of hole current density (logarithmic plot): (a) absorbing collectors, (b) floating control collector with metal contact, (c) floating control collector with oxide surface.

stages. The design problem is to lay out a mosaic of p-layers with proper dimensions suitable for representing the desired logic and leading to the highest possible functional density.

A design model taking its strong dependence on geometry into account is needed to solve the problem of current distribution in the device. Therefore a numerical simulation is carried out resulting in basic concepts for CHL modeling.

NUMERICAL SOLUTION AND INJECTION MODEL

The logic structure of the basic CHL element to be investigated by numerical methods is shown in Fig. 1(a), (b). Two-dimensional analysis of a monolithic p-n-p transistor with buried layer, substrate, and isolation diffusion [6] has justified the simplification of the cross section of this element to the structure under consideration [Fig. 3(a)]. The base contact is assumed to being placed in the center of the buried layer. This simplification is justified, especially in the case of a highly doped buried layer. Current loss due to vertical injection into the substrate of the parasitic p-n-n⁺p transistor can be modeled by the integral charge of majorities stored in the active base of the vertical transistor [6]. Its influence in the design of CHL will be considered in the Appendix.

Symmetry allows one to treat only one half section of a structure [Fig. 3(a)]. The thick epitaxial layer and the deep junctions correspond to standard bipolar technology for linear applications. In Fig. 3(b) input data are given. Lifetimes were measured in the epitaxial bulk material and were assumed to be independent of impurity concentration. The doping profiles were taken from actual devices and approximated by different Gaussian functions. Field and impurity dependent mobilities were taken into account. Hence, due to the relative low impurity concentrations, high doping effects were neglected. For the numerical calculations, Poisson's equation and the continuity equations for electrons and holes have been solved under steady-state conditions by an algorithm converging nearly independent of the injection level.

To understand device performance, the distribution of hole current flow is discussed first. Fig. 4(a) shows a logarithmic plot of the absolute value of hole current density for medium-level injection for an absorbing control collector. The indi-

cated xy plane gives the level of 1 A/cm². At first, current flows essentially from the emitter edge to the adjacent collector edge spreading almost uniformly into the whole depth of the epitaxial layer. Maximum current densities of 10 A/cm² occur at the contact edges. Underneath the emitter, vertical current injection is small due to the buried layer and is essentially forced aside by the retarding field of the buried layer. Further on one observes that nearly all the current is absorbed at the control collector and only a negligible portion

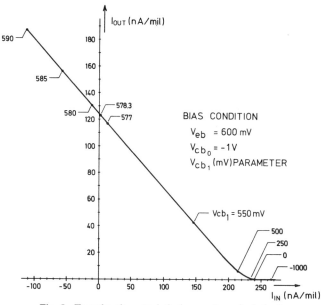

Fig. 5. Transfer characteristic (computer calculation).

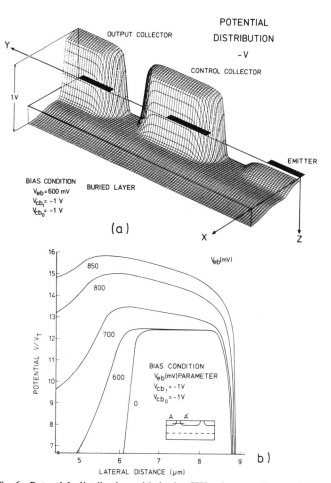

Fig. 6. Potential distribution: (a) basic CHL element (linear plot), (b) lateral cross section A–A' through the base, $x = 1$ μm.

passes the control collector and leaves the device at the output collector. This portion is in the order of the leakage current.

Fig. 4(b) shows hole current flow in the case of a floating control collector. Essentially the same injection pattern can be observed at the emitter. However, current is absorbed at one edge of the control collector contact and is reinjected into the base at the other edge. This collection and reinjection performance of the floating control collector causes a region underneath the control collector where current becomes very small. Nearly no current is carried in the epitaxial layer underneath the control collector. Underneath the control collector contact current is very small too, due to the shunt effect of the contact itself. If the control collector surface is covered by oxide only, current crosses completely the high-doped regions, as the simulation in Fig. 4(c) shows. Again nearly no current underpasses the floating control collector.

To study the current hogging effect of the control collector the computed current transfer characteristic of the device is given in Fig. 5. I_{OUT} flows out of the biased output collector. I_{IN} enters through the control collector. At a control collector bias of $V_{cb1} = -1$ V, only leakage current remains at the output. If the control collector reaches base potential ($V_{cb1} = 0$ V), it still prevents output transistor action. Significant output current begins to flow when the potential at the control collector is 100 mV less than at the emitter. It is interesting to notice that the transfer curve is strictly linear, except for a very small region at the maximum input current. Finally, the characteristic shows that under floating conditions the control collector is forward biased 21 mV less than the emitter, and that nearly half of the maximum input current is available at the output.

Fig. 6(a) shows a linear plot of the potential distribution in the case of an absorbing control collector for medium-level injection ($V_{el} = 600$ mV). The bias voltage drops completely at the emitter–base junction. The shape of the potential surface in the epitaxial layer remains flat even in the narrow base valley. There is no drift field; hence current flows by diffusion

only. With a further increase in voltage, the injected hole concentration reaches or even exceeds the level of the donor concentration in the base. In this case high-level effects are induced, which can be noticed in a lateral cross section of the potential surface through the base given in Fig. 6(b). If the biasing voltage exceeds a certain level, only depending on donor concentration in the base

$$V^K = 2 V_T \ln \frac{N_D^+}{n_i}, \qquad (1)$$

the rise of a drift field can be noticed. It supports current flow not only close underneath the surface but also deep in the epitaxial layer.

Finally, the distribution of mobile carriers is to be discussed. A logarithmic plot of the distribution of holes for medium-level injection and absorbing collectors is given in Fig. 7(a). Underneath the emitter a plateau of hole concentration reaching the buried layer onset can be observed. In the base valley the concentration decreases laterally towards the collector. To show this effect in more detail a linear plot of the same distribution is given in Fig. 7(b). Concentration of the highly doped regions of emitter and collectors are not drawn to show the distribution of holes more explicitly in the base region. In the base the concentration decreases nearly linearly before reaching the depletion layer of the control collector. Even

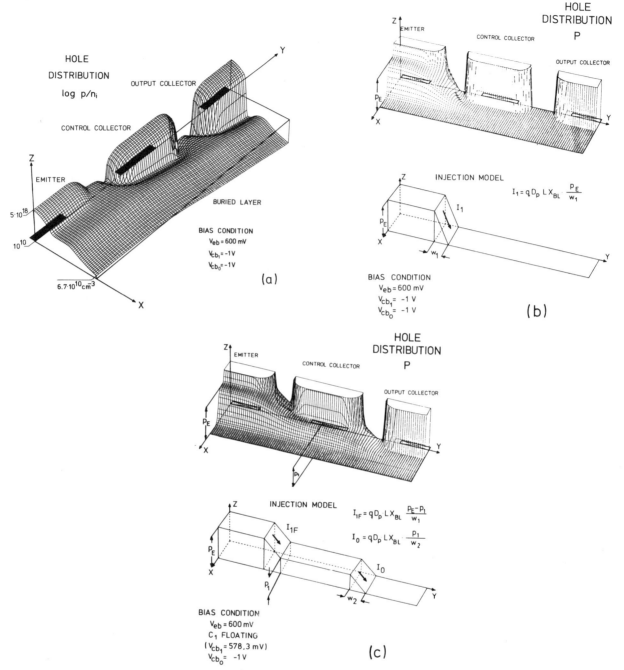

Fig. 7. Hole distribution and injection model: (a) absorbing control collector (log plot), (b) absorbing control collector (linear plot), (c) floating control collector (linear plot).

in the case of this very narrow base (the base width is 2.6 μ), linearity is clearly visible. In the rest of the device no significant excess concentration of holes can be seen. Current flows almost uniformly in the epitaxial layer from the emitter edge to the collector edge.

A one-dimensional injection model is a coarse, but justified, simplification for this injection performance. The principle idea of this model is illustrated in the lower part of Fig. 7(b). It is based on the almost triangular hole concentration in the active base, which holds even in case of high-level injection (Fig. 8).

A linear plot of the distribution of holes for a floating control collector is given in Fig. 7(c). The plateau of holes underneath the emitter can be observed in this linear plot, too. Fig. 4(b) and (c) has shown that the injected current is shunted by the highly doped control collector and is not carried in the epitaxial layer beneath. Therefore, it is not surprising to notice that the floating control collector causes a similar plateau of hole concentration in the epitaxial layer. This plateau, however, is at a lower level. Hence the potential at the floating control collector is somewhat lower than at the emitter, as the transfer curve in Fig. 5 has proven. The good

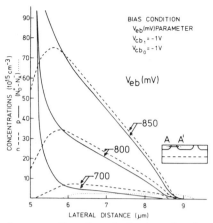

Fig. 8. Lateral cross section through the base ($x = 1$ μm) of mobile carrier and impurity concentrations (linear plot).

noise immunity of the CHL structure stems from the development of these carrier plateaus and their resulting large diffusion capacitances. Injection performance in case of a floating control collector leads to hole concentrations, which decrease almost linearly at both base valleys. The slope is nearly half as steep as in the case of an absorbing control collector because the effective base width is nearly doubled. Approximately half of the current which left the device at the biased control collector now leaves at the output collector, as has been indicated by Fig. 5. There is only a slight difference due to the influence of the depletion layers at the biased collectors. In the lower part of Fig. 7(c), a one-dimensional injection model which approximates this bias condition is shown. It is ruled by the indicated equations and enables the calculation of hole current at biased collectors, even if there are some floating control collectors placed in between. The variables in these equations are dependent on geometry and emitter–base voltage.

Before the model is applied to a real CHL structure it must be generalized by taking high-level effects into account. In this case the lateral current distribution remains essentially unchanged, but current is not carried by diffusion only and carriers depend no longer exponentially on emitter-base voltage. In Fig. 8 mobile carriers and impurity concentration are represented linearly to show high-level effects explicitly. It is obvious that in the active base electron density exceeds hole density by a constant amount for all injection levels. This amount is given by the donor concentration. Hence quasi-neutrality is preserved which in turn leads to an expression for current flow taking diffusion and drift into account.

$$I_L = q D_p L X_{BL} \frac{p_e - p_1}{W_1}$$
$$\cdot \left(2 - \frac{\ln\left((p_e + N)/(p_1 + N)\right)}{(p_e - p_1)/N} \right). \tag{2}$$

This equation derived in the Appendix gives the injection model. The second term is unity in case of low and two in case of high-level injection. In the latter case current is carried half by diffusion and half by drift. Actual CHL circuits are

operated with constant emitter–base voltage and therefore current ratios are of major interest. Nevertheless, absolute values of current might be of interest. Therefore, in the Appendix hole concentration at the emitter edge of the base is given as a function of emitter base voltage (5). The problem of vertical current loss due to substrate transistor action is considered in the Appendix.

Design Procedure

Computer simulation of the structure has resulted in and given justification for a simple model approximating device performance. This model now in turn can be applied to complex CHL structures. To illustrate this procedure and to compare it with experimental data a CHL structure is taken [Fig. 9(a)]. It obviously represents an AND–NOR function because current at the output collector C_O can be switched off by either biasing the control collector C_3 or the control collectors C_2 and C_1. To achieve this, the gap should not be larger than roughly 10 μ. In the figure the worst case condition delivering the smallest output current is given. The control collector C_1 is biased and the control collectors C_2 and C_3 float. The output and guard collectors are also biased. Device dimensions must be choosen such that the output current is still large enough to drive the output n-p-n transistor, which in turn drives the next stages. The injection model is applied to each transistor section corresponding to the current arrows in the figure. The emitter injects into the floating collector C_2, which in turn injects to the guard collector, to the collector C_1, and to the floating control collector C_3. The latter one injects partly to the guard collectors, partly back to the biased collector C_1, and partly to the output C_O. For the current of each transistor section the model leads to one equation in which the hole concentration of the floating collectors are the unknowns. The application of Kirchhoff's current law leads to two equations corresponding to the two floating collectors. The solution is done easily by hand and results in the output current as a function of geometry and hole concentration at the emitter edge. In actual circuits, however, only current ratios are of interest. Therefore hole concentration at the emitter edge is expressed by a reference current, as defined in Fig. 9(b). The resulting normalized output current is a function of device dimensions only [Fig. 9(c)]. Taking depletion layers at biased collectors into account the model can be improved. By means of that information the designer is enabled to obtain an optimal arrangement of p-layers and dimensions for the desired logical AND–NOR function with reasonable time and effort.

For the experimental verification the structure was built [Fig. 9(d)]. The spacings between the p-diffusions are 10 μ on the mask. The smallest contact windows are 7.5 μ^2. A comparison of measured and calculated output currents for all logical conditions is given in Fig. 10(a). The upper curve shows the measured signal current in case of all control collectors floating. Due to the symmetry of C_1 and C_2, the signal currents for biased C_1 or C_2 are nearly equal. In this case the signal current must be smaller because of the current loss at the biased control collector. The dashed lines show the level of the output current calculated from the simplified

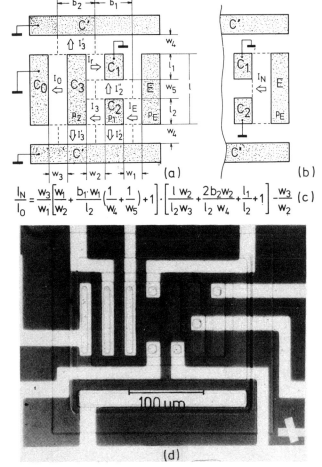

$$\frac{I_N}{I_0} = \frac{w_3}{w_1}\left[\frac{w_1}{w_2} + \frac{b_1 \cdot w_1}{l_2}\left(\frac{1}{w_4} + \frac{1}{w_5}\right) + 1\right] \cdot \left[\frac{l \, w_2}{l_2 w_3} + \frac{2 b_2 w_2}{l_2 \, w_4} + \frac{l_1}{l_2} + 1\right] - \frac{w_3}{w_2} \quad (c)$$

Fig. 9. CHL AND-NOR structure: (a) realization of logical function, (b) definition of reference current, (c) normalized output current, (d) chip photo.

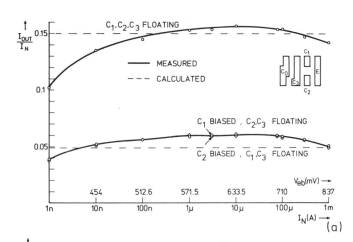

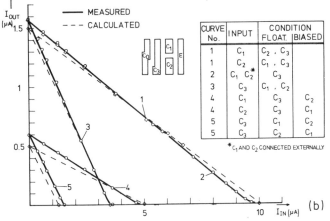

Fig. 10. Measurements and calculations of the AND-NOR structure: (a) normalized output current, (b) transfer curves for all logical conditions.

injection model. Despite the coarse simplification, accuracy is still good enough for quantitative design.

The transfer characteristics of the CHL AND-NOR structure are shown in Fig. 10(b). There are different curves depending on which control collector is taken, as the input and which collectors are floating or biased. The measured transfer curves are strictly linear as predicted by the exact numerical analysis. The simplified injection model is still good enough to yield transfer curves which are in good agreement with experimental data.

APPENDIX

A. Derivation of the Injection Model

Hole current density is described as a sum of drift and diffusion components.

$$j_p = -q\mu_p p \nabla\Psi - qD_p \nabla p.$$

The drift field which is built up by majorities can be calculated by only assuming the numerically justified constancy of the "quasi-Fermi level" of electrons Φ_n in the base.

$$-q\mu_n n\nabla\Psi + qD_n\nabla n = -q\mu_n n\nabla\Phi_n$$

$$\nabla\Psi = V_T \frac{\nabla n}{n}.$$

Assuming charge neutrality in the base $n = p + N$, $N = N_D^+ - N_A^-$ the equation for the hole current density reads

$$j_p = -qD_p \, 1/(p+N) \, \nabla(p(p+N)). \quad (3)$$

Accepting a one-dimensional current flow in the homogeneous doped base of the vertical thickness X_{BL} and the lateral width W_1, the equation can be integrated [12] and results in (2) giving the lateral current I_L as a function of hole densities at the emitter edge p_e and collector edge p_1. Only in case of high-level injection $p \gtrsim N$ must the second term describing the influence of the drift field be considered.

B. Calculation of the Hole Current Density

Numeric simulations show that the difference of the "quasi-Fermi levels" ϕ_n and ϕ_p differ at the emitter edge of the base by an amount of V_{eb}. Therefore the product of mobile carriers depends exponentially on the biasing voltage V_{eb}.

$$np = n_i^2 \exp(\Phi_p/V_T - \Phi_n/V_T) \approx n_i^2 \exp(V_{eb}/V_T). \quad (4)$$

The assumption of charge neutrality leads to an approximation for the concentration of minorities at the emitter edge.

$$p_e = (n_i^2/N) \exp(V_{eb}/V_T)$$
$$\cdot \{1 + (n_i/N)^2 \exp(V_{eb}/V_T)\}^{-1/2}. \quad (5)$$

C. Vertical Current Loss

Numerical simulations show that the vertical substrate current is nearly inversely proportional to the total base charge of the substrate transistor [6]. The charge is built up by electrons in the active base which reaches from the p-layer (X_{BE}) vertically to the substrate (X_{BS}). Therefore the application of the charge control model [2] to each vertical transistor is justified in spite of the influence of the buried layer. With the effective area of the parasitic transistor A_v, it results in an expression for the vertical substrate current essentially depending on doping profiles.

$$I_v = q n_i^2 A_v \cdot \frac{\exp\left(V_{eb}/V_T\right)}{\int_{X_{BE}}^{X_{BS}} n/D_n \, dX} \; .$$

The ratio of the vertical and the lateral current gives an estimation if and to which extent this vertical current loss must be taken into account. In the design procedure it can be handled in the same way as lateral current loss to some absorbing collectors.

REFERENCES

[1] J. J. Ebers and J. L. Moll, "Large signal behavior of junction transistors," *Proc. IRE*, vol. 42, pp. 1761–1772, Dec. 1954.

[2] H. K. Gummel and H. C. Poon, "An integral charge control model of bipolar transistors," *Bell Syst. Tech. J.*, vol. 49, pp. 827–852, May 1970.

[3] H. K. Gummel, "A self-consistent iterative scheme for one-dimensional steady-state transistor calculations," *IEEE Trans. Electron Devices*, vol. ED-11, pp. 455–465, Oct. 1964.

[4] H. H. Heimeier, "A two-dimensional numerical analysis of a silicon n-p-n transistor," *IEEE Trans. Electron Devices*, vol. ED-20, pp. 708–714, Aug. 1973.

[5] O. Manck, H. H. Heimeier, and W. L. Engl, "High injection in a two-dimensional transistor," *IEEE Trans. Electron Devices*, vol. ED-21, pp. 403–409, July 1974.

[6] A. W. Wieder, O. Manck, and W. L. Engl, "Two-dimensional analysis of a monolithic p-n-p transistor," in *1974 IEEE Int. Electron Devices Meeting, Dig. Tech. Papers*, pp. 414–417.

[7] A. W. Wieder, W. L. Engl, and H. Lehning, "Two-dimensional analysis and design procedure for current hogging logic," in *1975 IEEE Int. Solid-State Circuits Conf., Dig. Tech. Papers*, pp. 170–171.

[8] H. H. Berger and S. K. Wiedmann, "Merged transistor logic (MTL)–A low-cost bipolar logic concept," *IEEE J. Solid-State Circuits (Special Issue on Semiconductor Memories and Digital Circuits)*, vol. SC-7, pp. 340–346, Oct. 1972.

[9] K. Hart and A. Slob, "Integrated injection logic: A new approach to LSI," *IEEE J. Solid-State Circuits (Special Issue on Semiconductor Memories and Digital Circuits)*, vol. SC-7, pp. 347–351, Oct. 1972.

[10] H. Lehning, "Current hogging logic (CHL)–A new bipolar logic for LSI," *IEEE J. Solid-State Circuits (Special Issue on Semiconductor Memory and Logic)*, vol. SC-9, pp. 228–233, Oct. 1974.

[11] R. Müller, "Current hogging injection logic: New functionally integrated circuits," in *1975 IEEE Int. Solid-State Circuits Conf., Dig. Tech. Papers*, pp. 174–175.

[12] R. D. Middlebrook, "Effects of modified collector boundary conditions on the basic properties of a transistor," *Solid-State Electron.*, vol. 6, pp. 573–588, 1963.

Injection-Coupled Synchronous Logic

N. FRIEDMAN, C. ANDRE T. SALAMA, MEMBER, IEEE, AND PHILIP M. THOMPSON, MEMBER, IEEE

Abstract—A novel injector structure used in conjunction with an I^2L gate is proposed and its application to the design of current comparators and synchronous logic is described. The operation and fabrication of basic gates as well as current comparators, *SR*, and *T* flip-flops are discussed. The new gate structures exhibit similar power × delay products, but lead to a considerable increase in functional density when compared to standard I^2L in synchronous logic applications.

INTRODUCTION

A NOVEL injector structure used in conjunction with an I^2L gate [1], [2] is described in this paper and is shown to be particularly applicable to the design of synchronous logic. The new gate configuration shown in Fig. 1 provides, in addition to the regular I^2L base input, an injector control input tied to the collector of the p-n-p transistor.

The main differences between this structure and the current hogging injector logic structure (CHIL) [3] are that in the present case: 1) the power supply injector is never shunted to ground during operation [4], 2) the current in the injector control input can be used to provide a dynamic memory effect by controlling the storage time in the lateral p-n-p existing between the injector control input and the base of the inverted n-p-n, and 3) the additional injector control input increases functional density.

This paper describes the basic layout and operation of the new gate structure and its use in the design and fabrication of current comparators as well as synchronous logic elements such as *RS* and *T* flip-flops. The resulting circuits are shown to offer a 75 percent reduction in area when compared to standard I^2L [1], [2] while maintaining the same power × delay product.

BASIC GATE

The basic circuit diagram for the injection-coupled synchronous logic (ISL) gate is shown in Fig. 1(a), the layout of the gate is shown in Fig. 1(b), and the symbol used for the gate is shown in Fig. 1(c). The input signal to the base of the n-p-n transistor will be referred to as the clock input and the injector control input will be referred to as the data input.

The operation of the gate will be described with reference to Fig. 2 which shows a test gate driven and loaded by interfacing I^2L transistors. The base input of the test gate (clock input) is driven by a strobe transistor which is an I^2L inverter.

Manuscript received March 31, 1978; revised May 30, 1978.
N. Friedman and C. A. T. Salama are with the Department of Electrical Engineering, University of Toronto, Toronto, Ont., Canada.
P. M. Thompson is with Thompson Foss Inc., Ottawa, Ont., Canada.

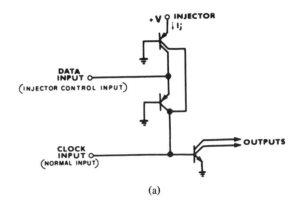

(a)

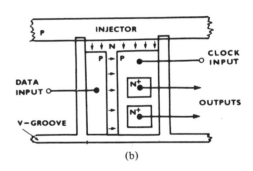

(b)

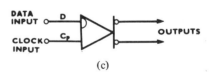

(c)

Fig. 1. Basic gate configuration. (a) Schematic diagram. (b) Layout. (c) Logic symbol.

Each of the I^2L interfacing transistors is injected with a current which is equal to the injector current of the test gate.

The basic gate can operate in two modes, the quiescent mode and the memory mode. The quiescent mode is used in the current comparator and the memory mode in the synchronous logic circuits. In the quiescent mode of operation, the data are changed from one logic level to the other while the clock $\overline{C_p}$ stays at "0" long enough for transients to stabilize before $\overline{C_p}$ goes to "1." In the memory mode of operation, the data inputs to all gates go to "1" shortly after $\overline{C_p}$ goes from "0" to "1," and the operation of the gate relies

Reprinted from *IEEE J. Solid-State Circuits*, vol. SC-13, pp. 549–555, Oct. 1978.

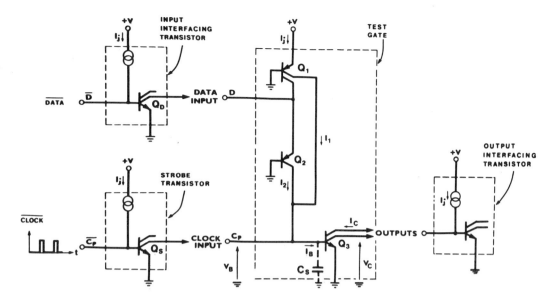

Fig. 2. The basic test gate with input and output interfacing I²L transistors.

on the "memory" of the p-n-p transistors Q_2 which will be discussed in the following paragraphs.

Fig. 3(a) shows the waveforms associated with the test gate when it is operated in the quiescent mode. Assuming $\overline{D}$ = "0" and $\overline{C_p}$ = "0," the base current of Q_3 is steady at $(I_1 + I_2)$ and the collector current is I_j where I_1 and I_2 are defined in Fig. 2 and I_j is the injector current of the test gate and the interfacing transistors. If Q_s is now turned on by changing $\overline{C_p}$ from "0" to "1," the potential at the base of Q_3 goes to ground, causing the base and collector currents of Q_3 to drop to zero. If Q_s is now turned off by changing $\overline{C_p}$ from "1" to "0," the voltage at the base of Q_3 rises from ground to the threshold of Q_3 at a rate I_B/C_s or $(I_1 + I_2)/C_s$ where I_B is the base current of Q_3 and C_s is the total capacitance at the base of Q_3. When this threshold is reached, the collector current of Q_3 rises from zero to I_j.

If we now assume that $\overline{D}$ = "1" and $\overline{C_p}$ = "0," then the base current of Q_3 is steady at I_1. When $\overline{C_p}$ goes from "0" to "1," Q_s is turned on and Q_3 is turned off. When $\overline{C_p}$ goes back from "1" to "0," the voltage of the base of transistor Q_3 rises from ground to the threshold of Q_3 at the rate of I_1/C_s. When this threshold is reached, the collector current of Q_3 rises from zero to I_j.

It follows that the delays T_1 and T_2 associated with the transition of the collector current of Q_3 depend on the logic state of the Data input when operating in the quiescent mode. The delays T_1 and T_2 are measured from the time $\overline{C_p}$ goes from "1" to "0" to the time when the base voltage V_B reaches the threshold of transistor Q_3 as shown in Fig. 3(a).

As mentioned previously, the operation of the gate in the memory mode is based on the fact that the lateral p-n-p transistor Q_2 has a turn-on time T_{pon} (including delay and rise times) which is significantly greater than the turn-on or turn-off times of the n-p-n transistor Q_3. In the memory mode of operation, the $\overline{D}$ input goes to "0" at time t_1 shortly after the application of $\overline{C_p}$. At time t_2, $\overline{C_p}$ returns to "0" and the previous[1] state of $\overline{D}$ is sensed by the delay in I_c. It can be

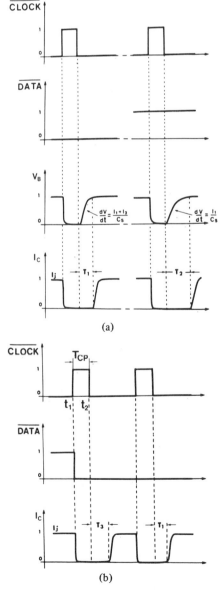

(a)

(b)

Fig. 3. Waveforms for the test gate. (a) Under quiescent mode of operation. (b) Under memory mode of operation.

---

[1]Previous state of Data is at time $(t_1 - \delta)$ where $\delta \to 0$.

seen from Fig. 3(b) that if the previous state of $\bar{D}$ was "1," the delay in I_c is T_3, and if the previous state of $\bar{D}$ was "0," the delay in I_c is T_1. For proper operation it is necessary to ensure that $T_3 > T_1$ which is possible if the width of the clock pulse T_{cp} is smaller than T_{pon}. If T_{cp} is increased and made equal to T_{pon}, then $T_3 \cong T_1$ and the state of $\bar{D}$ cannot be sensed through the collector current I_c. It should be noted that the lowest value of T_{cp} is limited by the inequality $T_{cp} > T_{nof}$ where T_{nof} is the total turn-off time of transistor Q_3 (including delay and fall time).

CIRCUIT REALIZATIONS

The current comparator shown in Fig. 4(a) consists of two ISL gates (Y and Z) and a conventional I^2L gate (X). The clock (normal) inputs are used to cross couple the Y and Z gates and the X gate is used as a strobe gate to clamp these inputs to ground. Fig. 4(b) shows the circuit diagram of the current comparator. The conventional I^2L gate (X) consists of the strobe transistor Q_s and its current source. This strobe transistor is initially turned on by $\bar{C_p}$ to ensure that both sides of the circuit can be turned off. At the instant comparison is required, the strobe transistor Q_s is turned off and the bases of transistors Q_1 and Q_2 are charged by the total injector currents. The transistor with the higher total injection current reaches its threshold first, turns on, and forces the other to stay off. It should be pointed out that the next comparison can only be performed when the circuit has reached its quiescent state. The circuit has two main limitations: 1) if I_A and I_B are much smaller than I_j, then the circuit may produce a false output, and 2) if I_A and I_B are much larger than I_j, then the circuit may change state without being strobed.

An *RS* flip-flop can be obtained directly from the current comparator by using the two data inputs as the set and reset terminals as shown in Fig. 5(a). Because of the difference in the storage time between the lateral p-n-p's Q_3, Q_4 and the inverted n-p-n's Q_1, Q_2, the state of the flip-flop when strobed will depend on the previous state of its inputs (memory mode of operation).

The input and output waveforms for the *RS* flip-flop are shown in Fig. 5(b) and illustrate the operation of the circuit. The time T_1 illustrated in Fig. 5(b) is the same delay time mentioned in conjunction with the basic test gate in Fig. 3(b).

The *RS* flip-flop can be used as a master–slave flip-flop, resulting in a 75 percent reduction in area over standard I^2L technology because a second flip-flop is not required for temporary memory and there is no need for additional gating circuitry. It should be noted that the maximum frequency of operation is determined by the turn-on time T_{pon} of the lateral p-n-p transistors.

A *T* flip-flop can be obtained by coupling the data inputs into the flip-flop itself as shown in Fig. 6(a). Assuming that Q_1 is initially off and Q_2 is on, then Q_3 will be on and Q_4 will be off. The applications of a short strobe pulse turns both Q_1 and Q_2 off, Q_3 remains on, and Q_4 starts turning on. If the strobe pulse is turned off before Q_4 has fully turned on, the base of Q_1 will charge faster than the base of Q_2 and Q_1 will turn on, holding Q_2 off. A new strobe pulse will reverse the state of Q_1 and Q_2. The input and output waveforms for the

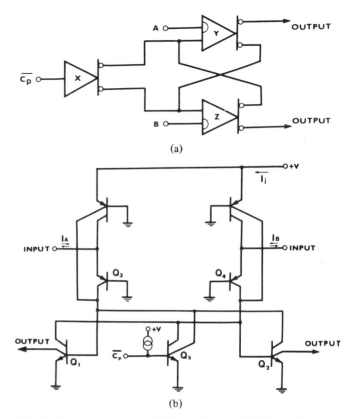

Fig. 4. Current comparator. (a) Logic diagram. (b) Circuit diagram.

T flip-flop are shown in Fig. 6(b) and illustrate the operation of the circuit.

The $\bar{C_p}$ pulses required can be generated on chip using the circuit shown in Fig. 7(a). The repetition rate of $\bar{C_p}$ is determined by the repetition of the input pulse V_{in} while the width of $\bar{C_p}$ is determined by T_{pon} of transistor Q_3. T_{pon} depends on the length of the collector of Q_2 as well as on the current injected in that transistor.

Fig. 7(b) shows the waveforms that are associated with the generator. The turn-on and turn-off delays of the various n-p-n transistors in the circuit are significantly smaller than those of the p-n-p transistors Q_2 and Q_3 and are not shown in the diagram. When V_{in} goes from "1" to "0," transistor Q_1 is turned off and transistor Q_3 starts to turn on. Because of the inherent delay in the p-n-p transistor Q_3, the base voltage of transistor Q_4 is delayed in its rise from "0" to "1." The collector voltage V_{C3} of transistor Q_5 goes from "1" to "0" when the input voltage V_{in} goes from "1" to "0," and it goes back from "0" to "1" only when V_{B1} reaches the threshold of transistor Q_4, thus producing a pulse with a width of T_{cp}. The voltage V_{C3} is inverted by the output transistors producing the desired $\bar{C_p}$ pulse at the output.

FABRICATION

In order to illustrate the operation of injection-coupled synchronous logic, current comparators, *RS* flip-flops, shift registers, as well as *T* flip-flops and binary counters were fabricated using a five mask *V*-groove isolation technology [5]. The starting material was (100) orientation n/n$^+$ epitaxial silicon. The resistivity of the n$^+$ substrate was 0.05 $\Omega \cdot$ cm. The resistivity and thickness of the n-epitaxial layer were 1 $\Omega \cdot$ cm and 4.5 μm, respectively. The *V*-groove oxide isola-

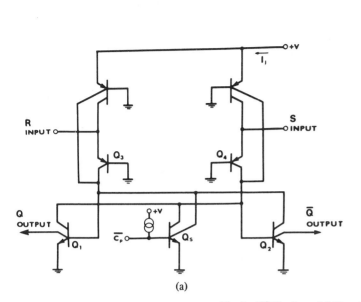
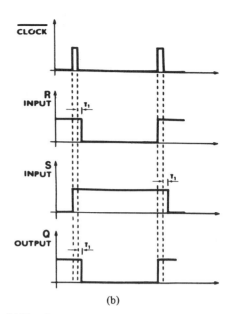

Fig. 5. RS flip-flop. (a) Circuit diagram. (b) Waveforms.

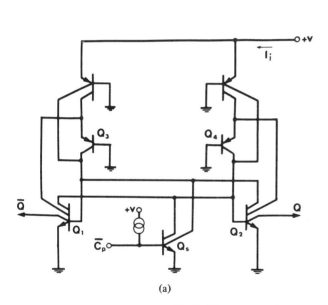
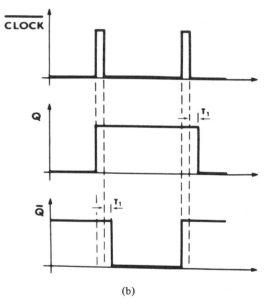

Fig. 6. Binary counter or T flip-flop. (a) Circuit diagram. (b) Waveforms.

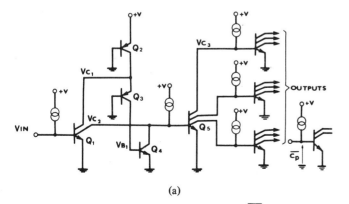
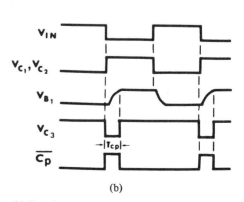

Fig. 7. $\overline{C_p}$ generator. (a) Circuit diagram. (b) Waveforms.

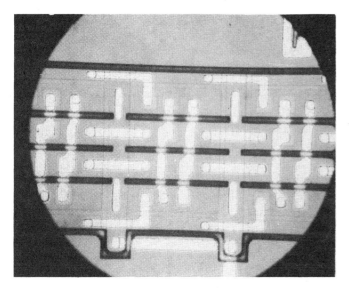

Fig. 8. Micrograph of *RS* flip-flops in a shift register configuration (layout rule 8 μm).

tion process was used to reduce lateral transfer between adjacent gates as well as speed–power product of the gates. The base diffusion was performed in a two-step process using a boron nitride source. The top collector was diffused using a phosphorus solid source. The p-base diffusion region was designed to have a sheet resistance of 200 $\Omega/\square$ and the n$^+$ collector diffusion was adjusted to provide a base width of 0.2 μm and a sheet resistance of 4 $\Omega/\square$.

A micrograph of three *RS* flip-flops in a shift register configuration is shown in Fig. 8. The layout of the flip-flops, in this particular case, was based on a 8 μm layout rule.

EXPERIMENTAL RESULTS

The various circuits were tested to verify the principle of the operation of the ISL gates as well as to establish typical power $\times$ delay $\times$ area figures of merit to be used for comparison purposes.

The operation of the basic gate shown in Fig. 2 was characterized by applying pulses to the $\overline{D}$ and $\overline{C_p}$ inputs and observing the output voltage as a function of the total injection current I_j in the range 1 μA–1 mA. The input–output waveforms of the basic gate for an injection current of 5 μA are shown in Fig. 9(a). The waveforms shown in this figure agree with the waveforms illustrated in Fig. 3(a) which were used to describe qualitatively the operation of the gate under quiescent conditions. The delay time T_1 was measured as a function of injection current I_j for the quiescent mode of operation with the $\overline{\text{Data}}$ input kept constant at "0." T_{pon} was also measured as a function of injection current in the memory mode of operation by increasing T_{cp} to a value $T_{cp\,max}$ at which $T_3 = T_1$. T_{pon} was then obtained from $T_{pon} = T_{cp\,max}$.

The delay T_1 determines the operational speed in the quiescent mode of operation (e.g., response time of comparator) and T_{pon} determines the maximum frequency for the memory mode of operation (e.g., maximum frequency of *RS* or *T* flip-flops). Both T_1 and T_{pon} are plotted in Fig. 9(b) as a function of I_j. These delays decrease for increasing injection current. When injection is above 200 μA, the delay times level

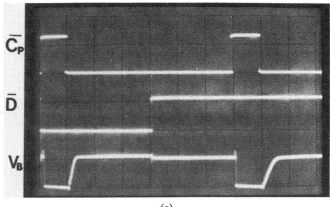

(a)

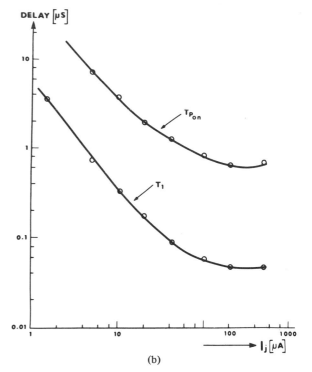

(b)

Fig. 9. Test gate characteristics. (a) Waveforms for quiescent mode of operation ($I_j = 5$ μA, vertical 0.5 V/div, horizontal 5 μs/div). (b) Delays T_1 and T_{pon} as a function of total injection current.

off in the same manner as observed in standard I^{2}L technology [6].

The current comparator shown in Fig. 4 was tested for speed of comparison at a variety of input current levels. Speed of comparison was defined as the time T_c taken for the comparator to provide a full output swing starting at the instant the comparator is strobed. For the purpose of testing, the two input currents I_A and I_B were directed into the comparator, I_B was set at 0.9 I_A, and the total injector current I_j to the circuit was adjusted such that $I_j = I_A + I_B$. The duration of the $\overline{C_p}$ pulse used was 0.2 μs for most of the measured range. The frequency of the $\overline{C_p}$ pulse was adjusted to allow operation of the comparator in the quiescent mode. Fig. 10(b) shows a plot of the comparison time T_c as a function of the injection current I_j.

The *RS* and *T* flip-flops fabricated were also tested for maximum frequency of operation. Typical injection current per flip-flop ranged from 5 μA to 1 mA and a constant clock

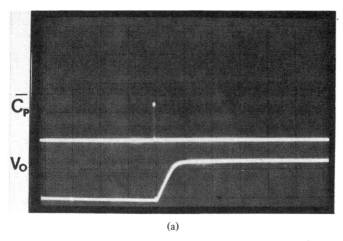

(a)

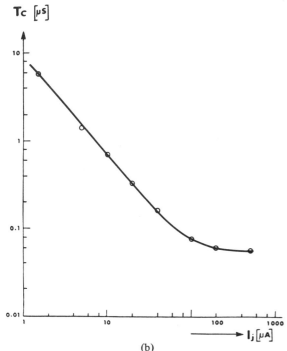

(b)

Fig. 10. Current comparator characteristics. (a) Waveforms (V_0 is the output voltage); $I_j = 5$ μA; vertical 0.5 V/div, horizontal 2 μs/div. (b) Comparison time T_c as a function of injection current per circuit I_j.

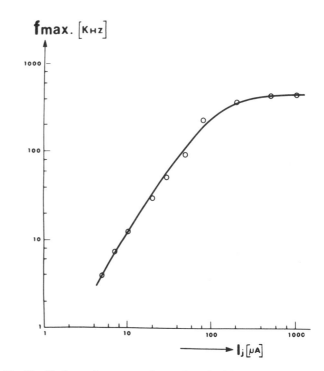

Fig. 11. Maximum frequency of operation of RS flip-flop as a function of total injection current I_j.

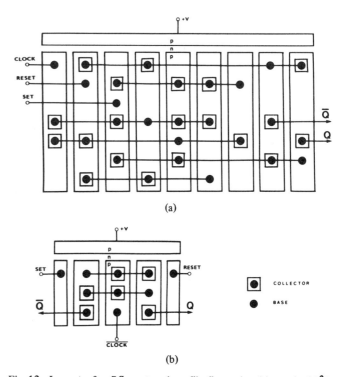

Fig. 12. Layout of a RS master–slave flip-flop using (a) standard I^{2}L technology (area = 4.3), (b) ISL technology (area = 1).

pulse width of 0.2 μs was used over most of the range of currents tested. Fig. 11 shows a plot of the maximum frequency of operation as a function of injected current I_j per flip-flop. As shown, a maximum frequency of operation of 400 kHz is reached at an injection current of 500 μA.

In order to compare ISL and standard I^{2}L technologies for synchronous logic applications, master–slave RS flip-flops using both technologies were tested. The flip-flops were found to exhibit the same maximum frequency of operation at any particular injection current;[2] however, as shown in Fig. 12, layouts for both of these flip-flops illustrate the reduction in area (75 percent) which results from the use of ISL rather than standard I^{2}L technology.

[2]It should be pointed out that the number of gates per flip-flop is smaller in ISL than in I^{2}L, and therefore for the same total injection current per flip-flop, the injection current per ISL gate is higher than that per I^{2}L gate.

Conclusion

In conclusion, the usefulness of the modified injector structure proposed in this paper has been demonstrated in the design of comparators and synchronous logic. The current comparator described can be used in analog to digital converters and as a state detector in dynamically coupled I^{2}L memories. The new structure offers a considerable reduction in area as compared to standard I^{2}L in the fabrication of synchronous logic while providing the same power X delay product per flip-flop.

REFERENCES

[1] K. Hart and A. Slob, "Integrated injection logic: A new approach to LSI," *IEEE J. Solid-State Circuits*, vol. SC-7, pp. 347–351, Oct. 1972.

[2] H. H. Berger and S. K. Wiedmann, "Merged transistor logic (MTL)—A low cost bipolar logic concept," *IEEE J. Solid-State Circuits*, vol. SC-7, pp. 340–346, Oct. 1972.

[3] R. Muller, "Current hogging injection logic," *IEEE J. Solid-State Circuits*, vol. SC-10, pp. 348–352, Oct. 1975.

[4] H. Lehring, "Current hogging logic (CHL)—A new bipolar logic for LSI," *IEEE J. Solid-State Circuits*, vol. SC-9, pp. 228–233, Oct. 1974.

[5] N. Friedman, C. A. T. Salama, and P. M. Thompson, "Realization of a multivalued integrated injection logic (MI^{2}L) full adder," *IEEE J. Solid-State Circuits*, vol. SC-12, pp. 532–534, Oct. 1977.

[6] N. C. de Troye, "Integrated injection logic—present and future," *IEEE J. Solid-State Circuits*, vol. SC-9, pp. 206–211, Oct. 1974.

Part III
Second Generation I²L:
Structures and Fabrication Techniques

The papers in this part present either new structures or fabrication process alterations which are aimed at improving the overall performance (especially speed and power-delay product) of conventional I²L. In general, the results have produced structures which are very similar to I²L as originally proposed. The resulting structures represent efforts to create I²L fabrication processes which could be placed in volume production during the time from 1975 to 1977. Consequently, the structures and techniques described do not represent the results of all-out efforts to achieve highest speeds and lowest power-delay products. In general, the structures do not push the limits of epi thickness, junction depths, nor photolithographic dimensions. In contrast, they rely mostly upon straightforward evolution of processing techniques or ingenuity in new approaches to the construction of conventional I²L-like structures. Efforts aimed at all-out speed improvements to I²L are described in the papers of part V.

The first paper in this part, by Herman *et al.* from Texas Instruments, describes a rather straightforward approach to improving I²L performance. The most striking difference between their approach and conventional I²L lies in the adoption of the technique of using a high-energy, deep, boron implantation to form the active, intrinsic base of the up-npn. This technique was first introduced by Bell Telephone Laboratories as described in paper III-4. The technique produces a base profile which can be precisely controlled and provides an aiding drift-field in much of the intrinsic base region, thereby improving device performance and manufacturability. The second and third most important aspects of the TI structure are the very low resistivity, extrinsic base region, and the thinner epitaxial layer. The low-resistivity extrinsic base region is crucial to the reduction of the series voltage drops along the length of gates of high fan-out which are operated at the high currents necessary for highest speed operation. The thinner epitaxial layer reduces the stored charge in the up-emitter and thereby reduces gate delays. The TI process/structure demonstrated that true LSI could be implemented in I²L with 20-ns gate delays over the −55 to 125°C temperature range using conventional (for 1976) processing techniques. One drawback to the TI structure (as well as many others) is that it does not permit super-thin epitaxial layers. The limitation is due to the variation in epitaxial-layer thickness (which is reported as 0.2 μ in the TI work) causing uncontrolled (for very thin layers) interaction between the intrinsic base doping and the n⁺ substrate out-diffusion.

Paper III-2 by Tokumaru *et al.* presents a novel technique (S²L) for obtaining near-optimum doping profiles for both the lateral pnp and the up-npn's of an I²L gate. The p-type epitaxial-layer base for the npn and the double-diffused lateral pnp, which fully encloses the npn, result in very high injection efficiency, high up-betas, large fan-out capability and good speed and power-delay performance. As is the case with the conventional lateral pnp form of injector, S²L will be susceptible to dynamic series base resistance effects during the turn-off portion of the gate's operation. This is true even though the gate is fully enclosed by its injector, a feature which diminishes the effects of series base resistance upon the turn-on delay. Thus for high fan-out gates, a low resistivity, extrinsic base diffusion will be required if highest speed is to be attained. The authors' statement concerning the effect of gate layout geometry upon packing density (i.e., with respect to Fig. 9) is not completely correct. The metal interconnection pattern will be negatively influenced by the square gate geometry in situations where the injector metal must be routed in a regular bus-type fashion. A second point which must be interpreted with caution is the power-delay curve of Fig. 13. The fan-out for the ring oscillator is not specified thus a fan-out of unity must be assumed and the speeds for larger fan-outs are not specified. Overall, S²L represents a significant second-generation I²L technique. The high injection efficiency is elegantly achieved and is in fact the feature which permits the fully injector-enclosed up-npn. The S²L structure also suffers from a dependence of the intrinsic npn base doping upon epitaxial-layer thickness variations. Consequently, the prospects for very thin epitaxial-layer structures are not good.

The third paper, on buried injector logic (BIL), by Yiannoulos, is a succinct account of an I²L form which achieves excellent performance in a standard analog bipolar process. One additional diffusion, the boron up-diffusion, is required to implement the structure which consists of a vertical npn current source and a vertical pnp switch. The vertical npn injector has good injection efficiency due to the profile of its diffused boron base. The characteristics of the analog, high-voltage portion of the circuit are not altered. The principal advantage of BIL is its good performance and simultaneous compatibility with high voltage analog processes. Thus the paper might have been presented in Part VII. Yet its structure is so unique as to warrant inclusion in the second generation category. It is worth noting that the author proposes (in Fig. 3) implementation of a merged vertical npn-vertical pnm which results as a natural consequence of the BIL structure.

The fourth paper, "Schottky I²L," by Hewlett, presents two novel ideas: 1) the insertion of a Schottky diode in series with the collector of an I²L gate in order to reduce signal swing, and 2) a technique for implanting an intrinsic p-type base doping profile deep below the surface of the n-type epitaxial layer.

Thus a thin n-type layer remains at the surface, and this feature permits the collector's series Schottky diode to be integrated directly into the usual contact position of an I^2L collector. The resulting parasitic Schottky-collector (pnm) transistor, whose emitter-base junction is merged with the npn's collector-base junction, was suppressed by increasing its integrated base doping in order to avoid current robbing from one output by an adjacent saturated output. This pnm device was later enhanced (Bibliography paper [IX-10]) and found application in a novel memory cell (paper IX-6). The implanted npn base doping permits precise control of the intrinsic up-npn's up-beta and improves the manufacturability of the I^2L structure. The effect of the series Schottky diode is to decrease the signal swing and thereby decrease the power-delay product. However, even though the Schottky collector offers overall advantages, the reduced signal swing reduces noise margins and makes the logical operation susceptible to the effects of n^+ crossunders. Consequently, the technique was implemented with a two-level metal interconnection scheme reported in bibliography paper [VIII-4].

Paper III-5 by Berger and Wiedmann presents various proposals for implementing I^2L with Schottky diodes integrated into the structures. The motives are to obtain a lower power-delay product by way of reduced signal swing and increased speed by reduction of stored charge when the down device goes into saturation. The authors claim that a factor of two reduction in the intrinsic delay time is possible. It must be pointed out here that such a reduction would only be realized if the stored charge which is to be eliminated contributes significantly to the total delay. That is, other regions of charge storage must not dominate the gate delay. The authors were the first to propose the use of a pnm device (a transistor with a Schottky junction as the collecting base-collector diode) as a means of implementing an I^2L-like gate. This structure appears to offer a compact layout and good power-delay performance. It has subsequently been proposed for incorporation in BIL of paper III-3 and adopted in paper III-7. Thus the pnm device holds promise for the future. The major drawback of this paper is the lack of actual implementation of the proposals in integrated circuit form. Only experimental results from breadboard-like circuits made up from discrete devices were demonstrated. In summary, the Schottky techniques look promising for future I^2L-like structures, and the ideas presented here are worthy of further exploration.

In the sixth paper, Walsh and Sumerling have labeled their vertical-pnp-injector configuration "Schottky I^2L," which is the same name as is used in paper III-4. However, in the vertical structure (or substrate-fed logic) the Schottky diodes are placed on the p-type base of the npn switch and are used to gain a reduced logical voltage swing as well as an isolated fan-in capability. The isolated fan-in permits a single collector output to drive multiple gate inputs, provided that the effective up-beta is adequate. The vertical pnp structure offers the advantage that each gate receives uniform injection of carriers over its entire area. Consequently, series resistance effects are diminished for the turn-on delay of the gate but are still important for the turn-off delay. Thus the extrinsic base needs to be of very low resistivity while permitting the fabrication of Schottky diodes on higher resistivity material. Even though the isolated fan-in capability offers significant layout advantages, it must be noted that each additional isolated fan-in increases the emitter-to-collector area ratio and thereby decreases the effective up-beta. Thus the isolated fan-in cannot be increased without limit. The vertical Schottky I^2L technique offers good second-generation performance yet may not be the best choice for future development as it also suffers from the seemingly everpresent drawback that the structure is sensitive to epitaxial-layer thickness variations. This sensitivity to epitaxial-layer thickness will increase with efforts aimed at more shallow structures and may limit the ultimate performance which can be achieved in a high-yielding process.

In the final paper in this part, Blackstone and Mertens present an implementation of the pnm structure proposed by Berger and Wiedmann. However, their approach is one of multiple collectors. They point out the current-hogging-related restrictions upon the fan-in and fan-out for this type of structure. Although the pnm approach looks promising, the multi-output Schottky collector upon a single intrinsic base region is not likely to be widely adopted, though it may find application in special instances.

It is noteworthy that five of the seven papers which describe second generation I^2L incorporate Schottky diodes in their structures. This fact suggests that the most successful I^2L techniques of the future may well rely upon Schottky diodes to attain third generation structures. Numerous other approaches to second generation I^2L structures have been reported and these publications are listed in the bibliography for Part III.

Second Generation I²L/MTL: A 20 ns Process/Structure

JOHN M. HERMAN, III, MEMBER, IEEE, STEPHAN A. EVANS, AND BEN J. SLOAN, JR., MEMBER, IEEE

Abstract—A high performance, second generation I²L/MTL gate for digital LSI applications with TTL compatibility has successfully been designed, characterized, and demonstrated fully functional over a wide current range and the military temperature range of −55 to 125°C. Performance is measured using an in-line five-collector gate having one end injector. The gate performed with the following characteristics at 100 μA injector current: $\beta_U^{eff} \geq 4$ for all collectors at 25°C and ≥ 2.5 at −55°C, $\alpha_{rec}/\alpha_F \cong 0.58$ and $\bar{\tau}_d$ = 18–20 ns from −55 to 125°C, and a speed–power product of 1.4 pJ at 25°C. At low injector currents, a constant speed–power product of 0.36 pJ at 25°C was obtained.

I. Introduction

FIRST generation I²L/MTL [1], [2] is basically a digital circuit technique, not a new technology [3], since it utilizes a basic four-mask, double-diffused bipolar process without junction isolation (n⁻ epi on n⁺ substrate) to build a gate consisting of a vertical n-p-n switching transistor and a lateral p-n-p load transistor. This gate has been extremely attractive for LSI applications since it has excellent functional density, a low speed–power product, and process simplicity. Its major shortcoming has been its absolute speed or performance at moderate current levels. To improve the absolute speed of the I²L/MTL gate, innovative process and device technology is required.

The purpose of this paper is to present a second generation I²L/MTL gate fabricated with a new process/structure and designed to operate at less than 20 ns for an input or injector current of 100 μA, while retaining the advantages of the first generation. This performance for both the far and near collectors is measured on a five-collector "stick"-type geometry with an injector at one end and is discussed using the standard I²L terminology [4].

The design of the second generation gate is described for both the structure and process, which includes a matrix on the p⁺ extrinsic base drive and implanted intrinsic base dose for the n-p-n transistor. A complete static and dynamic characterization then follows on the gates fabricated in the matrix. Finally, the second generation gate's performance is presented for a wide current range and the military temperature range of −55 to 125°C.

II. Gate Design and Characterization

The first generation [1], [2], double-diffused I²L/MTL gates suffer from a number of shortcomings which have limited their applications to low performance circuits in terms of absolute speed. A second generation I²L/MTL process/structure

Manuscript received October 4, 1976; revised December 2, 1976.
The authors are with the Semiconductor Research and Engineering Laboratory, Texas Instruments, Inc., Dallas, TX 75222.

is presented now which overcomes this low performance while maintaining the excellent functional density, low speed–power product, and process simplicity associated with the first generation.

A. Structure

The performance of the double-diffused gate is limited by the following key factors.

1) Low effective beta up per collector due to an unfavorable ratio of collector to emitter area, parasitic p-n-p transistor action between the bases of adjacent gates, and an inherently high value of down-beta which is difficult to control.

2) Emitter-base debiasing at high current levels for the "stick" geometry due to the high extrinsic base sheet resistance. This debiasing causes a significant reduction in the effective up-beta and an increase in the propagation delay for collectors far from the injector.

3) A positive gradient for the base impurity distribution which gives rise to an electric field that opposes minority carrier flow and increases the base transit time for the up-transistor.

4) Excess stored charge in the n⁻ epi region is a major source of diffusion capacitance for the n-p-n switching transistor which increases the propagation delay at high current levels.

The primary advantage of the first generation nonisolated I²L is its process simplicity, using the standard four-mask bipolar technology. The major disadvantage is the limitation on ac performance. In order to increase performance, it is necessary to design a new structure and process which overcomes the limitations previously described, while maintaining process simplicity.

Based on design curves and a clear understanding of the controlling factors for I²L gate performance, the gate in Fig. 1, shown with its structural cross section, was defined. The process used to build this structure will be described in detail in the next section. It requires a six-mask technology.

This structure has an intrinsic and extrinsic base which are introduced independently in the process. The intrinsic base is introduced by ion implantation, which allows precise control of the position and amount of active base charge. Since the up and down gains of the I²L n-p-n transistors are inversely proportional to this charge, the gains are predictably controlled with a very tight distribution. The output gate's breakdown requirement dictates the lower limit on implantation dosage ($\sim 1.0 \times 10^{12}$/cm²).

The extrinsic base region is heavily doped and is introduced by a conventional boron deposition. This base region is used to minimize lateral base debiasing and improves the effective

Reprinted from *IEEE J. Solid-State Circuits*, vol. SC-12, pp. 93–101, Apr. 1977.

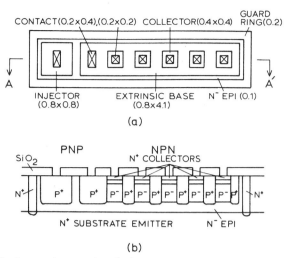

Fig. 1. A second generation I²L/MTL gate (a) and its structural cross-section at AA' (b). All dimensions for (a) are in mils.

TABLE I
MATERIAL PROCESS FLOW/MATRIX

PROCESS STEP	CONDITIONS
Getter Cycle	1075°C
Oxidation	1000°C (2500Å)
P+ Extrinsic Base O.R.	
P+ Extrinsic Base Deposition	BN, 980°C, 27Ω/□
P+ Extrinsic Base Diffusion (Matrix)	#1 10(O_2)-15(ST)-5(N_2) @ 1050°C #2 10-15-60 @ 1050°C #3 10-12-30 @ 1100°C #4 10-12-90 @ 1100°C
N+ Guard Ring O.R.	
N+ Guard Ring Deposition	5(O_2)-10(Source)-5(O_2)-10(ST)-5(N_2) @ 1050°C, $POCl_3$ @ 100cc Source
P⁻ Int. Base P.R. Mask/O.R.	1.5μm P.R.
P⁻ Int. Base Implant (Matrix)	¹¹Boron, 400 KeV 1,2,3,4x10¹²B/cm²
Collector P.R. Mask	
Collector Implant	⁷⁵Arsenic, 80KeV, 3.5x10¹⁵As/cm²
Oxidation	1000°C (1500Å Coll. Ox.)
Contact O.R.	
Metal Deposition - Pattern	PtSi, TiW, Al

ratio of the collector to emitter area. The latter is true because current injection into the extrinsic base is minimized when this region is heavily doped. Effectively, this reduces the parasitic component of the base current which increases the effective up-beta and reduces the charge stored in the base.

The parasitic p-n-p action is minimized by using a deep n⁺ diffused guard ring. This has an effect of increasing the effective up-beta [5] and isolating the bases of adjacent gates, thereby preventing crosstalk. The 0.1 mil space between the extrinsic base and guard ring is designed to reduce the peripheral emitter–base capacitance of the gate.

The starting material used to fabricate this structure is an n⁻ epitaxial film on an n⁺ substrate. The film resistivity is 1 Ω · cm, which was determined to be optimum for both the injection efficiency of the lateral p-n-p (0.2 mil base width) and the dynamic performance of the vertical n-p-n [6]. The film thickness is selected such that it equals the p⁺ extrinsic base junction depth plus the depletion region below it. This minimizes both the emitter–base depletion capacitance and the amount of charge that can be stored in the n⁻ epitaxial layer. In order to minimize the parasitic hole injection into the substrate [7] and the thermal up-diffusion during processing, an antimony-doped substrate with a resistivity of 0.01 Ω · cm is used.

B. Process Matrix

The process flow defined to fabricate the structure is given in Table I. The flow includes a matrix on the p⁺ extrinsic base drive and the p⁻ intrinsic base dose, while all other processing steps are identical. Fig. 2 illustrates the profiles for this structure, which for the p⁺ extrinsic base, p⁻ intrinsic base, and n⁺ collector were calculated using a process simulator [8]. This simulation takes into account all oxidations, including the initial getter cycle which consumes 0.2 μm of silicon when growing the masking oxide. If the getter step were omitted, it would be necessary to reduce the epitaxial film thickness accordingly.

The epitaxial film concentration and thickness are measured prior to processing using the Schottky C-V profile technique

on slices selected at random from the lot of epitaxial material. The thickness was also measured using an infrared interference measurement technique [9] (Epilog) on all slices prior to processing. The techniques correlated well, with the infrared measurement reading 0.5 μm greater than the thickness obtained from the C-V profile.

The C-V profile of a starting slice with an Epilog reading of 2.31 μm is shown in Fig. 2, and is accurate to ±10 percent

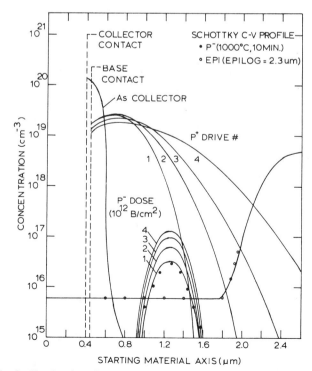

Fig. 2. Simulated profiles for process and matrix defined in Table I and measured C-V profiles for a nominal starting epitaxial film and p⁻ dose of 1 × 10¹² boron atoms/cm² at 400 keV. The origin for the measured p⁻ profile is 0.36 μm.

since the high-low transition occurs over many Debye lengths corresponding to the doping on the high side [10] and the circular Schottky diode diameter was optimized to minimize diode edge effects [11]. The up-diffusion into the epitaxial film during processing is approximately 0.1 μm, which results in a film thickness after processing of 0.6 μm less than the initial Epilog reading. This was determined experimentally by simulating the thermal cycle for all process variations in Table I on half of a given slice and then measuring the thickness on both halves of that slice. The spread in the actual epitaxial film thickness (*C-V*) is 1.8 ± 0.2 μm and concentration is 6 × 10^{15}/cm^3 ±15 percent over all slices processed in this study, with no measurable variation over any one slice profiled.

The matrix on the p$^+$ drive and p$^-$ dose is included in order to completely characterize the second generation I^{2}L/MTL gate. The p$^+$ drive variation will directly affect the junction characteristics of the n-p-n emitter–base and the injection efficiency of the p-n-p. The p$^-$ dose will determine the active base charge (Gummel number) or gain of an n-p-n switching transistor. In order to minimize the spreading out of the p$^-$ implant due to thermal cycling, it was introduced at the end of the process and activated during the final oxidation step at 1000°C.

The low dose, high energy boron implants are also characterized using the Schottky *C-V* profile technique. 12 Ω · cm boron-doped substrates were implanted with ^{11}B at 400 keV with doses up to 2 × 10^{12} B/cm^2. The boron was then activated in nitrogen at 1000°C for 10 min. The *C-V* profile for the dose of 1 × 10^{12} B/cm^2, correcting for the substrate concentration, is shown in Fig. 2. This profile, which was measured at 253 K, agrees with the true profile within ±20 percent since the Debye length for the measured concentrations is less than 400 Å [12]. The range and straggling are 0.9 and 0.12 μm, respectively, and agree well with experimental values reported in the literature [13].

C. Characterization

The key factors controlling the ac performance of the I^{2}L gate in Fig. 1 are the extrinsic base depletion capacitance, the total base diffusion capacitance, the extrinsic and intrinsic base sheet resistances, p-n-p alpha, and the n-p-n effective up-beta per collector. The results of a characterization on the matrix previously defined for all of these factors except the intrinsic base will be presented in this section along with the ac performance.

1) Extrinsic Base Depletion Capacitance and Sheet Resistance: The extrinsic base depletion capacitance and effective up-beta per collector are the two parameters having the greatest influence on the ac performance at low and medium current levels for the near collector of the gate in Fig. 1. For the other collectors, the extrinsic base resistance becomes important at higher current levels, since debiasing occurs along the emitter-base junction and results in a reduction of gain and ac performance.

The measured emitter–base zero-bias depletion capacitance of the n-p-n transistor in Fig. 1 versus the starting epitaxial thickness is given in Fig. 3. This capacitance, which was corrected for the parasitic metal lead and pad capacitance, is mainly a combination of the planar p$^+$-epi-substrate and

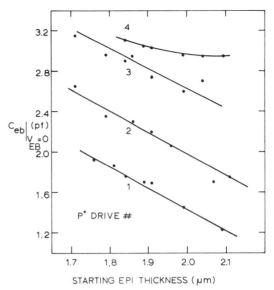

Fig. 3. Measured n-p-n emitter–base capacitance at zero-bias as a function of the actual starting epitaxial layer thickness for the four p$^+$ drive conditions.

peripheral p$^+$-n$^+$-guard ring capacitances. This figure illustrates the excellent correlation of the emitter–base capacitance and the measured epitaxial thickness for the four p$^+$ drive conditions where each point represents an average over a slice.

To extract the amount of peripheral capacitance associated with the emitter-base junction, the planar capacitance per unit area was calculated [14] using the simulated profiles in Fig. 2 for each p$^+$ drive condition and starting epitaxial thickness of 1.91 μm. The total capacitance was then measured on two other process monitors, one with the n$^+$ guard ring spaced 0.1 mil from the p$^+$ and the other with no guard ring. The results, which are presented in Table II, show that for p$^+$ drive condition 1, the peripheral p$^+$-n$^+$ guard ring capacitance is 60 percent of the total measured capacitance. This would be lowered to 45 percent with the p$^+$ side diffusion only into the n$^-$ epitaxial film, which agrees with calculations made by Buehler [15] for diffused junctions with geometries of this size. Theoretically, this peripheral capacitance could be eliminated with the use of an oxide guard ring.

The extrinsic base sheet resistance is also given in Table II for the four p$^+$ drive conditions. Since the base current and spreading resistance along the extrinsic base of the n-p-n is a function of this sheet resistance, it becomes important at higher current levels. In order to determine the approximate amount of debiasing, an assumption is made that the base current is linearly distributed down the extrinsic base. This results in an effective spreading resistance for the extrinsic base of [16]

$$REB \cong \frac{mR_s}{3} \qquad (1)$$

to the mth collector of the n-p-n transistor in Fig. 1 with an extrinsic sheet resistance of R_s. For the near collector, m=1 and for the far collector, m=5. For a sheet resistance of 100 Ω/□, there is approximately 33 μV of debiasing per collector for each microampere of n-p-n base current. This

TABLE II
p⁺ Extrinsic Base Zero-Bias Depletion Capacitance
and Sheet Resistance

P+ DRIVE CONDITION	SIMULATED	MEASURED		
	P+-SUBST. CAPACITANCE (pf/cm²)	PERIPHERAL CAPACITANCE		SHEET RESISTANCE (Ω/□)
		P+-N+ G.R. (pf/mil)	P+-N⁻ EPI (pf/mil)	
#1	2.6×10^4	0.11	0.07	100
#2	4.0×10^4	0.15	0.09	95
#3	6.9×10^4	0.15	0.09	90
#4	9.0×10^4	0.15	0.11	90

debiasing could be compensated for by scaling up the collector size to maintain an apparent gain for all collectors equal to that of the near collector.

2) DC Operation: The important parameters for characterizing the dc operation are the n-p-n gains, the p-n-p alphas, and the n-p-n breakdown voltages on a large single collector inverter used for interfacing with TTL circuitry.

As will be shown, the n-p-n up-gain, in conjunction with the extrinsic base depletion capacitance, have the most influence on the ac performance at low and medium current levels. The equivalent circuit for the five-collector gate in Fig. 1 is given in Fig. 4 where the various terminal currents and voltages and element currents are defined. The gains that have been measured in this characterization are defined with respect to these terminal voltages and currents. The definitions for the betas which apply to a single collector are

$$\beta_U' \equiv \frac{I_C}{I_B} \quad (I_{inj} = I_{C,M-1} = 0, V_E = 0, V_C = 0.5 \text{ V}), \quad (2)$$

$$\beta_U'' \equiv \frac{I_C}{I_B} \quad (I_{inj} = 0, V_E = 0, V_C = V_{C,M-1} = 0.5 \text{ V}), \quad (3)$$

$$\beta_U^{eff} \equiv \frac{I_C}{I_B} \quad (V_{inj} = V_E = 0, I_{C,M-1} = 0, V_C = 0.5 \text{ V}), \quad (4)$$

$$\beta_U^{comp} \equiv \frac{I_C}{I_{inj}} \quad (I_B = I_{C,M-1} = 0, V_E = 0, V_C = 0.5 \text{ V}), \quad (5)$$

and

$$\beta_D \equiv \frac{-I_E}{I_B} \quad (I_{inj} = I_{C,M-1} = 0, V_E = 0.5 \text{ V}, V_C = 0). \quad (6)$$

The results of the measurements for the up-betas as a function of the implanted intrinsic base dose for p⁺ drive 1 with an input current of 10 μA are given in Fig. 5. Extremely high intrinsic up-betas (>2000) are required in order to achieve the results presented in Fig. 5, since 99 percent of the input current is lost to the extrinsic elements [17].

β_U' measurement reflects the base current which is lost to the extrinsic base diode, I_{Diode}, the M-1 down-transistors for the open saturated collectors, $(M-1) I_D$, and the M-1 up-transistors, $(M-1) I_U$, with a small loss to the injector. β_U'' gives a measure of the amount of current hogging [1] since it has the same base current losses as β_U' except for the down-transistors which are eliminated by taking the $(M-1)$ collectors out of saturation. β_U^{eff}, which has the additional loss of base current to the p-n-p, I_{p-n-p}, over β_U', is a true measure of the up-beta in LSI circuit applications since a single injector tied in parallel with many injectors sees a constant voltage and not

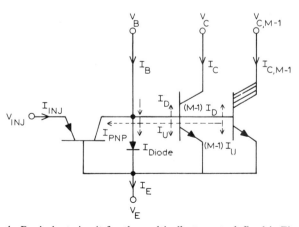

Fig. 4. Equivalent circuit for the multicollector gate defined in Fig. 1. The n-p-n base current components are indicated for the β_U^{eff} measurement condition by the dashed line.

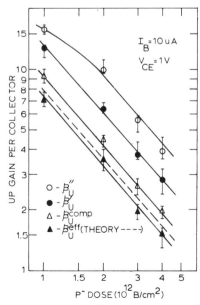

Fig. 5. Measured up gains per collector as a function of the p⁻ dose. Error bars represent the measured variation over many gates, and the dashed line is the calculated value for β_U^{eff}.

a constant current. β_U^{comp} is only the composite gain of a single gate driven with a current source and cannot be used to determine the effective up-gain for the gate in LSI applications. The calculated value for β_U^{eff} as a function of the intrinsic base dose is also presented in Fig. 5. The ratio of β_D/β_U^{eff} for the gates whose data are presented in Fig. 5 was 20 ± 10 percent at $I_B = 10\,\mu A$.

The injection efficiency of the lateral p-n-p depends on both the forward and recollection alphas, which from Fig. 4 are defined as

$$\alpha_F \equiv \frac{-I_B}{I_{inj}} \quad (I_C = I_{C,M-1} = V_E = 0) \tag{7}$$

and

$$\alpha_{rec} \equiv \frac{-I_{inj}}{I_B} \quad (I_{C,M-1} = 0, V_E = 0, V_C = 0.5\,V). \tag{8}$$

The process variable which affects the alphas is the p⁺ drive condition. The alphas measured as a function of input current are given in Fig. 6 for the four p⁺ drive conditions. The high recollection alphas for p⁺ drives 3 and 4 caused significant reduction in β_U^{eff} at lower current levels. Also, a large single emitter, double collector lateral p-n-p with mask dimensions of 0.2 mil base width and p⁺ strips of 0.6 × 5.5 mil was characterized by betas of 10-20 for p⁺ drives 1 and 2 and 20-40 for p⁺ drives 3 and 4.

The n-p-n breakdown voltage is punchthrough limited ($BV_{CES} < BV_{CBO}$) for this structure up to a dose of 3.5 × $10^{12}/cm^2$, as shown in Fig. 7. This was determined by measuring breakdown voltages on a single collector n-p-n transistor with a collector area of 0.16 mil², an intrinsic base area of 1.68 mil², and a minimum of 0.4 mil space between the extrinsic p⁺ base and n⁺ collector. The up-beta for this transistor with the implanted base dose of 1 × 10^{12} B/cm² was 400 for $I_C \leq 100\,\mu A$. A large single collector inverter designed to interface with TTL was also punchthrough limited for the implanted base dose of 1 × 10^{12} B/cm². A conservative limit on the base dose to guarantee a 5.5 V BV_{CES} would be 1.5 × 10^{12} B/cm².

3) AC Operation: The dynamic performance of the gate shown in Fig. 1 for the matrix previously described is charac-

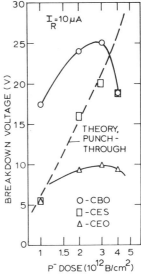

Fig. 7. n-p-n breakdown voltage as a function of p⁻ dose. Dashed curve is the calculated punchthrough breakdown voltage for collector-intrinsic base junction.

terized by the average propagation delay per gate, $\bar{\tau}_d$, as determined from the five-stage ring oscillators pictured in Fig. 8. The ring oscillator on the left has a near base, near collector hookup and the one on the right has a far base, far collector, all with respect to the injector. The sixth gate on each oscillator is a buffer gate which is used to eliminate capacitive loading on the oscillator. The average gate delay, which is defined as $(t_{on} + t_{off})/2$, where t_{on} is the time required to turn a gate on and t_{off} the time to turn it off, is equal to one-tenth the period of oscillation. The period of oscillation for both ring oscillators in Fig. 8 varied less than 5 percent at all input power levels.

The average delay per gate at 100 μA injector current is given in Fig. 9 as a function of the gate's extrinsic base capacitance for the four implanted intrinsic base doses. This figure, in conjunction with Fig. 3, clearly illustrates the importance of

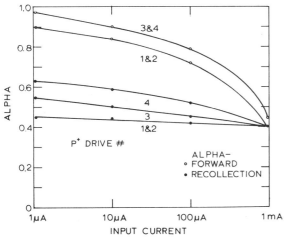

Fig. 6. p-n-p forward and recollection alphas as a function of current for the four p⁺ drive conditions.

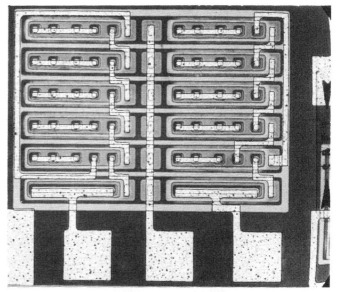

Fig. 8. Five-stage ring oscillators. Oscillator on the left has a near base, near collector and the one on the right has a far base, far collector, all with respect to the injector.

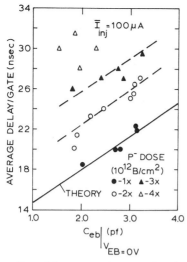

Fig. 9. Average time delay per gate as a function of the n-p-n emitter–base capacitance at zero-bias for an average injector current per gate of $100 \mu A$. The solid line is the calculated delay for a p^- dose of 1×10^{12} B/cm^2.

the epitaxial film thickness required in order to obtain high performance. The calculated average delay time versus emitter-base gate capacitance for a dose of 1×10^{12} B/cm^2 is also shown in Fig. 9. This was calculated by simulating a five-stage ring oscillator whose gate elements are shown in Fig. 4. The characteristics of the elements used in the simulation were obtained from both measured and calculated data [14].

Fig. 10(a) shows the effect an an implanted intrinsic base dose for p^+ drive 1 on the performance of the gate at medium and high current levels, while Fig. 10(b) shows the effect of the p^+ drive with a constant dose of 2×10^{12} B/cm^2 and an approximate starting epitaxial thickness of $1.91 \mu m$ for the same current levels. For this process/structure, both the extrinsic base capacitance and the effective up-beta per collector

are extremely important in order to achieve high performance in the medium to high current range.

III. SECOND GENERATION GATE PERFORMANCE

The results of the previous section demonstrate that high performance, specifically, an average gate delay of less than 20 ns at an injector current of $100 \mu A$, can be obtained for the gate defined in Fig. 1. The process designed to build this gate is given in Table I where the optimum p^+ drive condition is number 1, the implanted intrinsic base dose is 1×10^{12} B/cm^2 (1.5×10^{12} B/cm^2 for T^{2}L compatibility), and the starting epitaxial thickness (C-V) is 1.9–2.1 μm.

In order to completely characterize the performance of this 20 ns gate, the current and temperature dependence for both static and dynamic operation are measured. It will be shown that the I^{2}L gate is capable of performing over a wide current range and maintains high performance over the temperature range of -55 to $125°C$. This capability makes I^{2}L very attractive for LSI logic applications.

A. Gains

The dc gains for both the n-p-n and p-n-p are measured as a function of current and temperature. Fig. 11 shows the n-p-n gains for β_U^{eff} and β_D for both the near and far collectors in the gate of Fig. 1. From these results, it is seen that the gate is fully functional and able to sink two loads per collector for injector currents of up to approximately $200 \mu A$. Normally, each collector of the I^{2}L gate is designed to sink one load.

Fig. 12(a) compares β_U^{comp} and β_U^{eff}, which was presented in Fig. 11, as a function of temperature for three input current values. This comparison is made to illustrate the difference between the effective up-betas per collector for both a forced injector current and a forced injector voltage. The current dependence for each measurement condition at a given temperature can be explained by simply using the p-n-p characterization, which is given in Fig. 12(b), to determine the amount of base current driving the n-p-n. From Fig. 4, this current is defined as

$$I_{B,\text{n-p-n}} \equiv I_{\text{Diode}} + MI_U + (M-1)I_D. \qquad (9)$$

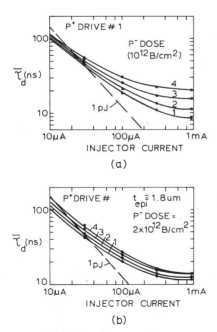

Fig. 10. Average gate delay as a function of injector current. (a) illustrates p^- dose dependence and (b) p^+ drive dependence for a p^- dose of 2×10^{12} B/cm^2.

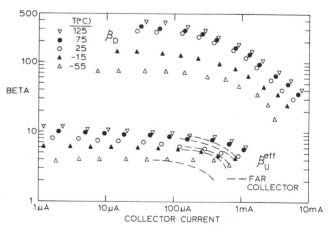

Fig. 11. Temperature dependence for down-beta and effective up-beta per near collector as a function of collector current. Dashed lines are for the far collector.

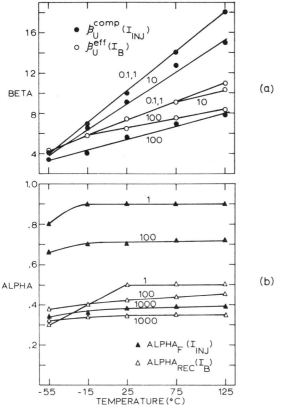

Fig. 12. Temperature and current dependence for the near collector composite up-beta and n-p-n effective up-beta (a) and for the p-n-p forward and recollection alphas (b). All current values are microamperes.

If a linear superposition is used for the p-n-p of an active forward-operated transistor and an inversely operated transistor [1] with *CB* current gains α_F and α_I, then the actual base current driving the n-p-n for the β_U^{eff} measurement is

$$I_{B,\text{n-p-n}}^{\text{eff}} = 1 - (\alpha_{\text{rec}}/\alpha_I)\, I_B \tag{10}$$

and for the β_U^{comp} measurement is

$$I_{B,\text{n-p-n}}^{\text{comp}} = \frac{(1 - \alpha_{\text{rec}}/\alpha_I)}{(1/\alpha_F - \alpha_{\text{rec}})}\, I_{inj} . \tag{11}$$

Combining these expressions for the same input current ($I_B = I_{inj}$),

$$I_{B,\text{n-p-n}}^{\text{comp}} = \frac{1}{(1/\alpha_F - \alpha_{\text{rec}})}\, I_{B,\text{n-p-n}}^{\text{eff}} . \tag{12}$$

Using the measured values of α_F and α_{rec} in Fig. 12(b), (12) predicts the gain dependence observed in Fig. 12(a) for both measurement conditions as a function of temperature and current.

The effective up-gain per collector is defined for a fixed injector current as the amount of current a collector for a gate which is on can sink divided by the current required to turn the gate off. β_U^{eff} as defined in (4) is the effective up-gain per collector when the injector sees a constant voltage, since the current a collector can sink is approximately $\alpha_F \beta_U^{eff} I_{inj}$ and the current it must sink is $\alpha_F I_{inj}$. For a forced injector current, the effective up-gain per collector

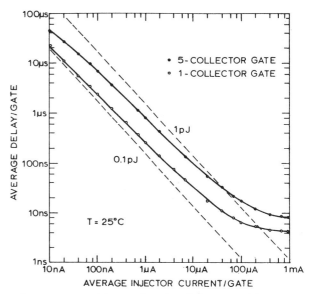

Fig. 13. Average gate delay as a function of the average injector current per gate for a five-collector and a one-collector gate. Dashed lines are the constant speed-power curves for 0.1 and 1.0 pJ.

would be $\beta_U^{\text{comp}}/\alpha_F$, which from the data presented in Fig. 12(a) and (b) clearly gives a much higher effective beta per collector than that obtained for a constant voltage at the input. Therefore, the β_U^{eff} measurement gives the actual effective gain per collector which will determine the dc gate performance in LSI applications.

B. Average Gate Delay

The average gate delay is measured for a five-collector gate using the ring oscillators in Fig. 8 and for a single collector gate laid out identically to the ring oscillator in Fig. 8. Fig. 13 shows the average gate delay versus average injector current per gate. The average gate delay varied less than 5 percent at all current levels and temperatures for both five-collector gates and both single collector gates.

The speed-power product for the five-collector gate at low current levels is 0.36 pJ and increases to 1.4 pJ (18 ns) at 100 μA injector current. The highest speed is 8 ns at 1 mA. The single collector gate has a speed-power product of 0.13 pJ at low currents and 0.5 pJ (6.5 ns) at 100 μA injector current with a maximum performance of 4.5 ns at 400 μA. Gates with two, three, and four collectors would have average gate delays of approximately 9, 12, and 15 ns, respectively, at 100 μA injector current.

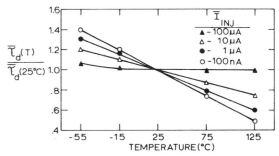

Fig. 14. Normalized average gate delay as a function of temperature for the average injector currents specified.

The temperature dependence of the average gate delay normalized to that at 25°C is given in Fig. 14, and holds for both the single and five-collector gates. At 100 μA injector current, the average gate delay is independent of temperature over the range changes shown and varies less than 50 percent for currents down to 100 nA/gate.

IV. SUMMARY

A high performance, second generation I^2L/MTL gate with TTL compatibility has been successfully designed and characterized over a wide current range and temperatures of -55 to 125°C. This gate maintains the first generation's excellent functional density, low speed-power, and process simplicity, while improving the absolute speed at medium current levels.

The process and structure for the gate is defined by 1 $\Omega \cdot$ cm, 1.9-2.1 μm (C-V) starting n^- epitaxial layer on an antimony-doped 0.01 $\Omega \cdot$ cm n^+ substrate, a p^+ extrinsic base sheet resistance less than 100 $\Omega/\square$, p^+ extrinsic base capacitance per unit area of $< 3 \times 10^4$ pF/cm^2 with complete carrier depletion in the n^- layer under the extrinsic base, and a boron-implanted intrinsic base dose of 1-1.5 $\times 10^{12}$ B/cm^2 at 400 keV.

It has been demonstrated that in order to achieve high performance for this structure in the medium current range, the n-p-n extrinsic base capacitance must be minimized, the n-p-n effective up-beta per collector maximized within breakdown voltage constraints, and the p-n-p gain ratio $\alpha_{\text{rec}}/\alpha_F$ minimized.

The second generation gate with five collectors in-line has the following performance at 100 μA injector current: $\beta_U^{\text{eff}} > 4$ for both the far and near collectors at 25°C and >2.5 at -55°C, $\alpha_{\text{rec}}/\alpha_F \cong 0.58$ and an average gate delay of 18-20 ns from -55 to 125°C, and a speed-power product of 1.4 pJ at 25°C. It also performs well at low injector currents with a measured speed-power product of 0.36 pJ at 25°C.

The ac performance of this second generation gate could theoretically be doubled by replacing the n^+ guard ring with an oxide guard ring which would result in a considerable increase in process complexity. Second generation I^2L/MTL with an n^+ guard ring is a highly manufacturable process because of its controllability and simplicity. When coupled with the high performance of the gate, it makes this type of logic very attractive for LSI applications. Recently, Texas Instruments, Inc. announced a 16-bit microprocessor implemented in a single LSI circuit using the second generation I^2L/MTL technology [18].

ACKNOWLEDGMENT

The authors would like to thank W. Banzhaf, J. Englade, W. Ray, and R. Martin for many valuable discussions, J. Manica for assistance with the test bar, C. Fuller for the metal depositions, E Alford for processing the material, and S. White for measurement assistance.

REFERENCES

[1] H. H. Berger and S. K. Wiedmann, "Merged-transistor logic (MTL)—A low cost bipolar logic concept," *IEEE J. Solid-State Circuits*, vol. SC-7, pp. 340–346, Oct. 1972.

[2] K. Hart and A. Slob, "Integrated injection logic: A new approach to LSI," *IEEE J. Solid-State Circuits*, vol. SC-7, pp. 346–351, Oct. 1972.

[3] N. C. deTroye, "Integrated injection logic—Present and future," *IEEE J. Solid-State Circuits*, vol. SC-9, pp. 206–211, Oct. 1974.

[4] H. H. Berger and S. K. Wiedmann, "Terminal oriented model for merged transistor logic (MTL)," *IEEE J. Solid-State Circuits*, vol. SC-9, pp. 211–217, Oct. 1974.

[5] A. Schmitz and A. Slob, "The effect of isolation regions on the current gain of inverse NPN-transistors used in integrated injection logic (I^2L)," in *Int. Solid-State Circuits Conf. Dig.*, 1974, pp. 508–510.

[6] F. M. Klaassen, "Device physics of integration injection logic," *IEEE Trans. Electron Devices*, vol. ED-22, pp. 145–152, Mar. 1975.

[7] M. S. Mock, "Transport equations in heavily doped silicon, and the current gain of a bipolar transistor," *Solid-State Electron.*, vol. 16, pp. 1251–1259, Nov. 1973.

[8] P. Shah and W. Schroen, "A process model for sequential diffusions and redistributions in silicon LSI technology," *J. Electrochem. Soc.*, vol. 122, p. 840, Mar. 1975.

[9] P. F. Kane and G. B. Larrabee, *Characterization of Semiconductor Materials*. New York: McGraw-Hill, 1970, pp. 226–228.

[10] W. C. Johnson and P. T. Panousis, "The influence of Debye length on the C-V measurement of doping profiles," *IEEE Trans. Electron Devices*, vol. ED-18, pp. 965–973, Oct. 1972.

[11] J. A. Copeland, "Diode edge effect on doping-profile measurements," *IEEE Trans. Electron Devices*, vol. ED-17, pp. 404–407, May 1970.

[12] C. P. Wu, E. C. Douglas, and C. W. Muller, "Limitations of the C-V technique for ion-implanted profiles," *IEEE Trans. Electron Devices*, vol. ED-22, pp. 319–329, June 1975.

[13] D. H. Lee and J. W. Mayer, "Ion implanted semiconductor devices," *Proc. IEEE*, vol. 62, pp. 1241–1255, Sept. 1974.

[14] S. A. Evans and J. S. Fu, "Application of a new, accurate bipolar simulator to correlate device performance to process selection," in *Extended Abstracts of the Electrochem Soc. Meeting*, May 1975, pp. 394–395.

[15] M. G. Buehler, "Peripheral and diffused layer effects on doping profiles," *IEEE Trans. Electron Devices*, vol. ED-19, pp. 1171–1178, Nov. 1972.

[16] A. B. Phillips, *Transistor Engineering*. New York: McGraw-Hill, 1962, pp. 216–220.

[17] S. A. Evans, J. M. Herman, III, and B. J. Sloan, "On The electrical properties of the I^2L n-p-n transistor," *IEEE Trans. Electron Devices*, vol. ED-23, pp. 1192–1194, Oct. 1976.

[18] L. A. Chamberlin and J. M. Hughes, "The SBP9900 microprocessor," *N.A.E. C.O.N.*, Wright-Patterson AFB, Dayton, OH, May 1976.

I²L with a Self-Aligned Double-Diffused Injector

YUKUYA TOKUMARU, MASANORI NAKAI, SATOSHI SHINOZAKI, SHINTARO ITO, AND YOSHIO NISHI

Abstract—This paper reports the structure, topology, and characterization of integrated injection logic (I²L/MTL) with a self-aligned double-diffused injector. It is shown that using the new structure, a lateral p-n-p transistor with effective submicron base width can be realized even by using standard photolithographic techniques. One of the features of the approach is the high injection efficiency. Another feature is the high current gain capability for n-p-n transistors. A power-delay product of 0.06 pJ, a propagation delay time of 10 ns at the power dissipation of 80 μW, and a packing density of 420 gates/mm² have been obtained by single layer interconnections of 6 μm details. A *J-K* flip-flop with clear and preset terminals has been fabricated to demonstrate the superiority of S²L to conventional I²L.

Manuscript received September 2, 1976.

The authors are with the Semiconductor Engineering Department, Toshiba Research and Development Center, Tokyo Shibaura Electric Company, Ltd., Kanagawa, Japan.

I. INTRODUCTION

THE performance of integrated injection logic (I²L) is determined by the characteristics of upside-down operated n-p-n transistors with multicollector and lateral

Reprinted from *IEEE J. Solid-State Circuits*, vol. SC-12, pp. 109–114, Apr. 1977.

75

p-n-p transistors [1], [2]. In order to obtain large fan-out capability, high speed, and large noise margin in I^2L circuits, high current gain for the n-p-n transistor is required in an upside-down operated mode [3]. But the current gain realized with standard bipolar processes is very low because of hole injection in the n-type epitaxial layer and the presence of a retarding electric field in the base region of the n-p-n transistor.

Higher injector efficiency and low parasitic capacitance result in an excellen   wer–delay product. Present I^2L devices are limited in injector efficiency by the attainable minimum base width of the lateral p-n-p transistor being influenced by the accuracy of photolithography, undesirable lateral hole injection in the direction away from the base of the n-p-n transistor, and vertical hole injection into the n-type epitaxial layer under the p^+ injector. This undesirable lateral hole injection can be suppressed by using an n^+ guard ring. However, the junction formed between the n^+ guard ring and the p^+ base region of the n-p-n transistor introduces a parasitic capacitance which slows down the extrinsic propagation delay time [4].

In this paper, a new approach will be described which offers I^2L structures having both a self-aligned double-diffused injector and an epitaxial base layer for the n-p-n transistor. One of the features of the approach is the high injection efficiency. Thus, it is being identified as S^2L for self-aligned super-injection logic. Another feature is a high current gain capability for n-p-n transistors. Feasibility in topology and packing density will also be discussed, as well as several experimental results to support the discussion.

II. DEVICE STRUCTURE

The basic gate of S^2L is characterized by complementary pair transistors with optimized impurity profiles. The structure in which the upside-down operated n-p-n transistor involved in an inverter is surrounded with the self-aligned double-diffused injector with a submicron base width is shown in Fig. 1. The p-type epitaxial layer acts both as a collector of the lateral p-n-p transistor and as a base of the n-p-n transistor. The n-type well acts effectively as the base of the lateral p-n-p transistor, and the n^+ substrate acts as the common emitter of the upside-down operated n-p-n transistor. The injector structure allows one to independently choose impurity concentrations for the emitter and collector of the lateral p-n-p transistor, which essentially results in a heavily doped emitter. The base width, which is defined by the subsequent diffusions of phosphorus and boron

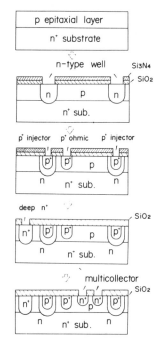

Fig. 2. Process flow chart of S^2L.

through the same silicon nitride opening, is easily controlled with better accuracy than that of the lateral p-n-p transistor in conventional I^2L. Submicron base width, four sides of injection without loss of minority carriers injected from the injector, and optimized impurity profile are features, all of which improve the injection efficiency. Since the n-p-n transistor has a lightly doped uniform base with a heavily doped emitter in contrast to having the retarding field with a lightly doped emitter found in conventional I^2L, it can be expected to exhibit a large value of upward current gain βu while retaining the adequate value of the downward current gain.

And it is also possible to reduce the junction capacitance of the n-p-n transistor by introducing the lightly doped epitaxial layer. As a result, the S^2L structure simultaneously improves the performance of complementary pair transistors, which is not possible with the conventional I^2L structure.

Fig. 2 is the process flow chart of S^2L. Fabrication starts with a p-type epitaxial layer growth on the n^+ substrate. Then the surface of the wafer is oxidized and silicon nitride film is deposited. The silicon nitride film and the oxide film are engraved for the base diffusion of lateral p-n-p transistors. The n-type well, which is formed by phosphorus diffusion, reaches the n^+ substrate at the bottom. After the base ohmic contact holes of n-p-n transistors are made by the same masking technique, boron is diffused. In the next step, the deep n^+ region is formed by phosphorus diffusion. The multicollectors of n-p-n transistors are made finally by conventional preferential diffusion. It may be noticed that the resistivity of the p-type epitaxial layer is chosen to meet the requirements for the n-p-n transistor only. The p^+ region must be heavily doped to guarantee a good injection efficiency, a low resistance of injector line, and a high current gain βu of the n-p-n transistor. Optimized impurity profiles of S^2L are indicated in Fig. 3 in comparison with the conventional I^2L.

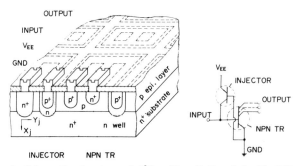

Fig. 1. Schematic structure of I^2L with self-aligned double-diffused injector.

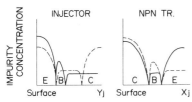

Fig. 3. Impurity profiles of complementary pair transistors with S^2L structure (solid lines) compared with those of conventional I^2L (broken lines).

III. TOPOLOGY

The *J-K* flip-flop, composed of 15 inverters with 3 buffer transistors shown in Fig. 4, exemplifies the layout technique to demonstrate the superiority of S^2L to conventional I^2L. The base region of the lateral p-n-p transistor or the n-type well concurrently acts as a separating region for isolating the respective inverter elements from each other. This eliminates the necessity of intentionally providing a separating region and, in consequence, simplifies the pattern of I^2L devices. An injector is formed in the n-type well all along the outer periphery of the inverter elements by the self-aligned double-diffusion technique, which leads to no additional injector area.

Furthermore, as described previously, the S^2L structure permits a higher impurity concentration for the injector, which ensures the very low series resistance of the injector line. As a result, it is possible to minimize the area of metal interconnection for the injector. The advantages of this approach are as follows: designing of large circuits is easy because the minimized interconnection for injector hardly disturbs the logic wiring, and the self-aligned injector structure, in spite of injection from four sides, can attain high packing density superior to conventional I^2L.

Practical packing densities including injector area are indicated in Fig. 5. When 6 μm mask rules are used, packing densities are 420 gates/mm^2 and 250 gates/mm^2 for fan-out = 1 and 3, respectively. Since a one-side injector structure can also be used in S^2L, an oxide wall structure can be easily applied to make the separating region. The broken line in the figure shows the packing density of one-side injector S^2L with a three-sided oxide wall.

In addition to high packing density, the oxide wall structure improves the ratio of base and collector area of the n-p-n transistor, which results in high upward current gain. But it must be noticed that the interconnection area for the injector has

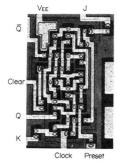

Fig. 4. Photomicrograph of a *J-K* flip-flop with clear and preset terminals fabricated by S^2L technologies.

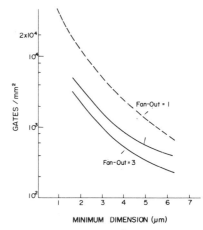

Fig. 5. Practical packing densities of S^2L. The solid lines indicate the case with a four-side injection structure. A one-side injector structure with a three-sided oxide wall is represented by the broken line.

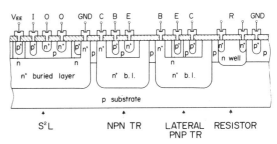

Fig. 6. Cross section of a chip which shows the possibility of combining S^2L gates with different types of bipolar devices on the same chip: CDI type n-p-n transistor, new lateral p-n-p transistor, and self-isolated n-type resistor.

been increased on a chip and that the oxide wall needs a complicated process. S^2L can be combined with different types of isolated bipolar devices: an n-p-n transistor of collector diffusion isolation (CDI) type [5], that of oxide-isolated monolithic (OXIM) type [6], a lateral p-n-p transistor with a self-aligned double-diffused emitter, and an n-type well resistor on the same chip, as shown in Fig. 6. This leads to high functional density.

IV. CHARACTERISTICS

Fig. 7 shows a typical example of the current gain characteristics of complementary pair transistors for the basic S^2L gate with a single collector of 14 by 14 μm. The upward current gain βu of the n-p-n transistor ranges from 30 to 100 under normal operating conditions, and the injector efficiency α of the lateral p-n-p transistor is higher than 0.9.

In spite of the decrease in the ratio of collector area to base area in a multicollector configuration, large values of βu have been obtained in the multicollector structure of S^2L, as shown in Fig. 8. Thus, the combination of the high efficiency injector and high βu n-p-n transistor exactly meets the requirements for low power dissipation, large fan-out capability, and reduction of the minimum delay time per gate.

Here, one might suspect that the fairly high sheet resistivity of the p-type epitaxial layer would cause a certain voltage drop in the base region remote from the base contact. But this

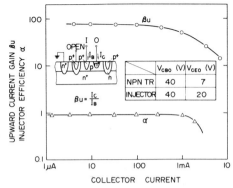

Fig. 7. Characteristics of the upside-down operated n-p-n transistor with a single collector and the injector in S^2L.

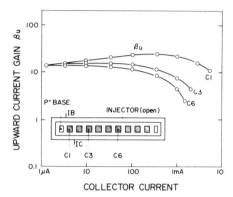

Fig. 8. Characteristics of the multicollector n-p-n transistor. Base current is directly injected from the p^+ base ohmic terminal.

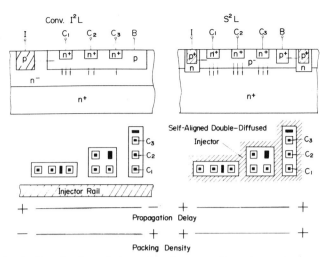

Fig. 9. Contributions of the multicollector configuration to the propagation delay time of inverters and packing density.

problem can be easily solved by introducing a heavily doped path in the base region. Moreover, the heavily doped path should also contribute to reducing the collector series resistance of the lateral p-n-p transistor and the storage of electrons in the extrinsic base region of the n-p-n transistor. In the conventional I^2L structure, the storage of holes in the low doped n-type epitaxial layer is the largest factor in determining the minimum delay time [7]. S^2L has a highly doped n^+ substrate as an emitter for the n-p-n transistor. Here lies one of the main differences between conventional I^2L and S^2L where the storage of electrons in the p-type epitaxial base layer may be important. Thus, the heavily doped path introduced in S^2L structure would improve the minimum delay time. In addition to reduction in charge storage, the extrinsic contribution to base current also decreases, leading to an increase in the current gain βu.

Fig. 9 indicates the contributions to the propagation delay time of inverters by the multicollector configuration in S^2L compared with conventional I^2L. It has been pointed out in conventional I^2L that the propagation delay time is strongly influenced by the layout of inverters [8]. When the base region is laid out perpendicular to the injector, inhomogeneous current density due to the base resistance of the n-p-n transistor results in different propagation delay times for the different collectors. A layout with inverters parallel to the injector ensures the minimum delay time for all collectors,

but decreases the packing density. Since all collectors in S^2L receive equal amounts of current from the self-aligned p^+ injector, the delay time should be the same for all collectors. Furthermore, the packing density of S^2L is not influenced by the layout. Fig. 10 demonstrates that different collectors in S^2L concurrently have the same value of sink current.

As stated in Section III, the S^2L structure ensures a smaller area of interconnection for the injector because of low series resistance. This effect will again be discussed using the test structure composed of 24×25 latticed inverters with 16 interconnection points of the injector laid out at the periphery of the block, as shown in Fig. 11. The currents injected into the base region of inverters in the block from the injector pad are shown as a function of the number of injector pads m in Fig. 12. In this case, the currents are measured for the inverters on a diagonal of the block. The result of $m = 8$ shows that all inverters in the block can concurrently obtain equal amounts of base current. To guarantee logic operation in the block, the current gain of the inverter having the minimum current injected must be greater than the ratio of the maximum injected current to the minimum value. High βu of S^2L also contributes to minimizing the area of interconnection for the injector.

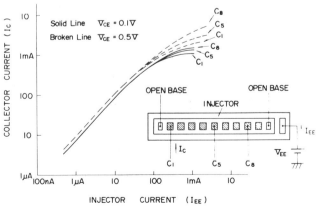

Fig. 10. Characteristics of the multicollector n-p-n transistor. Base current is injected from the self-aligned double-diffused injector.

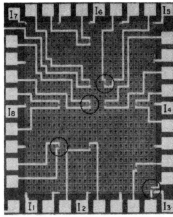

Fig. 11. Photomicrograph of a test structure composed of 600 inverters and one self-aligned double-diffused injector. I_1–I_8 are injector pads.

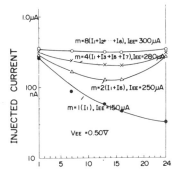

Fig. 12. Injected current characteristics of inverters as a function of the number of injector pads m. The inverters with the ○ mark have been measured under the condition of V_{BC} (for the lateral p-n-p transistors) = 0.

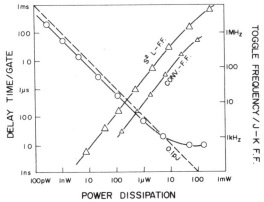

Fig. 13. Power–delay product of a 25-stage ring oscillator in S^2L and toggle frequency characteristics of S^2L *J-K* flip-flop in comparison with those of conventional I^2L.

V. Performance

To evaluate the basic performance of S^2L gates, a 25-stage ring oscillator has been fabricated using the minimum pattern size of 6 μm. The power–delay product is shown in Fig. 13. The value associated with the operating power level has been observed to be in the range of 0.06–0.1 pJ/gate with a minimum delay of 10 ns and a power dissipation of only 80 μW. Compared to conventional I^2L circuits, the performance is improved by up to a factor of 5. The toggle frequency characteristics of a *J-K* flip-flop with clear and preset terminals are also shown in Fig. 13 in comparison with those of a conventional I^2L version also fabricated in the present study. It is clear that an S^2L *J-K* flip-flop is significantly improved as far as the power dissipation is concerned.

VI. Summary

A novel I^2L structure with a self-aligned double-diffused injector and an epitaxial base layer for the n-p-n transistor has been described. High efficiency of the injector and high current gain capability of the n-p-n transistors have successfully given a power–delay product of 0.06 pJ/gate, a minimum propagation delay time of 10 ns at the power dissipation of 80 μW, and large fan-out capability. The advantage of an S^2L configuration was demonstrated by a *J-K* flip-flop with clear and preset terminals with a packing density of 420 gates/mm^2 and an excellent layout simplicity.

Acknowledgment

The authors are most grateful to J. Nakamura, H. Amano, and A. Ohmichi for helpful discussions and technical assistance.

References

[1] H. H. Berger and S. K. Wiedmann, "Merged-transistor logic (MTL)—A low cost bipolar logic concept," *IEEE J. Solid-State Circuits*, vol. SC-7, pp. 340–345, Oct. 1972.

[2] K. Hart and A. Slob, "Integrated injection logic: A new approach to LSI," *IEEE J. Solid-State Circuits*, vol. SC-7, pp. 346–351, Oct. 1972.

[3] F. M. Klaassen, "Device physics of integrated injection logic," *IEEE Trans. Electron Devices*, vol. ED-22, pp. 145–152, Mar. 1975.

[4] R. A. Allen and K. K. Schuegraf, "Oxide-isolated integrated injection logic," in *1974 IEEE Int. Solid-State Circuits Conf., Dig. Tech. Papers*, Feb. 1974, pp. 16–17.

[5] B. T. Murphy and V. J. Glinski, "Transistor–transistor logic with high packing density and optimum performance at high inverse gain," *IEEE J. Solid-State Circuits*, vol. SC-3, pp. 261–267, Sept. 1968.

[6] W. J. Evans, A. R. Tretola, R. S. Payne, M. L. Olmstead, and D. V. Speeney, "Oxide-isolated monolithic technology and applications," *IEEE J. Solid-State Circuits*, vol. SC-8, pp. 373–379, Oct. 1973.

[7] H. H. Berger, "The injection model—A structure–oriented model for merged transistor logic (MTL)," *IEEE J. Solid-State Circuits*, vol. SC-9, pp. 218–227, Oct. 1974.

[8] N. C. deTroye, "Integrated injection logic—Present and future," *IEEE J. Solid-State Circuits*, vol. SC-9, pp. 206–211, Oct. 1974.

Buried Injector Logic: Second Generation I^{2}L Performance

Aris A. Yiannoulos

Bell Laboratories

Reading, PA

THE RELATIVE MERITS of a vertically structured I^{2}L gate have been propounded earlier[1] in a SFL (*Substrate Fed Logic*) approach. This paper will discuss the integration of a SFL-type gate as a SBC (*Standard Buried Collector*) element, affording a versatile vehicle for integrating I^{2}L with linears. The structure is shown in Figure 1. The role played by the substrate and the first epitaxial layer in SFL is presently assigned to double buried diffusion and throughout the structure the function of P-type and N-type material has been interchanged. The gate is in the PNP-inverter/NPN-source arrangement, which is the reverse of the usual configuration. The SBC NPN transistor shown alongside the gate (Figure 1) shares the buried-N layer, the epitaxy, and the P$^+$ surface diffusion. The buried-P diffusion, not normally a part of the SBC process, is the only source of deviation, or addition, presently required. The advantages:

(*a*)   No conflict between the need for high upward gain in the I^{2}L inverter and the need for high breakdown in the linear device (the SBC NPN). The two can be independently adjusted.

(*b*)   Optimally graded impurity profiles (Figure 4), and favorably constituted parasitics.

(*c*)   Choice of Schottky-clamped, Schottky-collector, Schottky-base, or standard I^{2}L function as in SFL (Figure 3), and elsewhere.

(*d*)   High packing density afforded by the advantages inherent to a buried injector; i.e., (1) – versatility in keeping power busses from interrupting logic ties, and (2) – the gates need not line up to face a rail.

(*e*)   High fan-out and matching collector characteristics, since all collectors face the injector in a like manner.

(*f*)   Means to isolate electrically the logic portion of the circuit from the linear portion, or one logic portion from another to power gate or to stack.

The test chip uses P-type substrate, $<100>$, boron doped, $\rho > 10\Omega$-cm, and N-type epitaxy, arsenic doped, $\rho = 2\Omega$-cm.

The diffusion sequence is:

N-type buried layer – as implant and drive-in . . .

P-type buried layer – B implant and drive-in . . .

Collector and injector contact diffusion from POCl$_3$ predeposit . . .

Isolation diffusion from BN predeposit . . .

Base diffusion – B implant and drive-in . . .

Emitter diffusion and gate-base contacts from POCl$_3$ source . . .

Gate collectors from nonselective B implant and anneal . . .

Plantinum silicide and Metal (Ti, Pt, Au).

The process requires a minimum of seven photoresist steps excluding metal pattern definition. Table I (Figure 2) summarizes the essential features of both the logic and of a typical NPN device.

---

[1] Blatt, V., Walsh, P.S., and Kennedy, L.W., "Substrate Fed Logic," *IEEE J. Solid-State Circuits*, Vol. SC-10, p. 336-343; Oct., 1975.

GATE CHARACTERISTICS (NON–SCHOTTKY)	FO=5	FO=2
DENSITY	110 GATES/MM^2	185 GATES/MM^2
$\alpha'_u \beta$ (PER COLLECTOR)	12	20
α'_u (NPN)	0.65	0.65
β_d (PNP)	180	200
$\tau_D \cdot P$	0.22 pJ	0.17 pJ
τ_D (MIN)	30 ns	25 ns

NPN CHARACTERISTICS (MIN. GEOMETRY SBC LINEAR DEVICE)

BV_{EBO}	7.0V (MIN.)
BV_{CBO}	60.0V (MIN.)
BV_{CEO}	30.0V (MIN.)
BV_{CIO}	80.0V (MIN.)
β_{peak} (I$_C$ = 3mA)	70 (TYP.)
f$_{T peak}$	400 MHz (TYP.)
r'_c	18 Ω (TYP.)

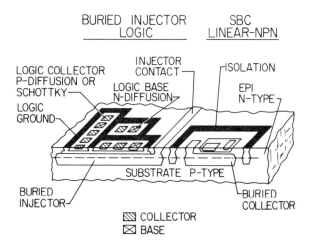

BURIED INJECTOR LOGIC   SBC LINEAR-NPN

LOGIC COLLECTOR P-DIFFUSION OR SCHOTTKY
LOGIC
LOGIC GROUND
INJECTOR CONTACT
LOGIC BASE N-DIFFUSION
ISOLATION
EPI N-TYPE
SUBSTRATE P-TYPE
BURIED INJECTOR
BURIED COLLECTOR
⊠ COLLECTOR
⊠ BASE

FIGURE 1–Cross section of BIL and NPN device structure.

FIGURE 2–Table of essential performance characteristics.

Reprinted from *IEEE Int. Solid-State Circuits Conf. Digest Tech. Papers*, Feb. 1978, pp. 12–13.

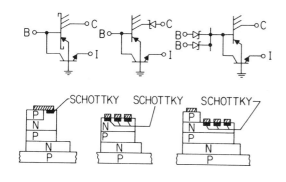

[Above]

FIGURE 3--Potential Schottky configurations.

[Right]

FIGURE 4—BIL impurity profile.

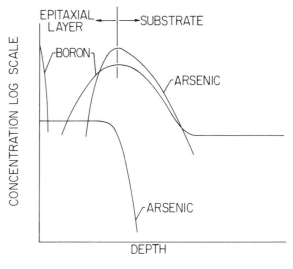

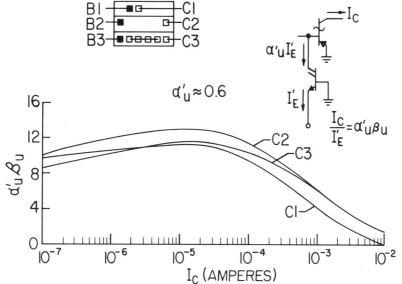

$\alpha'_u \approx 0.6$

$$\frac{I_C}{I'_E} = \alpha'_u \beta_u$$

FIGURE 5—Gate gain characteristics.

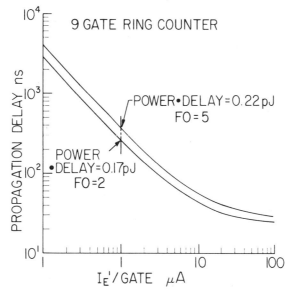

FIGURE 6—Nine gate ring counter propagation delay characteristics.

Schottky I²L

FRANK W. HEWLETT, JR., MEMBER, IEEE

Abstract—Schottky I²L uses the principles of integrated injection logic (I²L/MTL) and the properties of ion implantation to obtain improved performance at the same densities as conventional I²L. Schottky diodes are formed in the multicollectors of the switching transistor and reduce the signal swing, thus improving the power delay efficiency. An increase in the intrinsic speed limit is also feasible.

The Schottky I²L structure and characteristics are described and contrasted with conventional I²L. A model which is useful for its design is discussed. Integrated test structures which provide direct comparison between conventional and Schottky I²L performance have been fabricated. The experimental results demonstrate a factor of 2 improvement in power-delay efficiency of Schottky I²L over conventional I²L.

I. INTRODUCTION

INTEGRATED injection logic (I²L) [1] or merged transistor logic (MTL) [2] is a digital circuit technique in which base drive is injected into the base of the switching transistor from an adjacent p-n diode. The high functional density (~100 gates/mm² with 10-μm lines and spaces) and power-delay efficiency (~1.0 pJ) achievable make I²L attractive for large-scale integration (LSI).

As first described [1], [2] this technique was implemented in a standard bipolar technology which provides manufacturability and compatability with analog and other digital circuits on the same chip.

This paper describes Schottky I²L [3] which uses the principles of I²L and the properties of ion implantation to obtain improved performance at the same densities as conventional I²L. Schottky diodes are formed in the multicollectors of the switching transistor as proposed by Agraz Guerena and Fulton [4]. These Schottky diodes reduce the signal swing which improves the power-delay efficiency.

Schottky I²L retains compatability with other bipolar circuitry. Improved manufacturability of devices which operate at or near their intrinsic speed limit is feasible with the control of ion implantation.

The Schottky I²L structure and characteristics are described and contrasted with conventional I²L. A model which is useful in its design is discussed. Integrated test structures which provide direct comparison between conventional and Schottky I²L performance have been fabricated. A factor of 2 improvement in power-delay efficiency has been demonstrated by Schottky I²L over conventional I²L.

II. LOGIC UNIT

The logic units for conventional [1], [2] and Schottky I²L [3] are shown for comparison in Fig. 1. Each is an inverter implemented as a multicollector n-p-n transistor.

Manuscript received April 10, 1975; revised June 9, 1975.
The author is with Bell Laboratories, Allentown, Pa. 18103.

Base drive is supplied by injection from the emitter of a lateral p-n-p transistor whose collector is merged with the base of the n-p-n. The outputs are self isolating.

Logic functions are obtained by direct coupling of the transistors in each case. The Schottky I²L unit has Schottky diodes in series with each collector. These diodes reduce the signal swing which improves power-delay efficiency. Improvement of the intrinsic speed limit is also feasible.

The following description of the topography and cross section shows how these Schottky diodes are obtained.

A. Topography and Cross Section

The topography and cross section of a Schottky I²L unit with fan-out (FO) equal to 3, are shown in Fig. 2. The three outputs lie on a center line normal to the injector stripe. This unit is of the type described by deTroye [5] which provides efficient packing density.

The unit is fabricated in an n⁻ epitaxial layer upon an n⁺ substrate or buried layer. The deep collector diffusion forms a collar around the unit which improves the upward gain and separates one unit from another. The collar is open on the side adjacent to the injector. As in conventional I²L, an oxide collar may be used to reduce capacitance and improve packing density. The p-type diffusion forms the emitter and collector of the lateral p-n-p as well as the extrinsic base of the n-p-n. The intrinsic n-p-n base is ion implanted boron (Fig. 2). Contact window and metallization operations complete the process. The use of ion implantation permits a buried p layer (intrinsic n-p-n base) with good control of sheet resistance and junction depth and is essential in the fabrication of Schottky I²L.

The metallization must provide Schottky barrier contact to the n⁻ epitaxial layer above the ion implanted intrinsic base and ohmic contact to the diffused n⁺ and p regions. The extrinsic n-p-n base surrounds each unguarded Schottky diode. Alternatively, the Schottky diode cathodes may occupy a common n⁻ region [3] as proposed by Pedersen [6] and subsequently by Berger and Wiedmann [7]. This device is represented in Fig. 3. In this case, the extrinsic base diffusion must be inhibited in the region between the Schottky barrier contacts. The fabrication sequences for Schottky I²L and the common cathode version are identical. The Schottky I²L implementation, Figs. 1(b) and 2, was selected here because it is less susceptible to malfunction than the common cathode implementation, Fig. 3, which can have device interaction due to leakage current in the unguarded Schottky diodes. Care must be taken in the design of Schottky I²L to avoid parasitic Schottky collector action and current hogging. A discussion of these undesirable effects and a design which avoids them are deferred to the model section. In the common cathode implementation, a restriction on input placement avoids these ef-

Reprinted from *IEEE J. Solid-State Circuits*, vol. SC-10, pp. 343–348, Oct. 1975.

82

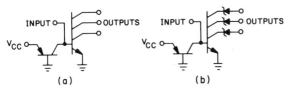

Fig. 1. Conventional and Schottky I²L logic units.

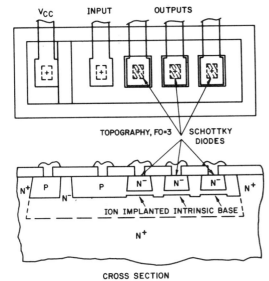

Fig. 2. Schottky I²L topography and cross section.

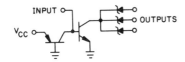

Fig. 3. Common cathode Schottky I²L.

fects. The input of a logic unit may not lie between two outputs. However, a severe reduction in wiring flexibility results in a single level metallization system.

An additional n⁺ diffusion provides ohmic contact to the n⁻ expitaxial layer above the ion implanted base in which high value resistors 3.3 kΩ/□ and low-resistance low-capacitance crossunders may be fabricated. This additional n⁺ diffusion is necessary in order to retain compatability with analog and other digital bipolar circuitry which operate in the normal mode.

Independent control of the n-p-n intrinsic and extrinsic base sheet resistances and junction depths provides design flexibility. For example, if an oxide collar instead of the n⁺ collar is used, the extrinsic base sheet may be lowered[1] well below that of the standard process, typically 200 Ω/□. (The Gummel number, or integrated-base dopant, of the n-p-n is determined by the ion implantation and not affected by a change in the extrinsic base sheet resistance.) For a given geometry, a reduction in base resistance occurs, allowing each output to switch at a more nearly equal speed [5]. Further-

<hr/>

[1]The p⁺n⁺ junction in the case of the n⁺ collar could result in large values of depletion capacitance and tunnel junctions.

more, the extrinsic base may be diffused to the n⁺ buried layer or substrate, which would reduce or eliminate the n⁻ epitaxial layer below the extrinsic base (see Fig. 2). Berger [8] has shown that charge storage in this region constitutes the dominant component of emitter time constant which determines the intrinsic speed limit of conventional I²L. Thus, improvement in the intrinsic speed is possible. The deeper and more heavily doped p region should improve the lateral p-n-p transistor characteristics. The attendant reduction of breakdown voltages must be acceptable in the specific application.

B. Characteristics

The common-emitter characteristics of a test device with a PtSi Schottky diode, FO = 1, and a base large enough to accommodate five outputs, is shown in Fig. 4. The voltage shift provided by this diode is ~530 mV at $I_B = I_C = 10 \mu A$. The characteristic is that of an n-p-n transistor with an ideal Schottky diode in series with its collector except for the negative collector current at voltages less than about 450 mV. This negative current is a result of collection by the Schottky diode of carriers injected by the collector–base diode of the saturated n-p-n transistor. A model which describes this behavior is contained in Section III. The device is designed to maintain the unwanted Schottky collection at an acceptable level.

The common-emitter characteristic of the same unit in which Pd_2Si formed the Schottky diode is shown in Fig. 5. The voltage shift provided by the Pd_2Si Schottky is less than that of the PtSi Schottky, Fig. 4, for two reasons. First, the barrier height of the Pd_2Si Schottky is ~100 mV less than that of the PtSi Schottky. Second, the emission coefficient (the emission coefficient characterizes the slope of the Schottky diode I-V characteristic) of the Pd_2Si Schottky is ~2 compared with ~1 for the PtSi Schottky.

The common-emitter characteristic of the Pd Schottky I²L unit, Fig. 6, demonstrates the value of upward gain attainable with the ion implanted base. β_u is greater than 12 for this device. The value of composite β_u, which increases approximately linearly with fan-out, would be greater than 60 for FO = 5.

The transfer characteristics, V_{out} versus V_{in}, of conventional and Schottky I²L are shown for comparison in Fig. 7. In conventional I²L, a low voltage at the input V_{SAT} results in a high voltage V_{BE} on the output. As the input rises to V_{BE}, the output falls to V_{SAT}, as indicated by the clear circles in Fig. 7. In Schottky I²L, a low voltage at the input $V_{SAT} + V_S$ results in a high voltage V_{BE} at the output. As the input rises to a V_{BE}, the output falls to the low level, $V_{SAT} + V_S$. The signal swing of conventional I²L,

$$\Delta V_{CON} = V_{BE} - V_{SAT} \qquad (1)$$

is reduced in Schottky I²L,

$$\Delta V_s = V_{BE} - V_{SAT} - V_S \qquad (2)$$

by the forward Schottky voltage.

The average propagation delay, which is directly proportional to the signal swing [9] in the extrinsic region of operation (linear region of power-delay characteristic), is reduced and

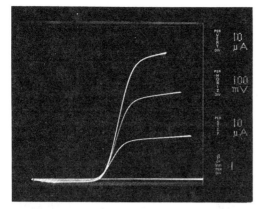

Fig. 4. Common-emitter characteristics of PtSi Schottky I²L.

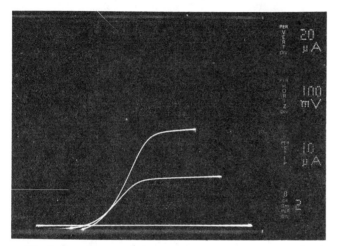

Fig. 5. Common-emitter characteristics of Pd₂Si Schottky I²L.

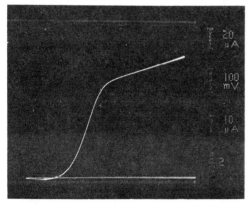

Fig. 6. Common-emitter characteristics of Pd₂Si Schottky I²L ($\beta_u > 12$).

power-delay efficiency improved as shown in Section IV. The delay is less for Pt than Pd because of its larger barrier height.

III. MODEL

Each output of a conventional I²L unit has been represented as an n-p-n transistor with an additional quasi constant base current source [9]. In this section, the conventional I²L model is extended to incorporate the presence of the Schottky diode.

The Schottky diode fabricated in the collector of the n-p-n

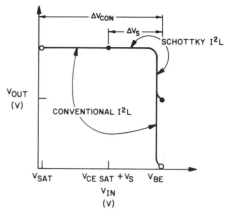

Fig. 7. Transfer characteristics.

transistor in Schottky I²L forms the collector of a parasitic p-n-p transistor, Fig. 8(a). The emitter of the Schottky collector p-n-p is the n-p-n base. The n-p-n collector forms the parasitic p-n-p base. The design parameters which suppress parasitic p-n-p action are identified in terms of the Schottky I²L model.

The model for a Schottky I²L output is shown in Fig. 8(b). Current flow across each junction is represented as the sum of an injected and collected current, after Ebers and Moll [10]. The diodes represent injection and the current sources represent minority carrier collection. The diodes have the usual dependence on saturation current and junction voltage. The Schottky diode may also be characterized in this way.

A Schottky diode and two current sources have been added to the conventional representation. The current source $\alpha'_{FS}I_R$ represents collection by the Schottky of minority carriers injected by the n-p-n collector–base junction. $\alpha'_{IS}I_{SS}$ represents collection by the collector–base junction of minority carriers injected by the Schottky diode. The device is designed to suppress parasitic p-n-p action as follows.

Using the relationship among junction saturation currents and alphas for a multijunction structure [9], an expression for the alphas in terms of intercept currents [11], [12] may be obtained:

$$\frac{\alpha_d}{\alpha'_{FS}} = \frac{I_s}{I'_s} \equiv \gamma \tag{3}$$

where I_s and I'_s are the n-p-n and parasitic p-n-p intercept currents, respectively. Each is directly proportional to its collector area and inversely proportional to its integrated-base dopant [13]. Large values of the ratio γ suppress parasitic p-n-p action and enhance the downward gain. An expression for γ in terms of device morphology is contained in the Appendix. In Schottky I²L, as in conventional I²L, adequate values of α_d are required to avoid current hogging.

In the case of low recombination, most of the carriers injected by the junction represented by I_R are collected. Therefore,

$$\alpha'_{FS} + \alpha_d \cong 1 \tag{4}$$

is valid. Combining (3) and (4), α_d may be written as

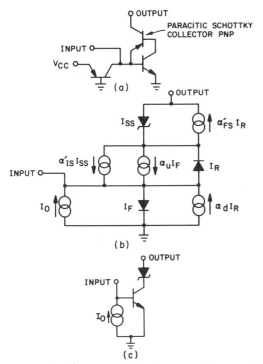

Fig. 8. (a) Schottky I^2L output showing parasitic p-n-p Schottky collector transistor. (b) Model for a Schottky I^2L output. (c) Simplified model of Schottky I^2L output for $\gamma > 10$.

$$\alpha_d \cong \frac{1}{1 + \dfrac{1}{\gamma}}. \tag{5}$$

Values of $\gamma > 10$ suppress parasitic p-n-p action and allow sufficient values of α_d ($\beta_d > 9$) to avoid current hogging [2]. $\alpha'_{IS}I_{SS}$ represents collection by the n-p-n collector–base junction of minority carriers injected by the Schottky diode. The Schottky diode is a majority carrier device whose minority carrier injection ratio is low [14]. Thus, this current source may be neglected under normal operating conditions. It may become important at high temperatures and high current densities resulting in latchup.

The Schottky I^2L model for $\gamma > 10$, is an n-p-n transistor with an additional quasi-constant base current source and a Schottky diode in series with its collector, Fig. 8(c).

IV. Experimental Results

A. Test Structure

A photomicrograph of the test structure which has been fabricated in both the conventional and Schottky I^2L technologies is shown in Fig. 9. Pertinent fabrication parameters and mask feature dimensions are contained in Tables I and II, respectively. The device is a gated inverter chain which permits yield study, measurement of average propagation delay, and determination of the effect of the condition of adjacent outputs on the driving output. Each unit in the chain has a FO = 5. The driving output is adjacent to the injector. The unused outputs are tied together and brought out to a contact pad (refer to Fig. 9).

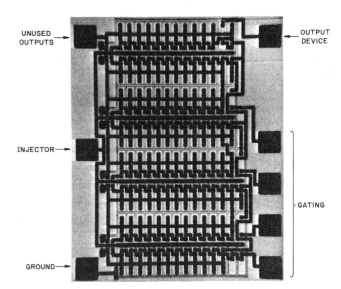

Fig. 9. Photomicrograph of a test structure processed in both conventional and Schottky I^2L technologies.

TABLE I
Pertinent Fabrication Parameters

		Conventional	Schottky	Unit
Epitaxial layer	Thickness	6	11[a]	μm
	Resistivity	0.5	0.25	$\Omega \cdot$ cm
Extrinsic base	Junction depth	1.65	1.65	μm
	Sheet resistivity	200	200	$\Omega/\square$
Intrinsic base	Dose	–	$3.0\,E+12$	cm^{-2}
	Energy	–	600	keV
Collector	Junction depth	1.0	0.75[b]	μm
	Sheet resistivity	7.0	3.3K	$\Omega/\square$

[a]For test purposes only.
[b]Calculated value based on extrapolation of data by Seidel [15] to 600 keV ion implanted boron.

TABLE II
Mask Feature Dimensions

Feature	Dimension
Minimum geometry contact window (area of Schottky diode)	6 × 8
Injector contact window width	6
n-p-n collectors	16 × 16
p-n-p basewidth	8
n$^+$ collar width	8
Metal linewidth	10
Metal spacing	12 (8 min)

All dimensions are in microns.

B. Performance

The average propagation delay $\bar{\tau}_{PD}$ versus gate current or power dissipation per volt is shown in Fig. 10 for both conventional and Pd$_2$Si Schottky I^2L. These data were taken on the test structure, Fig. 9, with the unused outputs floating. Pd$_2$Si Schottky I^2L shows about a factor of 2 improvement in delay over conventional I^2L. The unused outputs of a unit in the chain which is "on" are saturated which is the worst case in

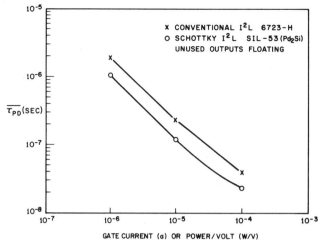

Fig. 10. Average propagation delay versus gate current or power/volt
for both conventional and Schottky I²L.

normal operation for robbing of base drive from the driving output.

When a positive 1.0 V is applied to the unused output terminal, the average propagation delay decreases by ~13 percent for conventional I²L, and 4 percent for Schottky I²L at a gate current of 1 μA. The unused outputs may not saturate in this case. The effective collector–base junction capacitance is reduced which in turn reduces the average propagation delay. The effect of the positive voltage on the average propagation delay is smaller for Schottky I²L because its collector–base junction capacitance is less than conventional I²L, and therefore, has a smaller effect on the delay.

At higher currents (~100 μA), $\bar{\tau}_{PD}$ of Schottky I²L increases by 21 percent when a positive 1.0 V is applied to the unused output terminal. This effect is a result of charge storage in the saturated parasitic p-n-p transistor which is driven into harder saturation with the increase in voltage.

A negative voltage, −1.0 V, causes a reduction in $\bar{\tau}_{PD}$ from the floating voltage case of about 1 percent at 1.0-μA gate current. This voltage does not occur in normal operation. It is a severe test of current hogging and would cause the inverted chain to malfunction if current hogging were a problem.

V. Summary

Schottky I²L uses the principles of I²L and the properties of ion implantation to obtain improved performance at the same densities as conventional I²L. Integrated test structures which permit direct comparison between conventional and Schottky I²L performance have been fabricated. A factor of 2 improvement in power-delay efficiency was demonstrated by Schottky I²L in which Pd₂Si formed the Schottky barrier contacts.

Appendix

An expression for γ in terms of device morphology is developed in this Appendix.

The intercept current for the n-p-n transistor may be written:

$$I_s = \frac{q\bar{D}_n A_c n_i^2}{N_G} \tag{A1}$$

where

q electronic charge,
$\bar{D}_n$ effective electron diffusivity in the n-p-n base,
A_c n-p-n collector area,
N_G n-p-n integrated-base dopant (Gummel number),
n_i intrinsic carrier concentration.

Assuming an expression similar to (A1) for I'_s, the parasitic p-n-p intercept current, yields γ, the ratio of I_s to I'_s:

$$\gamma = \frac{\bar{D}_n A_c N'_G}{\bar{D}_h A_s N_G} \tag{A2}$$

where

$\bar{D}_h$ effective hole diffusivity in the parasitic p-n-p base,
A_s parasitic p-n-p collector area (area of contact window),
N'_G parasitic p-n-p integrated-base dopant (Gummel number).

Acknowledgment

The author wishes to thank A. W. Fulton, J. Agraz Guerena, and R. A. Pedersen for illuminating discussion, and E. G. Parks for processing support.

References

[1] K. Hart and A. Slob, "Integrated injection logic: A new approach to LSI," *IEEE J. Solid-State Circuits (Special Issue on Semiconductor Memories and Digital Circuits)*, vol. SC-7, pp. 346–351, Oct. 1972.
[2] H. H. Berger and S. K. Wiedmann, "Merged-transistor logic (MTL)—A low-cost bipolar logic concept," *IEEE J. Solid-State Circuits (Special Issue on Semiconductor Memories and Digital Circuits)*, vol. SC-7, pp. 340–346, Oct. 1972.
[3] F. W. Hewlett, Jr., "Schottky I²L," presented at the IEEE Solid State Circuits Committee Meeting, United Engineering Center, N.Y., N.Y., Feb. 10, 1975.
[4] J. Agraz Guerena and A. W. Fulton, private communication.
[5] N. C. deTroye, "Integrated injection logic—present and future," *IEEE J. Solid-State Circuits (Special Issue on Semiconductor Memory and Logic)*, vol. SC-9, pp. 206–211, Oct. 1974.
[6] R. A. Pedersen, private communication.

[7] H. H. Berger and S. K. Wiedmann, "Schottky transistor logic," in *ISSCC Dig. Tech. Papers*, Feb. 1975, pp. 172–173.

[8] H. H. Berger, "The injection model–A structure-oriented model for merged transistor logic (MTL)," *IEEE J. Solid-State Circuits* (*Special Issue on Semiconductor Memory and Logic*), vol. SC-9, pp. 218–227, Oct. 1974.

[9] H. H. Berger and S. K. Wiedmann, "Terminal-oriented model for merged transistor logic (MTL)," *IEEE J. Solid-State Circuits* (*Special Issue on Semiconductor Memory and Logic*), vol. SC-9, pp. 211–217, Oct. 1974.

[10] J. J. Ebers and J. L. Moll, "Large-signal behavior of junction transistors," *Proc. IRE*, vol. 42, pp. 1761–1772, Dec. 1954.

[11] H. K. Gummel and H. C. Poon, "An integral charge control model of bipolar transistors," *Bell Syst. Tech. J.*, vol. 49, pp. 827–857, May–June 1970.

[12] I. Getreu, "Modeling the bipolar transistor," *Electronics*, pp. 114–120, Sept. 19, 1974.

[13] H. K. Gummel, "Measurement of the number of impurities in the base layer of a transistor," *Proc. IRE* (Corresp.), vol. 49, p. 834, Apr. 1961.

[14] S. M. Sze, *Physics of Semiconductor Devices*. New York: Wiley, 1969, p. 390.

[15] T. E. Seidel, "Ion implantation in semiconductors," in *Proc. 2nd Int. Conf. Ion Implantation*, 1971, p. 47.

Advanced merged transistor logic by using Schottky junctions

by H. H. Berger and S. K. Wiedmann†

The power-delay product, an essential figure of merit for logic circuits, is proportional to the logic swing. In MTL, the latter is given by the forward voltage of a base-emitter junction (≈ 750 mV). Since about 150 mV are sufficient to obtain a satisfactory current ratio in the switching device, it is beneficial to reduce the swing in MTL. This is achieved by the use of Schottky diodes.
Another benefit from this approach is the possibility of reducing the charge storage and thus to improve the speed limit. Furthermore, by using a metal (Schottky) collector transistor, the number of active silicon regions can be reduced from 4 to 3.

1. Introduction

Merged Transistor Logic (MTL)[1], or Integrated Injection Logic (I²L)[2], has found great interest, as it offers power delay product below 1 pJ at medium performance and more than 1,000 gates/chip, when utilizing conventional bipolar production processes.

One may ask, whether with the additional freedom of tailoring production processes one could devise MTL circuit modifications for even better results. Possible areas for such improvements are shown in Table 1. The table focuses on improvements by circuit and device modifications, implying the production process tailoring. Although it is not directly matter of this discussion, one has to be also aware, that the general progress of technology, e.g. decreasing of line widths, adds to these circuit/device improvements.

The power delay product ($P \cdot t_d$), first item in Table 1, is portional to the logic swing $\triangle V$, which in MTL is about 750 mV. Because of the high transconductance of bipolar transistors one could as well operate internal circuits with a swing as low as 150 mV. Hence, provided that a scheme is conceived for such a swing reduction, power delay can be improved by a factor of 5.

The second item in Table 1 is the intrinsic delay t_{di} which represents the speed limit of the logic gate. The intrinsic delay in MTL is larger than in conventional logic circuits because of excessive charge storage in the upside-down operated npn transistor. One part of this excessive charge storage is caused by parasitic junctions and adverse doping profiles[3]. This part can be reduced by technological means which are not the main subject of this paper. Another part of the charge storage originates from the high inverse current gain β_i of the upside-down operated npn transistor[4]. In the basic MTL circuit this high inverse current gain* – which is the forward current gain in conventional circuits – is absolutely necessary to eliminate current hogging (1). Figure 1 shows the dependence of t_{di} on inverse current again. From this diagram one can conclude that t_{di} can be decreased by about a factor of 2, if the current hogging problem can be solved by means other than high inverse current gain, so that $\beta_i \leqslant 1$ may be chosen.

An essential feature of MTL is the small number of active silicon regions (Table 1). It contributes indirectly to the small power delay product via capacitance savings. Thus, the legitimate question is, whether one can obtain an even further reduction of active regions from 4 to 3.

Following the sequence indicated in Fig. 2, we will show that MTL can be improved according to Table 1 by introducing Schottky junctions. First, the MTL scheme with its multicollector output will be briefly recapitulated, then the multicollectors will be replaced by Schottky diodes. This approach is called Schottky Coupled Transistor Logic (SCTL)[5]. It gives the desired swing reduction and speed enhancement and can be implemented with relatively small extensions, e.g. with a deep implanted base. Nevertheless, a further step has been made to Schottky Transistor Logic, which, in addition to Schottky diodes, uses a metal Schottky collector. This reduces the number of active silicon regions from 4 to 3.

Feature	Basic MTL Circuit	Improved Circuit
$\triangle V (\sim P \times t_d)$	750 mV	150 mV
t_{di} (Speed Limit)	$t_{di1} = f(\beta_i)$	$t_{di2} \neq f(\beta_i)$ $\approx t_{di1}/2$
Number of active Si-regions	④	③

Table 1 Possible MTL improvements by circuit/device modifications.

*In [3] and [4] the terms "upward" and "downward" current gain have been introduced to describe the current gains in relation to the device structure. In this paper we discuss primarily circuit aspects and, therefore, will use the terms "forward" and "inverse". Forward current gain applies to an operation in which that transistor junction is forward biased, across which the control signal would be applied in the respective circuit.

†IBM Laboratories, Boeblingen, Germany.

Reprinted with permission from *Microelectronics*, vol. 7, pp. 35–42, Mar. 1976. Copyright © 1976 Mackintosh Publications Ltd.

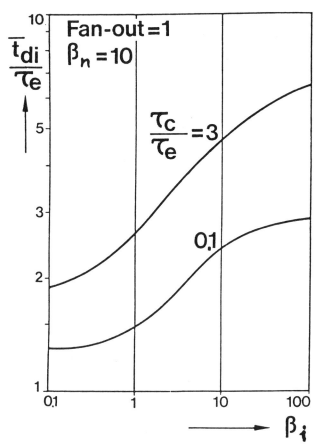

Fig. 1   Intrinsic delay t_{di} (determining speed limit) normalized with emitter time constant τ_e as a function of inverse current gain β_i. Collector time constant τ_c normalized with τ_e is parameter.
Inverse current gain below 1 is desirable for small t_{di}.

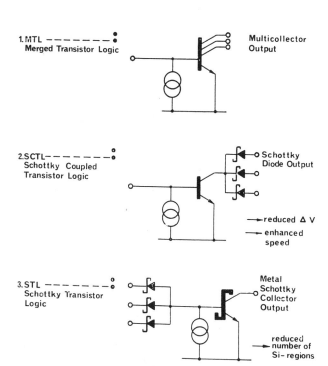

Fig. 2   MTL and its extension that are subject of this paper.

2. Merged Transistor Logic (MTL)

Figure 3 shows a section of some random logic built of MTL devices. One can either define a NOR gate similar to DCTL by the inputs I_{11}, I_{12} and the output 0_1, or define a NAND gate by the inputs I_{21}, I_{22} and the output 0_2. The latter definition has the advantage of referring only to a single MTL device. This device is an upside-down operated npn transistor having multicollectors and a base current source. The base current source is actually made up by a pnp transistor that is merged with the npn transistor[1].

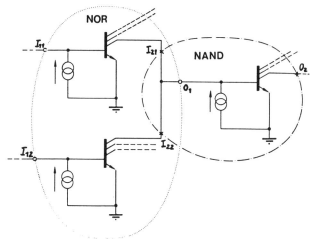

Fig. 3   Section of some random logic built with MTL showing the possibilities of defining a basic gate.

The necessity of a good decoupling of the multicollector outputs becomes clear from the NOR gate description. Those collectors C' that are not part of this particular gate are normally used to provide other NOR combinations with other devices. The current drawing capability of either one of the collectors must not be affected by the state of the other collectors. In other words, one must avoid the current hogging effect known from DCTL.

In MTL with conventional technology, this is automatically achieved by the inherently high inverse current gain of the upside-down operated npn transistor[1], which is the forward current gain in conventional circuits. The arising ping-pong game with minority carriers in the device stabilizes V_{be} against the saturation of collector outputs as wanted, but it also produces excessive charge storage. This is represented in Fig. 1 by the increase of intrinsic delay t_{di} with increasing β_i. Therefore, one would like to have some other decoupling scheme that would allow a reduction of inverse current gain to a value below 1, thereby enhancing the maximum speed by about a factor of 2.

3. Schottky Coupled Transistor Logic (SCTL)

In Fig. 4 the multicollectors are replaced by a single one plus Schottky diodes that now decouple the outputs[5,6,7]. Hence, one is free now to use a low inverse current gain. NOR and NAND gates are defined analogous to MTL.

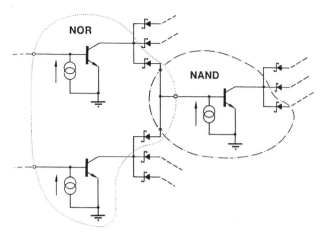

Fig. 4   Introducing Schottky diode output decoupling in MTL (Schottky Coupled Transistor Logic-SCTL) definition of basic gates.

An embodiment closest to MTL is described in Fig. 5. As in MTL, there is a pnp transistor for the base current supply, merged with the npn switching transistor. The Schottky diodes are merged with the collector of the npn transistor that now requires low doping. The low doping is also important for getting small inverse current gain and thus higher speed.

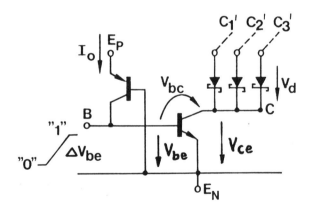

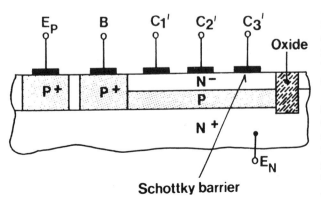

Fig. 5   Basic device of Schottky Coupled Transistor Logic (SCTL), (a) equivalent circuit (b) cross-section of a possible monolithic realization.

Since the diodes lie in series with the transistor, the logic swing $\triangle V_{be}$ at the base-emitter input of the following gate is reduced resulting in an improved power delay product.

$$\triangle V_{be} = V_{be\ on} - V_{be\ off}; \quad . \quad . \quad . \quad . \quad . \quad . \quad . \quad . \quad 1$$

$V_{be\ on}$ is determined by the operation current of the switching transistor, and $V_{be\ off}$ appears at the Schottky diode output (=input of the next stage), when the transistor is in its on-condition:

$$V_{be\ off} = V_{ce\ on} + V_{d\ on} \quad . \quad . \quad . \quad . \quad . \quad . \quad . \quad 2$$

where $V_{d\ on}$ is the Schottky diode forward voltage drop. The saturation voltage $V_{ce\ on}$ of the npn transistor on the other hand is given by

$$V_{ce\ on} = V_{be\ on} - V_{bc\ on} \quad . \quad . \quad . \quad . \quad . \quad . \quad . \quad 3$$

neglecting ohmic series resistance.
By combining equations (1)-(3) one gets the simple equation

$$\triangle V_{be} = V_{bc\ on} - V_{d\ on} \quad . \quad . \quad . \quad . \quad . \quad . \quad . \quad 4$$

indicating that the logic swing equals the difference of base-collector and Schottky diode forward voltages under the operating conditions of the circuit.

In order to estimate what differences can be practically achieved, one may write equation (4) in terms of barrier heights ϕ, assuming about equal* current densities in both diodes:

$$\triangle V_{be} \approx \phi_{c\ eff} - \phi_d \quad . \quad . \quad . \quad . \quad . \quad . \quad . \quad 5$$

ϕ_d is here the Schottky barrier of the output diodes, $\phi_{c\ eff}$ is an effective barrier for the collector-base pn junction, that can be defined by comparing pn diode and Schottky equations[7] (see Appendix). $\phi_{c\ eff}$ is typically about 1 Volt. It can become a real Schottky barrier as well, if the npn transistor is Schottky clamped (Fig. 6). The Schottky clamp in conjunction with the circuit Fig. 4 has also been used by Peltier in a more conventional monolithic realization[8].

Figure 6b shows the range of possible barriers of Schottky diodes on n-type Si[9] including the effective barrier of the unclamped collector p-n junction. The barriers have to be chosen in such a way, as to provide at least about a 150 mV . . . 200 mV swing. A straightforward solution would be aluminium for the Schottky diodes combined with an unclamped npn transistor, resulting in a swing of about 300 mV. Schottky barrier technology is still progressing, and many other interesting combinations may become attractive.

In summary, this SCTL approach yields small logic swing, and thus the power-delay improvement, and it allows the use of an npn transistor with small inverse current gain (by a proper collector and base profile or a Schottky clamp) giving the improvement in maximum speed. Although SCTL is very interesting for these features, development has been taken one step further in order to reduce the basic device to one that requires only 3 active silicon regions instead of 4.

*This assumption is useful only for a very rough orientation; a more accurate analysis is given in the appendix.

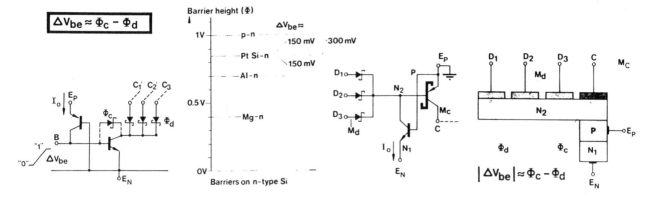

$$\boxed{\Delta V_{be} \approx \Phi_c - \Phi_d}$$

Fig. 6   Choices of diode barriers ϕ to obtain a certain logic swing ΔV_{be}.

Fig. 8   (a) Circuit of a basic STL device that is complementary to that in Fig. 7 for easier monolithic realization; (b) basic monolithic structure.

4. Schottky Transistor Logic (STL)

Figure 7 shows this Schottky Transistor approach. The switching transistor now has a genuine Schottky collector. That means, the collector region consists solely of metal[10]. Therefore, one cannot further superintegrate the Schottky diodes into the collector. Instead, the diodes are assigned to the base of the transistor[11] and accordingly the NAND gate is defined by the diode inputs I_1, I_2 and collector output O. For a random logic network that makes no difference.

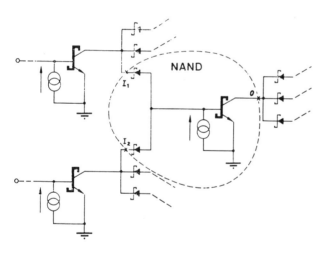

Fig. 7   Schottky Transistor Logic (STL) circuit using metal collector transistors; NAND gate definition referring to the basic monolithic device.

If one sticks to the n-type emitter and p-type base for the switching transistor, one would have to provide Schottky barriers on the p-type base. As technology is more advanced with Schottky barriers on n-type Silicon, the complementary structure has been chosen with a p-type emitter, an n-type base and metal collector, in other words, a pnm transistor. The transistor arrow and the Schottky diodes then have to be reversed as shown on Fig. 8a. Accordingly, the transistor for base current supply becomes now the npn type instead of pnp.

Figure 8b depicts the basic semiconductor structure for this Schottky Transistor Logic. The silicon layers N_1, P and N_2 make up the npn transistor for base

current supply; P and N_2 are furthermore part of the p-n-metal transistor. The N_2 layer, which is both the base of the pnm and the collector of the npn transistor, also carries the input Schottky diodes.

As with SCTL, the voltage swing at the base of the switching transistor is equal to the difference of collector and diode barriers. PtSi for the collector and Al for the diodes would be a possible choice. The inverse current gain of the pnm transistor is inherently small, so that no excessive charge storage can occur in saturation.

Possible realizations of STL are shown in Fig. 9. Figure 9a utilizes a vertical transistor for base current supply[1,11,12], Fig. 9b utilizes the more conventional lateral transistor for this purpose. The N^+ buried layer in both cases not only provides a low ohmic extension of the pnm transistor's base, but also prevents parasitic pnm transistors from occurring with the input diodes.

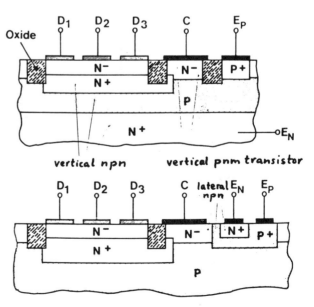

Fig. 9   Possible practical realization of the structure Fig. 8b in present technology (a) with vertical npn transistor for base current supply (b) with a lateral npn transistor.

5. Experiments on STL

For our feasibility study we used discrete devices whose dc– parameters come close to the monolithic case. To represent the pnm switching transistor, a lateral pnp transistor was used with a high barrier Schottky clamp. Low barrier Schottky diodes were taken for the input.

Figure 10a shows the forward characteristics of these two diode types exhibiting a forward voltage or barrier difference of 200 mV or somewhat less. The grounded emitter characteristics (Fig. 10b) of the high-barrier clamped pnp transistor show an offset voltage of about 75 mV and a current gain around 50. Inverse current gain was 0·1.

The transfer characteristics of such a STL gate are presented in Fig. 11. Also V_{be} as a function of input voltage is shown. The base-emitter voltage swing ΔV_{be} is 200 mV as expected from the Schottky barrier difference of the diodes. The transfer curves for fan-out of 1 and 3 show a noise sensitivity of about 150 mV. This is a good value, as for internal circuits it has to be seen relatively to the voltage swings that are the main noise contributors here. Driver and receivers, however, would have to be provided usually with larger swings to overcome the larger external noise.

Diodes

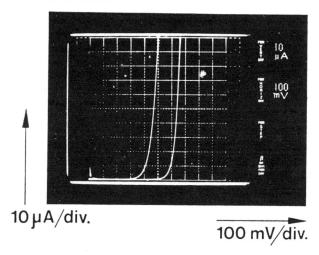

10 µA/div.

100 mV/div.

Transistor

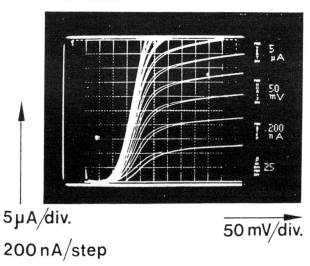

5 µA/div.

200 nA/step

50 mV/div.

Fig. 10 (a) Characteristics of Schottky diodes used in the feasibility experiment showing a forward voltage difference of about 200 mV (b) grounded emitter characteristics of the lateral pnp transistor clamped with the high-barrier Schottky diode to represent the pnm transistor.

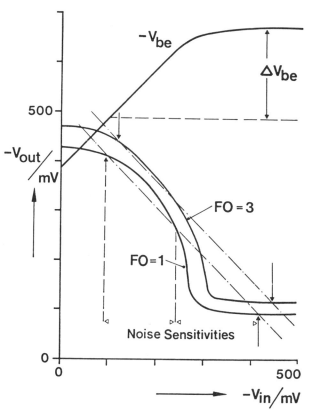

Fig. 11 Measured transfer characteristics of a STL gate built of discrete components.

A closed loop oscillator has also been built; the delay per stage vs. supply current per stage has been plotted in Fig. 12. For comparison, a curve with unclamped pnp transistors was also taken. Here, the relevant voltage swing at the emitter base junction is about 1·4 times larger. Accordingly, the power-delay curve moved up by the same factor. The intrinsic delay that limits the speed can be determined at higher supply currents from the difference between the actual curve and the ideal constant power-delay line. We get 4·5 ns for the clamped version, that represents STL, vs. 9 ns when the clamp is removed.

The improvement by a factor of 2 is here due to the combined effect of inverse current gain reduction and storage reduction in the collector. The 4·5 ns intrinsic delay is, of course, not necessarily representative for a monolithic realization. where faster vertical transistors would be used. Also the rather good power delay figure of 1·4 pJ obtained here would improve at least by an order of magnitude because of much less stray capacitance.

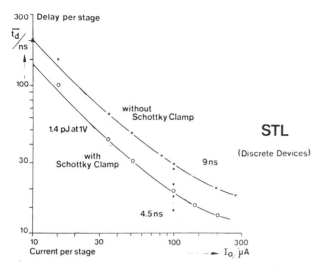

Fig. 12 Delay t_d vs. power supply current I_o of a STL gate built of discrete components obtained from a 5-stage closed loop oscillator. Influence of Schottky collector (simulated by the clamp diode) is shown on power delay product (via logic swing) and on limiting speed.

Samples have been made also of genuine vertical pnm transistors according to the pnm part of Fig. 9b. Figure 13 shows a typical grounded emitter characteristic. Current gains in the order of 50 and emitter time constants $\tau_e \leqslant 1$ ns have been achieved. This emitter time constant is more than 4 times smaller than that of the lateral pnp transistor used in the experiment (Fig. 12). Intrinsic delay would be reduced accordingly.

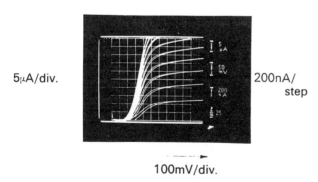

Fig. 13 Grounded emitter characteristics of an experimental genuine metal collector (pnm) transistor showing its feasibility.

6. Conclusions

The original Merged Transistor Logic is tailored for simple conventional bipolar processes.

If one is not bound to a conventional process, one can get even better circuits by adding Schottky diodes as decoupling devices according to the SCTL scheme. They allow an increase in speed by a factor of 2 and an improvement in power-delay by a factor of 5. If one goes one step further and uses metal collector Schottky transistors one gets Schottky Transistor Logic that requires only 3 active silicon regions and maintains the other advantages.

It should be stressed that general technological progress will always add to these circuit/device improvements so that one may expect a very impressive progress in the field of bipolar superintegrated logic.

7. References

[1] Berger, H. H. and Wiedmann, S. K., "Merged Transistor Logic (MTL) – A Low-Cost Bipolar Logic Concept", *IEEE J. Solid-State Circuits*, vol. SC-7, pp.340-346, Oct., 1972.

[2] Hart, K. and Slob, A., "Integrated Injection Logic: New Approach to LSI", *ibid.*, pp.346-351.

[3] Berger, H. H., "The Injection Model – A Structure Oriented Model for Merged Transistor Logic (MTL)", *IEEE J. Solid-State Circuits*, vol. SC-9, No. 5, pp.218-227, Oct., 1974.

[4] Berger, H. H. and Wiedmann, S. K., "Terminal Oriented Model for Merged Transistor Logic (MTL)", *ibid.*, pp.211-217.

[5] Berger, H. H. and Wiedmann, S. K., "Schottky Transistor Logic", *IEEE ISSCC 75*, Digest of Technical Papers, pp.172 and 173.

[6] Schuenemann, C. L. and Wiedmann, S. K., IBM Technical Disclosure Bulletin 15, p.509, 1972.

[7] Berger, H. H., "Bipolar devices for low power digital application-progress through new concepts", Solid-State Devices 1973, Conference Series No. 9, pp.118 and 119, The Institute of Physics, London and Bristol.

[8] Peltier, A. W., "A New Approach to Bipolar LSI: C³L", *IEEE ISSCC 75*, Digest of Technical Papers, pp.168 and 169.

[9] Attalla, M. M., "Metal-semiconductor Schottky Barriers, Devices and Applications", *Mikroelektronik*, **2**, R. Oldenbourg Verlag Munich/Vienna, 1967.

[10] Noyce, R. N., *et al*, "Schottky diodes make IC scene", *Electronics*, vol. 42, No. 15, July 21, 1969, Figure on p.79.

[11] Blatt, V., *et al*, "Substrate Fed Logic – an Improved Form of Injection Logic", *IEEE* International Electron Devices Meeting, 1974, Technical Digest, pp.511-513.

[12] Berger, H. H. and Wiedmann, S. K., "Monolithically Integrated Logical Basic Circuit", IBM Technical Disclosure Bulletin, vol. **16**, p.650, July, 1973.

[13] Phillips, A. B., Transistor Engineering, McGraw-Hill, New York, 1962.

8. Appendix

Definition of effective barrier for p-n diode and evaluation of deviations from the ideal case $V_{be} = \phi_c - \phi_d$ (5).

According to 13 the equation of a p-n diode is of the form

$$j = \text{const.}_1 \cdot D \cdot n_i^2 \cdot [\exp(qV_D/kT) - 1] \quad \text{A.1}$$
$$\approx \text{const.}_1 \cdot D \cdot n_i^2 \cdot \exp(qV_D/kT),$$

since

$$\exp(qV_D/kT) \gg 1 \text{ in forward operation}$$

j	=	current density
D	=	Diffusion constant for injected minority carriers
n_i	=	intrinsic carrier density
V_D	=	diode voltage
k	=	Boltzmann constant
T	=	absolute Temperature
q	=	elementary charge
$\frac{k \cdot T}{q}$	=	V_T = temperature voltage (26 mV @ 25°C)

Again according to[13],

$$n_i^2 = \text{const.}_2 \cdot T^3 \cdot \exp(-qV_G/kT) \ , \quad \ldots \ldots \quad A.2$$

where a bandgap voltage of $V_G = 1.21$ V has to be taken in the case of Si.

The Einstein relationship allows the replacement of D in equation A.1 by

$$D = \mu \cdot \frac{k \cdot T}{q} \quad \ldots \ldots \ldots \ldots \ldots \quad A.3$$

where μ is the minority carrier mobility.

The temperature dependence of μ can be approximated for the purpose of this evaluation by

$$\mu \sim T^{-2} \quad \ldots \ldots \ldots \ldots \ldots \ldots \quad A.4$$

With equations A.2, A.4 inserted in A.1 we get

$$j = C \cdot T^2 \cdot \exp\left[\frac{q(V_D - V_G)}{k \cdot T}\right] \ldots \ldots \ldots \quad A.5$$

A Schottky diode on the other hand can be described by the equation 8

$$j = A \cdot T^2 \cdot \exp\left[\frac{q(V_D - \phi)}{n \cdot k \cdot T}\right], \quad \ldots \ldots \quad A.6$$

where

ϕ	=	Schottky barrier height
A	=	Richardson constant
(AT^2	=	10^7 A/cm² @ room temperature)
n	=	dimensionless constant ≥ 1 ("ideality factor")

Equations A.5 and A.6 are of the same form. The differences lie in the constants (C vs. A) and the n-factor in equation A.6, which often is slightly larger than 1. For simplicity one assumes in the following the ideal case (n=1).

Now one defines an effective barrier $\phi_{c\,eff}$ for the base-collector p-n diode, by setting its current density j_{bc} equal to that of an imaginary Schottky diode (j_{sd}) having the barrier $\phi_{c\,eff}$

According to equations A.5 and A.6 we write

$$j_{bc} = C \cdot T^2 \cdot \exp\left(\frac{V_D - V_G}{kT/q}\right), \ldots \ldots \ldots \quad A.7$$

and

$$j_{sd} = A \cdot T^2 \cdot \exp\left(\frac{V_D - \phi^{eff}}{kT/q}\right), \ldots \ldots \ldots \quad A.8$$

with $j_{bc} = j_{sd}$ we get

$$\phi_{ceff} = V_G - \frac{kT}{q} \cdot \ln\left(\frac{C \cdot T^2}{A \cdot T^2}\right) \ldots \ldots \ldots \quad A.9$$

In order to determine the term C · T² we may take measured emitter current densities (j_{be}) of typical npn transistors at a given base-emitter voltage V_{be}. We take into account the Ebers-Moll relation of saturation current densities to extrapolate to the base-collector junction, thereby assuming the desirable inverse current gain of $\alpha_i \approx 0.1$:

$$j_{bc} \approx \frac{1}{\alpha_i} \quad j_{be} = 10 \cdot j_{be} \ldots \ldots \ldots \quad A.10$$

For a typical intrinsic base sheet resistance of

$$R_{si} = 5k \ \Omega/\square \text{ and } V_{be} = 660 \text{ mV}$$

one usually measures

$$j_{he} = 6 \text{A/cm}^2 \text{ (25°C)}$$

Introducing these figures with equation A.10 into equation A.7 we get at 25°C

$$C \cdot T^2 = 9.23 \cdot 10^{10} \text{ A/cm}^2 \ldots \ldots \ldots \quad A.11$$

This, with $A \cdot T^2 = 10^7$ A/cm$r$ yields with equation A.9

$$\text{or } \phi_{c\,eff} \begin{array}{ll} = & 0.97 \text{ V at } 25°C \\ = & 0.93 \text{ V at } 85°C \end{array}$$

Now, having all diode equations, including that of the collector-base diode, written in the form of equation A.6 with n=1,

$$\triangle V_{be} = \phi_c - \phi_d \qquad \text{(equation (5))}$$

immediately follows for equal current densities. With constant ϕ's as for Schottky diodes, V_{be} is also independent on temperature, again for equal current density.

Practically, however, current densities become different due to layout restrictions and due to varying fan-out F_o and fan-in F_i. The fan-out is defined as the number of Schottky diodes fed by the collector of the switching transistor, whereas fan-in is given by the number of diodes tied to its base (Fig. A.1). The consequences of fan-in and fan-out will be discussed first.

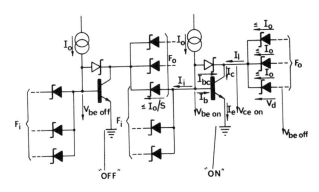

Fig. A1 Schottky MTL (SCTL or STL) circuit chain for a more rigorous analysis of worst case conditions on logic swing.

In order to ensure safe operation, it is required that the off-condition of the switching transistor be defined by the collector current being less than I_o/s $(s \gg 1)$, in other words (use general diode equation):

$$V_{be\ off} \leqslant V_{be}(I_o) - \frac{kT}{q} \ln s \quad \ldots \ldots \quad A.12$$

Using equations (2) and (3) one may write

$$V_{be\ off} = V_{be\ on} - V_{bc\ on} + V_{d\ on} \quad \ldots \ldots \quad A.13$$

In order to determine $V_{be\ on}$ and $V_{bc\ on}$ we have to evaluate the emitter current I_e and respectively the current I_{bc} forward biasing the base-collector junction. For simplicity, I_{bc} has been shown in Fig. A.1 as the current through the clamp diode. From this Figure follows:

$$I_e = I_b + I_c, \quad \ldots \ldots \ldots \ldots \quad A.14$$

$$I_{bc} = I_o - I_i - I_b, \quad \ldots \ldots \ldots \quad A.15$$

$$I_c (= \beta \cdot I_b) = I_{bc} + I_l. \quad \ldots \ldots \ldots \quad A.16$$

From the latter two equations one gets:

$$I_b = \frac{1}{\beta+1}\left(I_o + I_l - I_i\right), \quad \ldots \ldots \quad A.17$$

or $$I_{bc} = \frac{\beta}{\beta+1}(I_o - I_i) - \frac{1}{\beta+1} \cdot I_l. \quad \ldots \quad A.18$$

Finally, equations (A.16, A.17, and A.14) yield

$$I_e = I_o + I_l - I_i. \quad \ldots \ldots \ldots \ldots \quad A.19$$

By expressing currents I_l and I_i through multiples of I_o:

$$I_l = l \cdot I_o, \quad \ldots \ldots \ldots \ldots \quad A.20$$

$$I_i = i \cdot I_o, \quad \ldots \ldots \ldots \ldots \quad A.21$$

one gets for equations A.18 and A.19

$$I_{bc} = I_o \left[\frac{\beta}{\beta+1}(1-i) - \frac{1}{\beta+1} \cdot l\right], \quad \ldots \quad A.22$$

$$I_e = I_o(1 + l - i). \quad \ldots \ldots \ldots \quad A.23$$

Accordingly, equation (A.13) may be written as

$$V_{be\ off} = V_{be}(I_o) - V_{bc}(I_o) +$$

$$\frac{kT}{q} \ln \left(\frac{1 + l - i}{\frac{\beta}{\beta+1}(1-i)\frac{l}{\beta+1}}\right) + V_{d\ on}, \quad \ldots \quad A.24$$

with $\beta \gg 1$ and equation A.12 we get

$$\frac{k.T}{q} \cdot \ln\left(s \cdot \frac{1 + l - i}{1 - i - l/\beta}\right) \leqslant V_{bc}(I_o) - V_{d\ on} \quad \ldots \quad A.25$$

This equation has to be fulfilled also with worst case operation condition leading to (compare with Fig. A.1)

$$(V_{d\ on})_{max} = V_d(I_c) \quad \ldots \ldots \ldots \quad A.26$$

$$l = (F_o)_{max} \cdot \alpha. \quad \ldots \ldots \quad A.27$$

$$i = (F_i)_{max} \quad \ldots \ldots \ldots \quad A.28$$

Thus we get with equation A.25

$$V_{bc}(I_o) - V_d(I_o) \geqslant \frac{kT}{q} \cdot \ln\left[s \cdot \frac{1 + (F_o)_{max} - (F_i)_{max}/s}{1 - (F_o)_{max}/\beta - F_{i\ mav}/s}\right],$$

$$\geqslant \frac{kT}{q} \cdot \ln\left[s \cdot (1 + F_o)_{max}\right] \quad \ldots \quad A.29$$

Reasonable numbers would be:
$(F_i)_{max} = 4$, $(F_o)_{max} = 4$, $S = 16$, $\beta = 20$.
so that at an operating temperature of 85°C

$$V_{bc}(I_o) - V_d(I_o) \geqslant 154\ mV, \quad \ldots \ldots \ldots \quad A.29a$$

would be required.

To write equation A.29 in terms of barriers one has to introduce the ratio of collector base-diode area A_c and of the Schottky diode A_d:

$$\phi_c - \phi_d \geqslant \frac{kT}{q} \ln\left(\frac{A_c}{A_d} \cdot s \cdot \frac{1 + F_{o\ max} - F_{i\ max}/s}{1 - F_{i\ max}/s - F_{o\ max}/\beta}\right). \quad A.30$$

In case of the SCTL-structure in Fig. 5 the ratio $\frac{A_c}{A_d}$ is unavoidably larger than unity by at least the fan-out number. Assuming

$$\frac{A_c}{A_d} \sim 2\cdot5 \times F_{o\ max} = 10,$$

another

$$\frac{k.T}{q} \cdot \ln 10 = 72\ mV\ \text{at } 85°C$$

would have to be added to the figure of 154 mV in equation A.29a. Thus, an unclamped npn transistor combined with an Al-Schottky barrier diode would be a good solution.

Schottky I²L (Substrate Fed Logic)— An Optimum Form of I²L

PHILIP S. WALSH AND GEOFFREY W. SUMERLING

Abstract—A modified form of Schottky I²L (originally called substrate fed logic) has been developed, differing from the earlier process mainly in the extrinsic n-p-n base profile. Heavier boron doping in this region has lead to reduced charge storage so that minimum delays as low as 8 ns/gate at a power of 50 μW are now achieved in ring oscillator circuits. The reduced minimum delay also applies to more complex gates, as demonstrated by a *D*-type flip-flop which operated at 20 MHz with a power dissipation of 70 μW/gate. The excellent yield and high packing density which have been obtained on trial circuits demonstrate that the process is capable of very large scale integration.

INTRODUCTION

SCHOTTKY I²L (described in an earlier publication [1] as substrate fed logic or SFL) is an extension of the injection logic principle. It provides a multiinput, multioutput gate by the incorporation of Schottky barrier diodes to the base of the n-p-n switching transistor and uses a vertical p-n-p transistor for the injector. The earlier publication described the basic process, which is illustrated in Fig. 1. The substrate is the

Manuscript received November 15, 1976; revised December 7, 1976. This work was supported by the Procurement Executive, Ministry of Defence, sponsored by CVD.

The authors are with the Allen Clark Research Centre, The Plessey Company Ltd., Caswell, Towcester, Northants., England.

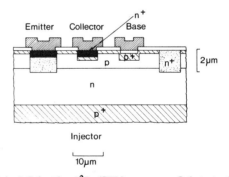

Fig. 1. Original Schottky I²L (SFL) process. Substrate doping 5×10^{18} cm^{-3}. Epitaxial emitter doping 1×10^{17} cm^{-3}. Epitaxial base doping 3×10^{15} cm^{-3}.

emitter of a p-n-p device whose base and collector are epitaxial layers; the n-p-n device uses the layers as emitter and base, while the collectors are diffused n-type regions. Each gate is defined by a deep n-type diffusion that reaches down to the n-type layer. The p-type layer is lightly doped to allow the fabrication of Schottky barrier diodes.

The required doping profile in the p-type layer is determined by several factors. In the intrinsic n-p-n base, light doping is required to provide a high gain. In the Schottky barrier con-

Reprinted from *IEEE J. Solid-State Circuits*, vol. SC-12, pp. 123–127, Apr. 1977.

96

tact region, a low doping is required to avoid tunneling currents. However, as discussed in [1], under open circuit conditions the Schottky diode can act as a collector; injected minority carriers flow to the contact where they are balanced by an equal flow of holes. This effective recombination leads to a fall in collector current. In the process originally described, this effect was minimized by locally increasing the doping of the p-type layer under the Schottky barrier using ion implantation after cutting the contacts. In oxide covered regions, the tail of this implant increased the doping level at the surface to act as a channel stopper and to reduce base series resistance.

Performance of the Original Process

The process described above has been shown to be capable of a minimum delay of 20 ns and a power–delay product of 0.03 pJ [1]. These performance figures compare favorably with those achieved by I^2L manufactured on a shallow diffused process. For example, Plessey Process III I^2L, with a base junction depth of 0.6 μm, a base width of 0.2 μm, and a 2.5-μm-thick epitaxial layer produces gates with a minimum delay of 15 ns and a power–delay product of 0.5 pJ. The power–delay product is an order of magnitude lower in the Schottky I^2L structure owing to a combination of the following:

1) a reduced voltage swing arising from the addition of a Schottky diode in the base lead

2) a higher p-n-p gain because transistor action has been moved away from the sensitive surface region

3) a smaller emitter–base capacitance due to smaller device size

4) a smaller collector–base capacitance because of the smaller collector size and because the doping of the epitaxial base is significantly lower than the doping of a diffused I^2L base at the collector junction edge.

The gate delay of a four-collector Process III I^2L gate is of the order of 15 ns, but can rise to 30 ns in particular configurations of collectors and bases owing to base resistance between collectors. This is not a problem in Schottky I^2L because the vertical injector is equidistant from all collectors [1].

It is instructive to calculate the minimum gate delays of both structures on a simple first-order basis. The minimum gate delay t_d can be expressed as the product of the collector time constant τ_c and a function of the upward current gain:

$$t_d = \tau_c \cdot f(\beta u) \tag{1}$$

where

$$\tau_c = \frac{\text{total charge stored in the gate}}{\text{collector current per collector}} = \frac{Q}{I_c}. \tag{2}$$

In this analysis, charge stored in the depletion regions may be ignored as it does not contribute to the minimum delay. Moreover, it may be assumed that charge storage in the collector regions is negligible and that all semiconductor regions are in a low injection regime. The three main charge storage regions are the intrinsic base (i.e., under the collectors), the extrinsic base, and the emitter. These regions differ in volume and doping density for conventional I^2L and Schottky I^2L.

Each region can be represented by an effective volume v' and an effective doping density N', and it can be shown that (see Appendix) τ_c is given by

$$\tau_c = m \frac{W_c^2}{D_n} \left(1 + \frac{v'_{EX}}{v'_{IN}} \frac{N'_{IN}}{N'_{EX}} + \frac{v'_{EM}}{v'_{IN}} \frac{N'_{IN}}{N'_{EM}} \right) \tag{3}$$

where

m = number of collectors per gate
W_c = n-p-n base width
D_n = electron diffusion constant in the intrinsic base
$v'_{IN}, v'_{EX}, v'_{EM}$ = the effective volumes of the intrinsic base, extrinsic base, and emitter regions
$N'_{IN}, N'_{EX}, N'_{EM}$ = effective doping densities of the intrinsic base, extrinsic base, and emitter.

In I^2L, effective doping density of the extrinsic and intrinsic bases is usually provided by a single diffusion; the intrinsic base has a lower effective doping density because the shallow collector overdopes the most heavily doped region of the p-diffusion. The effective doping density of the emitter is determined by the lightly doped n-epitaxial layer. In the original Schottky I^2L process, both the extrinsic and intrinsic effective doping densities were determined by the p-epitaxial layer and the emitter doping by the n-epitaxial layer.

The minimum delay t_d can be calculated from the collector time constant using (1). The function $f(\beta_u)$ has been determined from a computer model of a delay line. The function varies slowly and a value of 1.5 has been used in the calculation of t_d. Fig. 2 illustrates the contribution of each region to the total minimum delay for I^2L and for the original Schottky I^2L process. The predicted gate delay in the Schottky I^2L structure is lower than that measured, owing to the onset of high current effects, principally high injection in the lightly doped p-epitaxial layer which causes charge storage in the emitter to increase in importance. In the I^2L structure, the bulk of the delay arises from charge storage in the large volume of epitaxial emitter. It is difficult to reduce the epitaxial charge storage of an I^2L gate; the effective volume is determined by photolithographic tolerances and epitaxial thickness control, whereas the epitaxial doping cannot be raised without detriment to both the emitter–base capacitance and the p-n-p gain which combine to increase the power–delay product. In

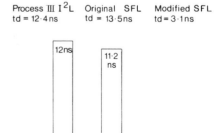

Fig. 2. Comparison of minimum gate delay of Process III I^2L and the original and modified Schottky I^2L (SFL) processes showing the relative contributions due to charge storage in the intrinsic base (a), the extrinsic base (b), and the emitter (c).

Schottky I²L, charge storage in the n-type epitaxial region has been drastically reduced by raising the doping by more than an order of magnitude. This is possible in the Schottky I²L structure because the emitter-base capacitance is determined by the p-type epitaxial layer doping, and the p-n-p gain is inherently higher because transistor action has been moved away from the sensitive surface region. The bulk of the delay in the Schottky I²L structure thus originates from the lightly doped p-type epitaxial base. A reduction in the amount of charge storage in this region would provide much lower gate delays. Equation (3) indicates that raising the p-type epitaxial base doping, and hence N'_{IN} and N'_{EX}, would not give any advantage; the only result would be an increase in the emitter-base capacitance.

A disadvantage of the original Schottky I²L process was a compromise between base resistance and Schottky diode breakdown voltage. The shallow penetration of the boron implantation through the oxide gave a high base resistance. The dose could not be increased, however, without reducing the Schottky diode breakdown voltage, which was determined by tunneling currents arising from the steep gradients in the sidewall of the diode. The breakdown voltage of ~2 V was already lower than desired for interface circuitry.

MODIFIED PROCESS

In order to achieve a lower minimum gate delay and avoid the compromise between base resistance and Schottky diode breakdown voltage, a modified process was developed as illustrated in Fig. 3. In this scheme, boron was implanted at higher energy before cutting contacts but was masked from the collector regions by photoresist. Earlier work [2] had shown that there was a range of surface doping concentrations which prevented surface inversion and at the same time allowed the formation of Schottky diodes. This structure gives several advantages.

In the original process, there was high doping under the Schottky diodes to minimize electron collection, but this heavier doping has now been extended over the whole extrinsic base, reducing charge storage. As the calculations for a four-collector gate, illustrated in Fig. 2, show, charge storage in the extrinsic base has been reduced from 80 to 30 percent of the total. The heavier extrinsic base doping has also reduced the base resistance from ~10 kΩ/sq to ~1 kΩ/sq.

The sharp gradient of dopant atoms at the Schottky diode perimeter has been removed, resulting in an increase of Schottky diode breakdown voltage to over 5 V. Finally, the intrinsic base doping remains unaffected by implant conditions or subsequent annealing treatments. Thus, in the modified process, the doping in the intrinsic base, the extrinsic base, and the emitter are controlled independently and this versatility allows the process to be tailored for specific applications.

The reduction in charge storage using the modified process is evident from the power-delay characteristics shown in Fig. 4. The minimum delay has been reduced by more than a factor of two to 8 ns, but is significantly larger than the 3 ns predicted from simple calculations. This is because of the onset of high current effects, not considered in the simple model, which begin at higher injector currents before minimum delay is achieved. The onset of high injection in the p-type epitaxial layer causes the collector current and charge storage in that layer to increase at a slower rate than the charge stored in the more heavily doped extrinsic base and n-epitaxial layer, resulting in an increase in the collector time constant (2) at higher currents. This effect can also be observed in the comparison of measured and calculated delays in the original process, but the effect is less pronounced because the charge stored in the more heavily doped regions initially contributes a smaller fraction of the total (Fig. 2). The power-delay product has been increased from 0.03 to 0.2 pJ because of the intersection of the tail of the deep p-implant with the n-type epitaxial layer. However, the power-delay product at 10-ns gate delay is only 0.3 pJ, which is extremely competitive with other LSI processes.

The gate delay of 8 ns was measured on a ring oscillator composed of minimum size gates. The gate delay of a larger gate is similar because, unlike I²L, each Schottky I²L gate receives a current proportional to its size [3]. This can be demonstrated by measuring the toggle frequency of a D-type flip-flop. Fig. 5 shows the toggle frequency of the flip-flop as a function of the power consumed by a minimum size gate. This flip-flop contains six gates, the largest of which has two Schottky contacts and three collectors. The flip-flop requires six gate delays per clock cycle, and therefore the maximum observed frequency of 20 MHz implies a gate delay of 8 ns. The power-delay product at this toggle frequency is 0.6 pJ.

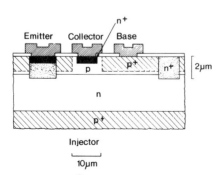

Fig. 3. Modified Schottky I²L process. Doping levels are the same as in the original process, but the heavily doped region of the base is implanted at a higher energy before cutting contacts.

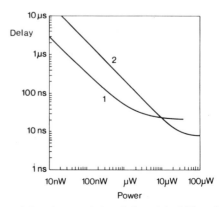

Fig. 4. Power-delay characteristics of the original (1) and modified (2) Schottky I²L processes.

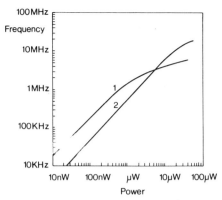

Fig. 5. Toggle frequency versus power consumed by a minimum size gate as measured on a D-type flip-flop for the original (1) and modified (2) processes.

Yield

The high performance of Schottky I^2L has been achieved with a structure specifically designed for high yield. Two factors are important in the design of a process for high yield. The first is the simplicity of the processing. Schottky I^2L uses six masking stages, two of which involve only the definition of the photoresist without subsequent etching. High temperature heat treatments have been kept to a minimum. The second factor is the insensitivity of the process to crystal defects. A major cause of failure in bipolar circuits is known to be collector–emitter leakage, which is related to structural defects in the silicon. Such leakage currents are strongly dependent on basewidth. Schottky I^2L, with a base-width approaching 1 μm, will give far higher yields than conventional forms of I^2L at the same defect densities.

The yield of Schottky I^2L has been evaluated with the aid of a specially designed test mask, shown in Fig. 6. On this mask

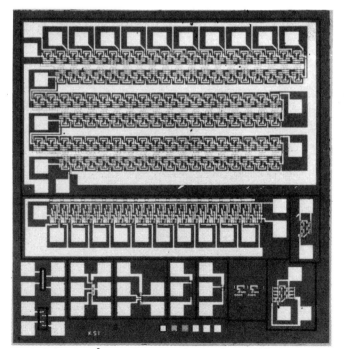

Fig. 6. Schottky I^2L yield test mask showing a 111-element shift register, a 20-element shift register composed of single output/multi-input gates, and various test components.

there is a long shift register made from 111 D-type flip-flops, with a toggle on the first stage and tapped at intermediate stages. The circuit contains 666 gates at a local packing density of nearly 800 gates/mm^2, and has demonstrated that the process is capable of giving high yield on LSI circuits.

A second, shorter shift register composed of 120 gates having only one collector and several Schottky diode inputs is also shown on the mask. By comparing the yield of equal lengths of the two registers, it has been shown that Schottky diode failures account for only a small proportion of gate failures.

Summary

A modified form of Schottky I^2L has been described which increases the flexibility of the process by allowing independent variation of the doping in the n-type epitaxial layer and the intrinsic and extrinsic regions of the p-type epitaxial base. This flexibility has been utilized to reduce the minimum gate delay below 10 ns for both large and small gates. Additional advantages include 5 V Schottky diode breakdown voltages and reduced base resistance. Simple processing has led to low defect levels, and the wide basewidth of the n-p-n device, compared with conventional I^2L, has made the process insensitive to residual defects. The resultant high yields make Schottky I^2L a very attractive proposition for high-speed LSI circuits of the future.

Appendix
The Collector Time Constant

The total minority carrier charge stored can be expressed as the sum of the charge stored in the intrinsic base Q_{IN}, the extrinsic base Q_{EX}, and the emitter Q_{EM}. This enables the collector time constant to be rewritten as follows:

$$\tau_c = \frac{Q}{I_c} = \frac{Q_{IN} + Q_{EX} + Q_{EM}}{I_c}. \tag{4}$$

The charge stored in each region can be simply expressed by assuming low injection conditions and by using a one-dimensional approximation:

$$Q = \int_0^W \frac{qA_J F n_i^2}{N} \exp\left(V_{BE}/V_T\right) dx$$

$$= qA_J n_i^2 \exp\left(V_{BE}/V_T\right) \int_0^W \frac{F}{N} dx \tag{5}$$

where A_J is the junction area, W the width of the region, F a function dependent on the minority carrier distribution in that region, and N the doping density. F is unity at the emitter-base junction; its value in the bulk of the region depends on recombination and the boundary condition at $x = W$. For the purposes of this analysis, (5) is approximated to

$$Q = qn_i^2 \exp\left(V_{BE}/V_T\right) \cdot A_J W \overline{F} \cdot \int_0^W \frac{1}{N} \frac{dx}{W}.$$

This enables the charge storage to be expressed in terms of an effective doping density N', which can be easily determined from the doping profile, and an effective volume v', which includes a factor $\overline{F}$ dependent on the minority carrier distribution

$$Q = q n_i^2 \exp(V_{BE}/V_T) \cdot \frac{v'}{N'} \qquad (6)$$

where

$$\frac{1}{N'} = \int_0^W \frac{1}{N} \frac{d_x}{W}; \quad v' = A_J W \overline{F}.$$

If the diffusion length is longer than the width of the region, then the value of $\overline{F}$ depends on the boundary condition at $x = W$. If the charge storage volume is the intrinsic base of a saturated transistor, then $\overline{F}$ is unity. If the volume is bounded by a "reflective" interface, such as a high–low junction, then $\overline{F}$ is again unity. If the region is bounded by a reverse bias junction, $\overline{F}$ is assumed to be $\frac{1}{2}$. For an oxide covered region, $\overline{F}$ will be between $\frac{1}{2}$ and 1, depending on the surface recombination velocity; a value of 1 has been assumed for the calculations in this paper. A value of $\frac{1}{2}$ has been assumed for the volume of the n-emitter which also forms the intrinsic base of the p-n-p transistor because only the charge stored in the inverse p-n-p transistor is changed during a switching transition (i.e., the injector is at a constant voltage).

The collector current can also be expressed in terms of the effective doping density of the intrinsic base N'_{IN} and the effective volume of intrinsic base charge v'_{IN}. Assuming the intrinsic base region is in a low injection regime,

$$I_c = \frac{q A_c D_n n_i^2 \exp(V_{BE}/V_T)}{\int_0^{W_c} N d_x}.$$

Assuming that in the intrinsic base

$$\int_0^{W_c} N d_x = \left[\int_0^{W_c} \frac{1}{N} \frac{d_x}{W_c} \right]^{-1} W_c = N'_{IN} W_c$$

and that the effective charge storage volume can be expressed as

$$v'_{IN} = m A_c W_c$$

(where m is the number of collectors, all assumed to be saturated when the gate is "ON", i.e., $\overline{F} = 1$), the collector current becomes

$$I_c = \frac{q v'_{IN} D_n n_i^2 \exp(V_{BE}/V_T)}{m W_c^2 N'_{IN}}. \qquad (7)$$

Using (6) and (7), the collector time constant can be rewritten as follows:

$$\tau_c = \frac{v'_{IN}/N'_{IN} + v'_{EX}/N'_{EX} + v'_{EM}/N'_{EM}}{(D_n v'_{IN})/(N'_{IN} m W_c^2)}$$

$$\tau_c = m \frac{W_c^2}{D_n} \left(1 + \frac{v'_{EX}}{v'_{IN}} \frac{N'_{IN}}{N'_{EX}} + \frac{v'_{EM}}{v'_{IN}} \frac{N'_{IN}}{N'_{EM}} \right). \qquad (8)$$

ACKNOWLEDGMENT

The authors are grateful to Dr. V. Blatt for stimulating much of this work, to R. C. Ashford for performing the experimentation, and to the Directors of The Plessey Company Ltd. for permission to publish.

REFERENCES

[1] V. Blatt, P. S. Walsh, and L. W. Kennedy, "Substrate fed logic," *IEEE J. Solid-State Circuits*, vol. SC-10, pp. 336–342, Oct. 1975.
[2] V. Blatt *et al.*, "Substrate fed logic—An improved form of injection logic," in *IEDM Tech. Dig.*, 1974, pp. 511–514.
[3] V. Blatt and G. W. Sumerling, "Schottky I²L (substrate fed logic)—An analysis of the implications of the vertical injector structure and Schottky collection," this issue, pp. 128–134.

Schottky Collector I²L

S. C. BLACKSTONE, STUDENT MEMBER, IEEE, AND R. P. MERTENS

Abstract—A new I²L gate which promises increased packing density and increased speed is discussed. It incorporates the use of a Schottky contact as the collector of the vertical switching transistor of an I²L gate. Calculations and experiments show that the problems associated with this structure (low downward beta) can be controlled by limiting both the fan-out and the fan-in. Delays of less than 10 ns have been measured using a 10-μm technology and a 6-μm-thick epi. A divide-by-two circuit with a maximum toggle frequency of 12.5 MHz has been built. The additional fan-in limitation of the logic is described.

I. INTRODUCTION

IT HAS BEEN SHOWN [1], [2] that the minimum propagation delay of an I²L gate is an increasing function of the upward transit time and the upward and downward current gains. The power-delay product, on the other hand, decreases with decreasing voltage swing and decreasing gate capacitance. It has been demonstrated [3] that by substituting the collector-

base junction of the switching transistor by a Schottky contact, it is possible to reduce both the voltage swing and the downward current gain and thus to increase the speed of the gate over the entire power range.

Since from a technological viewpoint it is easier to make Schottky contacts on n-type material, the switching transistor must have an n-type base [Fig. 1(a), (b)]. This device, then, is a transistor whose emitter–base junction is a p-n junction, but whose base–collector junction is an n-metal Schottky contact. This gives rise to Berger and Wiedmann's connotation [3] of a PNM transistor.

This paper describes the properties of the merged structure obtained by combining the PNM switching transistor with a lateral n-p-n injector [Fig. 1(c), (d)].

The second section deals with the transfer characteristics of the gate and describes the influence of the Schottky collector on these characteristics. The fabrication of the devices is described in the third section and the main advantages and disadvantages, from a technological viewpoint, are given.

The fourth section discusses the problems of logic, built with multiple Schottky-collector outputs, and mainly deals with the current hogging problem as discussed in [4].

Manuscript received November 10, 1976; revised February 8, 1977. R. P. Mertens is sponsored by the Belgian National Science Foundation (NFWO).

The authors are with the Laboratory for Electronics, Systems, Automatization and Technology, Catholic University of Leuven, Heverlee, Belgium.

Reprinted from *IEEE J. Solid-State Circuits*, vol. SC-12, pp. 270–275, June 1977.

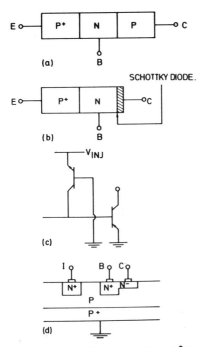

Fig. 1. Evolution of Schottky-collector I²L gate.

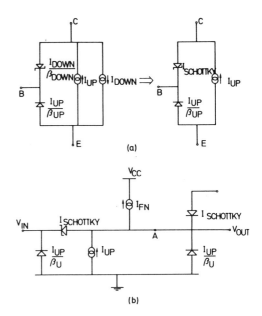

Fig. 2. Modified Ebers–Moll model of Schottky-collector transistor and I²L gate.

In the fifth section, experimental results on ring oscillators and divide-by-two's are presented.

Section VI deals with the potential of the present approach. The last section, finally, gives a summary of the paper and its main conclusions.

II. TRANSFER CHARACTERISTICS OF THE BASIC INVERTER

The switching transistor in the basic inverter of Fig. 1(c), (d) has two unique properties as a result of the Schottky barrier. The large saturation current of the Schottky causes the forward voltage drop across the base–collector junction to be small and the resulting absence of substantial minority carrier injection results in a very low value of downward current gain. The transistor will have a larger saturation voltage from the equation

$$V_{EC} = V_{EB} - V_{CB} = V_{sat}. \tag{1}$$

If we simply start with the Ebers–Moll model [5], it is easily fitted to this transistor by making the base–collector junction a Schottky diode and by making the downward current gain very low or for a simplified model, eliminating it [Fig. 2(a)].

If a current-source transistor is now added, it is possible to derive the transfer characteristics of the Schottky-collector I²L gate. Starting with the simplified model and adding the current source without the emitter–base loss diode and another gate as load, the following model is obtained [Fig. 2(b)]. The subscript P refers to the p-n-p, whereas the subscript N refers to the n-p-n-transistor. The loss diode associated with the forward mode of operation of the lateral n-p-n has been omitted. The β_U is now the β_{UP} of Fig. 2(a) reduced by the back injection of the base to the injector as defined in [1].

Using Kirchhoff's current law about A [Fig. 2(b)] yields

$$I_{FN} - I_{SP} \Phi_{-V_{in}} - I_{SS} \Phi_{(V_{in}-V_{out})} - \frac{I_{SP}}{\beta_U} \Phi_{-V_{out}}$$

$$+ I_{DS} \Phi_{(V_{out}-V_{in})} = 0 \tag{2}$$

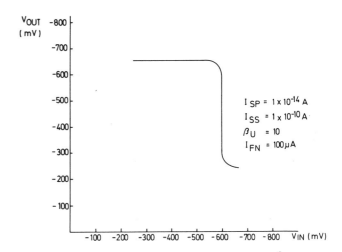

Fig. 3. Transfer characteristics of Schottky-collector I²L gate.

in (2) the symbol Φ_V stands for $(\exp((q/kT) V) - 1$; I_{SP} is the saturation current of the p-n-p; I_{SS} is the saturation current of the Schottky barrier; β_U is the beta of the vertical p-n-p with injector grounded; and I_{FN} is the injector current = $I_{SN} \Phi_{-V_{cc}}$.

Solving (2) numerically, one can plot the transfer characteristics of the I²L gate (Fig. 3). From this plot, one can see the conventional I²L characteristics in the off state. However, in the on state, it saturates at a higher voltage as a result of the Schottky diode.

III. DEVICE FABRICATION

The fabrication of the basic Schottky-collector I²L inverter gate is as follows (Fig. 4). As Schottky diodes are less difficult to fabricate on n-type material, and because A1 metallization was desired, the starting material was a 6-μm epi p/p⁺ with an epi resistivity of about 1–2 Ω · cm. The epi thickness and concentration are not optimized and had to be chosen out

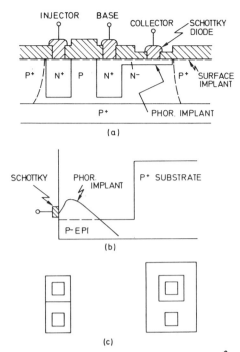

Fig. 4. Fabrication and layout of Schottky collector I^2L inverter.

of the available supply. To prevent the problem of surface inversion commonly associated with p-type material, a shallow p-implantation is done over the entire wafer. This could also be avoided by choosing a lower resistivity epi material. Next, the field oxide is grown and then a p^+-diffusion is done to reduce lateral injection. Following that, an n^+-diffusion is done to form the injector and inactive base. Now the active base region is defined and opened and a 1200-Å chlorine oxide is grown. To form the active base, a phosphorus implant of 400 · keV, 4×10^{12} cm^{-2} is performed over the entire wafer (the field oxide over the base of the lateral n-p-n shields it from the implant) and annealed at 920°C for 30′ to preserve the profile. Finally, contact holes are opened and the wafer is metallized, the pattern defined, and the wafer sintered at 450°C 30′.

This is then a 5-mask technology with fewer critical steps than normal I^2L. The main advantages of this technology are the following.

As a result of the high doping in the inactive base, the base resistance will be lower, the current injected into the inactive base region will be small, and the charge stored in the inactive base region will also be reduced. The same advantages can be obtained in conventional I^2L by using two base diffusions.

Two, by ion implanting the active base, one can achieve a higher degree of control over the profile of the active base than by diffusion. This not only means good uniformity but it also allows one to adjust the electric field in the base creating an aiding field. It is recognized, however, that this aiding field only has a minor practical impact on the speed performance.

Three, by not doing a collector diffusion, the problem of spikes or of a very highly doped collector, preferencially diffusing along a dislocation through the base into the emitter and shorting the device, does not exist. For small circuits, this is not a problem, but for LSI this becomes a major advantage.

Finally, for the same ground rules, the device will be as small as using the "washed-emitter" technique as a result of the fact that the collector contact hole (Schottky contact) need be only one tolerance from the isolation region [Fig. 4(c)]. This not only leads to a higher packing density, but reduces the capacitance of the gate, allowing for a lower power-delay product.

A disadvantage of this device is that the switching transistor, being a p-n-p rather than an n-p-n, will have a lower f_T as a result of the higher saturation current for the n-p-n for identical and complementary structures. This is a consequence of the higher electron mobility. However, this theoretical disadvantage will be offset by the lower charge storage in the n-inactive base and the Schottky barrier producing both a low downward current gain and a clamping effect. As a result, in the actual device, the Schottky-collector p-n-p transistor, for the same layout rules and profiles, turns out to be faster than the conventional unclamped n-p-n I^2L structure.

As a final point on technology, an additional boron implant can be performed through a photoresist mask to form a collector and thus a normal I^2L gate or, with a p^+ buried-layer mask, an isolated transistor. It should be pointed out that this would not be a normal I^2L gate in that it would have a very highly doped injector which would allow metal lines to cross it with a minimal voltage drop allowing a more versatile circuit design, and the highly doped extrinsic base would allow the collector, far from the injector, to switch at nearly the same speed as the collector near the injector which in conventional I^2L can differ by a factor of 4 [6].

IV. LOGIC WITH MULTIPLE SCHOTTKY COLLECTORS

Thus far, only the inverter has been examined, which is insufficient for performing logic. The problem with performing in the normal I^2L mode (i.e., multiple collectors) is the same point which makes this logic fast: low downward current gain. The two approaches to this problem have been, 1) to introduce a lightly doped collector and put a Schottky barrier on top of it [7], or 2) to add Schottky barriers of a lower barrier height on the base to decouple the input and only use one Schottky collector [3]. Our approach is between these two, we use multiple pure Schottky collectors but add a special surface treatment to enhance the downward current of each collector. By doing this, we found that we could build certain structures in which current hogging is a controllable problem. To examine this problem, consider the case of a gate with a fan-out of two. The worst case, which will have to be avoided, is if one collector is floating. In this case, all of the current injected into the floating collector will have to be recombined with base current and the current gain of the nonfloating collector will drop below one. Thus the question is one of fan-in or how many collectors can be "wired anded" to the first collector such that the second can still sink one base current.

The simplest example is the ring oscillator with many gates of one collector and one gate of two collectors. Using a simplified Ebers–Moll model (no downward current gain) one can draw Fig. 5(a) where one collector is connected to the following gate and the other is connected to a fractional base current.

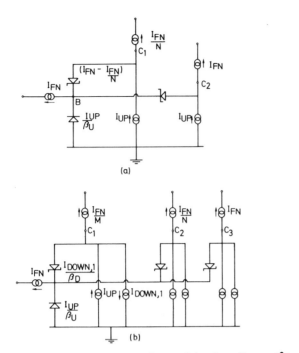

Fig. 5. Models of two- and three-collector Schottky-collector I²L gates.

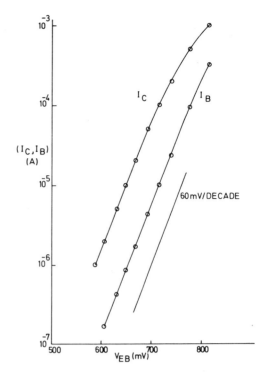

Fig. 6. Plot of I_c and I_b versus V_{EB} for a Schottky-collector transistor in an I²L gate. The injector is grounded and the collector is $10 \times 10\,\mu m$.

If we assume as a limiting condition that collector C_2 is just out of saturation then both current sources, assuming identical collector characteristics, will be supplying a current of I_{FN}. This will result in zero current flow across the Schottky collector of C_2. Thus the current flowing across the Schottky collector of C_1 will be $I_{FN} - I_{FN}/N$. The current flowing through the base-emitter loss diode will then, by Kirchhoff's law about point B, be

$$I_B = I_{FN} - I_{FN} + I_{FN}/N = I_{FN}/N. \qquad (3)$$

The limiting β_U necessary to satisfy this condition will then be

$$\beta_U = \frac{I_{FN}}{I_B} = N \qquad (4)$$

or the condition on β_U is

$$\beta_U > N. \qquad (5)$$

Thus, in the case of a two-collector structure, the fan-in of the first collector is limited by the value of the upward current gain. So, theoretically, it is possible even without inverse beta to perform a limited amount of logic, the voltage noise immunity being extremely small.

To try to extend this approach to greater fan-in and fan-out capabilities, one quickly finds it impossible without some downward current gain. As the excess hole concentration in the n-region just at the Schottky barrier follows the same Boltzmann relationship as for a p-n junction [10], the only way to increase downward beta is to decrease the saturation current of the Schottky barrier or, in other words, to increase the barrier height of the Schottky barrier. It has been demonstrated that the barrier height of an Al Schottky barrier on n-type material increases as a function of heat treatment [8].

Thus, using this technique, it is possible at high currents to achieve a significant injection of minority carriers producing a downward current gain. Now, redoing the calculations including downward current gain, it is possible to achieve better results.

To examine this question, consider the following situation; where there are two collectors with a fan-in of M and N and then calculate the beta of the third collector. Drawing the Ebers–Moll model [Fig. 5(b)] and performing the calculations yields the following effective beta of the third collector:

$$\beta_{\text{eff}} = \frac{\beta_U(\beta_D + 1 + 1/N + 1/M)}{1 + \beta_D + 2\beta_U} \qquad (6)$$

where β_U and β_D are the upward and downward current gains, respectively, as defined in [1].

V. Experimental Results

Schottky-collector I²L gates have been fabricated and Fig. 6 is a plot of I_c and I_b as a function of V_{EB} for a Schottky-collector transistor incorporated in an I²L gate (injector grounded). One can readily see that the collector current follows the 60 mV/decade typical of a bipolar transistor. Fig. 7 is a plot of current gain as a function of collector current showing flat characteristics out to about 100 μA.

Using a seven-stage ring oscillator with six single-collector transistors and one two-collector transistor with collectors of $10 \times 10\,\mu m$ and a 10-μm minimum linewidth, gate delays of less than 10 ns have been measured.

By going to higher sintering temperatures, it was possible to obtain downward betas of up to one-half at higher current levels. Fig. 8 is a photograph of the upward I_c versus V_{CE} of a Schottky-collector transistor after such a heat treatment,

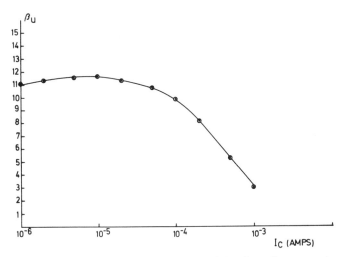

Fig. 7. Plot of effective beta versus I_c for a Schottky-collector transistor incorporated in an I^2L gate. The collector is 10×10 μm.

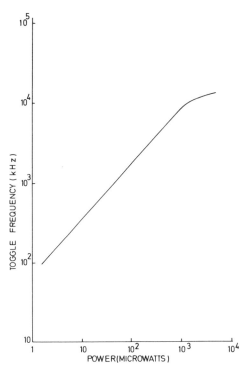

Fig. 9. Plot of toggle frequency versus power for a D-type flip-flop connected as a divide-by-two. This is using a 6-μm epi and a 10-μm technology.

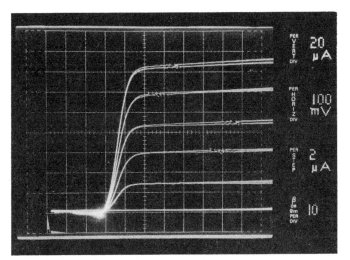

Fig. 8. Photograph of I_c versus V_{EC} for a Schottky-collector transistor after heat treatment.

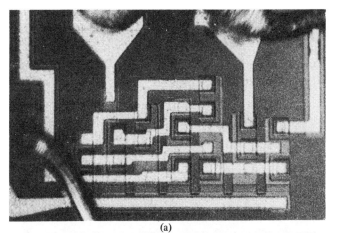

(a)

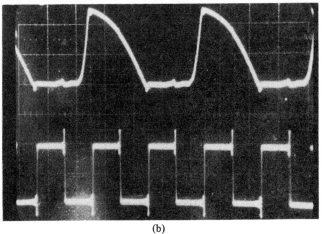

(b)

Fig. 10. Photographs of (a) the divide-by-two and (b) the waveforms. Top is the output and bottom is the input. Horizontal, 0.5 μs; vertical, lower 500 mV/div and upper 200 mV/div.

showing that the base–collector junction is still a Schottky barrier as a result of the high saturation voltage.

This suggested that if the upward beta was high enough, it should be possible to fabricate a conventional seven-gate divide-by-two. Although the different fan-in values for the worst case gate (fan-out three) are two and three, respectively, one can show that for the gate in the ON state two collectors have to sink one base current each, whereas the remaining collector sinks only half a base current. Thus the worst case collector will be one of the collectors sinking one base current. From (6), making $M = 1$ and $N = 2$, and using the measured value of $B_D = 0.5$, to have an effective beta of greater than one (condition of operation), one needs an upward beta in excess of 1.5.

VI. POTENTIAL OF PRESENT APPROACH

As shown in the previous section, using multiple Schottky collectors, D-type flip-flops can be fabricated. Consequently, counters and shift registers could be fabricated using this technology. To perform random logic on the same circuit, an additional p⁺-implant can be done into the active base region. This will then form normal I²L gates or, with a buried-layer mask, isolated transistors. Such isolated transistors have been fabricated and exhibit downward betas of one (f_T) at approximately 1 GHz. This is readily comparable with the f_T of conventional n-p-n transistors. Thus it would allow digital and linear circuits on the same chip. A case in point might be the superintegrated memory of Wiedmann [9]. The memory cell could be made of cross-coupled Schottky-collector transistors resulting in reduced size, and the encoding and decoding could be done using the isolated p-n-p transistors.

VII. CONCLUSIONS

Schottky-collector I²L as a technology and as a logic concept has been discussed and experimentally verified. It is based on using Schottky barriers as the collector-base junctions of the vertical transistors in an I²L gate. This allows for a simple technology which displays speeds better than conventional I²L and packing densities comparable to oxide isolation. The logic is limited by fan-in and fan-out due to current hogging; however, it has been shown that a limited fan-in and fan-out capability is available.

ACKNOWLEDGMENT

The authors wish to thank Mr. Kennedy of the Plessey Company and Mr. Goser of Siemens for supplying p-epi material and Mr. Mattheus of the Catholic University of Leuven for many helpful discussions.

REFERENCES

[1] H. H. Berger and S. K. Wiedmann, "Terminal-oriented model for merged transistor logic (MTL)," *IEEE J. Solid-State Circuits*, vol. SC-9, pp. 211–217, Oct. 1974.
[2] F. M. Klaasen, "Device physics of integrated injection logic," *IEEE Trans. Electron Devices*, vol. ED-22, pp. 145–152, Mar. 1975.
[3] H. H. Berger and S. K. Wiedmann, "Advanced merged transistor logic by using Schottky junctions," *Microelectron.*, vol. 7, pp. 35–42, 1976.
[4] ——, "Merged transistor logic (MTL)–A low cost bipolar logic concept," *IEEE J. Solid-State Circuits*, vol. SC-7, pp. 340–346, Oct. 1972.
[5] J. J. Ebers and J. L. Moll, "Large-signal behavior of junction transistors," *Proc. IRE*, vol. 42, pp. 1761–1772, Dec. 1954.
[6] W. Mattheus and R. Mertens, "Dynamic modeling of I²L," to be published.
[7] F. W. Hewlett, "Schottky I²L," *IEEE J. Solid-State Circuits*, vol. SC-10, pp. 343–348, Oct. 1975.
[8] H. C. Card, "Schottky diode clamping in silicon integrated circuits and distress caused by thermal processings," in *IEDM 1975 Tech. Dig.*, pp. 288–290.
[9] S. K. Wiedmann, "Injection-coupled memory: A high density static bipolar memory," *IEEE J. Solid-State Circuits*, vol. SC-8, pp. 332–337, Oct. 1973.
[10] A. Y. C. Yu, "The metal-semiconductor contact: An old device with a new future," *IEEE Spectrum*, pp. 83–89, Mar. 1970.

Part IV
I²L Device Physics, Models, and LSI Simulation

By far the most interesting, controversial, and fruitful efforts in I²L research have delved into the device physics and modeling of the basic I²L gate. In this regard the appearance of I²L upon the IC scene ushered in wholly new approaches to device modeling and stimulated rethinking of the classical approaches to bipolar device physics. These efforts have resulted in improved modeling techniques and in general a better understanding of devices which are founded upon minority carrier injection. Indeed, the insight gained from such research has provided the direction for the development of a host of improved I²L structures.

Paper IV-1 by Klaassen was the first publication to provide a comprehensive treatment of the overall aspects of I²L device physics and circuit operation covering the dc, transient, and noise properties of the basic, original, analog-compatible I²L gate structure. This paper combines the results of analytic and numerical solutions to arrive at generally useful approximations for conventional I²L gate performance. However, for efforts aimed at all-out speed optimization, Klaassen's analyses could not be used directly. Specifically Klaassen does not treat the effects of series base resistance upon either the dc beta or the turn-on and turn-off delays for an I²L gate.

Paper IV-2 by Berger and Wiedmann presents an organized, systematic application of the dc Ebers–Moll bipolar transistor model to the multijunction I²L gate structure. As a result, they clearly identify a set of terminal parameters for an I²L gate, and the correct techniques for the measurement of those parameters are unambiguously established. The now widely adopted terminology of "upward" and "downward" operation introduced by these authors greatly aids the readability of their paper. The newcomer to I²L would benefit from the exercise of directly reconfirming the dc analyses presented by Berger and Wiedmann in order to gain familiarity with and understanding of the interrelations within the multiple-junction structure of an I²L gate. The authors state that all injectors (pnp emitters) on a die are at an equipotential, and consequently the pnp can be replaced by an equivalent constant current source. This statement certainly applies under the conditions that the injector is voltage driven and low-current operation with metal interconnections is used for a single injector bus and all ground buses. For higher current operation of large circuits, the alternative technique of on-chip injector-ballast-resistors is frequently adopted in order to avoid voltage drops in the power supply buses. Consequently, the voltages of the then decoupled individual injectors can differ substantially as a result of the states of the logic gates supplied by those injectors. The situation arises by way of the current which is recollected by the injector from the npn's, and the net negative consequence is that an I²L gate in one portion of the circuit may lack current drive capability to "sink" the cur-

rent of an I²L gate in a second portion of the circuit. Thus a proper understanding of Berger's and Wiedmann's recollection factor is essential for the design of successful I²L circuits. The authors point out that their gate-delay-model-generated curves for the intrinsic gate delay as a function of the up and down betas are only indicators for circuit design and do not relate directly to the physical device structure. This is an important point and their Fig. 9 should be interpreted with this veiwpoint in mind.

Berger's paper (IV-3) on the injection model represents a landmark along the road toward truly structure-oriented modeling of the physical mechanisms in bipolar devices. The highly distributed nature of I²L demands such a modeling approach if ultimate circuit performance is to be properly related to the geometric and process-structure-related parameters of the composite I²L gate/device. The highlight of Berger's work is the clever scheme which is presented for the experimental extraction of the parameters which describe the building blocks of the injection model. The ability to directly evaluate the base current contributions due to recombination in the various regions of the gate structure permits the direct evaluation of process or structural changes upon I²L gate performance. Additionally, the technique permits the acquisition of physically meaningful parameters for use in distributed-gate models in circuit simulation programs. It should be pointed out that the dimensions of Berger's test devices may not be adequate for some processes and the geometric design of such test layouts should be optimized for the particular process/structure which is to be characterized.

One of Berger's conclusions is that the vertical injection of holes into the epitaxial emitter region accounts for only a small fraction of the total base current. This conclusion is in conflict with later results presented by other workers, and the differing viewpoints have resulted in a controversy as to the magnitudes of the various current components, the governing physical mechanisms, and the experimental techniques for the determination of the I²L base current components. Papers IV-5–7 address this question in greater detail. Nonetheless, Berger's results clearly demonstrated the effects of the boundary conditions at a metal contact or oxide-covered region upon p-n junction injection of minority carriers. Such an experimental technique had not been previously reported and has since become a widely adopted tool for I²L investigation.

Another of Berger's conclusions is that the base contact of an I²L gate should be placed near the injector to avoid voltage drops along the gate caused by the current which flows to support recombination at the contact. However, it should be noted that this choice of location is not necessarily optimum for the turn-off delay of the gate, especially for the far collectors of a multiple fan-out gate. Berger also proposes an oxide-walled structure in which the only current path to the far collectors is by way of the very high resistivity intrinsic base regions. Such a structure would be limited to operation at very low current levels (and therefore low speed) because of the severe voltage drops along the gate at higher currents. Berger correctly applies his injection model to the most important consideration of the effect of device structure upon the speed (or propagation delay) of an I^2L gate. The dominant dependence of the emitter time constant upon stored charge in the epitaxial emitter is clearly demonstrated, and the weak dependence upon the up-beta is described.

Paper IV-4 by Jaeger provides a confirmation of the applicability of Berger's injection model. The noteworthy result is that injection modeling is found to be adequate for graded-base-profile devices but as a result of two-dimensional effects the technique is not applicable to homogeneously doped base regions.

The paper by Heimeier and Berger presents an experimental investigation of the injection model for injection into a p-type base region beneath a metallic contact or a collecting p-n junction. The specific goal of this work was to relate the carrier injection to the sheet resistivity of the layer into which injection occurs. The authors found a direct proportionality between carrier injection and sheet resistivity. However, the experimental data could only be reconciled with theory by invocation of bandgap narrowing due to heavy doping. Thus application of the injection model to I^2L modeling would benefit from the inclusion of bandgap-narrowing effects.

Wulms, in paper IV-6, presents a detailed experimental study of the origins of the base current components in an I^2L gate. He arrives at conclusions which are generally in conflict with Berger's conclusions with respect to the relative importance of the contributions to base current due to electron and hole recombination. The overall lesson to be derived from the many differing reports upon the relative magnitudes of I^2L base current components is that these base current components will be different for different structures and, furthermore, will even be different for apparently similar structures which are implemented in different laboratories. Wulms points out the need for paying careful attention to the design, fabrication, and testing of the test devices which are intended to extract the base current components. Small oversights in this regard can lead to erroneous conclusions. In particular, Wulms points out the need for controlled and reproducible surface effects upon the electron recombination in the p-type base and space-charge regions. Secondly, the effects of localized gettering by phosphorous must be taken into account in the design of the test structures. Finally, statistically meaningful quantities of data must be gathered and reduced by standard techniques in order to rule out material and processing variations. Wulms found that it was necessary to include the effects of bandgap narrowing in order to reconcile the experimentally measured base current components with the theoretically predicted values. He found the vertical hole current into the epitaxial emitter to be responsible for 80 percent of the measured base current. However, it must be noted that Wulms has quoted base current components as percentages of the net base current

with the effects of the injector recollection removed whereas such percentages are typically quoted so as to include the effects of the injector recollection. When the injector recollection is taken into account (from Table I) the vertical hole current is found to be between 60 and 65 percent of the total base current which is in general agreement with typical results for I^2L structures fabricated in a clean bipolar process similar to that used by Wulms.

Paper IV-7 by Mattheus et al., is the last paper in Part IV which treats the subject of I^2L base current components. This paper pays special attention to the operation of an I^2L gate at very low current levels. Their experimental data does not fully support the conclusions of Wulms with respect to the effects of phosphorous gettering. However, since different geometries were used, Wulms' data is not invalidated. A major result of this work is that the experimentally measured components of base current due to injection of electrons under an oxide-covered p-type region of the extrinsic I^2L base could not be reconciled with theoretical calculations. An explanation for this discrepancy has been proposed by Heasell in bibliography paper [IV-9]. Heasell provides a detailed treatment of recombination beneath metallic contacts and oxides, and the interested reader is referred to that paper for further information on the subject. An important conclusion from the work of Mattheus et al. is the need for a special low-temperature final annealing step in the fabrication of I^2L devices intended for use in very low current applications.

Many other authors have provided analyses of the conventional I^2L gate operation. The publications are too numerous to even mention here and are included in the Bibliography for Part IV. Papers IV-1-5, when taken together, constitute a sufficient exposition of those aspects of I^2L device physics which are crucial for a complete understanding of the process and structurally related dependencies of I^2L static performance.

The use of Schottky diodes in the collector region of I^2L gates has received much attention. Paper IV-8 by Blackstone and Mertens presents a largely theoretical exploration of the single-collector, multiple Schottky-collector-contact implementation of an I^2L gate. These authors conclude that the multiple (nonisolated) Schottky-collector-contact structure is a viable (and even desirable) approach to the fabrication of I^2L gates. The major shortcoming of their paper lies in the lack of a treatment of the effects of Schottky diode reverse leakage currents. Such leakage currents can have devastating effects upon the gate performance, especially at elevated temperatures. Simulation results were presented for a Schottky-clamped version of the structure but no experimental results were reported. The claims made here for the common-collector, multiple Schottky-contact structure should be treated with caution in situations where Schottky diode reverse leakage currents are expected, and the Schottky clamped version is even more susceptible to limitations due to the Schottky diode characteristics at elevated temperature. Finally, a severe layout limitation is that the structure does not permit the location of the base contact to be freely exchanged with each collector contact location as does conventional I^2L.

The ultimate performance of I^2L gates is frequently related to a physical mechanism which is spatially distributed in nature. The two seemingly everpresent examples are the base resistance and stored charge. Papers IV-9-12 treat the subjects of laterally distributed base resistance, vertically distributed stored charge in the epitaxial emitter, the laterally distributed RC nature of the gate and the effects of the base contact location upon gate delay and transient response.

In paper IV-9 Kirschner presents an analytical investigation of the effects of the distributed base resistance upon the dc up-beta of an I^2L gate. Kirschner's analysis demonstrates the effects of "current crowding" toward the injector end of the gate. Consequently, at higher current levels, the collectors near the injector receive (relatively) increased carrier injection. A further (and serious) consequence not mentioned by Kirschner is that, as injection is crowded toward the injector end of the gate at high current operation, the (relative) reverse injection to the injector is dramatically increased. The resulting strong fractional increase in the recollected component of the base current is equivalent to a reduced current drive for the complete I^2L gate. This phenomenon has been accurately modeled in bibliography paper [IV-43]. Kirschner's paper is of limited practical value for actual quantitative calculation of I^2L gate performance. However, the contribution of the work lies in the presentation of an analytic solution which provides insight into the consequences of the extrinsic base resistance and the attendant lateral voltage distribution.

Paper IV-10 is a condensed abstract of an ISSCC presentation by Lohstroh. The paper presents the results of a numerical simulation of the dynamics of vertically distributed stored charge in an I^2L gate. A complete account of the work is presented in bibliography paper [IV-21]: however, the essential results are contained in the ISSCC abstract. It must be stressed that Lohstroh's simulation does not take into account the effects of the laterally distributed base resistance of an I^2L gate. The major insights gained from the dynamic simulations are as follows. 1) The stored charge in the epitaxial layer is dominant. This is to be expected for the epitaxial layer thickness of 6.5μ used in the simulation. 2) The spatial distribution of the stored charge is time dependent and, consequently, would be difficult to represent accurately by a simple first-order model. 3) The I^2L npn takes a relatively long time to saturate, and consequently the gate propagation delay as deduced from ring oscillator experiments may be sensitive to the number of stages included in the ring oscillator test structure. In general, these conclusions would be valid for designs where the base resistance is important yet quantitative agreement could not be expected unless the base resistance effects were included. Lohstroh's results are applicable to the typical analog compatible I^2L structure. However, I^2L logic implementations will normally take advantage of thinner epitaxial layers which greatly diminish the emitter stored-charge distribution which was found in this work.

Paper IV-11 is unique in its application of steady-state sinusoidal techniques for the characterization of the distributed RC transmission-line-like nature of an I^2L gate. The input impedance as a function of frequency is observed to deviate from the 20-dB per decade which would be expected for a

purely lumped device representation. In contrast to Lohstroh's work, Mattheus *et al.* conclude that the vertically distributed hole concentration in the epitaxial emitter is not of relative importance in their structures. It should be noted that Lohstroh simulated a structure with an epitaxial resistivity of approximately $0.5 \Omega \cdot cm$ and an epitaxial layer thickness between the base and the n^+ buried layer of approximately 4.0μ, while these quantities were $0.5 \Omega \cdot cm$ and 1.0μ, respectively, for the Mattheus *et al.* structure. Furthermore, the magnitude of the series resistance in the I^2L base region can strongly influence the relative importance of the two possible explanations (i.e., lateral or vertical distributed nature) for the observed near 10-dB per decade input impedance. Lohstroh did not consider the effects of lateral base resistance. Nonetheless, for the Mattheus *et al.* structure, the vertically distributed holes cannot account for the observed behavior.

In this paper, Mattheus *et al.* correctly point out that the small-signal beta is the product of the input impedance and the transconductance for a bipolar transistor. This decomposition of small-signal beta recognizes that the input current to the I^2L gate can advantageously be viewed as driving the emitter-base diode to generate a voltage (V_{be}) which in turn controls a current source (I_c). This separation of I_b and I_c by way of V_{be} (which is explicitly contained in the early work of Ebers and Moll) represents a valuable aid in the visualization of bipolar device operation and especially I^2L. Unfortunately, such a decomposition is frequently overlooked and attention is focussed upon beta directly.

Mattheus *et al.* provide an analytic solution for their distributed RC model of the I^2L gate and the asymptotic solutions provide excellent qualitative confirmation of the validity of the model and the correctness of the solution. They show that classical techniques cannot be used directly to find the transit time of an I^2L gate device from a $(1/2\pi f_T)$ versus $(1/I_c)$ plot. Alternatively, they present a technique to extract the transit time by using their distributed analysis. It should be pointed out that the authors are correct in the strict sense that the classical technique does not apply directly to the I^2L gate structure. However, well-designed single devices can be used to accurately extract the upward transit time from f_T measurements. Subsequently, such measurements can be combined with measurements of series resistance and junction capacitances in order to establish a complete model. The result should not differ greatly from that obtained by the distributed analysis technique presented by these authors. The distinction is that the technique of Mattheus *et al.* applies to the I^2L gate directly, whereas the classical technique requires special test devices. The distributed model yields simulation results which are in good agreement with experimental ring oscillator measurements. An important contribution of this paper is contained in Fig. 15 and the description pertaining thereto. The authors used their model to investigate the effects of the location of the base contact upon the propagation delay. They found substantially higher propagation delays when the base contact is located near the injector in contrast to lower propagation delays when the contact is located at the far end of the base (away from the injector). The authors explain the "slow" operation as being due to the need to remove excess charge stored under the gate contact and that the device which is to remove this charge has diminished current drive capability.

I prefer the viewpoint that the solid curve of Fig. 15 (curve R11) should be considered to be the reference, and it is the faster operation (lower delays of curves R21 and R22) which needs interpretation. The propagation delay deduced from an experimental (or simulated) ring oscillator experiment is the average of the turn-on and the turn-off delays. Consequently, ring oscillator frequency observations do not permit the separation of these two contributions to the total propagation delay. However, simulations can yield the two delays directly. In order to understand the curves of Fig. 15 it must be noted that the effects of the series base resistance upon turn-on delay depend upon the location of the collector relative to the injector, and the location of the base contact is relatively unimportant. In contrast, the effects of the series base resistance upon turn-off delay depend upon the location of the collector relative to the base contact, and the proximity of the injector is somewhat unimportant. Thus the fast operation observed in curves R21 and R22 of Fig. 15 is best explained by the short turn-off delay which results due to the base contact being adjacent to the collector (i.e., series resistance effects are minimized during turn-off). Additionally, since the base contact has been displaced from its usual position between the collector and the injector, the collector is nearer the injector, and a relatively short turn-on delay is also achieved (in comparison with the alternative situation represented in curves R11 and R12).

From this discussion it can be concluded that the lowest turn-on delay will result when the collector is nearest the injector. Analogously, the lowest turn-off delay will result when the collector is nearest the base contact. Consequently, the overall fastest gate operation (i.e., the minimum spread in the speeds of the various collectors) will occur when the base contact is located at the far end of the gate (away from the injector) since this configuration improves both turn-on and turn-off delays. The above discussion together with Fig. 15 deserves careful study since the effects of gate layout upon the turn-on and turn-off delays and the underlying mechanisms have gone largely unrecognized since the introduction of I^2L and still are not widely understood.

Paper IV-12 by Kerns presents circuit model simulations of the turn-on and turn-off delays for an I^2L gate for various locations of the base contact. Kern's results confirm that the turn-on delay is dominated by the position of the collector relative to the injector while turn-off delay is dominated by the position of the collector relative to the base contact. Kern's results deserve careful study.

The overall insight to be gained from papers IV-9-12 is that the base resistance of an I^2L gate must be taken into consideration when developing an I^2L process/structure, or when a logic circuit is to be designed in an existing I^2L process. If the effects of the series resistance represent an obstacle to achieving the desired goals, and most straightforward solution is to decrease the extrinsic base resistance by way of an addi-

tional p^+ diffusion. Typical analog bipolar processes exhibit extrinsic base sheet resistivities in the range from 150 Ω/square to 300 Ω/square, while a process optimized for I^2L may exhibit a value less than 50 Ω/square. The ultimate reduction in series base resistance effects would be realized by the incorporation of multiple base contacts. The layout would place one base contact near the injector and each collector adjacent to an additional base contact. All base contacts would then be metalized together. The effects of series base resistance would then be minimized for both the turn-on and turn-off delays. Such an approach (which obviously requires a dual-level metalization scheme) is presented in paper V-5.

Although the vertical injector configuration of I^2L known as substrate-fed logic (SFL) has not received wide attention, it is worthwhile to include an account of the physics and models for the structure in the present text. Paper IV-13 by Blatt and Sumerling provides a treatment of the dc operation of this somewhat unfamiliar structure. Although (in this later publication) the authors have renamed their structure "Schottky I^2L." I will use the term "substrate fed logic" or SFL in order to avoid confusion with the Schottky I^2L as introduced by Bell Laboratories in paper III-4. The authors point out the all-important feature of their vertical injector structure, that is, as fan-out is increased by the addition of collectors, there is an attendant (and unavoidable) increase in injector current delivered to the gate's base region. It is incorrectly stated that conventional or lateral-injector I^2L does not possess this feature. Conventional I^2L is usually laid out with the collectors in a row perpendicular to the lateral pnp injector, and in this configuration the current delivered by the injector is constant and independent of gate fanout. However, the I^2L gate can be readily laid out with the collectors in a row parallel to the injector in which case conventional I^2L shares (with SFL) the feature of an automatic increase in injector current with an increase in fan-out. In contrast to SFL, I^2L enjoys the ability to selectively take advantage of this auto-biasing feature. The SFL structure incorporates Schottky diodes on the p-type base as isolated inputs to the gate. This feature permits increased functional density. However, the Schottky contact can act as either a collector of minority carriers (reverse biased) or as a recombination surface for minority carriers (forward biased). In this regard, the Schottky contact (when saturated or forward biased) has the same effect upon cell performance as would an ohmic contact in the same location. The authors find that, for their typical device parameters, their gate can safely drive five unit sections of similar SFL cells. Thus in the simplest sense SFL offers the potential for a factor of five improvement in functional density over I^2L. However, typical logic implementations will not be able to fully exploit this potential advantage. The authors conclude that the current collected at the Schottky contacts must be small to avoid a limitation upon the current drive capability of the cell. A heavily doped region is introduced beneath the Schottky collector to reduce the current collected (and therefore possibly recombined) by the Schottky contact. The effect of the introduction of the heavy implant beneath the Schottky collector can most readily be viewed as effecting an increase in the integrated base doping of an (undesired) npm parasitic transistor. Consequently, the minority carrier collection (and thereby minority carrier recombination) at the Schottky collector is reduced.

The two final papers in Part IV address the application of computer aids to LSI design with I²L. Paper IV-14 by Wittenzellner deals with a broad range of CAD techniques, from calculation of basic gate electrical properties to the generation of the actual circuit layout. A serious shortcoming of his approach is the use of a logic simulator which cannot accurately include the effects of gate propagation delays. This is especially true for I²L operated at higher current levels where the delays associated with different collectors of a high fan-out gate are substantially different.

Boyle's paper IV-15 addresses the need for a simple, logic-timing simulator for I²L. A simulation program for injection logic (SIMPIL) is described which can accurately and efficiently (in terms of computer memory and execution time) simulate the time-dependent internal node variables of an I²L LSI circuit design. Such logic-timing simulators have been available for MOS logic circuits for quite some time (see Boyle's references [1] and [2]). The techniques used in the MOS timing simulators were not applicable to I²L because of the differing delays associated with the different collector positions of an I²L gate. The problem is compounded by the dependence of the collectors' delays upon injector current level.

Boyle presents a unique solution to the variable (current dependent–position dependent) delay problem. He has introduced a "stiffness" factor which was derived from an analytic solution of the *RC* transmission-line-like nature of the I²L gate. This stiffness factor takes into account the current dependence of each collector's delay and permits accurate timing of node waveforms without expensive circuit simulation techniques as are employed in circuit programs such as SPICE. A second innovative and important feature of Boyle's work is the use of charge (rather than voltage) as an independent variable in the simulation. This technique avoids problems

associated with the exponential relationship between voltage and current in bipolar devices. The internal charge variables are mapped into voltages only for the purpose of presentation to the user of the program.

It should be noted that Boyle's equation (2) is in error and should read

$$V_{cdc} = \frac{V_b/G_{eq}}{R + 1/G_{eq}}.$$

The results obtained with SIMPIL compare favorably with those from a SPICE simulation, while the computation time required is over 100 times less. The availability of fast, inexpensive LSI simulation programs such as SIMPIL is crucial to the wide application of I²L in digital LSI or VLSI. However, even those applications which implement I²L on a much smaller scale, e.g., analog compatible I²L, can greatly benefit from the capabilities of programs like SIMPIL. Boyle's paper is a condensation of a part of a much broader effort in bibliography paper [IV-43] in the modeling and simulation of I²L. Anyone who is actively involved in I²L development, design, modeling, or simulation would benefit from a thorough reading of Boyle's complete work. Detailed modeling and simulation techniques and results are presented so as to offer excellent insight into the operation of conventional I²L.

The fifteen papers contained in this part cover almost all aspects of I²L device physics, models, and LSI simulation. The bibliography for part IV contains many additional publications for those workers interested in an exhaustive search of the literature. However, the papers reprinted here provide the insight necessary to approach any I²L-like structure from the viewpoint of providing an explanation of the relevant mechanisms which dictate device and gate performance and their relationships to the structure-process related model parameters. A thorough understanding of the material in these fifteen papers will permit an easy grasp of all other material contained in this text.

Device Physics of Integrated Injection Logic

FRANÇOIS M. KLAASSEN

Abstract—After a brief review of relevant device parameters, characterizing the inversely operating multicollector n-p-n transistor and the lateral p-n-p transistor which make up an I^2L basic cell, some electronic circuit properties of this gate are discussed quantitively. Analytic expressions are derived for the transfer characteristics, the noise margin and the propagation delay time per gate in relation to the cell geometry, fan-out, doping profiles, and recombination properties. These expressions are compared with experimental and numerical circuit simulation results.

LIST OF SYMBOLS

β_n	Current gain of n-p-n transistor.
β_p	Current gain of p-n-p transistor.
β_{eff}	Effective current gain of I^2L cell.
C_{eb}	Emitter depletion capacitance.
C_{cb}	Collector depletion capacitance.
f_T	Frequency with unity current gain.
F	Number of collectors of n-p-n transistor.
i_B	Base current.
i_c	Collector current.
I_n	Collector current of n-p-n transistor in I^2L cell.
I_p	Normal injector current.
i_p	Inverse injector current.
n	Electron density.
N_{epi}	Doping density of epilayer.
$\int N_B{}' dx$	Integral base dope under collector area.
$\int N_B dx$	Integral base dope besides collector area.
p	Hole density.
Q_{epi}	Hole charge density in epilayer.
R_b	Base resistance.
s_p	Hole recombination velocity at n-n$^+$ boundary.
S_B	Base area of n-p-n transistor.
S_C	Collector area of n-p-n transistor.
$S_{e,\text{inj}}$	Emitter area of p-n-p transistor.
$S_{C,\text{inj}}$	Effective collector area of p-n-p transistor.
τ_{del}	Propagation delay time per gate.
τ_{eff}	Effective hole lifetime in epilayer.
V_{bias}	Bias voltage of I^2L injector.
V_{in}	Base input voltage.
V_{o}	Collector output voltage.
V_{tr}	Transition voltage between the binary states of the I^2L cell.
ΔV	Noise margin.
W_B	Base width of p-n-p injector.

Manuscript received March 12, 1974; revised November 5, 1974.
The author is with the Philips Research Laboratories, Eindhoven, The Netherlands.

Reprinted from *IEEE Trans. Electron Devices*, vol. ED-22, pp. 145–152, Mar. 1975.

W_{epi} Thickness of epilayer under base area.
W_{inj} Length of p-n-p injector.
x_j Diffusion depth of base.

INTRODUCTION

INTEGRATED injection logic, which has been recently introduced [1], [2], is a bipolar logic comparable with dynamic MOST logic in density and power dissipation. The basic cell (Fig. 1) is made up of a multiemitter n-p-n transistor and a lateral p-n-p transistor, whose base and collector are common to the collector and the base of the first transistor, respectively. In order to avoid unwanted lateral hole diffusion in the n-epitaxial layer, the cell has been surrounded by an n+-diffusion collar. For logic operation, the p-n-p transistor is used both as an injector of base current for the n-p-n transistor in the same cell and as a current source load for a n-p-n transistor in an adjacent cell (Fig. 2). Moreover, the n-p-n transistors are operating in the inverse mode by using the n+-substrate as a common emitter.

Referring to Fig. 2, it is readily shown that the basic cell operates as a simple inverter. When V_{in} is high, all current from the p-n-p transistor is used up by the n-p-n transistor T_1, operating in the saturated mode, and no current is left for the base of the n-p-n transistor T_2. Hence V_{01} is low and V_{02} is high. When V_{in} is low, the opposite situation applies.

Due to the construction of Fig. 1, I^2L is characterized by the following features. a) The density is high (approximately 250 gates/mm² for a 7-μm process) because of the simple layout and the reduction of metal interconnections on the slice [1], [2]. b) The dissipation is low, since a forward diode drop is the highest potential in the circuit. Moreover, the dissipation can be easily varied over several orders of magnitude.

In this paper, I^2L electronic circuit properties such as the noise margin, maximum fan-out, and propagation delay time per gate will be discussed quantitively in relation to well-known device parameters such as the current gain (β) and the transition frequency (f_T). Since these parameters strongly deviate from the usual values in normal transistors, their relation to the cell geometry, the doping profile, and the recombination properties are discussed in a separate chapter. In order to keep the discussion clear and to gain insight, high-injection effects and low-current recombination effects have been omitted.

RELEVANT DEVICE PARAMETERS

A. The Current Gain of the n-p-n Transistor

An essential property of integrated injection logic is the operation of the n-p-n transistors in the inverse mode. It is well known that the current gain for most i.c. transistors in that mode is very low. This is mainly caused by hole injection in the n-type epitaxial layer, which results in a low emitter efficiency. In order to increase β_n for I^2L, some special measures have to be taken and will be discussed later on. One of these measures, for instance, is

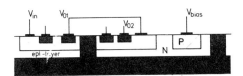

Fig. 1.   Cross section of I^2L gate, in which the white n-region is the remaining epilayer.

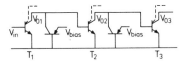

Fig. 2.   Electrical equivalent circuit of I^2L gate.

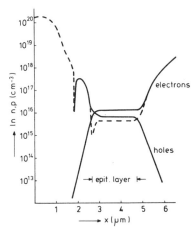

Fig. 3.   Electron and hole distribution of n-p-n transistor operating in the inverse mode ($V_{cb} = 700$ mV, $V_{eb} = 600$ mV). The dashed line is the doping profile.

the enclosure of the basic cell by an n+-diffusion collar (Fig. 1). The injection of holes in the epitaxial layer is illustrated by Fig. 3, in which a distribution of electrons and holes perpendicular to the surface have been given for an n-p-n transistor operating in the inverse mode[1]. Typical of the inverse mode is that $dp/dx \approx 0$ in the epitaxial layer between base and substrate. From an analytical solution of the transport equations, we have confirmed that this property applies exclusively to the inverse mode for a wide variety of current densities.

When we consider the n-p-n transistor shown in Fig. 1, two factors contributing to the base current in the inverse mode have to be taken into account: a) recombination of holes in the epitaxial layer and the substrate; b) recombination of electrons in the base layer outside the collecting emitter areas (parasitic p-n-n+ junction). However, from an independent study of the transient and small-signal behavior of p-n-n+ structures incorporated in the I^2L slices we concluded that the recombination of holes in the substrate is much more important than volume recombination in the epitaxial layer [3], [5]. The hole recombination can be characterized by an interface recombination velocity $s_p \approx 10$–20 m/s.

Calling henceforth the emitter areas of Fig. 1 the col-

---

[1] Numerical results from a transistor-simulation program by J. W. Slotboom [7].

lectors and the substrate the emitter, we divide a multi-collector n-p-n structure with F collectors (F = fan-out) in ($F + 1$) equal sections with an elementary base area S_B (compare also Fig. 4). In this case, the base current in the medium collector current range (100–1000 A/cm²) is given by

$$i_B \approx q S_B n_i^2 \left[\frac{D_n \{1 + F(1 - S_C/S_B)\}}{\int N_B \, dx} + \frac{(F+1)s_p}{N_{epi}} \right]$$

$$\cdot \exp qV/kT \quad (1)$$

in which $\int N_B \, dx$ is the integral base dope per unit area outside the collectors, N_{epi} is the dope of the epitaxial layer, and S_C is the area of one collector. The first term in (1) represents the electron recombination in the base outside the collector areas and the second term the hole recombination in the interface between epitaxial layer and substrate. For the derivation of the first term, an infinite surface recombination velocity has been assumed.

Although (1) suggests that N_{epi} should be increased for optimum inverse current gain, it should be realized that this will reduce the injection current from the p-n-p transistor, which may be disadvantageous as will be shown later on. Moreover in many applications, where I^2L is combined with other electronic circuits [1], a high value of N_{epi} would cause an unwanted collector breakdown. In practice, $N_{epi} \approx 5 \times 10^{15}/$cm³ has been taken as a good compromise. In this case, the electron current component in (1) may be neglected for $F > 3$ and for not-too-shallow base diffusions.

Because of the symmetry of the Ebers–Moll equations, the normal equation for the collector current applies in the inverse mode. However high-injection effects have to be taken into account, when at high bias voltages, the number of holes injected into the epitaxial layer no longer can be neglected compared to that in the base [4]. For the test circuits studied this situation occurred at bias voltages in excess of 750 mV and current densities of 1000 A/cm². In practice, this effect may be left out in the discussion. Combining (1) with the well-known equation for the collector current

$$i_c = q S_C n_i^2 D_n \exp (qV/kT) [\int N_B' \, dx]^{-1}$$

the value of the inverse current gain per collector is given by

$$\beta_n \approx \left(\frac{S_C}{S_B} \right)$$

$$\cdot \frac{[\int N_B' \, dx]^{-1}}{[1 + F(1 - S_C/S_B)][\int N_B \, dx]^{-1} + (F+1)s_p/D_n N_{epi}}$$

$$(2)$$

in which S_C is the effective area of one collector (compare Fig. 4) and $\int N_B' \, dx$ is the integral base dope under the emitter. From a two-dimensional analysis program [7], we have observed that S_C may be computed by adding a value of approximately $3\times$ the basewidth to the geo-

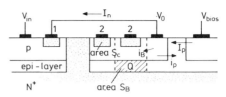

Fig. 4. Current gain and transition frequency of a n-p-n transistor in I^2L as a function of the number of collectors (F) for the intermediate current range.

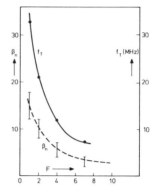

Fig. 5. Elaborate version of Fig. 1, in which the n-p-n transistor is split in ($F + 1$) sections with a hole store Q.

metrical collector dimensions. Taking $\int N_B' \, dx = 3 \times 10^{12}$ cm⁻², $\int N_B \, dx = 3 \times 10^{14}$ cm⁻² for a standard process, we obtain for $S_C/S_B = 0.7$, $F = 1$, $N_{epi} = 5 \times 10^{15}$ cm⁻³, $D_n \approx 10$ cm² s⁻¹, and $s_p = 10$–20 m/s, thus

$$10 < \beta_n < 20.$$

These values have also been found experimentally as illustrated in Fig. 5. The interrupted line corresponds to (2).

B. The Frequency Limit of The Current Gain

Compared with the normal current mode the maximum transition frequency f_T of the inverse mode is also much smaller. This is caused by the retarding field in the base and the injected hole charge in the epitaxial layer. Writing formally $i_c = Q_{epi}/\tau_t$, in which

$$Q_{epi} \approx \frac{q n_i^2}{N_{epi}} (F+1) S_B W_{epi} \exp qV/kT$$

is the total hole charge in the epitaxial layer and $\tau_t = (2\pi f_T)^{-1}$, the transition frequency f_T is given by

$$f_T \approx \left(\frac{S_C}{S_B} \right) \frac{D_n N_{epi}}{2\pi (F+1) W_{epi} \int N_B' \, dx} \quad (3)$$

where W_{epi} is the width of the epitaxial layer between base and substrate. Taking the same value for the parameters as for the computation of β_n, we obtain for $W_{epi} = 1 \; \mu$m and $F = 1$:

$$f_T \approx 25 \; \text{MHz}.$$

Of course, this value will only apply in the intermediate current range (100–1000 A/cm²). For our samples, transition frequencies between 20 and 50 MHz have been found experimentally (see also Fig. 5). Later on it will be shown that this low value of f_T limits the switching speed of the gates considerably.

C. The Current Gain of the Injector

In the same way as for the n-p-n transistor, the hole injection in the epitaxial layer under the p-injector causes a low value of the current gain and the transition frequency of the p-n-p transistor. The effect upon f_T is not so important, since the hole charge under the injector remains constant during switching; however, the dc recombination of this hole charge contributes to the efficiency of the I^2L system. Using (1) in which S_B has been replaced by the lateral area $S_{e,\text{inj}}$ of the injector for the base current of the p-n-p transistor, the current gain is given by

$$\beta_p \approx \left(\frac{S_{C,\text{inj}}}{S_{e,\text{inj}}}\right) \frac{D_p[N_{\text{epi}}W_B]^{-1}}{D_n[\int N_B \, dx]^{-1} + s_p N_{\text{epi}}^{-1}} \quad (4)$$

in which $S_{C,\text{inj}}$ is the effective collector cross section of the lateral p-n-p transistor [6] and W_B is the basewidth of the p-n-p transistor. Generally $(S_C/S_e)_{\text{inj}} \approx x_j/W_{\text{inj}}$, in which x_j is the diffusion depth of the p-layer and W_{inj} is the injector width, has a low value. For $W_B = 4 \ \mu\text{m}$ and $(S_C/S_e)_{\text{inj}} = 0.10$, the value of the current gain in the medium current range is

$$1.5 < \beta_p < 3.$$

These values have been confirmed experimentally. Due to the relatively low dope of the epitaxial layer, the p-n-p

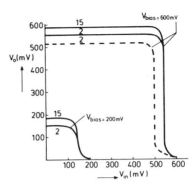

Fig. 6. Transfer characteristics of I^2L gate for $V_{\text{bias}} = 200$ and 600 mV; $I_{po}/I_{no} = 0.10$ (fully drawn curves) and 0.02 (interrupted curve) with $\beta_n(F)$ as a parameter.

the p-n-p transistor is being charged, a hole current $i_p(V_o)$ flows back to the injector where

$$i_p = I_{po} \exp qV_o/kT. \quad (8)$$

Moreover, a base current

$$i_B(V_o) = \frac{I_{no} \exp qV_o/kT}{\beta_n(F)} \quad (9)$$

is necessary to provide the recombination losses. In the last equation, the excess base current for an inverse-saturated n-p-n transistor has been neglected because of the high collector dope. By substituting (6)–(9) in (5), a relation between input and output voltage is obtained

$$\exp qV_{\text{in}}/kT = \frac{(I_{po}/I_{no})[\exp qV_{\text{bias}}/kT - \exp qV_o/kT] - \beta_n^{-1} \exp qV_o/kT}{1 - \exp - qV_o/kT} \quad (10)$$

transistor current gain already decreases at rather low values of injection currents (100 A/cm²). Generally, a high value of the current gain is not necessary; for $\beta_p > 3$ the p-n-p transistor hardly contributes to the dissipation of the system.

TRANSFER CHARACTERISTICS AND NOISE MARGIN

Considering Fig. 4, which is a more elaborate version of a multicollector cell as introduced in Fig. 1, the following fundamental current equation applies at the base node with voltage V_o

$$I_p - i_p(V_o) - I_{n1}(V_o,V_{\text{in}}) = i_B(V_o). \quad (5)$$

In this equation, I_p is the injector current, which can be written formally as

$$I_p = I_{po} \exp qV_{\text{bias}}/kT \quad (6)$$

in which I_{po} is a well-known current constant, provided that the current density is not too high. I_{n1} is the collector current from an n-p-n transistor in an adjacent cell, which is given by

$$I_{n1} = I_{no}[\exp qV_{\text{in}}/kT - \exp q(V_{\text{in}} - V_o)/kT]. \quad (7)$$

When the base of the n-p-n transistor in the same cell as

In Fig. 6, the transfer characteristics arising from (10) have been given for the following data: $V_{\text{bias}} = 200$ mV, 600 mV; $I_{po}/I_{no} = 0.10$, 0.02, with $\beta_n(F)$ as a parameter. What is striking in this plot is the small voltage range needed for the transition from one stable binary level to the other. This is due to the fact that the transition region with high gain represents the balance of the two competing exponential current sources I_{no} and I_{po}. Moreover, on inspecting the 200-mV characteristics, it must be concluded that I^2L is still operating in principle as a useful logic element at extreme low current levels. However, in practice, at LSI, 500 mV has appeared to be a lower limit because of possible current gain degeneracy at low currents (<100 nA).

Besides the numerical results of Fig. 6 some specific values of the characteristics can be estimated from (10):

a) when V_{in} is low, V_o may be approximated by

$$V_o(V_{\text{in}} \text{ low}) \approx V_{\text{bias}} - (kT/q) \ln [1 + I_{no}/\beta_n I_{po}]; \quad (11)$$

b) when V_{in} has a value given by (11), the output voltage is low and is approximately given by

$$V_o(V_{\text{in}} \text{ high}) \approx (kT/q)[I_{po}/I_{no} + \beta_n^{-1}]; \text{ and} \quad (12)$$

c) the two binary states characterized by (11) and

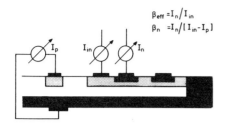

Fig. 7. Definition of several current gains in multicollector n-p-n transistors.

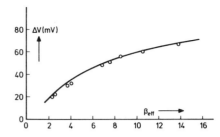

Fig. 8. The noise voltage margin as a function of the effective current gain.

(12) and within which the small signal voltage gain $\ll 1$, are separated by a small transition region with a typical width of kT/q and a high gain.

The center voltage of this high gain transition is given by

$$V_{\text{tr}} \simeq V_{\text{bias}} - (kT/q) \ln (I_{no}/I_{po}). \quad (13)$$

From the last expression we conclude that

$$I_{no}/I_{po} > 1$$

is a necessary condition for binary operation.

However, this is not a sufficient condition. The system as a whole no longer operates when the $V_o -$ value as given by (11) is insufficient to turn on next sections. From the condition $V_o > V_{\text{tr}}$ and (11) and (13), we then obtain as a fundamental requirement for the current gain $\beta_n(F)$ of the multicollector cell

$$\beta_n(F) > [1 - (I_{po}/I_{no})]^{-1}. \quad (14)$$

In combination with (2), this relation restricts the fan-out F of the system. However, using the standard process results of Fig. 5, we observe that even for an extreme value $I_{po}/I_{no} = \frac{1}{2}$, the fan-out is limited to $F < 7$. In fact, F is much more limited by the delay time, as we will show in the next section.

Comparing the estimation for the binary levels and the transition voltage, a noise margin ΔV may be defined as given by the difference between (11) and (13)

$$\Delta V \approx (kT/q) \ln [I_{po}/I_{no} + \beta_n^{-1}(F)]^{-1}. \quad (15)$$

In this formula, the factor between brackets is significant, since this factor may be interpreted as an effective current gain (β_{eff}) of the cell

$$\beta_{\text{eff}} \approx \frac{I_{no}}{I_{no}/\beta_n(F) + I_{po}}. \quad (16)$$

In practice, this current gain can be measured by short circuiting the injector with respect to the substrate (compare Fig. 7). In this way, (15) may be written in a form already given in [1],

$$\Delta V \approx (kT/q) \ln \beta_{\text{eff}}. \quad (15a)$$

The ratio I_{po}/I_{no} is mainly determined by the geometry of the cell and the base doping profiles, whereas β_n is also a function of the fan-out (F) and the recombination properties. In Fig. 8, (15a) has been compared with experimental results. When F has a low value, ΔV may be mainly determined by the ratio I_{no}/I_{po}. For $F = 1$ and

$$I_{no}/I_{po} = 20,$$

$$\Delta V \approx 60 \text{ mV}.$$

Although this value is a relatively small voltage margin, it corresponds to a large current range within the chip. Obviously the noise margin improves slightly with the increase in temperature.

DYNAMIC PROPERTIES

For an analysis of the transient behavior of inverter stages as given in Fig. 2, all charge stores in the circuit have to be considered. For low values of the current provided by the current sources only the charge in the depletion layers of the n-p-n transistor is important. Since the collector voltage practically varies between 0 and V_{bias}, the depletion layer charge on both sides of the p-type base should be considered. The main contribution to the emitter-base capacitance C_{eb} comes from the p-n$^+$ sidewall boundary. For low currents, the charge stored in C_{eb} and C_{cb} is only a very weak function of the current and consequently the delay times will vary inversely with the current level. On the other hand, when V_{bias} is increased, the current provided by the p-n-p transistors may reach a value for which the active hole charge stored in the epitaxial layer is much larger than the charge stored in the depletion layers. In this case, the charge, which has to be stored or removed by the currents, is proportional to the current level and consequently the delay time will be current-independent. The circuit operates at maximum speed. First we will compute the minimum delay time per gate, which can be obtained with I^2L.

A. The Minimum Delay Time

Generally, the delay time per inverter may be computed by considering a number of inverter stages in cascade (compare Fig. 2). Starting from a situation with the n-p-n transistor T_1 and T_3 conducting, T_2 nonconducting at $t = 0$, transistor T_1 is suddenly discharged. After some time t', transistor T_3 will also become nonconducting. Usually the delay time per gate is defined as $\tau_{\text{del}} = \frac{1}{2}t'$.

In order to calculate t', we start with the basic charge control equations for an I^2L cell, which can be considered as a generalization of (5). Referring to Fig. 4, the charge control equation for a multicollector cell reads as

$$I_p - i_p(V_o) - I_n = (F + 1)\{Q/\tau_{\text{eff}} + dQ/dt\}. \quad (17)$$

In this equation, Q is the hole charge, being stored in one of the $(F + 1)$ sections of the multicollector n-p-n tran-

116

sistor. The recombination current as introduced in (1) has been expressed in a term $(F + 1) \cdot Q\tau_{\text{eff}}^{-1}$ for convenience. Possible electron recombination current in the parasitic p-n-p⁺ junction may also be expressed in terms of Q, since the electron injection is proportional to the hole injection for the medium current range. The effective lifetime τ_{eff} may be calculated from (1) and the formula for Q_{epi} introduced above (3). For our samples, τ_{eff} has a value between 100–200 ns.

Since the current $i_p(V_o)$ is proportional to the hole charge Q, we formally write

$$i_p + \frac{(F + 1)Q}{\tau_{\text{eff}}} = \frac{(F + 1)Q}{\tau_{\text{eff}}'}.$$

The effective lifetime τ_{eff}' introduced in this way may be calculated, by using the dc-relation $(F + 1)Q/\tau_{\text{eff}} = \beta_n^{-1}I_n$. The result is given by

$$\tau_{\text{eff}}' \approx \tau_{\text{eff}}[1 + \beta_n(F) I_{po}/I_{no}]^{-1}. \quad (18)$$

For $F = 4$, $I_{po}/I_{no} = 0.10$, $\tau_{\text{eff}}' \approx 50–100$ ns. Introducing τ_{eff}' in (17), this relation may be simplified into

$$I_p = I_n + (F + 1)\{Q/\tau_{\text{eff}}' + dQ/dt\} \quad (19)$$

in which equation I_p is a constant current delivered by the injector. We use (19) for the computation of the delay time t' introduced previously.

When the n-p-n transistor T_1 in a cascade of inverters is suddenly discharged at $t = 0$, the n-p-n transistor T_2 will be charged according to (19) with the (extra) condition $I_n = 0$. Making use of the charge control relation $I_n = 2\pi f_T Q(F + 1)$ (compare (3)), the unsaturated collector current $I_n(T_2)$ is given by the solution of (19):

$$I_n(T_2) = 2\pi f_T I_p \tau'_{\text{eff}}[1 - \exp - t/\tau_{\text{eff}}']. \quad (20)$$

In this way we tacitly assume that the collector-base depletion capacitance does not retard the increase of the collector current. In contrast to normal bipolar logic, we have reason to neglect this effect upon I^2L for two reasons. In I^2L no resistive collector load is present to introduce a time constant in the system in combination with the collector depletion capacitance. Also, the logic swing is so small that transport of the total depletion layer charge would demand very little base current. Moreover, no Miller effect at all has been observed in detail results of the transient in I^2L circuits which have been obtained in a circuit simulation program.

The collector current $I_n(T_2)$ will immediately discharge transistor T_3, which process is also described by (19). Substituting (20) in (19) the time t', at which the n-p-n transistor T_3 is completely discharged may be obtained from the solution of (19) and is given by the transcendental equation

$$t' = \tau_{\text{eff}}' \ln \frac{t' + \tau_{\text{eff}}'}{\tau_{\text{eff}}' - (2\pi f_T)^{-1}}. \quad (21)$$

Since both f_T and τ_{eff}' are functions of the fan-out F, the

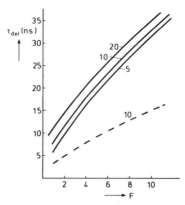

Fig. 9. The minimum propagation delay time per gate as a function of the fan-out F with the ratio (I_{no}/I_{po}) as a parameter. The dashed line is the result according to (22a).

propagation delay time $\tau_{\text{del}} = \frac{1}{2}t'$ will depend on F. In Fig. 9 τ_{del} has been plotted as a function of F with the ratio I_{po}/I_{no} as a parameter and $\beta_n(F = 1) = 15$, $f_T(F = 1) = 40$ MHz and $\tau_{\text{eff}} = 100$ ns. Roughly the delay time varies proportionally to the fan-out, which indicates that F is seriously limited by the delay time allowed.

When $t' < 4\tau_{\text{eff}}'$, (20) may be simplified and τ_{del} is given directly by the relation

$$\tau_{\text{del}} \approx [4\pi f_T(F)]^{-1}\{\beta_n^{-1}(F) + I_{po}/I_{no}\}^{-1/2} \quad (22a)$$

or

$$\tau_{\text{del}} \approx \beta_{\text{eff}}^{1/2}/4\pi f_T. \quad (22b)$$

Equation (22a) has been plotted in Fig. 9 as an interrupted line. Obviously, in most cases, (22a) is only a poor approximation. Since in most cases, (22a) differs from (21) by a factor 2, a better approximation to (21) will be

$$\tau_{\text{del}} \simeq [\beta_{\text{eff}}(F)]^{1/2}/2\pi f_T(F). \quad (23)$$

Equation (23) is very useful in practice, since the parameters $\beta_{\text{eff}}(F)$ and $f_T(F)$ can be measured from simple test structures on the slice. Excluding a small effect on β_n, τ_{del} *is apparently independent of the hole recombination time* τ_{eff}. *In this respect, I^2L is quite different from other types of saturated logic.* Moreover, this result justifies the approximation of the recombination process by a time constant τ_{eff} for convenience.

In the derivation given earlier, high-injection effects upon the charge-control equation have been omitted. However, in some cases, a cell running at high current will approach this complicated situation. From circuit simulation analysis we have observed that in this case the base resistance in particular effects the delay time of the n-p-n transistors. We will discuss this later on in relation to experimental results.

B. The Delay Time at Low Currents

For low-current operation, where the depletion capacitances dominate the charge-discharge process, the same procedure for the computation of τ_{del} can be repeated. When the n-p-n transistor T_1 is suddenly discharged, the

TABLE I
COMPARISON OF MEASURED AND COMPUTED RESULTS OF THE
MINIMUM DELAY TIME FOR SEVERAL I^2L GATES

f_T(MHz)	I_{no}/I_{po}	β_n	β_{eff}	τ_{del}(calc)(ns)	τ_{del}(meas.)(ns)
33	22	20	10.5	16	15
34	12	18	7.3	14	14
45	5	17	3.9	7	7.5
46	2.7	14	2.2	5.5	6
15	22	8	6	27	30
15	12	7	4.5	22	24
18	5	5	2.5	14	14

current source I_p starts to charge the capacitances C_{cb} of T_1 and $(C_{eb}, + FC_{cb})$ of T_2. When the base voltage of the n-p-n transistor of the last stage reaches a voltage V_o, given by (11), the charging process comes to a stop at t_1, approximately given by

$$t_1 \approx [C_{eb} + (F + 1)C_{cb}]V_o/I_p. \tag{24}$$

Before that time, no electron current will be observed at the collector of T_2 because part of I_p will flow to the collector via the collector-base capacitance. For $t > t_1$, an electron current $I_n \approx \beta_{eff}(I_p + C_{cb} \cdot dV/dt)$ passsing the collector starts to discharge transistor T_3. However, a hole current I_p from the injector of T_3 will cancel part of the electron current. Effectively, only a current

$$I_n' \approx \beta_{eff}\left(I_p + C_{cb}\frac{dV_{o2}}{dt}\right) - I_p$$

is useful for the discharge of T_3. Since, at low currents, this process is limited by the discharge of the capacitance $FC_{cb} + C_{eb}$, T_3 has been discharged after a time t_2, which according to $I_n' = -(FC_{cb} + C_{eb})(dV_{o2}/dt)$ is approximately given by

$$t_2 \approx \{(F + \beta_{eff})C_{cb} + C_{eb}\}V_o/(\beta_{eff} - 1)I_p. \tag{25}$$

Using the approximation $V_o \approx V_{bias}$ and $\beta_{eff} \gg F$, we finally obtain for the propagation delay time $\tau_{del} = (t_1 + t_2)/2$ at low currents

$$\tau_{del} \simeq [C_{eb} + (F + 2)C_{cb}]V_{bias}/2I_p. \tag{26}$$

From this equation, it may be concluded that the delay time is inversely proportional to the current level and proportional to the fan-out F, since the depletion capacitance varies roughly with F.

For the intermediate current range, at which depletion layer charge and storage charge are in the same order of magnitude, no analytical solution for the delay time can be given. However, comparing the approximation given above with experimental results, we may conclude that the sum of (23) and (26) is valid for the whole current range.

EXPERIMENTAL RESULTS AND CONCLUSION

The experimental results have been obtained from the oscillation frequency of ring oscillators with 5 I^2L cells in cascade. Moreover, cells with different geometries and

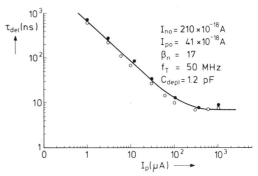

Fig. 10. Propagation delay time per gate versus injection current. Fully drawn curve corresponds to approximation (23) and (26), open circles to experimental values, and closed circles to numerical simulation results, with a base resistance $R_b = 300\ \Omega$ assigned to the n-p-n transistors.

diffusion profiles have been constructed, resulting in a wide variety of the I_{no}/I_{po} ratio and the cutoff frequency f_T. A comparison between theory and experimental results has been given in Table I in relation to the minimum delay time, and in Fig. 10, where measured results, analytic expressions (23) and (26), and numerical results from a circuit analysis program have been plotted for a large current range. For both cases, the agreement is fair. Only at high currents is (23) likely to deviate from the experimental results when the delay time again increases with current. The same phenomenon has also been observed on introducing high injection parameters into the numerical circuit analysis program[2] and it has been found that it is mainly the base resistance which is responsible for this phenomenon. In the program PHILPAC, a base resistance of 300 Ω for the n-p-n transistors has been used. This is a realistic value, which has been obtained from noise measurements. However, the increase of τ_{del} due to R_b can also be argued. Referring to the procedure for the derivation of (23), the electron current of the n-p-n transistor T_2 will deviate from the current-time relation (20), since the injector current I_p has to pass the base resistance R_b. The voltage difference over R_b will cause a much higher back current i_p to flow in the injector, so that less hole current for charging the base of T_2 becomes available. As a result, the collector current increases much slower than according to (20) and consequently the discharging of T_3 takes longer.

Finally, we remark that, in some extreme cases of cell

[2] Private communication by H. E. J. Wulms.

construction, the relatively simple description of I^2L given here is no longer accurate and consequently a numerical circuit analysis program has to be used. Some cases which deserve mention are, for instance, an I^2L cell in which the epitaxial layer underneath the base diffusion has been eliminated, or a cell with very shallow diffusions where the electron injection in the parasitic p-n-n$^+$ diode under the base contact is very important. However, in most practical cases with rather conventional transistor structures, the analytic results given here are useful for understanding and designing I^2L circuits.

ACKNOWLEDGMENT

The author wishes to thank F. J. B. Smolders, J. W. Slotboom, W. de Groot, and H. E. J. Wulms of Philips Research Laboratories and H. Grooten of the Eindhoven Technical University.

REFERENCES

[1] K. Hart and A. Slob, "Integrated injection logic," *IEEE Trans. Solid State Circuits*, vol. SC-7, pp. 346–351, 1972.
[2] H. H. Berger and S. K. Wiedman, "Merged transistor logic," *IEEE J. Solid State Circuits*, vol. SC-7, pp. 340–346, 1972.
[3] F. M. Klaassen, to be published.
[4] H. K. Gummel, "A charge control relation for bipolar transistors," *Bell Syst. Tech. J.*, vol. 49, pp. 115–120, 1970.
[5] R. W. Dutton and R. J. Whittier, "Forward current–voltage characteristics of p$^+$-n-n$^+$ diodes," *IEEE Trans. Electron Devices*, vol. ED-16, pp. 458–467, 1969.
[6] S. Chou, "Investigation of lateral transistors," *Solid State Electron.*, vol. 14, pp. 811–826, 1971.
[7] J. W. Slotboom, "Computer-aided two-dimensional analysis of bipolar transistors," *IEEE Trans. Electron Devices*, vol. ED-20, pp. 669–679, 1973.

Terminal-Oriented Model
for Merged Transistor Logic (MTL)

HORST H. BERGER AND SIEGFRIED K. WIEDMANN

Abstract—A simple device model is derived to represent merged transistor logic (MTL) circuit behavior. Using the Ebers–Moll equations, the proper definitions of the various current gains are derived, and it is shown that MTL devices can be basically interpreted as n-p-n transistors having an additional base current source. The relations between the intensity of this source and the current actually supplied are derived. Time behavior is modeled according to the charge control concept. Using this model, circuit delays are given as a function of current gains, collector and emitter time constants, supply current, and of fan-out.

I. Introduction

IN PREVIOUS papers a new bipolar logic concept called merged transistor logic (MTL) [1] or integrated injection logic (I²L) [2] has been described. Power-delay products below 1 pJ per gate, high functional density of about 100 gates/mm² for 10-μm line widths, and compatibility with usual bipolar processing are the most attractive features of this concept. Furthermore, it is level compatible with other saturated bipolar logic families like transistor-transistor logic (T²L).

The basic unit of MTL is a superintegrated device that consists of an upside-down operated n-p-n transistor having multicollectors which is merged with a p-n-p transistor. Naturally, the behavior of a circuit built of such devices is not as transparent as it used to be with isolated components.

The purpose of this paper is to represent the terminal behavior of the MTL device by a simple model for circuit simulation. This includes the proper definition of device parameters such as current gains. Delay curves that have been computed via this model are given as a function of the device parameters.

The discussion proceeds along the following outline. First, the complete set of Ebers–Moll equations for the MTL device will be discussed. From these the corresponding equivalent circuit will be derived and then be reduced to that of a single transistor having an additional base current source. The relation between the intensity of this source and the current actually supplied is then established.

Based on this model, circuit delays have been computed and are presented in this paper as a function of device parameters. Measurement conditions for the determination of the device parameters are explained in the course of the model derivation.

Because confusion is so easy in MTL with the usual designations of vertical n-p-n transistor current gains (*forward, inverse*), new designations are introduced in this paper that are oriented on the device structure, and not on the prevailing operation mode. Accordingly, the current gain shall be called *downward* (β_d, α_d) when

Manuscript received July 23, 1973; revised March 26, 1974.
The authors are with the IBM Laboratories, Boeblingen, West Germany.

Reprinted from *IEEE J. Solid-State Circuits*, vol. SC-9, pp. 211–217, Oct. 1974.

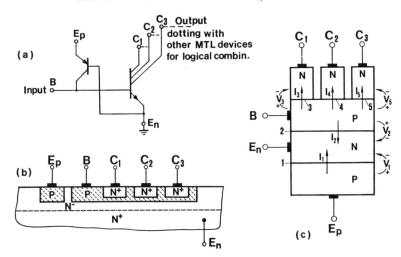

Fig. 1. Basic MTL device, example with three collectors. (a) Circuit representation. (b) Structure in standard buried layer process. (c) Principal representation as a multijunction device with junction current and voltage notations.

the associated minority carrier injection into the base is directed downward from the semiconductor surface. This corresponds to the *forward* current gain in regular monolithic circuits. With the minority carrier injection into the base directed upward towards the semiconductor surface, the associated current gain shall be called *upward* (β_u, α_u). This corresponds to the *regular* operation of the MTL n-p-n transistor.

II. EBERS–MOLL EQUATIONS FOR THE MULTICOLLECTOR MTL DEVICE

In Fig. 1(b) a basic MTL device structure having three collectors in this example is shown for a standard buried layer process. Fig. 1(c) presents a more schematical drawing of the same device. According to Ebers and Moll [3][1], the total junction current I_i crossing junction i may be considered to be a linear superposition of partial currents I_{ik}, being either injected ($i = k$) or collected ($i \neq k$) across the junction.[1] The *injected* current of junction i is[2]

$$I_{ii} = I_{is}\left(\exp\frac{V_i}{kT/q} - 1\right). \qquad (1)$$

The *collected* minority carrier current of junction i is some fraction α_{ik} of the current injected at another junction k that shares a region with the collecting junction

$$I_{ik} = \alpha_{ik} \cdot I_{ks}\left(\exp\frac{V_k}{kT/q} - 1\right) \qquad (i \neq k)$$

$$= \alpha_{ik} \cdot I_{kk}. \qquad (2)$$

For the three-collector device example of Fig. 1 it results in

$$\begin{bmatrix} I_1 \\ I_2 \\ I_3 \\ I_4 \\ I_5 \end{bmatrix} = \begin{bmatrix} 1 & \alpha_{12} & 0 & 0 & 0 \\ \alpha_{21} & 1 & \alpha_{23} & \alpha_{24} & \alpha_{25} \\ 0 & \alpha_{32} & 1 & \alpha_{34} & \alpha_{35} \\ 0 & \alpha_{42} & \alpha_{43} & 1 & \alpha_{45} \\ 0 & \alpha_{52} & \alpha_{53} & \alpha_{54} & 1 \end{bmatrix} \cdot \begin{bmatrix} I_{11} \\ I_{22} \\ I_{33} \\ I_{44} \\ I_{55} \end{bmatrix}. \qquad (3)$$

In the α matrix some positions are filled by zeros because only minority carriers that originate from neighboring junctions can be collected. The interpretations of the remaining α's is as follows.

With the collectors C_1, C_2, C_3 shorted to base, one effectively obtains a p-n-p transistor E^x, B^x, C^{x*}[3] (compare Fig. 2), and has to introduce the condition $V_3 = V_4 = V_5 = 0$ into (3). According to (1) it means $I_{33} = I_{44} = I_{55} = 0$ so that only

$$\begin{pmatrix} I_1 \\ I_2 \end{pmatrix} = \begin{pmatrix} 1 & \alpha_{12} \\ \alpha_{21} & 1 \end{pmatrix}\begin{pmatrix} I_{11} \\ I_{22} \end{pmatrix} \quad (V_3 = V_4 = V_5 = 0) \qquad (4)$$

remains as the essential ingredient.

The forward grounded base current gain of this partial p-n-p transistor is, according to the usual definition,

$$\alpha_n = -\frac{I_2}{I_1} \quad (V_2 = 0 \to I_{22} = 0)$$

$$= -\alpha_{21}. \qquad (5)$$

Similarly,

$$\alpha_i = -\alpha_{12}. \qquad (6)$$

By consistently keeping $V_1 = 0$ and by permutating the

---

[1] The extension of the Ebers–Moll equations to multijunction (more than two junctions) devices has been described by D. K. Lynn [7]. H. C. Lin [8] showed an application to multiple collector or multiple emitter structures.

[2] It can be measured by shorting all other junctions.

[3] The asterisk is used here to indicate the p-n-p transistor in contrast to the partial n-p-n transistor discussed later on.

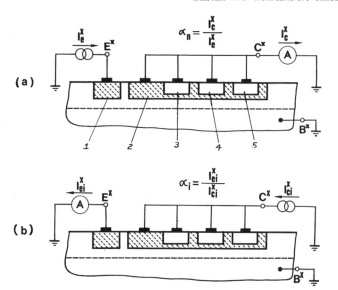

Fig. 2. Circuits for defining and measuring (a) forward current gain α_n, and (b) inverse current gain α_i of the partial p-n-p transistor of the MTL device in Fig. 1.

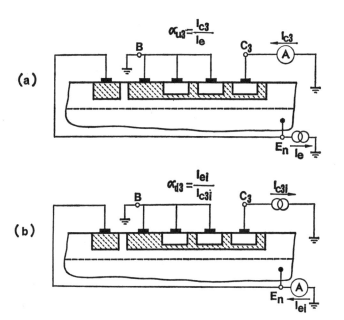

Fig. 3. Circuits for defining and measuring (a) upward current gain α_u, and (b) downward current gain α_d of one of the partial n-p-n transistors of the MTL device in Fig. 1.

remaining junctions on the condition that two of them be shorted (see Fig. 3), the other α's can be related to the grounded base current gains of the partial n-p-n transistors

$$
\begin{bmatrix} I_1 \\ I_2 \\ I_3 \\ I_4 \\ I_5 \end{bmatrix} = \begin{bmatrix} 1 & -\alpha_i & 0 & 0 & 0 \\ -\alpha_n & 1 & -\alpha_{d1} & -\alpha_{d2} & -\alpha_{d3} \\ 0 & -\alpha_{u1} & 1 & 0 & 0 \\ 0 & -\alpha_{u2} & 0 & 1 & 0 \\ 0 & -\alpha_{u3} & 0 & 0 & 1 \end{bmatrix} \cdot \begin{bmatrix} I_{11} \\ I_{22} \\ I_{33} \\ I_{44} \\ I_{55} \end{bmatrix}. \quad (7)
$$

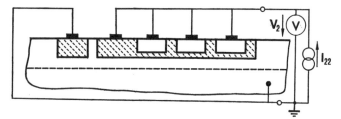

Fig. 4. Measurement circuit for determining the saturation current of junction 2 according to (1). This example illustrates that all junctions but the measured one must be shorted.

The numerical indices of the α's indicate the collector involved (compare Fig. 3). The coupling between the collectors represented by (α_{34}, α_{43}), (α_{35}, α_{53}), and (α_{45}, α_{54}) in (3) has been assumed to be negligible, so that these places have been filled by zeros in (7). This is justified by the following consideration.

For each column of the matrixes (3) or (7) the condition exists that

$$
\sum_{i=1}^{5} |\alpha_{ik}|_{(i \neq k)} \leq 1 \quad (8)
$$

as no more minority carriers can be collected than have been injected. On the other hand, MTL devices require downward current gains α_d very near to unity in order to avoid current hogging problems [1]. This, with condition (8), dictates that the intercollector coupling will be negligible.

Another conclusion from (8) in conjunction with (7) is that the upward current gains α_u and the inverse current gain α_i of the p-n-p transistor are interdependent.

According to Ebers and Moll an additional condition exists relating the saturation currents I_{is}, I_{ks} to the partial current gains

$$
\frac{\alpha_{ik}}{\alpha_{ki}} = \frac{I_{is}}{I_{ks}}. \quad (9)
$$

This condition is helpful for checking device parameters put into a computer simulation.

The saturation currents can be determined via the voltage-current characteristics of the junctions [compare (1)]. To assure that no collection current flows across the junction being measured, all other junctions must be shorted. This condition also follows from (3). As an example, the circuit for measuring $I_{22} = f(V_2)$ is shown in Fig. 4 [compare with Fig. 1(c)].

III. Equivalent Circuit

The equivalent circuit described by Le Can [4] (compare also Ashar *et al.* [5]) is a representation of the Ebers–Moll equations, and takes into account minority carrier storage by introducing capacitances that are related to charge-control parameters [6]. Extended for the MTL device according to (7) it assumes the form shown in Fig. 5. The diffusion capacitances C_d, repre-

122

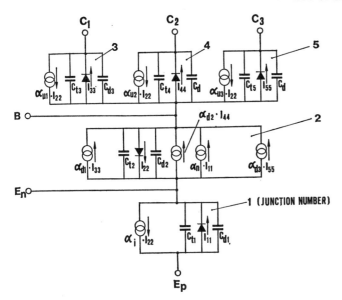

Fig. 5. Equivalent circuit for a three-collector MTL device.

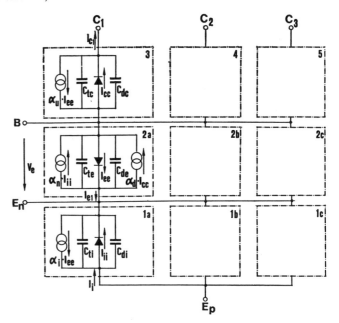

Fig. 6. Splitting of junctions 1 and 2 of Fig. 5 to obtain three single collector MTL devices in parallel.

senting the minority carrier charge storage, vary with injection current I_{ii} according to (10)–(12).

$$C_{di} = \frac{\tau_i}{r_i}. \qquad (10)$$

$$r_i = \frac{kT/q}{I_{ii}}. \qquad (11)$$

$$\tau_i = \frac{Q_i}{I_{ii}} = \text{constant}. \qquad (12)$$

(Q_i = minority carrier charge caused by injection current I_{ii}.)

The depletion layer capacitances C_{ti} vary according to the voltages across the junctions

$$C_{ti} = C_0\left(1 - \frac{V_i}{V_D}\right)^{1/n}. \qquad (13)$$

C_0 capacitance for zero junction voltage,
V_i junction voltage,
V_D contact potential,
$n = 2 \cdots 3$.

The equivalent circuit of Fig. 5 can be assumed to be the result of connecting single collector devices in parallel except with their collectors as shown in Fig. 6. The Ebers–Moll equations for one of the single collector devices then become

$$\begin{bmatrix} I_i \\ I_e \\ I_c \end{bmatrix} = \begin{bmatrix} 1 & -\alpha_i & 0 \\ -\alpha_n & 1 & -\alpha_d \\ 0 & -\alpha_u & 1 \end{bmatrix} \cdot \begin{bmatrix} I_{ii} \\ I_{ee} \\ I_{cc} \end{bmatrix}. \qquad (14)$$

Series resistances have not been included in Fig. 6. They require a more complicated subdivision of the device elements [9].

Assuming equal collector sizes of the multicollector

device,[4] the transition from Fig. 5 to Fig. 6 is made by splitting junctions 1 and 2 into equal parts according to the number of collectors, i.e., in our example into three parts. This means that the diode saturation currents and the junction capacitances have to be divided by three (e.g., $C_{te} = 1/3\ C_{t2}$). The reduced diode saturation currents automatically reduce the diffusion capacitances by the same amount since the time constant τ_i [compare (10), (11)] is invariable. The transition from Fig. 5 to Fig. 6 does not affect the current gains pertaining to the current sources in the split junctions. However, for the collector junctions

$$\alpha_u = 3 \cdot \alpha_{ux} \qquad (\alpha_{ux} = \alpha_{u1} = \alpha_{u2} = \alpha_{u3}) \qquad (15)$$

is valid. This relation can be understood by considering that the sum of injection currents of the split junctions 1 or 2 (Fig. 6) must equal those of the composite junctions (Fig. 5).

The new single device parameters can be measured on the actual (composite) device by connecting all collectors in parallel and thus treating it as a single collector device. For insertion into the circuit of Fig. 6, all thus measured junction capacitances and diode saturation currents must be divided by the number of (equal size) collectors. However, current gains must be inserted as measured[5] with these parallel connected

---

[4] In usual applications collector sizes would be equal. At least they can be reduced to a multiple of a unit size. The same procedures of junction splitting may be used for a single p emitter that pertains to more than one MTL device.

[5] Because of the difference of the upward current gain α_{ux} pertaining to a single collector and measured according to Fig. 3(a), and of the α_u used here and measured with all collectors in parallel, reference should be given to the measurement circuit when citing current gains α or $\beta = \alpha/(1 - \alpha)$.

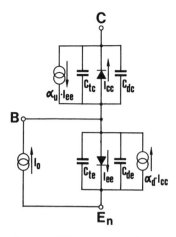

Fig. 7. Single collector MTL device of Fig. 6, simplified for the condition of a quasi-constant voltage source at the p emitter junction 1.

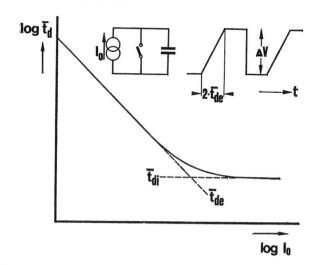

Fig. 8. Principal course of average delay $\bar{t}_d$ versus supply current I_o with a region of constant product $\bar{t}_d \cdot I_o$, a transition region, and a region of constant (intrinsic) delay. *Inset*: approximate equivalent circuit and waveform for the range of constant product $\bar{t}_d \cdot I_o$.

collectors. As with usual transistors, one gains accuracy by measuring the grounded emitter current gain β and then calculating α.

With the regular MTL supply mode all p emitters (injectors) are connected in parallel. This effectively provides a constant voltage source even when a constant dc current is actually supplied.[6] Therefore, the current source $\alpha_n \cdot I_{ii}$ (compare Fig. 6) is constant, and for the circuit operation the actual origin of this current is irrelevant. Thus, each of the three parallel connected devices in Fig. 6 can be represented by the simple equivalent circuit shown in Fig. 7. It comprises only an n-p-n transistor with an additional built-in base current source (compare [1] and [2]).

In order to relate this source current I_o of Fig. 7, which is $I_o = \alpha_n \cdot I_{ii}$ (compare Figs. 6 and 7), to the actual current I_i that is supplied from the E_p terminal (Fig. 6), two extreme cases may be considered (refer to Fig. 6).

Case 1: n-p-n transistor switched OFF ($V_e = 0 \to I_{ee} = 0$).

Case 2: n-p-n transistor switched ON and in deep saturation ($I_c = 0$ and thus because of no external current to terminal B: $I_{e1} = 0$).

Case 1 according to (14) simply yields $I_i = I_{ii}$ and thus

$$\frac{I_i}{I_o} = \frac{I_i}{\alpha_n \cdot I_{ii}} = \frac{1}{\alpha_n}. \tag{16}$$

Case 2 is more complicated. Solving (14) for I_{ii} with $I_e = I_c = 0$ yields

$$I_{ii} = I_i \frac{1 - \alpha_u \cdot \alpha_d}{1 - \alpha_u \cdot \alpha_d - \alpha_n \cdot \alpha_i} \tag{17}$$

and this leads to

$$\frac{I_i}{I_o} = \frac{I_i}{\alpha_n \cdot I_{ii}} = \frac{1}{\alpha_n}\left(1 - \alpha_n \frac{\alpha_i}{1 - \alpha_u \cdot \alpha_d}\right). \tag{18}$$

[6] It can be a constant voltage source at the outset, if a voltage regulator controlled by a p-n-p reference device is spent.

This equation corresponds to (2) in [1] if one sets

$$\frac{\alpha_i}{1 - \alpha_u \cdot \alpha_d} = \alpha'_{\text{p-n-p}}. \tag{19}$$

$\alpha'_{\text{p-n-p}}$ has been called "recollection factor" [1]. It can be shown that the recollection factor for the nonsaturated n-p-n transistor corresponds to (19) but with α_d omitted.

IV. DELAY COMPUTATIONS

The delay of all known bipolar logic circuits consists of two basic parts.

Part 1: The intrinsic delay (t_{di}) of the switching device due to minority carrier storage in the device.

Part 2: The extrinsic delay (t_{de}) due to depletion layer, stray and load capacitances.

The intrinsic delay does not depend on the amount of dc power supplied when constancy of the device parameters is assumed. However, the extrinsic delay is inversely proportional to the charging current available, and thus inversely proportional to the supplied dc power (constant supply voltage assumed). Both delays are indicated in Fig. 8 as a function of source current I_o. With good accuracy, the total delay is the linear sum of the two delays.

The average extrinsic delay $\overline{t_{de}}$ can be estimated according to the inset of Fig. 8.

$$\overline{t_{de}} \approx \frac{1}{2} \cdot \frac{\sum C_{\nu\text{ eff}} \cdot \Delta V}{I_o}. \tag{20}$$

$\Sigma C_{\nu\text{ eff}}$ is the total effective node capacitance, ΔV is the logic voltage swing. The contribution $C_{\nu\text{ eff}}$ of a single capacitance can be determined by relating the total charge variation to the logic voltage swing

$$C_{\nu\text{ eff}} = \frac{1}{\Delta V}\int_{V_1}^{V_2} C_\nu(V)\, dV = m \cdot C_\nu(0). \tag{21}$$

TABLE I

COMPARISON OF EXTRINSIC DELAYS COMPUTED USING MODEL FIG. 7
WITH THOSE CALCULATED AFTER (20) AND (21). CAPACITANCES
HAVE BEEN VARIED FOR DIFFERENT COMBINATIONS OF C_{te} AND C_{tc}.

| Depletion Layer Capacitances | | | $\bar{t}_d$/ns | |
$C_{te}(OV)$/pF	$C_{tc}(OV)$/pF	Eq. (21)[a]	Computer Simulation	
1	0.001	4.6	4.6	
1	0.5	9.5	10	
0.2	0.9	9.7	10.3	

$I_o = 10^{-4}A$, $\beta_d = \alpha_d/(1 - \alpha_d) = 100$ $\beta_u = \alpha_u/(1 - \alpha_u) \approx 10$.

[a] $C_{te_{eff}} = 1.3\ C_{te}(OV)$ $\Delta V_{EB} = 0.7$ V
$C_{tc_{eff}} = 2.8\ C_{tc}(OV)$ $\Delta V_{BC} = 1.4$ V.

For capacitances between emitter and base it is

$$\Delta V = (V_2 - V_1)_{EB};$$

however, the voltage change $V_2 - V_1$ for capacitances between collector and base is about twice as large

$$2\ \Delta V \approx (V_2 - V_1)_{CB}.$$

The estimate according to (20) and (21) comes very close to an accurate computer simulation as the examples of Table I show for a variety of capacitances.

The computed extrinsic delay has been found to be independent of upward current gain in the examined range of 1.5 ⋯ 10 times fan-out. This says that the minimum upward current gain required is a question of noise immunity rather than speed.

The intrinsic delay t_{di} cannot be predicted as easily as the extrinsic one. Therefore, a set of curves has been generated (Fig. 9) that relates this delay to the current gains and the time constants of the model.[7]

MTL devices in standard buried layer process have ratios $\tau_c/\tau_e \ll 1$. Therefore, the delay increase due to τ_c is of minor importance. However, the delay clearly depends very much on the upward and downward current gains β_u, β_d. The reason is that the internal current feedback in saturated transistors, having relatively large current gains in both directions, leads to excess charge storage even with a small collector time constant.

The dependence of the intrinsic delay on current gain as demonstrated by Figs. 6–8 might lead to incorrect conclusions for the device design. The increase of delay by current gain increase is true only if the time constants are independent of current gains. However, in usual MTL devices

$$\tau_e \sim \frac{1}{\beta_u} \qquad (22)$$

[9], so that this effect of delay decrease is stronger.

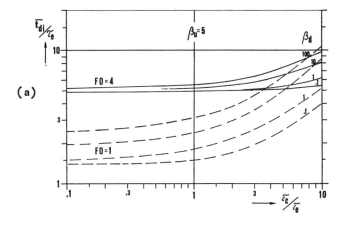
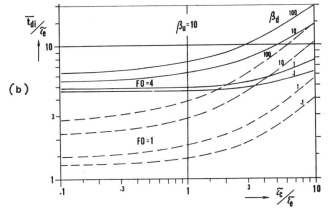
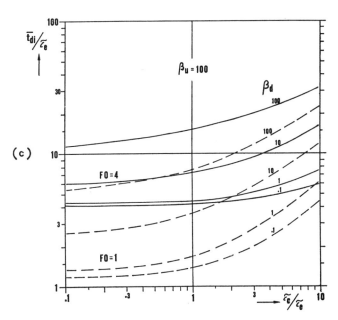

Fig. 9. Intrinsic delay $\bar{t}_{di}$ of inverter chain versus collector time constant τ_c, normalized with emitter time constant τ_e for an upward current gain of (a) $\beta_u = 5$, (b) $\beta_u = 10$, and (c) $\beta_u = 100$. Downward current gain β_d and fan-out (FO) are parameters. Current hogging at small β_d has not been considered. For definition of fan-out see [1].

This case demonstrates the limitations of a model describing primarily the terminal behavior of a device while giving a very weak replica of the physical device. It should, therefore, be used only for circuit analysis with given devices, but not as a tool for device improvement.

---

[7] Current hogging has not been included in the computation, so that for fan-out > 1, the curves applying to low downward current gain are only for reference purposes.

V. Summary

Starting out from the Ebers–Moll equations, it has been shown that for investigating the circuit behavior the MTL device may be modeled as a simple n-p-n transistor having an additional built-in current source. The intensity of this current source can be easily related to the current actually supplied to the p emitter of the MTL device.

The model has been used to compute data for diagrams relating the intrinsic circuit delay to transistor current gains and time constants. For the delay in the region of constant power-delay product $(\bar{t}_d \gg t_{d_i})$ a simple approximation has been shown to be useful. These results can be used for a first pass circuit delay estimate with given devices.

This model for circuit behavior is strictly terminal oriented. For device optimization, and for a proper consideration of series resistances within the device regions, a different model would be required which provides a more direct replica of the physical device structure and operation mechanisms. Such a structure-oriented model will be described in a subsequent paper [9].

Acknowledgment

Thanks are due to H. G. Pietrass for performing the computer simulation.

References

[1] H. H. Berger and S. K. Wiedmann, "Merged-transistor logic (MTL)—A low-cost bipolar logic concept," *IEEE J. Solid-State Circuits,* vol. SC-7, pp. 340-346, Oct. 1972; U.S. Patent 3 736 477, May 29, 1973.
[2] K. Hart and A. Slob, "Integrated injection logic: A new approach to *LSI,*" *IEEE J. Solid-State Circuits,* vol. SC-7, pp. 346-351, Oct. 1972.
[3] J. J. Ebers and J. L. Moll, "Large-signal behavior of junction transistors," *Proc. IRE,* vol. 42, pp. 1761–1772, Dec. 1954.
[4] C. Le Can *et al., Switching Devices of Diodes and Transistors* (Eng. Ed.). Eindhoven, The Netherlands: Philips Gloeilampenfabrieken, 1962.
[5] K. G. Ashar *et al.,* "Transient analysis and device characterization of ACP circuits," *IBM J. Res. Develop.,* vol. 7, pp. 207-223, July 1963.
[6] R. Beaufoy and J. J. Sparkes, "The junction transister as a charge-controlled device," *ATE J.,* vol. 13, pp. 310-324, Oct. 1957.
[7] D. K. Lynn, C. S. Meyer, and D. J. Hamilton, *Analysis and Design of Integrated Circuits.* New York: McGraw-Hill, 1967, p. 75 ff.
[8] H. C. Lin, "DC analysis of multiple collector and multiple emitter transistors in integrated circuits," *IEEE J. Solid-State Circuits,* vol. SC-4, pp. 20-24, Feb. 1969.
[9] H. H. Berger, "The injection model—a structure-oriented model for merged transistor logic (MTL)," this issue, p. 218.

The Injection Model—A Structure-Oriented Model for Merged Transistor Logic (MTL)

HORST H. BERGER

Abstract—The merged transistor device is represented by assigning separate diodes to the various electron and hole injections along the active p-n junctions. Where collection takes place, current sources are introduced. Measurement procedures are described that allow a quantitative separation of the various injections, and hence the determination of the model parameters. Results of such measurements are given. Device terminal parameters, like current gains and storage time constants, can be predicted from the measurements for devices of arbitrary horizontal geometry, so that the injection model can serve as a device optimization tool. As a circuit analysis model it allows representation of the internal device series resistances which would not be possible with an Ebers–Moll model. The injection model is significant beyond the merged transistor logic (MTL) aspects as it renders a better insight into bipolar devices, particularly into lateral p-n-p and saturated n-p-n transistors.

I. Introduction

CIRCUIT performance generally depends very much on the components used to build the circuit. This is even truer with merged transistor logic (MTL) [1], [2] where the merged transistors embody a substantial part of the circuit. All metallic interconnections besides the single supply line are primarily the matter of the logic design. Thus, the MTL circuit designer has to focus on the MTL device, on the design of a proper horizontal geometry or even vertical profile. For this he requires a model that describes the merged transistor from the viewpoint of physical structure and mechanism. The otherwise very useful Ebers–Moll model [3], [4] cannot serve this purpose as it is terminal oriented.

A structure-oriented model has been offered already with the first MTL publication [1], and is called here injection model. In this model separate diodes are assigned to the various parts of the emitter-base junction and its hole or electron injections. Where collection takes place, current sources are introduced. Structure-oriented models, however, have a severe disadvantage that hampers their application. Namely, the model parameters cannot be determined directly by measurements on the regular device terminals. Only lump sums can be measured there. Deduction of the constituents from the sum is usually ambiguous. Computations of the parameters from

the doping profiles and the geometry are possible in principle, but at least some measurement crosscheck is desirable. In some cases information on boundary conditions can be supplied only by measurement.

This paper describes a test structure and measurement procedures that allow one to separate the injections in the MTL device as required for the injection model. For a better understanding, an introduction into the model is given first. Examples of current densities obtained from two different processes giving different vertical profiles will be given and discussed. These examples show the influence of the various injections on current gain, and thus facilitate decisions on horizontal device geometry. Furthermore, the influence of the various injections on charge storage, and thus on speed limit, will be discussed.

The new designations for n-p-n transistor current gain (upward, downward)[1] introduced in [3], will be used in this paper to avoid the easily arising confusion with "forward" and "inverse."

II. The Injection Model

Fig. 1 shows the circuit representation of the MTL device and a typical device cross section. The blowups of its regions (a) and (b) drawn in Fig. 2 (a) and (b) serve to explain the basic idea of the injection model. Blowup (a) represents the forward biased emitter-base junction of the lateral p-n-p transistor and its collector (= base of n-p-n transistor); and blowup (b) represents the forward biased emitter-base junction of the upward n-p-n transistor, including the collector action of the p-n-p transistor's emitter ("injector"). The injections taking place along the forward biased junctions are discriminated after carrier type, and after doping profile and boundary condition of the region into which these carriers are injected. The simplifying assumption is made that the minority carriers flow either strictly vertically or strictly horizontally.[2] Furthermore, lateral injection at the outer device edges shall be suppressed by a collar

Manuscript received March 25, 1974; revised June 25, 1974. This is an extended version of the paper "Design Consideration for Merged Transistor Logic (Integrated Injection Logic) Circuits" presented at the International Solid-State Circuits Conference, Philadelphia, Pa., February 1974.

The author is with IBM Laboratories, Boeblingen, W. Germany.

[1] *Downward* current gain corresponds to the normal operation mode in regular circuits with the emitter at the semiconductor surface, where the injection into the base is directed *downward*.

[2] At the border between regions that have different injection current densities, one would actually expect the minority carrier paths to bend towards the region of higher current density, thereby enlarging the effective area of this region. So far, experiments (Section V) indicate that this effect is of minor practical importance.

Reprinted from *IEEE J. Solid-State Circuits*, vol. SC-9, pp. 218–227, Oct. 1974.

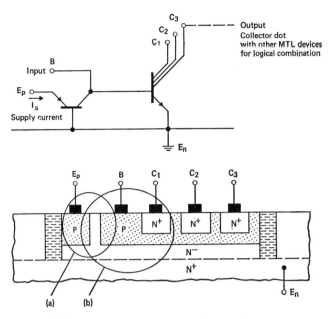

Fig. 1. MTL device—circuit representation and typical cross section with injection inhibiting collar. Regions (a) and (b) appear blown up in Fig. 2.

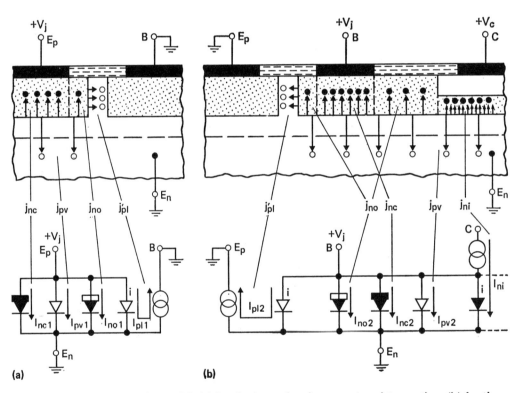

Fig. 2. Explanation of the injection model, (a) for the forward active p-n-p transistor section, (b) for the upward n-p-n transistor section, comprising inverse lateral injection and collection in the lateral p-n-p transistor.

of highly doped n region or better by recessed oxide (compare Fig. 1), so that noticeable lateral injection occurs only in the intrinsic base region of the lateral p-n-p transistor.

All vertical hole injection into the n^-/n^+ substrate is uniform along the junction because of uniform conditions in the n^-/n^+ substrate. Its current density is des-

ignated by j_{pv}. For the vertical injection of electrons into the p regions three different conditions exist: contact covered p region (injection current density j_{nc}), oxide covered p region (j_{no}), and intrinsic base region of the n-p-n transistor (j_{ni}).

Furthermore, a lateral hole injection occurs in the intrinsic base region of the p-n-p transistor, that is di-

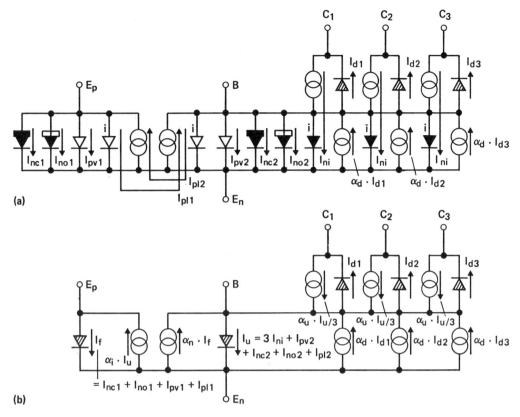

Fig. 3. (a) Injection model of total MTL device compared with (b) Ebers–Moll model. Explanation of diode symbols: hole injection—empty diode symbol; electron injection—symbol filled out; mixed injections and mixed boundaries—hatched symbol; metal boundary—roof of symbol filled out; isolator boundary—roof empty; collecting boundary or volume recombination—no roof.

rected "forward" [Fig. 2(a)] or "inverse" [Fig. 2(b)]. It is practical to normalize this current with the length of the injecting edge (j'_{pl}) and not like the other injections with the junction area.

The partial junction currents I_ν associated with the various injections of density j_ν are simply given by

$$I_\nu = A_\nu \cdot j_\nu (V_i) \qquad (1)$$

where A_ν is the junction area associated with the injection j_ν. For the lateral hole injection

$$I_{pl} = l \cdot j'_{pl}(V_i) \qquad (2)$$

holds, where l is the length of the emitting edge.

The currents depend on voltage with the well-known exponential relation of a diode

$$I_\nu = I_{s\nu}\left(\exp \frac{V_i}{n \cdot k \cdot T/q} - 1\right) \qquad (3)$$

where $I_{s\nu}$ is the saturation current, and kT/q is the temperature voltage (26 mV at room temperature). $n = 1$ for these diffusion currents.

Because of (3) the partial junction currents may be modeled by diodes, as shown in the lower part of Fig. 2. Modified diode symbols indicate the injection type (empty symbol: hole injection; filled out: electron injection), and the boundary condition (roof filled out:

metal boundary; roof empty: isolator boundary; no roof: collecting boundary or volume recombination). Where collection takes place (I_{pl}, I_{ni}), a current source is connected to the collector. The recombination in the intrinsic base regions may be neglected, and therefore the currents[3] in these current sources are set equal to those of the associated injecting diodes.

In Fig. 3(a) the partial models of Fig. 2 are assembled, making use of the principle of linear superposition of the forward and inverse injection in the lateral p-n-p transistor, as taught by Ebers and Moll [4]. Moreover, the n-p-n transistor part in Fig. 3(a) has been supplemented by the diodes and current sources for the downward operation under saturation condition. However, these diodes have not been split up according to injection types as this split-up would not depend much on device geometry. They have been represented by the crosshatched diode symbols for mixed injections. Consequently, the currents in the current sources and in the downward injecting diodes have been related by the downward current gain factor α_d.

Fig. 3(b) is the Ebers–Moll representation of the MTL

---

[3] The recombination current in the intrinsic base region can principally be modeled by an additional diode of proper saturation current.

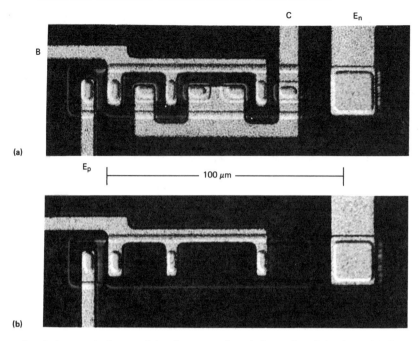

Fig. 4. Microphotographs of the test devices used for the separation of the various injections. (a) Complete MTL device. (b) Same device, but n+ collectors missing.

device [3]. One can deduce its terminal parameters from the injection model Fig. 3(a) simply by merging all parallel diodes into a single composite diode.

This leads to the current gain factors that relate the currents of the current sources to those of the associated composite diodes. The comparison of Fig. 3(a) and 3(b) yields

$$\text{p-n-p} \qquad \alpha_n = \frac{I_{pl1}}{I_{pl1} + I_{pv1} + I_{nc1} + I_{no1}} \qquad (4)$$

$$\alpha_i = \frac{I_{pl2}}{I_{pl2} + I_{pv2} + I_{nc2} + I_{no2} + m \cdot I_{ni}} \qquad (5)$$

$$\text{n-p-n} \qquad \alpha_u = \frac{m \cdot I_{ni}}{I_{pl2} + I_{pv2} + I_{nc2} + I_{no2} + m \cdot I_{ni}} \qquad (6)$$

where m is the number of collectors, in the example Figs. 1 and 3, $m = 3$.

III. APPLICATION OF THE INJECTION MODEL

For a specific vertical device profile as fixed by a given production process, a set of injection current densities can be determined as shall be shown in Section IV. Using this set and (1) $\cdots$ (3) the diode characteristics of the injection model can be readily calculated for devices of arbitrary horizontal geometry. Vice versa, one can use the injection model for optimizing a horizontal device geometry to fulfill particular parameter requirements like a certain current gain in terms of the Ebers–Moll representation.

In circuit analysis one would use either the injection model directly, or its Ebers–Moll derivation. The former has the principal advantage of allowing one to consider

the base series resistance of the device for operation at higher current levels. This can be done by properly splitting up the diodes that represent the extrinsic base region, and by putting lumped series resistors in between. However, suitable experiments have not been made yet. Even current gain fall-off at low current can be modeled by introducing another diode in parallel with the injection diodes that describes the recombination current in the space-charge layer. Its voltage-current characteristic would follow (3), however, with $n = 2$.

Most important for circuit analysis is the extension for ac modeling which shall be discussed in Section VI. But we shall proceed first with the determination of the key set of injection current densities.

IV. TEST DEVICES AND TEST CIRCUITS

Fig. 4 shows microphotographs of the test devices used, and Fig. 5 explains the cross sections of the devices, as well as the measurement circuit for the separation of injections. A typical set of voltages and currents is given in parentheses. The upper structure is a complete MTL device having four collectors. In order to reduce base series resistance effects in the measurements, three base contacts have been applied. The lower structure has exactly the same dimensions but does not carry the n+ collectors. Both structures have been laid out side-by-side on the same chip to ensure excellent tracking.

The nominal vertical dimensions are indicated in Fig. 5; the usual p substrate has been chosen with a regular n+ buried layer diffusion, on top of which the epitaxial layer was grown. A deeply diffused n+ collar has been used to practically eliminate sidewall injection. All side-

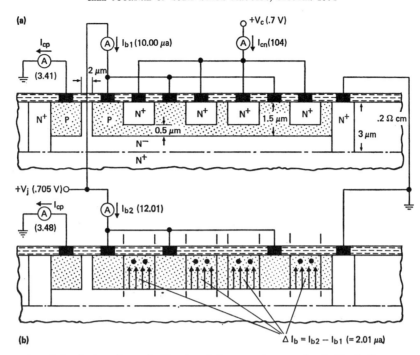

Fig. 5. Cross section of the devices shown in Fig. 4 and the measurement circuit. Typically measured currents and applied voltages in parentheses (units are μA and V, respectively).

wall junctions have been drawn vertically according to the assumption of only horizontal or vertical injection current flow. Upward current gain β_u of the n-p-n transistors is about 10 (104-μA collector current divided by 10-μA base current).

The current measured on the n+ collectors may be considered the total electron injection into the p regions beneath them, if one neglects recombination there. An estimate tells that the recombination current should be less than 0.1 μA in this example. Thus, the electron injection into these p regions practically does not contribute to base current.

However, if we omit the n+ collectors as in the lower structure [Fig. 2(b)], then the electron injection into these regions of now missing collectors adds to the base current. Hence, this increase of base current ΔI_b, divided by the area of the collectors, gives us the electron injection density into oxide covered p region. Contacts provide a different boundary condition, and a third structure with larger base contacts showed that the injection into contact covered p region is about ten times stronger. The currents I_{cp} measured at the grounded injectors represent the lateral inverse injection of holes towards the injector, again assuming negligible recombination in the intrinsic base of the lateral p-n-p transistor.[4]

Knowing now the vertical electron injections and the

lateral hole injection towards the injector, we can attribute the remaining base current to the vertical hole injection into the n−/n+ bottom layer. Hereby, the sidewall injection at the n+ collar is assumed negligible because of the high doping there.

V. DC Measurement Results and Discussion

Fig. 6 shows the current densities thus determined for the vertical structure of Fig. 5, and for another shallower one of 2-μm epitaxial thickness. In the column graphs relative numbers are used with the density of vertical hole injection j_{pv} as a reference. The lateral hole injection j'_{pl} can not be included in the column graph, because of the differing units. In contrast to the other ones, this injection density can be varied somewhat by the designer of the horizontal device structure by varying the basewidth of the lateral p-n-p transistor. A plot of $1/j'_{pl}$ versus basewidth on mask is given in Fig. 6 for the shallower structure. This curve follows a straight line that cuts the abscissa when the *actual* basewidth becomes zero.

Both sets of current densities contradict the widespread notion [5]-[8] that in a usual p+n−n+ diode structure, hole injection would prevail over electron injection. On the contrary, j_{no} and j_{nc} are much larger than j_{pv}, and thus it is not necessary to assume a high recombination velocity at the n−/n+ interface to account for the observed terminal current. Also S. Chou [9] has experimentally found prevailing electron injection. Interesting is also the high intrinsic upward current gain of the n-p-n transistor, which is given by the ratio of j_{ni} to j_{pv}. This means intrinsic β_u's of 180 or 226. They are about three times larger than the downward current gain β_d (= forward

---

[4] Here, some uncertainty arises from the inexactly known recombination velocity at the oxide interface of the base region. An argument for small recombination is the fact that the emitter current of the forward active p-n-p transistor can be sufficiently explained without the assumption of hole recombination in the base [see Fig. 7(a)].

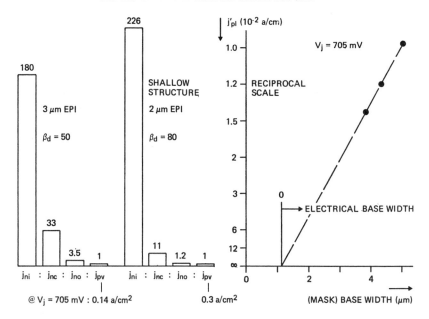

Fig. 6.   Column graphs of relative injection current densities (reference: j_{pv}) for the 3-μm structure of Fig. 5, and for a shallower one. For the latter also j'_{pl} is given as a function of (mask) basewidth.

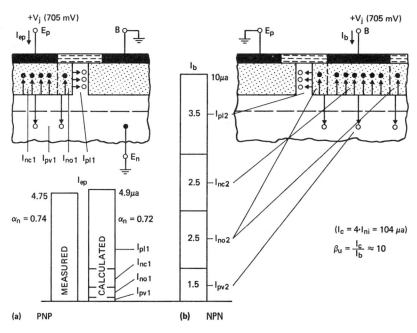

Fig. 7.   Current split-ups after injection type for the device of Figs. 4(a) and 5(a). (a) Split-up of emitter current of forward active p-n-p transistor section; comparison with actually measured current. (b) Split-up of base current of upward n-p-n transistor section.

current gain in regular circuits). The higher emitter efficiency in upward direction can be explained by the lighter doping [10] and the larger thickness of the buried n⁺ layer.

Fig. 7 shows the current split-up for our MTL test device of Figs. 4(a) and 5(a). On the n-p-n transistor [Fig. 7(b)], of the 10-μA total base current, 1.5 μA originate from the vertical injection of holes I_{pv} into the n⁻/n⁺ bottom. The injections of electrons into oxide covered (I_{no}) and contact covered p region I_{nc} contribute

2.5 μA each. The largest part, 3.5 μA, is caused by the lateral back-injection of holes towards the injector.

Similarly, the emitter current I_{ep} of the forward active lateral p-n-p transistor part can be split up now into its various contributors. Fig. 7(a) shows the result for the same voltage at the emitter as was applied to the base of the n-p-n transistor part. The thus obtained current (4.9 μA) is very close to the actually measured one (4.75 μA), as is the grounded base current gain. From the second set of current densities for the 2-μm structure the cur-

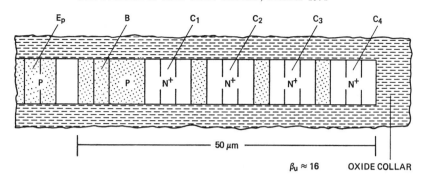

Fig. 8. Layout of a single-base contact MTL device having a recessed oxide collar that touches the n+ collectors. Layout ground rules as for the device of Figs. 4(a) and 5(a). Note the area reduction by a factor of 2 and the increased upward current gain β_u.

rent gain of the rather complex injection-coupled memory device [11] has been calculated. The result deviated by less than 15 percent from the measured value. These examples supply evidence for the validity of the model.

The relatively strong electron injection into the contact covered p region (j_{nc} in Fig. 6) suggests that a single-base contact device is better for current gain than the triple-contact test structure. Since also parasitic capacitances are smaller with a single-base contact, this is the natural choice as long as series resistances are not relevant. The effect of series resistance in the base region is the smallest when the single-base contact is put near the injector so that the parasitic current of the contact region need not traverse the whole p stripe.

A recessed oxide collar that may touch the n+ collectors reduces the other two injections into oxide covered p region, and into the n⁻/n+ bottom for better current gain. The layout example in Fig. 8 uses this option and a single-base contact. The layout ground rules are the same as for the test device of Figs. 4(a) and 5(a). For the same vertical 3-μm profile, upward current gain β_u would now be 16 instead of 10 with the test device.

The shallower (2 μm) vertical structure (compare current density column in Fig. 6) would yield even better values because of the better ratio of usable (j_{ni}) to parasitic (j_{nc}, j_{no}, j_{pv}) currents. These examples demonstrate that MTL fully partakes of the progress in technology.

VI. DISCUSSION OF AC MODELING

Of course, the injection model can also be extended for ac representation. We will not consider here the relatively trivial case of space-charge layer capacitances that determine the power-delay product at lower speeds [3]. These capacitances lie in parallel to the diodes that represent the corresponding junction.[5]

The more difficult and therefore interesting question is the speed limit (intrinsic delay) where the minority car-

rier charge storage governs. This charge-storage effect can be expressed by the emitter time constant

$$\tau_e = \frac{Q_{\text{total}}}{I_e} \qquad (7)$$

of the (extrinsic) upward n-p-n transistor (only the n-p-n transistor part is switched in MTL).

The influence of the much smaller time constant of the downward n-p-n transistor may usually be neglected in MTL. In addition to τ_e, upward and downward current gains influence the intrinsic delay as has been shown by using the Ebers–Moll model [3]. Fig. 9 gives the intrinsic delay versus upward current gain for different fan-outs (= number of collectors per device) and for different ratios of downward to upward current gain. This ratio is—for a given device and production process—rather independent of the absolute value of current gain.[6] According to this diagram, the key for determining intrinsic delay is τ_e.

Every one of the injection diodes [Fig. 2(b)] belonging to the n-p-n transistor part contributes to τ_e via the total charge Q_{total} in (7). Since we can define individual time constants τ_ν of these diodes

$$\tau_\nu = \frac{Q_\nu}{I_\nu} \qquad (8)$$

(7) becomes

$$\tau_e = \sum_\nu \tau_\nu \frac{I_\nu}{I_e}. \qquad (9)$$

This equation says that the time constants of the individual diodes have to be weighed by the ratio of the diode current to the total emitter current, to find their contribution to the emitter time constant.

Calculation of time constants from doping profiles is usually hampered by the unknown boundary conditions, which is the case particularly with the oxide covered p

---

[5] The space-charge layer capacitance logically belongs to the diode representing space-charge layer recombination current, which can be introduced for modeling the low current fall-off of current gain as mentioned in Section III.

[6] This observation can be readily explained by the injection model if variation of intrinsic basewidth only is assumed. For the explanation, the diode of the downward n-p-n transistor (Fig. 3) has to be split up also according to the various injections.

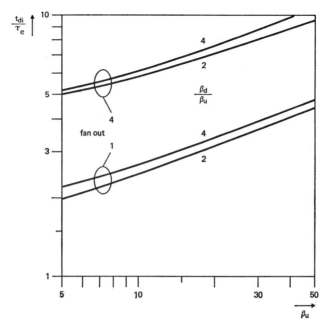

Fig. 9. Intrinsic delay t_{di} (maximum speed) as a function of upward current gain β_u, ratio of downward to upward current gain, fan-out and emitter time contant τ_e after [3]. Current hogging and time constant of the downward active n-p-n transistor have been neglected.

region and the n^-/n^+ bottom layer.[7] This gap is filled now by the measured injection densities at a given junction voltage, which give the sufficient boundary condition (p or n, dp/dx or dn/dx) at the front end of the semiconductor layers. Estimates of stored charges can readily be made by assuming a minority-carrier distribution as if no current would flow (worst case). This is a close approximation for the cases of limited recombination at the end of the layer, or of steeply increasing doping. With high recombination at the end of the layer and increasing doping the charge actually stored would lie between 50 and 100 percent of this worst case estimate.

Such estimates have been made for the structure of Figs. 4(a) and 5(a), and are shown in Fig. 10. Since the actual thickness W_e and doping N_e of the epitaxial layer beneath the p diffusion were least known, the associated time constant τ_{pv} for the injection of holes into the n^-/n^+ bottom was adjusted to fit the measured total time constant $\tau_e \approx 3$ ns.

Since

$$\tau_{pv} \sim \frac{W_e}{N_e} \qquad (10)$$

it can readily assume microseconds with low doping and thicker layer instead of the ≈ 150 ns estimated in our

case. This time constant, even when weighed with the current ratio (9) represents a substantial part of the emitter time constant as the column graph in Fig. 10 demonstrates. The second largest contribution comes from the electron injection into oxide covered p region, whereas the contact covered p region and the inverse lateral p-n-p transistor are of no concern. Also the contribution of charge storage (τ_{ni}) in the intrinsic bases of the n-p-n transistors is relatively small. From this it becomes clear that a recessed oxide collar would be helpful for reducing τ_e, as it was for increasing the current gain β_u. It cuts down those injections that are most detrimental. Also, shallower structures with thin epitaxial layers of relatively high doping would help, as well as a better adjustment of doping profiles by ion implantation.

With the recessed oxide collar, τ_e is reduced, but upward current gain β_u is increased. The intrinsic delay then improves less than τ_e would suggest, because of the influence of current gain shown in Fig. 9. However, β_u can always be reduced via the inverse lateral p-n-p transistor by prolonging the injecting edge or by reducing basewidth.

Equation (9) says that

$$\tau_e \sim \frac{1}{I_e} \approx \frac{1}{m \cdot I_{ni}} \sim \frac{1}{\beta_u} \qquad (11)$$

which means that a deeper drive-in of the n^+ collectors (reduction of intrinsic basewidth) would reduce τ_e via a relative increase of I_{ni}. This τ_e reduction is accompanied by an increase of β_u, which again can be countered by a proper lateral p-n-p transistor design.

---

[7] Measurements of time constants are also principally possible using a difference method similar to the dc method of Fig. 6. This has been tried for the time constant τ_{no} which came out $\approx$ 30 ns close to the estimated one [22 ns in Fig. 10]. However, the required high measurement accuracy is usually difficult to achieve.

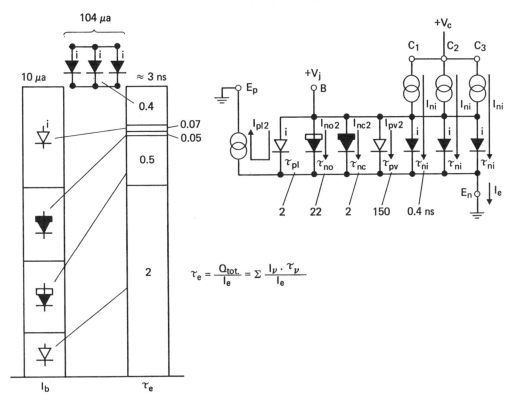

Fig. 10.   Individual time constants τ_ν of the device of Figs. 4(a) and 5(a), and their influence on the emitter time constant τ_e of the forward active n-p-n transistor. The column graphs show the base current split-up of Fig. 7 and the corresponding split-up of τ_e.

The effect on speed limit of such a collector drive-in without counteraction on β_u has been experimentally verified on a 7-stage closed-loop oscillator built from the devices in Figs. 4(a) and 5(a). A wafer containing such oscillators was cut into two halves, and one of these obtained a second collector drive-in before metalization. In the measured power-delay diagram (Fig. 11) there is no speed difference at low power.[8] But the intrinsic delay that shows up at high power is smaller for the device with the drive-in, which also has the higher current gain. The intrinsic speeds fit satisfactorily[9] according to the computer prediction (Fig. 9) if one assumes

$$\tau_e = \frac{30 \text{ ns}}{\beta_u} \qquad (12)$$

according to (11), and to the measurement of $\tau_e = 3$ ns for a device having $\beta_u = 10$ (Fig. 10).

[8] In comparing the power-delay product and intrinsic delay numbers of Fig. 11 with those of other publications, the large fan-out = 4 should be considered, as well as the fact that the test device used was not optimized for speed or power delay.

[9] The ratio t_{d41}/t_{d42} for the two cases corresponds exactly to the prediction of Fig. 9. However, the absolute values are somewhat off: t_{d41} calculated 15.5 ns, measured 13.5 ns; t_{d42} calculated 11.5 ns, measured 10.0 ns. Probably the reference taken for τ_e in (12) (30 ns) is somewhat too large.

VII. Conclusions

The circuit designer has to concentrate on the device when he wants to improve MTL circuit behavior. For this he needs a structure-oriented model. The injection model is such a tool. Proper test structures and procedures to determine its parameters have been described in this paper.

The injection model provides the detailed understanding of the relationships between device geometry and doping profiles on one side, and device behavior on the other side. This insight is essential for MTL device synthesis. But the model can be used as well for refined MTL circuit analysis, as it allows one to properly consider internal device series resistances.

Simplification of the injection model directly leads to the terminal-oriented Ebers–Moll model. Hence, such terminal parameters as current gains and storage time constants can be deduced from the device geometry via the injection model.

The injection model is important beyond MTL, as it provides insight into related memory devices [11], [12] and into lateral p-n-p transistors and saturated n-p-n transistors of regular circuits.

The discussion of possible MTL device improvements has shown, that MTL fully partakes of the progress in semiconductor technology, so that its features will im-

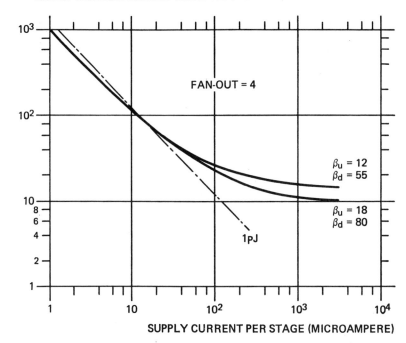

DELAY PER STAGE (NANOSECONDS)

SUPPLY CURRENT PER STAGE (MICROAMPERE)

Fig. 11. Delay-supply current diagram for 7-stage ringoscillators built from the devices in Figs. 4(a) and 5(a). The device with the larger current gain had received an additional collector drive-in. The diagram demonstrates the influence of collector drive-in on intrinsic delay (maximum speed).

prove concurrently with those of the other known logic circuits.

ACKNOWLEDGMENT

The author is indebted to F. Seidenschwann for taking care of the production of test samples, to H. G. Pietrass for measurement assistance, and to S. K. Wiedmann for helpful comments.

REFERENCES

[1] H. H. Berger and S. K. Wiedmann, "Merged-transistor logic (MTL)—A low-cost bipolar logic concept," *IEEE J. Solid-State Circuits*, vol. SC-7, pp. 340–346, Oct. 1972.

[2] K. Hart and A. Slob, "Integrated injection logic: A new approach to LSI," *IEEE J. Solid-State Circuits*, vol. SC-7, pp. 346–351, Oct. 1972.

[3] H. H. Berger and S. K. Wiedmann, "Terminal-oriented model for merged transistor logic (MTL)," this issue, pp. 211–217.

[4] J. J. Ebers and J. L. Moll, "Large-signal behavior of junction transistors," *Proc. IRE*, vol. 42, pp. 1761–1772, Dec. 1954.

[5] R. W. Dutton and R. J. Whittier, "Forward current-voltage and switching characteristics of p+-n-n+ (epitaxial) diodes," *IEEE Trans. Electron Devices*, vol. ED-16, pp. 458–467, May 1969.

[6] K. Venkateswaran and D. J. Roulston, "Recombination dependent characteristics of silican P+-N-N+ epitaxial diodes," *Solid-State Electron.*, vol. 15, pp. 311–323, 1972.

[7] O. W. Memelink, "Reflections about digital low-power IC's," presented at the Int. Symp. Low-Power Digital Circuits, Wildbad, Germany, May 1972.

[8] F. M. Klaassen, "Device physics of integrated injection logic," presented at ESSDERC 1973, Munich, Germany, paper A 6.

[9] S. Chou, "An investigation of lateral transistors—DC characteristics," *Solid-State Electron.*, vol. 14, pp. 811–826, 1971.

[10] R. P. Mertens, H. J. De Man, and R. J. van Overstraeten, "Calculation of the emitter efficiency of bipolar transistors," *IEEE Trans. Electron Devices*, vol. ED-20, pp. 772–778, Sept. 1973.

[11] S. K. Wiedmann, "Injection-coupled memory: A high density static bipolar memory," *IEEE J. Solid-State Circuits*, vol. SC-8, pp. 332–337, Oct. 1973.

[12] S. K. Wiedmann and H. H. Berger, "Superintegrated memory shares functions on diffused islands," *Electronics*, vol. 45, pp. 83–86, Feb. 1972.

AN EVALUATION OF INJECTION MODELING

Richard C. Jaeger

IBM Thomas J. Watson Research Center, Yorktown Heights, NY 10598, U.S.A.

(Received 8 September 1975; in revised form 22 December 1975)

Abstract—Charge storage in the base of an MTL structure is evaluated using two-dimensional simulation. The results are compared to those predicted by the method of injection modeling as developed by H. H. Berger. The results show that injection modeling yields pessimistic estimates of the stored base charge for a homogeneous base device. For the more important case of a graded base structure, injection modeling yields estimates which are very close to those computed in the two-dimensional simulation.

NOTATION

j_n electron current density
q electronic charge
D_n, D_h diffusion coefficient for electrons, holes
u_n, u_h electron, hole mobility
$n'(x)$ excess electron density
$E(x)$ electric field
$N_A(x)$ acceptor density
L diffusion length
w base width

1. INTRODUCTION

Berger[1] introduced injection modeling as a method for obtaining estimates of charge storage and current flow in bipolar device structures. The technique was used to predict the performance of Merged Transistor Logic (MTL), and consists of partitioning the structure into one-dimensional diode segments which may be easily analyzed. Charge storage and current flow in each segment are then combined to predict the performance of the overall structure.

The purpose of this work is to study the degree to which the injection model characterizes the MTL structure and to assess the errors which are introduced by the two-dimensional nature of the MTL device. The two collector MTL device structure of Fig. 1 is used as the vehicle for this study. The minority carrier distributions in the base of the device are computed numerically for the cases of homogeneous base and exponentially graded base devices. The results are compared with those predicted by use of injection modeling and extended to include other graded base profiles.

2. TWO-DIMENSIONAL SIMULATION

Charge storage in the base region of the MTL device becomes a significant contributor to the emitter delay time in structures in which the N- eptiaxial region has been eliminated[1]. Further, it is easily shown (see Appendix 1) that charge storage in the *pnp* base region does not represent a performance limit in typical MTL devices. The lateral *pnp* device has also received considerable attention from others[2–5]. The MTL emitter region is highly one-dimensional and injection modeling should adequately represent this region. On the other hand, the

two-dimensional geometry of the MTL base could significantly alter the minority carrier distributions from those predicted by the injection model.

For these reasons, the base region of the MTL device of Fig. 1 was chosen for analysis. The base region was analyzed by numerically solving the two-dimensional minority carrier transport equation, as described in Appendix 2, with the boundary conditions indicated in Fig. 2.

The emitter-base junction is assumed to be uniformly forward biased, and the minority carrier density along the bottom of the base region is normalized to unity. Along the collector-base junction of the lateral *pnp*, the minority carrier density is assumed to be unity for the homogeneous base device, and to decrease exponentially as one approaches the surface for the case of the graded base device. Zero excess minority carrier density is assumed to be maintained at the base contact and at the collector-base junctions. Surface recombination is neglected at the other boundaries, and the current crossing these surfaces is set to zero.

The graded base transistor is assumed to have an exponentially doped base region which is most heavily doped at the surface and decreases as one proceeds into the material. The doping is assumed to decrease by a factor of 1000 between the base surface and the base-emitter junction. The assumption of exponential doping is a reasonable approximation of a transistor base profile, and simplifies the one and two-dimensional analyses. Other profiles are considered in Section 5.

The devices are assumed to operate in low level injection, and voltage drops due to transverse base current flow are neglected. Finally, the minority carrier diffusion length was chosen to be ten times the base depth H. This assumption is valid for the shallow structures at which this work is directed. The computed minority carrier densities are given in Figs. 3 and 4.

3. INJECTION MODELING OF THE MTL DEVICE

Injection modeling of the MTL structure requires that the device be divided into diode elements which may then be analyzed in one-dimension. The MTL base region of Fig. 2 may be divided into two types[1] of one-dimensional regions. The first region is the oxide covered

Reprinted with permission from *Solid-State Electron.*, vol. 19, pp. 639–643, July 1976. Copyright © 1976, Pergamon Press, Ltd.

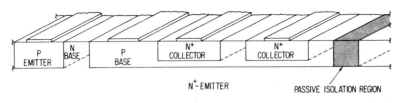

Fig. 1. 2-collector MTL device.

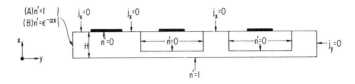

Fig. 2. NPN base region with boundary conditions.

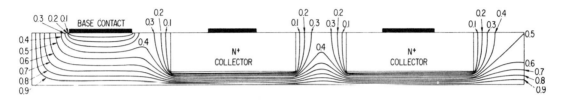

Fig. 3. Contours of constant minority carrier density for the homogeneous base device.

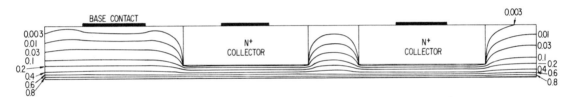

Fig. 4. Contours of constant minority carrier density for the graded base device.

base region which has boundary conditions of unity excess minority carrier density at the base-emitter junction and zero current flow at the base surface. The second diode region is characterized by unity excess minority carrier density at the base-emitter junction and zero excess minority carrier density at the other boundary. This diode represents both the intrinsic base region directly beneath the collectors and the contact covered base region. To simplify the analysis of the diode regions, recombination will be neglected. The minority carrier distributions in the diodes may then be determined by solving the equation:

$$\bar{j}_n = \frac{j_n}{qD_n} = \frac{dn'}{dx} + \frac{\mu_n}{D_n} n' E(x). \quad (1)$$

The electric field E is determined by the exponential grading of the base region and is given by[6]

$$E(x) = \frac{D_h}{\mu_h} \frac{1}{N_A(x)} \frac{dN_A(x)}{dx}$$

in which the acceptor density is

$$N_A(x) = N_0 \epsilon^{\alpha x}.$$

For the homogeneous base device, the constant α is zero and the solutions for the two diode regions are found to be:

(a) *Oxide covered base region* †

$$n'(x) = 1 \quad \bar{Q} = w \quad \bar{J}_n = 0$$

where

$$\bar{Q} = \int_0^w n'(x)\, dx.$$

(b) *Contact covered and intrinsic base regions* †

$$n'(x) = 1 - \frac{x}{w} \quad \bar{Q} = \frac{w}{2} \quad \bar{j}_n = -\frac{1}{w}$$

For the graded base device, $\alpha = (\ln K)/w$ in which w is the base width and $K = Na(w)/Na(0)$.

(a) *Oxide covered base region* †

$$n'(x) = \epsilon^{-\alpha x} \quad \bar{Q} = \frac{K-1}{K} \frac{w}{\ln K} \quad \bar{j}_n = 0$$

(b) *Contact covered and intrinsic base regions* †

$$n'(x) = \frac{K\epsilon^{-\alpha x} - 1}{K - 1} \quad \bar{Q} = w\left[\frac{1}{\ln K} - \frac{1}{K-1}\right] \bar{j}_n = -\frac{\ln K}{w(K-1)}$$

---

†Note that w refers to the width of the specific region under analysis and has different values for the various regions.

By extending the above results over the breadth of the various base regions, charge storage and current flow estimates are obtained for the total device.

4. RESULTS AND COMPARISON

Using the results of the one-dimensional models of Section 3, the charge storage and current flow estimates of Fig. 5 are obtained for the base region of the MTL device. Charge storage estimates are obtained from the two-dimensional analysis by integrating the minority carrier density over the diode regions of interest. Current flow is computed using eqn (1).

(a) The homogeneous structure

The estimates of charge storage in the intrinsic base region and contact covered base region are quite good. As can be seen in Fig. 3, the minority carrier distributions in these regions are highly one-dimensional in character. However, the stored charge in the oxide covered base region is over-estimated by 100%. The regions between the two collectors and at the right end of the base contain carrier distributions which are much lower in magnitude than that which the injection model predicts. The two-dimensional character of these regions strongly modifies the minority carrier distributions and total amounts of stored charge.

On the other hand, estimates of the current flowing in the device are good since the regions in which the majority of the current flows are one-dimensional in character. It is important to note that the base contact acts in the same manner as a collector. The current "collected" by this contact represents a portion of the MTL base current and would limit the upward beta[9] of the overall MTL device to less than seven per collector for this structure. The base current components caused by hole injection into the emitter and pnp base would further degrade the magnitude of upward beta.

The current collected by the base contact may be reduced by placing a heavily doped P region directly below the contact. The reflecting properties of the high-low junction[7] thus formed would cause some increase in the charge stored in the base, but significantly reduce the current flow to the base contact. Figure 6 shows the results of a simulation of this situation in which the P-region directly beneath the contact has a doping level twenty times that of the base region. The total charge stored in the base region increased by 6%. The base current was reduced by approximately an order of magnitude. This portion of the base current will no longer limit the upward beta of the MTL device.

One concludes from the above analysis that injection modeling provides reasonable estimates of the current flowing in the homogeneous base device, but greatly over-estimates the magnitude of the stored charge.

(b) The graded base device

The graded base device of Fig. 4 can be seen to be much more one-dimensional in nature. The retarding electric field which is set up by the base impurity profile causes the excess minority carrier density to decrease rapidly as one proceeds away from the base-emitter junction. By the time the regions in which the two-dimensional effects are the strongest are reached, the excess minority carrier density has decreased to a very low value. The contribution of the two-dimensional regions to the total stored charge is quite small. Thus, one would expect injection modeling to provide a more accurate estimate of charge storage for this case. This is evident in Fig. 5. Both the charge storage and current flow estimates agree well. Injection modeling provides a good estimate of conditions in the graded base device. Also, the retarding field of the graded base device effectively eliminates the base current which was collected by the base contact in the homogeneous base advice.

5. DISCUSSION AND EXTENSION

The injection models and two-dimensional simulation of the graded base device were based upon the assumption of an exponential base impurity profile. The built-in field caused by this profile is beneficial to the MTL device since it reduces the charge storage in the extrinsic base regions. Further, the field causes the stored charge to be compressed into a narrow region near the base-emitter junction. The charge distribution is very similar in both the intrinsic and extrinsic base regions, and spreads out only slightly in the extrinsic base region. As predicted by the injection models of Section 3, the distribution changes by a negligible amount when the boundary condition is changed from $j(0) = 0$ (oxide covered regions) to $n'(0) = 0$ (contact

	Q_i	Q_{ox}	Q_c	Q_{tot}	I_B	I_C
Homogeneous Base Device						
Injection Model	1000	5600	1000	7600	1.3	20
Two-Dimensional Simulation	1000	2900	1000	4900	1.9	26
Graded Base Device						
Injection Model	730	810	290	1800	.0086	7.5
Two-Dimensional Simulation	730	790	310	1800	.019	8.3

* Q_i – stored charge in the intrinsic base region
Q_{ox} – stored charge in the oxide covered base region
Q_c – stored charge in the contact covered base region
Q_{tot} – total stored charge
I_B – base current collected by the base contact
I_C – total collector current

Fig. 5. Comparison of the injection model and two-dimensional simulation.

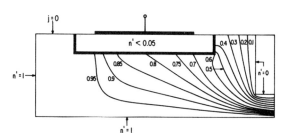

Fig. 6. Minority carrier density for P-region under the base contact.

covered region). This is again due to the built-in electric field. For $j(0) = 0$, a minority carrier gradient must be set up so that the diffusion current just balances the drift current. For $n'(0) = 0$ a current will flow, but this requires only a slight imbalance between the drift and diffusion components of current and only a slight redistribution of the minority carrier charge.

The above discussion also holds for other base impurity distributions. One-dimensional simulations of the minority carrier density are displayed in Fig. 8 for the base impurity distributions of Fig. 7. The impurity distributions are all normalized so that the integrated doping is the same. Thus, equal diode currents will flow for the boundary condition of $n'(0) = 0$. The minority carrier densities for the cases of Gaussian and complementary error function impurity distributions fall off even more rapidly than for the exponential case since the electric field is higher near the base-emitter junction. The total stored charge is somewhat less. Virtually no difference in the distributions exists for the boundary conditions of either $j(0) = 0$ or $n'(0) = 0$. The charge is again compressed to a narrow region near the base-emitter junction. One would expect injection modeling to provide good estimates of the base charge storage for base impurity

distributions which provide reasonably strong retarding fields near the base-emitter junction. A given impurity profile can easily be tested for this condition using a one-dimensional model.

In the homogeneous and graded base devices of Figs. 3 and 4, the charge stored in the intrinsic base region represents respectively only 20 and 40% of the total stored base charge, and hence a smaller percentage of the total charge stored when the emitter is forward biased. Altering the impurity profile and field in the intrinsic base region will not have a dominant effect on the stored charge. The main parameter of interest is the integrated base doping or Gummel number[8] of the intrinsic base region. For a given extrinsic base profile, the integrated doping of the intrinsic base controls the magnitude of the collector current flow and with it upward beta and emitter delay time. Thus, control of the total impurity concentration in the intrinsic base region is more important than it's shape!

6. SUMMARY

Charge storage and current flow estimates for the base region of an MTL device, using injection modeling, have been compared with those obtained from a two-dimensional simulation for both homogeneous base and graded base devices. Injection modeling has been shown to yield good estimates of these quantities for the graded base device and to yield a pessimistic estimate of charge storage in a homogeneous device. Extension of the results to include devices with other base profiles has been discussed. A retarding field in the extrinsic base region has been shown to significantly reduce the stored charge in the MTL device.

REFERENCES

1. H. H. Berger, *IEEE JSSC* SC-9, 218 (1974).
2. J. Lindmayer and W. Schneider, *Solid-St. Electron.* 10, 225 (1967).
3. D. E. Fulkerson, *Solid-St. Electron.* 11, 821 (1968).
4. S. Chou, *Solid-St. Electron.* 14, 811 (1971).
5. T. E. Demassa and L. Rispin, *Solid-St. Electron.* 18, 481 (1975).
6. D. K. Lynn, C. S. Meyer and D. J. Hamilton, *Analysis and Design of Integrated Circuits*, Chap. 4. McGraw-Hill, New York (1967).
7. R. W. Dutton and R. J. Whittier, *IEEE Trans. Electron Devices*, ED-16, 458 (1969).
8. H. K. Gummel, *Prod. IRE*, 834 (April 1961).
9. H. H. Berger and S. K. Wiedmann, *IEEE JSSC* SC-9, 211 (1974).
10. F. M. Klassen, *IEDM* (late news paper no. 24.6), (Dec. 1975).

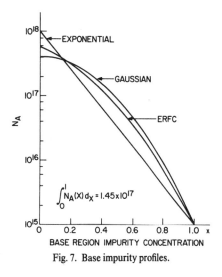

Fig. 7. Base impurity profiles.

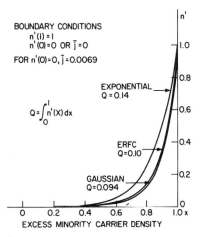

Fig. 8. Minority carrier densities for various base impurity profiles.

APPENDIX 1

The emitter delay time τ_e is expressed[1] as

$$\tau_e = \frac{Q_e}{I_e} = \frac{Q_{pnp} + Q_{npn}}{I_e}$$

or

$$\tau_e = \frac{\tau_{pnp} I_{pnp}}{I_e} + \tau_{npn}$$

But

$$\frac{I_e}{I_{pnp}} \geq \beta_u$$

and

$$\tau_e \leq \frac{\tau_{pnp}}{\beta_\mu} + \tau_{npn}.$$

I_e = total MTL emitter current
Q_e = total charge stored to support I_e
Q_{pnp} = charge stored in lateral pnp base region to support I_{pnp}
$\tau_{pnp} = Q_{pnp}/I_{pnp} = pnp$ base transit time
τ_{npn} = emitter delay of npn transistor
β_μ = MTL upward beta [9].

For typical values of β_μ and τ_{pnp}, the contribution of the pnp base transit time to τ_e is small relative to the npn emitter delay time. For example, assuming a pnp base width of $3\,\mu$, a diffusion constant of $10\,cm^2/sec$, and β_μ of 30, an estimate of the contribution of the pnp base transit time to τ_e is

$$\frac{1}{\beta_\mu} \frac{W^2}{2D} = 0.15 \text{ nsec.}$$

Only in structures with very low npn emitter delay times will the pnp transit time represent a performance limit. The above result is supported by the recent experimental data reported by Klassen[10], in which eliminating saturation of the lateral pnp transistor only slightly reduced the intrinsic MTL delay.

APPENDIX 2

The minority carrier transport equation

$$\nabla^2 n'(x,y) + E(x)\frac{u}{D}\frac{\partial n'(x,y)}{\partial x} - \frac{n'(x,y)}{L^2} = 0$$

was solved numerically using finite difference techniques. The standard five point difference approximation was used for the operator ∇^2, and centered difference approximations were used for the first derivatives. The resulting difference equation is given below.

$$n(i,j)\left[4 + \frac{h^2}{L^2}\right] = n(i,j+1) + n(i,j-1)$$
$$+ n(i+1,j)\left(1 - \frac{\alpha h}{2}\right) + n(i-1,j)\left(1 + \frac{\alpha h}{2}\right)$$

h = grid spacing

An APL program was used to solve the finite difference equations using iterative methods.

Evaluation of Electron Injection Current Density in p-Layers for Injection Modeling of I²L

HELMUT H. HEIMEIER AND HORST H. BERGER

Abstract—Proportionality between electron injection current density and sheet resistance of p-layers having a sink boundary has been found over a two orders of magnitude range of sheet resistance. This facilitates prediction of electron injection parameters for injection modeling and process control of I²L/MTL.

For modeling and optimizing MTL/I²L structures, the injection model has been proposed by Berger [1]. It is a one-dimensional physical model that uses a split-up of the internal currents and the associated charges. They are split according to the various regions into which currents are injected and according to the various boundary conditions. Two-dimensional computer simulations by Jaeger [2] have confirmed the validity of the one-dimensional injection model for the usual technology.

The main parameters of the injection model, the various current densities, have been measured by several authors for their production processes [1], [3], [4]. All these results agree in the relative magnitude of the injection parameters. Namely,

j_{ni} current density of electrons into the intrinsic base of the n-p-n transistor (collector current density!) is by far the largest value,

j_{nc} current density of electrons into contact covered extrinsic base is the next prominent one, and

j_{no} current density of electrons into oxide-covered extrinsic base, as well as

j_{pv} current density of holes into the buried n⁺-layer

are about an order of magnitude smaller than j_{nc}. j_{no}, however, is strongly sensitive to surface conditions.

This commonality seems to reflect the fact that, in spite of different peak dopings or diffusion depths used, today's manufacturing processes have very similar sheet resistance ratios of those various layers that are associated with the injection current density figures.

There is indeed an interrelation between the sheet resistance of a layer and its injection current density, as both are a function of the integral doping. Moll and Ross [5] used this interrelation to describe an injection ratio (emitter efficiency). According to an interpretation of their equation by Phillips [6], the injection ratio is equal to the sheet resistance ratio of the layers involved. Difficulties in this description arise from the neglect of possible mobility differences in the layers and the need for sheet resistance redefinition in case of strong volume recombination.

Moreover, in our case of injection modeling, we need the injection current densities separately first. Hence, it is an interesting question as to whether a simple relationship between individual injection current densities and the sheet resistances of the associated semiconductor layers also can be found.

Manuscript received October 26, 1976; revised November 22, 1976.

H. H. Heimeier was with the IBM Laboratories, Boeblingen, Germany. He is now with the IBM Corporation, East Fishkill Facility, Hopewell Junction, NY 12533.

H. H. Berger is with the IBM Laboratories, Boeblingen, Germany.

This paper answers this question for the current densities j_{ni} and j_{nc}. They have been selected for two reasons.

1) The condition of a complete sink for minority carriers is fulfilled, which is also an implicit condition for the Moll-Ross emitter efficiency description.

2) There is negligible volume recombination, so that a redefinition of sheet resistance (using diffusion length [6]) is not required.

The sink in case of j_{nc} is the base contact; in the case of j_{ni} it is the collector junction. For j_{nc}, volume recombination may be neglected, as the corresponding j_{no} (the same layer—however, incomplete surface sink) has been found to be at least an order of magnitude smaller. Hence, the neglect of volume recombination is even more reasonable for the thinner and more lightly doped layer associated with j_{ni}.

The main experimental material to be considered here originates from two different production processes. The first one ("A") gives a junction depth for the base diffusion of about 0.7 μm and an n-p-n transistor's base width (intrinsic base) of about 0.3 μm. The data were taken from various production lots. Some of these were intentionally produced out of specification in order to obtain a wider sheet resistance spread. The second one ("B") has a 1.5 μm junction depth and about 0.5 μm base width.[1] The current density figures were obtained in both cases according to the method of base current differences described in [1], but using larger devices (100 × 100 μm²) for better accuracy. The temperature was kept strictly at 25°C, and junction voltage was $V_j = 660$ mV.

The j_{nc} and j_{ni} values have been plotted in the same diagram versus the sheet resistance of the corresponding layers (Fig. 1). In order to supplement the material at the low sheet resistance end, a j_{nc} value reported by Mertens [4] and extrapolated to 660 mV has been included. It refers to a base diffusion having a junction depth of 3.3 μm. Fig. 1 shows a surprisingly simple proportionality of j_n and R_s over two orders of magnitude, indicated by the broken line. If one estimates j_n by approximating the diffusion profiles by box profiles of an average doping concentration $\bar{N}_A$ (no bandgap narrowing) and of an average minority carrier mobility $\mu_n(\bar{N}_A)$, one obtains much smaller junction current densities, particularly at the low sheet resistance end. Such an estimate for process "A" is shown by the heavy line in Fig. 1 ($n_i^2 = 1.02 \times 10^{20}$ cm⁻⁶ was used according to [7, eq. (4)]).

If one looks at the ratio j_n/R_s, one obtains

$$\frac{j_n}{R_s} \approx q^2 \cdot V_T \cdot \bar{\mu}_n \cdot \bar{\mu}_p \cdot n_i^2 \cdot \exp\left(\frac{V_j}{V_T}\right) \qquad (1)$$

where q is the elementary charge, n_i is the intrinsic carrier concentration and

$$V_T = \frac{kT}{q} = 25.7 \text{ mV at 298 K}$$

V_j = junction voltage (660 mV in our experiment).

For this ratio to be constant over such a wide range of doping concentrations $(N_A \approx 10^{17} \cdots 10^{19}$ cm⁻³), the well-established decrease of μ_n and μ_p with increasing doping N_A must be compensated somehow. The only explanation readily at hand is bandgap narrowing causing n_i^2 to increase while $\mu_n \cdot \mu_p$ decreases by the same amount.

[1]The authors are indebted to A. Bhattacharyya, IBM Corporation, Burlington, Essex Junction, VT, for providing the injection data from process "B."

Reprinted from *IEEE J. Solid-State Circuits*, vol. SC-12, pp. 205–206, Apr. 1977.

142

TABLE I

N_A / cm^{-3}	$\mu_p / cm^2 / V_s$	$\mu_n / cm^2 / V_s$	$\frac{\Delta V_G}{mV}$	$\mu_n \cdot \mu_p \cdot \exp\left(\frac{\Delta V_G}{V_T}\right) / \left(\frac{cm^2}{V_s}\right)^2$
$4 \cdot 10^{16}$	320	860	0	$2.75 \cdot 10^5$
$3 \cdot 10^{17}$	140	430	15	$1.08 \cdot 10^5$
$1 \cdot 10^{19}$	60	110	70	$1.01 \cdot 10^5$

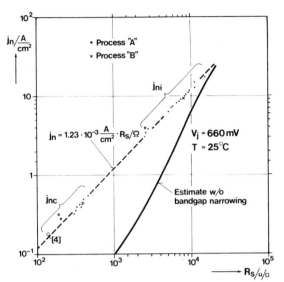

Fig. 1. Measured electron injection current densities versus sheet resistance of the corresponding p-layers for three different production processes.

Recently, Slotboom and de Graaff [7] evaluated bandgap narrowing versus doping in p-type layers. They measured j_{ni} as a function of doping and temperature, and from this deduced bandgap narrowing (ΔV_G). In order to check the consistency with our result on the proportionality of j_n and R_s, their results for three different doping levels have been listed in Table I. It says that at least at the boundaries of our measurement range ($N_A = 3 \times 10^{17}$ cm^{-3}, 1×10^{19} cm^{-3}), the required compensation of carrier mobility change with the deduced bandgap narrowing can indeed be shown with the Slotboom and de Graaff results. With (1) the proportionality factor j_n / R_s becomes now

$$\frac{j_n}{R_s} \approx q^2 \cdot V_T \cdot \bar{\mu}_n \cdot \bar{\mu}_p \cdot \exp\left(\frac{\Delta V_G}{V_T}\right) \cdot n_{io}^2 \cdot \exp\left(\frac{V_j}{V_T}\right) \quad (2)$$

where n_{io} is the intrinsic carrier concentration without bandgap narrowing.

Hence, with (compare Table I)

$$\mu_n \cdot \mu_p \cdot \exp\left(\frac{\Delta V_G}{V_T}\right) = 1.05 \cdot 10^5 \left(\frac{cm^2}{V \cdot s}\right)^2$$

and with $n_{io}^2 = 1.02 \times 10^{20}$/cm^6, we get

$$\frac{j_n}{R_s} \approx 10^{-3} \frac{A^2}{V \cdot cm^2}$$

which is very close to the line drawn in Fig. 1 (1.23×10^{-3} A^2/V $\cdot$ cm^2).

In summary, the injection into p-type layers (extrinsic and intrinsic base) that originate from different standard buried layer processes has been related to the sheet resistances of these layers. A direct proportionality has been found between the injection current densities and the sheet resistances in accordance with the bandgap narrowing deduced by Slotboom and de Graaff. Different thicknesses of the p-layers in the investigated range ($0.3 \cdots 3$ μm) have turned out to be of minor importance.

The proportionality factor is about

$$\frac{j_n}{R_s} = 1.2 \cdot 10^{-3} \frac{A^2}{V \cdot cm^2} \quad \text{at} \quad 660 \text{ mV}, 25^\circ C$$

or, in terms of saturation current density,

$$\frac{(j_n)_{sat}}{R_s} = 8.4 \cdot 10^{-15} \frac{A^2}{V \cdot cm^2} \quad \text{at} \quad 25^\circ C.$$

Besides confirming the bandgap narrowing theory, our results are important for I^{2}L/MTL design and processing as they give a simple rule of thumb for predicting j_{nc} or j_{ni} and for relating j_n variations to process variations specified in terms of sheet resistances.

REFERENCES

[1] H. H. Berger, "The injection model—a structure oriented model for merged transistor logic (MTL)," IEEE J. Solid-State Circuits, vol. SC-9, pp. 218–227, Oct. 1974.
[2] R. C. Jaeger, "An evaluation of injection modeling," Solid-State Electron., vol. 19, pp. 639–643, July 1976.
[3] H. E. Wulms, "Base current of I^{2}L transistors," in ISSCC Dig. Tech. Papers, Feb. 1976, pp. 92–93.
[4] R. Mertens, "I^{2}L at low power levels," Summer Course on I^{2}L and Bipolar LSI, Katholieke Universiteit, Louvain, Belgium, June 1976, and private communication.
[5] J. J. Moll and I. M. Ross, "The dependence of transistor parameters on the distribution of base layer resistivity," Proc. IRE, vol. 44, pp. 72–78, Jan. 1956.
[6] A. B. Phillips, Transistor Engineering. New York: McGraw-Hill, 1962, p. 192.
[7] J. W. Slotboom and H. C. de Graaff, "Measurements of bandgap narrowing in Si bipolar transistors," Solid-State Electron., vol. 19, pp. 857–862, Oct. 1976.

Base Current of I²L Transistors

HENK E. J. WULMS

Abstract—For the I^2L n-p-n transistor, a method is presented which allows the base current to be split into various components: electron recombination current in the oxide- and metal-covered p-region, hole recombination current in the high doped n^+-regions of the emitter, and hole leakage current to the p-type substrate. This has been achieved by comparing, at a fixed emitter–base voltage, the base current of I^2L devices, different in geometry. Several precautions against parasitic effects are described.

The measurements have been carried out in the emitter–base voltage range of 540–650 mV, and so the various base current densities are shown as a function of the applied emitter–base voltage. Mathematical expressions are derived for the measured current densities and are compared with theory. It is demonstrated that bandgap narrowing effects in the heavily doped regions of the device have to be taken into account in order to explain the difference between experimental values and theory.

Furthermore, it is shown that the experimentally determined base current of a four-collector I^2L gate is in good agreement with the calculations. For such a gate, the electron recombination current is only 20 percent of the base current, and so the hole recombination current is the dominant contribution to the base current.

Manuscript received September 6, 1976; revised November 16, 1976.
The author is with Philips Research Laboratories, Eindhoven, The Netherlands.

LIST OF SYMBOLS

A_{base}	Base area of the I^2L transistor.
$A_{b\,metal}$	Base contact area.
A_{coll}	Collector area of the I^2L transistor.
α_i	Inverse current amplification factor of p-n-p injector.
β_{up}	Common emitter current gain of I^2L transistor.
d	Mask distance between base diffusion and deep n^+-collar.
D_n	Diffusion constant of electrons.
i_b	Base current of I^2L transistor.
$i_{b\,metal}$	Electron recombination current in the base contact region.
i_{bn}	Electron recombination current in p-type base.
i_{b0}	$i_b - i_{recol}$.
i_{b0}^*	$i_{b0} - i_{b\,sub}$.
$i_{b\,ox}$	Electron recombination current in the oxide-covered base.
i_{bp}	Hole recombination current in the n^+-emitter regions.
i_{recol}	Recollection current to the injector.

Reprinted from *IEEE J. Solid-State Circuits*, vol. SC-12, pp. 143–150, Apr. 1977.

144

$i_{b\,\mathrm{sub}}$	Hole leakage current to the p-type substrate.
i_c	Collector current of vertical p-n-p transistor.
$j_{b\,\mathrm{metal}}$	Current density in the base contact region.
$j_{b\,\mathrm{metal}}(0)$	Extrapolated $j_{b\,\mathrm{metal}}$ at $V_{BE} = 0$ V.
$j_{b\,\mathrm{ox}}$	Current density in the oxide-covered base region.
$j_{b\,\mathrm{ox}}(0)$	Extrapolated $j_{b\,\mathrm{ox}}$ at $V_{BE} = 0$ V.
j_{bp}	Current density in the n^+-emitter regions.
$j_{bp}(0)$	Extrapolated j_{bp} at $V_{BE} = 0$ V.
$j_{b\,\mathrm{sub}}$	Hole current density to the p-type substrate.
$j_{b\,\mathrm{sub}}(0)$	Extrapolated $j_{b\,\mathrm{sub}}$ at $V_{BE} = 0$ V.
k	Boltzmann's constant.
m	Junction emission coefficient.
μ_n	Mobility of electrons.
μ_p	Mobility of holes.
N_{A0}	Acceptor concentration in p-region at the surface.
N_D	Donor concentration in buried layer.
N_{epi}	Donor concentration in n-type epitaxial layer.
n_i	Intrinsic carrier concentration ($1.58 \cdot 10^{10}$ cm^{-3}).
$\int N_A\,dx$	Integral base dope beside collector region.
q	Electron charge ($1.6 \cdot 10^{-19}$ C).
$R_\square$	Sheet resistance of buried layer.
s	Recombination velocity.
s_{eff}	Effective recombination velocity.
T	Temperature in degrees Kelvin.
V_{BE}	Emitter-base junction voltage of I^{2}L transistor.
w	Thickness of buried layer.

I. INTRODUCTION

SINCE the presentation of integrated injection logic (I^{2}L) [1], [2], several investigations have been conducted into the modeling of I^{2}L gates or the behavior of inverse operating n-p-n transistors, as is the case in I^{2}L gates [3]–[5].

At a moderate current level, in conventional n-p-n transistors the base current consists of recombination of electrons in the base and recombination of holes in the emitter. However, in n-p-n transistors of present-day manufacture, the latter is the dominant component [6], [7].

In I^{2}L gates, the conventional n-p-n transistor operates upside down; this changes the impurity concentration in emitter, base, and collector regions and the ratio of the emitter-collector area, which consequently affects the electrical characteristics. But, in principle, the same recombination mechanisms as mentioned for the conventional n-p-n transistor determine the base current of the I^{2}L transistor. In I^{2}L literature, however, conflicting conclusions are drawn concerning the component which is the dominant factor in the base current. For example, in [3] the statement is made that the main contribution is due to electron recombination, whereas in [4] and [5] the opposite conclusion is drawn, namely, that hole recombination, on which emitter efficiency depends, is dominant.

In order to bring more clarity to the situation, a further investigation has been made with the aid of a specially designed test chip. This paper reports on the measurement results and conclusions with this test chip. The chip contains 33 I^{2}L n-p-n transistors, each of different geometry. By comparing the base current of different geometries, determined at the same emitter-base and collector-base voltages, the contribution of each component can be determined. The measurement procedure is described. It is also indicated which transistor types are compared in order to find the electron recombination current densities in the oxide- and metal-covered p-region and the hole recombination current density in the n^+-emitter regions. Furthermore, this procedure is applied for different values of the emitter-base voltage in determining the voltage dependency of the current densities. Each density is represented by a mathematical expression making the measuring results suitable for modeling purposes. These expressions are compared with theoretical formulas.

Finally, for a four-collector I^{2}L gate, the experimentally found base currents are compared with the calculated values.

II. DEVICE STRUCTURE

A practical I^{2}L gate consists of a multicollector n-p-n transistor and a lateral p-n-p transistor as current source. As has been reported previously [2], [5], the base current of an I^{2}L transistor must be measured with the emitter-base junction of the p-n-p injector short-circuited. This is illustrated in Fig. 1 and we can conclude that i_{b0}, the base current of the n-p-n transistor itself, equals the measured current i_b at the base terminal minus i_{recol}, the recollection current to the injector. The current i_{recol} is due to the forward-biased collector-base junction of the p-n-p transistor. Making the assumption that all recombination currents in the collector and base region of the p-n-p transistor can be considered as a contribution to i_{b0}, then i_{recol} can be measured separately as a terminal current. This is also illustrated in Fig. 1.

If

$$\alpha_i = \frac{i_{\mathrm{recol}}}{i_b} \tag{1}$$

it is easily found that

$$\frac{1}{i_b} = \frac{1}{i_{b0}}(1 - \alpha_i). \tag{2}$$

Fig. 1 shows (2) in graphical form (drawn line) and also illustrates that the experiments are in good accord with the equa-

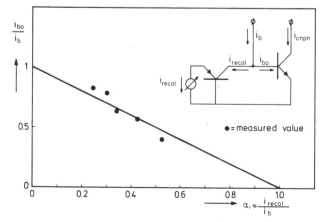

Fig. 1. Normalized reciprocal base current i_{b0}/i_b versus α_i of lateral p-n-p transistor. ($V_{BE} = 600$ mV and $i_{b0} = 270$ nA.)

tion. The variation of α_i has been obtained by changing the base width of the lateral p-n-p transistor (6-14 µm). In this way, characterization of the recollection current for a certain technology can be easily made.

In this paper we concentrate on i_{b0} which consists of recombination currents and substrate leakage current only. Therefore, the various transistors on the test chip were designed without an injector ($i_{recol} = 0$), thus allowing the components of i_{b0} to be determined, and afterwards the influence of the injector added with the aid of the characterization shown in Fig. 1.

The test structure used in this investigation is an n-p-n structure as in Fig. 2. A deep n⁺-collar is used to improve the β_{up} of the n-p-n transistor [1] and to provide contact with the buried layer which acts as an emitter. The dimensions of base and collector regions are not comparable with practical I²L gates, as can be seen in Fig. 3, but it should be emphasized that these structures have been designed to allow the base current to be split into its various components. Referring to Fig. 2, the base current i_{b0} here consists of the following components.

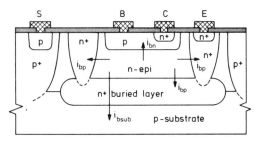

Fig. 2. Cross-sectional view of I²L transistor. The base current consists of three components: 1) electron recombination in the p-type base region (i_{bn}), 2) hole recombination in n⁺-emitter regions (i_{bp}), 3) leakage current to the substrate ($i_{b\,sub}$).

1) i_{bn} electron current in the p-type base region. It will be shown that i_{bn} can be further split into i_{box}, the recombination current in the oxide-covered base region, and $i_{b\,metal}$, the recombination current at the base contact.

2) i_{bp} hole recombination current in the deep n⁺-collar and in the n⁺-buried layer.

3) $i_{b\,sub}$ hole leakage current to the p-type substrate, due to the vertical parasitic p-n-p transistor.

Here it is assumed that recombination in the intrinsic base, the base region which is situated under the n⁺-collector, and volume recombination in the epitaxial layer may be disregarded [8]. Extra confirmation of the latter part of this assumption is seen in the fact that, as experiments have shown, the reciprocal current $1/i_{recol}$ is linearly proportional to the base width of the lateral p-n-p transistor, varying between 6 and 14 µm.

The hole current to the substrate ($i_{b\,sub}$) was measured separately and subtracted from i_{b0}. We therefore introduce $i_{b0}^* = i_{b0} - i_{b\,sub}$; consequently, i_{b0}^* consists of only $i_{bn} + i_{bp}$, which can be determined separately by comparing structures different in geometry.

The test devices were manufactured in a standard process: an n-type epitaxial layer of 0.3 Ω · cm and 8 µm thickness, 200 Ω/□ for the base region and 2.5 and 1.9 µm junction depth for the base and shallow n⁺-collector regions, respectively. The sheet resistance of the buried layer is 20 Ω/□. Concerning the process, the following observations must be made. In Fig. 4 two nearly identical configurations A and B are compared, the difference being that in configuration A, only a small part of the oxide-covered base region is covered by interconnection patterns, whereas in configuration B, nearly the entire region is so covered. Sizes of contact holes and all n- and p-regions are exactly the same.

Measuring the base currents of devices manufactured in a conventional way gives different values for the configurations A and B, indicating that the interconnecting metal does influence the base current (Fig. 4). However, in another part of

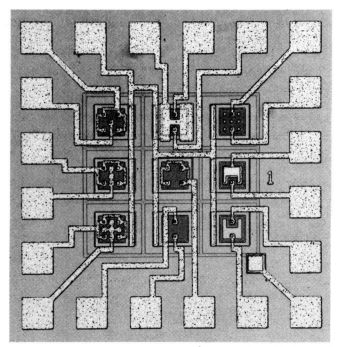

Fig. 3. Chip photomicrograph of some I²L test devices. Bonding pad dimensions are 100×100 µm².

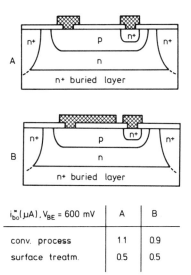

i_{b0}^*(µA), V_{BE} = 600 mV	A	B
conv. process	1.1	0.9
surface treatm.	0.5	0.5

Fig. 4. Influence on the base current of aluminum interconnecting patterns on top of the I²L device. Values are indicated for two ways of processing, one being the conventional and the other that in which an extra surface treatment is applied.

the same batch, where a special surface treatment was applied, the currents were found to be identical but lower than in the conventional process. This is due to the formation of active hydrogen at the Si–SiO$_2$ interface during this surface treatment, which decreases the number of recombination centers considerably [9], [10]. The conclusion is obvious: only devices which have undergone a proper surface treatment may be compared; otherwise, there is an unwanted influence introduced by the aluminum interconnections on top of the devices.

III. MEASUREMENT PROCEDURE

To ensure that the measured currents were representative for the whole batch, about 200 chips from each wafer were measured to eliminate statistical variations. Thus, all data (each measuring point) presented in this paper represent the mean value of 200 measurements. These measurements were performed with the aid of computer-controlled measuring equipment. During the measurements, upper and lower current boundaries were introduced to eliminate short circuits and open connections. Furthermore, pulsed measurements were carried out so as to avoid temperature effects.

It can be shown that even the position of the transistor on the test chip influences the base current. Referring then to Fig. 3, the photomicrograph of part of the test chip shows transistors arranged in a matrix of 3 × 3. Since the emitter contact is made on only one side of the transistor, not all positions in this matrix are identical with respect to the gettering effect of the phosphorus in the emitter contact. This gettering effect influences a limited area. It is illustrated by the fact that for identical devices situated in different positions of the matrix, not the same base current is measured, the central position, for example, being more favorable (lower base current) than the edge positions. Therefore, for the measurements described in this paper, only devices situated in identical positions of the matrix are compared with each other.

IV. EXPERIMENTAL RESULTS

First the measurement procedure for a fixed V_{BE} = 600 mV is discussed. The voltage dependency of the current densities is treated in the following section.

Electron Recombination Current in the Oxide-Covered Base Region

Fig. 5 shows a cross-sectional view of some of the I^{2}L structures which have been used to determine the electron recombination current in the oxide-covered base region (i_{box}). The size of the n$^+$-collector area (A_{coll}) is increased, the oxide-covered base area thus being decreased by the same amount. As all other dimensions are identical, it may be assumed that $i_{b\,metal}$ and i_{bp} are the same for these devices. Thus, an observed difference in i_{b0}^* is a measure of i_{box}.

The results are plotted in Fig. 6 (drawn curves) where i_{b0}^* is shown versus A_{coll}/A_{base} (A_{base} is base area). Fig. 6 gives the results for three transistor types with d as a parameter. This parameter d, which is indicated in Fig. 5, is the distance on the masks between the base diffusion and the deep n$^+$-collar.

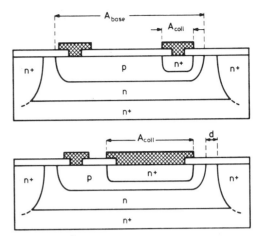

Fig. 5. Some of the I^{2}L structures used to determine the electron recombination current in the oxide-covered base region. d is the distance on the masks between the base diffusion and the deep n$^+$-collar.

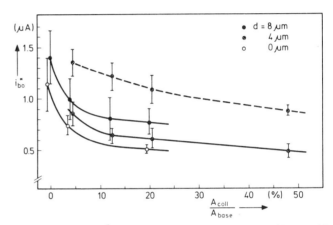

Fig. 6. Base current i_{b0}^* versus relative collector area A_{coll}/A_{base} with d as parameter. Drawn curves = extra surface treatment; dashed curve = conventional process. Measuring points and standard deviations are indicated.

The current density j_{box} can be determined from Fig. 6 in that part of the graph where the slope is constant (A_{coll}/A_{base} > 10 percent) because

$$j_{box} = \left| \frac{\partial i_{b0}^*}{\partial A_{coll}} \right|_{A_{base} = const.} \qquad (3)$$

For V_{BE} = 600 mV and taking into account the actual device geometries, one finds

$$j_{box} \approx 4 \text{ mA/cm}^2.$$

Three additional observations must be made with respect to Fig. 6. These are the following.

1) The curves show clearly that a comparison between a structure *without* and one *with* a collector (e.g., A_{coll}/A_{base} = 0 and A_{coll}/A_{base} = 10 percent) results in a higher value for j_{box} than given above. This is caused by the fact that the structure without a collector shows an extra high value of i_{b0}^* because there is no gettering effect of the collector.

2) Influence of the aluminum patterns. The drawn curves show the results for the devices processed with the extra surface treatment. The dashed curve shows the results for de-

vices from the same batch, but here the surface treatment has not been applied. As was shown in Fig. 4, the current i_{b0}^* is higher. This is also shown in Fig. 6, but here it can be seen that the slope of $j_{b\,ox}$ is steeper also. This is caused by the fact that the aluminum area on top of the transistor increases with increasing A_{coll}, resulting in a sharper decrease of i_{b0}^*.

3) Finally, it can be concluded from Fig. 6 that the hole recombination current is important. If d increases, then identical p-regions are situated in n-type pockets of increasing size. Because the p-regions are identical, current i_{bn} is the same for all configurations. Hence, the observed increase of i_{b0}^* is due to the increase of i_{bp}. Confirmation of this conclusion will be given later.

Electron Recombination Current in the Metal-Covered Base Region

Fig. 7 shows some of the structures used to determine the electron recombination current in the metal-covered base region (base contact): $i_{b\,metal}$. In the comparison, only the size of the base contact area $A_{b\,metal}$ is changed and so the variations of i_{b0}^* are a measure of $i_{b\,metal}$.

The drawn curve of Fig. 8 shows a linear increase of i_{b0}^* with $A_{b\,metal}$. However, if A_{base} is constant and $A_{b\,metal}$ increases,

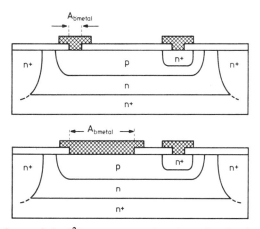

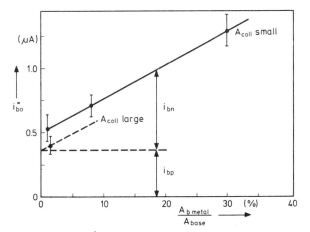

Fig. 7. Some of the I²L structures used to determine the electron recombination current in the metal-covered base region (base contact).

Fig. 8. Base current i_{b0}^* versus the relative base contact area $A_{b\,metal}/A_{base}$ for a small and a large collector area A_{coll}. Intersection with the Y-axis gives the hole recombination current i_{bp}. Measuring points and standard deviations are indicated.

the oxide-covered base area decreases by the same amount. So the increase of i_{b0}^* is caused by an increase of $i_{b\,metal}$ and a decrease of $i_{b\,ox}$.

The recombination current density at the base contact ($j_{b\,metal}$) can be determined from

$$j_{b\,metal} - j_{b\,ox} = \left| \frac{\partial i_{b0}^*}{\partial A_{b\,metal}} \right|_{\substack{A_{coll} \\ A_{base}} = const.} \quad (4)$$

From the actual device geometries, Fig. 8, and $j_{b\,ox} \approx 4$ mA/cm², it is determined that for $V_{BE} = 600$ mV

$$j_{b\,metal} \approx 40 \text{ mA/cm}^2.$$

Hole Recombination Current in n⁺-Emitter Regions

Fig. 8 can be used to determine the hole recombination current in the heavily doped parts of the emitter region (i_{bp}). Using a very large collector area A_{coll}, i.e., the dashed line in Fig. 8, the current $i_{b\,ox}$ can be ignored because $j_{b\,ox}$ is small and the oxide-covered base area is also very small. The current $i_{b\,metal}$, caused by the base contact, can be eliminated from i_{b0}^* by extrapolating the dashed curve until it intersects the Y-axis. The resulting current component is then i_{bp} which is constant for all devices simply because the emitter configuration is identical. So, for each device configuration, current i_{b0}^* can be split into an electron and a hole recombination part. Making the assumption that j_{bp}, the hole recombination current density, is the same in both the n⁺-collar (sidewall) and in the n⁺-buried layer (bottom), it can be found from Fig. 8 and the actual devices geometries that at $V_{BE} = 600$ mV

$$j_{bp} \approx 3.5 \text{ mA/cm}^2.$$

The structures on the test chip, however, were unsuitable for splitting i_{bp} into a sidewall and bottom component since devices with different bottom and sidewall areas were not available.

V. COMPARISON WITH THEORY

So far, the experimental results have been based upon measurements carried out with a fixed $V_{BE} = 600$ mV. In order to make the results suitable for modeling purposes, however, it is necessary to determine the current–voltage characteristic for the various current densities discussed. Expressions can then be derived which fit with the experimental results and a comparison with bipolar transistor theory can be made.

The procedure as described for $V_{BE} = 600$ mV was repeated for $V_{BE} = 540$ and 650 mV, covering the practical range of interest. Higher values for V_{BE} were not used. This was to ensure that the high current densities did not affect the measurements by parasitic voltage drops due to series resistances.

The results are summarized in Fig. 9 showing the current densities versus V_{BE}, in a semi-logarithmic plot.

Metal-Covered p-Region

By curve fitting it can be determined from Fig. 9 that the electron recombination current density can be expressed as

$$j_{b\,metal} = j_{b\,metal}(0) \{ \exp(qV_{BE}/kT) - 1 \} \quad (5)$$

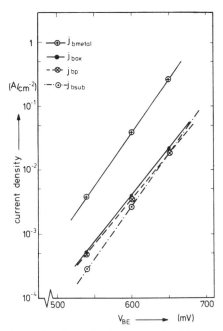

Fig. 9. Experimentally determined current densities of the various components of the base current versus the applied V_{BE}.

with

$$j_{b\,\text{metal}}(0) = 3.8 \cdot 10^{-12}\ \text{A/cm}^2$$

found by extrapolating the relevant curve of Fig. 9 until its intersection with the Y-axis at $V_{BE} = 0$ V. According to [11], one can derive

$$j_{b\,\text{metal}}(0) = \frac{qn_i^2 D_n}{\int N_A\, dx}. \tag{6}$$

In deriving (6), the simplifications are made that D_n is independent of the dope N_A. Bulk recombination effects in the p-region are ignored and an infinite recombination velocity is assumed at the metal contact. Substitution in (6) of $\int N_A\, dx = 3.8 \cdot 10^{14}$ cm^{-2}, $n_i^2 = 1.49 \cdot 10^{20}$ cm^{-6}, and $D_n = 6.5$ cm^2/s gives $j_{b\,\text{metal}}(0) = 0.41 \cdot 10^{-12}$ A/cm^2.

The large difference between this theoretical value and the experimentally determined value can be explained by bandgap narrowing effects in the high doped part of the p-region [12]. The actual dope concentration at the base contact is $3 \cdot 10^{18}$/cm^3. According to [12], n_i^2 increases for this concentration by a factor of 9. The theoretical value of $j_{b\,\text{metal}}$ (0) is then exactly the same as the experimentally determined value. If $j_{b\,\text{metal}}$ in Fig. 9 is extrapolated to 705 mV, one obtains $j_{b\,\text{metal}} = 3$ A/cm^2. Earlier reports [3] and [13] give for this current density 4.6 and 1 A/cm^2, respectively.

Oxide-Covered p-Region

From the current densities shown in Fig. 9, it follows that the electron recombination current density in the oxide-covered base region can be represented by

$$j_{b\,\text{ox}} = j_{b\,\text{ox}}(0)\ \{\exp(qV_{BE}/mkT) - 1\} \tag{7}$$

where $j_{b\,\text{ox}}(0) = 5.9 \cdot 10^{-12}$ A/cm^2 and $m = 1.12$.

It is not easy to derive a theoretical expression for this component of the base current because several contributions to

the recombination mechanism must be implemented: bandgap narrowing [12], oxide charge [13], and a finite value for the recombination velocity s at the Si–SiO$_2$ interface. However, all these effects can be taken into account by introducing an effective recombination velocity s_{eff} at the Si–SiO$_2$ interface:

$$j_{b\,\text{ox}}(0) = \frac{qn_i^2\, s_{\text{eff}}}{N_{A0}}. \tag{8}$$

Taking $j_{b\,\text{ox}}$ (0) = $5.9 \cdot 10^{-12}$ A/cm^2 and $N_{A0} = 3 \cdot 10^{18}$/cm^3, one obtains $s_{\text{eff}} = 7.5 \cdot 10^5$ cm/s. It must be emphasized that this very high value of s_{eff} is due to bandgap narrowing effects and oxide charge. However, the fact that $j_{b\,\text{ox}}$ (0) is determined by extrapolating the measured current density to $V_{BE} = 0$ V gives a further increase of s_{eff}. This is caused by the nonideal diode characteristic ($m = 1.12$) of this base current component. Comparing the measured $j_{b\,\text{ox}}$ of Fig. 9 with the literature, the value is seen to be in good agreement with [13] at 500 mV and much lower than reported in [3] at 705 mV. This disagreement may be due to differences in surface treatment.

Heavily Doped Parts of Emitter Region

The hole recombination current density can be represented according to Fig. 9 by

$$j_{bp} = j_{bp}(0)\ \{\exp(qV_{BE}/mkT) - 1\} \tag{9}$$

with

$$j_{bp}(0) = 10^{-11}\ \text{A/cm}^2\quad \text{and}\quad m = 1.15.$$

Introducing

$$j_{bp}(0) = \frac{qn_i^2\, s_{\text{eff}}}{N_{\text{epi}}} \tag{10}$$

and taking $N_{\text{epi}} = 2.5 \cdot 10^{16}$/cm^3, one obtains $s_{\text{eff}} = 10^4$ cm/s.

Such a high value of s_{eff} has been reported earlier [8], [14], while in [15] a lower value is given. The here determined high value of s_{eff} is due to its definition in (10) and the nonideal diode characteristic ($m = 1.15$). However, if j_{bp} in Fig. 9 is extrapolated to 705 mV, one obtains $j_{bp} = 0.135$ A/cm^2 which is very close to 0.14 and 0.1 A/cm^2, the values given in [3] and [13], respectively. It must be noted, however, that in [3] and [13] an n$^+$-substrate has been used, this in contrast with the n$^+$-buried layer and p-type substrate used in this investigation. Furthermore, in the literature where low values of s_{eff} are reported, it has been assumed that the current density concerned has the ideal diode characteristic. Fig. 9 and earlier reports [8], [13], however, clearly show this assumption to be unjustified. This implies that the value of s_{eff} determined from (10) depends strongly on the factor m in (9).

Substrate

Now all components of i_{b0}^* have been determined. Because $i_{b0}^* = i_{b0} - i_{b\,\text{sub}}$, the leakage current density to the substrate ($j_{b\,\text{sub}}$) is the last contribution to i_{b0} to be discussed. Current $i_{b\,\text{sub}}$ was measured separately and can be treated as the collector current of the parasitic vertical p-n-p transistor. From

Fig. 9, one can derive

$$j_{b\,\text{sub}} = j_{b\,\text{sub}}(0)\{\exp(qV_{BE}/kT) - 1\} \qquad (11)$$

where $j_{b\,\text{sub}}(0) = 3.2 \cdot 10^{-13}$ A/cm².

Due to the fact that the low doped parts of the buried layer do not contribute to either the i_c of the p-n-p or to $R_\square$ of the buried layer, the buried layer is simplified to a homogeneously doped region with dope N_D and thickness w. Then

$$j_{b\,\text{sub}}(0) = \frac{qn_i^2(kT/q)\mu_p}{N_D w} \qquad (12)$$

$$\frac{1}{R_\square} = q\mu_n N_D w. \qquad (13)$$

Consequently,

$$j_{b\,\text{sub}}(0) = q^2 n_i^2 (kT/q) R_\square \mu_n \mu_p. \qquad (14)$$

Substitution of $R_\square = 20$ Ω, $\mu_p = 37$ V · s/cm², and $\mu_n = 148$ V · s/cm² in (14) results in

$$j_{b\,\text{sub}}(0) = 1.1\,10^{-14} \text{ A/cm}^2.$$

Comparing this theoretical value with the experimentally determined value, one finds disagreement by a factor ≈ 25. The dope concentration in the buried layer is $N_D = 10^{19}$/cm³. Calculating according to [12] the bandgap narrowing for this dope concentration, one finds an effective increase of n_i^2 of 25 times. Theory and experiment are, therefore, in good agreement.

VI. PRACTICAL DEVICE GEOMETRY

Until now, the devices on the test chip have been used to determine the current–voltage characteristic of the various base current densities. Measurements on structures which have not been used for the above-mentioned purposes can be used to compare calculations and measurements. For this aim, a four-collector I²L gate has been used.

Fig. 9 shows the current densities. Multiplication of these calculated values by their respective areas in the four-collector gate results in the base current components. Addition of these components gives the calculated i_{b0} which is compared with the measured value. These results are summarized in Table I. It can be concluded from Table I that a good agreement exists between the calculations and the experiments. The expressions derived for the base current components can therefore be used to predict the base current of other configurations in the e–b voltage range of 540–650 mV. Furthermore, the contribution of $i_{b\,\text{metal}}$ for a practical configuration is negligible (<8 percent) in spite of the high current density. Current $i_{b\,\text{ox}}$ is about 15 percent of i_{b0} and the main contribution is due to i_{bp} (45–55 percent) and $i_{b\,\text{sub}}$ (25–35 percent). In general, the electron recombination current ($i_{b\,\text{metal}} + i_{b\,\text{ox}}$) for this I²L gate is 20 percent and the hole current ($i_{bp} + i_{b\,\text{sub}}$) is 80 percent of i_{b0}.

Table I also shows the influence of the injector on i_b. In these experiments, N_{epi} is relatively high, resulting in a low value of i_{recol}. However, for low values of N_{epi}, the current i_{recol} becomes an important part of i_b.

TABLE I
BASE CURRENT COMPONENTS OF A FOUR-COLLECTOR I²L GATE AS A FUNCTION OF THE APPLIED V_{BE}

V_{BE} (mV)	540		600		650	
	I²L gate (nA)	% of i_{b0}	I²L gate (nA)	% of i_{b0}	I²L gate (/uA)	% of i_{b0}
$i_{b\text{metal}}$	2.4	5	25	6	0.17	7
$i_{b\text{ox}}$	7.9	15	62	15	0.31	14
i_{bp}	28.6	56	202	50	1.06	45
$i_{b\text{sub}}$	12.4	24	119	29	0.80	34
i_{b0} (calculated)	51.3	100	408	100	2.34	100
i_{b0} (measured)	50		397		2.13	
i_{recol} (measured)	13.5		143		0.87	

$$i_{b0} = i_{b\text{metal}} + i_{b\text{ox}} + i_{bp} + i_{b\text{sub}}$$
$$i_b = i_{b0} + i_{\text{recol}}$$

VII. CONCLUSIONS

This paper has considered the base current of an I²L transistor. A special test chip has been designed with I²L structures different in geometry. The influence of the injector, phosphorus gettering, statistical variations, and aluminum interconnections on top of the structure have been eliminated.

By comparing i_{b0} of the devices at a fixed V_{BE}, current i_{b0} can be split into various components. For all these components, current densities are given as a function of V_{BE} in the practical range of interest (540–650 mV). By curve fitting, expressions have been derived for these current densities which have been compared with theory.

For $i_{b\,\text{metal}}$ and $i_{b\,\text{sub}}$, bandgap narrowing effects are taken into account according to [12]. In calculation of the bandgap narrowing using the actual dope concentrations, the intrinsic concentration n_i^2 increases by a factor of 9 and 25, respectively, and a very good agreement between theory and experiment is then found to exist.

Currents $i_{b\,\text{ox}}$ and i_{bp} show a deviation from the ideal diode characteristic ($m = 1.12$ and 1.15, respectively) which is in agreement with earlier reported measurements. These nonideal diode characteristics result in high values for s_{eff}, with $7.5\ 10^5$ and 10^4 cm/s for $i_{b\,\text{ox}}$ and i_{bp}, respectively. It has been shown that in the case of a nonideal diode characteristic, s_{eff} cannot be determined by a measurement at a fixed V_{BE} because s_{eff} is strongly dependent on the junction emission coefficient m.

Comparison of the measured and calculated i_{b0} reveals good agreement. For a practical I²L gate, it has been found that electron recombination is only 20 percent, but hole current is 80 percent of i_{b0}. This is due mainly to differences between the areas concerned because $j_{b\,ox}$, j_{bp}, and $j_{b\,sub}$ are about equal.

With the expressions derived for the base current components, one can predict the base current of other I^2L configurations produced by the same manufacturing process as used here.

ACKNOWLEDGMENT

The author wishes to thank A. Schmitz for processing the wafers and W. A. Jurgens for measurement assistance.

REFERENCES

[1] K. Hart and A. Slob, "Integrated injection logic: A new approach to L.S.I.," *IEEE J. Solid-State Circuits*, vol. SC-7, pp. 346–351, Oct. 1972.

[2] H. H. Berger and S. K. Wiedmann, "Merged-transistor logic (MTL)—A low-cost bipolar concept," *IEEE J. Solid-State Circuits*, vol. SC-7, pp. 340–346, Oct. 1972.

[3] H. H. Berger, "The injection model—A structure-oriented model for merged transistor logic (MTL)," *IEEE J. Solid-State Circuits*, vol. SC-9, pp. 218–227, Oct. 1974.

[4] A. Schmitz and A. Slob, "The effect of isolation regions on the current gain of inverse n-p-n transistors used in integrated injection logic (I^2L)," in *Dig. Int. Electron Devices Meeting*, Washington, DC, Dec. 1974, pp. 508–510.

[5] F. M. Klaassen, "Device physics of integrated injection logic," *IEEE Trans. Electron Devices*, vol. ED-22, pp. 145–152, Mar. 1975.

[6] D. P. Kennedy and P. C. Murley, "Minority carrier injection characteristics of the diffused emitter junction," *IRE Trans. Electron Devices*, vol. ED-9, pp. 136–142, Mar. 1962.

[7] H. C. de Graaff and J. W. Slotboom, "Some aspects of LEC transistor behaviour," *Solid-State Electron.*, vol. 19, pp. 809–814, Sept. 1976.

[8] R. W. Dutton and R. J. Whittier, "Forward current-voltage and switching characteristics of p^+-n-n^+ (epitaxial) diodes," *IEEE Trans. Electron Devices*, vol. ED-16, pp. 458–467, May 1969.

[9] J. Olmstead, J. Scott, and P. Kuznetzoff, "Hydrogen-induced surface space-charge regions in oxide-protected silicon," *IEEE Trans. Electron Devices*, vol. ED-12, pp. 104–107, Mar. 1965.

[10] P. L. Castro and B. E. Deal, "Low temperature reduction of fast surface states associated with thermally oxidized silicon," *J. Electrochem. Soc.*, vol. 118, p. 280, 1971.

[11] A. B. Phillips, Transistor Engineering. New York: McGraw-Hill, 1962, p. 192.

[12] J. W. Slotboom and H. C. de Graaff, "Measurements of bandgap narrowing in Si bipolar transistors," *Solid-State Electron.*, vol. 19, pp. 857–862, Oct. 1976.

[13] R. Mertens, "I^2L at low power levels," Summer course on I^2L and bipolar LSI, Katholieke Universiteit Leuven, Louvain, Belgium, June 1976.

[14] D. L. Scharfetter, "Minority carrier injection and charge storage in epitaxial Schottky barrier diodes," *Solid-State Electron.*, vol. 8, pp. 299–311, 1965.

[15] S. Chou, "An investigation of lateral transistors—D.C. characteristics," *Solid-State Electron.*, vol. 14, pp. 811–826, 1972.

Characteristics of I²L at Low Current Levels

WALTER H. MATTHEUS, ROBERT P. MERTENS, AND JAN D. STULTING

Abstract—The validity of the injection model is assessed in the low power range. Experimental evidence is given that the three base current components (I_{nc}, I_{no}, and I_p) can be determined from a three-gate experiment. The results are explained from the underlying device physics. Experimental data are presented for the temperature dependence of the upward current gain.

I. INTRODUCTION

THERE are several papers [1]–[5] in the technical literature dealing with the problem of upward current gain in I²L devices but only base–emitter voltages equal to or higher than 600 mV have been extensively considered. However, an important area for the application of I²L is battery operated logic with the digital watch circuits as the most outstanding example. To be competitive in that area with complementary MOS, I²L must operate safely down into the nanoampere current levels and over an extended temperature range.

The aim of this paper is to characterize the upward current gain in the low current range, to investigate its temperature dependence, and to determine which mechanisms are responsible for the observed behavior. The paper proceeds as follows. In a first section, the validity of Berger's injection model [1] is assessed in view of the results obtained by Wulms [4]. A second section is devoted to the description of the obtained results for the different current components. The third section describes the influence of the low temperature annealing step. Agreement between theoretical calculations and the observed current values is investigated in a next section. The temperature

Manuscript received January 3, 1977; revised May 20, 1977.
W. H. Mattheus and R. P. Mertens are with the E.S.A.T., Departement Elektrotechniek, Katholieke Universitiet Leuven, B3030 Heverlee, Belgium.
J. D. Stulting is with the South African Council for Scientific and Industrial Research.

dependence of the upward current gain is described next, and a final section is devoted to the main conclusions of the paper.

II. ASSESSMENT OF THE INJECTION MODEL

Berger's injection model [1] and its associated test pattern are based on the assumption that the intrinsic properties of the base region, such as the minority carrier lifetime and the surface recombination velocity underneath the oxide, are identical for the three gates in the pattern. Wulms [4] demonstrated that, for his test pattern, the absence of a collector in the base strongly increased the base current. When plotting the base current as a function of the ratio of the collector to base area, for I²L gates with identical base areas, he found a nonlinear curve. The base current increased strongly when no collector was present. The explanation was that the gate without collector was not influenced by the gettering action of the collector diffusion and that the corresponding lifetime in that gate would be lower than for the other gates.

To assess these statements, we designed a new test mask consisting of nine I²L gates with identical base geometries but with a different number of collectors and a different metal or oxide base top coverage (Fig. 1). As proposed by Wulms [4], no injector is present, since the back injected current from the base to the injector can be measured independently. The important difference from the pattern used by Wulms is that our test pattern consists of I²L gates as far as layout is concerned, whereas Wulms' test pattern consisted of upward operating transistors with much larger base dimensions. The pattern originally defined by Berger consisted of three gates (numbers 7, 8, 9 of Fig. 1). Before describing the measured results on our test pattern, we will define the different base current components present in an I²L gate (Fig. 2). We choose the notation used by Berger in his injection model [1]. The different components are

Reprinted from *IEEE Trans. Electron Devices*, vol. ED-24, pp. 1228–1233, Oct. 1977.

152

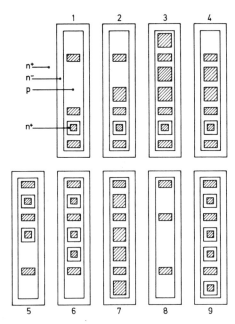

Fig. 1. Test pattern used to determine different base current components.

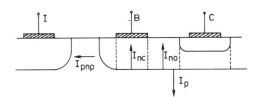

Fig. 2. Different components of base current in an I²L gate.

I_{pnp}: the back injected current from the base to the injector;

I_{nc}: the electron current injected underneath the base contact;

I_{no}: the electron current injected into the oxide covered base region;

I_p: the remaining part of the base current, which consists of a hole current injected into the n-n⁺ substrate and the recombination currents in the bulk and surface base–emitter space charge layer. The reason to take the three components together into a single current I_p has no theoretical background, since they are related to different loss mechanisms. The experimental pattern shown in Fig. 1, does not allow to make a direct distinction between these three components.

Since I_{pnp} can be measured independently, three gates with different collector–base area ratios and top metal coverage theoretically suffice to determine the three other base current components. To assess the statement made by Wulms [4], we used 5 test gates (with identical metal top coverage, but with a number of collectors equal, respectively, to 0, 1, 2, 3, and 4, corresponding to gates 8, 1, 5, 6, 9 of Fig. 1) to determine I_{no}, the electron current injected into the oxide covered base. The measured base currents

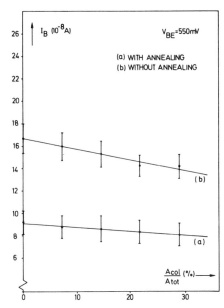

Fig. 3. Base current as a function of the collector to base area ratio (V_{BE} = 550 mV).

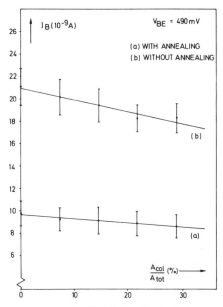

Fig. 4. Base current as a function of the collector to base area ratio (V_{BE} = 490 mV).

for these devices are given in Figs. 3 and 4, for two different V_{BE} values and for different surface annealing treatments. They are given as a function of the relative collector to base area. The points are average values obtained from, typically, 15 measurements. To exclude all processing variations, the processing runs have been repeated three times. The vertical segments represent the 95-percent confidence limits of the measurements. The important conclusion from these experimental data is that for our devices a straight line dependence is found and that all gates have been gettered by the phosphorous diffusion in an identical way. Our measured results thus differ from those reported by Wulms [4]. In our opinion, the explanation probably lies in the fact that the test patterns used by Wulms, are not typical for an I²L gate as far as area is concerned, since the

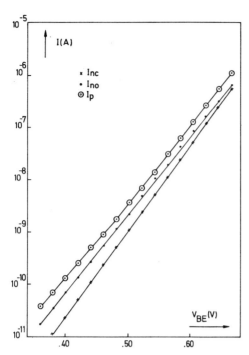

Fig. 5. Different base current components as a function of V_{BE} for an I²L gate with four collectors.

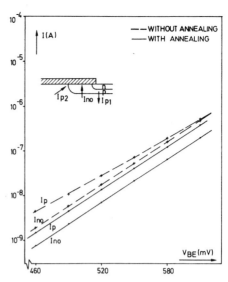

Fig. 6. Influence of an additional annealing on the nonideal base current components. Measurement on an I²L gate surrounded with deep isolation.

distance between the center of the base and the surrounding n⁺ collar is typically 80 µm. In our devices, the base width is only 30 µm, which is typical for 10-µm line width technology. Every point in the base in within 20 µm of the surrounding n⁺ collar. The small distance between the n⁺ collar and the base, makes all base islands in an actual I²L device being gettered in an identical way. For these devices the test pattern originally defined by Berger yields meaningful results. The slope of the straight lines allows us to determine I_{no} in a reliable way.

III. THE DIFFERENT CURRENT COMPONENTS AS A FUNCTION OF V_{BE}

By repeating the same measurements at other V_{BE} values we can determine $I_{no}(V_{BE})$. In the same manner of Wulms [4], by plotting the base current as a function of the top metal coverage for different voltages, we can determine the electron current I_{nc} injected underneath the metal covered base. The current injected back to the injector can be determined independently. The remaining current then is the current I_p, representing different losses: injection in the n-n⁺ and recombination in the bulk and surface space charge region, respectively.

The three base current components are plotted in Fig. 5 as a function of the base–emitter voltage. These refer to an I²L gate with a fan-out 4. The devices have been fabricated on an n-n⁺ substrate (2×10^{16} cm⁻³/10^{19} cm⁻³) with an initial epilayer thickness of 5 µm. A deep n⁺ collar [3] reaching the substrate was present. A low temperature aluminum annealing step [6] has been incorporated into the process.

A number of conclusions can be made.

1) As far as the magnitude of the different current components is concerned, no real dominant mechanism is present, and in order to accurately model the base current, the three components must be taken into account.

2) The component I_{nc} follows the ideal Boltzmann law, characterized by a 60 mV per current decade slope, over the entire current range. The reason is that I_{nc} is an injection current, independent of recombination. It only is determined by the impurity profiles and the device geometry. Moreover, one has to take high doping effects or bandgap narrowing effects into account [7], [8] in order to explain the observed current density.

3) The components I_{no} and I_p do not follow the ideal Boltzmann law. They cause the falloff of β_u at low current levels. Both these components are strongly dependent on the surface properties. This will be clarified in the next section.

IV. INFLUENCE OF THE ANNEALING STEP ON THE MAGNITUDE OF I_{no} AND I_p

Fig. 6 shows I_{no} and I_p as a function of the applied base-emitter voltage V_{BE}. The results are obtained for gate 9 of the test pattern of Fig. 1. The lower curves are obtained, including an additional low temperature annealing treatment into the processing. The upper curves give the results if this annealing step is omitted. The annealing treatment is a heat treatment in wet nitrogen ambient after aluminum metallization [6]. The importance of related treatments for I²L already has been pointed out by Wulms [4]. Fig. 6 clearly shows the influence of this treatment in the low current range. The total base current more than doubles if the treatment is omitted. The results of Fig. 6 are obtained if a deep n⁺ reaching the buried layer is present between the base regions.

The obtained results can, in a qualitative way, be explained as follows. As far as I_{no} is concerned, the result is a simple consequence of the lowering of the surface recombination velocity at the Si–SiO₂ interface, due to the annealing. Indeed, I_{no} is a current injected into a short base diode and thus is strongly dependent on the boundary condition at the contact. Clearly, I_{no} is influenced by about the same amount over the entire current range. For I_p, on the other hand, the bulk component (I_{p1} in Fig. 6) will be dominant at medium and higher current levels, whereas at low current levels, the surface recombination component in the emitter–base surface space charge region (I_{p2} in Fig. 6) will be more important. Since the surface component is strongly influenced by the treatment, and, to a first approximation, the bulk component remains unchanged, the behavior of I_p, as far as annealing treatment is concerned, is a strong function of the current level.

A somewhat different picture is found for the devices isolated by a shallow n^+ collector diffusion. In that case, I_p is rather strongly affected by the annealing treatment at medium current levels also. Without the additional annealing treatment a difference, ΔI_p, is found between the I_p values for the shallow and the deep n^+, respectively. This difference is given in the table below for three V_{BE} values.

V_{BE} (mV)	ΔI_p (A)
490	2.7×10^{-9}
550	2.4×10^{-8}
610	2.3×10^{-7}

Clearly, ΔI_p does not strongly deviate from the ideal Boltzmann relationship, which indicates that ΔI_p is due to additional recombination in a neutral region. We feel that this additional current component is due to surface recombination in the n region between the n^+ and p diffusions. This clearance is larger for the shallow n^+ which only diffuses 2 μm sideways, compared with 5 μm for the deep n^+ isolation. Further evidence for this supposition is given by the fact that the devices with the additional annealing treatment display only very small differences, when the deep n^+ is substituted by a shallow n^+ isolation. This statement, however, is only true when the sideways diffused deep n^+ does not touch the base, as is the case for our devices where we are dealing with a 10-μm clearance on the mask between the base and n^+ isolation.

V. Agreement with Theoretical Calculations

As already pointed out in Section II, a good agreement between experimental and theoretical values is obtained, for the component I_{nc}. It only depends on the impurity profiles and the geometry.

Let us now examine whether the current I_{no} is in agreement with theoretical calculations. Because of the high bulk lifetimes, it seems reasonable to assume that I_{no} is completely determined by the surface recombination underneath the oxide. In this case, a simple analytical expression can be derived

$$I_{no} = A_{ox} \frac{q s n_i^2}{N_{AO}} e^{(q/kT)\Delta E_g} e^{(q/kT)V_{BE}}. \quad (1)$$

In this expression, A_{ox} stands for the area of the oxide

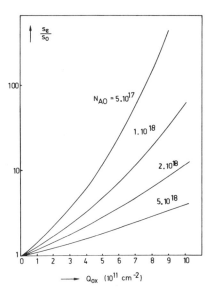

Fig. 7. Influence of the fixed oxide charge on the effective surface recombination velocity.

covered base region, N_{AO} is the base surface concentration, s is the surface recombination velocity, and ΔE_g stands for the bandgap narrowing present at the surface. The other symbols have their usual meaning.

By fitting this theoretical formula to the actually measured current, one finds that s values have to be assumed of several times 10^4 cm/s to explain the observed results. For ΔE_g, the values obtained by Slotboom and De Graaf [8] have been used. The value obtained for s must be considered as being very high for thermally oxidized silicon. This curve fitted value was obtained for devices with the additional annealing treatment. Measurements, using gated diodes, with the gate extending over the p-type base did not give very conclusive results, due to the high surface concentration. Measurements with the gate over the n-type epiregion yielded values lower than 10 cm/s, about 10^3 times smaller than the curve fitted value from the I_{no} data. Two effects contribute to make this discrepancy smaller. The first effect is the fact that, as measured by Grove and Fitzgerald [10], surface recombination velocity, while being independent of the impurity concentration at low doping levels, starts to increase with increasing doping for concentrations higher than 10^{17} cm^{-3}. The second effect is caused by the fact that due to the positive oxide charge, band bending is present at the silicon–silicon dioxide interface and the minority carrier concentration at zero bias at that interface will be higher than the thermal equilibrium value. This effectively enhances surface recombination [9]. The effective surface recombination, which takes this effect into account has been calculated and is represented in Fig. 7, as a function of the fixed oxide charge. The effective surface recombination velocity s_e, which must be used in formula (1), is represented, normalized with respect to the flat-band surface recombination velocity s_0, and is given with N_{AO} as a parameter. The direct measurement of q_{ox}, using $C(V)$ methods on top of the base region did not yield conclusive results. HF $C(V)$ measurements using MOS capacitors on top of an epiregion yielded q_{ox} values about 3×10^{11} cm^{-2}. According to Werner [11], the ratio of oxide charges on top of the base and on top of the ep-iregion is 4.3 for aluminium annealed devices in wet N_2 ambient and for (111), oriented material. Thus a rough estimate of q_{ox} on top of our base, with a 10^{18} cm^{-3} doping, will be 1.3×10^{12} cm^{-2}. Using that value for q_{ox}, we can estimate the s_e/s_0 value in our devices to be 100.

Taking into account the two effects: the increasing value of s at higher doping levels and the existance of a positive oxide charge, the discrepancy between the curve fitted value of s (several times 10^4 cm/s) and the estimated values becomes much smaller. However, we still find a rather large difference between the two values.

In theory, the component I_{no} also contains a bulk recombination component. We tried to evaluate the magnitude of that component by using an experimentally lifetime versus doping level relationship. This relation has been determined using n$^+$-p diodes with variable substrate concentration, fabricated in the same integrated circuit facility as the I^{2}L devices. The lifetime was obtained by measuring the spectral response of these diodes in the infrared. This measured relation turns out to be

$$\tau_n = \frac{15 \; \mu s}{1 + \dfrac{N_A}{5 \times 10^{16}}}. \tag{2}$$

Using these values, together with the estimated impurity profile in the base and the values for the bandgap narrowing of [8], we could actually calculate the bulk recombination in the extrinsic base. However, this bulk recombination component also turns out to be about one order of magnitude smaller than the actually measured current I_{no}.

As far as I_{no} is concerned, no straightforward calculations using the experimentally determined quantities (s_o, q_{ox}, τ_n, N_A, ΔE_g) seem possible at this moment. Further research seems necessary to clarify this point.

As far as I_p is concerned, the agreement seems better, at least when the proper annealing step has been done. In that case, the current recombining in the bulk n-n$^+$ will prevail. Neglecting recombination in the epiregion, this current can be roughly expressed by

$$I_p = A_{\text{Base}} \frac{q n_i^2 D_p e^{\Delta E_g/kT}}{N_B L_p} \exp\left(\frac{q}{kT} V_{BE}\right). \tag{3}$$

A_{Base} is the base area, N_B the donor concentration in the n$^+$ substrate, L_p the diffusion length of holes, and ΔE_g the bandgap narrowing present in the heavily doped substrate. The other symbols have the conventional meaning.

Formula (3) can be used to obtain a curve fitted value of L_p, the diffusion length of minority carriers in the heavily doped substrate, from the measured I_p values. Using these values of I_p at medium current levels (right-hand side values of Fig. 5) one finds diffusion lengths and hole lifetimes which are consistent with (2). However, this formula predicts a q/kT slope of I_p versus V_{BE}; whereas the experiments (Fig. 5) give a slight deviation of this slope even at higher current levels and with the additional an-

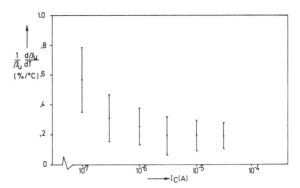

Fig. 8. Temperature coefficient of upward current gain for nonannealed devices.

nealing treatment. This deviation from the ideal Boltzmann law at higher current levels could be due to the fact that, even with the proper annealing, the emitter–base surface space charge recombination current is never completely eliminated. Measurements of the temperature dependence of the gain (next section) however indicate that this is not likely to be true. It is therefore suggested that the nonideal slope of I_p at higher current levels is due to the saturation of traps, which could cause an increasing lifetime with increasing current level.

The agreement between theoretical calculations and experimentally determined values for the different components is summarized in the following table.

I^{2}L Base Current Components	Agreement with Calculations
I_{nc}	good
I_{pnp}	good
I_{no}	?
I_p	moderate

VI. TEMPERATURE DEPENDENCE OF THE UPWARD CURRENT GAIN

It is a well-known fact in conventional bipolar transitor theory that downward current gain decreases with decreasing temperature [12], [13]. The effect is, most likely, related to the presence of a pronounced bandgap narrowing present in the heavily doped emitter. The temperature dependence of the downward current gain is typically 0.7 percent/°C. Fig. 8 shows the measured temperature coefficients of the upward current gain as a function of the collector current, for I^{2}L gates processed without an additional aluminium annealing step. The vertical segments, once again, represent the 95-percent confidence limits of the measurements. At medium and higher current levels, the temperature dependence of the upward current gain is much smaller than that of the downward mode. This is consistent with the lower emitter and extrinsic base impurity concentrations and the smaller associated bandgap narrowing. Similar conclusions have been reported by Mürrmann for poly-sil emitter structures [14]. At lower current levels, the temperature dependence of the upward current gain increases. The reason is that the surface recombination current, present in the emitter–base sidewall space charge region, becomes the dominant base current

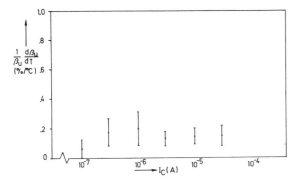

Fig. 9. Temperature coefficient of upward current gain for annealed devices.

component at low current levels. The base current will be a weaker function of the temperature than the collector current and the upward current gain will decrease with decreasing temperature. Thus in the region where we are dealing with the lowest current gain values (falloff of β_u at low current levels), we also have to deal with the strongest degradation with temperature. This observation could cause reliability problems. Fortunately, when using the low temperature annealing, the temperature dependence of the upward current gain is small over the entire current range (Fig. 9). The reason is that in this case the surface recombination component is virtually eliminated. The I²L gates then can be used over the entire military temperature range even in the nanoampere current range.

VII. CONCLUSIONS

The main conclusions of the paper can be summarized as follows.

1) The injection model and its associated test pattern can be used down into the nanoampere range.

2) The final annealing treatment at low temperatures strongly influences I_{no} over the entire current range, and I_p at low current levels. However, when a clearance between the n⁺ collar and the p base is left, I_p is also affected by the treatment at higher current levels.

3) Not only the surface recombination velocity, but also the fixed oxide charge, is influencing the I_{no} value.

4) The component I_{nc} is in good agreement with theoretical computations, whereas a moderate agreement is found for I_p. As far as I_{no} is concerned, no straightforward agreement using experimentally determined quantities

was obtained at this moment. More accurate measurements of these quantities on the I²L gates themselves could, perhaps, clarify this point.

5) The temperature dependence of the upward current gain can be made quite small over the entire current range.

ACKNOWLEDGMENT

Discussions with P. Bierbaum, P. Dartnell, and T. Caudell are deeply appreciated. The authors are indebted to J. Elen for assistance during the measurements.

REFERENCES

[1] H. H. Berger, "The injection model—A structure-oriented model for merged transistor logic (MTL)," *IEEE J. Solid-State Circuits*, vol. SC-9, pp. 218–227, Oct. 1974.

[2] F. M. Klaassen, "Device physics of integrated injection logic," *IEEE Trans. Electron Devices*, vol. ED-22, pp. 145–152, Mar. 1976.

[3] A. Schmitz and A. Slob, "The effect of isolation regions on the current gain of inverse NPN-transistors used in Integrated Injection Logic (I²L)," in *IEDM Digest Tech. Papers*, pp. 508–510, Washington, 1974.

[4] H. E. J. Wulms, "Base current of I²L transistors," in *ISSCC Digest*, pp. 92–93, 1976.

[5] C. A. Grimbergen, "The influence of geometry on the interpretation of the current in epitaxial diodes," *Solid State Electron.*, vol. 19, pp. 1033–1037, Dec. 1976.

[6] P. L. Castro and B. E. Deal, "Low temperature reduction of fast surface states associated with thermally oxidized silicon," *J. Electrochemic. Soc. 118*, p. 280, 1971.

[7] R. P. Mertens, H. J. De Man, and R. Van Overstraeten, "Calculation of the emitter efficiency of bipolar transistors," *IEEE Trans. Electron Devices*, pp. 772–778, Sept. 1973.

[8] J. W. Slotboom and H. C. de Graaff, "Measurement of bandgap narrowing in Si bipolar transistors," *Solid State Electron.*, vol. 19, pp. 857–862, 1976.

[9] W. Mattheus, R. Mertens, and J. Stulting, "Base current of I²L gates at low current levels," in *Digest Int. Electron Devices Meeting*, Washington, DC, Dec. 1976, p. 316.

[10] D. J. Fitzgerald and A. S. Grove, "Surface recombination in semiconductors," Surface Sci., vol. 9, pp. 347–369, 1968.

[11] W. M. Werner, "The influence of fixed interface charges on the current-gain fall off of planar n-p-n transistors," *J. Electrochem. Soc.*, vol. 123, no. 4, pp. 540–543, Apr. 1976.

[12] W. L. Kaufmann and A. A. Bergh, "The temperature dependence of ideal gain in double diffused silicon transistors," *IEEE Trans. Electron Devices*, vol. ED-15, pp. 732–735, Oct. 1968.

[13] D. Buhanan, "Investigation of current-gain temperature dependence in silicon transistors," *IEEE Trans. Electron Devices*, vol. ED-16, pp. 117–124, Jan. 1969.

[14] H. Murrmann, A. Glasl, and K. Lindemann, "Temperature dependence of current gain in Si-npn transistors with poly Sil Emitters," in *ESSDERC Conf.*, Münich, Germany, 1976, p. 25.

Modeling of Schottky Coupled Transistor Logic

SCOTT C. BLACKSTONE AND ROBERT P. MERTENS

Abstract—The SCTL gate which promises increased speed and reduced power is discussed. It involves the use of a single lowly doped collector incorporating Schottky diodes to decode the output. A complete electrical model is formulated and compared with experimental results. The model is then used to optimize this structure with respect to extrinsic and intrinsic base doping and collector doping, and it resulted in an 8.5 ns fanout four device on a 2.5 μm epi layer. Finally, the model is used to study the possibility of Schottky clamping the base collector, and it was found that higher collector doping was needed for a minimum delay.

I. INTRODUCTION

IN ORDER for I^2L to gain an advantage in the marketplace, it has to be able to achieve high speed at a low power dissipation. To obtain this high speed, several parameters can be varied [1]-[3]. A further speed improvement could also come about by reducing the downward gain, although in conventional I^2L this would lead to current hogging [4]. To reduce power dissipation, one can reduce either or both the capacitance or the voltage swing. A reduction in capacitance or the voltage swing, with a series Schottky diode, results in a direct reduction in power. In conventional I^2L, however, these diodes are impossible to integrate directly on the device as the regions are too highly doped.

A new structure was proposed by Berger and Wiedmann [4] which incorporates some of these new features and is called Schottky coupled transistor logic (SCTL). In SCTL, the multiple collectors of conventional I^2L are replaced by a single collector to which Schottky contacts are added to decouple the output. The collector is very lightly doped to allow both the fabrication of Schottky contacts directly on the collector and to achieve low downward current gain. The current hogging problem is solved here by having only one collector, which eliminates the problem, but thus demands Schottky decoding. This structure then has low power as a result of the reduced voltage swing and high speed as a result of the low downward current gain.

In this paper, this SCTL structure will be examined. First an electrical model will be formed and then compared with experimental results. This model will be used to optimize the device, and finally to predict the results of a possible extension of this SCTL gate by Schottky clamping the base collector junction.

Manuscript received March 31, 1978; revised June 5, 1978.
S. C. Blackstone is with BARCO-COBAR, Kortrijk, Belgium.
R. P. Mertens is with the Laboratorium E.S.A.T., Katholieke Universiteit Leuven, Heverlee, Belgium, and the Belgian National Science Foundation.

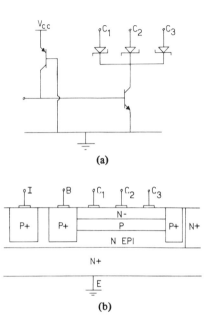

Fig. 1. The SCTL gate. (a) Electrical schematic and (b) physical cross section of gate.

II. THE SCTL GATE

The basic SCTL gate is shown in Fig. 1. As seen by the electrical schematic of part (a), the SCTL gate has the same lateral p-n-p injector and n-p-n switching transistor as in conventional I^2L, the only difference being the one large collector to which the Schottky contacts are made. The cross section of the gate is shown in part (b). This uses a heavily doped p^+ to form the injector and the extrinsic base region (base region not under the collector). This heavily doped extrinsic base helps to eliminate base debiasing effects resulting from the base resistance. To achieve the low surface concentration necessary for the formation of the Schottky contacts on the collector, both the intrinsic base region (base region under the collector) and the collector region are ion implanted. If the field oxide is made sufficiently thick, the only region that will be affected by the implantation will be the collector region. This means that no mask is needed for the implantation of either the intrinsic base or the collector; however, one mask is needed to open this region. Thus, with a deep n^+ isolation, this is only a five-mask technology as compared to six in conventional double base I^2L.

III. MODELING

To study the influence of the various parameters of this structure, a mathematical model must first be formulated. To

Reprinted from *IEEE J. Solid-State Circuits*, vol. SC-13, pp. 893–898, Dec. 1978.

158

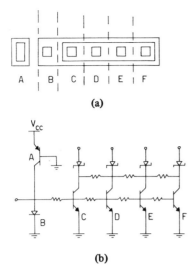

(a)

(b)

Fig. 2. Modeling the SCTL gate. (a) Breakup of gate and (b) simple electrical model of gate.

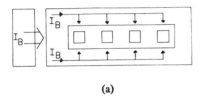

(a)

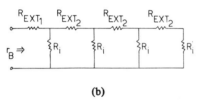

(b)

Fig. 3. Calculation of base resistance. (a) Assumption of current flow and (b) model of total base resistance for a fanout four gate.

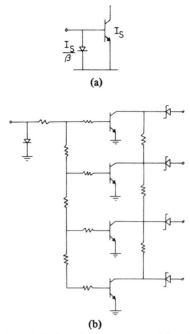

(a)

(b)

Fig. 4. Model for calculation of time constants (a) and complete electrical model (b).

correctly predict high speed performance, several authors have shown that the effects of base resistance must be included [1], [5]. So, to be able to include this effect, the device has to broken up as shown in Fig. 2(a). Here, the base contact is separated out as in conventional I^2L. The collector, however, being one region, is divided up symmetrically about the Schottky contacts to form separate common emitter transistors. Each collector then is in series with a Schottky diode, and as all collectors are common, they are connected by resistors. This simple electrical model is shown in Fig. 2(b).

The first parameter of this model to be determined will be the base resistance. In this structure, the base can be divided into two distinct regions, the extrinsic and the intrinsic. As the extrinsic base has a much lower resistivity than the intrinsic base, it is assumed that all of the base current flows down the extrinsic part, and then is perpendicularly distributed to different parts of the intrinsic base as seen in Fig. 3. Thus, one can use the extrinsic base model of Fig. 2(b) and add in parallel an intrinsic resistance between each node and the transistor as shown in the expanded model of Fig. 4(b). The extrinsic base

resistance can be determined by knowledge of the base sheet resistivity and layout of the cell. The intrinsic base resistance can be determined by the phase-cancellation technique of Sansen and Meyer [6]. The input impedance of a common base transistor can be made purely real by adjusting the collector current I_{CM}. When this condition is met

$$I_{CM} = \frac{V_T}{r_B}. \qquad (1)$$

Thus, the total base resistance r_B can be easily found. Assuming all intrinsic base resistances R_i equal, the total base resistance can be modeled as in Fig. 3(b). From this figure, the value of intrinsic base resistance can be calculated.

Just as there are two base regions, there are also two time contants. This is because the extrinsic base has a deeper junction depth and a different doping from the intrinsic base. Assuming the model of Fig. 4(a), this allows one to separate the delay of the extrinsic loss diode from the delay of the intrinsic diode. One can say that the total emitter charge is equal to the charge under the extrinsic diode plus the charge under the intrinsic diode, or assuming the current gain of the intrinsic transistor large and neglecting the additional base current component underneath the base contact which is small because of the small area of the contact and the large extrinsic base doping, gives

$$Q_{\text{total}} = \tau_{\text{int}} I_S + \tau_{\text{ext}} I_S / \beta \qquad (2)$$

or simply

$$\tau_{\text{total}} = \tau_{\text{int}} + \tau_{\text{ext}} / \beta. \qquad (3)$$

As this is a single collector device, one can take a gate with a fanout one and a gate with a fanout four, all outputs common, and measure the time constants (τ_{total}) of these two devices.

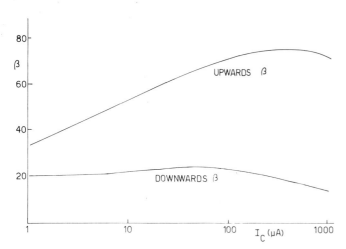

Fig. 5. Plot of upward and downward current gain versus collector current for a fanout four gate with all collectors common.

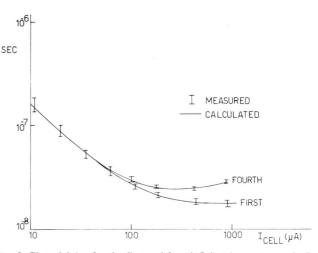

Fig. 6. Plot of delay for the first and fourth Schottky contacts of a fanout four SCTL gate versus cell current.

This represents a ratio of intrinsic of total area of 23 and 43 percent, respectively. Then, by measuring the upward current gain of each device and plugging into (3), the two results can be solved simultaneously to produce a value for the intrinsic and extrinsic delay. The advantage of this approach is that it allows one to calculate the time constant of a region with a given ratio of extrinsic and intrinsic regions. Thus, it allows the calculation of the time constant of the common emitter transistors which are separated out as was shown in Fig. 2(b). The delay of these transistors was assumed to be the same as the delay of the entire gate minus the base contact loss diode. To find this delay, (3) has to be modified to include the increase in upward current gain as a result of decreasing the base current by the amount lost to the base contact.

The resistance between the collectors was calculated by knowledge of sheet resistivity and layout. The space-charge capacitance was calculated from the profile using a device analysis program.

IV. Results

These devices were fabricated on a 5 μm thick epi n on n$^+$ with an epi resistivity of 0.5 $\Omega \cdot$ cm. The extrinsic base had a sheet resistivity of 60 $\Omega/\square$. The implant for the intrinsic base was $5 \times 10^{12}/cm^2$ at an energy of 350 keV. The phosphorus implant for the collector as a dose of $9 \times 10^{12}/cm^2$ at an energy of 300 keV. This results in a collector resistivity of 1.5 k$\Omega/\square$ and a base pinch resistivity of about 20 k$\Omega/\square$. The minimum line width and space was 8 μm.

Fig. 5 is a plot of the upward, with grounded injector, and downward current gain for a fanout four structure with all four collectors common. One can see that a rather large upward current gain is possible as a result of the narrow base width and the improved emitter-to-collector-area ratio. The upward current gain for a fanout one structure was 20.

The emitter time constant for a fanout one and four structure was 5.35 and 2.35 ns, respectively. These, when put into (3), gave an intrinsic delay of 1.25 ns and an extrinsic delay of 82 ns. To measure the delay of each transistor, structures were fabricated to determine the base current lost by the base contact

region [part B of Fig. 2(a)]. It was found that this base contact region is responsible for 30 percent of the total base current for a fanout four case. This is also its ratio of total extrinsic base area. This means that for the separate transistors, the extrinsic time constant divided by total upward current gain has to be multiplied by 0.7. Thus, the calculated delay of each common emitter transistor was 2.03 ns. The loss diode then had a delay of 82 ns and a saturation current of 0.3 times I_S/β.

These values were substituted into the model of Fig. 4(b) and run on a circuit simulation program. Fig. 6 is a plot of delay versus cell current for a fanout four first (Schottky contact near injector) and fourth (Schottky contact far from injector) Schottky contact. This figure shows a power–delay product of just under 1 pJ and a minimum delay for the first Schottky contact of about 17.5 ns at a current of 600 μA. This figure also shows the rather good agreement between the measured points and the calculated points. With this model, one can evaluate the various parameters which can be varied in order to optimize this gate.

The first parameter to be studied is the boron implantation for the intrinsic base region. By varying this boron implantation, one varies four parameters which are the downward and upward gains, the saturation current, and the emitter time constant. The emitter time constant is scaled with the saturation current. An additional parameter which is much more difficult to calculate is the intrinsic base resistance. Two possibilities are used. The first approximation is that the intrinsic base resistance at high current (minimum delay) is approximately constant, and only the on-set current (the current at which the base resistance becomes important) varies. Using this approximation, the intrinsic base resistance was held constant. The second approximation is that the intrinsic base resistance should be scaled inversely with the dose of the implant.

Fig. 7 is a plot of minimum delay (intrinsic delay) as a function of the saturation current. As expected, the minimum delay is an increasing function of base doping. The difference between holding the intrinsic base resistance constant and

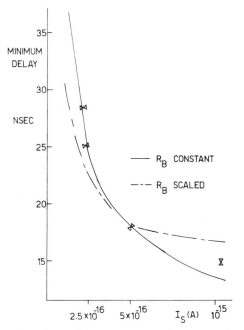

Fig. 7. Plot of minimum delay versus saturation current showing the effect of varying intrinsic base doping.

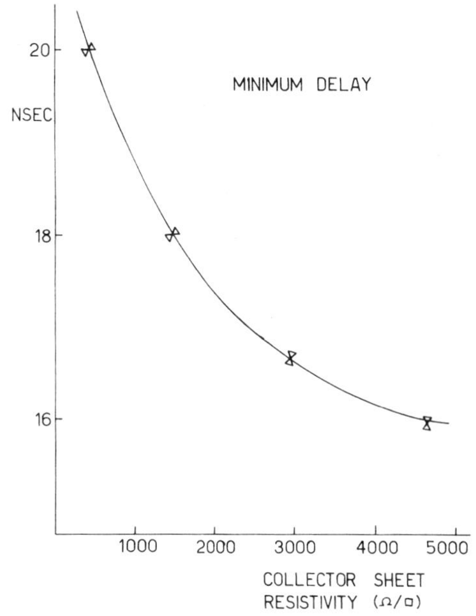

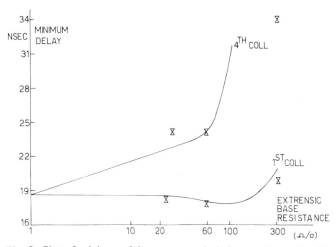

Fig. 8. Plot of minimum delay versus intercollector resistance showing the effect of varying collector doping.

scaling it is that at low I_S (high base doping), the scaled intrinsic base resistance gives lower delays than the constant intrinsic base resistance, and at high I_S (low base doping), the scaled intrinsic base resistance gives greater delays than the constant intrinsic base resistance. The previously measured values of intrinsic base resistance were used as a starting point for these calculations, which explains why the scaled and constant intrinsic base resistance curves intersect at these measured values. This plot shows that current crowding is strongly present in these devices, such that the assumption of a linearity increasing base resistance with increasing base pinch sheet resistance (dotted line) does not hold, the constant base resistance model agreeing better with the experimental data up to very high values of base pinch resistance.

The second parameter to be studied is the phosphorus implantation for the collector. Varying this implant varies the downward current gain and the collector resistance. A decrease in downward current gain results in increased speed; thus one would expect to see a decrease in minimum delay.

Fig. 8 is a plot of the minimum delay versus collector sheet resistivity as a result of varying the phosphorus implantation. As expected, the delay is proportional to the downward current gain. The measured values fit this curve rather well as it was possible to obtain a constant value of base pinch resistance. From this curve, one can see that the lower the doping of the phosphorus, the lower the minimum delay. This doping level is limited to about 3000 $\Omega/\square$ for a 5 V collector–emitter breakdown, which is one of the requirements for TTL compatibility.

The third parameter to be studied is the extrinsic base resistance. As in conventional I^2L, the effect of base resistance causes a difference in delay between the first and fourth collector as a result of debiasing the base. This effect can be

Fig. 9. Plot of minimum delay versus extrinsic base resistance for the first and fourth Schottky contacts of a fanout four SCTL gate.

reduced by an extrinsic base of highly doped material and thus low resistance. However, this increases the capacitance of the gate, and going to a lower sheet resistance has limitations.

Fig. 9 is plot of minimum delay for the first and fourth Schottky contacts as a function of extrinsic base resistivity. In this plot, it was assumed that the capacitance was independent of resistivity. Thus, this simple curve gives the expected result that at very low resistivities, the first and fourth Schottky contacts switch at the same speed, and at very high resistivities, the speed of the first and the fourth Schottky contacts can differ by a factor of three or four as in the case of conventional I^2L. The measured results also show this trend until rather low resistivities are reached when the delay actually starts to increase as a result of increased capacitance. As low power is one of the goals of this technology, one would like to choose the highest resistivity possible which still gives a small spread between the first and fourth Schottky contacts. This criterion is met by a value of around 60 $\Omega/\square$.

To show that this gate is an improvement on conventional I^2L, a mask was fabricated which included both an SCTL gate and a conventional I^2L on the same chip. The collector of the conventional I^2L gate was formed by an arsenic implant which was done in addition to the phosphorus implant such that the phosphorus implant determined the junction depth. This allowed both devices to have the same base–emitter parameters such as emitter time constant, upward current gain, etc. This mask was fabricated on a 2.24 μm epi n on n^+ wafer with an epi resistivity of 0.54 $\Omega \cdot$ cm. As a result of this analysis, an optimum gate was constructed using a boron implant of $5 \times 10^{12}/cm^2$, a phosphorus implant of $5 \times 10^{12}/cm^2$, and an extrinsic base sheet resistivity of 60 $\Omega/\square$. For the SCTL fanout four gate, this gave an average measured minimum delay of 7.7 ns for the first collector and 14.6 ns for the fourth collector. For the conventional I^2L fanout four gate, this gave an average measured minimum delay of 9.0 ns for the first collector and 21.0 ns for the fourth collector. This improvement is due to the lower downward current gain and better emitter-to-collector-area ratio of the SCTL gate over the conventional I^2L gate.

V. Extension of Approach

To improve this gate even further, one can use a second Schottky diode to clamp the base collector junction [4]. The resulting voltage swing will be the difference in forward voltage between the Schottky diode that is clamping the base collector and the Schottky which is decoding the output. This, by proper choice of Schottky diodes, allows the gate to be constructed with the minimum voltage swing possible, and thus the lowest possible dissipation for a given gate dimension. This also reduced the charge storage effects allowing high speed as in Schottky TTL.

These Schottky diodes can be formed by two metals which are widely used in the semiconductor industry—Al and Ti. These two metals have a barrier height of 0.74 and 0.53 eV, respectively, resulting in a voltage swing of 210 mV. This gate can be realized by extending the base contact over the collector region, resulting in only a small area increase and no problems of intercell metallization.

An electrical model for this structure is shown in Fig. 10. It is the same as the unclamped model except for the Schottky clamping diode and the series collector resistance. Fig. 11 is a plot of simulated delay versus current for the previously described 5 μm epi technology using this electrical model. One can see that for the fourth Schottky contact, the collector resistance not only prematurely limits the switching speed, but decreases the speed drastically afterwards. The first Schottky contact is also prematurely limited in switching speed. The reason for this is that even though the part of the collector near the clamping diode is clamped, the part far from the clamping diode is unclamped as a result of collector resistance. As the first Schottky contact has to discharge the entire collector, it is slowed down by the unclamped portion. This also explains

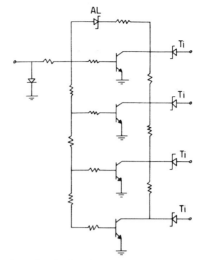

Fig. 10. Complete electrical model of Schottky clamped SCTL gate for a fanout four device using Al and Ti.

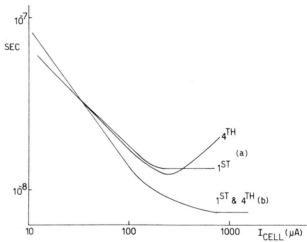

Fig. 11. Simulated delay versus cell current for a Schottky clamped SCTL fanout four gate for the first and fourth Schottky contacts (a) for a lowly doped collector and (b) for an order of magnitude higher collector doping.

why the fourth Schottky contact has a lower minimum propagation delay than the first. Here the fourth Schottky contact is drawing current, and the opposite end, the most heavily saturated and near the clamping diode, is unclamped. This is the best possible situation, and thus yields the highest speed.

To improve this situation, the collector resistance should be reduced. However, to reduce the collector resistance means to increase the downward current gain. This fortunately is not a drawback as the collector base junction can never become forward biased enough to inject significant current into the emitter due to the Schottky clamp. So, new simulations were run assuming an increase of eight in doping. This increase in doping still allows the fabrication of Schottky diodes [7]. Fig. 11(b) is a simulated plot of delay versus current for this new collector profile. Now, one sees that the collector resistance effects are no longer present, and that all Schottky contacts switch at the same speed. The minimum delay of 7.5 ns is almost a factor of two below the delay without clamping. Simulations have been done on even more highly doped collectors, and no improvement in maximum speed was observed. This 5 μm epi technology then has the performance of a conventional unclamped 2 μm epi technology.

VI. CONCLUSION

In this paper the SCTL approach was presented. As shown, this involves the use of a single lowly doped collector incorporating Schottky diodes to decode the output. An entire electrical model was constructed which involves separating each Schottky contact into an equivalent transistor. A simple method was used for the determination of delay which separates the delay into two regions, the intrinsic and extrinsic delay. Extrinsic and intrinsic base resistance were also determined. It was shown that a compromise has to be reached between capacitance and doping for the extrinsic base, and for the intrinsic base it was shown that the lighter the doping, the lower the minimum propagation delay. For the collector doping, it was also discovered that the lower the doping, the faster it is.

Finally, a possible extension of this approach was presented. This involves the use of a second Schottky diode to clamp the collector to the base. Simulations show that to obtain a low delay for all Schottky contacts, a higher doping must be used.

REFERENCES

[1] F. M. Klaassen, "Device physics of integrated injection logic," *IEEE Trans. Electron Devices*, vol. ED-22, pp. 145–152, Mar. 1975.
[2] D. P. Gaffney and A. Bhattacharyya, "Modeling device and layout effects of performance driven I^2L," *IEEE J. Solid-State Circuits*, vol. SC-12, pp. 155–162, Apr. 1977.
[3] J. M. Herman, III, S. A. Evans, and B. J. Sloan, "Second generation I^2L/MTL: A 20 ns process/structure," *IEEE J. Solid-State Circuits*, vol. SC-12, pp. 93–101, Apr. 1977.
[4] H. H. Berger and S. K. Wiedmann, "Advanced merged transistor logic by using Schottky junctions," *Microelectronics*, vol. 7, no. 3, pp. 35–42.
[5] W. H. Mattheus, R. P. Mertens, and L. De Smet, "Modeling the dynamic behavior of I^2L," *IEEE J. Solid-State Circuits*, vol. SC-12, pp. 163–170, Apr. 1977.
[6] W. M. C. Sansen and R. G. Meyer, "Characterization and measurements of the base and emitter resistance of bipolar transistors," *IEEE J. Solid-State Circuits*, vol. SC-7, pp. 492–498, Dec. 1972.
[7] L. Kennedy, private communication.

THE EFFECT OF BASE RESISTANCE
OF THE VERTICAL *NPN* TRANSISTOR
IN I²L STRUCTURES

N. KIRSCHNER

Solid State Electronics Division, National Electrical Engineering Research Institute, Council for Scientific and
Industrial Research, P.O. Box 395, Pretoria 0001, Republic of South Africa

(*Received 22 June 1976; in revised form 18 November 1976*)

Abstract—Expressions are derived for the lateral base current and for the base-emitter voltage by solving the differential equations obtained from a physical model of the base region of the vertical *npn* transistor. The theoretical and experimental results concur in showing that on the one hand the decrease of the upward current gain of the individual collectors at higher values of the collector current is due to the lateral voltage drop, and that high injection effects appear only for small values of current gain which have no practical importance. On the other hand the curves of current gain plotted against collector current show that the lateral voltage drop causes a point of inflexion followed by a maximum. This effect is evident at that collector nearest to the injector (or even at several such collectors, depending upon how many there are). Furthermore it is seen that the decrease of the current gain is almost entirely independent of the current gain of the intrinsic transistor.

NOTATION

A area of diode *pn* junction
A_v area of vertical diode *pn* junction
a depth of base-emitter junction
b width of base strip
C^2 constant of integration
D_n diffusion constant of electrons
D_p diffusion constant of holes
d length of base strip
d_p depth of diode *p* region
I_C collector current
I_d lateral current at end of base strip furthest from the injector ($x = d$)
I_v current of vertical diode
$I(x)$ lateral current in the base as a function of distance
i_n electron current density
i_p hole current density
i_{sl} lateral current density in the base-emitter diode
i_{sv} vertical current density in the base-emitter diode
$i_{sv,l}$ equal lateral and vertical current density in the base-emitter diode
k Boltzmann's constant
$N_A(y)$ impurity concentration in the base as a function of distance
n diode slope factor
n_i intrinsic carrier concentration
n_{0p} electron density in *p* region at equilibrium
$n(x)$ electron distribution as a function of distance
p_{0p} hole density in *p* region at equilibrium
q charge on the electron
r resistance of unity length of base
r_c resistance of unit length of base at the collector region
r_o resistance of unit length of oxide-covered base
r_p pinch resistance of unit length under the collector
r_s resistance of unit length of base beside the collector
T temperature in degrees Kelvin
V_d lateral base-emitter voltage at the end of the base furthest from the injector ($x = d$)
V_{EB} base-emitter voltage
V_T thermal voltage
$V(x)$ base-emitter voltage as a function of distance
w base width
x_n, x_{n+1} co-ordinates of the boundaries of the ($n + 1$) region in the base, as in Fig. 2
Δx width of element of the base region

y_1, y_2 optional depth in the base
z_1, z_2 co-ordinates of the collector
μ_n electron mobility
μ_p hole mobility
ρ_s sheet resistivity
ρ_{SB} sheet resistivity of base diffusion
ρ_{SP} sheet resistivity of base diffusion under the collector.

1. INTRODUCTION

Integrated Injection Logic (I^2L) is a bipolar logic technique for large-scale integration (LSI)[1]. The number of outputs of a stage, which corresponds to the number of collectors of the vertical *npn* transistor, is an important factor influencing the attainment of a high packing density, and is determined by various factors, the most important of which are speed and base resistance[2].

If the number of collectors is increased, the amount of charge stored in the vertical transistor will also increase, and as a result the storage time will become longer and the speed lower.

The base resistance causes a voltage drop along the base of that I^2L structure for which the packing density is optimal and injection takes place through the short side of the base of the vertical *npn* transistors, as shown in Fig. 1. As a result the base-emitter voltage is not constant and also the various collector currents differ from each other. The smallest of these currents flows through the collector furthest from the injector, i.e. each additional collector is in a less favourable position. This effect becomes more pronounced as the base current increases.

In order to investigate this effect of the base resistance, an attempt will be made to construct a physical model of the base region. Differential equations for the model will be established and used to calculate the base voltage drop. When this is known, the upward current gains—which will, in what follows, be referred to simply as current gains—of the various collectors have to be

Reprinted with permission from *Solid-State Electron.*, vol. 20, pp. 641–646, July 1977. Copyright © 1977, Pergamon Press, Ltd.

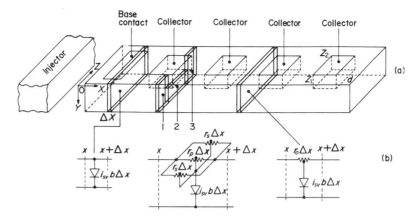

Fig. 1(a). A pictorial view of an I^2L structure with 4 collectors. (b) Equivalent circuits of the different base regions.

evaluated. In this way it will be possible to explain current gain as function of collector current, and to show that the effects of high injection levels become apparent only at small values of current gain in the region—unimportant from the point of view of applications—in which current gain decreases as collector current increases.

2. DETERMINATION OF THE VOLTAGE DROP IN THE BASE OF THE VERTICAL *npn* TRANSISTOR

2.1 *Physical model of the base*

To evaluate the effect of the base resistance, the base region with the base-emitter junction will be regarded as a distributed resistance-diode line[3]. The three different elements of the base region are shown in Fig. 1. These are: the region under the base contact, the base region in the vicinity of a collector and the oxide-covered base region.

The equivalent circuit for the base contact region consists of the diode of the base-emitter junction, since the metal base contact short-circuits the sheet resistivity. The other two equivalent circuits consist of the same diode and a resistance in the collector region being the result of a number of resistances connected in parallel.

The values of the resistances can be calculated using the following formula for the sheet resistivity[4].

$$\frac{1}{\rho_s} = \int_{y_1}^{y_2} q\mu_p N_A(y)\,\mathrm{d}y. \tag{1}$$

The value of the resistance of the oxide-covered region, to be used in the equivalent circuit, will be given by the following formula:

$$r_0\Delta x = \rho_{SB}\frac{\Delta x}{b} = \frac{\dfrac{\Delta x}{b}}{\displaystyle\int_0^a q\mu_p N_A(y)\,\mathrm{d}y}. \tag{2}$$

At a collector, the base resistance has three components: the pinch resistance of the active base region and, to the left and right of the collector, the sheet resistance of the base diffusion, which are equal if the mask alignment error is disregarded. The resistance r_c is

given as follows:

$$r_c\Delta x = \frac{\Delta x}{\dfrac{1}{r_s}+\dfrac{1}{r_p}+\dfrac{1}{r_s}} = \rho_{SB}\frac{\Delta x}{b}\frac{1}{1-\dfrac{z_2-z_1}{b}\left(1-\dfrac{\rho_{SB}}{\rho_{SP}}\right)} \tag{3}$$

where

$$\frac{1}{\rho_{SP}} = \int_a^{a-w} q\mu_p N_A(y)\,\mathrm{d}y.$$

The edge effects due to lateral out-diffusion can be taken into account by suitably choosing the geometrical dimensions.

The diode characteristics are given by:

$$I_v = i_{sv}A_v\left(\exp\left[\frac{qV_{EB}}{nkT}\right]-1\right) \cong i_{sv}A_v\exp\left[\frac{qV_{EB}}{nkT}\right]. \tag{4}$$

In using this formula, it will be assumed that $n = 1$[5]. Both this assumption and the approximation are justified within the region of lateral voltage drop.

The saturation current density i_{sv} differs in each of the three regions. Of the two components comprising the saturation current, the hole current is the same throughout, but the electron current changes owing to the different boundary conditions. If the recombination in the active base region is neglected, the electron current of the collector region consists only of the recombination currents in the emitter-base space charge region and in the oxide-covered base region on either side of the collector. In the oxide-covered base region the electron current is determined by recombination in the base and at the silicon/silicon dioxide interface. At the base contact the electron current is the same as before, but the recombination velocity at the metal-silicon interface is infinite.

In determining the electron current, only a vertical component will be assumed. This assumption is justified up to that region where the voltage drop begins. Here the lateral current is a hole current.

2.2 *Mathematical description of the base*

In the mathematical formulation of the equivalent circuits it is assumed that the lateral voltage drop occurs only in the direction of the x-axis.

165

The region of the base contact is described by eqn (4), as no lateral voltage drop exists. The following differential equations are valid for the other two regions, which qualitatively have the same equivalent circuits:

$$-\frac{dI(x)}{dx} \cong i_{sv}b \exp\left[\frac{qV(x)}{kT}\right] \quad (5)$$

$$-\frac{dV(x)}{dx} = rI(x). \quad (6)$$

The approximation in eqn (5) is justified, in the same way as that in eqn (4), at current levels high enough to cause a voltage drop.

The boundary conditions of the differential equations can be chosen either at the edge of the base region nearest to the injector, or at the other end of the base. In the first case the relationship between the base-emitter voltage and the lateral current will also be influenced by the characteristics of the lateral *pnp* transistor. At the other end of the base this relationship is simpler, and is given by eqn (4). Here the boundary conditions are as shown in Fig. 2.

$$V(x = d) = V_d \quad (7)$$

$$I(x = d) = I_d \cong i_{sl}ab \exp\left[\frac{qV_d}{kT}\right] \quad (8)$$

$$-\frac{dI(x)}{dx}\bigg|_{x=d} \cong i_{sv}b \exp\left[\frac{qV_d}{kT}\right]. \quad (9)$$

Appendix *A* shows how these differential equations were solved, using the above boundary conditions. The equations for the lateral current and voltage drop are then:

$$I(x) = C \tan\left[C\frac{qr}{2kT}(d-x) + \arctan\frac{I_d}{C}\right] \quad (10)$$

$$V(x) = V_d - \frac{2kT}{q}\ln\left|\cos\left[C\frac{qr}{2kT}(d-x)\right]\right.$$
$$\left.-\frac{I_d}{C}\sin\left[C\frac{qr}{2kT}(d-x)\right]\right| \quad (11)$$

$$C^2 = \frac{2kT}{qr}i_{sv}b \exp\left[\frac{qV_d}{kT}\right] - \left(i_{sl}ab \exp\left[\frac{qV_d}{kT}\right]\right)^2. \quad (12)$$

The physical meaning of the constant of integration C^2 is investigated in Appendix *B* and it is found that the case $C = 0$ corresponds to the limit of high injection.

2.3 Calculation of the voltage drop in the base and of the current gain of an I^2L structure

Using eqns (10)–(12) and boundary conditions (7)–(9) it is possible to calculate the voltage drop throughout the base region of the I^2L structure, and thus also the separate collector currents of the vertical transistors and the whole base current. Next to be determined are the current gains of the separate collectors, as functions of the collector current.

For this purpose the base is divided into regions, as shown in Fig. 2. The regions are characterized by the values i_{sv} and r. If the value of the base-emitter voltage at $x = d$ is selected, this value is used to calculate the base-emitter voltage and the lateral current at the left edge of the region 11. These values in turn will be used as boundary conditions at the right of region 10. This procedure is then repeated for each successive region until the whole base current has been determined.

It should be noted that the boundary conditions should be selected at that end of the regions where the base-emitter voltage and the lateral current are smallest. For this reason a check should also be made every time as to whether the limit of high injection has not been reached at the other end of the regions, since the equations given are no longer valid in the case of high injection. The check can be made by determining the sign of the constant of integration.

The separate collector currents are then calculated with the aid of the following formula[6]

$$I_C = \frac{qD_n n_i^2}{\int_a^{a-w} N_A(y)\,dy}(z_i - z_1)^2 \int_{x_n}^{x_{n+1}} \exp\left[\frac{qV(x)}{kT}\right]dx. \quad (13)$$

The results of calculations for I^2L structures with 1, 2, 3 and 4 collectors are given in Fig. 3. In each case the current gain is defined as the quotient when the collector current is divided by the whole base current; this obviates the necessity for subdividing the base current among the separate collectors, which creates a problem under conditions of significant lateral voltage drop.

3. COMPARISON BETWEEN THE THEORETICAL AND EXPERIMENTAL CURRENT GAIN vs COLLECTOR CURRENT CURVES

Current gain curves obtained experimentally from an I^2L chip with 4 collectors made in the laboratory[7], are shown in Fig. 4. These curves deviate from the theoretical ones at small collector current because the cal-

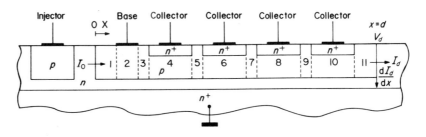

Fig. 2. Cross-section of an I^2L structure.

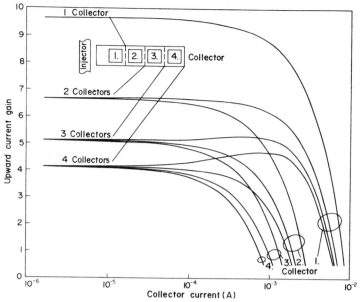

Fig. 3. Theoretical curves of current gain plotted against collector, current, for I^2L chips with 1, 2, 3 and 4 collectors.

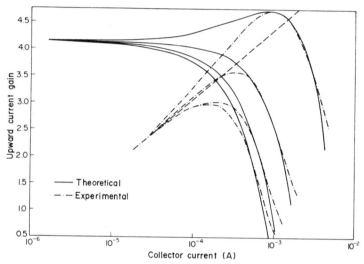

Fig. 4. Theoretical and experimental curves of current gain plotted against collector current, for an I^2L structure with 4 collectors. (The dashed line is the estimated current gain curve of the transistors without lateral base voltage drop.)

culations were based on the assumption that the current gain of the intrinsic transistor was independent of the collector current, the term "intrinsic transistor" being here taken to denote the active transistor region below the collector area in question.

On the other hand the calculated decrease of current gain at higher collector currents agrees very well with the measured results: the slopes of the curves and the distances between the curves are nearly the same.

For the two collectors nearest to the injector, the theoretical curves show an increase of current gain compared with the current gain at low collector currents. This effect, which is considerably more pronounced in the case of the first collector, can be explained by the fact that the base-emitter voltage and the base current of these collectors exceed their average values, as shown in Fig. 5. If the lateral voltage drop increases further, a continually increasing part of the base current flows through that region of the base-emitter junction situated in front of the corresponding collector. This will cause

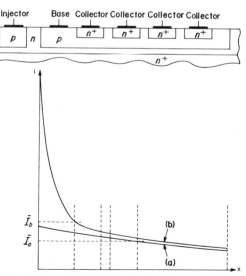

Fig. 5. Distribution of base current in the I^2L structure. (a) In the region of maximum current gain at the first collector. (b) In the region of decreasing current gain at the first collector.

167

the base-emitter voltage and the base current first to decrease until they have values more nearly approaching their respective averages, and then to fall below these average values. This explains the point of inflexion and also the maximum observed in the current gain curve. These points of inflexion and maxima can also be observed in the experimental curves for the first two collectors in Fig. 4, but are less marked owing to the increase of the intrinsic current gain.

The discrepancy between the experimental and theoretical curves at very high currents is due to high injection effects. These effects become evident in the collector regions earlier than in the other base regions, because the doping concentration is usually lower, and they can be taken into account when the collector currents are calculated[8]. In addition, the lateral voltage drop increases less steeply with current owing to conductivity modulation: at large currents the injection of minority carriers into the base is so high that the minority carrier concentration is also increased, and consequently the conductivity. In addition the electron paths are no longer vertical but curve towards the injector side of the base, thus affecting the saturation current.

4. CONCLUSIONS

As the theoretical investigation has shown, the decrease of current gain at higher collector currents is not due to high injection as in the case of bipolar transistors, but is a result of the lateral voltage drop in the base, being almost independent of change of current gain in the intrinsic transistor. High injection occurs only at the end of the decrease in current gain, and reduces the decreases by conductivity modulation and the change of electron current through the base-emitter junction.

At one or more of the collectors situated nearest to the injector, the lateral voltage drop, as may be observed from Fig. 3, causes the current gain curves to have a point of inflexion followed by a maximum. This maximum, which will occur even though the intrinsic transistor may be assumed to have a constant current gain, may be explained by uneven distribution of the base-emitter voltage and base current.

At all collectors on the structure, the cause of the reduction in current gain is that most of the entire base current drains off through the region of the base-emitter junction at the injector side of the corresponding collector. For this reason the current gain curves of those collectors which are at an equal distance from the injector, approach each other within the region of decrease, independently of the number of collectors on the structure, as shown in Fig. 3.

Actually the current gain of the intrinsic transistors increases with increasing collector current, prior to high injection. If a logarithmic relationship is assumed, it is possible to estimate the variation in current gain without lateral voltage drop in the base. The shape of the curve can be approximated to by the straight line shown in Fig. 4, whose slope is that of the current gain curves before they have been influenced by the lateral voltage drop.

Acknowledgements—The author wishes to thank Mr. F. R. Baudert for editing the language of the manuscript; Mr. R. F. Greyvenstein

for useful discussion in the completion of this paper, Dr T. C. Verster of NEERI, CSIR and Prof. A. G. K. Lutsch of Rand Afrikaans University, Johannesburg, for helpful suggestions and for their encouragement of this work; thanks are also due to the Rand Afrikaans University for granting permission to publish at this stage results which are to be included in a Ph.D. thesis.

REFERENCES
1. N. C. de Troye, *IEEE J. Solid-St. Cir.* **SC-9**, 206 (1974).
2. H. H. Berger, *IEEE J. Solid-St. Cir.* **SC-9**, 218 (1974).
3. H. N. Ghosh, *IEEE Trans. Electron Dev.* **ED-12**, 513 (1965).
4. J. C. Irwin, *Bell Syst. Tech. J.* **41**, 387 (1962).
5. S. M. Sze, *Physics of Semiconductor Devices*, p. 104. Wiley, New York (1969).
6. H. K. Gummel, *Bell Syst. Tech. J.* **49**, 115 (1970).
7. M. Crooke and R. F. Greyvenstein, *Trans. SAIEE* **67**, 118 (1976).
8. C. S. den Brinker and A. N. Morgan, *ESSCIRC '75*, IEE Conference Publication Number 130.
9. A. Möschwitzer and K. Lunze, *Halbleiterelektronik-Lehrbuch*, p. 166. Hüttig, Heidelberg (1973).

APPENDIX A
Derivation of the equations for the lateral base current and for the base-emitter voltage

In order to derive the expressions, the differential equations (5) and (6) have to be solved.

If eqn (5) is differentiated once more and eqn (6) substituted for the derivative of the voltage, we get the following second-order differential equation for the current:

$$-\frac{d^2 I(x)}{dx^2} = \frac{qr}{2kT}\frac{dI^2(x)}{dx}.$$ (14)

This can be reduced to a first-order equation by integrating:

$$-\frac{dI(x)}{dx} = \frac{qr}{2kT}[C^2 + I^2(x)].$$ (15)

The constant of integration C^2 is determined from the given boundary conditions (7)–(9):

$$C^2 = \frac{2kT}{qr}i_{sv}b\exp\left[\frac{qV_d}{kT}\right] - \left(i_{sl}ab\exp\left[\frac{qV_d}{kT}\right]\right)^2$$ (12)

Equation (15) can be solved by integration but the result of the integration depends on the sign of the constant of integration. As is shown in Appendix B, the positive sign yields the physically meaningful solution.

Equation (11) for the base-emitter voltage can be derived by integration after $I(x)$ from eqn (10) has been substituted in eqn (6).

APPENDIX B
Determination of the sign of the constant of integration, C^2

To determine the physically meaningful sign of the constant of integration, the case $C = 0$ will be investigated making certain approximations which will not invalidate the results. A simple case is examined: a *p*-base region in an *n*-epitaxial layer. In this case the lateral and vertical current densities, i_{sl} and i_{sv}, are equal at the end of the region. Therefore the expression for the constant of integration can be rewritten as follows:

$$C^2 = i_{sl,v}ab\exp\left[\frac{qV_d}{kT}\right]\left(\frac{2kT}{qra} - i_sl_1vab\exp\left[\frac{qV_d}{kT}\right]\right).$$ (16)

In the case of $C = 0$ the following relationship holds:

$$i_{sl,v}ab\exp\left[\frac{qV_d}{kT}\right] = \frac{2kT}{qra}.$$ (17)

The left-hand side is the expression for the lateral current at the end of the base region. Substitution of the resistivity r for the case where the minority carrier concentration cannot be neglected, yields the following:

$$I_d = ab \frac{2kT}{qa} \frac{1}{a} \int_0^a [q\mu_p p(y) + q\mu_n n(y)] \, dy. \quad (18)$$

If the mobility is assumed constant, and the diffusion constant is introduced by the Einstein relation, the current density which is the sum of the electron and the hole current is given by

$$i_d = i_p + i_n = qD_p \frac{2\frac{1}{a}\int_0^a p(y)\,dy}{a} + qD_n \frac{2\frac{1}{a}\int_0^a n(y)\,dy}{a}. \quad (19)$$

To investigate the minority carrier current, the electron distribution in the p-region at a condition of high injection can, according to the literature[9], be described as:

$$n(x) = -\frac{1}{2}p_{0p} + \sqrt{\left(\frac{1}{2}p_{0p} + n_{0p}\right)^2 - p_{0p}\frac{i_n}{qD_n}}. \quad (20)$$

At the onset of high injection the electron density according to definition is equal to the thermal equilibrium density of the holes:

$$n(d_p) = p_{0p}. \quad (21)$$

If condition (21) is incorporated in eqn (22), and the minority carrier density is neglected, the following experession for hole current density results:

$$i_n = qD_n \frac{2p_{0p}}{d_p}. \quad (22)$$

If d_p and the average minority carrier concentration are equal to "a", i.e. to the thermal equilibrium density of the holes, a comparison between eqns (19) and (22) shows that the case $C = 0$ describes the onset of high injection.

If the lateral base current is less than that given by eqn (20), which is the interesting case, the constant of integration is positive.

Dynamic Behavior of Active Charge in I^{2}L Transistors

Jan Lohstroh

Philips Research Laboratories

Eindhoven, The Netherlands

SEVERAL PUBLISHED I^{2}L models[1,2] give the terminal behavior of I^{2}L gates, but they present only minimal information about the dynamic behavior of electrons and holes inside the gates. Lumped transistor models[3] can provide this information, because in these models, transistors are split up in a number of sections each containing an individual number of minority carriers. Very large circuits cannot be calculated with lumped models; they are too complicated and therefore time-consuming. However lumped models can successfully be used to calculate the internal switching behavior of the I^{2}L gate itself.

A cross section of a typical I^{2}L structure with arbitrary dimensions is shown in Figure 1. For both the PNP and NPN transistor one-dimensional lumped models have been developed. The vertical NPN is split up in three parts[4]: I is the intrinsic NPN transistor, II is a loss diode with a low recombination velocity of electrons at the surface, and III is a loss diode with a high recombination velocity at the surface. Figure 2 illustrates, as an example, the lumped model of the intrinsic part I of the NPN transistor; both the epilayer and base are split up in 6 sections; there is a retarding field in the base. In all of the models it is assumed that all the transistor actions fulfill the conditions of the low injection case. In addition it is assumed that no recombination takes place in the bulk of the epilayer and in the bulk of the P-diffusion[4].

To calculate the minimum delay time an approach with two I^{2}L stages is taken[5]; see also Figure 3. There are two identical I^{2}L stages, preceded by a switch and terminated by a current source with a diode as load. The switch is closed for $t < 0$. At $t \geqslant 0$ the switch is opened; then transistor T1 is charged and consequently T2 is discharged by T1. To calculate the transient with the minimum delay time, the passive charges (stored in the junction capacitances C_j) is neglected with respect to the active charges.

The transient calculation has been made using a Philpac program. Figure 4 gives the calculated voltages on the nodes 1, 2 and 3 (Figure 3) as a function of time. Figure 5a and b show the calculated normalized excess minority carrier concen-

trations in the transistors T1 and T2 with time as parameter. For the parts I, II and III, the hole concentrations in the epilayer are equal; the electron concentrations in the several P-areas are drawn separately.

The most obvious conclusions are:

(A)– Most of the active charge is stored in the epilayer.

(B)– During the transient, the hole concentrations in the epilayer cannot be approximated by lines parallel to the steady state case, especially not for T2 which is switched off. Here the need for the lumped model becomes evident.

(C)– After the voltage pulse leading edge has been propagated (96 ns) and T2 is switched off (106 ns), T1 is not yet fully saturated and requires a relatively long time to do so; $t_{sat.}$ with 95% full charge = 600 ns. This means that if a trailing edge is applied to T1 within $t_{sat.}$, this transistor will be switched off in a shorter time than will be expected from a fully-saturated transistor. This conclusion predicts that ring oscillators with a small number of stages will oscillate with a shorter delay time per stage than ones which have a larger number of stages.

The measured results of ring oscillators with an increasing number of stages is shown in Figure 6. The stages are built up with typical I^{2}L gates without a deep N$^+$ diffusion; in this case the active charges dominate for reasonable currents. For low currents the passive charges dominate and all the oscillators give the same delay time per stage. For high currents the active charges dominate and now short time oscillators give values for $\tau_{min.}$/stage that are too optimistic. Hence, ring oscillators must have enough stages to measure the proper minimum delay time.

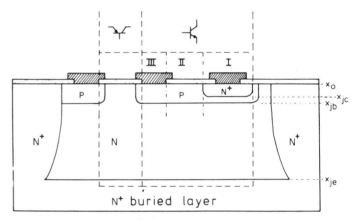

FIGURE 1—Typical I^{2}L structure with arbitrary dimensions. For the dashed sections, lumped models have been developed. Section II and III are loss diodes with different surface recombination velocities.

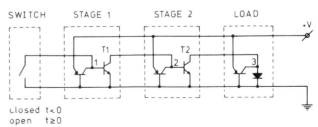

FIGURE 3—Electrical circuit to calculate minimum delay time. For all of the five transistors lumped models have been introduced.

[1] Berger, H. H., and Wiedman, S. K., "Terminal-Oriented Model for Merged Transistor Logic (MTL)", *IEEE J. Solid-State Circuits*, vol. SC-9, p. 211-217; Oct., 1974.

[2] Berger, H. H., "The Injection Model, a Structure-Oriented Model for Merged Transistor Logic (MTL)", *IEEE J. Solid State Circuits*, Vol. SC-9, p. 218-227; Oct., 1974.

[3] Linvill, J. G., "Transistors and Active Circuits" *McGraw-Hill Book Company*, New York; 1961.

[4] Wulms, H. E. J., "Base Current of I^{2}L Transistors", *ISSCC Digest of Technical Papers*, p. 92-93; Feb., 1976.

[5] Klaassen, F. M., "Device Physics of Integrated Injection Logic", *IEEE Transactions on Electron Devices*, Vol. ED-22, p. 145-152; March, 1975.

Reprinted from *IEEE Int. Solid-State Circuits Conf. Digest Tech. Papers*, Feb. 1976, pp. 94–95.

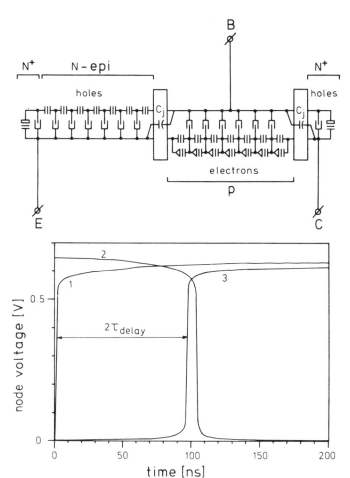

[Left]

FIGURE 2—Lumped model of section I of NPN transistor. Both holes in epilayer and electrons in the base are distributed in six sections. A retarding field in the base is included.

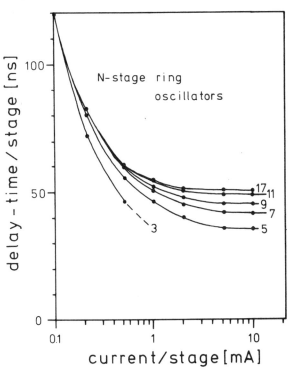

FIGURE 4—Calculated node voltages of circuit in Figure 3. Time between two leading transients corresponds with 2τ delay.

FIGURE 6—Measured delay times in ring oscillators with an increasing number of stages. For high currents active charges dominate; thus short ring oscillators give too optimistic values for $\tau_{min.}$/stage.

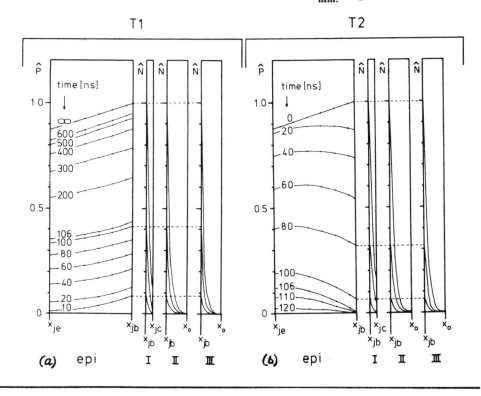

FIGURE 5 (*a and b*)—Calculated normalized excess minority carrier concentrations in transistors T1 and T2 versus location with time as parameter: x_{jc}, x_{jb} and x_{je} = 6.5, 1.5 and 1.0 μm, respectively.

Modeling the Dynamic Behavior of I²L

WALTER H. MATTHEUS, ROBERT P. MERTENS, AND LUK DE SMET

Abstract—The validity of the charge control approach is checked for the normal (upward) operation of an I^2L gate, leading to the conclusion that deviations are mainly due to the distributed nature of the base resistance. An alternative method is presented to determine the relevant device parameters, starting from experimental data. An equivalent model, incorporating the distributed base resistance, is proposed and verified by simulating the power delay characteristics of ring oscillators.

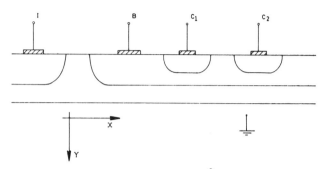

Fig. 1. Cross section of an I^2L gate.

I. INTRODUCTION

MODELS which allow one to characterize I^2L gates from terminal measurements [1] and structure-oriented models [2] have been presented and the methods to determine the parameters for these models have been established.

For transient analysis, these models rely on a one-dimensional charge control equation. In reality, the I^2L geometry is essentially two-dimensional (Fig. 1), but time domain analysis in two dimensions is not feasible. Therefore, one must obtain the least complex model with sufficient accuracy. First-order models describing the switching of saturated transistors are the charge control model and the large signal Ebers–Moll model. These models assume a quasi-static distribution of charge and current [3]. In principle, these models fail because the distributions both in the X (horizontal plane) and in the Y (vertical) directions are non-quasi-static.

It will be demonstrated in this paper that for conventional I^2L structures, the assumption of a quasi-static behavior fails in the X direction prior to the Y direction (Section II). The influence of the distributed nature of the base resistance on the small-signal characteristics of the I^2L gate is investigated in Section III. A method to determine the device parameters will be established in Section IV, and it will be shown that the determination of the time constants from $f_{T,\max}$ (upward) is invalid. In Section V, the least complex model incorporating the distributed base resistance will be presented. The validity of this model will be checked by comparing the results of the simulations with experimental results (Section VI). The model will allow the study of the influence of the interconnection pattern on the minimum propagation delay of ring oscillators.

II. THE VALIDITY OF THE ASSUMPTION OF QUASI-STATIC DISTRIBUTIONS

One of the basic assumptions of charge control theory is the existance of a quasi-static charge distribution. This reflects in the presence of a dominant pole in the small-signal input im-

pedance versus frequency characteristics of a bipolar device [4]. Although the charge control model is used in switching problems, this one-pole approximation remains a valid measure for the applicability of the charge control model.

However, when one plots the measured input impedance of an I^2L gate versus frequency, curves emerge which strongly deviate from the ideal behavior, characterized by a -20 dB/dec rolloff (Fig. 2). This discrepancy is not found for the downward mode of a conventional bipolar transistor since, in this case, the input impedance versus frequency curves behave much more ideally. Theoretically, non-quasi-static behavior, both in the X and in the Y directions, can give rise to the observed deviation from charge control theory. To investigate whether the non-quasi-static behavior in the Y direction can be important, it will first be assumed that no base resistance is present. More generally, all two-dimensional effects in the X direction will first be excluded.

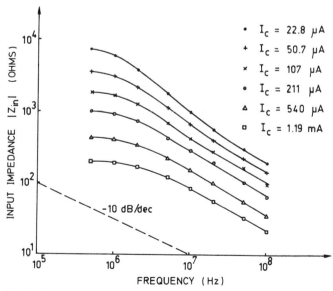

Fig. 2. Frequency characteristics of the magnitude of the input impedance, measured on a two-collector I^2L gate, with the dc collector current as a parameter.

Manuscript received September 1, 1976; revised November 25, 1976.

W. H. Mattheus and L. De Smet are with the Department Elektrotechniek, Laboratorium Elektronica, Systemen, Automatisatie en Technologie, Katholieke Universiteit Leuven, Heverlee, Belgium.

R. P. Mertens is with the Departement Elektrotechniek, Laboratorium Elektronica, Systemen, Automatisatie en Technologie, Katholieke Universiteit Leuven, Heverlee, Belgium, and the Belgian National Science Foundation.

Reprinted from *IEEE J. Solid-State Circuits*, vol. SC-12, pp. 163–170, Apr. 1977.

Since most of the charges are stored in the epitaxial layer, one should look for the variation of that charge with time. It has been reported [5] that this charge distribution is, in principle, non-quasi-static. However, it is important to find out how large the deviation is and how much this affects the characteristics of the device. The criterion at hand to check the validity of the charge control principles in the Y direction is the slope of the input impedance (or admittance) versus frequency characteristics.

The small-signal admittance of a p-n-n$^+$ diode is calculated in the Appendix.

$$Y(\omega) = \frac{q}{kT} \, q \, p_0(0) \frac{D_p}{W} \sqrt{\frac{\tau}{\tau_p} (1 + j\omega\tau_p)}$$

$$\times \frac{1 + \frac{D_p}{sW} \sqrt{\frac{\tau}{\tau_p}(1+j\omega\tau_p)} \tanh \sqrt{\frac{\tau}{\tau_p}(1+j\omega\tau_p)}}{\tanh \sqrt{\frac{\tau}{\tau_p}(1+j\omega\tau_p)} + \frac{D_p}{sW} \sqrt{\frac{\tau}{\tau_p}(1+j\omega\tau_p)}}$$

(1)

with the parameters

$p_0(0)$ dc hole carrier concentration at the n side edge of the space-charge layer, related to the applied voltage

D_p, τ_p diffusion constant and lifetime of holes in the epitaxial layer

W net width of the epitaxial layer

$\tau = \frac{W^2}{D_p}$ transit time of the epitaxial layer.

The effective n-n$^+$ interface recombination velocity s is determined by the recombination and the bandgap narrowing effects [6], [7], and by the doping levels in the n$^+$ layer. In deriving (1), it has been assumed that the base current entirely consists of holes injected into the n and n$^+$ layer. However, in actual I^{2}L devices, electron injection may be important [2], but then the quasi-static behavior of the p-n-n$^+$ diode is enhanced [8]. Therefore, since interest is focused on the importance of non-quasi-static charge and current distribution, it will be assumed that no electron injection is present.

The expression (1) indicates that the small-signal admittance is a complicated function of frequency. At frequencies below the first pole, i.e., $\omega\tau_p < 1$, a constant admittance is found, determined by the device parameters τ/τ_p, D_p/sW, and s and by the external conditions through $p_0(0)$. At higher frequencies, $\omega\tau_p > 1$, the influence of the bulk recombination disappears and the small-signal admittance reduces to

$$Y(\omega) \simeq \frac{q}{kT} \, qp_0(0) \frac{D_p}{W} \sqrt{j\omega\tau} \, \frac{1 + \frac{D_p}{sW} \sqrt{j\omega\tau} \tanh \sqrt{j\omega\tau}}{\tanh \sqrt{j\omega\tau} + \frac{D_p}{sW} \sqrt{j\omega\tau}}.$$

(2)

Two extreme cases can be considered:

1) $s \ll D_p/W$. The admittance becomes

$$Y(\omega) \simeq \frac{q}{kT} qp_0(0) \frac{D_p}{W} \sqrt{j\omega\tau} \tanh \sqrt{j\omega\tau}.$$

(3)

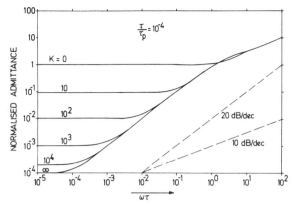

Fig. 3. Normalized input admittance as a function of normalized frequency with $K = D_p/sW$ as a parameter.

The frequency characteristic is illustrated in Fig. 3 by the curve $K = D_p/sW = \infty$. The one-pole admittance of the quasi-static behavior, with a slope of +20 dB/dec, is clearly a good approximation up to frequencies determined by $\omega\tau < 1$. For still higher frequencies, the slope reduces to +10 dB/dec.

2) $s \gg D_p/W$. The admittance now reduces to

$$Y(\omega) \simeq \frac{q}{kT} \, qp_0(0) \frac{D_p}{W} \sqrt{j\omega\tau} \coth \sqrt{j\omega\tau}.$$

(4)

The frequency characteristic is represented in Fig. 3 by the curve $K = D_p/sW = 0$, which is constant for frequencies such that $\omega\tau < 1$. Beyond the frequency $\omega = 1/\tau$, the curve displays a slope of 10 dB/dec.

Hence, the question of whether for practical I^{2}L structures a quasi-static one-lump model in the Y direction suffices is reduced to the problem of determining whether in these devices case 1) or 2) prevails.

Let us first take the example of the I^{2}L devices presented in this paper. The net epi-thickness W between the bottom of the base and the top of the n$^+$ is about 1 μm. The resistivity of the epitaxial layer is 0.5 $\Omega \cdot$ cm. Hence, the transit time turns out to be $\tau = 10^{-9}$ s. A maximum value of the effective surface recombination velocity s can be experimentally determined. Assuming a hole lifetime $\tau_p \gg \tau = 10^{-9}$ s in the epitaxial layer, the dc hole current density can be approximated by

$$j_{p0}(0) \simeq q \, s \, \frac{n_i^2}{N_{\text{epi}}} e^{qV_{BE}/kT}.$$

(5)

where N_{epi} is the donor concentration in the epitaxial layer and V_{BE} is the voltage applied to the p-n-n$^+$ diode.

At $V_{BE} = 0.6$ V, the base current density of the devices under consideration equals 5 mA/cm^2. Assuming that all base current is hole current, a maximum value of s can be derived from (5): $s_{\max} = 160$ cm/s. Since, on the other hand, $D_p/W = 10^5$ cm/s, case 1) prevails for the measurements presented in this paper. The one-pole approximation holds for frequencies up to about $1/(2\pi\tau) = 160$ MHz.

Referring to Fig. 2, it can be concluded that over the entire measured range, a quasi-static one-lump model in the y direction may be assumed. Hence, the shape of the measured curves must be explained by a nonideal behavior in the X direction, which will be treated in the next section.

The above-mentioned condition for case 2), i.e., $s \gg D_p/W$, and the expression (5) also indicate that only for very thick epilayers, not commonly used for I^{2}L, non-quasi-static behavior in the Y direction must be taken into account.

III. SMALL-SIGNAL CHARACTERISTICS OF THE DISTRIBUTED BASE RESISTANCE

It should be pointed out that the upward current gain of an I^{2}L gate, plotted as a function of frequency (Fig. 4), seems to follow the -20 dB/dec rolloff imposed by the charge control model. These results seem to indicate that a single pole charge control model can be used. However, a more detailed analysis shows that this is not the case. The current amplification β indeed equals the product of the input impedance and the transconductance:

$$\beta = Z_{\text{in}} \times g_m . \tag{6}$$

According to the charge control model, the slope of the β characteristics is due to the slope of -20 dB/dec of the input impedance and a constant transconductance. However, the measurements of Z_{in} and g_m separately (Figs. 2 and 5) show that the slope of nearly -20 dB/dec of β originates from the sum of a slope between -10 and -20 dB/dec for Z_{in} and of less than -10 dB/dec for g_m. These data indicate that the use of the charge control model can introduce errors.

It will now be demonstrated that the observed characteristics can be explained if one takes the distributed character of the base resistance (Fig. 6) into account. The general distributed network (Fig. 7, insert) has been analyzed, using the following assumptions, which allow for an analytical solution.

1) The overall impedance R_B and the overall admittance $r_\pi//C_\pi$ are uniform over the length L. This implies that lateral variations of the base resistance are ruled out by adopting mean values for R_B, r_π, and C_π.

2) The voltage dependence of r_π and C_π along the base is neglected for the ac analysis. However, this dependence is taken into account to determine the dc biasing of the overall diode. This condition implies that the results of these calcula-

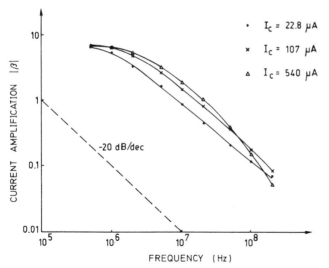

Fig. 4. Frequency characteristics of the upward current amplification, measured on the first collector of a two-collector I^{2}L gate, with the dc collector current as a parameter.

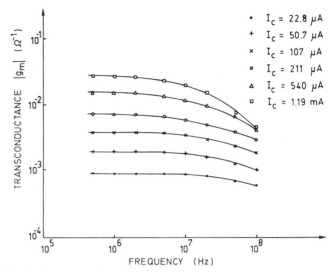

Fig. 5. Frequency characteristics of the transconductance, measured on the first collector of a two-collector I^{2}L gate, with the dc collector current as a parameter.

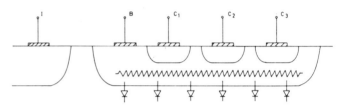

Fig. 6. Distributed base resistance in the I^{2}L gate.

tions will only apply for moderate dc biasing. A practical limit will be discussed in the next section.

Under these assumptions, the input impedance of the distributed base can be written as [9]

$$Z_{\text{in}} = \frac{R_B}{\sqrt{\dfrac{R_B}{r_\pi}(1 + j\,\omega r_\pi C_\pi)}\ \tanh\ \sqrt{\dfrac{R_B}{r_\pi}(1 + j\,\omega r_\pi C_\pi)}} . \tag{7}$$

The schematic characteristic of this impedance versus the frequency has been represented in Fig. 7. Depending on the dc biasing condition, two cases have to be considered.

A. $R_B < r_\pi$

This is represented by the upper curve in Fig. 7.

For $\omega < 1/r_\pi C_\pi$, the impedance is real and equals

$$Z_{\text{in}} \simeq \frac{\sqrt{r_\pi R_B}}{\tanh\ \sqrt{\dfrac{R_B}{r_\pi}}} . \tag{8}$$

For $1/r_\pi C_\pi < \omega < 1/R_B C_\pi$, the impedance is capacitive, and the amplitude rolls off with a -20 dB/dec slope:

$$Z_{\text{in}} \simeq \frac{1}{j\omega C_\pi} . \tag{9}$$

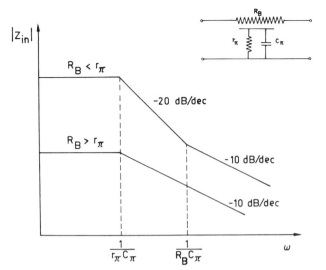

Fig. 7. General distributed network. Diagram of the magnitude of the input impedance as a function of pulsation.

For $\omega > 1/R_B C_\pi$, finally, the network behaves like a distributed line:

$$Z_{\text{in}} \simeq \frac{R_B}{\sqrt{j\omega R_B\, C_\pi}} \,. \tag{10}$$

The slope of the amplitude equals -10 dB/dec.

B. $R_B > r_\pi$

This case is given by the lower curve of Fig. 7.

For $\omega < 1/r_\pi C_\pi$, the impedance is real and is given by (8).

For $\omega > 1/r_\pi C_\pi$, the impedance is determined by the distributed nature of the base:

$$Z_{\text{in}} \simeq \frac{R_B}{\sqrt{j\omega R_B\, C_\pi}} \,. \tag{11}$$

The slope of the amplitude thus equals -10 dB/dec.

It should be stressed that the behavior of the input impedance as predicted by cases A and B is indeed experimentally found (Fig. 2). At high current levels (low r_π), a single breakpoint, separating a constant and a -10 dB/dec region, exists. However, at low current levels (high r_π), two distinct breakpoints with a middle region of approximately -20 dB/dec rolloff exist.

Also, the transconductances of the intrinsic transistors, located along the distributed base, strongly deviate from the constant (= frequency independent) value as predicted by charge control theory. This effect is caused by the ac voltage drop along the base, which is given by the relation [9]

$$\frac{v}{v_1} = \frac{\cosh\sqrt{\dfrac{R_B}{r_\pi}\left(1 - \dfrac{x}{L}\right)^2 (1 + j\omega r_\pi C_\pi)}}{\cosh\sqrt{\dfrac{R_B}{r_\pi}(1 + j\omega r_\pi C_\pi)}} \tag{12}$$

with v_1 the small-signal input voltage and v the small-signal voltage at a point x along the line.

The external transconductance of a transistor located at point x is given by

$$g_m = g_{m0}\,\frac{v}{v_1} \tag{13}$$

with g_{m0} the transconductance of the intrinsic transistor. The measured transconductance is represented in Fig. 5 for the first collector of a two-collector I^2L device.

The conclusion which can be drawn from the calculation is that the distributed nature of the base resistance has a profound influence on the small-signal characteristics of an I^2L gate. Moreover, in the next section it will be shown that the determination of the upward transit time through f_T measurements will result in erroneous results since the basic assumptions which lead to the definition of f_T are no longer valid.

IV. CALCULATION OF THE INVERTOR PARAMETERS FROM THE SMALL-SIGNAL PARAMETERS

The conventional way to determine the invertor parameters τ_F and C_{BE} makes use of the plot of $1/(2\pi f_T)$ as a function of $1/I_c$ and extrapolates $1/(2\pi f_T)$ to the zero value of $1/I_c$. For I^2L, this measurement gives rise to strongly inaccurate results (Fig. 8). The basic charge control assumptions, and hence the definition of f_T, are only valid for very low current levels, indicated by the presence of a -20 dB/dec slope in the frequency characteristics of the input impedance (Fig. 2). Only in this region, $1/(2\pi f_T)$ varies linearly with $1/I_c$ and extrapolation is feasible. However, in the indicated range, f_T will be largely dominated by the space-charge capacitances, making the measurement of τ_F inaccurate.

The alternative method for deriving τ_F and C_{BE} relies on the expressions (7), (12), and (13). The device parameters are determined using a square least squares fitting technique for the frequency characteristics of the input impedance and of the transconductance. The main approximation in this method is that the dc voltage drop along the base resistance is neglected to determine r_π and C_π (Section III). The voltage dependence of the diode characteristics is neglected to calculate the small-signal parameters, but not for the dc operating point of the total diode. To check the influence of this approximation, a

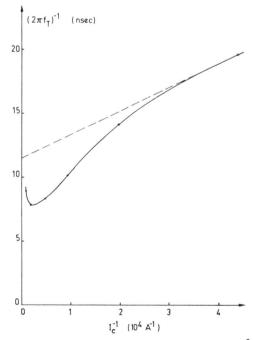

Fig. 8. $1/(2\pi f_T)$ versus $1/I_C$ measured on a two-collector I^2L gate.

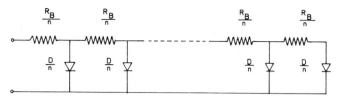

Fig. 9. Discrete model of the distributed network.

TABLE I
RESULTS OF THE DEVICE PARAMETERS OBTAINED BY THE LEAST SQUARES
FITTING METHOD DESCRIBED IN SECTION IV

V_{BE} (mV)	r_π (Ω)	τ (nsec)	R_{B1} (Ω)	$R_{B1} + R_{B2}$ (Ω)
660	7910	145	197	461
680	3540	102	240	433
700	1730	85.4	243	441

distributed network has been simulated using a circuit analysis program. The network consists of 20 sections, as represented in Fig. 9. The characteristics of the diodes and the operating point are chosen such that, neglecting the base resistance, the r_π of the overall diode, respectively, equals 5 kΩ, 500 Ω, and 50 Ω. The frequency characteristics are given in Fig. 10. The solid lines represent the exact solution, whereas the dashed curves represent the result as obtained from formula (7). For $r_\pi = 5$ kΩ, both characteristics coincide. The deviation becomes important when r_π is smaller than R_B. For $r_\pi = R_B$, the error is 13 percent and for $r_\pi = 0.1 R_B$, it is already 26 percent. Analogous results are found for the transconductance. It therefore will be assumed that the analytical formulas (7) and (12) are valid if $r_\pi \geqslant R_B$. Other approximations in the derivation of (7) and (12) are the assumption of low level injection and the fact that one assumes the base resistance to be uniform along the length of the cell. The variation of the base resistance caused by the presence of the collectors is neglected and a mean value for the base resistance per unit length has been assumed. Furthermore, the influence of a lateral electric field in the epilayer is neglected.

The method to derive the invertor parameters proceeds as follows. From the frequency characteristic of the input impedance, the small-signal resistance r_π and the time constant $\tau = r_\pi C_\pi$ of the emitter–base diode are determined, using a least squares fitting method for expression (7). This procedure is repeated for every V_{BE}. In principle, the total base resistance R_B also could be derived from this curve-fitting method. However, an approximate analysis of the expression of the input impedance Z_{in} shows that the base resistance mainly influences Z_{in} at higher frequencies. Using a least squares approach, R_B will be derived from a limited number of points in the region where the experimental error starts to be impor-

tant. It is, therefore, inappropriate to derive the value of R_B from the fitting of Z_{in}. For this reason, all calculations have been performed with a value of R_B determined from dc measurements. This rough estimate suffices since the influence of R_B on the value of the other parameters will be small.

With these values for r_π and C_π, the base resistance $R_{Bx} = R_B(1 - x/L)$ can be determined for each collector by a least squares fitting approach on the transconductance versus frequency characteristic using expression (12) for every V_{BE} value. The method, described above, has been tested on a two-collector invertor. Some results are summarized in Table I.

The resistor R_{B1} stands for the base resistance between the base contact and the first collector, and R_{B2} is the base resistance between the first and the second collectors. The time constant $\tau = r_\pi C_\pi$ is determined by the diffusion capacitance and by the space-charge capacitances:

$$\tau = \tau_E + r_\pi(C_{je} + C_{jc}) \qquad (14)$$

with

τ_E time constant of the emitter–base diode
C_{je} space-charge capacitance of the emitter–base diode
C_{jc} space-charge capacitances of the base–collector diodes.

Fig. 11 shows the derived time constant τ as a function of r_π. It should be stressed that this characteristic indeed displays the linear relationship predicted by (14). The determination of $\tau_E = 69$ ns from the intersection with the vertical τ axis thus is meaningful, provided that the extrapolation is done in the region $R_B \leqslant r_\pi$. This is not the case when using the classical method as represented by Fig. 8. Finally, the emitter tran-

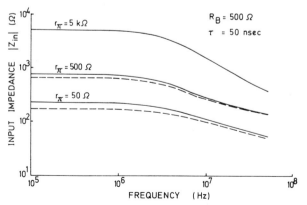

Fig. 10. Simulation of the frequency characteristics of the magnitude of the input impedance of a distributed system. (a) Without dc voltage drop over R_B (solid lines). (b) With dc voltage drop over R_B (dashed lines).

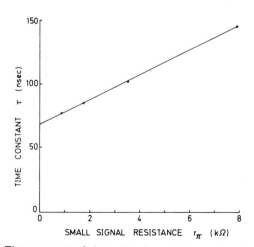

Fig. 11. Time constant of the emitter–base diode as a function of the small-signal emitter base resistance r_π.

sit time for the upward operation of the transistor is $\tau_F = \tau_E/\beta_u$, with β_u the upward current amplification of the intrinsic transistor. However, the value of β_u depends on the model being used for the I^2L gate.

V. Equivalent Model of an I^2L Inverter

For use in practical circuit analysis programs, the distributed base resistance must be represented by a number of discrete branches. To limit the number of nodes, the number of lumps must be as small as possible. The influence of the number of lumps has been checked by comparing the small-signal characteristics of a set of discrete uniformly distributed networks with a varying number of branches. The conclusion is that a lumped model with two sections can be accepted up to current levels where $r_\pi \geqslant R_B$; this result agrees with the conclusions of the previous sections.

To investigate the influence of the discretization on the switching properties, a cell with fan-out 4 has been simulated with a circuit analysis program for transient analysis. Each collector is loaded by the base of the following invertor. At $t = 0$, a switch is opened and the invertor is charged through the p-n-p transistor. Since interest is focused on the relative rather than on the absolute switching performances of the different collectors, this p-n-p transistor is simulated by a constant current source. The simulations have been performed assuming a distributed base resistance with (4×20) sections in the first case and with a model where each base impedance has been represented by a single resistor in the second case. The results are given in Fig. 12 for an injection current equal to 100 μA. The agreement is better towards the fourth collector because the last collectors in the discrete case are a better representation of the distributed nature due to the presence of the different resistances.

Other computer runs with a two-collector structure have shown that the representation with one resistance per collector is adequate up to current levels corresponding to $r_\pi \geqslant R_B$. For larger injection currents, the deviation strongly increases and equals 100 percent at 1 mA.

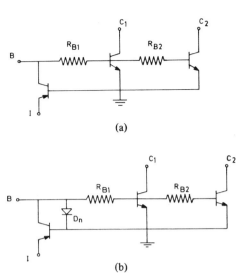

Fig. 13. Equivalent model of a two-collector I^2L gate. (a) Terminal-oriented model. (b) Structure-oriented model.

However, since such high current levels are of no practical interest for I^2L, the models of Fig. 13 are adequate for most practical problems. A minimum of two lumps is necessary. This requirement is met since the minimum fan-out equals two, except for a simple invertor. In this case, an additional lump is necessary.

Fig. 13(a) gives the model for the case where only terminal measurements are available. The parameters can be determined by the method described in the previous section. The resistance R_{B1} is determined from the transconductance versus frequency plot for the first collector; the resistance R_{B2} equals the difference between the base resistance determined from the transconductance versus frequency plot of the second and first collectors, respectively.

On the other hand, if detailed information about the structure and technology is available, the representation of Fig. 13(b) can be used. The diode D_n stands for the losses underneath the base contact; the other loss currents are incorporated in the β_u values of the different collectors. To determine the model parameters completely, other measurements, in addition to terminal measurements, are necessary [2]

VI. Simulation of Ring Oscillators

To check the validity of the proposed model, ring oscillators with fan-out 2 and with fan-out 4 have been measured and simulated, and the resulting power-delay characteristics are compared in Fig. 14. The base contact of the invertors is located at the injector side. The model parameters have been determined by the method presented in Section IV.

The lateral p-n-p transistor is simulated by a Gummel–Poon model, which allows us to take high injection effects into account [10]. The correction introduced this way is very important in the range of interest for this paper, i.e., beyond 10 μW. Indeed, when high injection effects are present in the injector, more power will be consumed from the source for the identical current injected into the base of the invertor. The net result is that the power-delay curves are spread out in the high power range.

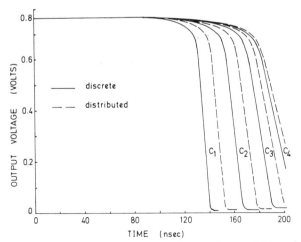

Fig. 12. Variation of the collector voltages when switching a four-collector I^2L gate. (a) Discrete base resistances (solid lines). (b) Distributed base resistance (dashed lines).

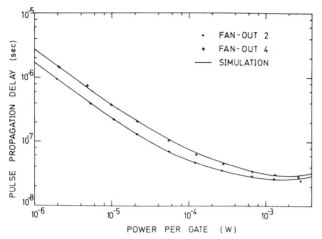

Fig. 14. Measured and simulated power delay characteristics of a two-
and a four-collector I²L gate.

The agreement between measured and simulated results is good up to very high power levels. Beyond 10^{-3} W/gate, the deviation becomes important, but then the proposed model is no longer valid ($r_\pi < R_B$). However, the point 10^{-3} W/gate is also a practical limit since higher power levels will rarely be used in I²L.

The model also has been used to investigate the influence of the position of the base contact on the propagation delay. Ring oscillators have been tested and simulated using I²L invertors with the base contact located near the injector or at the end of the cell. The different connection patterns are summarized in the insert in Fig. 15. The calculated power-delay plots are represented in Fig. 15. For sufficiently low power levels, in this case smaller than 20 μW/gate, the characteristics coincide because the voltage drop across the base resistance is too small to have any effect on the performance.

For high power levels, the voltage drop across the distributed base resistance causes a different switching time, the structures with the base contact on the injector side being slower. The

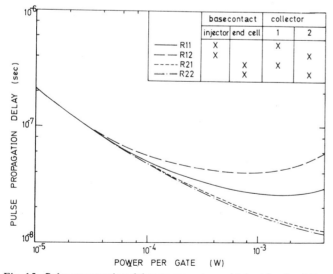

Fig. 15. Pulse propagation delay versus power, obtained by simulation of ring oscillators composed of two-collector I²L gate structures. The four interconnection patterns are summarized in the insert.

reason is that, in this case, the switching collector must evacuate a higher charge, stored underneath the base contact region of the following gate, than corresponding to its own current level. This effect is more pronounced if the collector is located further from the injector.

The presented results of the simulations are in good agreement with the characteristics measured on the actual devices. It can thus be concluded that the models of Section V allow us to take the geometry dependence of the propagation delay into account.

VII. CONCLUSIONS

It has been demonstrated in this paper that the distributed nature of the base resistance in I²L devices has to be taken into account for accurate device modeling. The conventional definition of f_T and the commonly used measurement of the transit time do not now hold for I²L devices. An alternative model and a method to determine the device parameters relying on curve fitting of the small-signal characteristics have been represented. The model has been used to predict minimum propagation delays and power-delay curves for different ring oscillators. The model enables us to study the influence of the position of the base contact on the minimum propagation delay. The calculated values have been compared with measured values and sufficient accuracy is obtained.

APPENDIX

The admittance of the n-n⁺ part of the p-n-n⁺ diode of Fig. 16 will be calculated. The profile is assumed to vary stepwise, and at the n-n⁺ interface, an effective recombination velocity s is adopted to account for the hole current flowing through the plane $x = W$. Furthermore, low injection conditions are assumed. Let the net hole concentration be the sum of a dc and a small-signal part:

$$p = p_0 + p_1 e^{j\omega t} \tag{15}$$

with

p_0 dc net hole concentration
p_1 complex magnitude of the small-signal hole concentration
ω pulsation frequency.

The continuity equation for p_1 then becomes

$$\frac{d^2 p_1}{dx^2} - \frac{p_1}{L_p^{*2}} = 0 \tag{16}$$

with

$$L_p^{*2} = \frac{D_p \tau_p}{1 + j\omega\tau_p}. \tag{17}$$

The boundary conditions are as follows.
1) At $x = 0$, the net hole concentration is determined by the

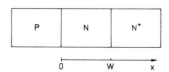

Fig. 16. Schematic of a p-n-n⁺ diode.

applied voltage v according to Boltzmann's law:

$$p(0) = p_e e^{qv/kT}. \tag{18}$$

For the ac part, this condition becomes

$$p_1(0) = \frac{q}{kT} p_0(0) v_1 \tag{19}$$

with v_1 the magnitude of the small-signal applied voltage.

2) At $x = W$, an interface recombination velocity s relates the hole current density with the net hole concentration. Expressed in ac variables,

$$j_{p1}(W) = qs p_1(W). \tag{20}$$

This condition can be expressed entirely in p_1 using

$$j_{p1} = -q D_p \frac{dp_1}{dx}. \tag{21}$$

Solving the differential equation (16) subject to the boundary conditions (19) and (20) enables one to calculate the admittance defined as

$$Y(\omega) = \frac{j_{p1}(0)}{v_1}. \tag{22}$$

This results in

$$Y(\omega) = \frac{q}{kT} q\, p_0(0) \frac{D_p}{L_p^*} \frac{1 + \dfrac{D_p}{sL_p^*} \tanh \dfrac{W}{L_p^*}}{\tanh \dfrac{W}{L_p^*} + \dfrac{D_p}{sL_p^*}}. \tag{23}$$

References

[1] H. H. Berger and S. K. Wiedmann, "Terminal-oriented model for merged transistor logic (MTL)," *IEEE J. Solid-State Circuits*, vol. SC-9, pp. 211–217, Oct. 1974.

[2] H. H. Berger, "The injection model–A structure oriented model for merged transistor logic (MTL)," *IEEE J. Solid-State Circuits*, vol. SC-9, pp. 218–227, Oct. 1974.

[3] C. S. Meyer, D. K. Lynn, and D. J. Hamilton, *Analysis and Design of Integrated Circuits*. New York: McGraw-Hill, 1968.

[4] R. Beaufoy and J. J. Sparkes, "The junction transistor as a charge-controlled device," *ATE J.*, vol. 13, pp. 310–327, 1957.

[5] J. Lohstroh, "Dynamic behavior of active charge in I^2L transistors," in *ISSCC Dig. Tech. Papers*, 1976, pp. 94–95.

[6] R. J. Van Overstraeten, H. J. De Man, and R. P. Mertens, "Transport equations in heavy doped silicon," *IEEE Trans. Electron Devices*, vol. ED-20, pp. 290–298, Mar. 1973.

[7] J. W. Slotboom and H. C. De Graaf, "Measurements of bandgap narrowing in Si bipolar transistors," *Solid-State Electron.*, vol. 19, pp. 857–862, 1976.

[8] L. De Smet and R. Mertens, "On the saturation time of an NPNN$^+$ bipolar transistor," presented at the ESSDERC Conf., Grenoble, France, 1975.

[9] H. C. Lin, *Integrated Electronics*. San Francisco: Holden-Day, 1967.

[10] H. K. Gummel and H. C. Poon, "An integral charge control model of bipolar transistors," *Bell Syst. Tech. J.*, vol. 49, pp. 827–852, May 1970.

The Effect of Base Contact Position on the Relative Propagation Delays of the Multiple Outputs of an I²L Gate

DAVID V. KERNS, JR., MEMBER, IEEE

Abstract—The multiple collectors of an I²L gate do not slew simultaneously, giving different propagation delays for the various outputs; the relative positions of the base contact, the injector, and the collector outputs affect these delays. In this paper, three possible configurations are modeled, simulated, and the results summarized.

INTRODUCTION

INTEGRATED injection logic (I²L) or merged transistor logic (MTL) has received considerable attention since it was introduced in 1972 [1], [2]. The now well-known structure in which a lateral p-n-p current source is merged with an inverted n-p-n device with multiple collectors (see Fig. 1) is challenging both conventional bipolar and MOS technologies in many applications.

The more or less standard layout for I²L circuitry is that shown in Fig. 2, where gates are placed along both sides of an injector stripe. This arrangement provides high packing density and ease of layout, since metal routes can be placed over unused positions in neighboring cells. Within a gate, the designer has the freedom to place the base contact at any of the cell positions, the position chosen usually governed by metal routing constraints.

In designing any digital system, certain critical paths require a knowledge of the gate propagation delays. For I²L gates, the minimum propagation delay has been shown approximately proportional to fan out [3]; however, for a given gate, the propagation delays from input to each of the multiple out-

Manuscript received January 20, 1976; revised June 6, 1976. A portion of this work was performed at Bell Laboratories.

The author is with the Department of Electrical Engineering, Auburn University, Auburn, AL 36830.

Reprinted from *IEEE J. Solid-State Circuits*, vol. SC-11, pp. 712–717, Oct. 1976.

180

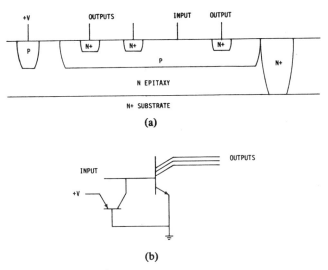

Fig. 1. (a) Basic I^{2}L gate structure and (b) circuit equivalent.

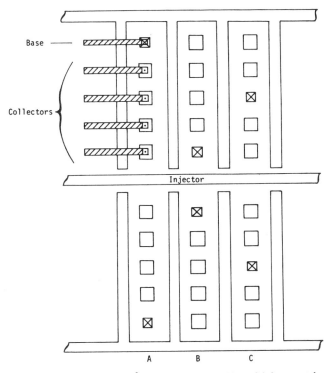

Fig. 2. Typical layout of I^{2}L gates on both sides of injector stripe.
(Gates A, B, and C on bottom row illustrate the three configurations
considered in this paper.)

puts will generally differ and the relative positions of the base
contact, the injector, and the collector outputs affect these
propagation delays. The effect of base resistance debiasing
has been mentioned previously by de Troye [4] and den
Brinker and Morgan [5]. In this paper, three possible configurations are modeled, simulated, and the results summarized
for a range of device parameters and conditions.

The three classes considered are illustrated on the bottom
line of gates in Fig. 2: A) the base contact at the opposite end
of the gate from the injector, B) the base contact adjacent to
the injector, and C) the base contact in the middle of the gate.
An equivalent circuit model of the three cases just described
is shown in Fig. 3 with all three gates driven by a common
source S.

THE MODEL

The most accurate measure of propagation delay for a gate
without a hard threshold (i.e., an I^{2}L gate) is obtained by
using a large number of cascaded stages or a ring oscillator. For
ease of simulation, the I^{2}L gates in this paper are driven by

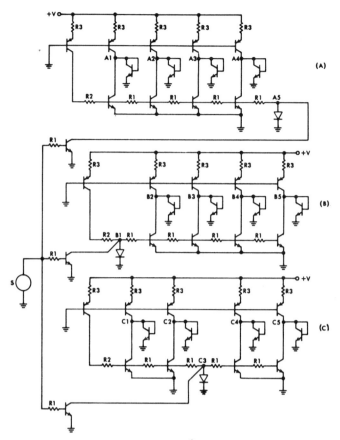

Fig. 3. Complete model of the three I^2L gate configurations and the driving circuitry.

one-transistor inverters which simulate the preceding gate, and the inverters are in turn driven by a single source with rise and fall times approximating those of the gate modeled. The source S must act as a current source when the input to the inverters is swinging positive (simulating the charging of the bases of the inverters by injector current), and must act like a current sink of compliance V_{ce}(sat) when pulling down (simulating the effect of a saturated device). To model this, separate computer runs were performed for the two cases with the sources as described.

Fig. 3 shows each of the gates modeled for a fan out of four by a five-section model. There are four transistors per gate, each associated with a collector output. In the fifth position, a diode is connected to model the parasitic junction under the base contact. The transport model was used in modeling all transistors, in slight contrast to previous work using an Ebers–Moll approach [6], [7].

The parameter β_u is the upward common-emitter current gain or inverse beta of a normal n-p-n structure. To ensure that the transistors modeling each section could be saturated, the device is designed for 100 percent base overdrive. Thus, for a five-section base, $\beta_u = 10$. Other pertinent transport model device parameters for these n-p-n transistors, the parasitic diode, and the p-n-p injector devices are listed in Table I, and are characteristic of devices from a standard n on n^+ 1 $\Omega \cdot$ cm epi I^2L technology.

Berger and Wiedmann [6] have shown that the p-n-p injector can be modeled as a current source. The value of this source

TABLE I
TRANSPORT MODEL PARAMETERS

n-p-n Transistor (each section)

$$I_s = 4.6 \times 10^{-16} \text{ A}$$

$\beta_u = 10$	$\beta_d = 70$
$\tau_u = 5$ ns	$\tau_d = 0.7$ ns
$C_{EJ} = 0.475$ pF	$C_{CJ} = 0.45$ pF

p-n-p Transistor (each injector)

$$I_s = 2.0 \times 10^{-17} \text{ A}$$

$\beta_F = 4$	$\beta_R = 4$
$\tau_F = 5$ ns	$\tau_R = 5$ ns
$C_{EJ} = 0.475$ pF	$C_{CJ} = 0.45$ pF

Diode (under base contact)

$$I_s = 4.6 \times 10^{-17} \text{ A}$$
$$C_D = 0.475 \text{ pF}$$
$$\tau_D = 5 \text{ ns}$$

is related to the actual injector emitter current by including the effects of finite transistor gains and back-injected current towards the injector. Simulations were done, both with the injector modeled as a current source, and with the complete p-n-p transistor structure. The discrepencies between these approaches are shown in the tabulation that follows later. Identical diodes of appropriate size are placed on all the collector outputs to simulate the inputs to the following gates,

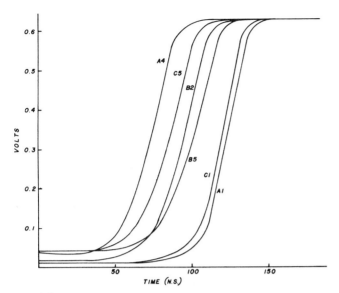

Fig. 4. I²L gate output waveforms for positive transitions (time measured from beginning of source s transition.)

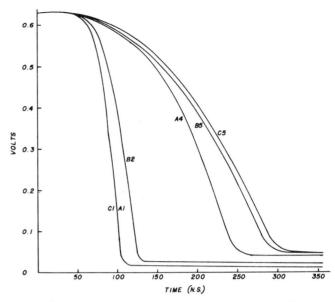

Fig. 5. I²L gate output waveforms for negative transitions (time measured from beginning of source s transition.)

and the p-n-p transistors connected to these nodes provide the injector currents for these gates. The resistance connecting the gate sections, the intersection resistance, is designated R_1, and R_2 is set at 0.8 of R_1. The resistance R_3 is adjusted to control the injector current.

THE SIMULATION

The computer simulations were done with both the NICAP and SPICE circuit analysis computer programs. The simulation seeks first to examine the *relative* delays in switching of the I²L gate outputs for the three configurations. A "benchmark" simulation (to which later variations will be compared) was done with a set of parameters typical of high-speed I²L. At higher injector currents, the series base drops are increased, giving a greater dispersion in propagation delays. For this reference simulation, the injector emitter current was set at 122 μA. The intersection resistance, R_1, was set somewhat lower than a typical value at 150 Ω to emphasize that, even for such a value, delay variations are significant.

The voltages at the collectors on opposite ends of the gates were plotted as a function of time (measured from the beginning of the source transition) for both positive and negative transitions; see Figs. 4 and 5, respectively. The time to first transition thus represents two average gate delays; the relative delays show the proper time differences for a single gate.

RESULTS OF THE REFERENCE SIMULATION

Consider first gate A in Fig. 3 with the base contact and injector on opposite ends of the gate. For positive transitions, collector A4 (nearest the base contact) shows the smallest propagation delay, while collector A1 shows the largest of all the outputs in all three configurations. The collectors A2 and A3 slow at times approximately evenly spaced between A1 and A4. For negative transitions (Fig. 5), output A1 switches (along with C1) the fastest of all the outputs, while A4 is the fastest of a slower group. Thus, configuration A shows the

greatest dispersion of positive transition propagation delays from slowest to fastest and the fastest negative transitions. Because of this spread in positive transition delays, care should be exercised when utilizing this arrangement to avoid race conditions in the logic. Configuration B with the injector adjacent to the base contact gives a positive transition propagation delay slower than A4, approximately midway between A4 and A1. The spread of these propagation delays, however, is very narrow, with B3 and B4 falling between B2 and B5. The spread in negative transition delays is about the same as for configuration A, with some penalty in absolute delay. Thus, if absolute speed is not of critical importance, configuration B appears most desirable because it more nearly gives simultaneous switching of the multiple outputs. The final arrangement C shows a relatively wide dispersion of positive transition propagation delays (output C4 switched slightly faster than C5, giving a slightly wider spread in delays than that shown in Fig. 4) and the most spread and slowest of negative transition delays. This configuration appears generally less desirable compared to A and B described above.

EXPLANATION OF RESULTS

The variation in delays can be explained by examination of the distributed network which comprises the base of the I²L gate. The series intersection resistance is shunted periodically by the emitter–base capacitance and junction of the section transistors. The devices nearest the injector end will be in heaviest saturation, as evidenced in Fig. 4 by the lower saturation voltages of A1, C1, and B2. Additionally, the base contact provides the path through which base charge is removed and the inverted device is switched "off." For positive output transitions, the device in heaviest saturation and furthest from the base contact (namely, A1) should show the longest propagation delay; conversely, the least saturated output and closest to a base contact (A4) should show the shortest delay. These conclusions are consistent with the simulation. Configuration

TABLE II

Condition	$\bar{t1}^+ = \dfrac{tA4}{2}$	$\Delta t^+ = tA1 - tA4$	$tC5$	$tB2$	$tB5$	$tC1$
	(ns)	(ns)	Positive Transitions (Fraction of Δt^+)			

Positive Transitions

Condition	$\bar{t1}^+ = \dfrac{tA4}{2}$ (ns)	$\Delta t^+ = tA1 - tA4$ (ns)	$tC5$	$tB2$	$tB5$	$tC1$
			(Fraction of Δt^+)			
Current Source Injector (100 μA)	41.5	52	0.288	0.423	0.577	0.923
*$IE_{\text{p-n-p}} = 122\,\mu$A	42	48	0.271	0.438	0.583	0.917
$IE_{\text{p-n-p}} = 87\,\mu$A	55	41	0.293	0.415	0.561	0.878
$IE_{\text{p-n-p}} = 51\,\mu$A	82	30	0.266	0.366	0.533	0.833
*$\beta_u = 10$	42	48	0.271	0.438	0.583	0.917
$\beta_u = 15$	45.5	42	0.357	0.404	0.643	0.905
$\beta_u = 20$	47.5	39	0.385	0.385	0.667	0.897
$R1 = 120\,\Omega$	44.5	52	0.286	0.429	0.571	0.906
*$R1 = 150\,\Omega$	42	48	0.271	0.438	0.583	0.917
$R1 = 180\,\Omega$	40	53	0.264	0.453	0.604	0.943
$R1 = 200\,\Omega$	38.5	57	0.246	0.474	0.596	0.930
$R1 = 220\,\Omega$	37.5	59	0.237	0.475	0.593	0.949

Negative Transitions

Condition	$t1^- = \dfrac{tC1}{2}$ (ns)	$\Delta t^- = tC5 - tC1$ (ns)	$tA1$	$tB2$	$tA4$	$tB5$
			(Fraction of Δt^-)			
Current Source Injector (100 μA)	34.5	80	0.000	0.113	0.813	0.888
*$IE_{\text{p-n-p}} = 122\,\mu$A	39	89	0.000	0.112	0.787	0.899
$IE_{\text{p-n-p}} = 87\,\mu$A	49	65	0.000	0.138	0.800	0.831
$IE_{\text{p-n-p}} = 51\,\mu$A	73	39	0.000	0.205	0.820	0.897
*$\beta_u = 10$	39	89	0.000	0.112	0.787	0.899
$\beta_u = 15$	37	55	0.000	0.164	0.818	0.873
$\beta_u = 20$	37	45	0.000	0.178	0.844	0.889
$R1 = 120\,\Omega$	38.5	68	0.015	0.132	0.794	0.853
*$R1 = 150\,\Omega$	39	89	0.000	0.112	0.787	0.899
$R1 = 180\,\Omega$	38.5	117	0.000	0.094	0.761	0.940
$R1 = 200\,\Omega$	38	143	0.000	0.084	0.727	0.979
$R1 = 220\,\Omega$	38	188	0.000	0.069	0.654	0.979

* = reference simulation. $\bar{t1}$ = average time to first transition. Δt = time interval from first transition to last.

B shows approximately equal positive transition propagation delays because of the offsetting effect of two phenomena—the distributing of injector current down the length of the base region and during turn off, and the removal of charge from the base, back through the same network (i.e., the device in heaviest saturation has base charge removed the fastest, etc.). This leads one to consider the possibility of an optimally designed structure similar to configuration B where all outputs would show equal positive transition propagation delays.

A similar type of reasoning can be used to explain the negative transitions of Fig. 5.

THE EFFECT OF VARYING INJECTOR CURRENT, INTERSECTION RESISTANCE, AND UPWARD BETA

Computer simulations were performed to determine the effects of varying injector current, intersection resistance, and upward beta on the propagation delays. In order to compare delay times without presenting excessive graphical infor-mation, an arbitrary voltage threshold of 0.5 V was selected to mark points in time to and from which delays could be measured. The actual switching waveforms for these additional simulations appeared similar to Figs. 4 and 5, except with different time scales. Table II summarizes these results for both positive and negative transitions.

The so-called reference simulation, as described earlier, is marked with an asterisk and repeated in each of the sections of Table II. The only parameter varied in the simulations described in each of the sections is that given in the first column. The second column gives a value for $\bar{t1}$, the average time to the first transition. This is obtained by halving the time-to-first-transition obtained from the simulation, since the simulation includes two gate delays. The third column presents the time spread Δt or the time interval from the first transition to the last transition for a particular simulation. Columns 4–7 mark the transition points of the other outputs expressed as a fraction of the time interval Δt.

Note that for both positive and negative transitions, there is the expected strong increase in time to first transition and decrease in delay spread Δt as injector current is reduced. Data are presented for one simulation where the p-n-p injector structure is replaced by an ideal current source of $100\,\mu$A. The results are reasonably close to the reference simulation.

Varying both upward beta and intersection resistance alters the time-to-first-transition only slightly; however, they have a substantial effect on Δt, as shown.

Of particular interest is the result that throughout the range of parameter variations described, the order of switching of the various outputs does not change, and the relative time positions of the transitions change by less than 10 percent with three exceptions. The exceptions are a 12 percent increase in the relative positive transition time for $C5$ as β_u is increased and a 13 percent change in both $tA4$ and $tB5$ for negative transitions as intersection resistance is varied. The nearly simultaneous negative transition switching of $A1$ and $C1$ proved interesting and consistent. The trends in the relative propagation delays of the other outputs as gate parameters are varied can be determined from Table II.

CONCLUSIONS

Configurations A and B offer widely different responses as described, and the choice of which would be more appropriate would depend on the timing requirements of the logic system being implemented. In reality, the base contact cannot always be placed at extreme ends of the gates due simply to layout constraints; however, the tendencies in propagation delay as base contact position is varied are illustrated. The model is generalized by varying three principal device variables: injector current, intersection resistance, and upward beta with no resulting change of significance in *relative* propagation delays.

These results were valuable in the design and layout of an I^2L microprocessor chip, and should prove useful to the designer of any I^2L circuit with critical timing requirements or potential race conditions.

ACKNOWLEDGMENT

The author would like to thank G. W. Kling for his assistance with the modeling and F. W. Hewlett, Jr. for supplying model parameters. Also, J. R. Griffith should be acknowledged for his help in running the computer simulations.

REFERENCES

[1] K. Hart and A. Slob, "Integrated injection logic: A new approach to LSI," *IEEE J. Solid-State Circuits*, vol. SC-7, pp. 346–351, 1972.
[2] H. H. Berger and S. K. Wiedmann, "Merged transistor logic (MTL) —A low cost bipolar concept," *IEEE J. Solid-State Circuits*, vol. SC-7, pp. 340–346, 1972.
[3] F. M. Klaassen, "Device physics of integrated injection logic," *IEEE Trans. Electron Devices*, vol. ED-22, pp. 145–152, 1975.
[4] N. C. de Troye, "Integrated injection logic–Present and future," *IEEE J. Solid-State Circuits*, vol. SC-9, pp. 206–211, 1974.
[5] C. den Brinker and A. Morgan, in *Proc. 1st European Solid-State Circuits Conf.*, Sept. 2-5, 1975, pp. 18–19, IEE Conf. Publ. 130.
[6] H. H. Berger and S. K. Wiedmann, "Terminal-oriented model for merged transistor logic," *IEEE J. Solid-State Circuits*, vol. SC-9, pp. 211–217, 1974.
[7] H. H. Berger, "The injection model–A structure-oriented model for merged transistor logic," *IEEE J. Solid-State Circuits*, pp. 218–227, 1974.

Schottky I²L (Substrate Fed Logic)—An Analysis of the Implications of the Vertical Injector Structure and Schottky Collection

VICTOR BLATT AND GEOFFREY W. SUMERLING

Abstract—The dc behavior of a Schottky I²L gate is analyzed by using the Ebers–Moll equations, modified to include Schottky diodes. The usual definition of I²L common emitter current gain is replaced by a new definition which is more suitable for the vertical injector structure of Schottky I²L. The analysis is general and can be applied to any multijunction structure containing Schottky diodes or having a distributed current source. This framework is used to examine the effect on the fan-out of minority carrier collection at the Schottky contacts. Equations are presented which relate both the recombination at the Schottky contacts and the vertical reinjection through the inverse p-n-p transistor to the device structure.

LIST OF SYMBOLS

α_d Downward common-base current gain for one collector of the n-p-n multisection transistor.

α_i Common-base current gain of inverse p-n-p injector transistor.

α_n Common-base current gain of the p-n-p injector transistor.

α_{uc} Upward common-base current gain for one collector of the n-p-n multisection transistor.

α_{us} Upward common-base current gain for one Schottky contact of the n-p-n multisection transistor.

β_d Downward common-emitter current gain for one emitter of the n-p-n multisection transistor.

β_{uc} Upward common-emitter current gain per unit section for one collector of the n-p-n multisection transistor.

β_{us} Upward common-emitter current gain per unit section for one Schottky contact of the n-p-n multisection transistor.

A_c Collector area.

A_R Injector area per unit section.

A_S Schottky contact area.

D_{nc} Electron diffusion constant in the p-base beneath the collector.

D_{ns} Electron diffusion constant in the p-base beneath the Schottky contact.

D_p Hole diffusion constant in the n-epitaxial layer.

I_b Base current arising from recombination in n-p-n emitter and base.

I_c Collector current.

I_c^* Collector current measured with all collectors and Schottky contacts in the same gate unsaturated.

I_o Current collected from the injector by a unit section of the n-p-n base.

I_R Reinjection current.

I_s Current collected by a reverse-biased Schottky contact.

I_s^* Current collected by a reverse-biased Schottky contact with all other collectors and Schottky contacts in the same gate unsaturated.

I_{11} Diode current of injector–n-p-n emitter junction.

I_{22} Diode current of emitter–base junction.

I_{cc} Diode current of collector–base junction.

I_{ss} Diode current of Schottky contact–base junction.

m Number of collectors per gate.

m' Number of saturated collectors per gate.

M Number of unit sections per gate.

n Number of Schottky contacts per gate.

n' Number of saturated Schottky contacts per gate.

n_i Intrinsic carrier concentration.

N Maximum number of units that a collector can drive.

N_{AC} Doping density of the base under the collector.

N_{AS} Doping density of the base under the Schottky contact.

N_D Doping density of the n-epitaxial layer.

q Electronic charge.

V_{BE} Emitter–base junction voltage of the n-p-n transistor.

V_T Thermal voltage ($= kT/q$).

W_c Base width of n-p-n transistor.

W_R Base width of p-n-p transistor.

W_S Base width below Schottky contact.

x Vertical displacement from the emitter–base junction.

INTRODUCTION

SCHOTTKY I²L (described in an earlier publication [1] as substrate fed logic, or SFL) is an extension of the injection logic principle; the structure of a typical gate is illustrated in Fig. 2(a); a more detailed description is given in [2]. The two major differences from the standard forms of I²L are the inclusion of Schottky diodes, which add a multiinput facility to the multioutput gate, and a vertical p-n-p structure, which allows significant improvements to be achieved in packing density and in dynamic performance. The multijunction Ebers–Moll model has been extended to incorporate these features. The nature of the Schottky I²L structure allows a wide variety of choice of doping density and dimensions of the various regions; however, care must be taken to ensure that parasitic minority carrier collection at the Schottky diode contacts and at the large area p-n-p injector is not significant in comparison with the collector current because, otherwise, the output driving capability may be reduced. Equations are de-

Manuscript received November 12, 1976; revised December 7, 1976. This work was supported by the Procurement Executive, Ministry of Defence, sponsored by DCVD.

The authors are with the Allen Clark Research Centre, The Plessey Company Ltd., Caswell, Towcester, Northants., England.

Reprinted from *IEEE J. Solid-State Circuits*, vol. SC-12, pp. 128–135, Apr. 1977.

186

rived which enable the gate structure to be designed to eliminate the problem.

DEFINITION OF SCHOTTKY I²L GAIN

The usual definition of gain in I²L as the ratio of the current of one collector in the gate to the total base current is not very meaningful in Schottky I²L. Before examining Schottky I²L, the dependence of gain on gate size will be reviewed for the I²L case.

Generally, in I²L designs the current received from the injector is the same for all gates. This current, the total base current, can be considered as the sum of a current reinjected through the inverse p-n-p transistor and a recombination current. As gate size is increased, the larger recombination volume absorbs more of the total base current, causing a fall in the emitter–base junction voltage and consequently in the collector current. The I²L gain falls in proportion to the collector current because the total base current remains constant. In addition, debiasing due to the series base resistance causes divergence of the gain connected with collectors adjacent to and remote from the injector. An overdrive factor, important for noise and speed considerations, can be defined as the ratio of the collector current to the current which has to be sunk from the following gate. In I²L each output is required to drive only one input, and since the total base current is the same for all gates, the overdrive factor is the I²L gain.

In Schottky I²L the current received from the injector scales with gate size because of the vertical injector structure, so that the additional recombination volume is matched by the supply of additional current. In addition, when the gate is "ON," there is no debiasing due to base resistance because the current received from the injector is distributed evenly. Therefore, it is clear that the emitter–base junction voltage, and hence the collector current, will remain substantially constant. The overdrive factor is not simply related to gain as in the I²L case because the current received from the injector is not the same for each gate. Moreover, each output may drive more than one gate because their inputs are isolated by Schottky diodes. Gain defined in the I²L manner falls with increasing gate size due to the increase in total base current; this is misleading because, for a fixed load, an increase in gate size does not affect the overdrive factor as it does not affect the collector current.

A very convenient method of analyzing Schottky I²L is to divide the gates into unit sections, where each section may contain a Schottky diode input, a collector output, or a crossover. The size of these three possible types of sections is almost identical because the gate is metal limited (Fig. 1). Each section of the base collects a current (I_o) from the injector. A gain β_{uc}, can be defined as the collector current I_c divided by the total base current of a single unit (I_o), and the gain so defined gives an indication of the maximum number of unit sections each collector can drive:

$$\beta_{uc} = \frac{I_c^*}{I_0}. \qquad (1)$$

This definition assumes that in the "ON" state there is no lateral flow of current from one section to the other, which is

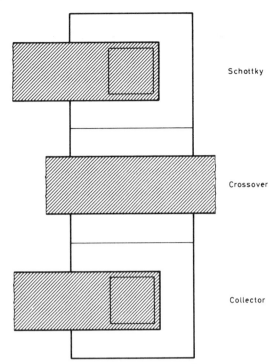

Fig. 1. A three-unit Schottky I²L gate.

a reasonable assumption when neither collectors nor Schottky contacts are saturated. Under these conditions, the collector current will be represented by I_c^*. Further analysis is required because, in operation, Schottkys are left floating and collectors saturate.

A Schottky diode sustains a depletion layer, and when the emitter–base junction is forward biased, minority carriers will be collected at the depletion layer edge. A Schottky current gain can be defined in a similar manner:

$$\beta_{us} = \frac{I_s^*}{I_0}. \qquad (2)$$

I_s^* is the minority carrier current collected at the Schottky contact when all collectors and Schottky contacts in the gate are reverse biased. The measurement of β_{uc}, β_{us} and other important parameters is described in Appendix I.

SATURATION OF COLLECTORS AND SCHOTTKY CONTACTS

The multicollector Ebers–Moll model described by Wiedmann and Berger [3] can be conveniently extended to include the effects of Schottky diodes by adding them as extra junctions, but acknowledging the fact that their diode currents consist of majority carriers and therefore cannot be collected by other semiconductor junctions in the vicinity. As an example, Fig. 2 depicts a Schottky I²L gate with two collectors and two Schottky contacts. The nomenclature used corresponds with that introduced by Wiedmann and Berger with the exception of an extra suffix c or s to distinguish between α_u for collectors or Schottkys. The nonsaturated collector current of a Schottky I²L gate with m collectors, m' of them saturated, n Schottkys, n' saturated, and M unit sections can be expressed in terms of the upward collector current gain β_{uc}, the upward Schottky current gain β_{us}, the downward collector gain β_d, and the common-

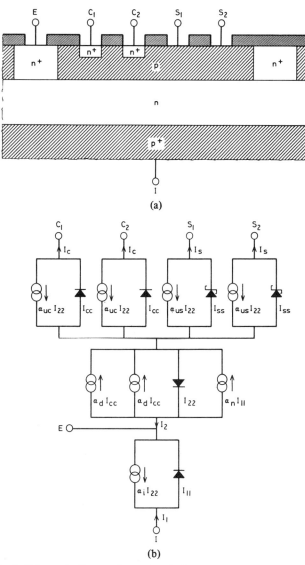

Fig. 2. Schematic diagram (a) and equivalent circuit (b) of a Schottky I^2L gate. A gate with two collectors and two Schottky diodes is shown as an example.

base current gain of the vertical p-n-p transistor α_n (Appendix II):

$$I_c = \frac{\beta_{uc} I_o}{1 + \frac{m'}{M} \frac{\beta_{uc}}{(1+\beta_d)} + \frac{n'}{M} \beta_{us}}. \tag{3}$$

Compare (3) with (1), which can be rewritten as follows:

$$I_c^* = \beta_{uc} I_o.$$

The collector current has been reduced because of the saturation of the collectors and Schottky contacts. The maximum number of unit sections N that a collector can drive is given by

$$\frac{I_c}{I_o} = \frac{\beta_{uc}}{1 + \frac{m'}{M} \frac{\beta_{uc}}{(1+\beta_d)} + \frac{n'}{M} \beta_{us}} = N. \tag{4}$$

In practical designs, the number of units driven has to be reduced by a factor of at least 2 because of speed and noise immunity considerations.

Although formula (4) can be solved for any combination of saturated inputs, saturated collectors, and crossovers, it is especially useful to consider two worst cases which are for large gates with either a large number of saturated collectors or saturated Schottky contacts. The number of sections per gate is unrestricted in Schottky I^2L, and therefore a gate with an infinite number of sections is considered as a theoretical example.

1) A gate with one unsaturated collector, one saturated input, and an infinite number of saturated collectors:

$$m \to \infty, m' \to \infty, n = 1, n' = 1, M \to \infty.$$

Equation (4) reduces to

$$N = \frac{\beta_{uc}}{1 + \frac{\beta_{uc}}{1 + \beta_d}}. \tag{5}$$

N has been plotted in Fig. 3 as a function of β_{uc} with β_d as a parameter. This is essentially the same as [4, fig. 10] except that the graph is plotted for an infinite number of collectors.

2) A gate with one unsaturated collector and an infinite number of saturated inputs:

$$m = 1, n \to \infty, n' \to \infty, M \to \infty.$$

In this case

$$N = \frac{\beta_{uc}}{1 + \beta_{us}}. \tag{6}$$

A plot of this formula is shown in Fig. 4, where it can be seen that relatively modest Schottky gains have a strong influence on the driving capability of a collector; gains of unity would halve it. When typical measured values of β_{uc}, β_{us}, and β_d (Table I) are inserted, it is found that the worst case is given by an infinite number of inputs when N becomes 10. This means that if an overdrive factor of 2 is used, each collector can drive up to five sections. It must be remembered that this applies to a basic collector size of $6 \times 6 \ \mu m^2$, and that if more than five sections are required to be driven, the collector area can be increased. This will give a linear increase in collector current since the emitter–base junction voltage is independent of gate size.

VERTICAL REINJECTION THROUGH THE INVERSE P-N-P TRANSISTOR

When one looks at the large injector area of Schottky I^2L, the first impression is that reinjection accounts for such an enormous proportion of the base current that achieving high

TABLE I
PROCESS PARAMETERS

β_{uc} (npn)	per unit land	12	at 600 mV injector
β_d (npn)	per unit land	170	at 600 mV injector
β_{us} (Schottky)	per unit land	0.2	at 600 mV injector
α_n (pnp)		0.8	at 600 mV injector

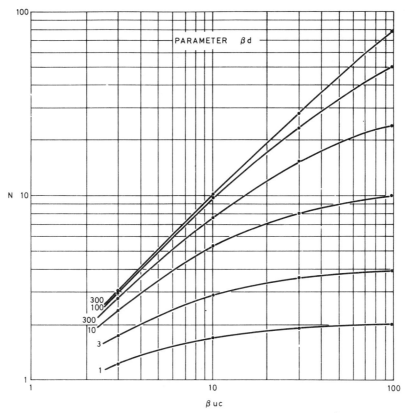

Fig. 3. Number of units N that can be driven by a Schottky I^2L gate containing a large number of saturated collectors as a function of upward current gain β_{uc} and downward current gain β_d.

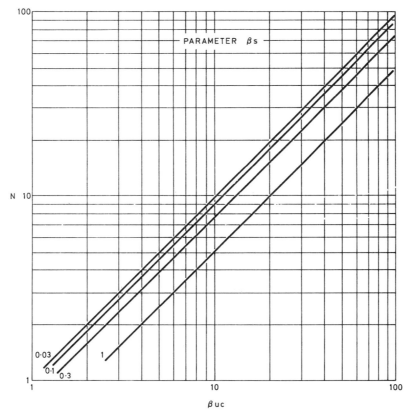

Fig. 4. Number of units N that can be driven by a Schottky I^2L gate with a large number of saturated Schottky diode inputs as a function of upward current gain β_{uc} and upward Schottky current gain β_{us}.

upward gains is almost impossible. Although there is a large reinjection current, a detailed analysis of the parameters affecting β_{uc} shows that sufficient gains can be achieved easily. The unit base current I_o can be split into two components: the reinjected current I_R and the recombination current I_b:

$$I_o = I_R + I_b. \tag{7}$$

The gain can be expressed as

$$\beta_{uc} = \frac{I_c^*}{I_R + I_b}. \tag{8}$$

Equation (8) can be rewritten as

$$\beta_{uc} = \left[\left(\frac{I_c^*}{I_R} \right)^{-1} + \left(\frac{I_c^*}{I_b} \right)^{-1} \right]^{-1}. \tag{9}$$

From the above equation it is apparent that sufficient upward gain cannot be achieved unless the ratio of the collector current to the reinjected current is greater than the β_{uc} required. Even in the limiting case of zero recombination current, the ratio must be at least equal to β_{uc}. If the ratio is made significantly greater than β_{uc}, then the achievement of a sufficient upward gain is only dependent on the ratio of the collector current to the recombination current.

I_c^* and I_R are given by

$$I_c^* = \frac{q A_c D_{nc} n_i^2}{\int_0^{W_c} N_{AC}\, dx} \exp\left(V_{BE}/V_T \right) \tag{10}$$

$$I_R = \frac{q A_R D_p n_i^2}{\int_0^{W_R} N_D\, dx} \exp\left(V_{BE}/V_T \right) \tag{11}$$

where $\int N\, dx$ is the integrated base doping of the n-p-n or p-n-p transistor:

$$\frac{I_c^*}{I_R} = \frac{A_c}{A_R} \times \frac{D_{nc}}{D_p} \times \frac{\int_0^{W_R} N_D\, dx}{\int_0^{W_c} N_{AC}\, dx}. \tag{12}$$

This ratio is determined solely by the dimensions and doping densities of the epitaxial p-base under the collector and that part of n-epitax which forms the p-n-p base. If it is required that each collector should sink five units, then the ratio must be significantly greater than ten. In the present Schottky $I^2 L$ structure, using conservative figures, the ratio becomes

$$\frac{I_c^*}{I_R} = 0.2 \times 3 \times 60 = 36.$$

This ratio of 36 is more than adequate. β_{uc} can approach this ratio if recombination is small.

ELECTRON COLLECTION AT SCHOTTKY CONTACTS

Electron collection at floating Schottky contacts reduces the number of unit sections that a Schottky $I^2 L$ gate can drive. The "worst case" condition of (6) shows that the number N is

a function of β_{uc} and β_{us}. Both these parameters are recombination dependent and, as such, the equation does not provide guidelines for choosing doping levels which ensure that electron collection at the Schottky contact is unimportant. β_{us} can be expressed in terms of β_{uc} and the ratio of the Schottky to collector current (measured when both are reverse biased). This ratio is determined by doping levels and dimensions within the gate:

$$\beta_{us} = \frac{I_s^*}{I_o} = \frac{I_c^*}{I_o} \frac{I_s^*}{I_c^*} = \frac{\beta_{uc} I_s^*}{I_c^*}. \tag{13}$$

If it is required to drive N sections with an overdrive factor of 2, then substituting for β_{us}, (6) can be rewritten as follows:

$$\frac{\beta_{uc}}{1 + \beta_{uc} I_s^*/I_c^*} \geq 2N.$$

In a worst case, when heavy recombination (or reinjection) has caused β_{uc} to be reduced close to the minimum desirable value of $2N$, then the ratio of I_c^*/I_s^* must be small to satisfy the above equation:

$$\beta_{uc} \frac{I_s^*}{I_c^*} < 1$$

$$\frac{I_s^*}{I_c^*} < \frac{1}{\beta_{uc}} \simeq \frac{1}{2N}. \tag{14}$$

I_c^* is given by (10); I_s^* can be expressed as follows:

$$I_s^* = \frac{q A_s D_{ns} n_i^2 \exp V_{BE}/V_T}{\int_0^{W_s} N_{AS}\, dx} \tag{15}$$

where $\int_0^{W_s} N_{AS}\, dx$ is the integrated doping in the p-region beneath the Schottky contact; the ratio of I_s^* to I_c^* becomes

$$\frac{I_s^*}{I_c^*} = \frac{A_s}{A_c} \times \frac{D_{ns}}{D_{nc}} \times \frac{\int_0^{W_c} N_{AC}\, dx}{\int_0^{W_s} N_{AS}\, dx} \tag{16}$$

where the subscript s applies to the Schottky and the subscript c to the collector. The electron diffusion constants are included because of the possibility of using different doping levels in the two regions. If five units are to be driven, this ratio must be less than 0.1 (14). This is achieved in Schottky $I^2 L$ by implanting a heavily doped region beneath the Schottky contact; in the present structure the ratio is

$$\frac{I_s^*}{I_c^*} = 1 \times 0.7 \times 0.06 \simeq 0.04.$$

CONCLUSIONS

The usual definition of gain in $I^2 L$ is misleading when applied to Schottky $I^2 L$, and therefore a new definition has to be introduced whereby the gate is divided into separate units and the gain is expressed per unit land. The newly defined gain determines the maximum number of unit lands N that can be driven from one output.

N is reduced by the saturation of the collectors and by recombination at saturated Schottky contacts. The reduction can be quantified in terms of the number of unit lands of the gate, the downward current gain, and an upward Schottky current gain defined in the same manner as the upward collector current gain.

It has been shown that reinjection through the inverse p-n-p transistor and recombination at the Schottky contacts can be controlled by careful choice of doping densities and dimensions within the gate so that a sufficient number of unit lands can be driven by each gate output.

APPENDIX I

MEASUREMENT METHOD

As the base region of the n-p-n device is not directly accessible, the measurement of the most important parameters of Schottky I^2L has been made using an indirect approach based on the following two basic measurements, both realized with constant injector voltage. Consider the gate illustrated in Fig. 2.

1) With one Schottky grounded (S_1) and all other Schottkys and collectors floating, measure the injector current (I_{inj1}) and the current through the grounded Schottky (I_{s1}) [Fig. 5(a)].

2) With all Schottkys and collectors reverse biased, measure both currents (I_{s2} and I_{c2}) and the new injector current (I_{inj2}) [Fig. 5(b)].

In measurement 1, I_{s1} is the collector current of the p-n-p as the small Schottky voltage drop is insufficient to forward bias the p-n-p collector base junction. This current becomes the base current of the n-p-n device when the Schottky is allowed to float. The two measurements combine to yield all

the ratios and currents required:

$$I_o = \frac{\alpha_n I_{11}}{M} = \frac{I_{s1}}{M} \tag{17}$$

$$\alpha_n = \frac{\alpha_n I_{11}}{I_{11}} = \frac{I_{s1}}{I_{inj1}} \tag{18}$$

$$\beta_{uc} = \frac{I_c^*}{I_o} = \frac{\alpha_{uc} I_{22}}{\alpha_n I_{11}/M} = \frac{M I_{c2}}{I_{s1}} \tag{19}$$

$$\beta_{us} = \frac{I_s^*}{I_o} = \frac{\alpha_{us} I_{22}}{\alpha_n I_{11}/M} = \frac{M I_{s2}}{I_{s1}} \tag{20}$$

$$\frac{I_c^*}{I_R} = \frac{\alpha_{uc} I_{22}}{\alpha_i I_{22}/M} = \frac{M I_{c2}}{(I_{inj1} - I_{inj2})} \tag{21}$$

$$\frac{I_c^*}{I_s^*} = \frac{\alpha_{uc} I_{22}}{\alpha_{us} I_{22}} = \frac{I_{c2}}{I_{s2}}. \tag{22}$$

APPENDIX II

As described in the text, Schottky diodes can be incorporates into the multijunction Ebers–Moll model by introducing them as diodes in parallel with current sources representing minority carrier collection from other forward biased junctions. However, unlike a p-n junction diode, the Schottky diode is a majority carrier device, and therefore no current sources are included to represent minority carrier collection at other junctions from a forward biased Schottky diode. The equivalent circuit of a typical gate and the nomenclature used are shown in Fig. 2.

The following analysis applies to a gate with m collectors, n Schottky contacts, and M unit sections. The collectors and Schottky contacts are assumed to be either heavily saturated or reverse biased; a dash is used to indicate saturation and, therefore, m' is the number of saturated collectors, n' the num-

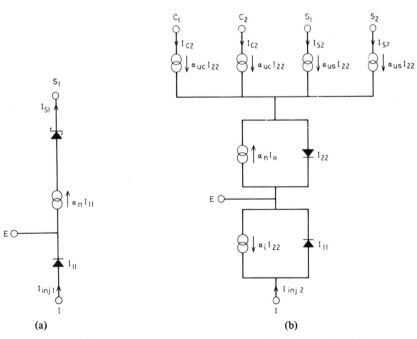

(a)   (b)

Fig. 5. Measurement of Schottky I^2L gate parameters. (a) Measurement 1—one Schottky diode grounded. (b) Measurement 2—all collectors and Schottky diodes reverse biased.

ber of saturated Schottky diodes, and I_c', I_s' the saturated collector and Schottky currents.

Assuming that all collector junctions are identical, that all Schottky diodes are identical, and that there is no interaction between adjacent collectors, the equations corresponding to the model are

$$I_1 = I_{11} - \alpha_i I_{22} \tag{23}$$

$$I_2 = -\alpha_n I_{11} + I_{22} - m'\alpha_d I_{cc} \tag{24}$$

$$I_c' = 0 = -\alpha_{uc} I_{22} + I_{cc} \tag{25}$$

$$I_c = -\alpha_{uc} I_{22} \tag{26}$$

$$I_c = \frac{-\alpha_n \alpha_{uc} I_{11}}{1 - (m - m')\alpha_{uc} - m'\alpha_{uc} + m'\alpha_{uc} - (n - n')\alpha_{us} - n'\alpha_{us} + n'\alpha_{us} - m'\alpha_d \alpha_{uc}}.$$

$$I_s' = 0 = -\alpha_{us} I_{22} + I_{ss} \tag{27}$$

$$I_s = -\alpha_{us} I_{22}. \tag{28}$$

From (25) and (26)

$$I_c = -\alpha_{uc} I_{22} = I_{cc}$$

$$\therefore \ I_{22} = -\frac{I_c}{\alpha_{uc}}. \tag{29}$$

$$I_c = \frac{-\alpha_n \alpha_{uc} I_{11}}{(1 - m\alpha_{uc} - n\alpha_{us})\left[1 + \dfrac{m'\alpha_{uc}(1 - \alpha_d)}{1 - m\alpha_{uc} - n\alpha_{us}} + \dfrac{n'\alpha_{us}}{1 - m\alpha_{uc} - n\alpha_{us}}\right]}$$

Similarly,

$$I_s = -\alpha_{us} I_{22} = \frac{\alpha_{us}}{\alpha_{uc}} I_c. \tag{30}$$

I_2 is the sum of the terminal currents of all collectors and Schottkys:

$$I_2 = -(m - m') I_c - (n - n') I_s. \tag{31}$$

Replacing (29), (30), and (31) in (24),

$$-(m - m') I_c - (n - n') I_s = \alpha_n I_{11} - \frac{I_c}{\alpha_{uc}} + m'\alpha_d I_c$$

$$-(m - m') I_c - (n - n')\frac{\alpha_{us}}{\alpha_{uc}} I_c + \frac{I_c}{\alpha_{uc}}$$

$$-m'\alpha_d I_c = -\alpha_n I_{11}$$

$$I_c\left[-(m - m') - (n - n')\frac{\alpha_{us}}{\alpha_{uc}} + \frac{1}{\alpha_{uc}} - m'\alpha_d\right] = -\alpha_n I_{11}$$

$$I_c = \frac{-\alpha_n \alpha_{uc} I_{11}}{1 - (m - m')\alpha_{uc} - (n - n')\alpha_{us} - m'\alpha_d \alpha_{uc}}. \tag{32}$$

This equation gives the value of the collector current as a function of the injector diode current and the α parameters of the gate. It is useful to express this equation in terms of the current gains defined in (1) and (2). This can be achieved by writing the collector and base currents in terms of the emitter-base diode current I_{22}. The base current I_o can be expressed as the difference between the total emitter base diode current and the current collected by the unsaturated collectors and Schottky diodes divided by the number of unit sections M. The reinjection current $\alpha_i I_{22}$ is not subtracted because it is

considered as part of the base current:

$$\beta_{uc} = \frac{I_c^*}{I_o} = \frac{\alpha_{uc} I_{22}}{(I_{22} - m\alpha_{uc} I_{22} - n\alpha_{us} I_{22})/M}$$

$$\beta_{uc} = \frac{\alpha_{uc} M}{(1 - m\alpha_{uc} - n\alpha_{us})}. \tag{33}$$

Similarly, for the Schottky diode

$$\beta_{us} = \frac{\alpha_{us} M}{(1 - m\alpha_{uc} - n\alpha_{us})}. \tag{34}$$

Equation (32) can be rewritten as

Rearranging,

$$I_c = \frac{-\alpha_n \alpha_{uc} I_{11}}{1 - m\alpha_{uc} - n\alpha_{us} + m'\alpha_{uc}(1 - \alpha_d) + n'\alpha_{us}}$$

or

and using (33) and (34),

$$I_c = \frac{-\beta_{uc} \alpha_n I_{11}/M}{1 + \dfrac{m'}{M}\beta_{uc}(1 - \alpha_d) + \dfrac{n'}{M}\beta_{us}}.$$

Substituting for α_d $(= \beta_d/(1 + \beta_d))$,

$$I_c = \frac{-\beta_{uc}\alpha_n I_{11}/M}{1 + \dfrac{m'}{M}\dfrac{\beta_{uc}}{(1 + \beta_d)} + \dfrac{n'}{M}\beta_{us}}. \tag{35}$$

The group of terms $\alpha_n I_{11}/M$ is the total base current received by a unit section I_o. Taking collector current into the device to be positive [cf. Fig. 2(b)], (35) can be rewritten as

$$I_c = \frac{\beta_{uc} I_o}{1 + \dfrac{m'}{M}\dfrac{\beta_{uc}}{(1 + \beta_d)} + \dfrac{n'}{M}\beta_{us}}. \tag{36}$$

ACKNOWLEDGMENT

The authors would like to thank Dr. P. S. Walsh for supplying process and performance data and the Directors of the Plessey Company Ltd. for permission to publish.

REFERENCES

[1] V. Blatt, P. S. Walsh, and L. W. Kennedy, "Substrate fed logic," *IEEE J. Solid-State Circuits*, vol. SC-10, pp. 336–342, Oct. 1975.
[2] P. S. Walsh and G. W. Sumerling, "Schottky I²L (substrate fed logic)–An optimum form of I²L," this issue, pp. 123–127.
[3] H. H. Berger and S. K. Wiedmann, "Terminal-orientated model for merged transistor logic (MTL)," *IEEE J. Solid-State Circuits*, vol. SC-9, pp. 211–217, Oct. 1974.
[4] ——, "Merged-transistor logic (MTL)–A low cost bipolar logic concept," *IEEE J. Solid-State Circuits*, vol. SC-7, pp. 346–351, Oct. 1972.

Computer-Aided Design of Large-Scale Integrated I²L Logic Circuits

E. WITTENZELLNER

Abstract–Thanks to the simple, regular structure of its basic gates, integrated injection logic (I²L) is particularly suited to automated design (CAD) procedures for evolving large-scale integrated digital circuits. This paper describes CAD methods for I²L circuits that permit the use of existing, tried CAD programs, and illustrates their application in the design of the I²L basic gate, computer simulation of I²L logic circuits, interconnection pattern generation, and preparation of a final layout plan.

I. INTRODUCTION

DURING the past two years or so, bipolar I²L technology has been used to an increasing extent, as well as MOS technology, in the production of large-scale integrated digital circuits. One of the advantages of this technology is the simple, highly regular geometry of its basic gate, a structure that suggests itself as particularly suitable for the application of computer-aided design (CAD) methods. A large-scale integrated I²L circuit contains only a few variants of this basic gate.

In the following, CAD methods for I²L circuits are described, which permit the utilization of existing and tried CAD programs.

If we consider the sequence of stages in the development of a large-scale integrated I²L circuit from the initial product idea to the generation of masks for the doping processes (Fig. 1), the work can be divided into four phases, to each of which the computer can be applied specifically.

1) Calculation of the electrical properties of the I²L basic gate from the geometrical dimensions and the characteristics of the chosen manufacturing process.

2) Computer simulation of the logic circuit plan for fault-free generation of a logic plan. (If suitable logic symbols are used, the logic plan of I²L circuits can simultaneously serve as a "circuit diagram" and be used directly for interconnection pattern generation.)

3) Interconnection pattern generation, usually in two planes (preparation of macroartwork = pattern generation for circuit subsections or "macros".).

4) Generation of the mask plan or layout (synthesized from gate elements) followed by production of the masks.

II. DETERMINING THE ELECTRICAL CHARACTERISTICS OF THE I²L BASIC GATE

A. Technology and Electrical Equivalent Circuit

Fig. 2(a) shows a cross section of an I²L gate with two outputs (collectors) in the technology that is usual today.

Manuscript received September 6, 1976; revised November 22, 1976. This work was supported by the German Federal Ministry of Research and Technology. The author alone is responsible for its contents.
The author is with Siemens AG, Munich, Germany.

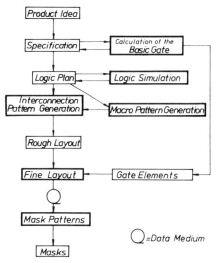

Fig. 1. Development stages for large-scale integrated I²L circuits from the product idea to production of the doping masks (thickly bordered items indicate computer aid).

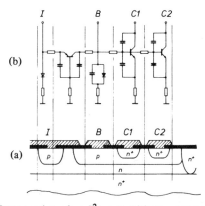

Fig. 2. (a) Cross section of an I²L gate with two outputs (collectors). Described in the text. (b) Electrical equivalent circuit of the I²L gate.

For generating an equivalent electrical circuit, this "functionally integrated" gate structure can be divided into several sections, as shown in [1] and [2]. The more the structure is divided up, the more exactly the electrical terminal characteristics can be determined over a wide working range. On the other hand, an increasing number of individual components means that measuring their electrical parameters becomes increasingly difficult and inexact. The required programming and computer time are also increased, of course.

The equivalent circuit in Fig. 2(b) has just about as many individual components as can be coped with. The assignment of the gate areas to the elements of the equivalent circuit is represented by the vertical dividing lines. The region of parasitic injection into the substrate under the injector (I) is simulated by a diode, the injection towards the base region (B) of

Reprinted from *IEEE J. Solid-State Circuits*, vol. SC-12, pp. 199–204, Apr. 1977.

the I^2L gate by a p-n-p transistor, the regions around the collectors ($C1$, $C2$) by n-p-n transistors, and the base connection region by a further diode. The bulk resistance in the base and emitter regions are also taken into consideration; in the collector region it is negligible. With this means of representation, I^2L gates with any number of collectors and any sequence of collectors and base connections can be simulated.

The circuit calculations are made with the aid of the network analysis program SPICE [3], [4]. This permits representation of the transistors by the Ebers-Moll model [5], as well as by the more exact Gummel-Poon model [6], which was used for the following calculation. The SPICE program system permits dc, ac, and transient analysis and can be operated in the on-line mode in time-sharing systems so that calculation and output of results may be made directly on a data display terminal.

B. Calculating the Signal Delay and Power Dissipation of an I^2L Gate

Measuring the signal delay of a single I^2L gate is fraught with difficulty, especially in the case of low injector currents. For measuring the delay and power dissipation, we therefore use multistage integrated ring oscillators with a decoupling stage for the frequency output. Fig. 3 shows a microphotograph of two ring oscillators whose gate delay was calculated by the model described above for various injector current values and power dissipations and compared with measured values.

Standing vertically in the center of the picture is the common injector, to the left and right of it two five-stage ring

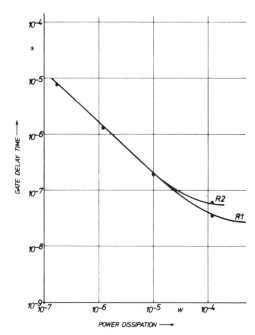

Fig. 4. Gate delay as a function of gate power dissipation for one gate (inverter) of each of the ring oscillators $R1$ and $R2$. Curves: measured values. Circles: calculated values.

oscillators, each with "five-position" gates; below these are the decoupling stages. The oscillators differ in the positioning of the collectors used for the ring circuit. This makes it possible to show the influence of the bulk resistances on the gate delay.

The electrical parameters for the elements of the equivalent circuit were partly derived from geometrical estimates (resistances, depletion layer capacitances) and partly from measurements made on integrated model structures constructed especially for this purpose.

First of all, the static (dc) behavior of the I^2L gate was exactly simulated over several decades of injector current and tested with measuring instruments. Thereafter, capacitance values necessary for the dynamic behavior were introduced into the calculation. This procedure permitted a very exact calculation of the gate delays, both in the proportional range and in the saturation range, as shown in Fig. 4. The solid curves, which overlap in the proportional range, were measured on the ring oscillators $R1$ and $R2$; the circles are calculated values. We can see how the values are split up in the saturation range because of the mentioned different bulk resistances.

III. LOGIC SIMULATION IN I^2L CIRCUITS

A. Logic Definition and Logic Symbol

If we wish to work on I^2L circuits with existing logic simulation programs, a logic definition of the I^2L gate is necessary which will permit simple conversion of the I^2L logic plan into a conventional logic plan. In practice, it is then only necessary to observe certain rules of conversion.

The I^2L transistor can be defined as a logic element, the base representing the input and the separate collectors representing individual outputs. Logic functions are therefore possible in the same way as the usual "wired AND" functions (e.g., for TTL). Fig. 5(a) shows an example of this, represented with I^2L transistor symbols. Although there is a standard symbol

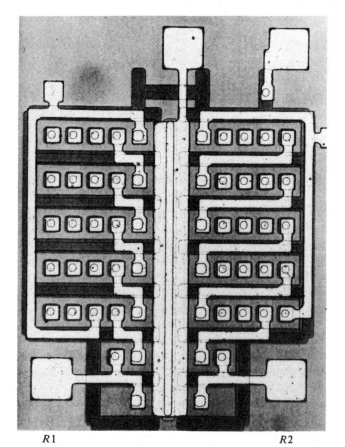

R1   R2

Fig. 3. Microphotograph of two I^2L ring oscillators $R1$ and $R2$.

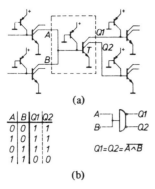

(a)

A	B	Q1	Q2
0	0	1	1
1	0	1	1
0	1	1	1
1	1	0	0

$Q1 = Q2 = \overline{A \wedge B}$

(b)

Input: 0 ≙ voltage low and current
flowing at input
(A,B)   1 ≙ no current at input

Output: 0 ≙ transistor T on
(Q1,Q2) 1 ≙ transistor T off

Fig. 5. (a) Simplified electrical equivalent circuit ("circuit diagram") for an I²L gate (bordered part) with inputs A and B driven and outputs $Q1$ and $Q2$ loaded. (b) Truth table, logic symbol, and logic definitions for the I²L gate shown in Fig. 5(a).

for this type of function, it has only one output and thus is not suitable for I²L gates. A new symbol was therefore defined, which represents *one* I²L transistor with several collectors as *one* I²L gate, including the wired function at the input [Fig. 5(b)]. The logic states can be defined as follows:

For the inputs (A, B):

logic 0 ≙ low voltage (referred to ground) and current flow out from input
logic 1 ≙ no current at input.

For the outputs (Q1, Q2):

logic 0 ≙ transistor T on, i.e., output impedance low
logic 1 ≙ transistor T off, i.e., output impedance high.

For an I²L gate, framed by a broken line in Fig. 5(a), we thus obtain the truth table as per Fig. 5(b). It fulfills the requirements for a NAND function, i.e.,

$$Q1 = Q2 = \overline{A \wedge B}.$$

The logic symbol [Fig. 5(b)] was accordingly designed with separate inverting outputs, following the practice adopted for the usual standard symbols.

B. Rules of Conversion for Logic Simulation

Conventional logic simulation programs, e.g., RATEG [7], can process logic elements in which the inputs, not the outputs, are electrically decoupled. This is the case with all usual logic families and large-scale integrated MOS circuits. At a nodal point in a logic network, it is permissible for several gate inputs to be connected to just one gate output.

In I²L circuits, however, the opposite node rule applies: several collectors (gate outputs) may be connected to just one base. This corresponds to the above definition of a wired function.

For programming an I²L circuit, it is therefore first of all necessary to convert the I²L logic diagram into a diagram with conventional gate descriptions. Fig. 6 shows this, taking a

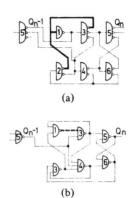

(a)

(b)

Fig. 6. I²L Divide-by-two circuit. (a) Representation in I²L symbols. (b) Representation in standard symbols for logic simulation.

divide-by-two circuit as an example. The flip-flop in Fig. 6(a) is represented with I²L symbols, and the same circuit in Fig. 6(b) with conventional symbols. It is immediately obvious that I²L NAND gates can be converted into conventional NAND gates quite formally: the outputs of the I²L symbols are linked and the inputs are separated. Instead of the I²L node rule, the conventional node rule then applies. The overall function remains the same, as can easily be checked, and likewise the number of gates.

The logical voltage level at a certain node in the I²L diagram equals the inverted logical level at the output of the corresponding gate in the conventional diagram. (See the thickly drawn lines and the dotted line in Fig. 6(a) and (b), respectively.)

IV. INTERCONNECTION PATTERN GENERATION

A. Pattern Generation Program

As shown above, an I²L gate corresponds to an I²L transistor, so that the logic plan can be used directly as a circuit diagram. For automatic pattern generation with acceptable programming outlay, the circuit elements must be standardized on as few basic cells as possible. In the case of large-scale integrated MOS circuits, it has already been possible to define standard cells that permit automatic pattern generation. For this purpose, the programming system AVESTA [8] was developed and successfully tested.

The standard cells (so-called "macros") are arranged in rows, every two rows being followed by a wiring channel. The cells have uniform width and variable length. Their position with respect to each other, i.e., their position in the rows, is varied until minimum wiring length is obtained.

This programming system is ideally suited to I²L circuits since the gates are already arranged in "rows" along an injector. By restricting the number of collectors per gate for electrical reasons, a uniform cell width can be obtained without much loss of area. A standard cell consists, for example, of a number of parallel, adjacent I²L gates.

B. Interconnection Pattern Generation for Standard Cells

The design and artwork of these standard cells (macros) are normally prepared manually (e.g., for MOS circuits). The program AVESTA can, however, also be utilized in designing I²L standard cells. In this case, the individual I²L gate is defined as the standard cell, and the gates are arranged in a row. The area over the gates themselves serves as the "wiring channel."

For the wiring, we need almost only aluminum lines; n⁺-crosslinks are scarcely necessary since the base and collector terminals of the gates can be exchanged as desired. They can be arranged in such a way that the crosslinks are formed by the base diffusion of the I²L gates. Figs. 7 and 8 show an example of pattern generation for a standard cell.

This is a synchronous 4-bit binary counter with parallel carry and reset features. Fig. 7 shows the logic network of the counter. The individual gates of each flip-flop are numbered, and likewise the line nodes.

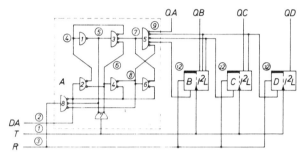

Fig. 7. Logic network of a synchronous 4-bit binary counter in I²L technology.

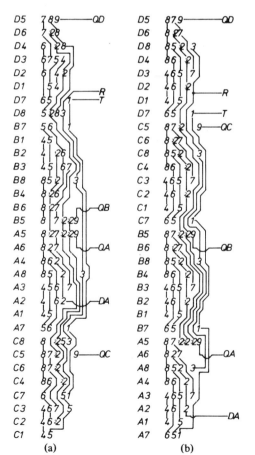

(a) (b)

Fig. 8. (a) Interconnection pattern of the 4-bit counter as per Fig. 7 by computer. (b) Interconnection pattern of the 4-bit counter as per Fig. 7 by hand.

The AVESTA output information is given as a row of gate numbers, representing the gate positions along the injector strip. With this information, a layout scheme has been drawn by hand in a simplified form [Fig. 8(a)]. The base and collector terminals are represented by the associated node numbers to the right of the gate numbers. All similar numbers are linked by an aluminum structure line (solid lines). No difference need be made at the pattern generation stage between base and collector connections. Lines which cross over the gates are run via the base diffusion. For the terminals QA, QB, and DA, additional n⁺-tunnels are required.

In order to test the effectiveness of this method, the counter circuit pattern was also prepared without computer aid [Fig. 8(b)]. The quality of the generated patterns using the two methods was shown to be approximately equal:

	CAD	Manual
Aluminum line length (grid units)	374	380
Total gate positions, including vacant positions for crossovers	132	137

If we take into account the time consumed for programming and evaluation of the calculated results, the computer method leads in time saved after about 10 or 20 gate patterns have been generated.

V. LAYOUT WITH I²L GATE ELEMENTS

A. Layout Generation via an Interactive Graphics Terminal

As a mechanical aid for mask plan generation, computer-controlled graphics terminals are used, as in other engineering sectors requiring drawings (e.g., mechanical engineering). They consist of a central computer and an interactive graphics terminal (BAP) or an interactive digitizer/plotter as an input/output device. With this equipment, layout drawings are generated and modified in the computer and then stored. The result is a control tape for an automatic mask-cutting setup.

Based on the computer-generated interconnection pattern proposal, a rough layout is first drawn by hand. There are always additional design considerations and restrictions which have to be introduced "manually." In order to keep manual work to a minimum, this rough layout should represent the circuit elements in a simplified, standardized form. It must, however, contain so much information about the correct arrangement and final configuration of the circuit elements that the relatively expensive work on the graphics terminal is kept as short as possible. It is therefore imperative to introduce standardized circuit elements that can be used in the same form for a series of circuits. In the rough layout, only their outlines or symbols are shown. All further details are stored in a components library and are added automatically by the computer.

It would be theoretically possible to combine the same circuit parts into a standard element as were combined into a standard cell for the interconnection pattern generation described above. In practice, however, it has been shown that for almost every new large-scale integrated circuit, these standard cells must be newly defined or at least varied in order to

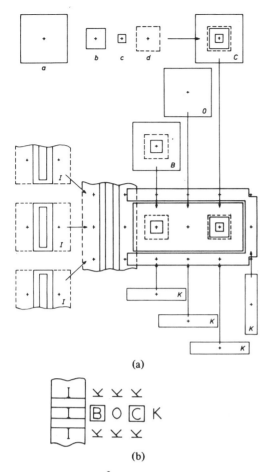

(a)

(b)

Fig. 9. (a) Breakdown of an I²L gate into "gate elements" for generation of a layout plan. (b) Layout of an I²L gate: symbolic representation.

With the gate shown in Fig. 9, this corresponds to a packing density of 280 gates/mm².

The described grid arrangement permits the I²L gate to be split up into a small number of standard elements from which

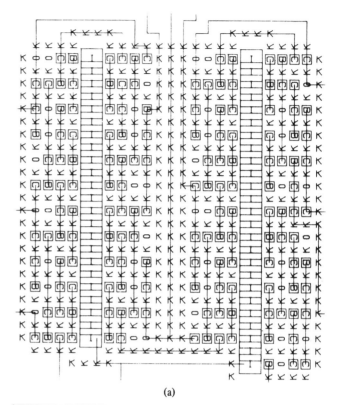

(a)

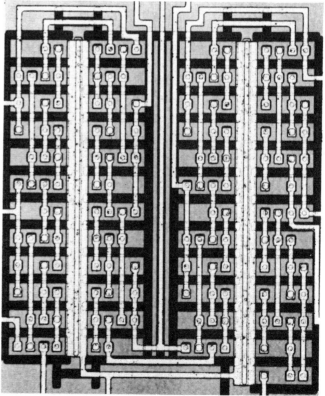

(b)

Fig. 10. (a) Layout of an I²L frequency divider (plotter drawing). (b) Microphotograph of the frequency divider as per Fig. 10(a).

arrive at an optimum electrical solution. We have adopted the approach of constructing the I²L basic gate, with the corresponding part of the injector strip, from standard elements.

B. I²L Gate Elements in Standard Grid

If we consider the geometry of an I²L gate, we see that the gate could be dimensioned in such a way that the base and collector terminals of all the stages of a logic circuit lie on the crosspoints of a standard grid. This would permit a simplified, symbolic form of representation in the rough layout and make the paths of the Al lines clear to follow, as well as simplifying the layout programming on the graphics terminal. On the latter, lengths and areas are always digitized in a grid pattern anyway. A square grid has been adopted in order to permit "horizontal" and "vertical" gate arrangement with equal facility. Fig. 9(a) (center) depicts an I²L gate with a base connection, one vacant position (for a line crossover), and a collector, the grid points being marked by crosses. The screen collars between the base regions are likewise symmetrically positioned with respect to a grid line, and each belong jointly to two adjacent gates. The injector strip lies symmetrically between the grid lines. In this way, it is possible to represent gates with any number of connections and in any sequence with maximum packing density. The connections can also lie side by side relative to the injector (for high switching speeds). The grid spacing is, at present, depending on the technology, 18-22 μm.

it is possible to construct almost all types of gate. Fig. 9(a) shows these elements:

C   collector element consisting of p-region (a), n^+-region (b), contact window (c), and section of A1 line (d);

B   base element with contact consisting of p-region, contact window, and section of A1 line;

O   base element without contact consisting of p-region;

I   injector element consisting of p-region, contact window, and A1 line;

K   collar element consisting of n^+-region.

The entire base region of a gate is formed by an overlapping sequence of *C*, *B*, or *O* elements. Likewise, an injector strip or a collar is formed by an overlapping sequence of *I* or *K* elements.

In the rough layout as well as in the overall drawing prepared by the computer, these elements are marked by letters, as shown in Fig. 9(b). The A1 line sections are drawn as rectangles in order to simplify the "wiring" which is represented by unbroken lines. In preparing the layout on the BAP, the required element is called out by name at the coordinates of the respective grid point and automatically stored in all mask planes. Wiring is done in the usual manner. This procedure does not, of course, preclude the combining of large complexes into standards. Fig. 10(a) shows the computer drawing of an I^2L frequency divider, comprising about 50 gates. Fig. 10(b) is a microphotograph of the frequency divider.

ACKNOWLEDGMENT

The author wishes to thank Dr. Barba, Dr. D'Andrea, Dipl. Ing. Scheckel, and Dipl. Ing. Zietemann of Siemens AG, Munich, Germany, for their cooperation in the development of the described procedures.

REFERENCES

[1] H. H. Berger and S. K. Wiedmann, "Terminal oriented model for merged transistor logic," *IEEE J. Solid-State Circuits*, vol. SC-9, Oct. 1974.

[2] H. Berger, "The injection model—A structure oriented model for merged transistor logic," *IEEE J. Solid-State Circuits*, vol. SC-9, Oct. 1974.

[3] L. W. Nagel and D. O. Pederson, "Simulation program with integrated circuit emphasis (SPICE)," presented at the 16th Midwest Symp. on Circuit Theory, Waterloo, Ont., Canada, Apr. 12, 1973.

[4] E. Cohen and D. O. Pederson, *Users Guide for SPICE*, version 2C, 2, edited by the College of Eng., Univ. California, Apr. 19, 1976.

[5] J. J. Ebers and J. L. Moll, "Large signal behavior of junction transistors," *Proc. IRE*, vol. 42, Dec. 1954.

[6] H. K. Gummel and H. C. Poon, "An integrated charge control model of bipolar transistors," *Bell Syst. Tech. J.*, vol. 49, May/June 1970.

[7] D. Ernst and D. Ströle, *Industrieelektronik*. Berlin, Heidelberg, New York: Springer Verlag, 1973.

[8] K. W. Koller and U. Lauther, "Computer-aided design of topography for MOS-standard cell circuits using the AVESTA program system," in *Proc. IEEE Int. Symp. Circuits and Syst.*, 1976, p. 666.

SIMPIL: A SIMULATION PROGRAM FOR INJECTION LOGIC

Graeme R. Boyle[*]

Department of Electrical Engineering and Computer Sciences
University of California, Berkeley, Ca., 94720

ABSTRACT

SIMPIL is a computer program for the simulation of large-scale Integrated Injection Logic (I^2L) circuits. The analysis techniques used in SIMPIL are based on those used in MOTIS-like timing simulators; however, SIMPIL is written for the specific analysis of multi-collector bipolar transistor circuits. The program is written in FORTRAN for a CDC CYBER computer and can handle up to 4096 I^2L gates. SIMPIL is over one hundred times faster than SPICE2.

1. Introduction

Programs MOTIS [1] and MOTIS-C [2] are timing simulators used for the simulation of Large-Scale Integrated (LSI) MOS transistor circuits. SIMPIL (simulation program for injection logic) is a new timing simulator for LSI circuits composed of bipolar Integrated Injection Logic (I^2L) gates.

Timing simulators are circuit simulators with simple models and relaxed convergence criteria that take advantage of the properties of digital circuits to enhance execution speed and decrease memory requirements. A table lookup scheme is used in place of function evaluation for device models and SIMPIL uses a gate macromodel for the multi-collector transistor.

I^2L is a bipolar logic technique suitable for large-scale integration. An equivalent circuit of an I^2L gate is shown in Fig. 1. For a bipolar device, the collector current is an exponential function of the base voltage and hence the simple table lookup schemes used in MOTIS and MOTIS-C cannot be used without a substantial loss of accuracy. SIMPIL formulates its lookup tables in terms of base charge rather than base voltage to overcome this problem.

The RC-transmission-line effects present along the distributed base of an I^2L gate, when high-current operation is used, can significantly affect the characteristics of the gate. To maintain analysis speed, SIMPIL uses an analytic solution for the RC-transmission-line characteristics which is included in the tables generated prior to analysis.

SIMPIL is written in FORTRAN for a CDC CYBER

_____
[*]Now with Tektronix Inc., Beaverton, Oregon.

computer and its analysis speed is over one hundred times faster than SPICE2 [3,4]. Circuits of over 500 I^2L gates have been analyzed by the program and the timing simulation results agree with measured performance to within 20%. The present version of the program can analyze circuits containing up to 4096 I^2L gates.

2. SIMPIL

SIMPIL has four main sections: the model preprocessor, circuit setup, analysis, and output. The circuit input consists of a gate-level description of the circuit in a SPICE2-like format [3,4]. Subcircuits similar to those allowed in SPICE2 may be used. The model inputs are process-related parameters and gate geometries. The circuit-level models are calculated internally from these data as described elsewhere [5]. During the transient analysis, a simple logic simulation is performed to predict whether or not a node voltage will change over the next timestep. If no change is indicated the analysis of that node is skipped. This is generally worthwhile since in many digital circuits a high proportion of the nodes are stable at any time (often as high as 90%) so significant analysis time can be saved by eliminating this unnecessary computation. All node voltage updates are stored on a disc file during the analysis phase. This file is then used in conjunction with the interactive plotting section of SIMPIL to display up to eight waveforms on a Tektronix graphics terminal. Either the entire duration of the analysis may be displayed or any portion may be windowed for a close look at critical timing. The initial state of the circuit may either be set by the user or specified as the state of the circuit at a specified time in a previous run. In the latter case, the program reads the specified file to find the node voltages at the given time. SIMPIL presently uses seven 60-bit words per gate with the data packed into these words. This feature can be easily changed to eliminate the packing requirement for machines with smaller word sizes.

3. Circuit Description

A circuit can be input to SIMPIL directly from an all-NAND logic diagram or a device layout since there is a one-to-one correspondence between a NAND logic gate and an I^2L device, as indicated in Fig. 2. For low current levels, the circuit operation and analysis is almost independent of collector position since all collectors of a given

Reprinted from *Proc. IEEE Int. Symp. Circuits and Systems*, May 1978, pp. 890-894.

area in an I^2L transistor exhibit identical performance. At high current levels where the effect of the distributed resistance and capacitance of the base becomes significant, the behaviour of each collector (each output from the NAND gate) is different and so the operation of the circuit will depend upon the location of each collector. Hence for accurate simulation of high-current operation, it is essential that the location of the collectors in the circuit description correspond to that in the layout. At present, only gates which can be modeled as a string of transistors and diodes, such as shown in Fig. 1, can be simulated. For reference purposes, the nodes within the model of each gate are numbered in a consistent manner. The first node of the gate description is always assigned to the base contact (see Fig. 1) independent of its physical location. The remaining nodes define collectors sequentially away from the injector with the second node refering to the collector nearest the injector end of the gate.

4. Model Description

The model description requires two kinds of data. The first is the process characterization data, which is common to all gates and consists of saturation current densities, planar capacitances per unit area, minority charge storage per unit area, base sheet resistance and contact resistance. Saturation current per unit length and capacitance per unit length for the sidewalls are also required. These parameters can be obtained from measurements on a number of test devices fabricated in the process to be used for the circuit [5]. The second type of input for the model is the geometrical and dimensional description of each gate configuration in the circuit to be simulated.

5. Analysis Technique

The objective in developing SIMPIL was to enable a very fast simulation of the dynamic operation of large I^2L circuits. In order to accomplish this goal, the calculation required to update each node voltage at each timepoint must be minimized. For high-current operation the base-emitter region of the I^2L device behaves as a lossy, non-linear RC line. The shunt capacitance of the line is mainly due to minority charge storage in the base and emitter and so is very strongly voltage dependent. The shunt conductance of the line models the base-emitter diode and so is also strongly voltage dependent. Since tables are to be used to represent the bias dependence of conductances, currents and capacitances, these must be expressed in terms of an independent variable that makes the functions reasonably smooth. Base-emitter voltage is unsatisfactory since all of the three abovementioned quantities are exponentially dependent upon voltage and so for tables formed using equal steps of voltage, only a small fraction of the entries would contain non-negligible values. Hence the accuracy would be poor for reasonably-sized tables. Base-emitter charge was used as the independent variable for the analysis since the conductances, currents and effective capacitances are all smooth functions of charge.

The first step in the table setup is to determine the incremental equivalent circuit at the base contact terminals. The circuit is obtained by approximating the distributed RC line with a multi-lump resistor-diode-capacitor network then using Newton-Raphson linearization and Backward-Euler integration to produce a linear current-source-resistor ladder. By approximating the dynamic state of the base with the static state corresponding to the state of the base-contact region at the previous timepoint, the network may be reduced to a linear resistive ladder with a single current source at the base terminals as in Fig. 3. This may be further reduced to a single equivalent-current source and a single equivalent conductance at the base contact terminals as shown in Fig. 4. This equivalent circuit is dependent only upon the state of the base-contact region and so may be evaluated over the range of possible states before the transient analysis and stored in tables. The incremental voltage over the timestep is then calculated from this very simple circuit and the base-terminal current. The base-terminal current is the sum of the collector currents for all collectors driving this base.

Now that the new state of the base-contact section has been calculated, the new states of each collector section for the I^2L device can be found. To do this, the base is considered as a voltage divider as shown in Fig. 5. R represents the base resistance from the base-contact node to the base node of the adjacent collector section, or the base resistance from one collector to the next collector. G_{eq} and C_{eq} represent the effective conductance and effective capacitance of the remaining base sections respectively. Assuming V_b remains constant over the analysis time interval, the incremental base voltage at the collector section, v_c, may be evaluated analytically as given in (1).

$$v_c(t_n) = S [V_{cdc} - V_c(t_n)] \qquad (1)$$

$$V_{cdc} = \frac{V_b}{R + 1/G_{eq}} \qquad (2)$$

$$\tau = \frac{R/G_{eq}}{R + 1/G_{eq}} C_{eq} \qquad (3)$$

$$S = 1 - e^{-\Delta t/\tau} \qquad (4)$$

S represents the electrical stiffness of the I^2L base subregion since $\Delta t/\tau$ is the ratio of the analysis timestep to the base subsection differential time constant (time constant of one section of the base with respect to the next). For low-current operation, any increment of voltage at the base contact is transmitted to all sections of the base in a time much less than the time constant of the base considered as a whole (dominant time constant). In this case the base appears to be very stiff and S is very nearly equal to unity. That is, the voltages at all points on the base appear to move together. For high-current operation the voltage dropped along the base is not negligible. The current which causes this voltage is due to dc base current plus the current required to charge minority carrier storage. This means the base dominant time constant approaches the differential time constants and so an increment of voltage at the base contact may take a time on the order of the dominant time constant to propagate to the end of the base. It will also be attenuated as it propagates. In this case the base is electrically flexible and S is less than unity. With the approximation that the dynamic state of the remaining base sections is almost equal to the static state corresponding to the state of the previous section, then the stiffness (S) is a function of the bias point only and so may be calculated, for a given injector voltage, prior to the transient analysis and stored in tables. Since charge is being used as the state variable, the formula actually used is expressed in terms of charge as given by

$$Q(t_n) = S(Q) [Q_{cdc} - Q_c(t_n)] \qquad (5)$$

where Q_{cdc} is the base-section charge if the subsection were statically biased to the level corresponding to that of the adjacent section on the base-contact side. Equation (5) is first used to calculate the charge increment in the base subsection using the new state of the base-contact section. Then (5) is used to calculate the incremental charge for each remaining collector section in turn using the state of the section on the base-contact side of it. The simulation results obtained using the algorithm described are reasonably accurate, despite all of the approximations, for two reasons. 1) Logic circuits have well defined high and low stable states due to saturation of the transistors, so any error in the node state introduced in calculating the transition is lost when the transition is complete. 2) Any timing error is due to the signal propagating through only a small number of gates so the absolute timing error does not compound over a long time.

6. Simulation Results

SIMPIL has been used to simulate a number of I^2L circuits and the results of some of these simulations are presented. Figure 6 shows a comparison of waveforms predicted by SIMPIL and

SPICE2 for a three-collector gate. The minimum toggle periods for a divide-by-two and a decade counter as simulated by SIMPIL and measured are shown in Figs. 7-8. Table 1 gives a comparison of the required cpu time for these simulations.

7. Conclusions

SIMPIL provides a means of simulating circuits consisting of up to thousands of gates over the entire operating bias range of I^2L (which can be up to six orders of magnitude in current) in a reasonable time. The analysis techniques rely on the voltage limiting characteristics of a digital circuit and a relatively small reverse transmission through the gates.

8. Acknowledgements

The author wishes to thank D. O. Pederson, J. Smith, I. Getreu and L. Gagliani for their helpful suggestions and A. R. Newton for many discussions and for providing the program MOTIS-C which served as the starting point for SIMPIL. This work was supported by Tektronix Inc.

9. References

[1] B. R. Chawla, H. K. Gummel and P. Kozak, "MOTIS: An MOS Timing Simulator," IEEE Trans. Circuits and Systems, vol. CAS-22, no. 12., pp. 901-910, Dec. 1975.

[2] S. P. Fan, M.Y. Hsueh, A. R. Newton and D. O. Pederson, "MOTIS-C: A New Simulator for MOS LSI Circuits," ISCAS Proc. pp. 700-703, 1977.

[3] L. W. Nagel, "SPICE2: A Computer Program to Simulate Semiconductor Circuits," ERL Memo No. ERL-M520, Electronics Research Laboratory, University of California, Berkeley, May 1975.

[4] E. Cohen, "Program Reference for SPICE2," ERL Memo No. ERL-M592, Electronics Research Laboratory, University of California, Berkeley, June 1976.

[5] G. R. Boyle, "Simulation of Integrated Injection Logic," Ph.D. dissertation, University of California, Berkeley, 1978.

CIRCUIT	SPICE2		SIMPIL	
	no. of transistors	CPU time (s)	no. of gates	CPU time (s)
Divide-by-2 501 points	32	120	12	1.48
Decade counter 2001 points	149	5745	47	13.0

Table 1. SPICE2 and SIMPIL comparison for two circuits

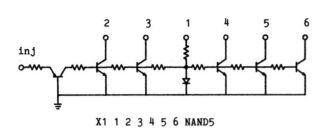

X1 1 2 3 4 5 6 NAND5

Fig. 1. Five-output gate model and
example input

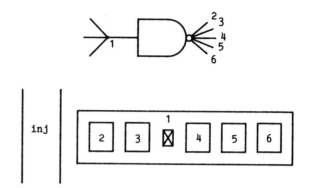

Fig. 2. Five-output gate logic diagram
and example layout

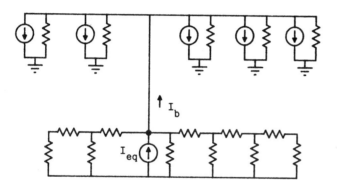

Fig. 3. Linearized base equivalent circuit

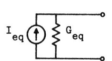

Fig. 4. Reduced linearized equivalent circuit

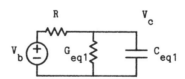

Fig. 5. Base-signal voltage divider

202

Fig. 6. Comparison of SIMPIL and SPICE2
voltage waveforms

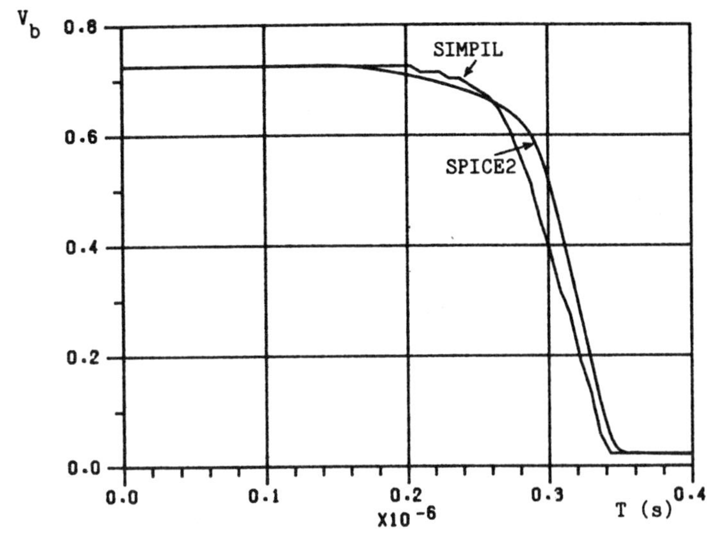

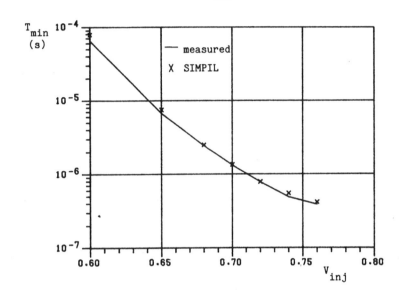

Fig. 7. Divide-by-two minimum toggle
period vs injector voltage

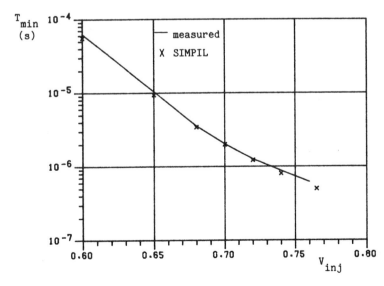

Fig. 8. Decade-counter minimum toggle
period vs injector voltage

Part V
High Performance I²L Structures

The papers presented in this part present either detailed investigations into the performance limiting mechanisms of I²L or structures which are aimed at achieving such fundamentally limited performance.

Paper V-1 by Davies and Meindl provides a comprehensive analysis of the absolute speed limiting mechanisms for ideal I²L as well as for more realizable I²L forms. A major conclusion which they propose is that I²L will always be slower than the MOS based LSI technologies. The treatment is rather complete and the arguments are convincing. The authors address the question of analog compatibility for I²L and propose a figure of merit which is breakdown voltage divided by I²L gate delay. They show that conventional I²L fabricated in a double diffused bipolar process will not exhibit a figure of merit greater than about 1.5 V/ns. In contrast, their so-called poly-I²L or a double-epi technique can lead to figures of merit near 8 V/ns. These results bear careful consideration by anyone wishing to implement high-speed I²L along with high-voltage analog circuits.

The second paper (V-2) by Berger and Helwig also provides a detailed investigation of the speed limiting mechanisms for I²L. However, these author's investigation is more aligned with experimental measurements and simulation of a specific I²L structure. Nonetheless, many of their conclusions agree with those of Davies and Meindl, (paper V-1). For example, both papers present evidence which says that the contribution to the gate delay due to the injector pnp is not important for realistic devices. These conclusions are in conflict with those reached by Klaassen in bibliography paper [V-1]. However, Klaassen's predictions do not appear to be confirmed by experiment. Berger and Helwig present a novel gate structure with injectors at both ends which helps to reduce the effects of base series resistance and thereby helps to equalize the turn-on delays of all collectors in the gate. Such a dual-injector I²L gate has been proposed previously in bibliography paper [IV-43] and shown there (by simulation) to yield improved gate delays due to the improved turn-on delays. Berger and Helwig conclude that such a dual-injector structure is sufficient to eliminate series resistance effects. However, their test structure contained only one collector even though its base area could accomodate four collectors. Consequently, the increased series resistance which would result from the addition of the remaining three collectors was not present in their measurements. Therefore, their conclusion is optimistic in this regard and should be taken cautiously. These authors investigate a down-diffused p-type base form of I²L and they conclude that the stored charge in the emitter cannot be reduced arbitrarily without adverse effects upon the control of the integrated base doping of the npn switching device. This conclusion is somewhat pessimistic, since the so-called up-diffused I²L structure circumvents the problem of integrated base doping interference by the n⁺ buried layer.

Paper V-3 by Evans presents examples of scaling the photolithographic dimensions of I²L. Devices with features on the order of 1.5μ were fabricated and the expected improvements in power-delay product and intrinsic speed limits were observed. The largest benefits to be derived from such scaled I²L are in the power dissipation and packing density. The speed improvements alone do not justify the effort involved in the fabrication of such fine-line structures.

Paper V-4 by Blackstone and Mertens presents a speed comparison of three forms of I²L: 1) the common-collector, Schottky diode output, 2) the isolated-collector, Schottky diode output, and 3) conventional n⁺ collector I²L. The authors demonstrate only a slight speed advantage for the common-collector Schottky output structure relative to the isolated Schottky output structure. Thus the most important insight to be gained here is that there is little to be gained in terms of speed by adopting the common-collector structure with its attendant layout limitations and potential Schottky diode reverse leakage current problems at high operating temperatures.

Paper V-5 by Mulder and Wulms presents an approach for the fabrication of I²L which is aimed at high-speed operation. Their structure incorporates such features as a very thin epitaxial layer, an implanted p-type base with an aiding drift field in the base, oxide isolation, and a dual-level metalization for interconnections. All of these features represent straightforward, well-known techniques for improving the speed of bipolar devices. Two unique features presented in this work are 1) the electrical and physical separation of the injector pnp from the switching npn, and 2) spatial separation of the npn collectors in order to facilitate layout. The authors suggest (indirectly) that the ability to take advantage of the second feature requires implementation of the former. The separation of the pnp and npn devices is supposed to improve speed by eliminating the need to switch the charge stored in the base of the (inverse) injector pnp. However, such separation of the npn and pnp in turn requires the use of a clamping npn in order to prevent deep saturation of the npn. The authors found that the collector area of the needed npn clamp device should be three times smaller than the npn switch collectors. This requirement could place limitations upon the minimum size which could be used for the switch npn in a given technology and thereby negatively affect the power-delay performance. Furthermore, it was found that the separation of the pnp and npn only resulted in a small (15 percent) decrease in the minimum propagation delay. Other workers have discounted the importance of the pnp stored charge, and the value of the pnp-npn separation for speed purposes is therefore dubious.

A careful consideration of the requirements for the use of the technique of separating the switching npn devices for layout convenience shows that the electrically separated pnp is not a requirement. In this regard the comparison shown between the layouts of Figs. 9 and 10 is not fair. The merged pnp–npn approach of Fig. 9 could take equal advantage of the layout scheme shown in Fig. 10. Consequently, the layout of Fig. 9 suffers unnecessarily from excessive extrinsic base-emitter junction area. Had the layout scheme of Fig. 10 been used for the merged pnp–npn structure, the performance would have been comparable to that found for the separated pnp approach. The slight gain in speed performance derived from the separated pnp approach does not justify the added complexity needed to implement the electrical separation, and the ultimate influence upon total system performance may even be negative under conditions of a fairer comparison.

Paper V-6 presents a novel solution to the sensitivity of I^2L performance to epitaxial layer thickness. In this paper, Roesner and McGreivy describe an I^2L implementation which relies upon the up-diffusion of boron from the n^+ buried layer in order to create a base doping profile which is referenced to the lower boundary rather than the upper boundary of the epitaxial layer. Thus epitaxial layer thickness variations do not influence the emitter-base junction doping profile. The up-diffused technique had been previously introduced in [V-5] of the bibliography. Roesner and McGreivy also investigated the experimental performance of a Schottky collector contact and a Schottky clamp diode across the collector-base junction of their structure. The Schottky collector contact reduces voltage swing, thereby reducing the power dissipation. The Schottky clamp diode helps to reduce the stored charge by limiting the turn-on of the high up-beta devices achieved by the up-diffused process. This work demonstrates that excellent I^2L speed performance can be achieved without consideration for the stored charge in the injector pnp. It should be noted that the fan-out is not specified for the power-delay curves of Fig. 8. Therefore, the effects of series base resistance upon fan-outs greater than one in the proposed structure cannot be deduced from the data presented.

Paper V-7 by Agraz-Guerena et al. presents an oxide-isolated, up-diffused process for an upward bipolar technology. Crucial to the successful implementation of this upward technology is the use of high pressure oxidation in order to limit the high temperature-times required in the process and thereby maintain the desired impurity doping profiles. The authors have adopted Mulder's and Wulms's technique of separating the individual output npn's and interconnected their bases with metal. In addition to providing layout convenience this technique offers the advantage of virtually eliminating the usual series resistance effects of an I^2L gate. Consequently, the turn-on and turn-off delays are independent of fan-out position, and all outputs offer the same propagation delay. I believe that the upward technology presented here is the most nearly optimum approach yet disclosed which can be realistically applied in commercial applications requiring high performance I^2L.

Paper V-8 by Bahraman et al. describes an unusual configuration for an I^2L gate. These authors have elected to implement an npn injector merged with a pnp switch. The primary motive here has been to achieve an isolated fan-in capability. Schottky diodes are used to achieve the isolated fan-in in a manner analogous to that employed in substrate fed logic (SFL). In this work, the authors have avoided the technological problems associated with fabricating their input Schottky diodes on p-type material. Their desire to fabricate the input Schottky diodes on n-type material dictated the pnp switch approach. As in SFL, the isolated, multiinput gate offers substantial layout advantages and increased functional density. In contrast to the SFL approach, Bahraman et al. implement their gate with a single output collector. It should be noted that an isolated, multiinput capability eliminates the need for a multioutput gate. The authors describe the limitations upon the fan-out of their structure in terms of the effective up-beta of the pnp switch and conclude that a fan-out of five can easily be supported. In this analysis, they do not mention the effects of a multiple fan-in upon the effective up-beta of the pnp. Since each additional isolated fan-in to a gate increases the extrinsic emitter area (and recombination at the Schottky contact) the fan-in and fan-out are interrelated in a fashion similar to that found in SFL. The notable exception is that the Schottky-base approach described here does not necessarily accrue additional injector current drive with the addition of each input as does SFL. A notable feature of the Schottky-base structure is the relatively high forward common-base current gain of the injector npn. The Schottky-base structure would most appropriately be compared with SFL, and such a comparison would perhaps favor the Schottky-base structure because of the relative ease of implementation in a standard bipolar fabrication facility. Two major drawbacks of the Schottky-base approach are 1) the dependence of the pnp-switch base-width upon epitaxial layer thickness, and 2) the high series-collector-resistance associated with the vertical npn injector.

The final paper in this part (V-9) by Perlegos and Chan presents another alternative to achieving an isolated, multiinput-gate capability. These authors also (as in paper V-8) promote the use of a single output collector on their switching transistor with fan-out capability achieved by way of a sufficiently high effective up-beta. In contrast to Bahraman et al., Perlegos and Chan retain the npn switch of typical I^2L and implement their input Schottky diodes in separately isolated n-type islands. This approach offers the advantages of fabricating the Schottky diodes upon n-type material while not requiring additional extrinsic base area for the input diodes as does SFL and the Schottky-base I^2L of paper V-8. Since a single output collector is used, the effects of series base resistance are minimized. The authors present simulation results which predict that high-speed performance with excellent functional packing density could be achieved with the diode input I^2L structure. Results from experimental devices were not reported in their paper.

There have been reported many other approaches aimed at achieving high performance I^2L. The papers reprinted here present a somewhat complete spectrum of the schemes which have been attempted. The optimum high performance I^2L will probably draw ideas from several of these works. My prediction for the form which a future high performance I^2L structure might assume is outlined below:

1) an oxide-isolated, up-diffused process as proposed in the "upward" technology of Bell Laboratories, paper V-7;

2) a multiinput, isolated Schottky diode approach as described in paper V-9;

3) a separated output npn scheme as introduced by Mulder and Wulms when multiple output gates are desired;

4) a highly efficient (i.e., probably asymmetrical) pnp injector (this could perhaps be a double diffused device);

5) multilevel metal interconnect capability; and

6) compatibility with TTL, ECL, and high voltage analog circuits could easily be maintained with the "upward" bipolar technology.

Finally it should be noted that the applicability of a digital logic technique for use in LSI or VLSI does not depend upon speed alone. The maximum power dissipation capability of conventional device packages represents an absolute limit which cannot be violated in cost-conscious applications. Thus speed, power dissipation, and packing density all must be addressed simultaneously in the selection of a high-performance digital logic structure.

Considerations for High-Speed and Analog-Circuit-Compatible I²L and the Analysis of Poly I²L

RODERICK D. DAVIES, MEMBER, IEEE, AND JAMES D. MEINDL, FELLOW, IEEE

Abstract—Expressions are derived for minimum propagation-delay time and dc operational conditions in the I²L circuit configuration, and are applied to several kinds of I²L limitations. 1) Ultimately achievable (roughly 0.34 ns, fan-out of 2) and reasonably expected minimum propagation-delay values (0.75–1.0 ns considering simple two-dimensional n-p-n limitations) are estimated. 2) Speed improvement of the standard I²L structure via doping level adjustment is shown to be minimal (it is primarily useful for ensurance of dc operation). 3) Requiring analog compatibility further constrains performance; a figure of merit of about 1 to 2 V/ns is derived and experimentally confirmed for the product of analog device BV_{CBO} and I²L speed for standard epitaxial I²L processing. Radical techniques using dual buried layers, dual epitaxial layers, or Poly I²L offer considerably enhanced performance by attacking the parameter with primary leverage on these tradeoffs: base-to-buried layer spacing W_{epi}. Analysis of Poly I²L reveals these specific advantages: 1) "removal" of W_{EPI} in the I²L devices and lowered emitter-to-collector area ratio, yielding n-p-n transit time $\simeq 0.8$ ns, 2) a large n-p-n saturation current I_{SN} which suppresses the reverse-p-n-p transit-time contribution, and 3) a very shallow epitaxial layer, obtained by elimination of an explicit isolation diffusion of standard processes, providing a shallower epitaxial layer for equivalent W_{epi}.

I. Introduction

THIS paper is intended to reveal several aspects of I²L [1], [2] maximum switching speed, dc operational performance, and analog-circuit compatibility, and to relate them to the Poly I²L [3] configuration.

In Section II, a self-consistent review of dc and intrinsic-ac integrated injection logic performance is presented in which minimum delay results as the product of an effective transit time and a current-gain parameter. The further inclusion of downward-n-p-n transit time is shown to have minor impact. In Section III, a technology-independent absolute lower limit on propagation delay of roughly 0.34 ns is predicted (fan-out of two), resulting solely from the effect of one-dimensional, upward-n-p-n base/emitter-limited transit time in the I²L circuit configuration. The contribution of the p-n-p injector is shown to be suppressable by providing a large saturation current ratio I_{SN}/I_{SP}. Inclusion of simple two-dimensional n-p-n transit time considerations results in a lower limit estimate of about 0.75–1.0 ns.

Manuscript received January 15, 1979; revised May 24, 1979.
R. D. Davies was with the Xerox Palo Alto Research Center, Palo Alto, CA. He is now with the Central Research Laboratories, Texas Instruments Inc., Dallas, TX 75265.
J. D. Meindl is with the Stanford Electronics Laboratories, Stanford, CA 94305.

Requiring analog compatibility (Section IV) further constrains performance; a figure of merit of about 1–2 V/ns is derived for the product of analog device BV_{CBO} and I²L speed using standard epitaxial I²L processing. Experimental data confirm this and demonstrate that limited improvements are available through doping-profile adjustments to the standard structure (doping-profile adjustment is instead shown to be primarily useful for ensurance of dc operation). Radical techniques using dual buried layers, dual epitaxial layers, or Poly I²L offer considerably enhanced performance at the risk of unfamiliar (but not necessarily much more difficult) processing. They attack the parameter with primary leverage on these tradeoffs: base-to-buried layer spacing W_{epi}.

Analysis of the Poly I²L structure (Section V) shows these specific advantages: 1) "removal" of W_{EPI} in the I²L devices, yielding n-p-n transit time $\simeq 0.8$ ns, 2) a large n-p-n saturation current I_{SN} which suppresses the reverse-p-n-p transit-time contribution, and 3) a very shallow epitaxial layer, obtained by elimination of an explicit isolation diffusion needed in standard processes; this allows a shallower epitaxial layer for an equivalent W_{epi}. The much smaller epitaxial thickness requirement reduces analog-device collector resistance and isolation capacitance and provides higher value on-chip epitaxial resistors.

The Appendix provides specific processing and technology information for Poly I²L.

II. Self-Consistent Analysis of I²L Minimum Delay and DC Operational Conditions

The I²L circuit configuration [1], [2] is described in Fig. 1. Terminal parameters for separated n-p-n's and a p-n-p will be used because they represent the ideally obtainable I²L (for example, the base contact arising from the normal gate layout is discounted as it is not intrinsic to the I²L circuit configuration, and some processes such as Poly I²L provide essentially ohmically separated devices [3]). Minimum propagation delay limits are then calculated neglecting depletion capacitances and base spreading resistances. We initially neglect n-p-n downward transit time and define

$$I_L = FI_{SN}/\beta_u + I_{SP}/\alpha_R \tag{1}$$

$$\tau^* = [FI_{SN}\tau_N + I_{SP}\tau_P]/I_L \tag{2}$$

$$x_i = \exp(v_i/V_T) - 1 \tag{3}$$

Reprinted from *IEEE J. Solid-State Circuits*, vol. SC-14, pp. 876–887, Oct. 1979.

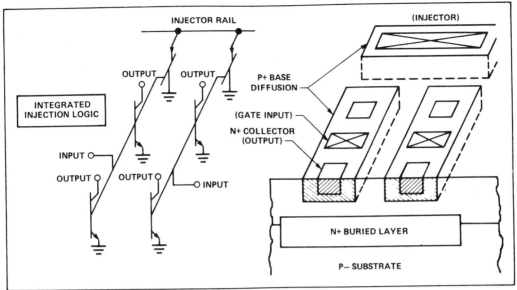

Fig. 1. I²L circuit schematic and corresponding cross-sectional view in the standard I²L structure.

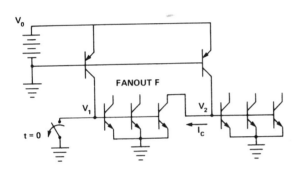

I_{SN}, I_{SP} NPN AND PNP SATURATION CURRENTS
τ_N, τ_P UPWARD NPN, REVERSE PNP TRANSIT TIMES
β_U, α_R NPN UPWARD BETA, PNP REVERSE ALPHA

Fig. 2. Schematic for determination of minimum delay time and dc operational conditions, with definition of relevant n-p-n and p-n-p Ebers–Moll parameters.

with the relevant Ebers–Moll transport version n-p-n and p-n-p parameters summarized in Fig. 2. Charging of the first gate after switch opening at time $t = 0$ (Fig. 2), and the subsequent discharge of the second gate (part of which occurs simultaneously with first-gate charge-up) is then described by

$$I_{SP}x_0 = I_L[x_1(t) + \tau^* dx_1(t)/dt] \tag{4}$$

$$I_{SP}x_0 - I_{SN}x_1(t) = I_L[x_2(t) + \tau^* dx_2(t)/dt]. \tag{5}$$

The first right-hand side terms in (4) and (5) express dc current flowing into the gates as represented by the proportionality factor I_L. The second represents displacement current flowing to stored minority charge in the p-n-p and n-p-n's as represented by the normalization τ^*. Solving for x_1 and x_2 by Laplace transformation and defining two propagation delays as having occurred when $v_1(t) = v_2(t)$ (or alternately, taking $I_{C2} \simeq 0$) yields

$$[1 - (I_L/I_{SN})] \cdot \exp[2\tau_{min}/\tau^*] = 1 + [2\tau_{min}/\tau^*]. \tag{6}$$

This transcendental relation is plotted as a parametric equation [4] in Fig. 3 for the explicit variation of delay time τ_{min} to

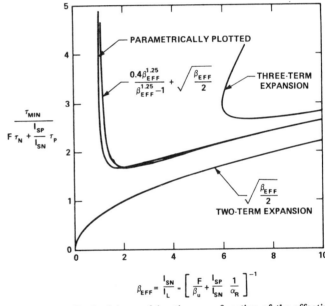

$$\beta_{EFF} = \frac{I_{SN}}{I_L} = \left[\frac{F}{\beta_u} + \frac{I_{SP}}{I_{SN}} \frac{1}{\alpha_R}\right]^{-1}$$

Fig. 3. Normalized minimum delay time as a function of the effective current gain β_{eff} using several analysis approaches.

the dc parameter I_{SN}/I_L. Also plotted are

1) an approximate analytical solution obtained expanding the exponential as two Taylor-series terms (similar to [5]); this yields a propagation delay proportional to the square root of I_{SN}/I_L

2) a similar approximation using the first three Taylor-series terms

3) a fitting formula derived by observing the first two and searching for a two-term response of τ_{min} to I_{SN}/I_L.

I_{SN}/I_L in (6) is conveniently called the effective current gain β_{eff} of the I²L gate (consistent with [5]):

$$I_L/I_{SN} = 1/\beta_{eff} = F/\beta_u + [I_{SP}/I_{SN}][1/\alpha_R]. \tag{7}$$

β_{eff} must be >1.5-2 for guaranteed operation [both from Fig. 3 and by inspection of (6)]; the resulting n-p-n upward current gain must exceed

$$\beta_u = 2F/[1 - 2(I_{SP}/I_{SN})(1/\alpha_R)]. \qquad (8)$$

This analysis yields a minimum delay which may be written as the product of an effective transit time τ_{eff} and a function $G(\beta_{eff})$:

$$\tau_{min} = \tau_{eff} \cdot G(\beta_{eff}) \qquad (9)$$

$$\tau_{eff} = F\tau_N + (I_{SP}/I_{SN})\tau_P \qquad (10)$$

$$G(\beta_{eff}) \simeq 0.4\beta_{eff}^{5/4}/(\beta_{eff}^{5/4} - 1) + [\beta_{eff}/2]^{1/2}. \qquad (11)$$

The saturation-current ratio in (10) and the existence of (11) arise specifically from the I^2L circuit-environment context and are transparent to "total-charge/total-current" analysis approaches.

The G-function has a minimum value of 1.7 which may be used to estimate an *upper bound* on I^2L speed, with consideration *only* to the transistor transit times and saturation currents (parameters which are unambiguously measurable).

The product $[2\tau_{min}/\tau^*] \cdot \exp[-2\tau_{min}/\tau^*]$ in (6) arises from a repeated root in the Laplace domain which physically represents the simultaneous discharge of the second gate with charge-up of the first gate. If we now extend the above analysis to include the *downward* n-p-n transit time τ_{ND}, then the time constants τ^* of the first and second gates become unequal because while the n-p-n downward transit time has no effect on the charge-up of the first gate, it enters into the differential equation of the second gate as an additional displacement current. This is a worst case simplifying assumption in that the forward bias (saturation) of the second-gate collector–base junctions cannot exceed x_2. By realizing that the voltage at the collectors of the second gate does not rise appreciably as most of the discharge occurs, a nonlinear differential equation is avoided; to replace (2) we now define for the first and second gates

$$\tau_1^* = [FI_{SN}\tau_N + I_{SP}\tau_P]/I_L \qquad (12a)$$

$$\tau_2^* = [FI_{SN}(\tau_N + \tau_{ND}) + I_{SP}\tau_P]/I_L. \qquad (12b)$$

Actually, two values of I_L also now exist, but this is neglected because they differ only by the addition of a small term β_{down}^{-1} (n-p-n) to the second-gate I_L. Solution of the new relations that are similar to (4) and (5) yields a product of the roots of (12) in the Laplace domain. Identification of an overall propagation delay that is strictly normalized to a single effective time constant is no longer possible; however, a two-term Taylor-series expansion similar to that done for (6) yields

$$\tau_{min} \text{ (down-n-p-n included)} \simeq [1 + \tau_{ND}/\tau_{eff}]^{1/2}$$
$$\cdot \tau_{min} \text{ (down-n-p-n excluded)}. \qquad (13)$$

This approximate result implies that the n-p-n downward transit time does not simply add to the other transit times, but enters in a square-root fashion. This effect has been confirmed by computer simulation with SPICE [6]. It implies that clamping the collectors of the I^2L gate out of saturation in the fashion of Schottky TTL will have a minor effect on maximum speed as compared to efforts reducing τ_{eff} (clamping may raise extrinsic-region efficiency by reducing the voltage swing, however).

III. ACHIEVABLE I^2L SPEED

A. Absolute Minimum (Technology-Independent) Value

An estimate for the ultimately achievable minimum delay of an I^2L gate is obtained ignoring n-p-n downward transit time and taking the minimum value of $G(\beta_{eff}) = 1.7$. Then

$$\tau_{min} = 1.7[F\tau_N + (I_{SP}/I_{SN})\tau_P]$$
$$= 1.7[W_{bn}^2/2D_{np}] \cdot [F(1 + Q_E/Q_B)$$
$$+ (A_{cp}/A_{cn})(W_{bp}/W_{bn})] \qquad (14)$$

with A_{cp}, A_{cn}, W_{bp}, and W_{bn} the respective n-p-n and p-n-p collector areas and base widths, with Q_E/Q_B the ratio of emitter and base stored charge. The well-known n-p-n base-limited transit time resulting from charge storage needed to support a dc collector current is factored out, and the hole and electron diffusivities are brought outside their respective base-doping integrals in the saturation currents I_{SN} and I_{SP} [7]; then the p-n-p transit-time contribution resembles that of another physical-dimension-scaled n-p-n transistor. The p-n-p delay contribution is seen to be suppressable, even for p-n-p (lateral) basewidths greater than the minimum possible, by taking a favorable n-p-n-to-p-n-p collector area ratio.

Hoeneisen and Mead calculated the minimum realistic bipolar basewidth as that value trading base punchthrough and collector avalanche breakdown, and then allowed for statistical fluctuations in base doping to assure that LSI yields will be available [8]. We take minimum basewidth $W_{bn} \simeq 0.20~\mu m$ at $5 \times 10^{18}/cm^3$ base doping by doubling their value to ensure a well-defined, β-controlling undepleted basewidth that is equal to the total depleted width.

B. Limitation by n-p-n Emitter Charge Using Epitaxial-Layer Processing

The amount that $(1 + Q_E/Q_B)$ in (14) exceeds unity represents the contribution of emitter charge storage to n-p-n transit time; a lower bound is estimated as follows. 1) Assume that the n^+ emitter cannot be doped higher than $5 \times 10^{19}/cm^3$ because of autodoping considerations in fabricating epitaxial layers [9]. 2) Assume that the resulting hole lifetime of about 20 ns [10] and diffusivity of about 1.5 cm^2/s dictate a stored charge that is not smaller than that value residing within a diffusion length of the emitter–base junction (triangular charge profile taken). 3) Recognize that effects such as bandgap narrowing only degrade these transit-time estimates by increasing Q_E/Q_B. This yields the lower bound of

$$Q_E/Q_B \simeq [p_{no}/n_{po}] \cdot [(D_{pn}\tau_p)^{1/2}/W_{bn}] \simeq 1. \qquad (15)$$

For a fan-out $F = 2$ and neglecting the p-n-p contribution, a lower bound delay estimate of roughly 0.34 ns results from (14) and (15). This is impressive by production standards, but lags the best reported experimental MOS 0.23 and 0.4 ns [11], [12] performance which represent devices that are buildable in LSI. This suggests that I^2L realizations will always be slower than such competing Si technologies.

C. Limitation by Two-Dimensional n-p-n Effects

A serious technological constraint is the departure from one-dimensional behavior of a practical I^2L (i.e., upside down) n-p-n transistor. The n-p-n transit time is actually no smaller than

$$\tau_N = Q_{\text{base\&emitter}}/I_{\text{collector}}$$

$$= [A_e/A_c(\text{effective})]\,[W_{bn}^2/2D_{np}]\,[1 + Q_E/Q_B]$$

even assuming an infinite recombination velocity at the silicon surface surrounding the (arbitrarily shallow) n⁺ collector.

This effective area factor is very nearly unity for conventional downward-operated double-diffused transistors because there is debiasing of the emitter–base junction along the junction sidewall approaching the heavily doped surface. For alignment of an I²L collector inside an intrinsic base diffusion, however (Fig. 1), with the alignment registration tolerance ranging between full and one half of the collector side, the degradation factor is between 4 and 9. This yields 1–3 ns minimum practical delay.

Advanced techniques that self-align the collectors to the masking edge of an extra surrounding "extrinsic" heavily doped base can be expected to decrease the effective A_e/A_c at the expense of degrading extrinsic efficiency (increase of emitter–base depletion capacitance). A possible alternate decrease of the effective A_e/A_c by using walled-collector oxide isolation (i.e., beyond intergate isolation) has previously been rejected because of a resulting experimentally observed serious increase in base spreading resistance [13]. The only obvious improvement of A_e/A_c is to simply increase the n-p-n size and compromise packing density and extrinsic efficiency. Unless reduction of effective A_E/A_C can be obtained below present values about 2:1 or 3:1, the expected achievable $\tau_{\min}$ from this analysis is roughly in the range of 0.75–1.0 ns.

D. Response of the Standard Structure to Doping Variations

Equations (9)–(11) can reveal the effect on the speed of standard-structure, epitaxial-emitter I²L (Fig. 1) for: 1) varying n-p-n base doping via diffusion sheet-resistivity modification or via extra n⁺ collector drive-in, or 2) varying epitaxial doping N_{epi}. With the standard-structure dominant stored charges being in the n-p-n emitter and the p-n-p base (Fig. 1), the sensitivities of Fig. 4 result; here the p-n-p transit time is base-limited and the well-known emitter-limited n-p-n transit time [5] is taken by

$$Q_{\text{EMITTER}} \simeq [qn_i^2 A_e/N_{\text{EPI}}]\,W_{\text{EPI}}x_1 \qquad (16a)$$

$$I_C = I_{SN}x_1 = \left[qn_i^2 A_c D_{np}\Big/\int N_B\,dx\right]x_1 \qquad (16b)$$

$$\tau_N = Q_{\text{EMITTER}}/I_C \simeq [A_e/A_c]\,[W_{\text{EPI}}/N_{\text{EPI}}]$$
$$\cdot\left[\int N_B\,dx/D_{np}\right]. \qquad (16c)$$

Although the two terms of the effective transit time τ_{eff} decrease linearly as "n-p-n base doping integral over epitaxial doping," the function $G(\beta_{\text{eff}})$ response approaches an inverse square-root law for practical values of $G(\beta_{\text{eff}}) > 2$. The overall predicted response then approaches a square-root law, as can be seen by inspection of data [14] for variation of the base-doping integral by varying collector drive-in (Fig. 5).

For an extreme case of deep drive-in of the I²L n-p-n col-

$$\tau_{\min} \sim \left[\tau_N + \frac{I_{SP}}{I_{SN}}\,\tau_P\right]\,G(\beta_{\text{EFF}})$$

PARAMETER	DOPING SENSITIVITY
$\tau_N = Q_{EN}/I_{CN}$	$\int N_b\,dx/N_{\text{epi}}$
$\tau_P = Q_{BP}/I_{CP}$	NONE
I_{SP}	$1/N_{\text{epi}}$
I_{SN}	$1/\int N_b\,dx$
β_u and $\left(\dfrac{I_{SP}}{I_{SN}}\dfrac{1}{\alpha_R}\right)^{-1}$	$N_{\text{epi}}/\int N_b\,dx$
$G(\beta_{EFF})$	$\sqrt{\dfrac{N_{\text{epi}}}{\int N_b\,dx}}$
τ_{EFF}	$\int N_b\,dx/N_{\text{epi}}$
$\longrightarrow \tau_{\min}$	$\sqrt{\dfrac{\int N_b\,dx}{N_{\text{epi}}}}$

Fig. 4. Calculated variation of standard-structure minimum delay time with n-p-n integrated base doping and with epitaxial doping.

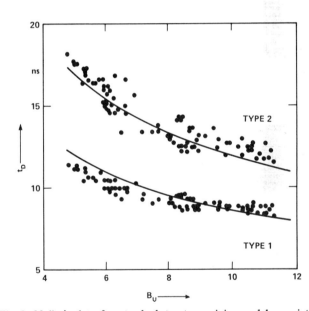

Fig. 5. Muller's data for standard-structure minimum delay variation with n-p-n collector drive-in, showing predicted square-root law.

lectors to drastically reduce integrated base doping (similar to "super-gain" transistors with associated downward current gains of 2000–10 000 [15]), this orchestrated linear variation of *both* terms of τ_{eff} along with inverse-square-root variation of *both* terms of β_{eff} precludes dramatic reduction of $\tau_{\min}$. For example, assuming that downward-β and integrated base doping track, deep collector diffusion to increase downward-β from 250 to 2500 would be expected to decrease $\tau_{\min}$ by a little more than 3:1.

Equations (9)–(11) and Fig. 4 analytically supplement Muller's CAD result [14] which was obtained by supplying transit times and current gains to a circuit simulator. The result of [16] differs somewhat from (9)–(11) and Fig. 4 in that

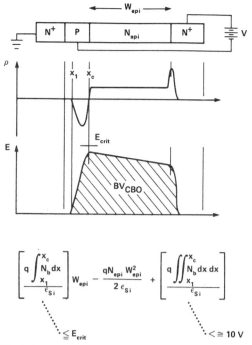

$$\left[\frac{q\int_{x_1}^{x_c} N_b\,dx}{\epsilon_{Si}}\right]W_{epi} - \frac{qN_{epi}W_{epi}^2}{2\,\epsilon_{Si}} + \left[\frac{q\iint_{x_1}^{x_c}N_b\,dx\,dx}{\epsilon_{Si}}\right]$$

$$\underset{\displaystyle \leqq E_{crit}}{} \qquad\qquad\qquad \underset{\displaystyle <\cong 10\ V}{}$$

Fig. 6. Calculation of breakdown voltage BV_{CBO} for an epitaxial-collector *BJT*.

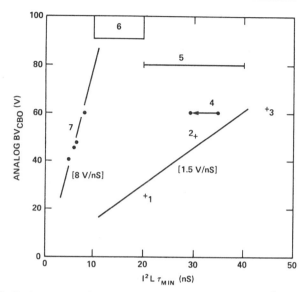

Fig. 7. Performance of various analog-circuit-compatible I²L approaches: analog-device breakdown voltage versus logic propagation delay.

it excludes variation of I_{SP}/I_{SN} that tracks the recognized variation of β_u. Because second-order effects such as high-level injection reduce collector currents and increase n-p-n base current injection into the emitter, this should be valid as a best case analysis. In short, the variation of minimum propagation delay will not be better than "square root of n-p-n integrated base doping divided by epitaxial doping."

IV. ANALOG-CIRCUIT COMPATIBILITY

A. Breakdown Voltage and the Breakdown-Over-I²L-Delay Figure of Merit BV/τ

The collector–base breakdown voltage of an analog-circuit buried-collector epitaxial transistor may be calculated as shown in Fig. 6. The mechanisms called base punchthrough [17], collector avalanche [18], reachthrough [17], and "premature punchthrough" [19] can be regarded in a unified manner by directly envisaging the integration of Poisson's equation from the emitter to a point inside the buried layer.

The first (and dominant) term in the BV_{CBO} expression of Fig. 6 represents a rectangle of electric field in the (width = W_{epi}) epitaxial collector region. The second term corrects overestimation in the first term by subtracting a triangle of electric field proportional to N_{epi} in the epitaxial region. The third term is the voltage stood off in the base region (typically less than 10 V); a fourth term would be the small voltage in the highly doped buried layer.

The breakdown is limited by the critical field of silicon $\mathcal{E}_{crit} \simeq 5 \times 10^5$ V/cm if this field strength is reached without some other limit occurring first. The coefficient of W_{epi} in the first term of Fig. 6 therefore cannot be larger than this value. If depletion into the base region reaches the edge of the emitter-depletion region before this occurs, however, then breakdown is limited by the integrated base doping (punchthrough). From Fig. 6 the minimum value is about $3 \times 10^{12}/$ cm². Note that the "punchthrough" breakdown voltage can be a function of epitaxial thickness, even though the ultimate breakdown mechanism is in the base [19]. This analysis differs with [19], however, in that Fig. 6 does not imply the existence of a W_{epi} value beyond which BV_{CBO} decreases.

Combining this with the minimum I²L delay [substituting in (9)–(11) and (16c)], which for the standard structure is assumed to be n-p-n emitter-charge-storage limited,

$$\tau_{min} = 1.7\,[FA_e/A_c]\left[\int N_B\,dx\,W_{epi}/D_{np}N_{epi}\right] \qquad (17)$$

an *upper-bound* figure of merit is then obtained by dividing the dominant first term of the breakdown voltage in Fig. 6 by the best case standard-I²L delay of (17):

$$BV_{CBO}\ (\text{analog device})/\tau_{min}\ (\text{I}^2\text{L})$$

$$= [q/\epsilon_{Si}]\,[D_{np}N_{epi}]\,[A_c/1.7\,FA_e]$$

$$= 1\ \text{to}\ 2\ \text{V/ns}. \qquad (18)$$

The fundamental nature of this figure of merit is suggested by a general absence of processing or structural variables. The chance to increase N_{epi} is limited by serious decrease of BV_{CBO} for $N_{epi} > 7.5 \times 10^{15}/\text{cm}^3$ (middle term of Fig. 6); N_{epi}'s lower limit, on the other hand, is set by the dc operation condition of (8) to about $2.5 \times 10^{15}/\text{cm}^3$ [20] (Section IV-B). Standard-process experimental data [21] in Fig. 7 confirm the validity of BV/τ as a figure of merit.

The actual-case result of varying n-p-n base-dope integral and epitaxial doping to *perturb* this figure of merit are evaluated by also considering variation of $G(\beta_{\text{eff}})$ [recall that *bestcase* $G(\beta_{\text{eff}}) = 1.7$ is used in (18)]; substituting (11) yields a square-root law in a manner similar to Fig. 4:

$$BV_{CBO}/\tau \sim \left[N_{\text{epi}} \cdot \int N_b \, dx^{\pm 1} \right]^{1/2} \quad (19)$$

where the sign of ± 1 depends on whether punchthrough or reachthrough breakdown occurs. The optimal base-dope integral just causes onset of punchthrough (as opposed to collector-avalanche) breakdown; larger values will not significantly increase BV_{CBO}, but will degrade $\tau_{\min}$, while smaller values degrade BV_{CBO} faster than they improve $\tau_{\min}$ (note the first term of Fig. 6). On the other hand, while W_{epi} is absent from (18), it is the processing variable having significant leverage to *traverse* the $BV/\tau = 1-2$ V/ns line. This is because it alone proportionally affects both I²L speed and analog-device breakdown voltage.

Also shown in Fig. 7 are experimental data for a process perturbation providing separate n⁺ surface diffusions (a shallow analog-device emitter to avoid punchthrough along with a deeper I²L collector to lower integrated base doping) [22]. A minor but noticeable improvement in BV/τ is seen by the arrowed path traversed through inclusion of this scheme; actually, the viability of this approach is mainly to ensure dc operational ability rather than to obtain high performance [22].

A second improvement is phosphorus implantation just after epitaxial deposition to selectively raise the doping N_{epi} in the entire epitaxial layer of I²L sections of the chip by a factor of 10 from 1×10^{15} to $1 \times 10^{16}/\text{cm}^3$ [23]. The amount of improvement obtained in implementing this procedure was not reported, probably because the dc operational condition [(8) and (20)] would almost certainly be violated were the selective doping left out in attempting to obtain *A-B* comparison data. Such implies that [23] is also a viable approach for assuring dc operation. Degrading performance in Fig. 7 by the square root of 10 (19) would put BV/τ back in the 1-2 V/ns range, as predicted by (18).

Larger improvements in BV/τ are available via separate epitaxial depositions to establish separate effective values of W_{epi} [24] (to multiply (18) by $[W_{\text{epiAnalog}}/W_{\text{epiLogic}}]$) or with Poly I²L [3] which utilize an optimized I²L n-p-n via out-diffused base. These techniques have the disadvantage of unfamiliar (but not necessarily much more difficult) processing; experimental $BV/\tau \simeq 8$ V/ns has been obtained with them.

B. DC Operational Limits

Equation (8) reveals the condition for dc operation of an I²L gate; for n-p-n current gain β_u smaller than some number approximately in the range of 2-10 (depending on F, I_{SP}/I_{SN}, and α_R), switching cannot occur. Calculation of n-p-n base current and hence β_u is difficult because the injection of holes into the n-n⁺ high-low emitter doping profile requires knowledge of the effective buried-layer recombination velocity s_p [5]. Estimates of this value, however, can be used to show that low values of epitaxial doping tend to make standard-

process I²L not operational; the inequality [20]

$$\left[\int N_B \, dx / (N_{\text{EPI}} D_{np} A_C) \right]$$
$$\cdot \left[(D_{pn} \cdot \text{Base Depth} \cdot \text{Gate Width}/W_{bp} \alpha_R) \right.$$
$$\left. + (F + 1) A_c s_p \right] \leqslant 2 \quad (20)$$

must be satisfied to ensure I²L operation. Taking typical values

$A_c = 225 \ \mu\text{m}^2$	$D_{np} = 10 \ \text{cm}^2/\text{s}$
Base Depth $= 1.75 \ \mu\text{m}$	$D_{pn} = 5 \ \text{cm}^2/\text{s}$
Gate Width $= 30 \ \mu\text{m}$	$W_{bp} = 10 \ \mu\text{m}$
$\alpha_R \simeq 1$	$\int N_B \, dx \simeq 3 \times 10^{12}/\text{cm}^2$

N_{EPI} must exceed about 2.5×10^{15} atoms/cm³ (effective s_p between 1000 and 2000 cm/s was used). I²L has not been reported using epitaxial resistivity >2-3 $\Omega \cdot$ cm ($\simeq 3 \times 10^{15}$ atoms/cm³), and in the Stanford Integrated Circuits Laboratory, I²L slices of higher resistivity have not been operational.

V. POLY N-P-N

A. Structure

Fig. 8 is a cross section of the Poly n-p-n; it is an inverted bipolar transistor with the active base region abutted directly against the heavily doped arsenic buried emitter without intervening n⁻ epitaxy. This essentially eliminates W_{epi} in (16); transit time is limited by base transport charge and by minor emitter charge storage. The extrinsic base regions consist of low-resistivity polysilicon (helping to minimize high-current debiasing) that are deposited on oxide along with the epitaxial layer and then doped during the analog-device optimal base diffusion. Dielectric bottom-wall isolation of the extrinsic base results from the $\simeq 0.8 \ \mu\text{m}$ SiO₂ polynucleating layer; dielectric-like sidewall isolation results from the very high resistivity as-deposited 10^{15} atoms/cm³ As-doped polysilicon (extrinsic efficiency of 0.25 pJ, using 10 μm line-space layout, have been achieved on ring oscillators [3]). Fig. 9 presents cross sections of the standard I²L epitaxial-emitter n-p-n, an oxide-isolated high-energy implanted base n-p-n, and a Poly n-p-n. These devices compare as follows.

Transit time between 10 and 100 ns results for standard processes [Fig. 9(b) and (16)] with $W_{\text{EPI}} = 1$-2 μm and $N_{\text{EPI}} = 1$-5×10^{15} atoms/cm³, assuming the effective emitter-to-collector area ratio $[A_e/A_c] \simeq 3$-4. The implanted-base n-p-n, on the other hand [Fig. 9(c)], utilizes the deepest boron implant typically attainable (B⁺⁺ at 400 keV) to place the peak of the profile just at the buried layer, thereby removing the lightly doped epitaxial emitter. A second, heavily doped base diffusion is introduced which surrounds the collectors to suppress upward electron injection in extrinsic regions, giving an effective value of $A_e/A_c \simeq 2$-3. The resulting base-transport-limited transit time reported by Klaassen [25] is $f_t \simeq 190$ MHz ($\tau_t \simeq 0.8$ ns) for this structure. τ_N in all three is not a strong function of linewidth because of the somewhat one-dimensional

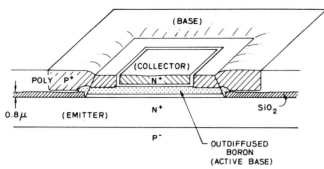

Fig. 8. Poly n-p-n cross section.

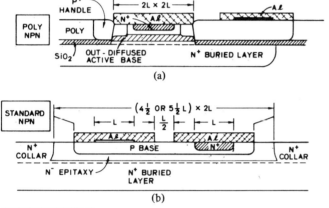

Fig. 9. Comparison of I^2L n-p-n's. (a) Poly. (b) Standard. (c) Oxide-isolated implanted base.

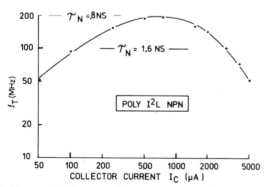

Fig. 10. Measured Poly n-p-n frequency response f_t from a network analyzer and S-parameter test set.

(vertical) nature of these devices. Indeed, Klaassen's value is for a device apparently realized using 4–6 μm layout rules (30 × 60 μm base area for FO = 2) [25], while measured Poly n-p-n f_t (Fig. 10) peaks at the same frequency despite a 10 μm line-space layout.

Base–Emitter Junction Area: The base input contact must be included in both conventional schemes [Fig. 9(b) and (c)]; $A_{BE} = (4.5L \times 2L)$ for linewidth L and overlap $L/2$. The cor-

responding Poly n-p-n A_{BE} is only $(2L)^2$ because the extrinsic base area is dielectrically bottom-wall isolated, and a "washed n^+" collector is employed. The junction-isolated n-p-n also incurs sidewall area ($18L \times$ base depth). Although Poly n-p-n base–emitter capacitance is dominated by a peripheral diode component along the epi–poly interface [3], the device has very little isolation sidewall parasitics because of the "dielectric-like" nature of lightly doped poly. Measured base–emitter capacitances for Poly I^2L show a factor of 2 reduction from those of 10 μm standard I^2L.

Base Resistance: The standard n-p-n requires approximately one square of 200 Ω/sq intrinsic base diffusion between input contact and the active device. The Poly and implanted-base n-p-n structures require a single square of extrinsic base material (55–75 Ω/sq); the Poly n-p-n obtains a low base resistance without extra processing steps because the poly is doped simultaneously with the on-chip 200 Ω/sq analog-circuit-device bases.

Packing Density: The 20 × 20 μm Poly n-p-n requires a 5 μm p^+ overlap on either side of the epitaxial "tub" to ensure low intragate resistance, resulting in a 30 μm minimum gate width. This is the same dimension as the I^2L gate width (based on 10 μm layout rules) in which a 10 × 10 μm contact hole must be spaced 5 μm inside the n^+ collector, which in turn is spaced 5 μm inside the p^+ gate diffusion. In the orthogonal direction, metallization spacing of 10 μm with 5 μm contact-hole overlaps determines equivalent collector-to-collector spacing for both Poly and standard I^2L. The packing densities of standard and Poly I^2L are therefore equivalent when using 10 μm layout rules. The densest structure is the oxide-isolated gate, especially if the n-p-n collectors can touch the oxide and avoid base spreading resistance increase [13] and base inversion along the oxide surface.

Process Complexity: The Poly I^2L process (see Appendix) requires four diffusions and seven masks, comparing favorably to five diffusions and seven masks for deep-n^+ collar I^2L. Four diffusions, a deep local oxidation, and up to 12 masks [26] may be necessary for implanted-base oxide-isolated I^2L. A drawback of Poly I^2L, however, is its novelty, both by use of polysilicon for extrinsic-device regions and by use of out-diffusing buried layers. Although the overall process is the least complex of the three discussed above, it may appear to be the most imposing.

Operating Current Range: The Poly n-p-n contains a parasitic poly diode in parallel with the base–emitter junction [3], limiting operation to above about 1 μA n-p-n collector current (Fig. 11). The parasitic diode is offset by a very low integrated base doping through adjustment of the out-diffused buried-boron-layer surface concentration; typical resulting saturation current $I_{SN} \simeq 1$–2×10^{14} A. (Most other forms of I^2L allow micropower operation down to about 1–10 nA. Further work is necessary to fabricate and evaluate I^2L on the Poly I^2L process that uses out-diffused boron, but which locally omits poly. The resulting logic would probably be relatively slow (minimum delay above 10–15 ns), but would function at micropower supply levels, be compatible with existing Poly I^2L, and would function on very high resistivity epitaxial layers.)

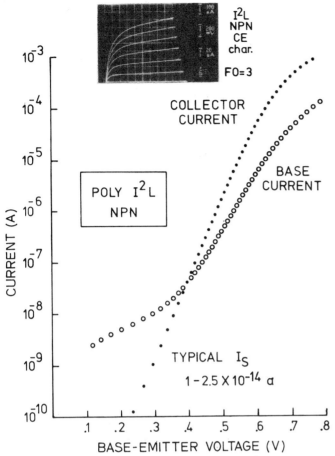

Fig. 11. Measured Poly 400 μm² n-p-n dc characteristics showing large saturation current I_{SN} with accompanying low current gain.

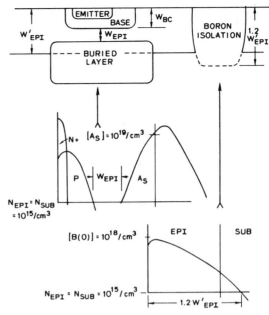

Fig. 12. Profiles and definitions for determination of the base-buried layer spacing W_{epi} of an epitaxial-collector BJT.

B. Removal of I^2L-W_{epi} and Provision of Large I_{SN} with Moderate β_u

From the above discussion, Poly I²L provides a very fast n-p-n ($\tau_N \simeq 0.8$-1 ns). Unlike other second generation I²L process structures with p-n-p basewidth as narrow as 3.5 μm [25], however, Poly I²L is constrained to p-n-p transit time $\tau_P \simeq 35$-45 ns with 10 μm analog-circuit layout rules. An important factor contributing to high–speed operation is the large value of I_{SN}/I_{SP}, typically 50–100, along with a low n-p-n current gain β_u. The following examples demonstrate the relative importance of τ_N, I_{SN}/I_{SP}, and β_u.

Consider an I^2L structure producing negligible τ_N and retaining typical standard-I^2L saturation current ratio I_{SN}/I_{SP} of 5. A 7.5 μm p-n-p effective basewidth and $\beta_{eff} \simeq 5$ then yields $\tau_{min} \simeq 14$ ns via (9)–(11), which is one third experimentally achieved Poly I^2L speed. Indeed, preliminary runs of Poly I²L with nonoptimal processing and mask layout yielded some slices with such tendencies. Although this level of performance is twice standard analog-compatible-I²L speed, reduction of the weighted τ_P term in Poly I²L can result in an additional factor of 2 increase in performance.

With saturation-current ratio $I_{SN}/I_{SP} \simeq 50$, the weighted p-n-p contribution to delay (10) is $\simeq 0.8$ ns which is close to the value of Poly p-n-p τ_N measured by scatter parameters on a network analyzer; the two contributions to delay are equal. For a saturation current ratio of 100, which is the upper limit

experimentally found with Poly I²L, the n-p-n dominates p-n-p-caused delay by a factor of 2, making Poly I²L delay essentially independent of layout rules (i.e., p-n-p basewidth scaling would provide little extra speed).

Consider an I^2L structure with a saturation-current ratio $I_{SN}/I_{SP} = 50$-100, n-p-n with a small transit time $\tau_N \simeq 0.8$ ns, but having a current gain that would be commensurate with such large I_{SN} were the poly loss diode absent ($\beta_u \simeq 500$-1000). Equation (7) would yield $G(\beta_{eff}) \simeq 5$ because of the large value of β_u, which is about twice typical Poly I²L $G(\beta_{eff})$. A predicted τ_{min} from (9)–(11) would then be about twice its actual value. A fast n-p-n alone is not sufficient, and even a fast n-p-n along with high saturation current ratio has drawbacks if achieved at the expense of high n-p-n current gain. Apparently, the parasitic poly diode serves a useful purpose in providing high-speed operation.

C. Eliminating Analog-Device Isolation Diffusion via Enhanced-Poly-Diffusion

The limitations of diffused junction-isolation in obtaining analog-device BV_{CBO} can be determined by considering the amount of n⁺ buried layer out-diffusion caused by the normal large amount of post-epitaxy high-temperature processing in an analog-circuit process. The epitaxial thickness directly determines the required post-epitaxy Dt for p⁺ isolation diffusion (to reach the substrate), and hence also determines the amount of resulting buried layer outdiffusion. Referring to Fig. 12, consider base–collector junction depth W_{BC}, epitaxial thickness W'_{epi}, and base-buried layer distance W_{epi}. Assume that the calculated isolation diffusion surface concentration $[B_{ISO}(0)]$ after all processing is not less than about 10^{18}-10^{20} atoms/cm³ to ensure that device regions cannot interact as a result of surface inversion after boron leaching, and further assume that the isolation diffusion depth is $1.2 \times W'_{epi}$ (20 percent safety margin) to ensure isolation. The resulting time

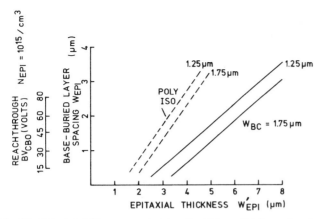

Fig. 13. Calculated W_{epi} versus total epitaxial layer thickness for standard diffused isolation (solid lines) and for Poly I^2L (dashed lines), with base–collector junction depths W_{BC} of 1.25 and 1.75 μm.

square root to diffuse isolation is approximately

$$[B_{ISO}(x)] = [B_{ISO}(0)] \exp(-x^2/4D_B(T)t) \quad (21)$$

$$(t)^{1/2} = (0.18 \text{ to } 0.23) W'_{epi}/(D_B(T))^{1/2} \quad (22)$$

if the substrate concentration is 10^{15} atoms/cm³. The buried layer is assumed to be a semi-infinite source with a peak doping $[As(W_{epi'})] \simeq 10^{19}$ atoms/cm³; 5×10^{16} atoms/cm³ will be taken as the arbitrary level of out-diffused doping concentration (at out-diffusion depth $[W_{epi'} - W_{As}]$) that compromises collector-reachthrough breakdown by reducing W_{epi}.

$$[As(W'_{EPI} - x)] = [As(W'_{epi})] \text{ erfc } [x/2(D_{As}(T)t)^{1/2}] \quad (23)$$

$$W_{As} = 2 [D_{As}(T)]^{1/2}(t)^{1/2}(2.45). \quad (24)$$

Slow-diffusing arsenic is the best case buried-layer dopant in the absence of autodoping. The resulting out-diffusion and base-to-buried layer distance W_{EPI} (with a diffusivity ratio of about 9:1 at 1200°C) are

$$W_{As} \simeq (0.9 \text{ to } 1.1) [D_{As}(T)/D_B(T)]^{1/2} W'_{epi} \quad (25)$$

$$W_{epi} = W'_{epi} - W_{As} - W_{BC} \simeq (2/3) \cdot W'_{epi} - W_{BC} \quad (26)$$

which is plotted in Fig. 13 for base–collector junction depths of 1.25 and 1.75 μm. A reachthrough BV_{CBO} of 30–60 V (Fig. 6) can only be obtained for epitaxial thickness greater than 4.5–6 μm. This compares to measured Poly I^2L analog-device $BV_{CBO} = 45$–60 V for epitaxial thickness of 2.75–3.5 μm, even including autodoping [27] because the large amount of post-epitaxial deposition high-temperature processing required for standard-process junction isolation is eliminated.

Alternately, using a phosphorus buried layer, the P/B diffusivity ratio of about 1.0 in (25) shows that each increment of isolation drive-in produces an essentially equal increment of buried-layer out-diffusion. In the above analysis, a still higher boron isolation-region surface concentration is required, and an approximate epitaxial layer thickness $\simeq 12$–15 μm is required for $BV_{CBO} > 50$ V. In such a case, a dramatic reduction of epitaxial thickness (and collector resistance and isolation capacitance) is available using the Poly I^2L enhanced-diffusivity isolation scheme (essentially that of [28]) to eliminate an explicit isolation diffusion.

VI. Conclusions

Minimum propagation delay and current gain requirements for the I^2L circuit configuration have been presented in which an upper bound on I^2L speed exists as expressed by an effective overall transit time multiplied by a postfactor $G(\beta_{eff})$ whose minimum value is 1.7. The absolute minimum achievable delay follows as roughly 0.34 ns (FO = 2); simple two-dimensional inverted-n-p-n considerations raise this estimate to 0.75–1.0 ns. The limited (square-root law) improvement of standard-structure I^2L with n-p-n base or epitaxial doping variations is shown to arise from competing transit time decrease with $G(\beta_{eff})$ increase.

Analog compatibility requirements impose constraints on simultaneously achievable standard-process analog-device breakdown voltage and I^2L speed with a theoretical and experimental figure of merit BV/τ of about 1.5 V/ns. Significant improvement in this figure of merit has been achieved experimentally by creating two effective epitaxial thicknesses W_{epi} for the I^2L and analog devices, either by employing two physical epitaxial depositions [24] or by using outdiffused n-p-n base technology [3]; such is explained theoretically by the treatment of this paper.

Poly I^2L provides excellent speed performance, not only because the n-p-n transit time τ_N is small (0.8 ns versus 10–100 ns for standard I^2L), but also because a large saturation current ratio I_{SN}/I_{SP} suppresses the contribution of the p-n-p transit time. A second factor yielding high Poly I^2L speed is the parasitic Poly diode forcing a low n-p-n current gain β_u despite the low integrated base doping of the device.

Further optimization of Poly I^2L should not be expected to provide much more than about a factor of two decrease of propagation delay from present experimental 5 ns (measured with ring oscillators and flip-flops); at that point, the "fundamental" two-dimensional limitations of the inverted n-p-n transistor will begin to dominate. The slow Poly p-n-p ($\tau_P \simeq$ 35–45 ns) is not of real concern because its contribution to delay is arbitrarily suppressable by selection of the n-p-n to p-n-p collector-area ratio and sacrificing some layout density.

Shallow epitaxial layers (2.75–3.5 μm) have yielded 45–60 V BV_{CBO} with the Poly process. This is possible because there is no isolation diffusion, which eliminates >98 percent of the post-epitaxial high-temperature processing diffusivity time product [27] and heavily reduces buried-layer out-diffusion. Using arsenic buried layers, it was shown that this essentially halves required epi thickness; for phosphorus buried layers, about a 5:1 reduction is achievable. This provides a 2:1 to 5:1 reduction in analog-device collector resistance, lowers isolation capacitance, and provides higher value on-chip epitaxial resistors as compared to standard diffused-isolation technology.

Appendix

Process Technology of Poly I^2L

The fabrication schedule for Poly I^2L (Fig. 14) is a seven-mask four-diffusion process, as compared to six masks and four diffusions for standard analog-device processing. Cross sections are on the left and the corresponding surface geometries are immediately on the right. The starting material is a

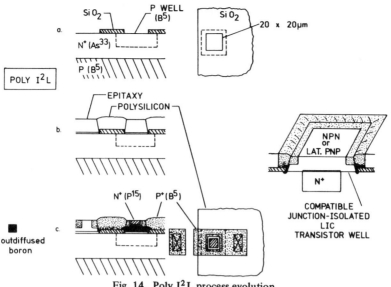

Fig. 14. Poly I²L process evolution.

boron-doped p⁻ wafer of ⟨100⟩ orientation [Fig. 14(a)]. After the introduction and drive-in of a heavily doped ($\sim 1.5 \times 10^{15}$ atoms/cm²) arsenic (n⁺) buried layer for the I²L ground plane and analog-circuit device buried collectors, a second (boron) buried layer is introduced at sites intended for Poly n-p-n transistors. This much lighter diffusion (1–4×10^{14} atoms/cm²) "disappears" behind the heavily doped arsenic layer ($[As(0)] \sim 10^{19}$ atoms/cm³). The $\simeq 0.8$ μm silicon dioxide layer grown during boron drive-in is next defined to selectively expose the single-crystal substrate in small (20×20 μm) regions contained within the boron n-p-n sites and also in larger regions intended for I²L injector "tubs" and analog-device "wells." In Fig. 14(b), a silane (SiH_4)-sourced epitaxial layer is deposited $\simeq 3$ μm thick at $1050°C$ (optically measured temperature). The amorphous SiO_2 layer forces the nucleation of polysilicon selectively located by the previous masking step. The approximately equal rates of deposition of poly and epitaxy result in a step height equal to the SiO_2 thickness (Fig. 15).

A p-type base and n-type emitter that are optimal for analog-circuit devices are then introduced [Fig. 14(c)]. The base diffusion selectively dopes the polysilicon to contact the intrinsic n-p-n base which outdiffuses from the substrate during this high-temperature processing; the p-n-p collector region is formed by overlapping the diffusion onto the larger epitaxial injector "tub," and a region of doped poly is allocated for the gate-input contact. This analog-device optimal base diffusion also provides junction isolation for the analog-circuit n-p-n's and lateral p-n-p's by overlapping a ring across the epitaxy/polysilicon interface that surrounds each transistor "well" (Fig. 14). Enhanced diffusion in the poly provides contact with the p-type substrate so as to form a p-n junction that isolates each transistor "well" and passivates the crystal-defect region at the SiO_2 edge [28].

The boron out-diffusion (Fig. 16) is self-aligned to the Poly n-p-n region by the underlapped SiO_2 cut. A single boron region can service a number of Poly n-p-n's; the only restriction is avoidance of the injector "tub" epitaxial region. Masking

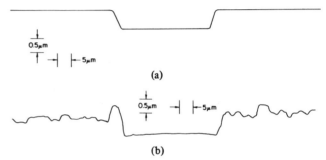

Fig. 15. Profilometer measurements showing very nearly equal rates of epitaxy and poly-silicon deposition. (a) Before deposition showing substrate-to-oxide step. (b) After deposition.

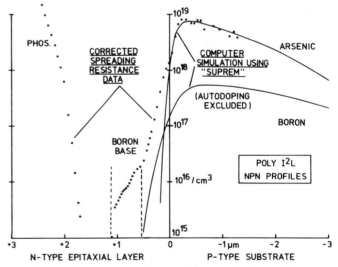

Fig. 16. Measured and simulated Poly n-p-n doping profiles.

alignment tolerance, therefore, does not degrade achievable device size and packing density for this step.

The selective doping of poly to define extrinsic gate and gate-isolation regions is determined by a single masking edge. These two regions self-align because the high-resistivity "isolation material" poly is directly converted to low resistivity "extrinsic conductor" by a single processing step. In comparison, standard I^2L processing requires separate masking operations to convert n^- epitaxy so as to define both the extrinsic p^+ gate and a deep or shallow n^+ collar [Fig. 9(b)]. An additional space equal to the minimum level-to-level registration distance (typically 5 μm with analog-circuit layout rules of 10 μm line-space masking, or 2.5 μm for LSI masking rules) must be observed to guarantee separation of the n^+ collectors from the isolation regions, and an even greater space is lost if the collar and gate are separated to minimize periphery capacitance [5].

REFERENCES

[1] K. Hart and A. Slob, "Integrated injection logic: A new approach to bipolar LSI," *IEEE J. Solid-State Circuits*, vol. SC-7, pp. 346–351, Oct. 1972.

[2] H. H. Berger and S. K. Wiedmann, "Merged-transistor logic (MTL)—A low-cost logic concept," *IEEE J. Solid-State Circuits*, pp. 340–346, Oct. 1972.

[3] R. D. Davies and J. D. Meindl, "Poly I^2L—A high-speed linear-compatible structure," *IEEE J. Solid-State Circuits*, vol. SC-12, pp. 367–376, Aug. 1977.

[4] R. C. Fisher and A. D. Zeiber, *Calculus and Analytic Geometry*. Englewood Cliffs, NJ: Prentice-Hall, 1959.

[5] F. M. Klaassen, "Device physics of integrated injection logic," *IEEE Trans. Electron Devices*, vol. ED-22, pp. 145–152, Mar. 1975.

[6] D. O. Pederson and L. W. Nagel, "SPICE—A general-purpose circuit simulation program," *IEEE J. Solid-State Circuits*, vol. SC-6, Aug. 1971.

[7] J. L. Moll and I. M. Ross, "The dependence of transistor parameters on the distribution of base layer resistivity," *Proc. IRE*, vol. 40, p. 1401, 1952.

[8] B. Hoeneisen and C. A. Mead, "Limitations in microelectronics—II, Bipolar technology," *Solid-State Electron.*, vol. 15, pp. 819–831, 1972.

[9] F. C. Eversteyn, P. J. W. Severin, C. H. J. van den Brekel, and H. L. Peek, "A stagnant layer model for the epitaxial growth of silicon from silane in a horizontal reactor," *J. Electrochem. Soc.*, vol. 117, pp. 925–931, July 1970.

[10] H. C. DeGraaff, "Emitter effects in bipolar transistors," in *Dig. Tech. Papers, NATO Advanced Study Inst. on Process and Device Modeling for Integrated Circuits Design,* Univ. Catholique de Louvain, Belgium, July 1977.

[11] J. Tihanyi and D. Wiedmann, "DIMOS—A novel IC technology with submicron effective channel Mosfets," in *Int. Electron Devices Meeting Tech. Dig.*, Dec. 1977, pp. 399–401.

[12] R. Jecmen, A. Ebel, R. Smith, V. Kynett, C-H. Hui, and R. Pashley, "A 25 nsec 4K static RAM," in *Int. Solid-State Circuits Conf., Dig. Tech. Papers*, Feb. 1979, pp. 100, 101.

[13] F. Hennig, H. K. Hingarh, D. O'Brien, and P. W. Verhofstadt, "Isoplanar integrated injection logic: A high-performance bipolar technology," *IEEE J. Solid-State Circuits*, vol. SC-12, pp. 101–108, Apr. 1977.

[14] R. Muller, "The simulation of charge storage in I^2L circuits," in *Dig. Tech. Papers, 1977 European Solid-State Circuits Conf.*, pp. 133–135.

[15] R. J. Widlar, "Super-gain transistors for IC's," *IEEE J. Solid-State Circuits*, vol. SC-4, pp. 249–250, Aug. 1969.

[16] T. E. Hendrickson and J. T. Huang, "A stored-charge model for estimating I^2L gate delay," *IEEE J. Solid-State Circuits*, vol. SC-12, pp. 171–175, Apr. 1977.

[17] A. Grove, *Physics and Technology of Semiconductor Devices*. New York: Wiley, 1967.

[18] K. McKay and K. McAfee, "Electron multiplication in silicon and germanium," *Phys. Rev.*, vol. 94, pp. 877–844, May 1954.

[19] F. Hewlett, F. Lindholm, and A. Broderson, "The effect of a buried layer on the collector breakdown voltages of bipolar junction transistors," *Solid-State Electron.*, pp. 453–457, 1973.

[20] R. Davies, D. Estreich, J. D. Meindl, and R. Dutton, "I^2L dc functional requirements," *IEEE J. Solid-State Circuits*, vol. SC-12, pp. 208–210, Apr. 1977.

[21] J. Saltich, W. George, and J. Soderberg, "Process technology and AC/DC characteristics of linear compatible I^2L," *IEEE J. Solid-State Circuits*, vol. SC-11, pp. 485–490, Aug. 1976.

[22] G. Bergmann, "Linear compatible I^2L technology with high voltage transistors," *IEEE J. Solid-State Circuits*, vol. SC-12, pp. 566–572, Oct. 1977.

[23] D. Allstot, S. Lui, T. Wei, P. Gray, and R. Meyer, "A new high-voltage analog-compatible process," *IEEE J. Solid-State Circuits*, vol. SC-12, pp. 479–482, Aug. 1978.

[24] T. Okabe, T. Watanabe, and M. Nagata, "A controller with high-speed I^2L and high-voltage analog circuits," in *Int. Solid-State Circuits Conf., Dig. Tech. Papers*, Feb. 1978, pp. 44–45.

[25] F. M. Klaassen, "Some considerations on high-speed injection logic," *IEEE J. Solid-State Circuits*, vol. SC-12, pp. 150–155, Apr. 1977.

[26] A. Anzai, private communication.

[27] R. D. Davies, "Poly I^2L: Integrated circuit technology for compatible analog and digital signal processing," Stanford Electron. Lab., Stanford, CA, Rep. SEL-78-008.

[28] I. Kobayashi, "Technology for monolithic high-power integrated circuits using polycrystalline Si for collector and isolation walls," *IEEE Trans. Electron Devices*, vol. ED-20, pp. 399–404, Apr. 1973.

An Investigation of the Intrinsic Delay (Speed Limit) in MTL/I²L

HORST H. BERGER AND KLAUS HELWIG

Abstract—This paper identifies and analyzes the main mechanisms that determine the intrinsic delay (speed limit) of today's MTL/I^2L devices. Experimental devices have been fabricated with different epitaxial thicknesses to find out to what extent the charge storage can be reduced by shallow epitaxy. Such a shallow-epitaxy device is investigated using computer simulation. Hereby, the injection model is used, into which new charge storage parameters are introduced. According to the analysis, the majority of the stored mobile charge is associated with the bottom junction of the n-p-n transistor part, while the charges in the p-n-p's intrinsic base are minor. However, the lateral p-n-p transistor contributes to the intrinsic delay by its high-level-injection current gain falloff. Furthermore, the significance of high intrinsic base sheet resistance of the n-p-n transistor for high speed is pointed out. Using the insight gained, a device is laid out that assumes only existing technologies, yet in the simulation yields intrinsic delays as low as 2 ns for a fan-out of 4.

I. INTRODUCTION

MERGED transistor logic (MTL) [1] or I^2L [2] is known as a strong bipolar candidate for VLSI because of its small power-delay product and its high density. The power-delay product, however, deteriorates considerably when the circuit is operated near its speed limit, also called the intrinsic delay t_{di}. State-of-the-art devices (fan-out of 4) typically have at large delays a power-delay product of 0.2 pJ which increases to almost 1 pJ at a 10 ns delay [3].

While there is little doubt that finer line resolution of lithography will nearly quadratically improve the density and the associated low-speed power-delay product, little can be readily said about the possible evolution of the intrinsic delay. For any prediction, one would at least need a good quantitative knowledge of the mechanisms that contribute to the intrinsic delay t_{di} of today's devices. Recently, a few publications have appeared on this subject. Some rely strongly on terminal parameters [4]–[6], whose translation into physical reality and back is difficult or even ambiguous. Another one emphasizes more empirical approaches [7]. In contrast, our present work has been based on the injection parameters [8] that have been complemented by similarly defined charge storage parameters. This keeps the relations transparent between device geometry on one side and the device currents and charge storages on the other side. Also, the relations to process parameters can be more easily identified.

Our analysis of the intrinsic delay has been tied to a state-of-the-art experimental device in order to have a realistic reference point. The geometry of this device and its fabrication process are described first in the following exposition. Then, the simulation model and its input parameters are presented. Since it is undisputed that shallow epitaxy should be used for high-speed MTL, an experimental investigation combined with computer simulation follows to show the charge storage dependence of epitaxial thickness and the limits of thinning the epitaxial layer. It serves to find an experimental sample of the "shallow-epitaxy device" to be taken as a good representative of the state of the art. A quantitative analysis of the intrinsic delay is performed on this sample using the simulation tools described.

Manuscript received September 11, 1978, revised October 26, 1978.

The authors are with IBM Laboratories Germany D/3200, D-703 Boeblingen, Germany.

Reprinted from *IEEE J. Solid-State Circuits*, vol. SC-14, pp. 327–337, Apr. 1979.

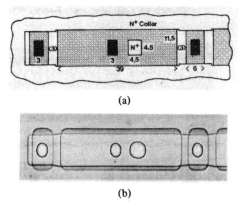

Fig. 1. (a) Design dimensions of the experimental MTL device. (b) Photomicrograph of an actual device (base diffusion mask overlaps the n^+ collar).

The results then permit a discussion of improvement possibilities. Particularly, the potential of the application of polycrystalline silicon [34] is investigated. This leads to the conclusion that devices with a propagation delay of 3 ns at 100 μW (0.3 pJ) with a fan-out of 4 are feasible using present technological capabilities only. Device scaling would yield further improvements. However, it is beyond the scope of this article.

II. Experimental Device and Process

For our investigation, an experimental device was laid out using a minimum linewidth of 3 μm. The design dimensions and a photomicrograph are shown in Fig. 1. Though the device carries only a single collector ("top n^+"), the prolonged base strip could accommodate up to four collectors and the base contact in an optional positioning. This provides a maximum fan-out of 4 per device for the widely used MTL interconnection scheme [1], [9] which corresponds to Weinberger's scheme for FET's [10]. Such a device, though less fast, is more representative for the practical application than the minimum-base devices with a fan-out of 1 which are often cited in performance evaluations.

In order to keep the series resistance effects on speed small, injectors have been provided on each end of the base strip. One of them has been assigned also to the base strip of an adjacent device. The collector was chosen larger than the minimum dimension in order to assure an upward current gain[1] $\beta_u \approx 2$.

For power/performance measurements, a 15-stage loop oscillator has been designed using a sixteenth device for output buffering as shown in the photomicrograph of Fig. 2. The devices have been realized with a conventional process using a p^- substrate, buried n^+ diffusion ("bottom n^+"), n^- epitaxy, base, top n^+ (collector), and deep n^+ collar diffusions. The main data characterizing the process are listed in Table I.

III. Simulation Model and Model Parameters

As is illustrated in Fig. 3, the MTL device has been represented by a lumped model, dividing the base strip into 5 sec-

[1] β_u is defined, as [38], i.e., it includes the effect of the back injection towards the injector.

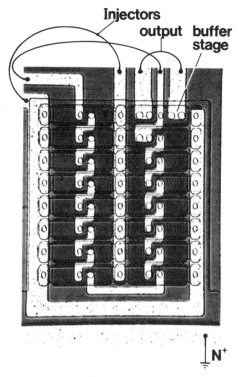

Fig. 2. Photomicrograph of a loop oscillator that uses devices of Fig. 1. For load adaption, the number of collectors is staged up at the output.

TABLE I
MAIN NOMINAL DATA OF THE EXPERIMENTAL PROCESS THAT WERE USED IN THE INVESTIGATION OF t_{di}

Region	Resistivity	Thickness or Depth
P^- Substrate	15 Ωcm	0.4 mm
Buried N^+ Diff.	7 Ω/□	$\approx$ 1 μm 1) 1.3 μm 2)
Epitaxy	0.3 Ωcm	$\approx$ 2 μm
Base Diffusion	400 Ω/□	0.7 μm
Top N^+ Diffusion	16 Ω/□	0.4 μm
N^+ Collar Diff.	25 Ω/□	0.9 μm
Intrinsic Base	10 kΩ/□	0.3 μm

1) measured upward from Epi/Substrate interface
2) " downward " " "

tions. This approach has been widely used for modeling the series resistance effects [11]–[17]. The transistor sections have been expressed in the transport model form, which alleviates the application of injection parameters, particularly for modeling the effect of process variations [18].

Fig. 4 repeats for convenience the definitions of the injection parameters j_ν and I'_ν according to [8]. They have been supplemented by parameters for the downward operation of the

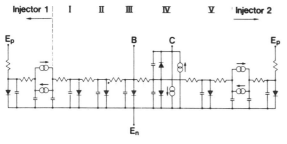

Fig. 3. Lumped model for device simulation. Input parameters are depletion layer capacitances, series resistances, and—according to the injection model—saturation injection currents and saturation charge storages.

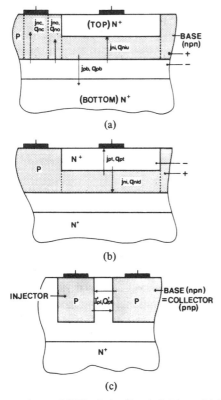

(a)

(b)

(c)

Fig. 4. Cross sections of MTL device for definition of injection and charge storage parameters according to [8]. (a) n-p-n upward operation. (b) n-p-n downward operation. (c) p-n-p forward and inverse operation. Units are $j\,[\text{A/cm}^2]$, $I'\,[\text{A/cm}]$, $q\,[\text{As/cm}^2]$, and $Q'\,[\text{As/cm}]$.

n-p-n transistor and by charge storage parameters q_ν. For the computer simulation it is practical to have the injection parameters in terms of saturation current densities $j_{\nu s}$. Since for speed investigations the low-current β_u falloff is unimportant, all currents have been assumed to follow the ideal characteristic [2]

$$j_\nu = j_{\nu s} \cdot \left[\exp\left(\frac{V_j}{V_T}\right) - 1 \right] \qquad (1)$$

where V_j is the junction voltage.

[2] The current density term $j_{p\nu}$ is known to have a less than ideal slope in the $\ln j$ versus V_j curve [19], [20]. We determined it at relatively high junction voltage ($V_j = 660$ mV) to reduce the extrapolation error.

TABLE II
INJECTION AND CHARGE STORAGE PARAMETERS FOR NOMINAL PROCESS CONDITIONS

Region		(for 25° C)	
		Injection Currents	Charges
Top N⁺		$j_{pts} = 9 \cdot 10^{-13}\,\frac{A}{cm^2}$	$q_{pts} \simeq 0.6 \cdot 10^{-21}\,\frac{As}{cm^2}$
Extrinsic Base	Contact	$j_{ncs} = 3.5 \cdot 10^{-12}\,\frac{A}{cm^2}$	q_{ncs} ⎫
	Oxide	$j_{nos} \lesssim 2 \cdot 10^{-13}\,\frac{A}{cm^2}$	q_{nos} ⎬ $\approx 6.4 \cdot 10^{-21}\,\frac{As}{cm^2}$
Intrinsic Base	upward	$j_{nis} = 8.7 \cdot 10^{-11}\,\frac{A}{cm^2}$	q_{nius} ⎫ $\approx 1.5 \cdot 10^{-21}\,\frac{As}{cm^2}$
	downward		q_{nids} ⎭
Bottom N⁻/N⁺		$j_{pbs} = 3.5 \cdot 10^{-13}\,\frac{A}{cm^2}$	$q_{pbs} \approx 4 \cdot 10^{-21}\,\frac{As}{cm^2}$ [1]
Base of PNP		$I'_{pls} = 2.8 \cdot 10^{-15}\,\frac{A}{cm}$ [2] $V_k = 778$ mV [3]	$Q'_{pls} \approx 5 \cdot 10^{-24}\,\frac{As}{cm}$ [2]

[1] Integration started from $N_D = 10^{17}\text{cm}^{-3}$ down into N⁺
[2] given per unit length of effective injector edge and for an electrical base width $W_{bel} = 1.9\mu m$ ($W_{b\ design} = 3\ \mu m$)
[3] Gummel-Poon knee voltage

Since high injector currents are applied near the speed limit, the high-level injection effect in the lateral p-n-p transistor had to be considered. A formulation of this effect, using the Gummel–Poon knee voltage V_k, has been given in [21]

$$I'_{pl} = I'_{pls} \cdot \left[\exp\left(\frac{V_j}{V_T}\right) - 1 \right] \cdot F_i(V_k, V_j) \qquad (2)$$

where F_i is the high-level correction factor for current.

All injection parameters, as well as V_k, were obtained from measurements on test structures [8], [21] which were available on the same chip as the experimental device. Thus random process variations were directly taken into account. The current densities then had to be multiplied with the associated areas or lengths to obtain the current components that determine the currents in the diodes and the current sources of the model in Fig. 3. As is immediately obvious from the comparison of Fig. 1(a) with 1(b), the actual device dimensions had to be used, which can deviate considerably from the design dimensions due to processing effects (e.g., corner rounding). Also, lateral outdiffusions, e.g., of the n⁺ collar, had been considered. The first column of Table II lists the nominal injection parameters for the process of Table I. The depletion layer capacitances were calculated similarly, using large test structures on the same chip to derive the required values per unit area (C'') or unit length (C'). Nominal values are given in Table III.

For the minority carrier charge it was found convenient to directly follow the injection model by assigning a saturation charge per unit area ($q_{\nu s}$) or unit length (Q'_{pls}) to each of the

TABLE III
NOMINAL 0 V DEPLETION LAYER CAPACITANCES

Junction	$C''/\frac{pf}{cm^2}$	$C'/\frac{pf}{cm}$
Top N$^+$	$1.8 \cdot 10^5$	–
Bottom N	$5 \cdot 10^4$	–
N$^+$-Collar	–	10.4

injections, thereby using the same indexes for designation, as shown in Fig. 4. From

$$q_v = q_{vs} \cdot \left[\exp\left(\frac{V_j}{V_T} \right) - 1 \right] \qquad (3)$$

a diffusion capacitance per unit area was derived

$$C''_{v\,\text{diff}} = \frac{\partial q_v}{\partial V_j} = \frac{q_{vs}}{V_T} \cdot \exp\left(\frac{V_j}{V_T} \right) \qquad (4)$$

that complies with the usual input format of the ASTAP simulation program. For the high-level injection in the lateral p-n-p, a correction factor F_c had been applied similar to F_i in the current equation (2) (see [21]).

$$C'_{pl\,\text{diff}} = \frac{Q'_{pls}}{V_T} \cdot \exp\left(\frac{V_j}{V_T} \right) \cdot F_c. \qquad (5)$$

In contrast to the injection parameters, there is no method known for reliably separating the various charge storage terms by measurement, mainly because of the inherently worse accuracy of the required ac measurements. Therefore, the charge storage parameters were determined from measured doping profiles, using the bandgap narrowing data by Slotboom and de Graaff [22]. The method can be described briefly as follows.[3] The doping profile curves are first converted into minority carrier profiles (thermal equilibrium). Their integral, multiplied with the elementary charge, would give the maximum saturation charge per unit area. It has to be corrected according to the actual profiles under current flow conditions. In the case of the intrinsic bases (n-p-n and p-n-p transistors) where uniform doping is taken, this is simply done by applying triangular profiles (factor 0.5). In the extrinsic base region of the n-p-n transistor, no correction is applied because of the very small influence of current flow in the steep profile [24]. For the top and bottom n$^+$ regions, the diffusion length of the holes in the high doping region is estimated from the injection parameters, and the integration is carried out accordingly.

The second column of Table II lists the thus obtained charge storage parameters for nominal process conditions. It has to be noted that the integration that lead to the hole charge q_{pbs} in the bottom n$^+$ layer, started from a doping level of $N_D = 10^{17}$ cm^{-3} upward.

[3]Other than in Hendrickson and Huang [23], it considers the actual doping profiles.

The accuracy of the charge storage data of the downward operated transistor can be roughly checked by calculating the time constant τ_d from

$$\tau_d = \frac{q_{pts} + q_{nis}}{j_{nis}} = \frac{2.1 \cdot 10^{-21} \text{ As/cm}^2}{8.7 \cdot 10^{-11} \text{ A/cm}^2} = 24 \text{ ps.} \qquad (6)$$

This lies in the same order of magnitude which one usually measures on modern transistors.

The total charge storage that is associated with the base bottom junction is either

$$\text{(extrinsic base) } (q_{us})_e = q_{pbs} + q_{ncs} \approx 1 \cdot 10^{-20} \text{ As/cm}^2 \quad (7)$$

or

$$\text{(intrinsic base) } (q_{us})_i = q_{pbs} + q_{nis} \approx 0.55 \cdot 10^{-20} \text{ As/cm}^2. \qquad (8)$$

Since our experimental device has a prevailing extrinsic base area (see Fig. 1), we have used in the computer simulations a common value $q_{us} = (q_{us})_e$ for the whole base bottom junction. Its dependence on the epitaxial thickness will be investigated next in order to find a device that is a good representative of the state of the art and thus can serve as a reasonable reference in the analysis of the intrinsic delay.

IV. "SHALLOW-EPITAXY" DEVICE

An MTL device in which the n$^-$ gap between the base bottom junction and the bottom n$^+$ layer has vanished, has been called a "shallow-" or "thin-" epitaxy device [4], [5], [25]. It has been assumed that for such a device the hole charge q_{pb}(7) of the bottom junction becomes negligible.

Instead of this somewhat idealized view, we will introduce a more practical definition. Considering the relatively soft transition from the n$^-$ epitaxial doping to the n$^+$ doping of the buried layer, we define a reference point on this transition curve by a doping level of $N_D = 10^{17}$ cm^{-3} (see inset of Fig. 6). The gap between the base bottom junction and the $N_D = 10^{17}$ cm^{-3} plane shall be called W''_{epi}. We then have to find out how small W''_{epi} may be made without affecting the control of the sheet resistance R_{si} of the intrinsic base region, whose average doping lies in the order of $\overline{N}_A \approx 2 \cdot 10^{17}$ cm^{-3}. This determines the practical minimum of the hole charge q_{pb} for the given process and thus gives a practical definition of the shallow-epitaxy device.

Fig. 5 shows the power-delay curves of a set of our experimental devices that was produced with different epitaxial thicknesses. Capacitance/voltage measurements on test diodes, which were available on the chip with the MTL devices, allowed the determination of W''_{epi}. The curves in Fig. 5 indicate that a larger W''_{epi} gives a larger intrinsic delay t_{di} because of a larger hole charge storage, while the extrinsic delay (i.e., the delay at small currents) becomes smaller due to a reduced depletion-layer capacitance. The effect of random process variations is superimposed on this general trend, however.

Computer simulation permitted the extraction of $q_{us} = f(W''_{epi})$ (see Fig. 6) from the measured power-delay curves of Fig. 5 by varying the input parameter q_{us} in the simulation for a best curve fit. All other parameters were either determined

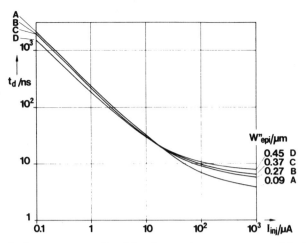

Fig. 5. Average propagation delay t_d per stage versus average injector current I_{inj} per stage obtained from loop oscillators of Fig. 2. They were fabricated on different epitaxial thicknesses leading to different gaps W''_{epi} between the base bottom junction and bottom n⁺ layer. Assuming 1 V supply voltage, the abscissa may be read as a power scale (μW).

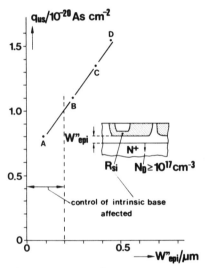

Fig. 6. Inset: definition of gap W''_{epi} between base bottom junction and bottom n⁺ layer. Diagram: bottom junction charge density q_{us} versus gap W''_{epi} as derived from Fig. 5 by means of simulation.

individually from the associated test devices, thus considering the random process variations or, as in the case of the remaining less significant charge storage parameters, were taken from Table II.

By comparing pinch resistors with and without the underlying buried layer, it could be monitored at which gap W''_{epi} the sheet resistance of the intrinsic base R_{si} was affected. $\Delta R_{si}/R_{si} > 10$ percent was found at $W''_{epi} < 0.2$ μm, giving a practical lower limit of the bottom junction charge parameter of

$$(q_{us})_{min} \approx 1 \cdot 10^{-20} \text{ As/cm}^2 \tag{9}$$

as seen in Fig. 6.

The slope of the q_{us} line in Fig. 6

$$\left(\frac{\Delta q_{us}}{\Delta W''_{epi}}\right)_{actual} \approx 2 \cdot 10^{-20} \frac{\text{As/cm}^2}{\mu\text{m}} \tag{10}$$

is much smaller than the pure epitaxial doping of

$$N_D = 2 \cdot 10^{16} \text{ cm}^{-3} \text{ would yield}$$

$$\left(\frac{\Delta q_{us}}{\Delta W''_{epi}}\right)_{theory} = 8 \cdot 10^{-20} \frac{\text{As/cm}^2}{\mu\text{m}}. \tag{11}$$

It indicates that, in the W''_{epi} range considered, the doping tail of the bottom n⁺ is quite effective. On the other hand, the data point for $W''_{epi} = 0.45$ μm most likely reflects the transition to a steeper slope (see Fig. 6).

Depending on the means used to extrapolate the curve in Fig. 6 to $W''_{epi} = 0$, the calculated value $q_{us} = q_{pbs} + q_{ncs}$ of Table II is 20–40 percent larger than the experiment gives. Considering the possible errors on the way from the doping profile measurement to the minority carrier profile determination, this is still a very satisfactory result.

According to our investigation above, device B (Figs. 5 and 6), having a $q_{us} = 1.1 \cdot 10^{-20}$ As/cm², is a good representative of a practical shallow-epitaxy device. It will be used in the following analysis of the intrinsic delay as our state-of-the-art reference device.

V. ANALYSIS OF INTRINSIC DELAY t_{di}

For consistency, we will now base all our analysis on the *simulated* power-delay curve of the shallow-epitaxy device B. The simulation results are shown in Fig. 7 together with the measured curve to indicate their accuracy. In Fig. 8, the simulated curve is shown once more, however, on an expanded scale for a derivation of the intrinsic delay t_{di}. For this purpose, the extrapolation of the straight low-current power-delay line has been drawn in addition. The extrapolation was checked by delay simulation, whereby charge storages, high-level injection, and resistors were omitted. The difference between the actual delay t_d and the extrapolation line t_{de} is, being fairly independent of the current level,

$$t_{di} = t_d - t_{de} = 5.8 \text{ ns}. \tag{12}$$

The individual contribution Δt_{di} of, e.g., the bottom charge storage Q_u to the intrinsic delay, can be found by setting the corresponding input parameter to zero ($Q_{us} = 0$) in the simulation and then by comparing the result $t_d(Q_{us} = 0)$ with the complete delay t_d:

$$\Delta t_{di}(Q_{us}) = t_d - t_d(Q_{us} = 0). \tag{13}$$

This is illustrated in Fig. 9, where the effects of some other input parameters are also shown. Table IV lists the individual contributions Δt_{di}. It turns out that $\Sigma \Delta t_{di} > t_{di}$, as the individual contributions are somewhat interdependent. The small difference found, however, confirms that the assumption of independence is an acceptable approximation.

According to Table IV, a column graph is shown in Fig. 10 to compare the individual contributors to the intrinsic delay. Probably most important is that, even in this shallow-epitaxy device, the charge storage of the n-p-n transistor clearly surpasses that of the p-n-p transistor. This is also obvious from a direct comparison of the relevant saturation charges:

$$\text{p-n-p: } Q_{pls} = 3.8 \cdot 10^{-27} \text{ As} \tag{14}$$

$$\text{n-p-n: } Q_{us} = 46 \cdot 10^{-27} \text{ As}. \tag{15}$$

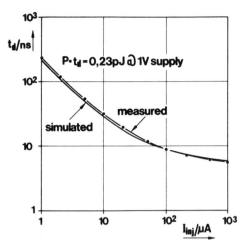

Fig. 7. Comparison of simulated with measured power-delay curve of shallow-epitaxy device (B) (see Fig. 5).

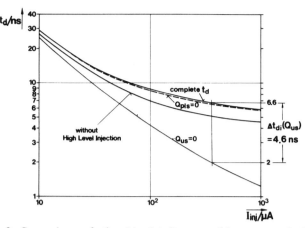

Fig. 9. Comparison of the (simulated) power-delay curve of the shallow-epitaxy device with simulations that do not consider 1) charge storage Q_{pl}, 2) charge storage Q_u, and 3) high-level injection in the lateral p-n-p transistor.

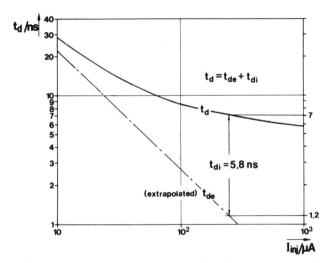

Fig. 8. Expanded power-delay curve of the shallow-epitaxy device (see Fig. 7) for derivation of intrinsic delay. Lower straight line is the extrinsic delay t_{de} as extrapolated from the low-current delay.

TABLE IV
LIST OF INTRINSIC DELAY CONTRIBUTIONS OF THE
SHALLOW-EPITAXY DEVICE

Parameter	Δt_{di} (ns)	$\dfrac{\Delta t_{di}}{\sum \Delta t_{di}}$ (%)
Charge storage, pnp (Q_{pls})	0.2	3
upward npn (Q_{us})	4.6	70
downward npn (Q_{ds})	·/·	·/·
High-level injection, pnp (HLI)	1.6	24
Series resistance, inject. (R_{inj})	0.4	6
base npn (R_{sb})	-0.2	-3
$\sum \Delta t_{di}$:	6.6 ns	
Measured t_{di} :	5.8 ns	

Considering that the effect of Q_{pls} is halved at a very high injection level, the observed 1:23 relation (Fig. 10) is well explained.

In contrast to our findings, Klaassen [13], [4], [5] assumed the dominance of p-n-p charge storage in a shallow-epitaxy device. Though a somewhat different process and device was considered (separated extrinsic and intrinsic base formation, oxide collar, larger p-n-p basewidth, fan-out of 1), there is no evidence that in a practical device Q_{pls} could become more than comparable with Q_{us}.[4]

Another argument against the dominance of p-n-p charge storage is supplied by Mulder and Wulms [25]. They obtained only a relatively small speed improvement ($\Delta t_{di} = 1$ ns out of $t_d = 7$ ns) when they experimentally separated the p-n-p transistor from their shallow-epitaxy device with a fan-out of 1. Moreover, the device operation mode that was chosen in the comparison [25, p. 384], in our opinion, led to an unnecessarily large base area in the I^2L mode, thus impairing the comparison in favor of the separated device.

[4]Also see our findings at the end of Section VI.

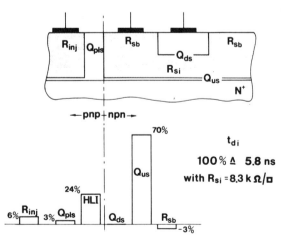

Fig. 10. Cross section of the MTL device and column graph of the various contributions to the intrinsic delay t_{di} according to Table IV. (HLI = high-level injection.)

Simulating the p-n-p/n-p-n separation for our device, we obtained the power-delay curve of Fig. 11. It shows an increased delay for the separated device over the whole power range. The simulation did not even consider that a separate collector of the p-n-p transistor would add some depletion layer capaci-

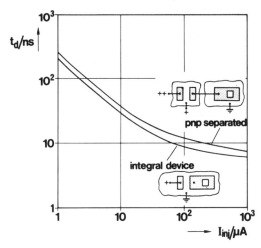

Fig. 11. Simulated power-delay curve for a device with separated p-n-p transistor compared with that of an integral device. Depletion layer capacitance increase in the separated device due to the required extra p-n-p collector area has not been considered yet.

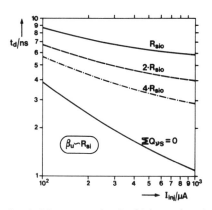

Fig. 12. Simulated delay curves in the high-speed region with sheet resistance R_{si} of the n-p-n's intrinsic base as a parameter and, as a reference, delay for vanishing charge storage ($\Sigma Q_{vs} = 0$).

tance. Hence, the worse power economy alone is sufficient to deteriorate the speed of the separated device which misses the power saving back injection of the p-n-p transistor. At higher currents the upward current gain increase of the n-p-n transistor also contributes.

Instead of trying to eliminate the charge storage Q_{pl} of the lateral p-n-p transistor, Fig. 10 suggests to reduce its high-level injection effect, as this gives the second largest contribution to the intrinsic delay. The double-diffused lateral p-n-p transistor [26], [27] might be a good step in this direction. Its reduced series resistance R_{inj} would also help somewhat according to Fig. 10.

In the n-p-n transistor part, the effect of the charge storage Q_d that is associated with the downward operation during saturation of the n-p-n transistor is barely noticeable (Fig. 10). Also the base series resistance R_{sb} has little effect in this double-injector design. Here, it gives even a small delay improvement. However, it is well-known that the effect of the series resistance on delay depends very much on the particular collector/base contact positioning relative to the injector [12], [15]; thus a delay deterioration can occur as well. It has been verified by additional experiments that for our double-injector device, these effects stay within a few percent.[5]

There is still another very important parameter to be looked at in the analysis of the intrinsic delay: the sheet resistance R_{si} of the n-p-n transistor's intrinsic base [18]. Using the relation by Heimeier and Berger [28],

$$j_{ni} \sim R_{si} \qquad (16)$$

further delay simulations were performed on our shallow-epitaxy device, now varying the $j_{ni}(R_{si})$ parameter only. Fig. 12 compares the power-delay curve for the original $R_{si0} = 8.3$ kΩ/sq with those for doubled and quadrupled R_{si}. Setting all charge storage parameters to zero yields a single reference curve $t_d(\Sigma Q_{vs} = 0)$ in all three cases of R_{si} (Fig. 12). In other words, R_{si} affects the charge storage only. Using the

reference curve, one can read out the charge storage portion of the intrinsic delay $\Delta t_{di}(\Sigma Q_{vs})$ as a function of R_{si}/R_{si0}:

$$\Delta t_{di}\left(\sum Q_{vs}\right) = f(R_{si}/R_{si0})$$

$$= t_d(R_{si}/R_{si0}) - t_d\left(\sum Q_{vs} = 0\right) \qquad (17)$$

which gives curve (a) in Fig. 14. The delay decrease with increasing R_{si} can be physically explained as follows. Because of (16) a certain collector current value, e.g., the base current (= forward injector current), of the following stage can be reached with a smaller base–emitter voltage and thus with a smaller charge storage (3) when R_{si} is larger. On the other hand, the charge storage at the end of the switching period for the given forward injector current is not reduced, as it is independent of R_{si}.

This charge, however, can be reduced as well to obtain a further delay reduction. It requires changing the p-n-p part of the MTL device to provide a larger back injection. This results in a smaller base–emitter voltage of the n-p-n transistor also in its full on condition. Though larger back injection reduces the upward current gain β_u, one can afford it with a larger R_{si}, since the constant back injection implies that

$$\beta_u \sim R_{si} \qquad (18)$$

because of (16). Hence it is reasonable to counteract the increase of β_u[6] by increasing, e.g., the length of the injector edge, thus obtaining the larger back injection. This (β_u = const.) has been assumed in the simulation of Fig. 13, which clearly shows the larger delay improvement over the case of $\beta_u \sim R_{si}$ in Fig. 12.

However, with a change of the device geometry, matters now become more complicated. The wider injector introduces a proportionally larger Q_{pls}, which in our case is insignificant because Q_{pls} is small relative to Q_{us} at the outset. Secondly, the high-level-injection effect of the lateral p-n-p transistor becomes less severe, and the power economy improves because of the larger back injection. This explains why the reference curve $t_d(\Sigma Q_{vs} = 0)$ now becomes R_{si} dependent (Fig. 13).

---

[5]Larger series resistance effects generally would not fit the concept of an intrinsic delay, as their delay contribution is usually strongly current dependent. They would deserve a separate analysis.

[6]This may also be interpreted as reducing the degree of saturation of the n-p-n transistor.

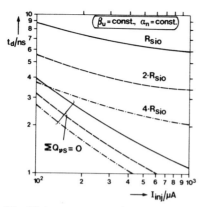

Fig. 13. As in Fig. 12; however, β_u was kept constant by increasing the back injection of the p-n-p transistor. The grounded-base forward current gain α_n of the latter was assumed not to change. Due to the varying p-n-p transistor, the reference line ($\sum Q_{vs} = 0$) splits up.

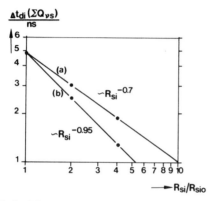

Fig. 14. Intrinsic delay portion that is caused by charge storage as a function of the n-p-n's intrinsic base sheet resistance R_{si}. Values taken from (a) Fig. 12 and (b) Fig. 13.

The contribution $\Delta t_{di}(\sum Q_{vs})$ versus R_{si}/R_{si0} now follows the steeper curve (b) in Fig. 14.

Klaassen [29] gives the charge storage induced delay in terms of terminal parameters. Using our designations, it is written

$$\Delta t_{di}\left(\sum Q_{vs}\right) = \beta_u^n \cdot \tau_u, \qquad (19)$$

whereby $n = 0.5$ or $n = 0.4$ [30]. The terminal parameters *per se*, however, do not permit any statement on the R_{si} dependence of Δt_{di}, unless additional physical insight is available. Using for this the injection model, one can derive simple expressions for β_u, $\tau_u = f(R_{si})$ and can write for (19)

$$\Delta t_{di} \sim R_{si}^{-0.6} \qquad (n = 0.4) \qquad (20)$$

and

$$\Delta t_{di} \sim R_{si}^{-1} \qquad (21)$$

for the $\beta_u \sim R_{si}$ and β_u = const. cases, respectively. This, as well as the so-obtained absolute value $\Delta t_{di} = 4.9$ ns (for R_{si0}), agree well with Fig. 14. Without the support from the physical model, however, one might have wrongly concluded from (19) that the delay *increases* with R_{si} because of an observed increase of current gain (unchanged geometry).

VI. DISCUSSION OF DEVICE IMPROVEMENT

From the analysis of the factors that determine the intrinsic delay on our device, the following conclusions can be drawn for device improvement.

1) Since the bottom junction charge Q_u has the biggest effect, it should be kept small. However, the corresponding saturation charge density q_{us} in the region of the intrinsic n-p-n transistor cannot be reduced below a certain value (shallow-epitaxy device) as, otherwise, the process control of the intrinsic base would be affected. Beyond that, the total saturation charge Q_{us} of the device can only be diminished by reducing the extrinsic base area or by forming the extrinsic and intrinsic base regions separately in the production process [31], [32], [6]. A separate extrinsic base permits stronger overlap of the base and bottom n+ profiles and thus a reduction of the charge storage parameter q_{us} in this region. However, the charge storage in the remaining relatively thick and highly doped p and n regions is still appreciable, particularly because of the bandgap narrowing effect. Moreover, the larger depletion layer capacitance of the then strongly overlapping base and n+ profiles would offset a part of the reduction of t_{di}. Hence shrinkage of the extrinsic base area should be the primary goal. It should also be mentioned that a reduction of vertical dimensions (vertical scaling) would reduce q_{us} accordingly.

2) While the charge storage of the lateral p-n-p transistor turns out to be negligible, its current gain loss at high currents (high-level injection region) considerably contributes to the effective intrinsic delay. Narrow basewidth and, accordingly, higher doping levels would help to improve the lateral p-n-p transistor. However, lithography sets a limit by the minimum permissible linewidth or by the dimension control problems. Double-diffused lateral p-n-p transistors [26], [27] seem to allow smaller base widths. However, little is known from the literature about the range of design freedom with this device. The power economy—and thus the delay at a given current—also depends very much on injector optimization, which is extensively discussed in [21].

3) Because of the associated reduction of intrinsic delay, the sheet resistance R_{si} of the intrinsic base of the n-p-n transistor should be made as large as possible. In pure MTL circuits, the operation voltages below 1 V do not impose a punch-through problem. Here, it is rather the process control that sets the limit. Namely, one should note that minimization of q_{us} for the bottom junction of the intrinsic base and a simultaneously well-controlled high-ohmic sheet resistance conflict. At least an excellent control of epitaxial thickness is required.

Relative to the above optimization rules, one may ask whether a new technology would yield some new freedom for applying these rules. There is, e.g., the polycrystalline silicon that has also been introduced in bipolar technology more recently [33]–[37]. Particularly interesting is the idea set forth by Middelhoek and Kooy [34] to use polysilicon in MTL devices simultaneously as a low-ohmic base bypass, as a base extension for contacting, and as a base diffusion source. This approach seems to have a high potential for improving

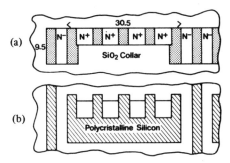

Fig. 15. Layout of a MTL device utilizing oxide collar, p-type poly-cristalline silicon, and top n⁺ self-alignment. (a) Shown without poly-silicon. (b) Corresponding polysilicon shapes.

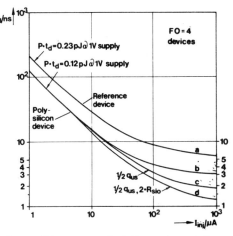

Fig. 16. (a) Power-delay curve of shallow-epitaxy reference device, compared with simulation results for the polysilicon device in Fig. 15 having (b) injection and charge storage parameters per unit area or unit length as with reference device (a), (c) halved charge storage at bottom junction (q_{us}), and (d) doubled sheet resistance R_{si} of intrinsic base.

the intrinsic delay when it is combined with other modern technologies as walled-oxide isolation, self-aligned collectors, and separate extrinsic and intrinsic base formation.

We have applied these assumptions to obtain by computer simulation an approximate picture of the polysilicon's potential in MTL. Basically following the design ground rules of our test device, as seen in Fig. 1, a layout was drawn accordingly (see Fig. 15). In this device, the polysilicon would overlap the oxide isolation. Thus it provides both a low-ohmic bypass for the base strip and an extra base contact area, without causing an extra bottom junction area. This saves the associated charge storage.

The lengths of the injector edges had to be larger than the active base strip in order to provide sufficient back injection, keeping β_u comparable with that of the test device of Fig. 1. The design in total is not necessarily optimized, as the primary goal was an easy comparison with the reference device, whose intrinsic delay has been analyzed above.

Fig. 16 shows the power-delay curves (b)–(d) obtained from a simulation of the design of Fig. 15 and the curve (a) of our shallow-epitaxy reference device. Curve (b) is obtained if the same vertical profiles as in our reference device are assumed, i.e., the same injection and charge storage parameters. The resulting intrinsic delay is

$$t_{di} \approx 3 \text{ ns}$$

i.e., a factor of 2 better than that of the reference device. This improvement is due to a 0.4-times smaller base area and an accordingly smaller charge storage Q_u. Also, the power-delay product decreased because of the similarly reduced depletion layer capacitance.

In the extrapolation, it should additionally be considered that for the polysilicon device the area of the intrinsic base would be 50 percent of the total base area. This gives more weight to the smaller q_{us} value of the intrinsic base region for the total Q_{us}. Also, since for the extrinsic base area the charge storage would probably be smaller than in the reference device, we used a common $q_{us} = 0.55 \times 10^{-20}$ As/cm²,[7] i.e., half of that of the reference device. Herewith [curve (c) in Fig. 16]

$$t_{di} \approx 2 \text{ ns}$$

[7]This is the value for the intrinsic base area of our reference device according to Table IV.

is obtained. Well-controlled intrinsic base sheet resistances $R_{si} = 16$ kΩ/sq can be imagined to be realized additionally in the future. This parameter would further improve the intrinsic delay to

$$t_{di} \approx 1.4 \text{ ns} \quad [\text{curve } (d) \text{ in Fig. 16}].$$

While experimental proof is still required, the extrapolation made is certainly not too far-reaching. Hence, there is some confidence that MTL devices with a fan-out of 4 and a delay limit as small as 2 ns can be realized using present technological capabilities.

Again, the point should be made that even in these devices the charge storage of the lateral p-n-p transistor would not be dominating:

$$Q_{pls} = 3.8 \cdot 10^{-27} \text{ As}$$
$$Q_{us} = 0.2 \cdot (Q_{us})_{reference} \quad (\text{see (14) and (15)}).$$
$$= 9.2 \cdot 10^{-27} \text{ As}.$$

VII. SUMMARY AND CONCLUSIONS

The charge storage parameters which have been introduced in this paper and the sensitivity analysis of the intrinsic delay have brought some important insights.

1) With shallow epitaxy, the *intrinsic* n-p-n transistor in the upward operation mode can be made nearly as fast as in the downward mode since the associated charge storage densities were found to differ only by a factor of ≈ 2 [see (6) and (8)].

2) In upward operation a charge storage also occurs, however, in the *extrinsic* base region, which in our typical device is nearly 10 times larger than that of the intrinsic transistor regions, spoiling the switching speed accordingly.

3) The charge storage in the intrinsic base of the p-n-p transistor can be neglected in present devices. However, the high-level-injection effect with its reduction of power economy has a noticeable effect on the intrinsic delay.

4) Series resistance effects of the base strip on delay can be kept sufficiently small by using double injectors.

5) The actual effect of the structure specific saturation charges on the intrinsic delay is directly determined by the sheet resistance of the n-p-n transistor's intrinsic base. The largest resistance gives the smallest delay.

Accordingly, improvement work should concentrate on

1) attaining a well-controlled high-ohmic intrinsic base for the n-p-n transistor,
2) reducing the extrinsic base area and the associated charge storage density,
3) diminishing of the high-level injection effect of the p-n-p transistor.

Only after efforts on the last two items would have had success, the charge storage of the lateral p-n-p transistor might become of interest again for further improvements. It depends, of course, on the ingenuity of the people working in the relevant areas, to what degree the wanted improvements can be realized. However, the evaluation of the polysilicon approach has already shown that devices operating in the very satisfactory 3 ns delay range are feasible within present technological capabilities.

ACKNOWLEDGMENT

The authors wish to express their gratitude to Prof. Dr. O. G. Folberth (IBM Fellow) for directing and supporting the work that led to this paper. Also the support of the pilot line under Dr. H. G. Jansen was greatly appreciated, particularly of E. Ebert who provided the epitaxial experiments. Furthermore, we wish to thank Dr. D. Hagmann for providing the doping profile measurements, Mrs. U. Dreckmann for pertinent device parameters, and B. Quiram for his assistance in the delay measurements.

REFERENCES

[1] H. H. Berger and S. K. Wiedmann, "Merged transistor logic (MTL)—A low-cost bipolar logic concept," *IEEE J. Solid-State Circuits*, vol. SC-7, pp. 340–346, Oct. 1972.
[2] K. Hart and A. Slob, "Integrated injection logic: A new approach to LSI," *IEEE J. Solid-State Circuits*, vol. SC-7, pp. 346–351, Oct. 1972.
[3] R. E. Crippen, D. O'Brien, K. Rallapalli, and P. W. J. Verhofstadt, "High-performance integrated injection logic: A microprogram sequencer built with I²L," *IEEE J. Solid-State Circuits*, vol. SC-11, pp. 662–668, Oct. 1976.
[4] F. M. Klaassen, "Some considerations on high-speed injection logic," *IEEE J. Solid-State Circuits*, vol. SC-12, pp. 150–154, Feb. 1977.
[5] ——, "Design and performance of micron-size devices," *Solid-State Electron.*, vol. 21, pp. 565–571, 1978.
[6] S. Shinozaki, T. Iizuka, F. Masuoka, K. Shinada, and J. Miyamoto, "Role of the external n-p-n-base region on the switching speed of integrated injection logic (I²L)," *IEEE J. Solid-State Circuits*, vol. SC-12, pp. 185–191, Apr. 1977.
[7] S. Shinozaki, K. Shinada and, J.-I. Miyamoto, "Effects of gate geometry on propagation delay of integrated injection logic (I²L)," *IEEE J. Solid-State Circuits*, vol. SC-13, pp. 225–230, Apr. 1978.
[8] H. H. Berger, "The injection model—A structure oriented model for merged transistor logic (MTL)," *IEEE J. Solid-State Circuits*, vol. SC-9, pp. 218–227, Oct. 1974.
[9] E. Wittenzellner, "Design of large-scale I²L logic circuits," *IEEE J. Solid-State Circuits*, vol. SC-12, pp. 199–204, Apr. 1977.
[10] A. Weinberger, "Large scale integration of MOS complex logic: A layout method," *IEEE J. Solid-State Circuits*, vol. SC-2, pp. 182–190, Dec. 1967.
[11] C. S. den Brinker and A. N. Morgan, "The effect of series resistance and distributed parasitic diode action on multicollector I²L structures," in *European Solid-State Circuits Conf.* (Canterbury/ G. B.) *Summaries*, Sept. 1975. pp. 18–19.
[12] D. V. Kerns, "The effect of base contact position on the relative propagation delays of the multiple outputs of an I²L gate," *IEEE J. Solid-State Circuits*, vol. SC-11, pp. 712–717, Oct. 1976.
[13] F. M. Klaassen, "Physics and models for I²L," in *Int. Electron Devices Meeting Dig. Tech. Papers* (Washington DC), pp. 299–302, Dec. 1976.
[14] D. B. Estreich and R. W. Dutton, "Modeling integrated injection logic (I²L) performance and operational limits," *IEEE J. Solid-State Circuits*, vol. SC-12, pp. 450–456, Oct. 1977.
[15] D. P. Gaffney and A. Bhattacharyya, "Modeling device and layout effects of performance driven I²L," *IEEE J. Solid-State Circuits*, vol. SC-12, pp. 155–162, Apr. 1977.
[16] L. J. Ragonese and N.-T. Yang, "Enhanced integrated injection logic performance using novel symmetrical cell topography," in *Int. Electron Devices Meeting Tech. Papers*, pp. 166–169, Dec. 1977.
[17] J. L. Dunkley, S. D. Kang, and P. A. Nygaard, "Modular bipolar analysis: Part II—Application," *IEEE Trans. Electron Devices*, vol. ED-25, pp. 306–313, Mar. 1978.
[18] H. H. Berger, "Modelling I²L/MTL cells," (tutorial paper), *Digest Journées D'Electronique*, 1977, Lausannes/Switzerland; *Ecole Polytechnique Fédérale de Lausanne*, pp. 119–140, Oct. 1977.
[19] H. E. J. Wulms, "Base current of I²L transistors," *IEEE J. Solid-State Circuits*, vol. SC-12, pp. 143–150, Apr. 1977.
[20] W. M. Mattheus, R. P. Mertens, and J. D. Stulting, "Characteristics of I²L at low current levels," *IEEE Trans. Electron Devices*, vol. ED-24, pp. 1228–1233, Oct. 1977.
[21] H. H. Berger and U. Dreckmann, "The lateral P-N-P transistor— A practical investigation of the dc characteristics," *IEEE Trans. Electron Devices*, to be published.
[22] J. W. Slotboom and H. C. de Graaff, "Measurements of bandgap narrowing in Si bipolar transistors," *Solid-State Electron.*, vol. 19, pp. 857–862, 1976.
[23] T. E. Hendrickson and J. S. T. Huang, "A stored charge model for estimating I²L gate delay," *IEEE J. Solid-State Circuits*, vol. SC-12, pp. 171–176, Apr. 1977.
[24] R. C. Jaeger, "An evaluation of injection modeling," *Solid-State Electron.*, vol. 19, pp. 639–643, July 1976.
[25] C. Mulder and H. E. J. Wulms, "High speed integrated injection logic," *IEEE J. Solid-State Circuits*, vol. SC-11, pp. 379–385, June 1976.
[26] Y. Tokumara, S. Shinozaki, M. Nakai, S. Ito, and Y. Nishi, "I²L with self-aligned double-diffusion injector," in *Int. Solid-State Circuits Conf. Dig. Tech. Papers*, pp. 100–101 Feb. 1976.
[27] W. B. Sander and J. M. Early, "A 4096 × 1 (I³L) bipolar dynamic RAM," in *Int. Solid-State Circuits Conf. Dig. Tech. Papers*, pp. 182–183, Feb. 1976.
[28] H. H. Heimeier and H. H. Berger, "Evaluation of electron injection current density in p-layers for injection modeling of I²L," *IEEE J. Solid-State Circuits*, vol. SC-12, pp. 205–206, Apr. 1977.
[29] F. M. Klaassen, "Device physics of integrated injection logic," *IEEE Trans. Electron Devices*, vol. ED-22, pp. 145–152, Mar. 1975.
[30] T. Poorter, "Electrical parameters, static and dynamic response of I²L," *IEEE. J. Solid-State Circuits*, vol. SC-12, pp. 440–449, Oct. 1977.
[31] F. Henning, H. K. Hingarh, D. O'Brien, and P. W. J. Verhofstadt, "Isoplanar integrated injection logic: A high-performance bipolar technology," *IEEE J. Solid-State Circuits*, vol. SC-12, pp. 101–109, Apr. 1977.
[32] J. M. Hermann, III, S. A. Evans, and B. J. Sloan, "Second generation I²L/MTL: A 20-ns process/structure," *IEEE J. Solid-State Circuits*, vol. SC-12, pp. 93–101, Apr. 1977.
[33] J. G. Graul, A. Glasl, and H. Murrmann, "High-performance transistors with arsenic-implanted polysil emitters," *IEEE J. Solid-State Circuits*, vol. SC-11, pp. 491–495, Aug. 1976.
[34] J. Middelhoek and A. Kooy, "Polycrystalline silicon as a diffusion source and interconnect layer in I²L," *IEEE J. Solid-State Circuits*, vol. SC-12, pp. 135–138, Apr. 1977.
[35] R. D. Davies and J. D. Meindl, "Poly I²L—A high-speed linear-compatible structure," *IEEE J. Solid-State Circuits*, vol. SC-12, pp. 367–375, Aug. 1977.

IEEE JOURNAL OF SOLID-STATE CIRCUITS, VOL. SC-14, NO. 2, APRIL 1979

[36] K. Okada, K. Aomura, J. Nokubo, and H. Shiba, "A 4k static bipolar TTL RAM," in *Int. Solid-State Circuits Conf. Dig. Tech. Papers*, pp. 100–101, Feb. 1978.

[37] J. Akazawa, H. Kodama, and T. Sudo, "A high-speed 1600 gate bipolar LSI processor," in *Int. Solid-State Circuits Conf. Dig.*

Tech. Papers, pp. 208–209, Feb. 1978.

[38] H. H. Berger and S. K. Wiedmann, "Terminal-oriented model for merged transistor logic (MTL)," *IEEE J. Solid-State Circuits*, vol. SC-9, pp. 211–217, Oct. 1974.

Scaling I²L for VLSI

STEPHEN A. EVANS

Abstract—Scaling integrated injection logic for high-density VLSI circuits is discussed. The basic principles governing the operation of an I²L device and the impact of specific process/design changes on performance are reviewed. A procedure for scaling I²L devices with geometries >1 μm is described and examples of scaled devices fabricated with e-beam slice writing techniques are given. It is shown that the I²L gate propagation delay can be scaled over the entire range of operating currents through a combination of scaling and sizing. The physical limitations that apply to submicron geometries are summarized and the performance attainable with a submicron device design is predicted.

I. Introduction

DEVICE SCALING for higher density and improved performance has been a blue-sky research and development topic for years. High-resolution lithography systems have been used in his effort to build a limited number of laboratory devices and circuits with micron and submicron geometries. The evolutionary development of high-speed e-beam writing techniques and more sensitive resists is on the threshold of making very large-scale integration (VLSI) a production reality. The push to upgrade all facets of device processing has gained enormous momentum in anticipation of handling VLSI class circuits.

With technology near at hand to build tens and hundreds of thousands of micron and submicron devices on a single chip, current device designs must be scaled and sized or redesigned to take the fullest advantage of the new VLSI capabilities. Of all the bipolar technologies, I²L has the best chance to meet the density, performance, and reliability requirements of VLSI.

Manuscript received August 21, 1978; revised November 11, 1978.
The author is with Texas Instruments Incorporated, Dallas, TX 75265.

In this paper, methods for scaling I²L devices for VLSI are discussed. The steady progress of I²L toward higher and higher density is summarized. The basic principles governing operation of an I²L gate are reviewed, and the design and optimization of a "full scale" device is described to make clear the impact of design and process changes on functionality and performance. A simple procedure for scaling devices with geometries >1 μm is described, and examples of scaled devices fabricated with the e-beam slice writing technique are given. Finally, physical limitations that apply to I²L devices with submicron geometries are summarized, and the performance attainable with a submicron I²L device design is predicted.

No attempt is made in this paper to compare I²L to other semiconductor device technologies since it is assumed that future systems will require several forms of both bipolar and unipolar circuits. However, many of the physical limitations discussed below are generally applicable to other technologies, particularly standard bipolar.

II. The Trend Toward High Density

Steady improvements in both density and performance have been achieved since the introduction of the first I²L device and circuit in 1972 [1], [2] through the utilization of improved lithography techniques and design innovations. Initially, I²L gates were designed with 10 μm minimum linewidths and had cell packing densities of ~100 gates/mm² (5 output collectors). Dropping the linewidth to 5 μm pushed the density up to ~400 gates/mm². Replacing the n⁺ guard ring with an oxide collar allowed the overlap of the base and base contact onto the oxide, permitting a shrinkage of device size without changing minimum feature size. Densities of ~600 gates/mm² have been reported for this type of structure

Reprinted from *IEEE J. Solid-State Circuits*, vol. SC-14, pp. 318–326, Apr. 1979.

230

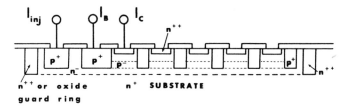

Fig. 1. I^2L device structure with deep implanted, intrinsic p^- base and five output collectors.

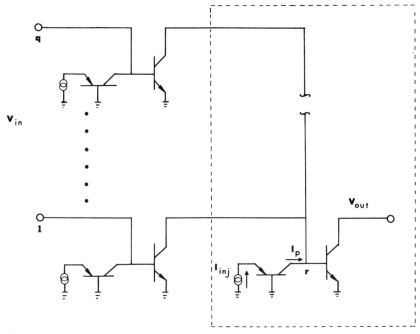

Fig. 2. Typical I^2L gate configuration. I_p is the source current (the unsaturated p-n-p collector current) for the gate labeled r. A NAND gate function can be implemented with the portion of the circuit set off by the dashed lines.

[3]. Eliminating the injector surface area altogether by using a substrate injector permitted even more cell compaction. Densities of ~800 gate/mm² have been reported using the substrate injection technique [4]. A dramatic improvement was reported recently for which the *e*-beam slice writing technique was used [5]. Gates were fabricated with 1.25 μm minimum linewidths giving a cell packing density of >2000 gates/mm². Going to submicron dimensions would, clearly, yield even more significant reductions.

The size-reduction techniques previously listed apply equally as well to standard bipolar technology, with the exception of the substrate injector. Transistors with $\frac{1}{2}$ μm wide emitters have already been built with *e*-beam lithography [6]. Utilizing high sheet-resistor technology, the ratio of standard bipolar to I^2L packing density should remain approximately constant.

III. OPERATION AND PERFORMANCE OF I^2L WITH CURRENT TECHNOLOGY

A. *Basic Principles of Operation*

The device physics of I^2L has been discussed quite extensively in the literature. A few examples are given in [7]–[11]. In the following paragraphs, the fundamental concepts are reviewed and the switching characteristics of a gate or unit cell are related to a few key parameters or observables with the objective of providing a formalism with which to discuss optimization and scaling.

The device structure of a nonisolated I^2L gate is shown in Fig. 1, and a typical gate hookup is shown in Fig. 2. The NAND function is realized by the portion of the circuit set off by the dashed lines [12]. The node labeled r is high when the input nodes of gates 1 through q are low. Node r is low when one or more of the nodes 1 through q are high. Switching node r from low to high requires charging all capacitances tied to r from V_{CESAT} to a V_{BE}. The charging current is supplied by the p-n-p and therefore determined by the injector voltage. In the reverse transition the voltage at node r goes from a V_{BESAT} to approximately a V_{BE} (this node is effectively off when the n-p-n transistor can no longer sink a unit of base current). Assuming nodes 2 through q are low during this transition, the average discharging current is a fraction of $\beta_{eff} I_p$, since node r is effectively off before V_{in_1} goes to a V_{BESAT}.

At very low current densities the turn-on time t_{on} is dominated by the voltage swing, junction-depletion capacitance, and interconnect capacitance. The turn-off time t_{off} is small compared to t_{on} in this current regime. t_{on} can be significantly reduced by 1) placing Schottkys on the output [13], [14] or input [4]; 2) replacing the n⁺ guard ring by oxide [3]; and 3) scaling down device geometries [5]. At high current densities,

231

t_{on} is assumed to be small compared to t_{off}. The volume of stored charge that is proportional to the p-n junction time constants and the saturation conditions dominates t_{off}. A large fraction of I^{2}L research and development has been directed toward ways of reducing stored charge in order to make I^{2}L competitive in speed with Schottky TTL while retaining its packing density advantage. The most obvious approach is to scale down all lightly doped regions [i.e., p-n-p basewidth and uncompensated epitaxial (epi) thickness] while holding the rest of the structure constant. This approach may require, in addition, changes in the epi resistivity and intrinsic base doping to maintain functionality. Other methods which require more or less major design changes are the following: 1) folded collector [15]; 2) decoupled p-n-p [16]; and 3) Schottky collector-base clamp [17]. Schottkys on the output, which reduce voltage swing, tend to reduce stored charge as well because down beta is much lower for a given design without the heavily doped collector [14].

B. Key Observables

While the device physics of integrated injection logic is fairly complicated due to complex current flows and interactive elements, one can write simple expressions that qualitatively predict switching speed and power consumption as a function of a few key parameters or observables. When the input current is low enough to make charge storage a negligible factor and β_{eff} (measured with the injector grounded) is large, the average propagation delay/gate is approximated by

$$t_D \sim t_{on}/2 \sim C_T V_{BE}/2I_p \tag{1}$$

where C_T represents the effective total capacitance at node r (Fig. 2). The speed power product SPP under the same conditions is given by

$$SPP \sim V_{inj} V_{BE} C_T/2 \propto {}_{\text{p-n-p}}. \tag{2}$$

In the operating range where charge storage is dominant, the minimum average propagation delay is approximated by an equation of the form [8], [10], [11]

$$t_D \sim t_{off}/2 \sim \bar{\tau}\beta_{eff}^{1/2}/2 \tag{3}$$

where β_{eff} is assumed large and

$$\bar{\tau} = (\tau_p I_{sp} + \tau_{pn} I_{spn} + M\tau_{ne} I_{sn} + (M-1)\tau_{nc} I_{sn})/I_{sn}.$$

The subscripts p, pn, ne, and nc label the time constants for the p-n-p, the parasitic p-n diode, the n-p-n emitter-base, and the n-p-n collector-base, respectively, and M is the collector fan-out. The time constant defined in (3) is simply the sum of the charges stored in each of the key elements of an I^{2}L unit cell normalized by the drive current.

The application of (3) to several specific I^{2}L structures is given below.

1) The lowest speed-power products have been achieved by increasing the area of the p-n-p relative to the vertical n-p-n [4], [18], [19]. One way to do this is to use injector isolated I^{2}L (i.e., injector on four sides). If the p$^+$ extrinsic base and thin epi are used, most of the charge storage will occur in the p-n-p base and the dominate component of n-p-n

base current will be back-injected current in the p-n-p. In this case, (3) reduces to

$$t_D \sim \frac{\tau_p}{2}\left(\frac{I_{sp}}{I_{sn}}\right)^{1/2} \sim \tau_p/(2\beta_{eff}^{1/2}). \tag{4}$$

Equation (4) shows qualitatively that for the injector-isolated structure, maximum speed is proportional to n-p-n gain. This behavior has been observed experimentally for I^{2}L gates with self-aligned, double-diffused injectors (S^{2}L) [20].

2) One of the fastest gate switching times has been obtained by decoupling the p-n-p from the n-p-n [16]. Assuming a heavily doped extrinsive base and thin epi, most of the charge will be stored in the n-p-n intrinsic base. In this case, (3) reduces to

$$t_D \sim M\tau_{ne}\beta_{eff}^{1/2}/2 \tag{5}$$

assuming that $\tau_{ne} \gg \tau_{nc}$. Equation (5) shows that when the intrinsic n-p-n dominates the device parameters, the speed will be inversely proportional to n-p-n gain.

Both (4) and (5) are simplified forms of (3) that apply to two extremes of I^{2}L gate design. For most of the structures discussed in this paper, the more general expression (3) is required to adequately predict the propagation delay as a function of gate design. The same functional relationships between delay and beta have been predicted by Klaassen [21].

C. Optimizing at Full Scale

Before attacking the problem of how to design a VLSI class device, it is instructive to first consider the design of an I^{2}L device using LSI design rules (5 μm). The best approach will, of course, depend on the design objective. For the purposes of this discussion, it is assumed that the design objective is a complex microprocessor chip. The goal in this case would be to achieve the highest possible packing density (both device and interconnect) and best performance while maintaining device functionality. Keeping in mind the principles of operation previously discussed, the following specific suggestions apply to a high-performance I^{2}L gate:

1) use a stick geometry (multicollector n-p-n perpendicular to the injector) with large fan-out when necessary;

2) separate extrinsic and intrinsic bases—employ the minimum geometry and heavy doping in the extrinsic base;

3) use the minimum-size collector consistent with design rules;

4) separate the devices with an oxide guard ring;

5) adjust the p-n-p basewidth, epi resistivity, and intrinsic base charge to ensure an efficient current source and an adequate beta.

The p$^+$ extrinsic base listed in item 2) not only inhibits electron injection from the substrate but also reduces base bulk resistance, allowing a larger fan-out.

The design procedure just described was developed to optimize the performance over a wide range of currents. To minimize the SPP in the low current regime where the junction capacitance is much greater than diffusion capacitance, reduce the epi concentration and widen the p-n-p base to keep the p-n-p base charge constant. Also, select an epi thickness equal to the sum of the p$^+$ junction depth and a zero bias depletion

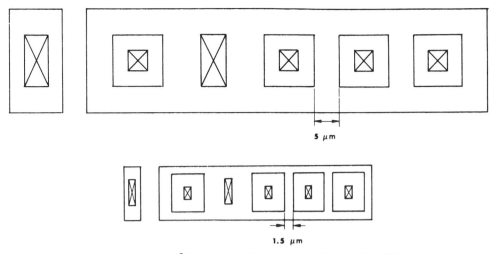

Fig. 3. Layout of I^{2}L gates using 5 and 1.5 μm minimum linewidths.

width. An alternative would be to keep the p-n-p basewidth constant and use an implant to maintain a constant base charge. To minimize the delay in the high current regime where the junction capacitance is much less than the diffusion capacitance, reduce the epi thickness to the p$^+$ junction depth. β_{eff} will remain approximately constant, since the hole injection into the substrate is almost independent of epi thickness (i.e., as long as a diffusion length in the epi is long compared to the thickness). In addition, increase the epi concentration and decrease the p-n-p basewidth such that I_{sp} and $\alpha_{\text{p-n-p}}$ remain constant. An adjustment to the intrinsic base implant dose may be necessary to keep the n-p-n active base charge constant.

IV. SCALING I^{2}L

A. Minimum Linewidth > 1 μm

The primary objective in scaling for VLSI is to increase the number of bits and logic functions per unit area while maintaining device functionality and yield. Power consumption per I^{2}L gate is, to first order, proportional to the square of the scale factor. The minimum delay is dependent on the details of the scaling.

A straightforward procedure for scaling is to simply shrink the x, y, and z dimensions simultaneously while holding the p-n-p basewidth constant. $\alpha_{\text{p-n-p}}$ and β_{eff} will remain approximately constant. τ_p will remain constant, while the other time constants will depend on the details of the vertical profiles. The IR drop to the far collector will be proportional to the scale factor. Since currents, not voltages, scale in I^{2}L, a smaller IR drop would allow a larger fan-out. It is assumed that the p$^+$ extrinsic base is tailored to minimize electron injection from the substrate and that diffusion lengths are less than the junction depths involved.

The impact of several scaling variations on the I^{2}L gate-level performance has been analyzed using a "second generation," full-size I^{2}L structure (5 μm minimum linewidth) as the baseline design [5], [10], [22]. It was demonstrated that scaling the lateral dimensions y and z, and the vertical junction depths x while holding the p-n-p basewidth constant results

in a lateral shift of the t_D versus I_{inj} curve along the current axis proportional to the change in area. In this calculation it was assumed that the junction capacitance per unit area and the junction time constants also remained constant. In addition, it was demonstrated that a reduction in the minimum delay requires sizing adjustments (i.e., independent variations of the p-n-p basewidth, extrinsic base, and collector areas) and/or reduction in junction time constants (i.e., changes in impurity profiles). For example, increasing the collector-to-base-area ratio reduces $\bar{\tau}$ [defined in (3)], since the intrinsic n-p-n time constant is normally much smaller than the p-n-p and parasitic p-n diode time constants; and reducing the uncompensated epi thickness reduces the time constants for both extrinsic and intrinsic elements of the n-p-n.

The guidelines given in the last section for minimizing SPP and delay apply to the scaled devices as well. However, when designing devices containing micrometer geometries, careful attention should be given to anticipated depletion widths, junction depths, and resist expansion properties.

B. Examples of Device Scaling Using e-Beam Lithography

I^{2}L gates with 1.25 μm minimum linewidths have previously been built using e-beam lithography and a "second generation," n$^+$ guard-ring process [5], [22]. Employing a similar process, gates utilizing 1.5, 3, and 5 μm minimum geometries for the extrinsic base were fabricated. A thick oxide guard ring was used instead of a phosphorus diffusion to separate devices. The extrinsic base was driven into the substrate to achieve maximum speed. The layouts of the 5 and 1.5 μm devices are compared in Fig. 3. A vertical profile through the intrinsic n-p-n is shown in Fig. 4. Also shown is the extrinsic base p$^+$ profile. A photomicrograph of experimental device structures with four output collectors organized in groups to form 25 gate-ring oscillators is shown in Fig. 5. The average propagation delay versus injector current is plotted in Fig. 6 for devices with the collector nearest to the injector connected to the base of the adjacent cell. Since all the gates were fabricated on one chip, the only difference between device structures is the lateral dimensions. It was found that the mea-

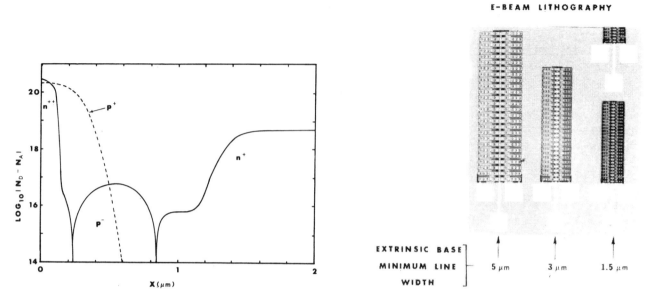

Fig. 4. Vertical diffusion profiles used with 1.2 μm epi. Solid line is the intrinsic n-p-n profile. Dashed line is the extrinsic p⁺ base profile.

Fig. 5. I²L ring oscillator circuits fabricated with *e*-beam lithography using 5, 3, and 1.5 μm minimum linewidths for the extrinsic base.

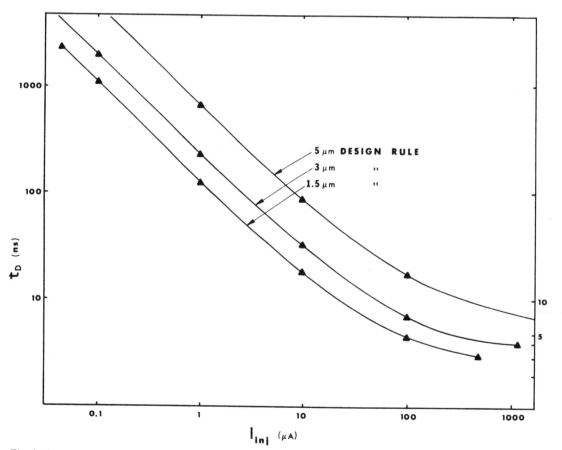

Fig. 6. Average propagation delay versus injector current per gate for I²L devices using 5, 3, and 1.5 μm minimum linewidths for the extrinsic base. A schematic of the device layout is given in Fig. 3.

TABLE I
E-Beam I²L Device Data, Oxide Guard Ring, 4 Collector Outputs

MINIMUM BASE DIMENSION (μm)	TOTAL GATE AREA (μm²)	GATES/mm²	SPP AT 1μA (pJ)	NORMALIZED SPP	NORMALIZED NPN AREA	MINIMUM t_D (ns)
5	2387	418	.38	4.7	4.0	7.0
3	1273	735	.15	1.9	1.9	4.0
1.5	686	1457	.08*	1.0	1.0	3.0

*<0.04 calculated for a structure optimized for *SPP* instead of speed.

I²L LSI Circuit

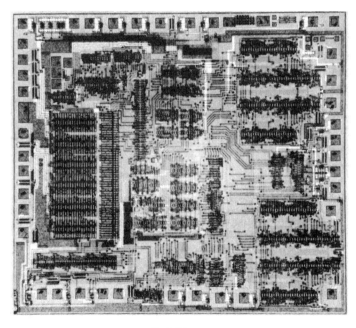

Full Size

Scaled 50% Linear Shrink

Fig. 7. Comparison of full-size and scaled version of I²L LSI circuit.

sured *SPP* scales roughly as the area of the n-p-n. The *SPP* for each design is given in Table I, along with the minimum delay. The reduction in minimum delay accompanying the device size reduction was achieved by implementing two size adjustments: 1) the ratio of the collector to the extrinsic base area was increased, and 2) the p-n-p basewidth was decreased. The net effect of these changes is to decrease $\bar{\tau}$ while keeping β_{eff} approximately constant [see (3)]. The delay, then, has been shifted over the entire range of operating currents, as demonstrated in Fig. 6, through a combination of scaling and size adjustments.

An LSI I²L bar design with about 1450 gates was shrunk to 25 percent of its original area to demonstrate the packing density and performance attainable with scaling. The procedure used is given as follows: 1) redesign input/output devices to meet voltage-breakdown specifications after shrink; 2)

shrink linear dimensions by 50 percent; and 3) size individual levels to optimize performance and satisfy *e*-beam machine and process limitations. The original and scaled bar designs are compared in Fig. 7. The original design is illustrated with a photomicrograph of an actual bar fabricated with photolithography. The scaled design is illustrated by the first-level metal pattern exposed with the *e*-beam writing technique. A comparison of performance and packing density is given in Table II. The data presented in this table were determined as follows.

1) Device parameters were calculated and used in an I²L gate model to predict the gate-level performance of the full-size bar [10], [23].

2) Comparisons were made with the experiment. Good agreement obtained between the experiment and theory

TABLE II
e-BEAM I²L LSI BAR DATA, OXIDE GUARD-RING PROCESS

	MINIMUM BASE DIMENSION (μm)	BAR SIZE (mm²)	SPP/GATE AT 1 μA (pJ)	t_D AT 100μA/GATE 4 COLLECTORS (ns)	GATES/mm² WITH INTERCONNECT
FULL SIZE	3.8	13.5	.17 - .23	10 - 12	107
SCALED	1.4	3.4*	.05	5.0	428

*Not including extra bond pads.

demonstrated that the calculated device parameters were reasonable for this device structure.

3) The device parameters were scaled to reflect the 50-percent shrink and the sizing adjustments. The scaled parameters were used to predict the gate-level performance of the scaled bar.

The predicted gate delay is a factor of 2 and the speed-power product is a factor of 4 better than the full-size bar. It should be noted that an additional 2 mm² had to be added on to the scaled bar for 20 4×4 mil I/O pads to facilitate bonding.

C. Fundamental Limitations Below 1 μm

Up to this point, the discussion has centered around scaling the lateral dimensions (except the p-n-p base) and junction depths while holding the epi concentration constant and the surface concentrations of the impurity profiles at the solid solubility limit. This procedure kept the device parameters β_{eff} and $\alpha_{p\text{-}n\text{-}p}$ approximately independent of the scale factor. Also to minimize the SPP after scaling, the epi thickness was set equal to the sum of the p⁺ junction depth and a zero-bias depletion width. Carrying this approach into the submicron region would eventually yield a negligible change in gate area, although the power consumption would continue to decrease. The limiting factors on area reduction are the p-n-p basewidth and the guard-ring lateral diffusion or oxidation. Clearly, the p-n-p as well as the n-p-n base doping level must be increased and the epi thickness decreased in order to make significant gains in gate packing density with submicron design rules. However, the power at low currents will no longer improve as the square of the scale factor because it is a function of both the area and the doping levels.

Increasing doping levels and shrinking basewidths forces consideration of a number of related nonlinear effects such as junction breakdown, punch-through, band shrinkage, Auger recombination, doping fluxuations, and narrow base effects. Given the junction breakdown and depletion width as a function of doping density, one can derive a curve showing the minimum basewidth as a function of the highest voltage required by the circuit [24]. For I²L, which operates at 1 V and below, the minimum basewidth is about 300–400 Å at a doping level of ~5 × 10¹⁸ cm⁻³. Taking into consideration doping fluxuations, this minimum goes to ~700 Å and ~3 × 10¹⁸ cm⁻³. It is assumed here that the base must be equal to or greater than the sum of the emitter-base and collector-base depletion widths. A second factor which must be figured into the equation is the effective bandgap shrinkage at high doping levels [25], [26] and Auger recombination [27]. The net

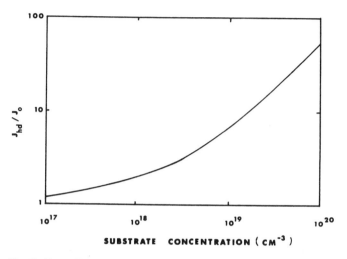

Fig. 8. Normalized hole current density injected into the I²L substrate emitter as a function of substrate concentration. The subscripts HD and o label the currents calculated with and without heavy doping effects, respectively.

effect is a larger base-current injection than is predicted by classical theory and a corresponding degradation of injection efficiency, making it more difficult to retain device functionality in the submicron regime. To demonstrate the importance of this heavy doping phenomenon, the hole current density injected into the I²L emitter has been calculated as a function of emitter doping level [23]. The ratio of J_{HD} to J_o is plotted in Fig. 8. The subscripts HD and o label the currents calculated with and without heavy doping effects, respectively. A third factor which has been given little attention due to the difficulty of obtaining explicit experimental evidence is the "thin base" effect. As the base of a bipolar transistor becomes thinner and thinner to achieve higher f_t, the number of probable collision events between a minority carrier and an impurity atom diminishes to the point where the classical diffusion equations are no longer applicable. Both classical [28] and quantum-mechanical [29] calculations have been carried out to estimate the impact on device parameters I_s and f_t. The results show that I_s tends toward independence of basewidth and f_t tends toward a first power dependence on basewidth. A more recent Monte Carlo calculation [30] concludes that deviations from classical theory are not great for basewidths down to 200 Å.

So far, the discussion has been limited to the simplest I²L structure. Structure modifications such as double-diffused injector, substrate injector, poly extrinsic base [31], and Schottkys have been implemented on full-size devices to ob-

TABLE III
PROCESS DESIGN SPECIFICATIONS ½ μm I²L

JUNCTION DEPTH, C_s { EXTRINSIC BASE / NPN COLLECTOR }	2000Å, 1x10²⁰(cm⁻³) / 1000Å, 2.3x10²⁰(cm⁻³)
EPI THICKNESS	2000Å
SUBSTRATE CONCENTRATION	3x10²⁰(cm⁻³)
BASE WIDTH, CONCENTRATION { PNP / NPN }	1000Å, 2x10¹⁸(cm⁻³) / 1000Å, 2x10¹⁸(cm⁻³)
TIME CONSTANT { NPN EMITTER-BASE / NPN COLLECTOR-BASE / PNP EMITTER-BASE / BASE-SUBSTRATE DIODE }	23 ps / 31 ps / 165 ps / 180 ps
CELL AREA (ONE OUTPUT COLLECTOR)	7 μm²

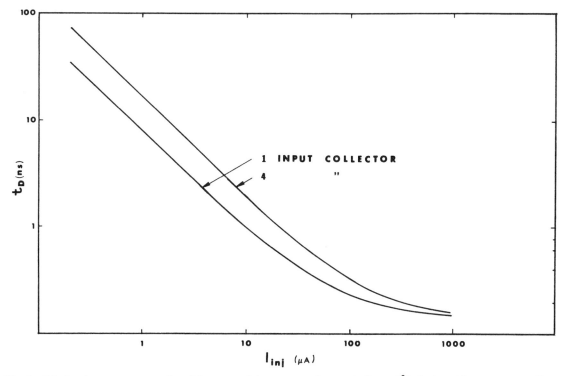

Fig. 9. Calculated average propagation delay versus injector current per gate for an I²L device with one output collector designed with ½ μm minimum linewidth. The impact of additional collectors tied to the input (see Fig. 2) is shown by the top curve.

tain significant performance gains without scaling. The question is how easily can these structures be scaled to submicron geometries? There are no basic problems with the double-diffused and substrate injectors. Using the present technology [31] for growing poly and good-quality epi simultaneously, the poly-grain size may be of the order of the minimum linewidth or larger which would present a problem in terms of patterning and metal coverage. The doping levels (~10¹⁸ cm⁻³) required for submicron geometries would make the fabrication of good Schottkys difficult; however, isolated Schottkys could be used in critical paths and I/O without seriously impacting the bar area.

D. Designing I²L with Submicron Linewidths

An I²L gate suitable for a VLSI-class chip (~10⁶ gates/chip) was designed with submicron lines and spaces to illustrate the speed and density possible with this bipolar technology. The capability to define ½ μm geometries and grow very thin epi (1000–5000 Å) was assumed. The scaling proce-

dures outlined for >1 μm gate designs are not applicable in this case because of the nonlinear effects previously described. Instead, an iterative approach was used: 1) design a minimum geometry device; 2) calculate device parameters; 3) predict ac/dc performance; and 4) modify design to ensure functionality and to obtain best performance. Table III summarizes the design specifications on an I²L device with ½ μm minimum feature widths. The vertical dimension (epi thickness) was kept small compared to the total device width to minimize the area required by the guard ring. The n-p-n profile was selected to minimize the base transit time while staying within the constraints on junction doping and basewidth previously listed. It was assumed that a diffusion length in the extrinsic base is longer than the base junction depth, so that the extrinsic base to substrate diode is dominated by electron injection under the base contact. The device parameters were calculated using a bipolar simulator which includes heavy doping effects and Auger recombination [23]. The calculated delay versus injector current is shown in Fig. 9 for devices with one output collector. Since the doping levels and base-widths used in this design are close to their limiting values, the minimum delay of 150 ps predicted here is close to the minimum possible with I^2L in its simplest form. The calculated *SPP* at 1 μA was 6 fJ.

V. SCALING INTERCONNECT

A key factor in the successful fabrication of VLSI circuits will be the interconnect technology, both in terms of yield and performance. Linewidth and thickness must be scaled to reduce capacitance and maintain reasonable aspect ratios. Also the interlevel dielectric must be scaled to reduce the area required by vias. Thinner metal lines will necessarily require scaling the device topology. The reduction in metal cross-sectional area will require the use of metal systems with inherently small grain size and high reliability. If one assumes that the power per unit area and the maximum current density remain the same, additional levels of interconnect may be required to accommodate power buses which will require the same cross-sectional area as before, assuming no major changes in conducting materials [24], [32].

An example of how interconnect capacitance can impact I^2L gate switching time is given in Fig. 9. The bottom curve represents a gate that has one collector tied to the base of the switching transistor with 4.5 μm of metal $\frac{1}{2}\mu$m wide on 3000 Å of oxide. The top curve represents a gate that has four collectors tied to the base with an average of 25 μm of metal per collector (see Fig. 2 for schematic). About half the shift in the curve is due to interconnect capacitance and about half due to the additional collectors.

VI. SUMMARY

The scaling of I^2L devices for VLSI circuits was discussed. It was demonstrated experimentally that I^2L can be scaled over the entire range of operating currents for minimum line-widths >1 μm. A minimum propagation delay of 3 ns was obtained for a 1.5 μm device fabricated with e-beam lithography. It was predicted that by scaling and sizing a "full-scale" LSI bar, a factor of 4 improvement in density and *SPP* can be realized without major redesign. The major problem areas in scaling to submicron dimensions were also discussed. A device with $\frac{1}{2}$ μm minimum geometries designed using process, device, and circuit simulators was described. Sub-nanosecond gate delays were predicted for this $\frac{1}{2}$ μm I^2L gate design.

REFERENCES

[1] H. H. Berger and S. K. Wiedman, "Merged-transistor-logic (MTL) –A low cost bipolar logic concept," *IEEE J. Solid-State Circuits*, vol. SC-7, pp. 340–346, Oct. 1972.

[2] K. Hart and A. Slob, "Integrated injection logic: A new approach to LSI," *IEEE J. Solid-State Circuits*, vol. SC-7, pp. 346–351, Oct. 1972.

[3] F. Hennig, H. K. Hingarh, D. O'Brien, and P. W. J. Verhofstadt, "Isoplanar integrated injection logic: A high-performance bipolar technology," *IEEE J. Solid-State Circuits*, vol. SC-12, pp. 101–109, Apr. 1977.

[4] V. Blatt, P. S. Walsh, and L. W. Kennedy, "Substrate fed logic," *IEEE J. Solid-State Circuits*, vol. SC-10, pp. 336–342, Oct. 1975.

[5] S. A. Evans, J. L. Bartelt, B. J. Sloan, and G. L. Varnell, "Fabrication of integrated injection logic with electron-beam lithography and ion implantation," *IEEE Trans. Electron Devices*, vol. ED-25, pp. 402–407, Apr. 1978.

[6] H. Yuan, Y. Wu, and J. B. Kruger, "A 2-watt X-band silicon power transistor," *IEEE Trans. Electron Devices*, vol. ED-25, pp. 731–736, June 1978.

[7] H. H. Berger, "The injection model–A structure-oriented model for merged transistor logic (MTL)," *IEEE J. Solid-State Circuits*, vol. SC-9, pp. 218–227, Oct. 1974.

[8] F. M. Klaassen, "Device physics of integrated injection logic," *IEEE Trans. Electron Devices*, vol. ED-22, pp. 145–152, Mar. 1975.

[9] S. A. Evans, J. M. Herman, III, and B. J. Sloan, "On the electrical properties of the I^2L NPN transistor," *IEEE Trans. Electron Devices* (Corresp.), vol. ED-22, pp. 1192–1194, Oct. 1976.

[10] S. A. Evans, "Analytic model for the design and optimization of ion implanted I^2L devices," *IEEE J. Solid-State Circuits*, vol. SC-12, pp. 191–198, Apr. 1977.

[11] T. Poorter, "Electrical parameters, static and dynamic response of I^2L," *IEEE J. Solid-State Circuits*, vol. SC-12, pp. 440–449, Oct. 1977.

[12] H. H. Berger and S. K. Wiedman, "Merged transistor logic–A low-cost bipolar logic concept," in *ISSCC Dig. Tech. Papers*, pp. 90–91, Feb. 1972.

[13] F. W. Hewlett, "Schottky I^2L," *IEEE J. Solid-State Circuits*, vol. SC-10, pp. 343–348, Oct. 1975.

[14] J. M. Herman, III, "High performance output Schottky I^2L/MTL," in *Int. Electron Devices Meet. Dig. Tech. Papers*, pp. 262–265, Dec. 1977.

[15] M. I. Elmasry, "Folded-collector integrated injection logic," *IEEE J. Solid-State Circuits*, vol. SC-11, pp. 379–385, June 1976.

[16] C. Mulder and H. E. J. Wulms, "High speed integrated injection logic (I^2L)," *IEEE J. Solid-State Circuits*, vol. SC-11, pp. 379–385, June 1976.

[17] B. B. Roesner and D. J. McGreivy, "A new high speed I^2L structure," *IEEE J. Solid-State Circuits*, vol. SC-12, pp. 114–118, Apr. 1977.

[18] N. C. deTroye, "Integrated injection logic–Present and future," *IEEE J. Solid-State Circuits*, vol. SC-9, pp. 206–211, Oct. 1974.

[19] Y. Tokumaru, M. Nakai, S. Shinozaki, S. Ito, and Y. Nishi, "I^2L with a self-aligned double-diffused injector," *IEEE J. Solid-State Circuits*, vol. SC-12, pp. 109–114, Apr. 1977.

[20] S. Shinozaki, K. Shinada, and J. Miyamoto, "Effects of gate geometry on propagation delay of integrated injection logic (I^2L)," *IEEE J. Solid-State Circuits*, vol. SC-13, pp. 225–230, Apr. 1978.

[21] F. M. Klaassen, "Some consideration on high-speed injection logic," *IEEE J. Solid-State Circuits*, vol. SC-12, pp. 150–154, Apr. 1977.

[22] J. M. Herman, III, S. A. Evans, and B. J. Sloan, Jr., "Second generation I^2L/MTL: A 20 ns process/structure," *IEEE J. Solid-State Circuits*, vol. SC-12, pp. 93–101, Apr. 1977.

[23] S. A. Evans and J. S. Fu, "Application of a new, accurate bipolar simulator to correlate device performance to process selection," *Extended Abstracts ECS Meet.*, vol. 75-1, pp. 394–395, May 1975.

[24] B. Hoeneisen and C. A. Mead, "Limitations in microelectronics– II. Bipolar technology," *Solid-State Electron.*, vol. 15, pp. 891–897, 1972.

[25] M. S. Mock, "On heavy doping effects and the injection efficiency of silicon transistors," *Solid-State Electron.*, vol. 17, pp. 819–824, Aug. 1974.

[26] A. H. Marshak and K. M. VanVliet, "Carrier densities and emitter efficiency in degenerate materials with position dependent band structure," *Solid-State Electron.*, vol. 21, pp. 429–434, 1978.

[27] J. Krausse, "Auger-Rekombination Im Mittelgebiet Durchlass-belasteter Silizium-Gleichrichter und Thyristoren," *Solid-State Electron.*, vol. 17, pp. 427–429, 1974.

[28] P. Rohr and F. A. Lindholm, "Questionability of drift-diffusion transport in the analysis of small semiconductor devices," *Solid-State Electron.*, vol. 17, p. 729, 1974.

[29] P. Rohr, "Modifications of drift-diffusion transport in the analysis of thin-base transistors," Ph.D. dissertation, Univ. of Florida, Gainesville, 1974.

[30] G. Baccarani, C. Jacoboni, and A. M. Mazzone, "Current transport in narrow-base transistors," *Solid-State Electron.*, vol. 20, pp. 5–10, 1977.

[31] R. D. Davies and J. D. Meindl, "Poly I^2L–A high speed linear-compatible structure," *IEEE J. Solid-State Circuits*, vol. SC-12, pp. 367–375, 1977.

[32] R. W. Keyes, "Physical problems of small structures in electronics," *Proc. IEEE*, vol. 60, pp. 1055–1062, Sept. 1972.

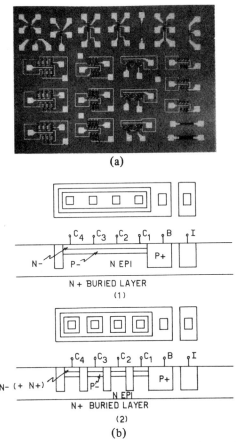

Fig. 1. (a) Microphotograph of chip containing all three technologies. (b) Layout and cross section of the SCTL (1) versus the multiple collector cells (2).

A Comparison of High-Speed I^2L Structures

S. C. BLACKSTONE AND R. P. MERTENS

Abstract—A comparison is made between the Schottky coupled I^2L structure, low downward beta I^2L, and conventional double base fully implanted I^2L. All of these were fabricated together on a single chip so that a direct comparison could be made. The results of both measured and predicted ring oscillators are presented. Finally, the results of a D-type flip-flop connected as a divide-by-two show that the SCTL gate is superior.

I. INTRODUCTION

In this correspondence three I^2L technologies designed for high speed will be compared. These are the Schottky coupled transistor logic or SCTL structure proposed by Berger and Wiedmann [1], the Schottky coupled isolated collector structure of Hewlett [2], and conventional double base fully implanted I^2L as used by Texas Instruments [3]. The SCTL approach as shown in part (1) of Fig. 1(b) uses one large lowly doped collector which serves as a common cathode for Schottky output decoding diodes. This allows low downward current gain without the problem of current hogging. The Schottky coupled isolated collector structure as shown in part (2) of Fig. 1(b) (with n^-) is essentially the same as the SCTL approach except that it isolates the collectors. This allows a more flexible circuit design as the base contact can be placed anywhere on the base; however, it requires a minimum downward current gain. The conventional I^2L as shown in part (2) of Fig. 1(b) (with n^- and n^+) employs the same heavily doped extrinsic base and implanted base and collector as the other two, but its downward current gain is very high. Various other approaches such as up diffusion, oxide isolation, and various arrangements of the p-n-p injector would affect all of these three structures somewhat equally, and thus will not be discussed.

The various parameters of these three structures will be compared and explained. The measured results of ring oscillators will be compared with predicted results using a model based on the SCTL structure.

Finally, the three technologies will be used to build D-type flip-flops and the results will be compared.

II. FABRICATION AND CHARACTERIZATION

To perform this comparison, a mask was fabricated [Fig. 1(a)] which included the three technologies on the same chip so that a direct comparison could be made. This mask was

Manuscript received April 20, 1978; revised June 15, 1978.

S. C. Blackstone is with the Laboratorium E.S.A.T., Katholieke Universiteit Leuven, Heverlee, Belgium.

R. P. Mertens is with the Laboratorium E.S.A.T., Katholieke Universiteit Leuven, Heverlee, Belgium and the Belgian National Scientific Foundation.

Reprinted from *IEEE J. Solid-State Circuits*, vol. SC-13, pp. 909–911, Dec. 1978.

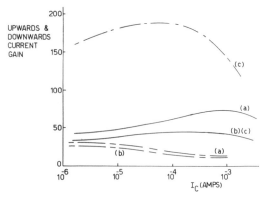

Fig. 2. Plot of measured upward (solid lines) and downward (dotted lines) current gain as a function of collector current for a fan-out four structure with all collectors common and injector grounded for (a) the SCTL case, (b) the Schottky coupled structure with isolated collectors, and (c) the conventional double base fully implanted I^2L.

made using an 8 μm minimum linewidth and space. This mask was fabricated on 2.24 μm epi n/n$^+$ wafer with an epi resistivity of 0.54 $\Omega \cdot$ cm. ʻ To allow all structures to have exactly the same base and emitter profiles, and thus emitter base parameters such as upward current gain, emitter time constant, etc., each technology received the same base and collector implant. The base was a boron implantation of 5×10^{12}/cm^2 at an energy of 350 keV and the collector was a phosphorus implant of 5×10^{12}/cm^2 at an energy of 300 keV. The collector of the conventional I^2L was formed with an arsenic implantation of 2.5×10^{15}/cm^2 at an energy of 180 keV. This arsenic implant is done in addition to the n$^-$ phosphorus implant such that the junction depth is determined by the n$^-$ phosphorus implant. The p$^+$ extrinsic base used by all three technologies was about 100 $\Omega/\square$. The n$^-$ had a sheet resistance of 1.5 k$\Omega/\square$, and the base pinch resistor was in the order of 25 k$\Omega/\square$.

Fig. 2 is a plot of the measured upward and downward current gain as a function of collector current for a fan-out four device with all four collectors common. From this graph one can see that the Schottky coupled structure with isolated collectors and the conventional I^2L structure have the same upward current gain showing that the n$^+$ does not change the junction depth. The difference in upward current gain between the SCTL and the multiple collector structures is due to the ratio of collector area to base area which in a fan-out four structure is 0.594, whereas the ratio of total collector area to base area in a fan-out four multiple collector structure is 0.372 [Fig. 1(b)]. This says that, ignoring back injection, the upward current gain of the SCTL structure should be higher than the multiple collector structure by the ratio of these two ratios. Thus, the SCTL structure should be 1.6 times higher than the multiple collector structure for a fan-out of four. From Fig. 2 the peak upward current gains are 72 for the SCTL structure and 44 for the multiple collector structure. This is a ratio of 1.6. The measured back injection for these structures was indeed small, as suggested by this result. The downward current gain clearly indicates that even though the arsenic implant does not come to the collector base junction, it forms a good emitter. That the downward current gains of the SCTL structure and the Schottky coupled structure with isolated collectors are the same is expected as the base buried layer diode is now reverse-biased.

The saturation current of the SCTL structure and the multiple collector structures will also be different due to the differing sizes of the intrinsic base area. For a fan-out four device

the ratio of total intrinsic base area for the SCTL structure to the total intrinsic base area of the multiple collector structure is 1.4. This implies that the saturation current of the SCTL structure is 1.4 times that of the multiple collector structures. The actually measured ratio of saturation currents was 1.45.

To find the emitter time constants, a plot of one over $2\pi f_T$ versus one over the collector current was measured for a fan-out one and fan-out four SCTL gate. This represents a ratio of intrinsic area to total area of 23 and 43 percent, respectively. The measured results gave approximately the same delay for both devices. The reason for this is a result of the thin epi used. For a thicker epi layer of, say, 5 μm, charge is stored under both the extrinsic base and the intrinsic base, giving a time constant equal to the intrinsic time constant plus one over the upward current gain times the extrinsic time constant. When one goes to a thinner epi layer the charge is stored entirely under the intrinsic base, and thus the emitter time constant is independent of fan-out. This is why the fan-out one and fan-out four have approximately the same time constant.

The result of the time constant measurement will mean that the comparison of these three technologies will be advantageous for the multiple collector structures. The reason for this is that after subtracting the base loss diode out, the multiple collector structures have 1.2 times as much loss diode per collector as the SCTL case. If one now calculates the ratio of active intrinsic area to loss diode area per collector, the SCTL collector has a ratio of 0.786 active to loss, whereas the multiple collector case has a ratio of 0.47 active to loss. This is a total improvement of almost 1.7 for the SCTL over the multiple collector structure. Here, however, as the extrinsic loss diode does not affect the time constant significantly, this improvement of active to loss area is not so important in terms of the emitter time constant. If thicker epi were used, for instance 5 μm, then this improvement would give lower emitter time constants for the SCTL structure than for the multiple collector structures [4].

III. RESULTS

To model the results, the model previously described by the authors [4] for the SCTL gate will be used. The resistor values were again calculated from the knowledge of the layout and sheet resistance values. The values for upward and downward current gains, saturation current, emitter time constant, etc., as previously discussed are also plugged in. From this, the minimum gate propagation delay was calculated for the first and fourth collectors of a four-collector device. For the multiple collector structures, the same model was used without the collector resistance and scaling the upward current gains by 1.6 and the saturation current by 1.4. Measured values of downward current gain and appropriate values of resistors were also used. Again, the minimum propagation delay was calculated for the first collector and fourth collector of a four-collector device. Table I is a summary of both the calculated results and the measured results for a fan-out four ring oscillator. All unused collectors were tied to a common supply.

Thus, one can see from Table I the rather good agreement between the calculated results of the model and the measured results. Due to the tight control of ion implantation and close physical proximity of the different technologies on the wafer, it was possible to establish a spread in measured minimum delay for a particular device in the order of 0.2 ns typically.

The results show that although the SCTL structure is slightly slower at the first collector, it is the overall fastest device. Next comes the Schottky coupled structure with isolated collectors which is faster than conventional I^2L as a result of lower downward current gain.

As the extrinsic base diode does not affect the emitter time

TABLE I

TYPE		Calculated Minimum Delay (nsec)	Average Measured Minimum Delay (nsec)
SCTL	1st	7.6	7.7
	4th	14.	14.6
Schottky Coupled	1st	7.5	7.4
Isolated Collectors	4th	16.	16.8
Conventional I²L	1st	8.5	9.0
	4th	20.	21.0

TABLE II

TYPE	Maximum Dividable Frequency
SCTL	17 MHz
Schottky Coupled Isolated Collectors	15 MHz
Conventional I²L	13 MHz

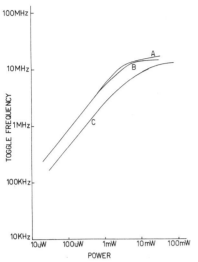

Fig. 3. Plot of toggle frequency versus power for a D-type flip-flop connected as a divide by two for all three technologies where A is the SCTL structure, B is the Schottky coupled structure with isolated collectors, and C is the conventional double base fully implanted I²L.

constant, one would expect that given the same values of current gain, the Schottky coupled structure with isolated collectors and the SCTL structure would switch at the same speed. The slight increase in speed of the first collector of the Schottky coupled structure with isolated collectors is a result of its lower upward current gain [5]. For the fourth collector this structure is limited by base resistance. For the SCTL, on the other hand, the base resistance is shunted by the single large collector, and thus results in a reduction of the fourth collector's minimum delay with respect to the Schottky coupled structure with isolated collectors. The poorer results of the conventional double implanted I²L are a result of its much greater downward current gain.

Although ring oscillators are useful in comparing different I²L technologies, a much more realistic approach is to fabricate an actual working circuit in each technology. So, along with the ring oscillators on the chip of Fig. 1(a), there are also three D-type flip-flops with the inverting output connected back to the input to make a divide by two.

These circuits were made and a plot of maximum dividable input frequency versus total power dissipated for all these technologies is shown in Fig. 3. All three circuits have exactly the same layout. In the case of the multiple collector structures, the collector areas were made as large as possible by extending them under crossovers to maximize their speed. The results show that at low power the SCTL and the Schottky coupled structure with isolated collectors have about the same power delay. This is a result of the reduced voltage swing and low base collector capacitance. At high power the SCTL shows superior performance as expected from the performance of the ring oscillators.

The conventional I²L structure has a much higher power dissipation as a result of its larger voltage swing, higher capacitance, and higher downward current gain. In the high power region, it saturates at a much higher power and a lower frequency than the other two approaches. The maximum dividable frequencies are listed in Table II.

Table II clearly shows that even in a circuit application which is not optimal for demonstrating SCTL (only one gate with a fan-out greater than two and one gate a simple inverter), it still shows faster performance.

IV. CONCLUSION

In this correspondence, a comparison was made between the SCTL structure, the Schottky coupled structure with isolated collectors, and conventional I²L. All of the above structures were fabricated on a single chip so that a direct comparison could be made.

First the dc characteristics were presented, and simple calculations from the layout of a fan-out four gate showed that the SCTL structure had a higher upward current gain by 1.6 and a higher saturation current by 1.4 over the other two multiple collector structures. Then the emitter time constant was measured and it was found to be independent of the extrinsic base as a result of the rather thin epi layer.

These parameters were used in a computer model to predict the SCTL case and were slightly modified to predict the two other multiple collector structures. The results of both measured and predicted minimum delay of fan-out four ring oscillators of first and fourth collectors are presented. Very good correlation was found between measured and predicted results. It was shown that the SCTL structure was the fastest of the three structures, followed by the Schottky coupled structure with isolated collectors, and then the conventional double implanted I²L.

Finally, the results of an actual circuit were presented. This was a D-type flip-flop connected as a divide by two. Again, it was shown that the SCTL was the superior structure with a maximum dividable frequency of 17 MHz. It was again found that the Schottky coupled structure with isolated collectors was the second fastest, followed by the double implanted conventional I²L structure. This suggests that to design high-speed I²L circuits, one should use a combination of SCTL when routing allows the base contact on one end and the Schottky coupled structure with isolated collectors when it does not.

REFERENCES

[1] H. H. Berger and S. K. Wiedmann, "Advanced merged transistor logic by using Schottky junctions," Microelectronics, vol. 7, no. 3, pp. 35–42.

[2] F. W. Hewlett, Jr., "Schottky I²L," IEEE J. Solid-State Circuits, vol. SC-10, pp. 343–348, Oct. 1975.

[3] J. M. Herman, III, S. A. Evans, and B. J. Sloan, "Second generation I²L/MTL: A 20 ns process/structure," IEEE J. Solid-State Circuits, vol. SC-12, pp. 93–101, Apr. 1977.

[4] S. C. Blackstone and R. P. Mertens, "Modelling of Schottky coupled transistor logic," to be published.

[5] F. M. Klaassen, "Some considerations on high speed injection logic," IEEE J. Solid-State Circuits, vol. SC-12, pp. 150–154, Apr. 1977.

High Speed Integrated Injection Logic (I²L)

COR MULDER AND HENK E. J. WULMS

Abstract—High speed integrated injection logic (I²L) circuits can be manufactured in a process using oxide separation involving a very thin epitaxial layer and ion implantation. Following a description of the process, electronic improvements which decrease the charge storage in both the p-n-p and n-p-n transistor are discussed.

Analytic expressions are derived which show the consequences for the minority charge stored in the base of the n-p-n transistor and for the influences on the current noise margin. A tradeoff between noise margin and speed is then made. Besides the reduction in delay time, another attractive aspect of this approach is that it allows a simple layout design. By using separate p-n-p and n-p-n transistors, the position of the n-p-n transistors can be adapted to the logic wiring because there is no limitation in the number of crossovers.

Finally, some experimental results are given. A minimum value of the propagation delay time of 3 ns has been measured.

I. INTRODUCTION

PRESENT DAY integrated injection logic (I²L) structures show a high packing density and an excellent power-delay product. This is achieved by the combination of lateral p-n-p transistors and multicollector n-p-n structures operating in the inverse mode [1], [2]. In addition to this, the attraction of using standard bipolar processes has resulted in the I²L technique finding widespread application in the LSI field. But, I²L circuits realized with these conventional processes have serious limitations in high speed applications. In practical LSI circuits, the minimum propagation delay time of conventional I²L gates is about 40–100 ns [2]. This is too high for those I²L applications which must be competitive with high speed circuits, e.g., TTL.

In this paper a new approach is described which offers I²L circuits having the same power-delay product as the conventional structures, but with a minimum propagation delay time, which is about a factor of 10 smaller.

The propagation delay time τ is a function of the gate dissipation. At higher dissipation τ becomes nearly constant and reaches the minimum value τ_{min}, which is closely related to the f_T of the inverse operating n-p-n transistor [3]. Generally it can be said that τ_{min} is determined by minority charge stored in the following regions:

1) low doped n-epi emitter of the n-p-n transistor,
2) base of the n-p-n transistor,
3) base of the p-n-p transistor.

What essentially has been done in the high speed I²L approach is that the conventional I²L process has been changed in such a way that the above-mentioned charges have been reduced or eliminated.

Manuscript received November 19, 1975; revised February 11, 1976.
The authors are with the Philips Research Laboratories, Eindhoven, The Netherlands.

Contribution 1) has been eliminated by employing a very thin epitaxial layer (1.25 μm). The low doped n-epi emitter has been avoided by converting this thin layer into a p-type base layer. Here lies one of the main differences between this and the conventional I²L process, where the dope in the epitaxial layer determines the emitter storage, the largest contribution to the total stored charge.

The fact that a thin epitaxial layer is employed allows LOCOS (local oxidation of silicon) [4] to be used as separation. In addition to the general advantages of LOCOS, in this case it improves the ratio of collector and emitter area, which results in a better ratio of β_{up} and β_{down} of the n-p-n structure. Here the same designations for current gain (upward, downward) will be used as in [5] to avoid confusion with "forward" and "inverse."

To reduce contribution 2), the retarding field in the base in upward operating n-p-n transistors has been changed into an aiding field, using the technique of ion implantation.

With an electronic improvement, the charge stored in the base of the p-n-p transistor [contribution 3)] can be eliminated by separating this base region from the common emitter region of the n-p-n structure. However, to benefit fully from this improvement it is necessary to keep the n-p-n transistor out of saturation. This is simply done by putting a diode between the emitter and base of the multicollector n-p-n structure. Another disadvantage of the conventional I²L structure is the considerable effort that must be put into the design of large circuits. A double layer of interconnections gives some improvement, but it will be shown that in this approach a simple design system can be obtained by separating the gate into individual transistors. Then, the logic wiring can be implemented in the second interconnection layer as single vertical strips.

The remarks above clearly illustrate that the manufacture of fast I²L circuits requires a new process. An extensive description of a suggested new process is given here. The impact of the electronic improvements on current noise margin, speed, and topology is also discussed. In addition, some experimental data are presented.

II. PROCESS CHARACTERIZATION

As stated previously, high speed I²L requires a more sophisticated manufacturing process than conventional I²L. Fig. 1 shows the cross-sectional view of the new p-n-p and n-p-n structure with an n⁺-type substrate, which acts as the common emitter for all n-p-n transistors and as the base for all p-n-p transistors. The process starts with the growth of a thin n-type epitaxial layer upon this substrate. This allows the size of the p-n-p and n-p-n transistors to be defined with the aid of the

Reprinted from *IEEE J. Solid-State Circuits*, vol. SC-11, pp. 379–385, June 1976.

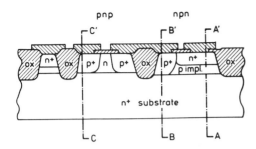

Fig. 1. Cross-sectional view of new I^2L structure. In the n-p-n zone, the n-type epitaxial layer has been overdoped with a boron implantation, so that an aiding field in the base exists when the n^+ substrate acts as emitter. Impurity profiles of the cross sections AA', BB', and CC' are shown in Fig. 2.

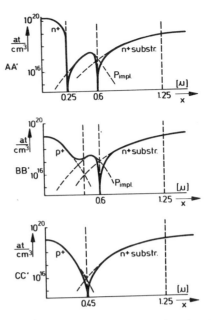

Fig. 2. Impurity profiles of the crosssections AA', BB', and CC' of the n-p-n and p-n-p structure of Fig. 1. Dashed lines indicate the concentrations due to implantation or diffusion. Drawn lines represent the net dope concentrations.

LOCOS technique. Thus, all parts of the n-type epitaxial layer outside the transistor regions are oxidized. In the next step the base of the n-p-n transistor is implemented.

Only in the n-p-n zones is the n-type epitaxial layer converted into p-type with a boron implantation, with this being done in such a way that in upward direction an aiding field in the base exists. The heavily doped p^+ regions are then made, again with a boron implantation step. The emitter and collector regions of the p-n-p transistors, and simultaneously the base contact regions of the n-p-n transistors, are now defined. In the last step, the n^+ collector regions are made by an arsenic implantation. Impurity profiles of the p-n-p and n-p-n structures are indicated in Fig. 2.

It may be noticed that

1) the resistivity of the n-type epitaxial layer is chosen to meet the requirements for the p-n-p transistor only. It has no further impact on the storage in the n-p-n transistor because the n-type epitaxial layer is completely overdoped into p-type.

2) the p^+ regions must be heavily doped to ensure a good emitter efficiency of the p-n-p and a high β_{up} of the n-p-n transistor. The high β_{up} is a consequence of the fact that the emitter now injects current only in the base region situated under the collector.

III. SEPARATION OF p-n-p BASE AND n-p-n EMITTER REGIONS

Until now it has been supposed that the p-n-p base region is the same as the n-p-n emitter(s). This implies that the c-b junction of the p-n-p transistor is always connected in parallel with the e-b junction of the n-p-n transistor.

This parallel connection has a big disadvantage at high currents: when the n-p-n transistor is conducting, the p-n-p transistor is in saturation. The minority charge in this saturated transistor is mainly stored in the low doped part of the base region, in this case the n-type epitaxial layer. Because the e-b voltage is constant, only the charge related to the c-b junction is of interest from the standpoint of speed. This switching charge is mentioned in the introduction as contribution 3). As has been explained, contribution 1) has been eliminated. Since 2), however, has been reduced, it is the charge in the p-n-p base region which now forms the obstacle to the obtainment of high speeds.

This part of the base storage can be eliminated completely when the p-n-p base is separated from the n-p-n emitter region and connected to a somewhat higher voltage. Then the c-b junction of the p-n-p transistor will be less forward biased. A voltage difference $\Delta V = 200$ mV will be sufficient because the charge involved will then be reduced by a factor of 2000 [$\approx \exp(0.2/(kT/q))$]. The separation can be easily realized by starting from a p-type substrate and, with the aid of an extra mask, making discrete n^+ buried layers. This is illustrated in Fig. 3.

The p-n-p transistor now acts as a real current source, supplying the same dc current at the input of each inverter, independent of the logic condition. However, this will not result directly in a faster device, because the n-p-n transistors will now come more into saturation and the base storage in the n-p-n transistor will increase considerably. It is necessary to take additional measures to limit this charge storage. As is shown in the following section this can be done in a controlled way by connecting a small diode in parallel with the e-b junction of the n-p-n transistors.

IV. EFFECT OF PARALLEL DIODE ON BASE STORAGE OF n-p-n TRANSISTORS

This effect will be discussed using the inverter circuit shown in Fig. 4. Due to the separation of the p-n-p base from the n-p-n emitter, the p-n-p transistors at input and output can be represented by simple constant current sources I. As an n-p-n model, the dc Gummel model [6], [7] has been used in its simplest form.

The currents in the saturated n-p-n transistor are

$$I_{up} = I_o(e^{qV_{BE}/kT} - 1)$$
$$I_{down} = I_o(e^{qV_{BC}/kT} - 1) \tag{1}$$

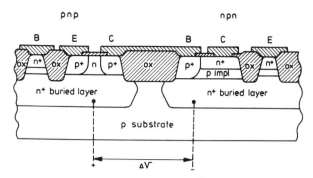

Fig. 3. Cross-sectional view of separated I^2L structure. Discrete n^+ buried layers must be used in order to separate the p-n-p base from the n-p-n emitter. In this case it is necessary to interconnect the collector of the p-n-p transistor and the base of the n-p-n transistor with an aluminum strip. To keep the p-n-p transistor out of saturation, a voltage difference ΔV must be applied between the two n^+ buried layers.

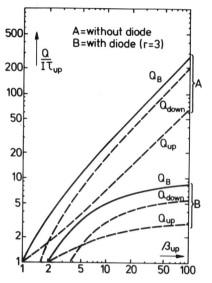

Fig. 5. Base storage of n-p-n transistor as a function of β_{up}. Q_{up} = storage due to forward biased e-b junction; Q_{down} = storage due to forward biased c-b junction; $Q_B = Q_{up} + Q_{down}$ = total base storage. Cases A and B correspond with the two cases indicated in Fig. 4. $\beta_{down} = 2 \beta_{up}$ and $\tau_{down} = 5 \tau_{up}$.

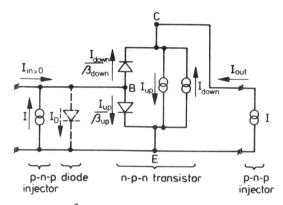

Fig. 4. High speed I^2L inverter model used for calculation of the base storage Q_B of the n-p-n transistor. For the n-p-n transistor, the Gummel model has been used and the p-n-p transistor is represented by a current source. Two cases must be distinguished: *Case A:* without diode; and *Case B:* with parallel diode at the input (indicated by dashed lines). The diode is realized by short-circuiting the c-b junction of an n-p-n transistor.

where I_o is the saturation current, which is equal in both equations. These currents are pure injection currents controlled by the forward biased e-b and c-b junctions, respectively.

Recombination effects in the various n- and p-type regions result in the following base currents:

$$I_{Bup} = I_{up}/\beta_{up}; \quad I_{Bdown} = I_{down}/\beta_{down} \qquad (2)$$

which are represented in the model by loss diodes.

Case A: Without Diode

From (1) and (2) the currents I_{up} and I_{down} can be solved as functions of I with the aid of the boundary conditions at input and output, which are, respectively,

$$I = I_{Bup} + I_{Bdown} \qquad (3)$$

$$I = I_{up} - I_{down} (1 + 1/\beta_{down}). \qquad (4)$$

Both currents contribute to the total base charge as follows:

$$Q_B = \tau_{up} \cdot I_{up} + \tau_{down} \cdot I_{down} = Q_{up} + Q_{down} \qquad (5)$$

where τ_{up} and τ_{down} are the base transit times in upward and downward direction, respectively.

The charges Q_B, Q_{up}, and Q_{down} are shown as a function of β_{up} in Fig. 5, where the assumption is made that $\tau_{down} = 5 \tau_{up}$ and $\beta_{down} = 2 \beta_{up}$. These calculated results are normalized to $\tau_{up} I$. It can be concluded from Fig. 5 that, due to the aiding field ($\tau_{up} < \tau_{down}$), the contribution of Q_{down} to the total base storage Q_B is very large, especially in the range for high values of β_{up}, where the transistor is heavy in saturation.

Case B: With Parallel Diode at the Input

The influence on Q_B of the parallel diode at the input will now be discussed. This diode is indicated by dashed lines in Fig. 4. The diode is obtained by short-circuiting the c-b junction of an n-p-n transistor. If r is the ratio of the collector area of the n-p-n transistor in the inverter and the diode (collector) area, then the diode current I_D can be expressed as

$$I_D = (I_{up} + I_{Bup}) \cdot \frac{1}{r} = I_{up} \left(1 + \frac{1}{\beta_{up}}\right) \cdot \frac{1}{r}. \qquad (6)$$

This means that (3), which describes the input condition, is now changed into

$$I = I_D + I_{Bup} + I_{Bdown} = I_D + \frac{I_{up}}{\beta_{up}} + \frac{I_{down}}{\beta_{down}}. \qquad (7)$$

In this case the currents I_{up} and I_{down} are reduced considerably, because the diode limits the effective upward current gain in the inverter to the area ratio r.

To illustrate the influence of the diode on the base charge, base charges Q_B, Q_{up}, and Q_{down} are depicted in Fig. 5 for the case $r = 3$. The conclusion is obvious: a small diode at the input is very effective in decreasing Q_B, and the propagation delay time will decrease accordingly. A disadvantage is that the current noise margin will also decrease. This is discussed in the next section.

V. RELATIVE CURRENT NOISE MARGIN

Since an I^2L inverter is fundamentally a current switch, it is better to express the noise margin in currents rather than in voltages. In the case of conventional I^2L, the calculation of current noise margin is complicated by the back-injection effect in the p-n-p transistor. In the present case, with separated p-n-p transistor and added parallel diode, the calculation is straightforward; this is because the p-n-p transistors supply equal and constant currents at each inverter input. For the sake of simplicity, spreads in transistor parameters, etc., will be disregarded.

The relative current noise margin N_c is defined in an infinite chain of identical inverters, as shown in Fig. 6. I_N is the maximum possible noise current source which can be connected to each input/output node, given that the logic states of the inverters do not change. The worst case situation is that, at the input of the inverter m, which is in the "ON" state, I_N tends to switch this inverter off. So the base current I_B is decreased from I to $I - I_N$. At the output I_N has the opposite direction, tending to switch inverter $m + 1$ to the "ON" state. This implies that the collector current of transistor T_1 in inverter m must have a minimum value of $I + I_N$ to keep inverter $m + 1$ in the "OFF" state. I_N can be calculated by making up the current balance at the input of inverter m:

$$I_B = I - I_N = I_{B1} + I_D + \sum_{k=2}^{n} I_{Bk}. \tag{8}$$

These terms can be determined as follows.

1) In the worst case situation, transistor T_1 is just out of saturation. Thus, for T_1: $I_{up} = I + I_N$ and $I_{down} = 0$. The base current I_{B1} is then

$$I_{B1} = \frac{I + I_N}{\beta_{up}}. \tag{9}$$

2) The diode current I_D is equal to the emitter current of T_1 divided by the collector area ratio r. Hence,

$$I_D = (I + I_N) \left(1 + \frac{1}{\beta_{up}}\right) \cdot \frac{1}{r}. \tag{10}$$

3) In an actual logic network the collector currents of the "load" transistors T_k ($k = 2, \cdots, n$) are in the worst case situation zero [1]. Then, for these transistors: $I_{down} = I_{up} = I + I_N$, because all transistors in inverter m are identical. Hence,

$$\sum_{k=2}^{n} I_{Bk} = (n - 1)(I + I_N) \left(\frac{1}{\beta_{up}} + \frac{1}{\beta_{down}}\right). \tag{11}$$

The *relative current noise margin* N_c is defined as the ratio of I_N and the nominal injector current I. Substitution of (9), (10), and (11) into (8) allows N_c to be calculated. Results are presented in Fig. 7 as a function of β_{up}, with $\beta_{down}/\beta_{up} = 2$ for different values of r and n. It can be seen that current noise margin increases, taking a higher value of r. So the extra

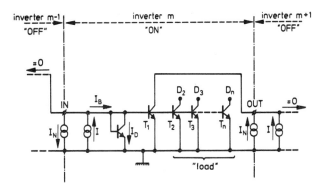

Fig. 6. Definition of relative current noise margin $N_c = I_N/I$. I_N is the maximum possible noise current source which can be connected to each input/output node, so that the logic states of the inverters do not change.

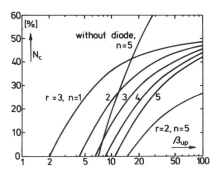

Fig. 7. Relative current noise margin N_c versus β_{up}, with the number of n-p-n transistors in one gate n and collector area ratio r as parameters.

diode at the input, which reduces the base storage, decreases the noise margin considerably. A tradeoff has to be made between noise margin and speed. In practice a value $r = 3$ is a good compromise.

The current noise margin can also be determined from the current transfer characteristic of a single inverter, in the same way as is usually done for voltage noise margins [8]. As shown in Fig. 8, N_c is the side of the maximum square which can be drawn between this calculated curve and its image. In this case, the transistor model is extended with parasitic series resistances. At this current level these parasitic resistances decrease N_c (compare with Fig. 7). However, the series resistances, if put in the correct place, can also serve to increase the current noise margin. This is demonstrated in Fig. 8 too, where a resistor R is added in series with the diode, resulting in a more bent transfer characteristic, and thus in a larger value of N_c.

VI. TOPOLOGY

The process allows different layout structures. To show the impact on the topology two extreme versions will be compared, namely, a conventionally designed structure (A) and a design optimized to speed (B). For each version a schematic layout of the same circuit was designed, and this is shown in Figs. 9 and 10, respectively.

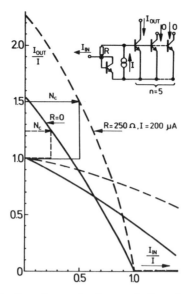

Fig. 8. Determination of current noise margin from the calculated current transfer characteristic. The drawn lines represent the case in which the resistor in series with the diode is 0. $R = 250 \ \Omega$ is represented by the dashed lines. $I = 200 \ \mu A$, $\beta_{up} = 40$, and $\beta_{down} = 80$.

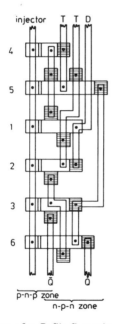

Fig. 9. Schematic layout of a D flip-flop using one layer of interconnection. For nearly all gates the base region is extended to allow crossover. (● = contact hole.)

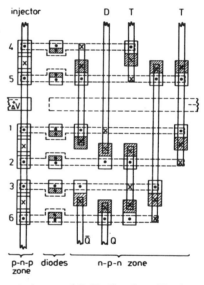

Fig. 10. Schematic layout of D flip-flop from Fig. 9. p-n-p and n-p-n transistors are separated and a diode is added at the input of each gate. A double layer of interconnection is used. (● = contact hole to first metallization layer. x = contact hole to second metallization layer.)

A. Version with Conventionally Designed I^2L Structures

The structure is about the same as for conventional I^2L, but the deep n^+ region is replaced by oxide and the position of the collectors is such that there exists a low ohmic connection between the base contact and the collector region in order to limit the base series resistance (Fig. 9). The advantages of this approach are as follows: the process is simple because one common n^+ substrate and one layer of metallization can be used; and the number of contact holes and implanted regions is minimized. Nevertheless, the designing of large circuits de-

mands much effort; this is because it is not easy to optimize the logic wiring. Moreover, the number of crossovers is limited, because each crossover increases the base area, resulting in an increase of the base series resistance and a decreasing value of β_{up}.

B. Version Optimized to Speed

The I^2L inverter consists of separate transistors (Fig. 10). The p-n-p is connected in the first metallization layer (dashed lines) to the n-p-n base regions and to a diode. This diode is an n-p-n structure which can be made smaller than the transistors, which are designed with minimum dimensions, because the short-circuited base–collector regions of the diode do not need separate contact holes. To guarantee that all n-p-n transistors operate at the same current level (0.1–0.5 mA), parasitic voltage drops must be avoided. Metal strips (indicated --) are therefore positioned at regular intervals, so ensuring good contact with the n^+ buried layer. In the same row contact has been made with the base of the p-n-p transistor (indicated -- + ΔV). This n^+ buried layer is connected to a ΔV higher voltage than in the common n-p-n emitter region to keep the p-n-p transistor out of saturation.

The logic wiring can be implemented in the second layer as single vertical strips (drawn lines). The position of the n-p-n transistor can be adapted to this wiring. The main feature of this approach is that the interconnecting pattern is simple. There is no limitation with respect to the number of crossovers. Simple design systems are therefore applicable.

The disadvantages are obvious. The number of contact holes has been increased. The process needs separated n^+ buried layers and has been extended with a second interconnection layer. It can be concluded that, although the inverters are much larger, the overall packing density increases to a lesser extent; this is because the inverters now incorporate a large part of the chip interconnections.

VII. EXPERIMENTAL RESULTS

The process outlined in Section II makes possible the manufacture of an almost symmetrical n-p-n transistor having a high value of β_{up} as well as β_{down}. The lateral p-n-p transistors must have sufficient emitter length to avoid high injection effects. Due to the thin epitaxial layer, only the sidewall component of the shallow p^+ regions is effective. Ring oscillators consisting of nine gates have been used to measure the propagation delay time τ.

On *homogeneous* n^+ *substrates* the following results have been obtained.

1) n-p-n transistors: $\beta_{up} \approx \beta_{down}$ ranging from 50 to 200 for collector currents up to 1 mA.

2) p-n-p transistors (60-μm emitter length, 4-μm base width on masks): $\alpha \geqslant 0.7$ for collector currents up to 100 μA.

3) For conventionally designed I^2L structures as described in Section VI-A, $\tau_{min} = 9$ ns (f.o. = 1) has been observed for transistors with a collector area of 270 μm^2. The speed-power product of this ring oscillator is 0.8 pJ/gate.

4) The addition of a parallel diode ($r = 2$) in this conventionally designed oscillator as suggested in [9] shows no speed improvement. On the contrary, τ_{min} decreases by 10 percent and the rings operate over a smaller current range. This is due to the fact that the current noise margin is reduced by two effects: by the parallel diode, as discussed at length in Section V, and by the recollection current to the injector (back injection) from the forward biased b–c junction of the p-n-p transistor. These two effects decrease the effective β_{up} of the n-p-n transistor. The reduction of β_{up} by increasing the lateral p-n-p base width has been proposed in [10].

Separated n^+ *buried layers* on p-type substrates have yielded the following results.

TABLE I
PROPAGATION DELAY TIME τ IN ns AS A FUNCTION OF p-n-p COLLECTOR CURRENT I, MEASURED IN 4 RING OSCILLATORS WITH DIFFERENT n-p-n COLLECTOR AREA AND FAN-OUT

	ΔV = 200 mV			
	Without diode ($r = \infty$)			diode ($r = 2$)
I (μA)	$A_c = 90\ \mu m^2$ f.o. = 1	$\cdot 210\ \mu m^2$ 3	$420\ \mu m^2$ 1	$420\ \mu m^2$ 1
28	14	75	35	30
120	5	15	11	9
350	3	8	6	5

1) Current gain factor β_{up} was rather low (10 to 20). This is marginal, but it allows some conclusions to be drawn.

2) Increasing the p-n-p base voltage from 0 to 200 mV with respect to the n-p-n emitter at constant p-n-p emitter currents gives the following results:

    a) a doubling of the p-n-p collector current I,

    b) a speed improvement of 20 percent ($0.1 < I < 0.4$ mA),

    c) a reduction of τ_{min} from 7 to 6 ns.

This speed improvement, due solely to the fact that the p-n-p transistor no longer comes into saturation, is the result of two opposite effects, namely, the elimination of the switching charge in the p-n-p [contribution 3)], and the elimination of the back injection by the p-n-p collector. Elimination of the back injection increases the effective β_{up}, resulting in a heavier n-p-n saturation.

3) Table I sets out typical results of the propagation delay time τ for ring oscillators with different collector area and fan-out, at $\Delta V = 200$ mV.

4) In the same table the influence of a parallel diode ($r = 2$) can be seen. A significant speed improvement has not been observed, partly due to the low β_{up} values. Here as well, however, two opposite effects apply, namely, the speed improvement gained by limiting the total base charge is partly cancelled by the fact that the discharge time of the base is longer in consequence of the reduced forward current gain.

5) The ring oscillators equipped with diodes ($r = 2$) did not operate at $\Delta V = 0$, because no current noise margin remains at these low β_{up} values.

Another important parameter to be discussed is the power-delay product. As has been stated, for the emitter-base junction of the n-p-n transistor there are now high doped regions on both sides of the junction. This results in a higher capacitance/unit area compared with the conventional process. However, using LOCOS, the sidewall capacitances may be ignored and this passive isolation allows smaller transistor geometries. The result is a power-delay product of 0.2 pJ for the smallest transistor structure.

VIII. CONCLUSIONS

With separated p-n-p transistors equal and constant currents are supplied to the inverter inputs, a fact which may be of interest from the standpoint of multivalue logic and other applications. The method yields some speed improvement and an increase in current noise margin.

In the separated version the addition of a small parallel diode gives some speed improvement too, but the p-n-p transistors must have high β values to guarantee sufficient current noise margin at a reasonable fan-out.

Finally, it can be said that designing the layout is easier. Using the double layer of interconnections, as in Fig. 10, the logic wiring consists only of vertical strips and the position of the n-p-n transistors can be adapted to this wiring. This is possible because there is no limitation on the number of crossovers. Through the use of separate n-p-n transistors instead of the multicollector structure, β_{up} is made independent of the number of crossovers, which is an advantage compared to the conventional approach, where each crossover reduces β_{up}.

ACKNOWLEDGMENT

The authors wish to thank P. de Haan and J. A. A. van Gils for processing the slices, and W. A. Jurgens for measurement assistance.

REFERENCES

[1] H. H. Berger and S. K. Wiedman, "Merged-transistor logic—A low cost bipolar logic concept," *IEEE J. Solid-State Circuits*, vol. SC-7, pp. 340–345, Oct. 1972.

[2] K. Hart and A. Slob, "Integrated injection logic: A new approach to LSI," *IEEE J. Solid-State Circuits*, vol. SC-7, pp. 346–351, Oct. 1972.

[3] F. M. Klaassen, "Device physics of integrated injection logic," *IEEE Trans. Electron Devices*, vol. ED-22, pp. 145–152, Mar. 1975.

[4] E. Kooi and J. A. Appels, "Selective oxidation of silicon and its device applications," *Semiconductor Silicon*, pp. 860–879, 1973.

[5] H. H. Berger and S. K. Wiedmann, "Terminal oriented model for merged transistor logic (MTL)," *IEEE J. Solid-State Circuits*, vol. SC-9, pp. 211–217, Oct. 1974.

[6] H. K. Gummel, "A charge control relation for bipolar transistors," *Bell Syst. Tech. J.*, pp. 115–120, Jan. 1970.

[7] H. K. Gummel and H. C. Poon, "An integral charge control model of bipolar transistors," *Bell Syst. Tech. J.*, pp. 827–851, May–June 1970.

[8] C. F. Hill, "Noise margin and noise immunity in logic circuits," *Microelectronics*, vol. 1, no. 5, pp. 16–21, Apr. 1968.

[9] M. I. Elmasry, "Nonsaturated integrated injection logic," *Electron. Lett.*, vol. 11, no. 3, pp. 63–64, Feb. 1975.

[10] H. H. Berger, "The injection model—A structure oriented model for merged transistor logic (MTL)," *IEEE J. Solid-State Circuits*, vol. SC-9, pp. 218–227, Oct. 1974.

A New High Speed I²L Structure

BRUCE B. ROESNER AND DENIS J. McGREIVY

Abstract—A new improved I^2L structure is discussed which has been shown to operate at high speeds with large fan-out capabilities while retaining low power operation. The new "up-diffused" structure is fabricated in such a fashion that Schottky diodes can be readily incorporated. With the addition of Schottky clamps between the collector and base of the n-p-n switching transistor, gate delays as low as 2.5 ns have been achieved.

LIST OF SYMBOLS

C	Capacitance (farads).
D_n	Electron diffusion constant in the base (cm²/s).
D_p	Hole diffusion constant in the emitter (cm²/s).
I_n	Emitter electron current (A).
I_p	Emitter hole current (A).
L_n	Diffusion length for electrons in the base (cm).
L_p	Diffusion length for holes in emitter (cm).
N_{AB}	Acceptor impurity density of the base region (cm⁻³).
N_{DE}	Donor impurity density of the emitter region (cm⁻³).
q	Magnitude of electronic charge (C).
V	Voltage (V).
W_B	Base thickness (cm).
γ	Emitter efficiency.
ϕ_B	Schottky barrier height (eV).

Manuscript received August 26, 1976; revised November 30, 1976.
The authors are with the Hughes Aircraft Company, Newport Beach, CA 92663.

INTRODUCTION

INTEGRATED injection logic (I²L) [1] or merged transistor logic (MTL) [2] is fast becoming a major digital circuit technique due to its high packing density and very low power

Reprinted from *IEEE J. Solid-State Circuits*, vol. SC-12, pp. 114–118, Apr. 1977.

dissipation. To date, I²L circuits have achieved only medium speed operation (gate delays greater than 10 ns). However, improvements in the basic structure allow I²L to seriously challenge high speed technologies such as Schottky TTL and even ECL while retaining its advantage of very low power operation. This paper describes two important aspects which, when considered, allow high speed I²L operation: 1) optimization of the doping profile of the vertical n-p-n transistor and 2) utilization of Schottky diode contacts.

An I²L gate, shown in Fig. 1, is composed of a p-n-p transistor. With a logic state "1" on the gate input (base of the n-p-n), a logic "0" occurs at the output (collector of the n-p-n). The maximum voltage drop across the gate is of the order of only 0.7 ~ 0.8 V, occurring across the forward-biased emitter-base junction of the p-n-p transistor. The standard I²L gate structure is fabricated by diffusing, or ion implanting, two adjacent p-type regions into an n-type silicon wafer, then diffusing a smaller, heavily doped n⁺ region into one of the p regions, as shown in Fig. 1(b). In this structure, the p regions form the emitter and collector of the p-n-p transistor, the n substrate acts as both the p-n-p base region and the n-p-n emitter region, and the n⁺ region acts as the n-p-n collector or output. It is the physical merging of the p-n-p device into the n-p-n and the absence of a top surface contact hole for the common p-n-p base and n-p-n emitter regions which yields the very high packing density characteristic of I²L circuits. To achieve I²L action, the common emitter current gain β of the n-p-n transistor must be greater than unity. Although this criteria is easily satisfied, the structure of Fig. 1(b) will not yield a high speed I²L gate. Since the function of the n-p-n device is to switch the logic state appearing at the base input for high speed operation, it is necessary that this transistor exhibit a short switching time. From an inspection of the n-p-n transistor doping profile, shown in Fig. 2(a), one readily recognizes several factors which inhibit high speed operation. First, since the n-type substrate is of lower doping concentration, N_{DE}, than the diffused p-base concentration, N_{AB}, this results in a low value for the emitter (substrate) injection

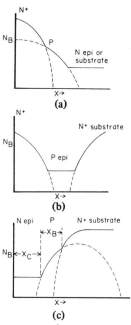

Fig. 2. n-p-n doping profiles for I²L structures. (a) Standard down-diffused. (b) p-epi base. (c) Up-diffused.

efficiency γ:

$$\gamma = \left[1 + \frac{D_p N_{AB} L_n}{D_N N_{DE} L_p} \tanh\left(\frac{W_B}{L_n}\right)\right]^{-1} \ll 1.$$

Also, a large capacitance and low breakdown voltage will exist at the collector–base junction because of the high n⁺ collector concentration.

Some improvement in the speed–power characteristics of I²L has been realized by growing a p-epi layer on an n⁺ substrate [3], [4], resulting in the n-p-n transistor doping profile shown in Fig. 2(b). A serious disadvantage of this structure is that the n-p-n base width is dependent upon the thickness variations in the p-epi layer. These thickness variations, typically $\pm 0.1\ \mu$, become important when fabricating submicron base widths.

The approach taken by these authors, and suggested by others [4], is to form a p-diffusion or implant into selected regions of the Sb-doped substrate ($\sim 10^{19}/cm^3$) prior to n-epi growth. During the n-epi growth ($\sim 1.0\ \Omega \cdot cm, \sim 1.4\ \mu$) and subsequent heat treatments, the p-type (boron) buried layer "up-diffuses" into the n-epi film, resulting in the profile shown in Fig. 2(c). A subsequent p⁺ diffusion forms both the injector and an annular top surface, low resistivity contact to the buried p-base region. With this up-diffused process, an improved n-p-n transistor doping profile is achieved which has: 1) a high emitter injection efficiency, 2) an aiding diffusion field in the graded p-base region, 3) a low collector capacitance, and 4) an improved collector–base breakdown voltage. A significant advantage of this structure is that the n-p-n emitter and base regions are formed from a single reference plane (the substrate–epi interface). The n-p-n base width, typically $0.4\ \mu$, is now independent of the n-epi film thickness, and variations in the epi thickness affect only the collector series resistance. Although the p-base region may also be formed by ion implanting boron through the n-epi film [5],

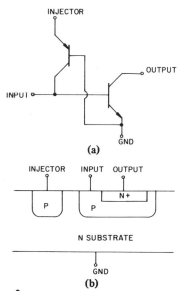

Fig. 1. I²L gate. (a) Schematic. (b) Cross section.

variations in the epi thickness will result in variations in base width and doping profile relative to the n^+ emitter (substrate) profile. In addition, if a thick epi film ($>1.5 \mu$) is required for the fabrication of other structures (e.g., TTL or ECL) on the same chip, extremely high energy (>500 keV) boron implants are required for the p-type base. Not only are the high energy implants difficult to achieve, but the width of the implanted p region increases, thereby increasing the base width, as the implant energy increases.

A second important consideration in optimizing the speed-power characteristics of I^2L circuits is the use of Schottky diode contacts. These devices can serve two purposes. First, if Schottky contacts are formed on the lightly doped n-epi collector [6], [7], as shown in Fig. 3(a), multiple fan-out is achieved. Not only does the presence of the Schottky barrier diode at each collector contact provide isolation between different collectors, but the Schottkys also reduce the capacitance, thereby reducing the power-delay product, PDP, where

$$PDP = CV^2.$$

A second Schottky diode may be used as a clamp between the base and the collector [3], as shown in Fig. 3(b). Schottky clamps reduce the "hard" forward biasing of both the base-emitter and collector-base junctions, resulting in less charge buildup, which allows for faster operation of the gate. Also, power consumption is reduced since the Schottky clamps decrease the voltage swing. It should be noted that the simultaneous usage of Schottky diodes for isolation (D_1) and clamps (D_2) requires careful choice of the metals used since the barrier height of D_1 (ϕ_{B1}) must be less than the barrier height of D_2 (ϕ_{B2}) in order for an I^2L circuit to operate. The difference in the two barrier heights determines the collector voltage swing, ΔV, where

$$\Delta V = q (\phi_{B2} - \phi_{B1}).$$

$I-V$ curves of the two Schottky's used in this work, titanium ($\phi_B = 0.53$ eV) and Al/(2 percent) Si ($\phi_B = 0.74$ eV), are

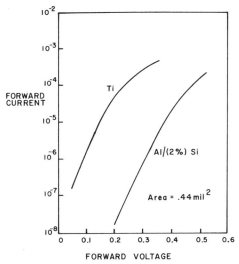

Fig. 4. $I-V$ curves for titanium and aluminum/(2 percent) silicon Schottky diodes.

presented in Fig. 4. Such a difference in barrier heights represents a voltage swing of 0.21 V. Both Schottkys were found to be of high reliability, with changes in barrier height of less than 0.025 eV after 500 h of life test at 250°C.

FABRICATION

Fabrication of the up-diffused structure in conjunction with double Schottky is simpler than would first appear. The first process step is to oxidize an n^+ (Sb) wafer, then mask for the p base and injector, followed by a light p diffusion or implant. The oxide is then removed and an n-epi is grown (see Fig. 5), at which time the p material "up-diffuses" into the n-epi film. An oxide is grown on the n-epi, then a p^+ deposition in selected areas forms contacts to the injector and active p-base region as well as serving to isolate the n^+ emitter and collector regions. Contacts are then opened and the first metal, M_1, is deposited. After selectively removing M_1, a second metal, M_2, is deposited and again selectively etched. The number of masking steps up

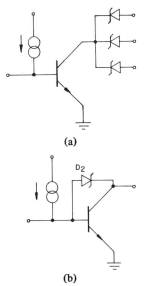

Fig. 3. I^2L structure with Schottky diodes. (a) Schottky collector for collector isolation. (b) Collector–base Schottky clamp.

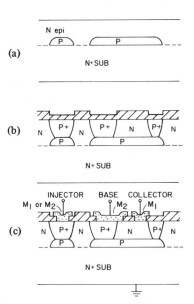

Fig. 5. Up-diffused process sequence. (a) After epi growth. (b) Following p^+ deposition. (c) Completed structure.

to and including contact is only three, while double Schottky requires an additional two masks. With overglass, the total number of masks required for the double Schottky up-diffused process is six, compared with five for standard I²L.

EXPERIMENTAL RESULTS

I²L transistors and 15-stage ring oscillators were fabricated using both the standard I²L and the new up-diffused I²L structures. These devices incorporated both single and double Schottky contacts and were processed using conventional contact photolithography, having an n-p-n emitter–base area of 0.66 mil² and a collector–base area of 0.2 mil². Typical *I-V* characteristics of the n-p-n transistors from both structures are displayed in Fig. 6(a) and (b). The value of $\beta_{\text{n-p-n}}$ is seen to increase from 12 for the standard I²L structure of Fig. 6(a) to 180 for the up-diffused structure of Fig. 6(b). One also observes an increase in the collector breakdown voltage. The substrate resistivity used in standard I²L fabrication affects these characteristics, as can be seen from the plots of $\beta_{\text{n-p-n}}$ versus breakdown voltage shown in Fig. 7.

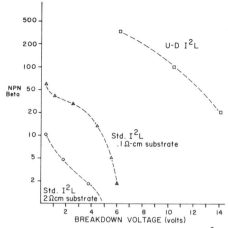

Fig. 7. Breakdown voltage versus n-p-n beta for various I²L structures.

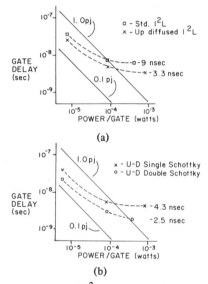

(a)

(b)

Fig. 8. Speed–power curves of I²L structures. (a) Standard versus up-diffused I²L. (b) Single Schottky versus double Schottky up-diffused I²L.

Ring oscillator measurements of power versus gate delay were then performed for both I²L structures. As seen in Fig. 8(a), the up-diffused process with Schottky diodes on the collector offers a considerable improvement over standard I²L in terms of reducing gate delays by a factor of almost 3 as well as reducing the power dissipation per gate. Further improvements in speed and power were realized when the base–collector clamped Schottky was incorporated into the up-diffused I²L

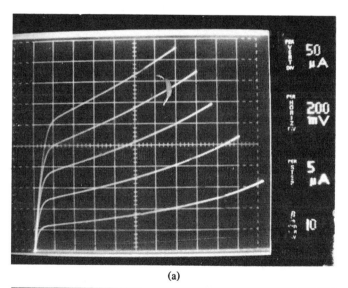

(a)

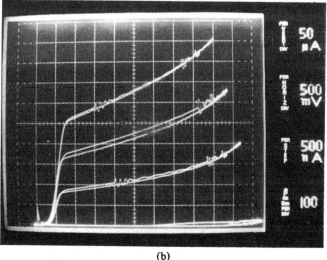

(b)

Fig. 6. *I-V* characteristic curves of standard I²L and up-diffused I²L transistors. (a) Standard I²L. (b) Up-diffused I²L.

TABLE I

STRUCTURE	(NORMALIZED)	
	PDP	MINIMUM GATE DELAY
Standard I²L	1	1
Up-Diffused I²L–Single Schottky on Collector	.62	.36
Up-Diffused I²L–Double Schottky	.45	.21

structure, as shown in Fig. 8(b). Gate delays as low as 2.5 ns were achieved on the double Schottky structures.

Table I compares the power–delay products and minimum gate delays (in normalized form) for each of the structures investigated.

CONCLUSIONS

Two important aspects for improving I^2L characteristics have been investigated—doping profile optimization of the vertical n-p-n transistor and the addition of Schottky diodes. The doping profile obtained by the up-diffused process produced a number of improvements over standard I^2L.

1) Higher n-p-n transistor betas for greater fan-out and drive capabilities.

2) Higher n-p-n transistor breakdown voltages for ease in interfacing with other technologies whether on or off chip.

3) Reduced power consumption.

4) Reduced minimum gate delay.

5) Capability by which Schottky diodes can be fabricated on the n-p-n transistor.

Schottky diodes further improved the I^2L characteristics by

1) reducing the power consumption,

2) reducing the minimum gate delay,

3) isolation of multiple outputs (Schottky diodes on the collectors).

It has been shown that double Schottky up-diffused I^2L structures with standard ($5\ \mu$) geometries can produce gate delays of 2.5 ns and PDP's of 0.2 pJ. This is by no means optimized, as further improvements can be expected by reducing the transistor geometry, further improving the doping profile during epi growth, and incorporating oxide isolation.

REFERENCES

[1] K. Hart and A. Slob, "Integrated injection logic: A new approach to LSI," *IEEE J. Solid-State Circuits*, vol. SC-7, pp. 346–351, Oct. 1972.

[2] H. H. Berger and S. K. Wiedmann, "Merged transistor logic (MTL)— A low-cost bipolar logic concept," *IEEE J. Solid-State Circuits*, vol. SC-7 pp. 340–346, Oct. 1972.

[3] ——, "Schottky transistor logic," in *ISSCC Dig. Tech. Papers*, Feb. 1975, pp. 172–173.

[4] B. Cook, S. H. McNally, and A. San, "I^2L II," in *Int. Electron Devices Meeting Tech. Dig.*, Dec. 1975, pp. 284–287.

[5] S. A. Evans and J. S. Fu, "Application of a new, accurate bipolar simulator to correlate device performance to process selection," *Elec. Chem. Soc. Abstr.*, pp. 394–396.

[6] V. Blatt, P. S. Walsh, and L. W. Kennedy, "Substrate fed logic," *IEEE J. Solid-State Circuits*, vol. SC-10, pp. 336–342, Oct. 1975.

[7] F. W. Hewlett, Jr., "Schottky I^2L," *IEEE J. Solid-State Circuits*, vol. SC-10, pp. 343-348, Oct. 1975.

HIGH PERFORMANCE "UPWARD" BIPOLAR TECHNOLOGY FOR VLSI

J. Agraz-Guerena, R. L. Pritchett, and P. T. Panousis

Bell Telephone Laboratories, Incorporated

Allentown, Pennsylvania 18103

The high-speed performance of MTL/ I^2L (1,2) circuits is limited by the fundamental diffusion vs. depletion capacitance trade off in PN junctions. However, it has been shown that significant improvements over the possibilities of conventional technology are attainable through advanced lithography, (3) oxide isolation techniques, (4,5) or updiffused impurity profiles. (6) The structure described here is a novel combination of updiffused profiles (6) and oxide isolation that produces a device with excellent upward transistor properties and high-density, high-performance I^2L circuits.

Figure 1 shows a cross-section of an MTL/I^2L inverter. The active, upward npn profile is obtained by selectively implanting and diffusing boron into the substrate. The boron impurities diffuse into the n-type epitaxial layer ahead of the antimony from the n^+ buried layer to form the profile shown in Figure 2. This produces a high-efficiency emitter junction, a favorably graded base region, and a lightly doped collector. With the updiffused base profile, the structure is not sensitive to the epi layer thickness. The p^+ extrinsic base region is formed by diffusion and its profile, shown in Figure 2, is chosen for minimum storage.

Oxide isolation is an essential feature of this structure because it substantially reduces the size and capacitance of the devices and allows for a better extrinsic to intrinsic base area ratio. High-pressure, low-temperature oxidation (300 psi steam, 700°C) (7) makes this structure possible because the heat treatment associated with atmospheric pressure oxidation is incompatible with the desired updiffused base profile.

As shown in Figure 1, the p^+ extrinsic base diffusion is used to form the injector of the lateral PNP; the epitaxial doping determines the PNP base doping as well as the NPN collector doping. The updiffused base is omitted in the lateral PNP base region and in areas used as buried layer contact. The collector contact may be a Schottky diode for Schottky I^2L (8) or an Ohmic contact. The latter is formed by preceding the silicide with a shallow, low dose donor implant. The contribution of a phosphorus implant is shown in Figure 2.

An isolated upward transistor that can be used as a general purpose device is shown in Figure 3, in this case the updiffused base serves as a channel stop between buried layers under the isolating oxide. The transistor of Figure 3 is minimum geometry in the x-direction and nominally 10 times minimum in the y-direction. This device is a four terminal device since the emitter-substrate junction collects holes injected downward by the intrinsic and extrinsic base. Figure 4 shows typical I_C, I_B, and $-I_S$ vs. V_{BE} for this transistor. Bulk recombination is a small effect and, to first order, the current densities are predicted by total majority charge in the layers involved.

The four terminal composite device can be modeled as a discrete updiffused NPN transistor and a low gain substrate PNP transistor connected as shown in Figure 5. Although it is heavily doped, the buried layer serves as the base of this PNP device, while the intrinsic and p^+ extrinsic NPN base regions form the emitter.

With this model an analysis can be made of minority carrier storage as measured by the emitter time constant τ_E. Figure 6 shows a plot of τ_E vs. $(\beta_U)^{-1}$. According to the injection model (9) the contributions to τ_E by the several injection phenomena can be summarized by:

$$\tau_E = \tau_i + \frac{\tau_e}{\beta_U}$$

where τ_i is the upward transit time through the intrinsic base and τ_e is the composite time constant of electrons stored in the extrinsic base and holes in the buried layer. A least square

Reprinted from *IEEE Int. Electron Devices Meeting Digest Tech. Papers*, Dec. 1978, pp. 209–212.

error fit to these data yields τ_i = 169 ps and τ_e = 15.7 ns. These results indicate that in an upward transistor of $\beta_U \sim 100$ the intrinsic transit time contributes $\sim 50\%$ of τ_E. The device in Figure 3 exhibits a peak f_T of 500 MHz, while a ring dot structure, which maximizes the ratio of intrinsic to extrinsic base area, shows values in excess of 900 MHz, approaching the theoretical maximum of 1 GHz indicated by the value of τ_i above.

Several I²L circuits were fabricated to evaluate the upward structure. For experimental purposes some of the I²L circuits employed the "High Speed I²L" approach of Mulder and Wulms, (5) where the base of the PNP injector is separated from the grounded NPN emitter and its potential lifted above ground. This keeps the injectors out of saturation, but we found that only on circuits with speeds below 3 ns was this an important factor. For most practical circuits a common buried layer for all regions is satisfactory. Retained from this approach, however, was the technique of interconnecting NPN bases with a 2nd level metal path. Figure 7 illustrates this for a FO = 6 circuit. This minimizes the area of the p⁺ extrinsic bases and thus minimizes capacitance and improves both f_T and beta.

Figure 8 and Table I summarize the results of 25 stage ring oscillators obtained for various I²L circuits and for a 51 stage ring oscillator of NTL inverters, (10) a non-saturating circuit shown in Figure 9 which illustrates the range of application for the up-transistor. The FO = 2 circuits use the layout of Figure 10 where an extended extrinsic base region is shared by the two collectors. These circuits were fabricated using 5 μm design rules and standard photolithographic techniques. The performance of 2.8 ns in the FO = 1 I²L circuit and the 1.7 ns NTL circuit indicate the high level of performance that can be achieved with this upward transistor. The breakdown voltages, current handling capability, and Schottky diodes are virtually the same to that of conventional buried collector structures, therefore high-performance interface and low voltage analog circuits can be supported.

TABLE I

SUMMARY OF TEST CIRCUIT PERFORMANCE

Circuit Type	$I \cdot \tau$ @ 1 μA	Near Minimum τ	Minimum τ
1. I²L, FO = 1	75 fc	3.1 ns @ 90 μA	2.8 ns
2. I²L, FO = 2	180 fc	7.5 ns @ 130 μA	6.8 ns
3. Schottky I²L, FO = 2	95 fc	7.7 ns @ 40 μA	6.9 ns
4. "High Speed I²L", FO = 6	280 fc	7.6 ns @ 170 μA	6.9 ns
5. NTL Inverters		1.7 ns @ 70 μA/cell	

REFERENCES

(1) H. H. Berger and S. K. Wiedman, "Merged Transistor Logic (MTL)--A Low Cost Bipolar Circuit Concept", IEEE J. of Solid State Circuits, Vol. SC-7, pp. 340-346, October, 1972.

(2) K. Hart and A. Slob, "Integrated Injection Logic: A New Approach to LSI", IEEE J. of Solid State Circuits", Vol. SC-7, pp. 346-351, October, 1972.

(3) S. A. Evans, J. L. Bartlet, B. J. Sloan, Jr., and G. L. Varnell, "Fabrication of Integrated Injection Logic with Electron-Beam Lithography and Ion Implantation", IEEE Transactions on Electron Devices, Vol. ED-25, pp. 402-407, April, 1978.

(4) F. Hennig, H. K. Hingarh, D. O'Brien, and P. W. J. Verhofstadt, "Isoplanar Integrated Injection Logic: A High Performance Bipolar Technology", IEEE J. of Solid State Circuits, Vol. SC-12, pp. 101-109, April, 1977.

(5) C. Mulder and H. E. J. Wulms, "High Speed Integrated Injection Logic (I²L)", IEEE J. of Solid State Circuits", Vol. SC-11, pp. 379-385, June, 1976.

(6) D. J. McGreivy and B. B. Roesner, "A New High Speed I²L Structure", IEEE J. of Solid State Circuits, Vol. SC-12, pp. 114-118, April, 1977.

(7) L. E. Katz and B. F. Howells, "Low-Temperature, High-Pressure Steam Oxidation of Silicon" Fall 1978 ECS Meeting, Pittsburg, Pennsylvania, Abstract 187.

(8) F. W. Hewlett, Jr., "Schottky I²L", IEEE J. of Solid State Circuits, Vol. SC-10, pp. 343-348, October, 1975.

(9) H. H. Berger, "The Injection Model-A Structure Oriented Model for Merged Transistor Logic (MTL)", IEEE J. of Solid State Circuits", Vol. SC-9, pp. 218-227, October, 1974.

(10) T. Sudo et al, "A Monolithic 8 pJ/2 GHz Logic Family ", IEEE J. of Solid State Circuits, Vol. SC-10, pp. 524-529, December, 1975.

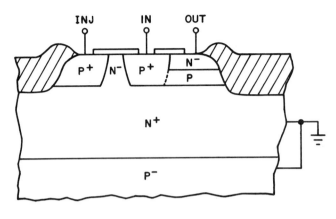

Fig. 1. MTL/I^{2}L Inverter

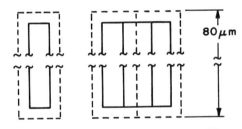

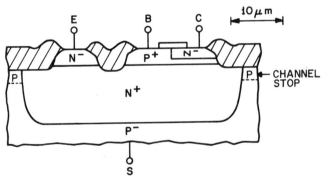

Fig. 3. Isolated Upward Transistor

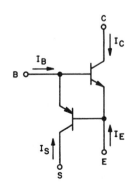

Fig. 5. Model for Upward Transistor

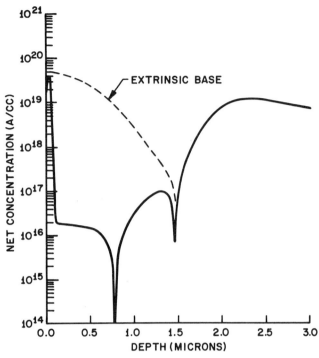

Fig. 2. Upward Transistor Profiles

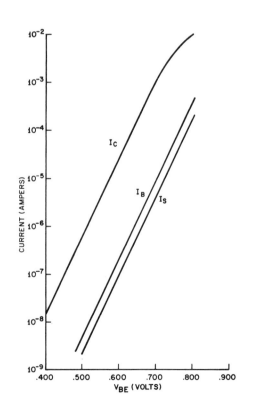

Fig. 4. I_C, I_B, and I_S for Isolated Transistor

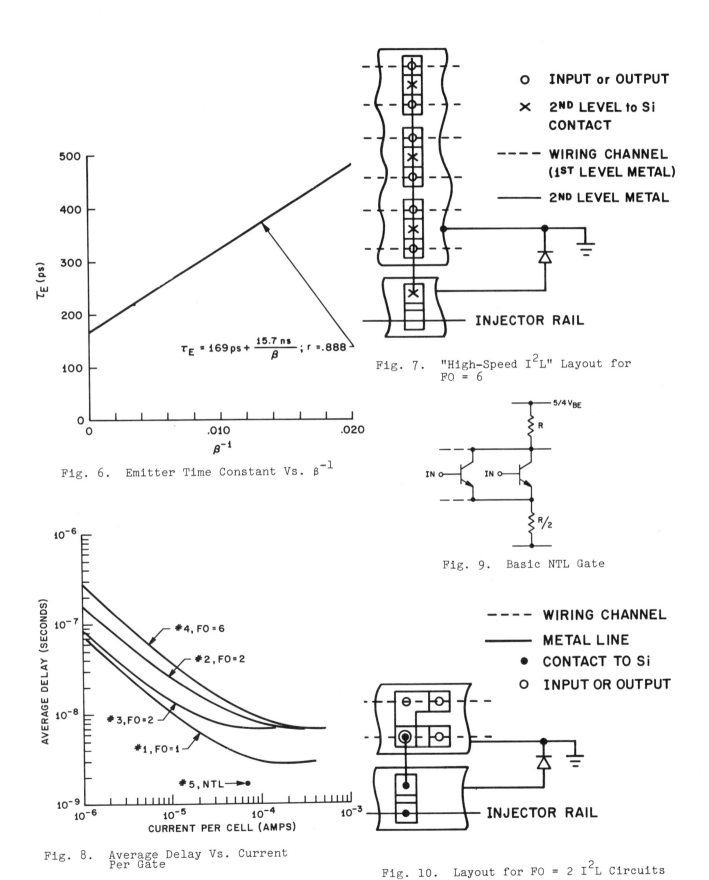

$$\tau_E = 169\,ps + \frac{15.7\,ns}{\beta}\ ;\ r = .888$$

Fig. 6. Emitter Time Constant Vs. β^{-1}

Fig. 7. "High-Speed I^2L" Layout for FO = 6

○ INPUT or OUTPUT

✕ 2ND LEVEL to Si CONTACT

---- WIRING CHANNEL (1ST LEVEL METAL)

—— 2ND LEVEL METAL

Fig. 9. Basic NTL Gate

#4, FO = 6
#2, FO = 2
#3, FO = 2
#1, FO = 1
#5, NTL

Fig. 8. Average Delay Vs. Current Per Gate

---- WIRING CHANNEL

—— METAL LINE

● CONTACT TO Si

○ INPUT OR OUTPUT

Fig. 10. Layout for FO = 2 I^2L Circuits

Schottky-Base I²L: A High-Performance LSI Technology

ALI BAHRAMAN, MEMBER, IEEE, S. Y. STEPHEN CHANG, DONALD E. ROMEO, MEMBER, IEEE, AND
KLAUS K. SCHUEGRAF, MEMBER, IEEE

Abstract—A new I²L technology is described which offers significant advantages in packing density, device performance, and reduced LSI circuit complexity as compared to the conventional I²L. The basic logic gate in this design is a multiinput, multioutput NAND gate which consists of a p-n-p switch and an n-p-n injector. Schottky diodes are formed on the p-n-p base which is merged with the n-p-n (injector) collector. This I²L technology also offers convenient interfacing with other standard IC parts. (Totem pole and 3-state logic levels can be made available on chip.) Experimental data on a test chip indicate a p-n-p current gain of ~50, TTL-type n-p-n current gain of ~80, a delay-power product of 0.5 pJ, and a minimum delay of 10 ns for devices using 7.5 μm minimum linewidths. Based on theoretical calculations, a minimum delay time of 1.5 ns at a power dissipation of 50 to 75 μW/gate is projected for oxide-isolated scaled-down Schottky-base I²L gates with 1 to 1.5 μm minimum linewidths.

I. INTRODUCTION

INTEGRATED injection logic (I²L) has found wide acceptance as a high-density, high-performance, and low-cost bipolar LSI circuit technology. Since the introduction [1], [2] of the I²L concept in 1972, a variety of advanced I²L structures have been developed in recent years, resulting in improved speed/power performance [3]–[7].

The incorporation of Schottky diodes for I²L structures has been reported in the literature [4], [5], [7]. The major benefit of Schottky diodes used in the collector node of the I²L switching transistor was a reduced voltage swing with an associated improvement in speed/power performance. Schottky diodes have also been used at the gate input to provide a multiple input capability [3]. However, the fabrication of Schottky diodes on the p-base region of an n-p-n switch results in very low barrier voltages.

This paper describes a novel approach to the design of a Schottky-base I²L (SBI²L) structure, utilizing an n-p-n current source and a p-n-p switch as the basic gate [8]. This structure offers a combination of circuit performance improvements resulting from device parameters, interconnect flexibility, delay/power product, and output buffer design, as described in the following sections.

Manuscript received October 23, 1978; revised January 4, 1979.
A. Bahraman and S. Y. S. Chang are with the Northrop Research and Technology Center, Palos Verdes Peninsula, CA 90274.
D. E. Romeo was with the Northrop Research and Technology Center, Palos Verdes Peninsula, CA 90274. He is now with the TRW Defense and Space Systems Group, Redondo Beach, CA 90278.
K. K. Schuegraf was with the Northrop Research and Technology Center, Palos Verdes Peninsula, CA 90274. He is now with the Hughes Aircraft Company, Culver City, CA.

II. DEVICE STRUCTURE AND DESIGN

For most LSI layouts, the metallization and crossunder paths usually consume a larger fraction of the chip area than the active gates. To meet the objectives of optimizing chip area and circuit complexity and improving circuit performance, a novel design, the Schottky-base I²L with p-n-p active gates, has been developed. It exhibits the following features.

1) A p-n-p switching transistor permits the fabrication of Schottky diodes on n-type epitaxial layers with aluminum metallization at no increase in design and process complexity.

2) The p-n-p switch transistor can be designed to offer better speed than the standard I²L n-p-n switch since the I²L gate delay time is controlled by the emitter/base storage time and not by the base transit time. Hence, the lower diffusion constant for holes does not limit the SBI²L speed.

3) A Schottky-base I²L design offers very significant advantages in terms of the following:

    a) increased density;
    b) good input/output isolation;
    c) a low power/delay product (due to reduced voltage swing);
    d) reduction of circuit propagation delay time;
    e) capability of high radiation tolerance;
    f) simplified circuit design and layout geometries;
    g) reduced metallization and gate-to-gate interconnects.

These advantages and some of the disadvantages of the design are discussed here and in Section III.

A p-n-p transistor fabricated in an n-type epitaxial layer on a p⁺ substrate forms the active switch. Schottky diodes are fabricated on the p-n-p base, which is merged with the n-p-n (injector) collector. A p-n-p transistor switch is chosen because Schottky diodes with sufficient barrier height are obtained readily on n-type silicon. The n-p-n injector can be defined by a self-aligned mask, as shown in Fig. 1(a), or by two separate masks, the latter providing a vertical n-p-n injector [Fig. 1(c)]. Fig. 1(b) shows the schematic of the basic gate. The p-n-p and n-p-n transistors are fabricated by separate diffusion steps, thus providing separate control of each device. Note that the device can operate with either a negative or a positive power supply. With a negative supply, the substrate is grounded and the injector (n-p-n emitter) is tied to the negative supply. Alternatively, the substrate may be tied to a positive supply and the injector terminals grounded. The latter is preferred for I²L/TTL interfacing.

Reprinted from *IEEE J. Solid-State Circuits*, vol. SC-14, pp. 578–584, June 1979.

258

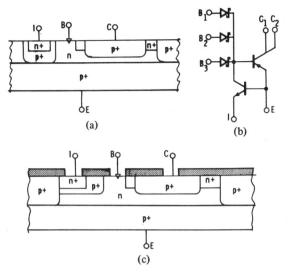

Fig. 1. Schottky-base I^2L structure. (a) Self-aligned Schottky-base I^2L. (b) Schottky-base I^2L gate schematic. (c) Vertical-injector Schottky-base I^2L.

TABLE I
MASK LEVELS AND PROCESS STEPS

MASK LEVEL	PROCESS DESCRIPTION
1: ISOLATION	BORON DEPOSITION – 1025°C
2: pnp COLLECTOR	BORON DEPOSITION – 920°C
	PARTIAL DRIVE IN – 1100°C
3: npn BASE	BORON DEPOSITION – 910°C
	DRIVE IN – 1100°C
4: npn EMITTER / pnp BASE COLLAR	PHOSPHORUS DEPOSITION AND DRIVE IN AT 900°C
5: CONTACT HOLES	ETCH CONTACTS
6: METAL	DEPOSIT AND ETCH METAL

The basic logic gate in this technology is a multiinput, multioutput NAND gate and is formed by only one inverter. (One or two outputs are sufficient for most designs, since the Schottky diode inputs are isolated.) In comparison, a multiinput NOR gate in conventional I^2L requires as many inverters as the number of its inputs. Therefore, there can be a substantial difference in logic-gate packing density between the two technologies. In addition, there is further improvement in packing density because inputs, being base Schottky contacts in SBI^{2}L, require less area than outputs, which are collectors in conventional I^2L.

The SBI^{2}L structure is fabricated using regular bipolar processing techniques. However, the actual process and the mask levels differ from the standard I^2L and TTL designs since a p-n-p switching transistor and a p^+ substrate are used in the SBI^{2}L design. Table I outlines the mask levels and process steps. Note that the p-n-p basewidth is defined by a single p-diffusion. Hence, with a fairly uniform epitaxial layer thickness across the wafer and from wafer to wafer, a good control of the p-n-p intrinsic base Gummel number is feasible. Since the injector is a right-side-up n-p-n transistor, fairly high n-p-n gains are possible without requiring very narrow basewidths.

These features minimize the collector/emitter short problem for both the p-n-p and n-p-n transistors.

The p-n-p basewidth control can become difficult if the p^+ substrate concentration is too high ($>5 \times 10^{18}/\text{cm}^3$) and if very high diffusion temperatures and long diffusion times are used. However, since the impurity concentration in the intrinsic base region of the p-n-p switch is constant, small variations in basewidth will only result in small variations in p-n-p gain. This is in contrast to the double-diffused n-p-n switch of the conventional I^2L, which shows large variations in gain due to small changes in basewidth.

Several steps may be taken to optimize the speed/power performance of the device. Reducing the minimum delay time requires an increase in the effective current gain β_{eff} and a decrease in the effective base storage time [9]–[11]. (Also, see Appendix I.) Neglecting series resistance and high-level injection effects, the effective gain and storage time are given by

$$\beta_{\text{eff}} = \frac{\beta}{1 + I_{N0}/I_{B0}} \tag{1}$$

$$\tau_s' = \frac{\tau_s}{1 + I_{N0}/I_{B0}} \tag{2}$$

where β is the p-n-p common-emitter current gain, τ_s is the p-n-p emitter-base storage time, and the parameters I_{B0} and I_{N0} yield the p-n-p base current and n-p-n (injector) collector current from the relations

$$I_B(\text{p-n-p}) = I_{B0} \exp(qV_B/kT) \tag{3}$$

$$I_C(\text{n-p-n}) = I_{N0} \exp(qV_I/kT) \tag{4}$$

where V_B is the p-n-p base voltage and V_I is the injector (n-p-n emitter) voltage.

Following Klaassen's analysis [9], we have collected the minimum delay time t_d in terms of the parameters in (1) and (2). Fig. 2(a) shows the dependence of t_d on β_{eff}. For large values of β_{eff}, t_d varies as $\tau_s'/\sqrt{\beta_{\text{eff}}}$. In Fig. 2(b), the normalized delay time is plotted versus I_{N0}/I_{B0}, with I_{B0} as the varying parameter.

Based on these results, t_d can be reduced by four different techniques: 1) if β is increased by achieving a narrower p-n-p basewidth, β_{eff} increases and t_d decreases as $1/\sqrt{\beta_{\text{eff}}}$; 2) if the n-p-n gain is increased by making I_{N0} larger while all other parameters are kept constant, both β_{eff} and τ_s' decrease [see (1) and (2)], but since $t_d \sim \tau_s'/\sqrt{\beta_{\text{eff}}}$, t_d also decreases—though not very substantially; 3) reducing I_{B0} can be very effective in minimizing t_d [as shown in Fig. 2(b)], since this will result in higher β and lower τ_s'; 4) if the storage time τ_s is decreased without reducing β, the delay time decreases as $t_d \sim \tau_s$. From the previous discussion, the minimum delay time is reduced most effectively by the design and processing steps that achieve a high β_{eff} and a low τ_s'. For a high β_{eff}, the p-n-p collector current must be much larger than the n-p-n collector current to allow a large fan-out and low delay times. This condition is easy to satisfy since: 1) the p-n-p integrated base concentration is controlled by the epitaxial-layer impurity concentration and the collector p-diffusion, which can be adjusted to obtain an optimum design; 2) the n-p-n base-

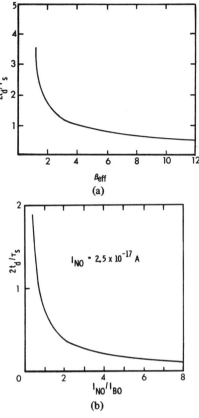

Fig. 2. (a) Variation of normalized delay time with β_{eff}. (b) Variation of delay time with the ratio I_{N0}/I_{B0}.

where τ_e is the electron recombination lifetime in the emitter, τ_h is the hole lifetime in the epitaxial region, Q_e and Q_{BS} are the corresponding stored charges, Q_C is the stored charge associated with recombination at the base contact, and Q is the total stored charge:

$$Q = Q_C + Q_{BS} + Q_e. \tag{7}$$

As mentioned previously, Q_{BS} is the largest component of stored charge. From (6) and (7) it can be shown that τ_s is much larger than τ_c, unless Q_{BS} is reduced appreciably. The latter is achieved by using a thin epitaxial layer and incorporating an n^+ collar in the extrinsic base region.

The previously stated charge and corresponding current components have been calculated from the basic device parameters and geometries. The results indicate a storage time of $\sim$30 to 50 ns for a 4-input gate with $X_B = 2$ μm and 5 μm minimum linewidth, as compared to $\sim$100 ns for conventional I^2L structures. The reduced input storage time for SBI^{2}L is primarily due to the Schottky inputs and low τ_c values. On the other hand, the Schottky inputs have the disadvantage of generating excess base current because of recombination at the Schottky contacts. In this case, the higher base current (lower gain) is traded off for a lower input storage time.

III. LSI DESIGN AND LAYOUT

High-density LSI layouts require not only a small area for the active gates but also techniques for minimizing the area required for interconnections. Double-layer interconnections are frequently required for complex LSI circuits. In conventional I^2L, the logic branching is accomplished with multicollector gates. This results in gate layouts with long and narrow base regions. The remote collector and the fan-out determine the minimum gate delay.

An important advantage of the Schottky-base I^2L is the capability of connecting several isolated gates to the input Schottky diodes of a single cell without jeopardizing the input/output isolation. A single collector can also be tied to several other Schottky inputs. This dual capability, not available in conventional I^2L designs, results in a much simplified logic design and layout, with a substantial savings in interconnect metallization lines and corresponding chip area. However, in any circuit design it is important to make sure that any collector tied to several bases has sufficient gain to source the injector currents associated with those bases. A large effective gain β_{eff} is needed for this purpose; e.g., a β_{eff} of 15 permits a fan-out of 15. However, in practical LSI designs one has to provide a 3:1 gain margin and reduce the fan-out to 5. As indicated in Table II, a β_{eff} of 15 can be readily obtained. (Table II is calculated for an epitaxial layer thickness of 2 μm for finished devices.) In addition, one can scale the collector area with the number of base contacts, which results in a large fan-out capability for multibase cells, as shown in Fig. 3. This is in contrast to other I^2L designs where β_{eff} drops dramatically as fan-out increases. Furthermore, the capability to drive 5 separate bases from a single collector should satisfy most logic circuit requirements.

Standard I^2L structures may require the connection of collectors in multicollector cells to distant bases through long

width is controlled by a double diffusion and its integrated base concentration is much larger than that of the p-n-p transistor; 3) the p-n-p collector area is larger than the n-p-n collector area.

A low τ_s' is achieved by reducing the base storage time and the base current (small I_{B0}). Let us now consider these briefly. The base current consists of electron injection into the emitter, hole injection into the epitaxial n-layer, and recombination current in the emitter/base junction space-charge region. Electron injection into the emitter is reduced by the highly doped p^+ substrate ($N_A \approx 2$ to 5×10^{18} cm^{-3}). Charge stored in the epitaxial layer is the primary stored base charge. To reduce this charge, an n^+ collar is used on four sides of the p^+ collector, as indicated in Fig. 1. This also reduces the base series resistance. The primary base current component is the recombination current at the contact region. The charge storage time for this component is equal to the transit time of holes for diffusion from the emitter/base junction to the base contact, which is given by

$$\tau_c = X_B^2/2D_h \tag{5}$$

where X_B is the emitter/base junction depth and D_h is the hole diffusion constant. For $X_B \sim 2$ μm and $D_h = 10$ cm^2/s, τ_c is 2 ns. Charge storage in the emitter and the epitaxial layer will increase the storage time. The general relation for the base storage time can be written as (see Appendix II),

$$\tau_s = \frac{\tau_c Q}{Q_C}\left[1 + \frac{Q_{BS}}{Q_C}\frac{\tau_c}{\tau_h} + \frac{Q_e}{Q_C}\frac{\tau_c}{\tau_e}\right]^{-1} \tag{6}$$

TABLE II
CALCULATED SCHOTTKY-BASE I²L PERFORMANCE PARAMETERS

pnp Gain	β	57
Effective Gain	β_{eff}	21
Propagation Delay	t_d (ns)	4
Speed-Power Product	$P \cdot t_d$ (pJ)	0.13

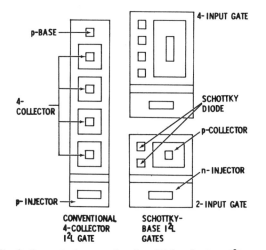

Fig. 3. Layout of conventional and Schottky-base I²L gate.

metal lines and/or crossunder connections for a chip of average complexity. Because of low gain, the collector current in multicollector cells may not be sufficient to sink the injector current of a distant gate at a reasonable speed due to the additional capacitive loading. Each collector may require an additional high-gain buffer. This increases the number of gates substantially and results in higher power consumption and layout complexity for standard I²L structures.

In the Schottky-base I²L design, the collector current for a multibase gate can source the injector currents of several bases, and for large fan-outs only one additional high-gain, single-input inverter is required for buffering. This provides a large fan-in and fan-out capability by using only two gates. Consequently, the number of metallization lines and active gates is reduced, resulting in lower power consumption and improvements in speed and effective gate packing density.

As mentioned previously, the NAND function is formed by a single SBI²L inverter. Consequently, most logic functions can be implemented with fewer gates in SBI²L than in other IC technologies. This results in a smaller circuit-propagation delay time and less power consumption.

The interfacing of I²L chips within a system requires careful consideration. The I²L/TTL interface is rather straightforward due to the logic level compatibility between the two families. At the I²L inputs, two types of interfacing have been commonly used: 1) TTL totem pole to an I²L n-p-n with an input resistor network; and 2) open collector TTL to an I²L buffer inverter with a high current p-n-p or pull-up resistor. I²L output interfacing to TTL is accomplished by using an open-collector I²L n-p-n to sink the TTL low-level input current. However, a TTL-type totem-pole output driver can be provided on-chip with Schottky-base I²L, since an n-on-p

structure is used. This provides for a very effective and high-speed interfacing to TTL loads. The n-on-p structure also allows the fabrication of the complementary n-p-n/p-n-p 3-state drivers discussed below.

For high data-rate applications, a signal transmission over properly terminated coaxial cables is desirable. In bus-oriented digital equipment, a 3-state capability is required. For these two applications, the Schottky-base I²L provides a simple solution.

Propagating I²L signals over coaxial cables requires termination of the line and results in fairly high drive currents. Schottky-base I²L permits the use of a complementary n-p-n/p-n-p I²L push/pull coaxial driver, to be used at each output to drive a terminated transmission line. Although the operating currents remain high, in this case both the n-p-n and the p-n-p transistors are high-gain vertical devices capable of high current operation. Hence, the SBI²L with terminated transmission lines provides a practical solution to higher speed signal propagation within a typical hardware system. Three-state output configurations have not been reported for nonisolated I²L. The SBI²L push/pull driver can be applied to the 3-state operation. This is made possible because the push/pull driver can be forced into any of three states: 1) low level with the n-p-n current sinking and the p-n-p at cutoff; 2) high level with the p-n-p current sourcing and the n-p-n at cutoff; and 3) high impedance with both n-p-n and p-n-p at cutoff. Current sourcing and sinking transistors are located at the driver end, and multiple low-current inputs can be tied to a given line. Since each output can be disabled by forcing it to the high-impedance state, multiple outputs may also be tied to the same line.

IV. EXPERIMENTAL RESULTS

A test chip was fabricated using design rules with 7.5 µm minimum linewidth. Included were test devices with Schottky inputs and ohmic base contacts. Values of β_{eff} of 15 to 20 for Schottky-input inverters and ~60 for devices with ohmic base contacts have been obtained, as indicated in Fig. 4. The primary base current of the Schottky-input devices is due to recombination at the base contact. In devices with an ohmic base contact, the recombination current is eliminated due to an n^+ diffusion in the contact area. However, the devices with Schottky inputs have a much smaller input storage time, as discussed in Section II. The injector α_F has been $\gtrsim 0.95$, as compared to ~0.7 for conventional I²L structures.

Fig. 5 shows ring-oscillator performance data for conventional I²L and the devices with Schottky and ohmic base contacts (single-collector inverters for conventional I²L; single-collector, 2-input inverters for SBI²L). These devices had 7.5 µm geometries. As shown in Fig. 5, all three devices have the same minimum delay time, but the Schottky-input device requires much less power for minimum delay. The increase in propagation delay at higher injector currents for the SBI²L device is due to series resistance in the epitaxial layer and can be eliminated with some design changes (phosphorus implantation in the n-p-n collector region and under the Schottky contacts). A reduction in delay time by a factor of 2 is expected for SBI²L by using 5 µm minimum linewidths. This expectation

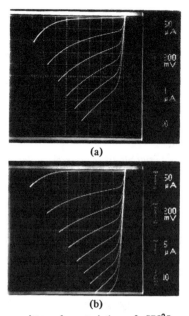

(a)

(b)

Fig. 4. Common emitter characteristics of SBI²L p-n-p transistor. (a) n⁺ base contact. (b) Schottky diode base contact.

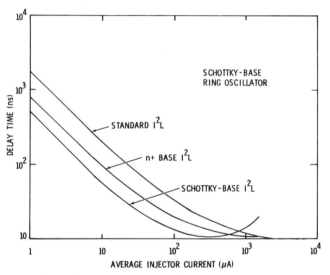

Fig. 5. Variation of delay time with injector current.

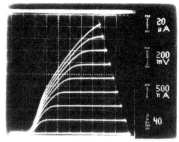

Fig. 6. n-p-n (injector) common-emitter characteristics (without n⁺ buried layer).

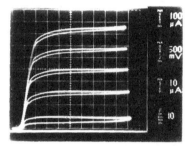

Fig. 7. n-p-n (injector) common-emitter characteristics (with n⁺ buried layer).

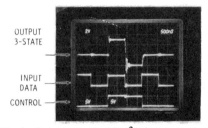

Fig. 8. Output signal of SBI²L 3-state buffer.

is based on theoretical calculation and on experimental data for conventional I²L devices with 7.5 and 5 μm geometries.

The n-p-n injector common-emitter characteristics are shown in Fig. 6. The device of Fig. 6 was fabricated on a 0.7 $\Omega \cdot$ cm epitaxial layer and shows a large collector resistance. This resistance has been reduced in two ways: 1) by using a lower resistivity epitaxial layer, and 2) by adding an n⁺ buried layer under the n-p-n collector. Fig. 7 shows the common-emitter characteristics for an n-p-n injector with an n⁺ buried layer. A very small collector series resistance has been obtained for this device. Note that a Schottky diode is in series with the collector of the n-p-n transistor. The buried-layer option has the disadvantage of increasing the input capacitance and process complexity. The more attractive option is to reduce the epitaxial-layer resistivity to 0.15 to 0.2 $\Omega \cdot$ cm.

Fig. 8 shows the output signal waveform of a SBI²L 3-state output buffer. When the 3-state control signal is high, the input data are transmitted to the output. When the control signal is low, the output floats at a high-impedance state and was set, in this case, at a level between the "1" and "0" voltage levels.

V. DEVICE SCALING CALCULATIONS

The Schottky-base I²L technology is especially suitable for VLSI applications and can meet the speed, power, and packing density requirements of a VLSI technology. By down-scaling the lateral and vertical dimensions of the device, the input capacitance and the charge components Q_C, Q_{BS}, and Q_e can be drastically reduced. In addition, down-scaling in the vertical dimension will result in a much smaller τ_c [see (5)]. From (6), a substantial decrease in τ_s should be feasible. Table III shows theoretically calculated delay/power performance data for scaled-down SBI²L structures. (N_{epi} is the epitaxial layer donor concentration, X_C is the p-n-p collector junction depth, W_B(p-n-p) and W_B(n-p-n) are the p-n-p and n-p-n basewidths, and the epitaxial thickness is equal to the sum $X_C + W_B$(p-n-p) for finished devices. Oxide isolation has been assumed in order to minimize the input capacitance.) As shown in Table III, minimum delay values of ~1.5 ns at power dissipation levels of 50 to 75 μW/gate appear feasible. The calculated delay/power product is about 0.02 pJ for a 4-input device with 1.5 μm minimum linewidth. These results com-

TABLE III
CALCULATED DELAY/POWER DATA FOR SCALED-DOWN SCHOTTKY-BASE
I^2L WITH OXIDE ISOLATION

Case	Min. Line-width (μm)	No. Base Inputs	Collector Area (μm^2)	Emitter Area (μm^2)	X_C (μm)	W_B(pnp) (μm)	W_B(npn) (μm)	t_d (ns)	P_d (μW)
1	5	4	17.5 x 55	42.5 x 80	1.6	0.4	0.5	5.4	600
2	2.5	4	10 x 29	22 x 40	1	0.25	0.3	2.5	200
3	2	2	7.5 x 10	16 x 16	1	0.25	0.3	2	116
4	1.5	2	4.5 x 6.5	11.5 x 11.5	0.8	0.2	0.2	2.4 / 1.4	23 / 152
5	1.5	4	4.5 x 10	14.5 x 15	0.8	0.2	0.2	3 / 2.1	28 / 67
6	1.5	4	4.5 x 10	14.5 x 15	0.6	0.2	0.2	2.3 / 1.6	23 / 54
7	1.5*	4	4.5 x 10	14.5 x 15	0.6	0.2	0.2	2.1 / 1.5	28 / 69

*N_{epi} = 2 x 10^{16}/cm^3; otherwise, N_{epi} = 3.5 x 10^{16}/cm^3

X_C = pnp collector junction depth

pare favorably with similar data for scaled-down conventional I^2L devices [12], [13].

Notice in Table III that a 4-input and a 2-input gate have comparable minimum delay times. This occurs for two reasons: 1) as mentioned previously, the collector area can be scaled with fan-in; hence, β_{eff} remains constant as the number of inputs increases; and 2) since the ratio of the base contact area to the active base area is the same for the 2-input and 4-input devices, the ratio Q_C/Q_{BS} is identical for the two devices. Therefore, from (6), the τ_s values for the two devices are about the same. Because τ_s and β_{eff} are the main device parameters that determine the minimum delay time, the 2-input and 4-input devices have nearly equal t_d values.

VI. SUMMARY

The design and performance of Schottky-base I^2L has been described. This structure uses an n-p-n current source and a p-n-p switching transistor. The Schottky-base I^2L achieves a very high logic-gate packing density and permits simplified layouts for LSI circuits. Push/pull output drivers for high-speed transmission-line terminations and 3-state capability for data bus operation are available.

Schottky-base I^2L lends itself very well to device scaling laws. For 1.5 μm minimum linewidths and 4-input gates, a delay/power product of 0.02 pJ and a minimum delay time of 1.5 ns at 50 to 75 μW power dissipation have been calculated.

APPENDIX I

In this Appendix, the dependence of the minimum delay time on the effective gain and storage time is derived. Starting with Klaassen's equation (21), the minimum delay time is given by the transcendental equation [9]

$$\frac{2t_d}{\tau_s'} = \ln\left[\frac{1 + 2t_d/\tau_s'}{1 - 1/(2\pi f_T \tau_s')}\right] \tag{A1-1}$$

where the transition frequency f_T is related to the inverter collector current by the relation

$$I_C(\text{p-n-p}) = 2\pi f_T Q. \tag{A1-2}$$

Using the relations

$$I_B = Q/\tau_s \qquad \beta = I_C/I_B \tag{A1-3}$$

and (A1-1), (1), and (2), it can be shown that

$$\beta_{eff} = 2\pi f_T \tau_s'. \tag{A1-4}$$

Hence,

$$\frac{2t_d}{\tau_s'} = \ln\left[\frac{1 + 2t_d/\tau_s'}{1 - 1/\beta_{eff}}\right]. \tag{A1-5}$$

This equation has been used to obtain the plots in Fig. 2. If $t_d \ll \tau_s'$ and $\beta_{eff} \gg 1$, (A1-5) can be expanded to obtain the solution

$$\frac{2t_d}{\tau_s'} \simeq \left(\frac{2}{\beta_{eff}} - \frac{1}{\beta_{eff}^2}\right)^{1/2}. \tag{A1-6}$$

This yields

$$t_d \simeq \tau_s'/\sqrt{2\beta_{eff}}. \tag{A1-7}$$

APPENDIX II

In this Appendix, the general relation for the base storage time is derived. Neglecting recombination in the emitter-base space-charge region, high-level injection, and series resistance effects, the components of base current are given by

$$I_{BE} = \frac{Q_e}{\tau_e} \tag{A2-1}$$

$$I_{BS} = \frac{Q_{BS}}{\tau_h} \tag{A2-2}$$

$$I_{BC} = \frac{Q_c}{\tau_c} \tag{A2-3}$$

where I_{BE}, I_{BS}, and I_{BC} are the current components associated with electron injection into the emitter, charge storage in the base, and recombination at the contact. The base current and total stored charge are

$$I_B = I_{BE} + I_{BS} + I_{BC} \tag{A2-4}$$

$$Q = Q_e + Q_{BS} + Q_c. \tag{A2-5}$$

We now define the base storage time by the relation

$$I_B = \frac{Q}{\tau_s}. \tag{A2-6}$$

Combining (A2-1) to (A2-6), one obtains the expression for τ_s given by (6).

REFERENCES

[1] H. H. Berger and S. K. Wiedmann, "Merged-transistor-logic (MTL)—A low cost bipolar logic concept," *IEEE J. Solid-State Circuits*, vol. SC-7, pp. 340–346, Oct. 1972.

[2] K. Hart and A. Slob, "Integrated injection logic: A new approach to LSI," *IEEE J. Solid-State Circuits*, vol. SC-7, pp. 346–351, Oct. 1972.

[3] V. Blatt, P. S. Walsh, and L. W. Kennedy, "Substrate fed logic," *IEEE J. Solid-State Circuits*, vol. SC-10, pp. 336–342, Oct. 1975.

[4] H. H. Berger and S. K. Wiedmann, "Schottky transistor logic," in *IEEE Int. Solid-State Circuits Conf. Tech. Dig.*, Feb. 1975, pp. 172–173.

[5] F. W. Hewlett, Jr., "Schottky I^2L," *IEEE J. Solid-State Circuits*, vol. SC-10, pp. 343–348, Oct. 1975.

[6] F. Henning, H. K. Hingarh, D. O'Brien, and P. W. J. Verhofstadt, "Isoplanar integrated injection logic: A high performance bipolar technology," *IEEE J. Solid-State Circuits*, vol. SC-12, pp. 101–109, Apr. 1977.

[7] B. B. Roesner and D. J. McGreivy, "A new high-speed I^2L structure," *IEEE J. Solid-State Circuits*, vol. SC-12, pp. 114–118, Apr. 1977.

[8] A. Bahraman, S. Chang, D. Romeo, and K. Schuegraf, "Schottky-base I^2L—A high performance LSI technology," presented at the 1978 European Solid State Circuits Conference, Amsterdam, The Netherlands.

[9] F. M. Klaassen, "Device physics of I^2L," *IEEE Trans. Electron Devices*, vol. ED-22, p. 145, 1975.

[10] A. Bahraman, S. Chang, D. Romeo, K. Schuegraf, and T. Wong, "Radiation-hardened, performance-optimized I^2L LSI," *IEEE Trans. Nucl. Sci.*, vol. NS-24, p. 2321, 1977.

[11] A. Bahraman, S. Chang, D. Romeo, and K. Schuegraf, "Design approach to radiation-hardened I^2L gate arrays," *IEEE Trans. Nucl. Sci.*, vol. NS-25, pp. 1494–1501, Dec. 1978.

[12] S. Evans, J. Bartelet, B. Sloan, Jr., and G. Varnel, "Fabrication of I^2L with electron-beam lithography and ion implantation," *IEEE Trans. Electron Devices*, vol. ED-25, p. 402, 1978.

[13] F. M. Klaassen, "Design and performance of micron-size devices," *Solid-State Electron.*, vol. 21, p. 565, 1978.

Modeling of the Diode Input I²L Structure

GUST PERLEGOS and SHU-PARK CHAN, senior member, ieee

Abstract—A high-speed single-collector multiinput Schottky diode I²L structure is presented. The structure features negligible p-n-p and a relatively low extrinsic base minority carrier storage, and lends to the near elimination of saturation. A theoretical model predicts that the structure produces circuit delays of better than 3 ns at 50 μA.

I. Introduction

THE basic integrated injection logic (I²L) [1], [2] has limited applications in the area of high-speed microprocessors due to its medium-speed performance. A number of major improvements have been made in the I²L structure [3]–[7] in order to reduce the speed–power product and the minimum propagation delay.

A substantial speed improvement is obtained by using an I²L structure having a single collector and separately isolated input diodes. Fig. 1(a) and (b) show the top and cross-sectional views of an oxide isolated n-p-n inverter with its merged p-n-p load and the separately isolated diodes. The circuit configuration is essentially identical to C³L [8] without the clamping diode and with the position of the diodes interchanged.

With oxide isolation and a single-collector structure, the extrinsic-to-intrinsic base area ratio can be made appreciably less than one and hence, the minority carrier storage contribution of the extrinsic regions is relatively low. In addition, the single-collector multiinput Schottky diode circuit configuration removes the high n-p-n inverse beta requirement of I²L. Therefore, a lightly doped collector is implemented in order to nearly prevent saturation of the n-p-n.

In this circuit configuration, a single n-p-n transistor drives a larger number of p-n-p transistors when compared to the basic I²L structure. However, the p-n-p minority carrier storage contribution is negligible.

In this paper, the oxide-isolated, diode input single-collector I²L structure is modeled. The analysis determines the minority carrier distributions in the different regions of the device. The simulations show that loaded circuit delays of better than 3 ns are obtained at an injector current of 50 μA.

II. The N-P-N and P-N-P Transistors

The impurity concentration profiles of the various regions are shown in Fig. 1(c). The electron carrier distribution, in the intrinsic base under the normal n-p-n region of operation, is

Manuscript received March 3, 1978; revised September 20, 1978.
G. Perlegos is with the Amdahl Corporation, Sunnyvale, CA.
S.-P. Chan is with the Department of Electrical Engineering and Computer Science, University of Santa Clara, CA, 95053.

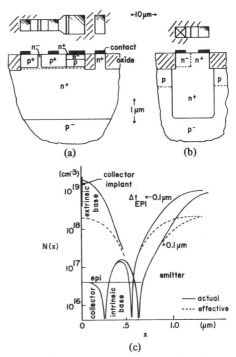

Fig. 1. Diode input I²L. (a) Top and cross-sectional views of the n-p-n and p-n-p transistors. (b) Input diode. (c) Impurity concentrations of different regions.

given by the following equation [9]:

$$n(x) = \frac{j_n}{q[N_A(x) + n(x)]} \int_{x_{C^+}}^{x} \frac{N_A(x) + n(x)}{D_n(x)} dx \qquad (1)$$

where j_n is the electron current density, N_A is the effective acceptor concentration, D_n is the electron diffusion constant, and q is the electronic charge. Equation (1) is solved iteratively and the results are shown in Fig. 2(a).

The back-injected hole distribution in the emitter is given by

$$p(x) = n_i^2 \, e^{v_{BE}/V_T} \int_{x_{E^-}}^{x} \frac{N_D(x)}{D_p(x)} dx \Bigg/ \left\{ [N_D(x) + p(x)] \int_{x_{E^-}}^{x_{B^+}} \frac{N_D(x)}{D_p(x)} dx \right\} \qquad (2)$$

where N_D is the effective donor concentration, D_p is the hole diffusion constant, and $V_T (= kT/q)$ is the thermal voltage. The base–emitter voltage is given by

$$v_{BE} = V_T \ln \left[\frac{j_N}{n_i^2 q} \int_{x_{C^+}}^{x_{B^-}} \frac{N_A(x)}{D_n(x)} dx \right] \qquad (3)$$

where j_N is the normal current density.

Reprinted from *IEEE J. Solid-State Circuits*, vol. SC-14, pp. 645–648, June 1979.

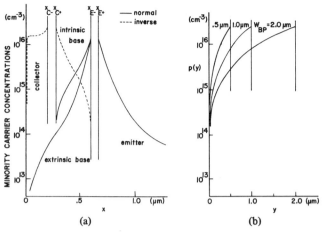

Fig. 2. Minority carrier distributions. Normal (or inverse) current = 0.5 mA, Δt_{EPI} = +0.1 μm, collector area = 50 μm². (a) n-p-n transistor. (b) Back-injected holes in the p-n-p base.

Similarly, the electron distribution in the contact-covered region is given by the following equation:

$$n(x) = n_i^2 e^{v_{BE}/V_T} \int_0^x \frac{N_A(x)}{D_n(x)} dx \bigg/ \left\{ [N_A(x) + n(x)] \int_{x_{C^+}}^{x_{B^-}} \frac{N_A(x)}{D_n(x)} dx \right\}. \quad (4)$$

The electron storage in the oxide-covered extrinsic base region is not appreciably higher than the storage under the base contact.

The n-p-n storage under the inverse mode of operation is determined by calculating the intrinsic base and collector minority carrier distributions. The electron distribution is calculated using (1) with a lower integration limit of x_{E^+}. The hole distribution in the collector region is given by

$$p(x) = \frac{n_i^2 e^{v_{BC}/V_T}}{[N_D(x) + p(x)]}. \quad (5)$$

The base–collector voltage is given by

$$v_{BC} = V_T \ln \left[\frac{j_I}{n_i^2 q} \int_{x_{B^-}}^{x_{C^+}} \frac{N_A(x)}{D_n(x)} dx \right] \quad (6)$$

where j_I is the inverse current density. These results are also shown in Fig. 2(a).

The p-n-p transistor enters high-level injection at high current levels. The back-injected hole distribution in the p-n-p base is calculated from the following equation [9]:

$$j_p y = q D_p \{2p(y) - N_D \ln [1 + p(y)/N_D] \} \quad (7)$$

where j_p is the lateral current density in the p-n-p base. Equation (7) is solved iteratively for $p(y)$ using the boundary condition [9]

$$p(W_{BP}) = \frac{n_i^2}{N_D + p(W_{BP})} e^{v_{BE}/V_T} \quad (8)$$

where W_{BP} is the p-n-p basewidth ($y = 0$ at the p-n-p E–B junction). The hole distributions for different p-n-p basewidths are shown in Fig. 2(b).

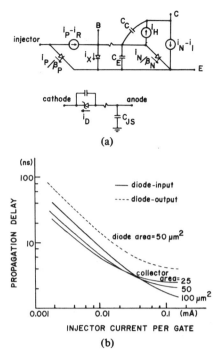

Fig. 3. (a) Large signal model of n-p-n and p-n-p transistors and of a separately isolated diode. (b) Propagation delay versus injector current of a single collector four-input NAND gate with a fan-out of 4 and an inverse n-p-n beta of 10; also of a diode output I²L with a fan-out of 4 and an inverse n-p-n beta of 10.

The minority carrier storage within the depletion layers are linearly approximated using the concentrations values at the edges. High doping effects are included in the calculation of the minority carrier distributions and currents of the highly doped regions [10].

III. THE SCHOTTKY DIODES

The Schottky diodes are selected to have a low reverse saturation current to prevent leakage and a low forward voltage in order to turn off the n-p-n transistor. For the device sizes shown in Fig. 1, a Schottky barrier height of less than 0.62 V is required to turn off ten gates at a junction temperature of 150°C and an injector current of 100 μA. The charging of a switching collector depends on the number of diodes connected to the collector and the reverse saturation current of the diodes. At 1 μA of leakage, a barrier height of more than 0.55 V is required. Molybdenum Schottky diodes have a barrier height of 0.59 V [11] which is within the desirable range.

IV. LARGE SIGNAL MODEL

A large signal model for the structure of Fig. 1(a) is shown in Fig. 3(a), where the device is partitioned in the intrinsic n-p-n transistor, the extrinsic base diode, and the p-n-p transistor regions [12].

The net transported electron current from the collector to the emitter of the intrinsic n-p-n is modeled with $i_N - i_I$. The back-injected hole currents into the emitter and collector regions from the intrinsic base are modeled with i_N/β_N and i_H, respectively. The electron current injected in the extrinsic base, plus the hole current injected from the extrinsic base

TABLE I
MINORITY CARRIER TIME CONSTANTS: Δt_{EPI} = +0.1 μm, w_{BP} = 2 μm

Collector area (μm^2)	25 μm^2	50	100
extrinsic diode (ns)	0.090	0.045	0.0225
p-n-p (ns)	0.0075	0.003	0.0015

into the emitter, is modeled with i_X. The current i_P-i_R is the net hole current transported from the injector to the n-p-n base and i_P/β_P is the electron current injected into the emitter region from the injector. The emitter and collector diffusion capacitances are related to i_N and i_I by the emitter and collector time constants. The junction capacitances, the bulk resistances, and the intrinsic n-p-n base resistance [13] are also included in the model.

The Schottky diode model is also shown in Fig. 3(a) where i_D is the diode current and C_{JS} is the substrate parasitic capacitance.

V. APPLICATIONS AND DISCUSSION

A number of circuit simulations were made to determine the performance of a typical gate. The minority carrier time constants are calculated by integrating the charges shown in Fig. 2 [9]. The collector and emitter time constants are equal to 0.093 and 0.114 ns, respectively, for a p-n-p basewidth of 1 μm. The intrinsic n-p-n contribution on the emitter time constant is equal to 0.067 ns. The extrinsic diode and p-n-p contributions are given in Table I for different collector areas and a p-n-p basewidth of 2 μm.

The results of collector area variations on the delay are shown in Fig. 3(b). Circuit delays of better than 2 ns are obtained at collector sizes of 100 μm^2. For comparison, an oxide-isolated output-diode I^{2}L of the same functional complexity was also simulated using identical parameters and feature sizes.

The contributing factors for higher speed are the considerable reduction of the extrinsic storage, the near elimination of saturation, and the effective reduction of the intrinsic n-p-n storage.

Comparing this structure with the standard I^{2}L configuration of the same functional complexity, the input minority carrier capacitance is reduced by a factor equal to the fan-out (all n-p-n transistors are turning on in a standard I^{2}L configuration). Furthermore, using the NAND versus an inverted "WIRED-AND" circuit configuration results in a smaller transient loading, since the probability of all the load gates being switched is less than unity.

The number of contacts is increased when separate diodes are used. A number of diodes can share the same n$^+$ contact (cathode) when the load gates are in the same location of the chip. Although the gate size is increased over the I^{3}L [7], the metal routings connecting the various logic blocks of the chip are reduced considerably.

REFERENCES

[1] H. H. Berger and S. K. Wiedman, "Merged-transistor logic (MTL)—A low cost bipolar logic concept," *IEEE J. Solid-State Circuits*, vol. SC-7, pp. 340–346, Oct. 1972.

[2] K. Hart and A. Slob, "Integrated injection logic: A new approach to LSI," *IEEE J. Solid-State Circuits*, vol. SC-7, pp. 346–351, Oct. 1972.

[3] H. H. Berger and S. K. Wiedman, "Schottky transistor logic," in *ISSCC Dig. Tech. Papers*, 1975, pp. 172–173.

[4] F. W. Hewlett, Jr., "Schottky I^{2}L," *IEEE J. Solid-State Circuits*, vol. SC-10, pp. 343–348, Oct. 1975.

[5] J. M. Herman, III, "High performance output Schottky I^{2}L/MTL," in *IEDM Tech. Dig.*, 1977, pp. 262–265.

[6] P. S. Walsh and G. W. Sumerling, "Schottky I^{2}L (substrate fed logic)—An optimum form of I^{2}L," *IEEE J. Solid-State Circuits*, vol. SC-12, pp. 123–127, Apr. 1977.

[7] F. Hennig, H. K. Hingarh, D. O'Brien, and P. W. J. Verhofstadt, "Isoplanar integrated injection logic: A high-performance bipolar technology," *IEEE J. Solid-State Circuits*, vol. SC-12, pp. 101–109, Apr. 1977.

[8] A. W. Peltier, "A new approach to bipolar LSI: C^{3}L," in *ISSCC Dig. Tech. Papers*, 1975, pp. 168–169.

[9] G. Perlegos and S. P. Chan, "Modeling and optimization of the oxide isolated substrate fed I^{2}L structure," *IEEE J. Solid-State Circuits*, vol. SC-13, pp. 491–499, Aug. 1978.

[10] R. J. Van Overstraeten, H. H. DeMan, and R. P. Mertens, "Transport equations in heavy doped silicon," *IEEE Trans. Electron Devices*, vol. ED-20, pp. 220–298, Mar. 1973.

[11] S. M. Sze, *Physics of Semiconductor Devices*. New York: Wiley, 1969, p. 399.

[12] H. H. Berger, "The injection model—A structure-oriented model for merged transistor logic (MTL)," *IEEE J. Solid-State Circuits*, vol. SC-9, pp. 218–227, Oct. 1974.

[13] J. R. Hauser, "The effects of distributed base potential on emitter current injection density and effective base resistance for stripe transistor geometries," *IEEE Trans. Electron Devices*, vol. ED-11, pp. 236–242, May 1964.

Part VI
Novel I²L Techniques:
Logic, Circuits, and Layouts

This part contains four papers which present novel and unusual schemes for expanding the usefulness of I²L beyond the more conventional applications. Paper VI-1 by Dao describes the application of I²L to threshold functions and multivalued logic. The multivalued logic approach permits increased on-chip functional density and thereby offers the potential for the application of I²L in the integration of very large digital logic designs. The major drawbacks to this scheme are the following:

1) the decreased noise immunity inherent in a multivalued logic system;
2) the reduced speed which results from the necessity of operating at lower current levels where series resistance effects do not substantially affect gate performance;
3) the more strict processing constraints which arise from the requirements for matched devices; and
4) typically, the application of I²L is not limited by packing density considerations but is limited by its speed.

Thus although the multivalued I²L technique may find application in special circumstances, it will not find general acceptance and wide application.

The second paper (VI-2) by Friedman *et al.* presents the realization of a specific multivalued logic function, the full adder. These authors' results verify that such an approach offers increased functional density at the expense of speed and more stringent processing requirements. The authors state that their approach offers the same area-delay product as a conventional binary I²L implementation. This statement is just another way of saying that speed must be traded for the increased functional density which is derived from the multivalued logic approach.

Paper VI-3 describes a novel technique for the "stacking" of different portions of an I²L circuit so as to place them in series with the power supply. The technique permits more efficient use of the power supply energy and is particularly attractive for low-power, battery-operated applications. It should be noted that the technique was first introduced in paper VIII-1.

Paper VI-4 by Ragonese and Yang presents a layout solution to the problems which arise due to the series base resistance of a conventional I²L gate. These authors recognized that the turn-on and turn-off delays of an I²L collector depend, respectively, upon the position of the collector relative to the injector and base contact. They show a gate layout which minimizes differences in the series resistances which affect the turn-on and turn-off of their four fan-out structure. The technique is valuable where a standard process must be used for the implementation of I²L yet the propagation delays of the circuit must be uniform through-out. The references for Part VI contain additional clever layout techniques.

Threshold I²L and Its Applications to Binary Symmetric Functions and Multivalued Logic

T. TICH DAO, MEMBER, IEEE

Abstract—I²L threshold gate using current mirrors providing weighting of inputs, summation, and comparison with a threshold is described and its practical realization is discussed. Application to binary symmetric functions shows significant area savings over standard I²L implementation. A complete multivalued logic family, using a four-level I²L threshold logic technique is introduced.

I. INTRODUCTION

THE USE OF threshold elements in logic circuits has been under investigation for some time. In fact several practical ECL implementations [1]–[3] have been proposed in the past. Threshold elements are rarely used in practice. They appear only where conventional logic implementation is unfeasible, e.g., partially or totally symmetric functions of many variables. Recently [4], they have been introduced as an efficient design tool for multivalued logic.

The threshold gate has binary inputs $x_1 \cdots x_n$ and a binary output y. Its internal parameters are input weights $w_1, \cdots, w_n$ and threshold T. The gate forms the linear weighted sum of inputs and compares it to the threshold. The resulting output is "1" if the sum exceeds the threshold, and "0" otherwise. With a wide range of weights and thresholds possible, many functions can be realized by a single threshold gate. The class of functions realizable is the well-known linearly separable functions.

II. I²L THRESHOLD GATE

I²L/MTL is in essence a current-mode direct-coupled transistor logic. Like ECL, I²L can implement the following functions which are essential to the threshold gates.

1) *Input replication*: create replicas of an input through current-mirror imaging.

2) *Weighted sums*: form arithmetic sum of several weighted replicas.

3) *Threshold detection*: determine if sum exceeds a predetermined threshold.

The I²L current mirror [4]–[5] constitutes the main building block. Fig. 1(a) shows the circuit diagram of a current mirror producing three replicas of an input. Figs. 1(b) and 1(c) give the top view and the cross section of the device.

It is known that since all I²L n-p-n collectors operate in the

Manuscript received April 26, 1977; revised June 20, 1977.
The author is with Signetics Corporation, Sunnyvale, CA 94086.

inverted mode, they are independent of each other in the sense that any of them may be saturated without affecting the others. The inaccuracy of the mirror due to the low beta can be corrected by undersizing the feedback collector with respect to the others.

The signal weighting is obtained by varying the size of the output collectors. Collectors of different sizes and from different current mirrors are connected together to form a weighted sum (Fig. 2). A more conservative design would use a Darlington current mirror, with an isolated n-p-n in front of the regular multicollector inverted n-p-n, thus providing high-loop gain to ensure both unity-current gain and larger fan-out. Also, the base of the p-n-p would be biased above ground to maintain the constancy of all current sources (Fig. 3).

A current differencing amplifier implements the threshold detection function. A fixed p-n-p current source injects current into the base of an n-p-n transistor, and a summing with a current drain equal to a weighted sum of several signals attempts to sink the injected current [Fig. 4(a)]. For threshold T, T units of current are injected. The transistor cuts off if the drain is T or greater. The threshold is physically controlled by the opening of the n⁺ suppression bar between the injector and the base region of the detector [Fig. 4(b)]. Better control of the threshold could be obtained by using an isolated multicollector p-n-p where the sizes of the separate collector are quantized to provide one half of the unit current. Several collectors are connected to produce the desired threshold. For sharper detection an isolated transistor [Fig. 4(c)] or a Schmitt trigger is used [Fig. 4(d) and 4(e)].

This latter circuit can be derived directly from the classic voltage Schmitt by taking the current dual of each element, as shown in Fig. 4(d) and 4(e).

Initially for $I_{in} = 0$, T_1 is cut off, the threshold current I_R is injected into the base of the current mirror T_2, current follower, or a dual of the emitter follower.

The feedback loop is kept closed. For $I_{in} \leqslant I_R$ all I_{in} is shorted to ground through T_2. For $I_{in} > I_R$, transistor T_1 starts to conduct. It saturates at the value of I_{in} such that $I_{in} - I_R \geqslant I_R/\beta$. T_2 then switches off, the feedback loop is disconnected, and the entire I_{in} flows into the base of T_1. In the return path, T_1 only switches off when I_{in} drops down below the level equal to I_R/β.

The trigger exhibits a hysteresis characteristic [Fig. 4(f)] directly related to the level of the threshold I_R. It is quite sim-

Reprinted from *IEEE J. Solid-State Circuits*, vol. SC-12, pp. 463–472, Oct. 1977.

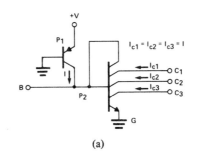

(a)

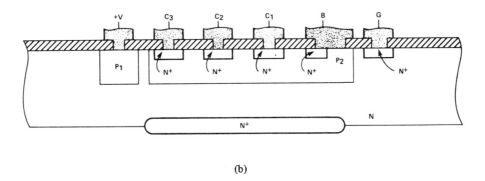

(b)

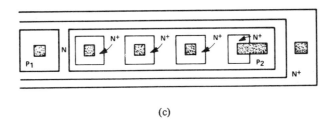

(c)

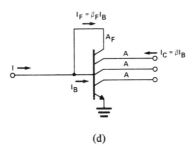

(d)

Fig. 1. (a) I^2L current mirror. (b) Side view. (c) Top view. (d) Low β I^2L mirror.

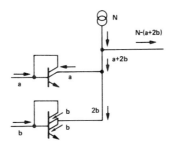

Fig. 2. Weighted sums.

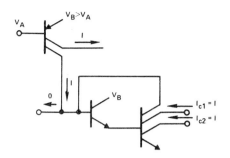

Fig. 3. Darlington current mirror.

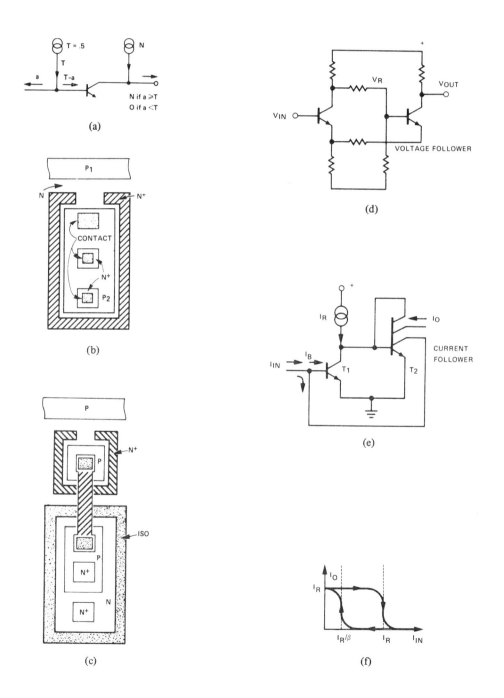

Fig. 4. Standard I²L threshold detector. (a) Threshold detector. (b) Layout. (c) Improved detector. (d) Voltage Schmitt. (e) Current Schmitt. (f) Current Schmitt hysteresis.

ple to control the hysteresis width by means of an additional delayed negative feedback loop or a controlled β.

III. I^2L Threshold Gate Sensitivity

The reliability of a threshold gate is strongly affected by the presence of unavoidable component variations and noise that corrupt the nominal values of the weighted sum and the threshold. More specifically, input current, current-mirror gain, and threshold current percentage fluctuation tolerances designated respectively by $\delta_I, \delta_B, \delta_T$, must be defined to ensure error-free operation on the "worst case" conditions. This situation occurs when the weighted sum S is 1) at its minimum for a true output, the threshold being at its upper limit $T(1 + \delta_T)$:

$$\sum_j I_j (1 - \delta_I) \beta_{mj} (1 - \delta_\beta) \geqslant T (1 + \delta_T);$$

2) at its maximum for a false output, the threshold being at its lower limit $T(1 - \delta_T)$:

$$\sum_j I_j (1 + \delta_I) \beta_{mj} (1 + \delta_\beta) \leqslant T (1 - \delta_T).$$

If we define by u and l the nominal value of the weighted sum corresponding respectively to true and false outputs of the threshold gate, then we can condense the two inequalities into:

$$(1 - \delta_I)(1 - \delta_\beta) u \geqslant T(1 + \delta_T)$$

$$(1 + \delta_I)(1 + \delta_\beta) l \leqslant T(1 - \delta_T).$$

Therefore the following constraint must be satisfied by a threshold gate in order to achieve error-free operation when parameter-fluctuation tolerances δ_I, δ_β, and δ_T are specified:

$$\frac{u - l}{(u + l)} \geqslant \frac{\delta_I + \delta_\beta + \delta_T + \delta_I \delta_\beta \delta_T}{\delta_I + \delta_I \delta_\beta + \delta_I \delta_T + \delta_\beta \delta_T}.$$

If we neglect second-order variations, and assume the same tolerances for the input and threshold currents $\delta_I = \delta_T = \delta$, then:

$$\frac{u - l}{u + l} \geqslant (2_\delta + \delta_\beta).$$

Furthermore, by setting the threshold T at the center of the gap, $(u - l)$ that means $2T = u + l$, tolerances on current sources and current gain must satisfy the following requirement:

$$2\delta + \delta_\beta \leqslant \frac{1}{2T}.$$

Assume that [Fig. 4(f)] A_F and A are, respectively, the areas of the feedback collector and the output collector, and β_F and β are their current gains. If base resistance effect is kept under control, then in first approximation, one can write:

$$\beta_F = \beta \frac{A_F}{A}.$$

Of course, the β's depend on the total number of collectors in the device. The current-mirror gain, defined as

$$\beta_m = \frac{I_c}{I}$$

can be expressed easily as

$$\beta_m = \frac{I_B \beta}{I_B \left(1 + \beta \dfrac{A_F}{A}\right)} = \frac{\beta}{\left(1 + \beta \dfrac{A_F}{A}\right)}.$$

It is desired that $\beta_m = 1$, therefore, one must have

$$\frac{A_F}{A} = \frac{\beta - 1}{\beta}.$$

Notice that

$$\frac{d\beta_m}{\beta m} \simeq \frac{d\beta}{\beta} \frac{1}{1 + \beta}, \quad \text{since} \quad \frac{A_F}{A} \simeq 1$$

and its variation is negligible. Typically, for $\beta = 5$, in a four-collector device, a 20 percent variation in β only results in about 3.3 percent variation in β_m. As an example for $\delta_\beta = 3.3$ percent as computed above, and if T is limited to 2.5, as in most of the following applications, then the tolerance of current source must be maintained better than:

$$\frac{1}{4T} - \frac{\delta_\beta}{2} = 8.3 \text{ percent}$$

which is achievable with I^2L technology and matched components.

Notice that the worst-case tolerance condition only occurs when input current sources and the corresponding threshold current source are distant from each other, or the level of current used is such that the drop along the injector bar contributes to the variation in α of the lateral p-n-p current source.

IV. Applications

A. Binary Symmetric Functions

Characterized by their independence over all permutations of input variables, they form a sizable family of logic functions which are most suitable for threshold gate implementation. Standard realization of those functions are often cumbersome or impractical. Functions such as arithmetic, parity checker, priority encoder, linear counting, etc.,... can be easily implemented.

As an example, two versions of a full adder are shown in Fig. 5(a) and 5(b). The area saving is about 20 percent when designed with threshold logic. Each input X, Y, C_o is triplicated through its corresponding mirror current. Triplicates of their linear sum are simultaneously compared to three thresholds (0.5, 1.5, and 2.5). The outputs of the threshold gates correspond respectively to an OR, a MAJORITY, and an AND of the inputs. A combination of their outputs provides the sum S and the carry C of the full adder.

In some applications where the use of a few threshold gates with a threshold much larger than 2.5 can save a large number of standard gates, then it is economically valid to incorporate them in the design, even at the cost of requiring trimming steps in the fabrication process to ensure their reliability.

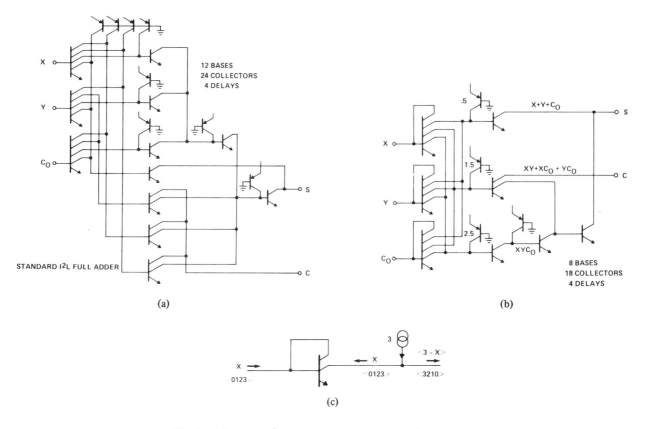

Fig. 5. (a) Standard I²L full adder. (b) Threshold I²L full adder. (c) Complement gate.

Such an approach has been adopted in the design of a deskewing FIFO which holds up to 16 two-bit data items. Status flags indicating $\frac{1}{4}$ full, $\frac{1}{2}$ full, $\frac{3}{4}$ full, full, empty conditions must be set.

They are derived by enumeration of the consecutive ONES or ZEROS in a 16-bit control register. For example, the $\frac{1}{4}$ full condition is true if four or more bits are ONES. To indicate such a condition with conventional two-level circuitry requires 13 AND gates. The $\frac{1}{4}$ full flag requires a four threshold. Practical realization of such a high threshold value was achieved by D. Preedy through the use of a multicollector lateral p-n-p injector, connecting three unit size collectors together with one of several optional collectors of fractional size [Fig. 5(c)].

B. Multivalued Logic

Multilevel digital circuits make feasible compact computers because such circuits have high logic density by the reduction of interconnection paths. The type of multivalued logic system to be implemented is determined by the basic function which can be realized reliably in modern technology. Such digital circuitry is based on the processing of signals with multiple discrete levels. Reliable means of level detection, i.e., threshold gate, must be provided to sense the true state of the signal, to restore, or requantize it to its nominal value before it drifts away too far, losing its information content. I²L threshold offers a relatively simple and reliable tool to implement multilevel logic functions of any radix.

TABLE I
BASIC MULTIVALUED LOGIC FUNCTIONS

Maximum:	MAX (x,y)	$= x$ if $x \geqslant y$ $= y$ if $y \leqslant x$
Minimum:	MIN (x,y)	$= x$ if $x \leqslant y$ $= y$ if $y \geqslant x$
Complement:	$\bar{x}$	$= 3 - x$ (four-valued logic)
Successor:	SUC (x)	$= (x + 1)$ modulo 4
Literals:	$a_x b$	$= 1$, if $a \leqslant x \leqslant b$ $= 0$, otherwise

A family of circuits for multilevel integrated injection logic is described here [6]. The specific values shown are for four-level realizations, but the technique is not limited to four levels.

It is well known [7] that if it is possible to realize certain basic functions, then any multivalued function can be realized by interconnections of these basic functions. A sufficient set of basic functions is listed in Table I.

The simplest of these basic functions to realize is the complement, for which a circuit is shown in Fig. 5(c). The notation used is that the symbol <0123> at the input terminal shows the four possible values of input current. The < > symbols elsewhere in the circuit show the corresponding currents which flow at these other points in the circuit. Thus, the

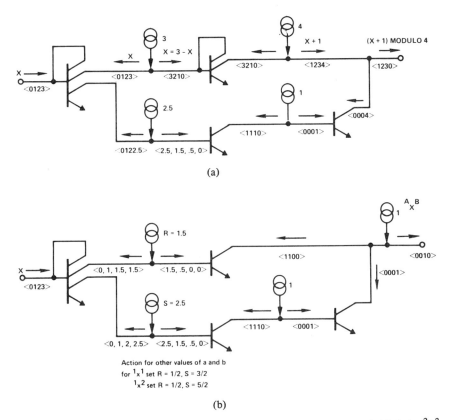

(a)

(b)

Fig. 6. Successor and literal circuits. (a) Successor circuit. (b) Literal circuit with labels for $^2X^2$.

symbol <3210> at the output means that there will be an output current of 3 when the input current is 0, an output current of 2 when the input current is 1, etc. The 3 next to the current source indicates that it sources three units of current. Circuits for the successor and literal functions are shown in Fig. 6. A circuit for the MAX function is shown in Fig. 7. This configuration was derived by E. J. McCluskey. Actually this circuit realizes the complement of the Maximum, $\overline{\text{MAX}(x, y)} = 3 - \text{MAX}(x, y)$. MAX (x,y) can be realized by using a complement circuit following the $\overline{\text{MAX}(x, y)}$ circuit to obtain $\overline{\overline{\text{MAX}(x, y)}} = 3 - (3 - \text{MAX}(x, y)) = \text{MAX}(x, y)$. The analysis in the figure shows that the output is $3 - (x + y - \text{MIN}(x, y))$, but it is easily demonstrated that $x + y - \text{MIN}(x, y) = \text{MAX}(x, y)$. A circuit for the MIN function is easily obtained by preceding each of the inputs by complement circuits since MIN $(x, y) = \overline{\text{MAX}(\bar{x}, \bar{y})}$, see Fig. 7.

Another type of basic building block is the multiplexer or T-gate shown in Fig. 8(a) and 8(b). It has been shown [8] that any multivalued function can be realized by appropriate interconnections of "T gates." The level of the control signal S is sensed by three parallel threshold detectors set at 0.5, 1.5, and 2.5, respectively. Their outputs are logically combined to provide a transmission path to one and only one selected data input (x, y, z, u); the nonselected inputs are shorted to ground. The column of current followers isolates inputs from each other and transmits the selected data to the outputs after a prior inversion.

A particularly important function in digital logic involves the addition of two base-b numbers. A full adder circuit for two base-4 digits is shown in Figs. 9 and 10.

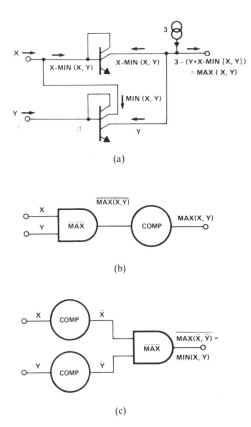

(a)

(b)

(c)

Fig. 7. Circuits for $\overline{\text{MAX}}$, MAX, and MIN functions. (a) Circuit for $\overline{\text{MAX}(x, y)}$. (b) Symbolic representation of circuit for MAX(x, y). (c) Symbolic representation of circuit for MIN(x, y).

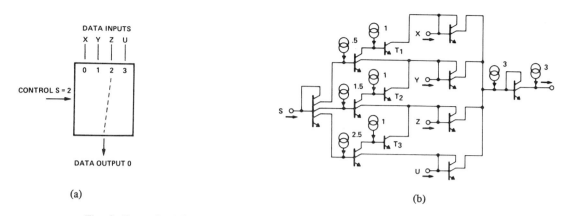

Fig. 8. Four-valued logic multiplexer of T-gate. (a) Block diagram.
(b) Circuit.

Y\X	0	1	2	3	Y\X	0	1	2	3	
0	0	1	2	3	0	0	0	0	0	
1	0	2	3	0.	1	0	0	0	1	$C_i = 0$
2	2	3	0	1	2	0	0	1	1	
3	3	0	1	2	3	0	1	1	1	

Y\X	0	1	2	3	Y\X	0	1	2	3	
0	1	2	3	0	0	0	0	0	1	
1	2	3	0	1	1	0	0	1	1	$C_i = 1$
2	3	0	1	2	2	0	1	1	1	
3	0	1	2	3	3	1	1	1	1	
			S					C		

Fig. 9. Truth table for quaternary adder.

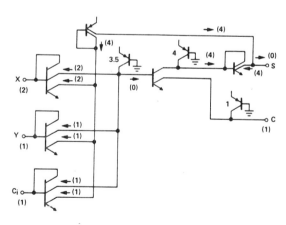

Fig. 10. Quaternary adder.

As an example, we pick the input value as

$X = 2$, $Y = 1$, and $C_i = 1$.

From the true table we must have as outputs

$S = 0$; $C = 1$.

By referring to Fig. 10, we notice that the arithmetic sum Σ of the three inputs are duplicated. One copy is transformed from current sinking to current sourcing at the logic sum output S, through a p-n-p mirror; the other is compared to a threshold 3.5.

If Σ is less than that value, then the detector remains in the on state, and we have:

$S = \Sigma$

$C = 0.$

If Σ is larger than the threshold, the detector is switched off

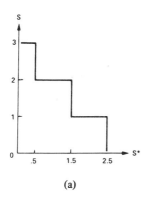

(a)

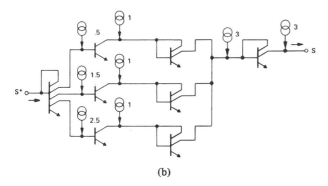

(b)

Fig. 11. Quaternary quantizer.

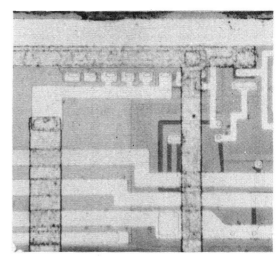

Fig. 12. Detector $T = 4$.

and liberates exactly four units of current into the current mirror, connected at the output S; the net current available at that terminal is

$$S = \Sigma - 4.$$

At the same time $C = 1$.

As mentioned earlier, signal restoration, in most of the circuits described, is achieved locally through level detection by threshold gates. However, in many instances, such as the complement, minimum and maximum gates, signals are linearly processed without the need for threshold gates. A signal going through a chain of those gates must be restored by a special circuit called a quantizer [Fig. 11(a) and 11(b)]. Such a circuit which is in essence a simple two-bit A to D converter, is obtained from the multiplexer or T gate.

The large family of gates, just described, allows realization of combinational functions, and sequential logic implementation. Storage elements such as D latch, D flip-flop, etc., are built around quantizers with output fed back to the input through several stages of control gates.

V. PROCESSING AND EXPERIMENTAL RESULTS

The test chips for both threshold functions, and the multivalued logic family were processed using industry-wide standard-technology Schottky T^2L, to which two minor variations were added: a more highly doped buried n^+ region to provide better n-p-n emitter injection efficiency, and a shallow n diffusion which is driven more deeply into the base to increase base transport efficiency. The result of both changes is forward current gains from 200 to 250 and reverse current greater than 4 for one of four collectors over a collector current range of 10

nA to 100 μA. Measurements of basewidth show typical widths of 0.2 μm and resultant BV_{CEO} of 5.0 V. The Schottky-like process was chosen because the thin epitaxy (3 μm) and shallow diffusion profiles permit dense surface technologies.

Relatively high base diffusion resistance 200 $\Omega/\square$ in the present process set an upper limit on the collector current in the current mirror, since its β_m must remain constant for the entire dynamic range of the signal. This constraint becomes more severe for a four-collector device. Means to minimize the base resistance effect have been devised at the cost of device size. For example, use the low resistivity of the p isolation of 4.5 $\Omega/\square$, by diffusing a long stripe of p isolation along the edge of the base. The solution was proposed by Slob and Bos.

Detailed description accompanied by experimental results of a few typical circuits will be given. Fig. 12 shows the photomicrograph of a threshold detector for a signal level 4, used in the FIFO. Four discrete collectors of normalized size (18-μm width) are lumped together to a common bus bar which connects all current mirrors contributing to the weighted sum. There is a provision for two additional collectors, one undersized and the other oversized, for trimming purposes. Once tests have determined the correct set of collectors, a final metal mask will freeze the design. This detector, and others, operate as part of a large system over a measurable dynamic range exceeding one decade from 19 μA to 290 μA per unit current weight, with switching time varying from 55 ns to 15 ns.

A quaternary logic signal has four distinct equidistant levels from 0, 1, 2, 3 corresponding here to nominal current values of 0, 10 μA, 20 μA, and 30 μA. Since it is found that with the present process and with standard design, excluding the use of Darlington and the p isolation stripe, as mentioned above, the β_m only varies about 5 percent within the current range (0–50 μA). Fig. 13(a) shows a current mirror with three outputs 0_1, 0_2, 0_3 having current loads corresponding to 1, 2, 3 units. Fig. 13(b) exhibits the dc characteristics of one collector, superposed with those of three common collectors, when the base is driven by four steps of base current (0, 10, 20, 30, 40 μA). It can be seen that the gain of a single collector is very close to unity, and that of three collectors is exactly triple.

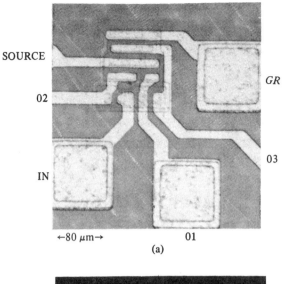

SOURCE

02

IN

GR

03

01

←80 μm→

(a)

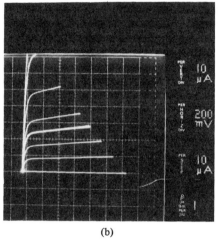

(b)

Fig. 13. Current mirror, current weighting.

SOURCE

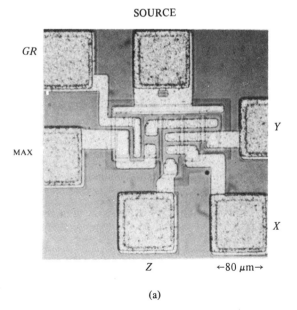

GR

MAX

Y

X

Z

←80 μm→

(a)

Max Output

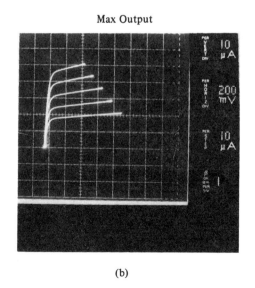

(b)

Fig. 14.

Fig. 14(a) represents an implementation of a three input maximum gate as described earlier. If input x is driven by the current steps (0, 10, 20, 30 μA), input y set at 10 μA, input z at 20 μA, then Fig. 14(b) shows that the output skips the first

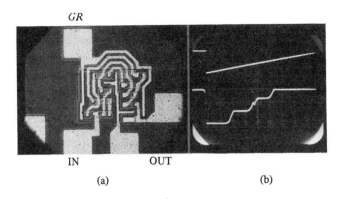

Fig. 15. (a) Quantizer 1. (b) Quantizer input/output.

two values 0 and 10 μA, and responds only to the running maximum, from 20 μA upwards.

Fig. 15 represents the photomicrograph of a quantizer. It illustrates the three design requirements that a circuit using threshold gate must satisfy, namely an input current mirror for triplication, three simultaneous detections (0.5, 1.5, 2.5), and a linear addition of currents to create the steps. The companion picture shows the current steps of 10 μA each when it is driven by a linear current input of 60 μA maximum.

VI. Conclusion

I^2L is essentially a current-mode logic, and relative amplitude of signal and reference are mainly defined by dimension of active base-injector interface. It lends itself, par excellence, with the use of current mirrors, to threshold gate implementation.

Significant advantage of the approach over standard I^2L, when applied to binary symmetric functions, has been shown. The use of I^2L threshold gate was extended into the virtually virgin domain of multivalued logic circuitry. A complete family of quaternary logic has been described. Test circuits fabricated with the present standard I^2L process show remarkable functionality, as predicted by computer simulation, and more importantly suggest few process modifications for higher performance. Circuit techniques used can be easily extended to higher valued logic, if lithography and processing permit.

Acknowledgment

The author wishes to thank L. K. Russell for having suggested, a few years ago, ECL threshold logic as a research project, which has led to this development in I^2L.

Many suggestions during the course of the study from P. Tucci, the practical implementation threshold gate from D. Preedy, and subsequent contributions for the enlargement of the quaternary logic family from E. J. McCluskey are duly appreciated. Stimulating discussions with A. Slob and I. Bos of Philips National Laboratory were shared later. Special thanks to D. Allison for fabrication of the devices, and to D. Kleitman for his sustaining support of this project since its inception.

References

[1] J. J. Amodei, R. O. Winder, D. Hampel, and T. R. Mayhew, "An integrated threshold gate," in *ISSCC Dig. Tech. Papers*, 1967, pp. 114–115.
[2] T. T. Dao, "Threshold logic gate," U.S. Patent 3 838 393, Sept. 24, 1974.
[3] B. A. Wooley and C. R. Baugh, "On integrated *m*-out-of-*n* detection circuit using threshold logic," *IEEE J. Solid-State Circuits*, vol. SC-9, pp. 297–306, Oct. 1974.
[4] T. T. Dao and P. A. Tucci, "Threshold integrated injection logic," Patent Appl. 591 400, June 30, 1975.
[5] M. I. Elmasry, "Folded-collector integrated injection logic," *IEEE J. Solid-State Circuits*, vol. SC-11, pp. 644–647, Oct. 1975.
[6] T. T. Dao, L. K. Russell, D. R. Preedy, and E. J. McCluskey, "Multilevel I^2L with threshold gates," in *ISSCC Dig. Tech. Papers*, Feb. 1977, p. 110.
[7] Z. G. Vranesic and K. C. Smith, "Engineering aspects of multi-valued logic systems," *Computer*, vol. 7, no. 9, pp. 34–41, Sept. 1974.
[8] T. Higuchi and M. Kameyama, "Ternary logic systems based on T-Gate," in *Proc. 1975 Int. Symp. Multivalued Logic*, Indiana Univ., Bloomington, IN, May 13–16, 1975, pp. 290–304, IEEE Cat. 75CH0959-7C.

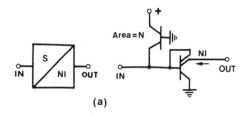

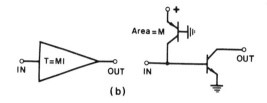

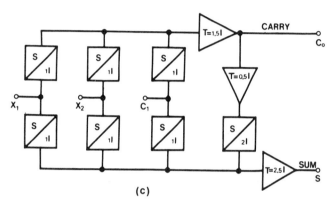

Fig. 1. (a) Current switch. (b) Threshold detector. (c) Multivalued full adder logic diagram.

Realization of a Multivalued Integrated Injection Logic (MI²L) Full Adder

N. FRIEDMAN, C. A. T. SALAMA, F. E. HOLMES, AND P. M. THOMPSON

Abstract—A multivalued integrated injection logic scheme and its application to the realization of a full adder is described in this correspondence. The integrated full adder is implemented and fabricated using V-groove isolated I²L technology. Results obtained on the experimental structures indicate that the multivalued full adder offers an increase in functional density while retaining approximately the same area x delay product as a binary full adder at identical power levels.

INTRODUCTION

Multivalued logic offers certain advantages over standard binary logic in the design of large-scale integrated circuits because it results in a significant increase in the functional density. The advent of high density current-mode threshold techniques as encountered in I²L [1], [2] can make multivalued logic a practical reality. The object of this work is to describe a multivalued integrated injection logic scheme and to discuss, as an example, its application to the implementation of an integrated full adder in which the input and output are binary while the logic within the adder is performed using a multilevel format, thus resulting in a considerable saving in area over standard I²L binary logic design.

Manuscript received March 24, 1977; revised June 6, 1977. This work was supported by the National Research Council of Canada.

N. Friedman, C. A. T. Salama, and F. E. Holmes are with the Department of Electrical Engineering, University of Toronto, Toronto, Ont., Canada.

P. M. Thompson is with Thompson Foss Inc., Ottawa, Ont., Canada.

LOGIC SCHEME

The logic scheme consists of transmitting the multivalued signal in the current mode while the binary signals are transmitted in the voltage mode (at conventional I²L levels). The advantage of using the current mode for multivalued signals is that it allows the supply voltage to be kept low without reducing the separation between logic values to a dangerously low level [3]. A similar scheme has been independently suggested by Dao *et al.* [4].

The two basic elements of the logic system are a current switch and a threshold detector. The current switch S is a binary controlled current sink shown symbolically in Fig. 1 (a). The realization of this switch in I²L technology is also shown in the figure. The value of the current sink NI can be controlled by the collector area of the p-n-p current source injector and is indicated on the switch symbol (I is an arbitrary reference current level and N is an area normalization constant). This particular realization of the current switch uses a folded collector connected to the base (current mirror). The area of the folded collector is chosen equal to that of the actual output collector. A number of switches can be realized simultaneously by adding extra output collectors, resulting in a very compact multiswitch structure.

The threshold detector T has a multivalued input and a binary output and is shown symbolically in Fig. 1 (b). For input currents smaller than the threshold detection level, the output current is zero. For input currents equal to or larger than the threshold level, the full required current (defined by the following stage) appears at the output. For the special

Reprinted from *IEEE J. Solid-State Circuits*, vol. SC-12, pp. 532–534, Oct. 1977.

case of a binary input, the threshold level is set midway ($0.5\,I$) between the "zero" and "one" levels and the detector acts as a binary inverter. The threshold detector can be realized using a single I^2L gate as shown in Fig. 1 (b). The threshold current level MI is set by the collector area (or length) of the p-n-p current source injector (M is an area normalization constant).

The combination of the switch and threshold detector can be used to realize a variety of logic functions. As an example of the application of the logic system, the logic diagram for a multilevel full adder with binary inputs and outputs is shown in Fig. 1 (c). The inputs of the full adder are X_1, X_2, and the carry C_1. The outputs of the adder are the sum S and the carry C_0. The full adder circuit operates internally with four current levels:[1] 0, $1\,I$, $2\,I$, $3\,I$, and three thresholds: $0.5\,I$, $1.5\,I$, and $2.5\,I$. The complete implementation of the adder consists of three unity area double collector switches, one double area single collector switch, and three threshold detectors. The threshold T_1 ($0.5\,I$) is tested when the sum output S changes from "0" to "1" while the carry output C_0 stays at zero. The threshold T ($1.5\,I$), which is the main threshold of the adder, is tested when both the sum output S and the carry output C_0 change state from "0" to "1." The threshold T_2 ($2.5\,I$) is tested when the sum output S changes state from "0" to "1" while the carry output C_0 remains constant at "1."

DESIGN REQUIREMENTS

As the number of levels in a multivalued logic circuit increases, the accuracy required from the threshold detectors in discriminating between logic levels increases. For the four-level full adder under consideration, the worst case tolerance margin occurs when a current weighted at $3\,I$ is to be detected by a $2.5\,I$ threshold detector. If θ is defined as the tolerance on the threshold level of the detector, i.e., for the $2.5\,I$ detector, then the threshold is assumed to be $2.5\,I\,(1 \pm \theta)$. Assuming the same tolerance on the input current to the detector, i.e., the input current is assumed to be $3\,I\,(1 \pm \theta)$, then under worst case conditions, for proper operation of the $2.5\,I$ detector, the following equation must be satisfied:

$$3\,I\,(1 - \theta) > 2.5\,I\,(1 + \theta). \qquad (1)$$

This implies that θ should be smaller than or equal to 9 percent, i.e., the tolerance on a unit current I processed through the system must be maintained to better than 9 percent. This tolerance is achievable using I^2L technology and matched components. For proper operation of an I^2L gate, the upward current gain β_μ must be larger than one. In addition, for proper operation of a multilevel I^2L circuit, the tolerance requirements on current levels must be achieved by: 1) close matching of currents using proper layout of the individual multicollector gate structures, and 2) proper scaling of the currents in the circuit.

In order to ensure current matching, the collectors must be laid out parallel to the injector rail rather than perpendicular to it in order to minimize lateral voltage drop due to the base resistance and ensure that all collectors receive equal amounts of currents. This type of layout leads to a decrease in packing density, but results in equal delays for all collectors. It should be pointed out that for large values of β_μ or low injection currents, the matching becomes less critical and a perpendicular collector structure may be used to achieve higher packing density.

Area scaling to control the current-handling capabilities of the switches and threshold detectors is carried out by scaling the

---

[1]The choice of four levels of operation for the full adder was made taking into consideration the limitations of the integrated circuit process.

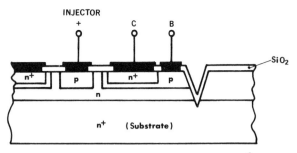

Fig. 2. Cross section of a typical V-groove isolated I^2L gate.

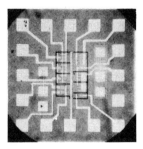

Fig. 3. Micrograph of the multivalued full adder.

collector area (or injecting length) of the p-n-p current source. The scaling of the injecting length in the current switches is straightforward, i.e., the injecting length for an NI current switch is normalized to N. However, due to the particular folded collector configuration of the current switch and the finite β_μ of the n-p-n transistors, it is necessary to scale the injecting area (or length) of the threshold detectors by a constant factor K given by

$$K = \frac{\beta_\mu}{1 + \beta_\mu}$$

where β_μ is the upside-down gain of the n-p-n transistor in the current switch.

FABRICATION AND EXPERIMENTAL RESULTS

The full adder was fabricated using a five-mask V-groove isolation technology [5]. The starting material was (100) orientation n/n^+ epitaxial silicon. The cross section of a typical I^2L gate is shown in Fig. 2. The base and injector diffusion was performed in a two-step process using a boron nitride source. The top collector was diffused using a phosphorus solid source. The vertical design parameters of junctions depths and impurity concentrations were selected to satisfy a variety of constraints. The n^+ substrate was 0.05 $\Omega \cdot$ cm. The resistivity and thickness of the n-epitaxial layer were 1 $\Omega \cdot$ cm and 4.5 μm, respectively. These parameters were chosen to optimize β_μ. The diffused base region was designed to have a sheet resistance of 200 $\Omega/\square$. The collector diffusion was adjusted to provide a base width of 0.2 μm and a sheet resistance of 1 $\Omega/\square$. The V-groove oxide isolation process was used to reduce the lateral transfer between adjacent gates as well as the speed–power product of the gates [5].

A micrograph of the integrated version of the full adder is shown in Fig. 3. The layout of the circuit was not optimized for minimum area, but rather was designed for ease of testing. A 7.5 μm layout rule was used. The areas of the threshold detectors were scaled to account for the finite value of β_μ.

The total area of the active circuit is 400 μm $\times$ 225 μm without layout optimization. An optimum design using the same layout rules and parallel collector structures would result in an area of about 270 μm $\times$ 90 μm. The corresponding area for a binary I^2L full adder fabricated using the same technology and layout rules and perpendicular collector structures was calculated to be 290 μm $\times$ 120 μm. This implies that an optimized multivalued I^2L full adder circuit occupies 70 percent of the area of the binary full adder. If the multivalued I^2L full adder is constructed using perpendicular collector structures, a further reduction in area would result. The I^2L threshold gates were characterized by measuring β_μ and β_d. A curve tracer was used for the measurements. The typical value of β_μ was 3 for collector currents ranging from 20 to 200 μA. In the same range of currents, the value of β_d was 600. The beta matching for a set of three collectors in a parallel structure with a unity area injector was found to be better than 3 percent over a range of current from 10 μA to 1 mA. The collector-to-emitter breakdown voltage for the upside-down n-p-n transistor was 1.6 V.

The full adder operation was successfully tested at low frequency using three synchronized input signals applied to terminals X_1, X_2, and C_1. A TTL-to-I^2L interface consisting of a single inverter stage was used at the input and an I^2L-to-TTL interface consisting of two inverters in series was used at the output.

The speed of operation of the circuit was tested with a stable dc level corresponding to a "one" at the X_1 input, a stable dc level corresponding to a "zero" at the X_2 input, and a pulse applied to the C_1 input. The delays of the sum and carry outputs are $t'_{ds} = 1.5$ μs and $t'_{dc} = 0.9$ μs, respectively, at an injector current of 75 μA. These delays include the delays of the input and output interfaces. The intrinsic values of the delays without the interfaces are $t_{ds} = 1.2$ μs and $t_{dc} = 0.6$ μs. In the multilevel full adder, all three inputs are interchangeable and the resultant delay is the same for any combination of a dc "zero" input, a dc "one" input, and a pulsed input. For comparison purposes, the corresponding intrinsic sum delay for a binary full adder operated at the same injection current and using the same interfaces was found to be approximately 0.8 μs. In the case of the binary full adder, all three inputs are not directly interchangeable and the delay depends on whether one of the inputs or the carry is clocked. The value 0.8 μs for the delay was obtained by averaging the delays for the case of a dc "zero" input, a dc "one" input, and a clocked carry and the case of a dc "zero" input, a clocked input, and a dc "one" carry. Therefore, it appears that for the same power dissipation, the area x delay product (in this case the delay refers to the delay associated with the sum output) for the multivalued full adder is approximately the same as for the binary full adder.

Conclusion

The multivalued full adder implemented using I^2L technology offers a sizable reduction in area while operating at approximately the same area x delay product as the binary version. The logic scheme described in this correspondence can be applied to the realization of a variety of other logic functions and, furthermore, can be extended to levels higher than four with improvements in processing technology.

Acknowledgment

The authors would like to thank Prof. K. C. Smith for his constant encouragement during the various stages of this work.

References

[1] K. Hart and A. Slob, "Integrated injection logic—A new approach to LSI," *IEEE J. Solid-State Circuits*, vol. SC-7, pp. 346–351, Oct. 1972.

[2] H. H. Berger and S. K. Wiedmann, "Merged transistor logic (MTL) —A low cost bipolar logic concept," *IEEE J. Solid-State Circuits*, vol. SC-7, pp. 340–346, Oct. 1972.

[3] N. Friedman, C. A. T. Salama, F. E. Holmes, and P. M. Thompson, "A multivalued integrated injection logic (MI^{2}L) full adder," *Electron. Lett.*, vol. 13, pp. 135–136, 1977.

[4] T. T. Dao, L. K. Russell, D. R. Preedy, and E. J. McCluskey, "Multilevel I^2L with threshold gates," in *1977 Int. Solid-State Circuits Conf., Dig. Tech. Papers*, Feb. 1977, pp. 110–111.

[5] M. J. Declerq, J. P. De Moor, P. G. Jespers, and A. M. Sevrin, "V-groove isolated I^2L circuits," *Electron. Lett.*, vol. 12, pp. 150–151, 1976.

Stacked I²L Circuit

KENJI KANEKO, TAKAHIRO OKABE, AND
MINORU NAGATA

Abstract—A new I²L circuit configuration is presented which cuts
down the effective power dissipation of conventional I²L circuits to
one third or even less. The basic idea of the new circuit concept is
stacking the multiple blocks of I²L circuit layers and operating them
in series connection.

INTRODUCTION

In the conventional I²L circuit, an injector current is supplied through a resistor or a constant current circuit [1], [2].

Manuscript received October 29, 1976.
The authors are with the Central Research Laboratory, Hitachi, Ltd.,
Tokyo, Japan.

The voltage necessary to operate the I²L circuit is about
0.7 V and the I²L circuit itself does operate with very low
power dissipation. This is a very desirable feature of the I²L
circuit. However, when the I²L circuit is used with another
circuit, a TTL circuit for example, the power is not effectively
utilized. The supply voltage of a TTL circuit is 5 V and almost
all the power is dissipated at the resistor or the constant current circuit, as shown in Fig. 1(a). It amounts to 86 percent of
the total power consumption.

CIRCUIT CONFIGURATION AND BIASING METHOD

The "stacked" I²L circuit is made by stacking m blocks of
I²L circuit layers, as shown in Fig. 1(b). In this circuit configuration, the dc bias current supplied to the first layer goes
through all the upper layers, effectively biasing the other
$(m - 1)$ circuits simultaneously [3].

Reprinted from *IEEE J. Solid-State Circuits*, pp. 210–212, Apr. 1977.

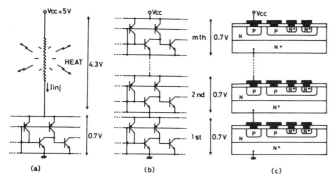

Fig. 1. Circuit construction of conventional and stacked I²L circuit. (a) Conventional I²L circuit construction. (b) Stacked I²L circuit construction. (c) Biasing principle of stacked I²L circuit.

Each I²L circuit block on the upper layers makes efficient use of the power that would be wastefully dissipated at the resistor or the constant current circuit. Consequently, dc power dissipation is reduced down to $(1/m)$ times that of conventional circuits for the same logic function. The total power can be decreased in proportion to the number of layers in the "stack."

When the supply voltage is m times the voltage of the I²L circuit, the wasted power becomes zero or the power efficiency is 100 percent. To get these benefits, however, it is necessary for the injector voltage of each layer to be biased correctly and to be able to transfer a signal between each layer. In other words, this stacked circuit concept is useful if the injector voltage of each layer is biased correctly and if the signal pulses are transferred from one layer to the others.

Because the base–emitter junction of the injector transistor in the I²L circuit is a p-n junction diode, the injector voltage of each layer is biased automatically, as shown in Fig. 1(c), since the diode string forms a voltage divider. There is no need for an additional component, although some adjustment of the injector diode area is required.

Of course, some isolated regions are required for making each I²L circuit block. However, the additional area is insignificant compared with the total chip area.

DRIVING CIRCUITS

The up and down driving circuits for transferring signal pulses from a lower to an upper layer and vice versa are shown in Fig. 2. The up-driving circuit, as shown in Fig. 2(a), is simple and the same as the standard I²L circuit.

Fig. 2(b) is a down-driving circuit. In this figure, a section of the thick line is a driving circuit which differs from standard I²L circuits. Transistor T_{12} is only used as a diode for shifting the signal level. When transistor T_{10} is on, all the current from transistor T_{11} flows to the collector of the transistor T_{10}. Hence, T_{12} is nonconductive or in the "off" condition. When transistor T_{10} is turned off, the current flows into the base of T_{12}. Since the collector voltage of T_{12} is low, the collector junction is forward biased and a part of the current flowing into the base flows through the base–collector junction of T_{12} into the base of T_{20}, turning on T_{20}. The equivalent circuit looks like that shown in Fig. 2(c), where T_{12} operates as two diodes.

Thus, the information can be transferred using the driving circuits, as shown in Fig. 2. It should be noted that these circuits take advantage of the inherent nature of I²L circuits. No additional component or diffusion region is necessary.

EXPERIMENTAL RESULTS

In order to demonstrate the concept, Fig. 3 shows the performance of a three-layered I²L circuit with a supply voltage of 5 V compared with that of the conventional I²L circuit.

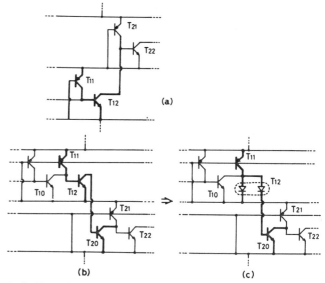

Fig. 2. Up and down driving circuit. (a) Up-driving circuit. (b) Down-driving circuit. (c) Equivalent circuit.

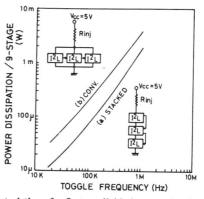

Fig. 3. Characteristics of a 9-stage divide-by-two circuit using a stacked I²L compared with a conventional I²L.

The 9-stage divide-by-two circuit was used for demonstrating the characteristics of the stacked I²L circuit. In this figure, curve (a) represents the characteristics of the three-layered stacked I²L circuit. There is a three-stage divide-by-two circuit in each layer and the signal pulses are transferred from the upper layer to the lower layer. Curve (b) represents the characteristics of the conventional I²L circuit of the same geometry. Although these two circuits realize the same logic function, it can be clearly seen that the power dissipation has been cut down to one third in the three-layered stacked I²L circuit.

ANOTHER CIRCUIT CONSTRUCTION

There is another interesting feature of this stacked I²L circuit, as shown in Fig. 4. This is the stacked I²L circuit in which the total number of the I²L unit circuits between each layer is different. When the number of the I²L unit circuits on the second layer from the top is two times that of the top layer, the injector current density of each unit circuit on the second layer is one half that on the top layer. Similarly, the injector current density of each unit circuit on the lowest layer is $(1/n)$ times that of the top layer. In this way, the current level of each unit circuit can be adjusted for its necessary value. In the conventional I²L circuit, the necessary injector current for each circuit has to be adjusted by using a current divider. For the stacked I²L circuit, the current of each unit circuit in the layers can be determined without the use of a

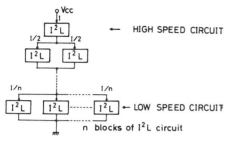

Fig. 4. Concept of dividing the injector current in stacked I^2L.

current divider. This means that it is possible for the different parts of a chip to consume the minimum necessary power in order to obtain the speed at which they have to operate. This configuration is especially useful for a counter circuit in time-keeping systems.

CONCLUSION

A new integrated injection logic circuit which consists of multiple layers of I^2L circuits is proposed. The stacked I^2L circuits are able to decrease the power dissipation in the system, that is, for the m-layer stacked I^2L circuit, the same logic function is realized using m times less power than the conventional I^2L circuit. Up and down driving circuits for transferring a signal from a lower to an upper and vice versa are easily made with a slight modification of the standard I^2L circuit. Moreover, the current supplied to a particular layer is determined by choosing the number of the I^2L unit circuit. Then the injector current is divided automatically without any additional current divider.

REFERENCES

[1] H. H. Berger and S. K. Wiedmann, "Merged-transistor logic (MTL)—A low-cost bipolar logic concept," *IEEE J. Solid-State Circuits*, vol. SC-7, pp. 340–346, Oct. 1972.
[2] K. Hart and A. Slob, "Integrated injection logic: A new approach to LSI," *IEEE J. Solid-State Circuits*, vol. SC-7, pp. 346–351, Oct. 1972.
[3] M. Nagata, K. Kaneko, and T. Okabe, "Stacked I^2L circuit," presented at the 2nd European Solid-State Circuits Conf., Toulouse, France, Sept. 1976.

ENHANCED INTEGRATED INJECTION LOGIC PERFORMANCE USING NOVEL SYMMETRICAL CELL TOPOGRAPHY

Louis J. Ragonese and Neng-Tze Yang

General Electric Company

Electronics Laboratory

Syracuse, New York

ABSTRACT

Contemporary I^2L logic gate structures use an in-line topography for the multiple collector npn transistor. Decoupling effects between adjacent segments introduce a spread in the relative performance of the outputs with respect to gain, maximum collector current, and propagation delay. A novel cell layout, which enables the base contact and pnp injector to be symmetrically positioned relative to every collector in a multiple collector device, was developed. In controlled experiments, using an industry compatible fabrication process, symmetrical quad output cells demonstrated a factor-of-20 increase in the magnitude of useful npn collector current and the degree of gain uniformity among outputs.

CONVENTIONAL IN-LINE TOPOGRAPHY

Background Information

As first described in 1972 (1), (2), Integrated Injection Logic (I^2L) was a digital circuit implementation that used, as its basic logic element, a multiple collector npn transistor that was biased "on" by a merged lateral pnp "current source". Figure 1 shows the cross-section of the basic logic element together with its circuit representation.

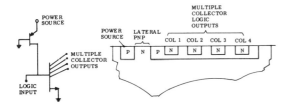

Figure 1. Basic I^2L Logic Element

Decoupling Effects Within the Logic Gate Structure

The npn transistor consists of multiple collectors positioned in a row, resulting in an in-line topography. The region below each npn incremental collector can be considered as independent intrinsic vertical npn transistors, which are decoupled from one another by the base region horizontal resistance. Figure 2 shows the resulting distributed lumped circuit representation of a quad output logic gate.

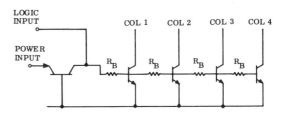

Figure 2. Distributed Lumped Representation of Logic Gate

Modeling of I^2L

The injection model for I^2L developed by H.H. Berger (3) can be slightly modified to reflect this decoupling effect. Figure 3 shows such a modified model, which is closely related to that reported by Klaason (4).

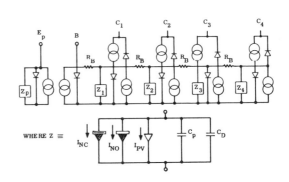

Figure 3. Modified Berger Model

Reprinted from *IEEE Int. Electron Devices Meeting Digest Tech. Papers*, Dec. 1977, pp. 166-169.

A qualitative inspection of this model shows a relatively complex ladder network with a number of shunt elements, including the parasitic and junction depletion capacitance, C_p, and the diffusion capacitance, C_D, associated with the stored charge effects. A further complication arises from the fact that each current component in Figure 3, in fact, represents the cumulative effect of a number of different sub-components. Figure 4 shows 23 different current sub-components, which contribute to the various vertical and horizontal current densities that influence the effective Z-shunt element in the ladder network.

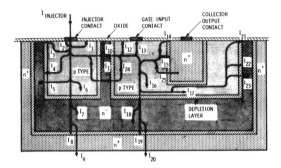

Figure 4. Flow of Hole Current in Basic I^2L Logic Gate

The relative significance of the various components depends on the specific fabrication process and cell layout as well as the environmental conditions of temperature and irradiation. As a result there is a significant variation in the apparent gain of a particular npn collector, and this variation depends on the location of the collector relative to the injector. Furthermore, the transient turn-on and turn-off of a particular output depends largely on its location relative to the "logic input" (npn base contact). This is especially apparent when the I^2L gates are operated at current levels above 50 μA/gate in many fabrication processes. The performance degradation effects are, therefore, especially noticeable at high current and/or high speed operation. Figure 5 shows the spread in gain as measured on an in-line quad gate fabricated with the Standard Linear Process. Figure 6 shows how the average propagation delay varies between "near" and "far" collectors for a particular fabrication process. At low current levels, the response is relatively matched. At current levels above 10 μA, however, there is a significant difference resulting in a minimum propagation delay -- about three times faster for the near collector in a quad output device.

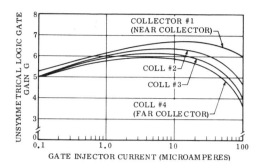

Figure 5. Unsymmetrical Quad Gain Variation with Location

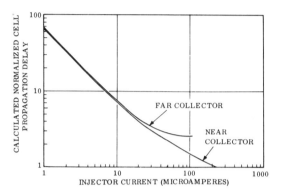

Figure 6. Comparative Propagation Delay of Near and Far Collectors in a Quad Output In-Line Device

SYMMETRICAL CELL TOPOGRAPHY

Design Considerations

The concept of a symmetrical logic cell topography was explored in response to the need for I^2L gate elements that demonstrated well-matched performance at relatively high current levels. One of the techniques used to achieve this objective was to develop topographies that minimize and equalize the base resistance between each npn collector and its base contact, and also betweeen each npn collector and the associated lateral pnp injector.

Specific Symmetrical Topographies

Figure 7 shows a test cell consisting of a dual output gate and a quad output gate. The dual out-

9.1

put gate uses a single pnp injector while the quad has two associated injectors. The four collectors in the quad output device are all symmetrically located and are near the npn base contact. This equalizes and minimizes the turn-off transient response of all outputs of the quad. The turn-on transient response is equalized and minimized by the combined effect of symmetrical npn base contacts and symmetrical pnp injectors. The fact that each pnp injector symmetrically supplies a pair of collectors within the quad also equalizes the npn collector current from any collector in the quad. The dual output device is designed to approximate one half of the quad. The result is

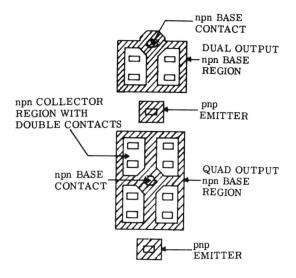

Figure 7. Rectangular Symmetrical Dual and Quad Gates

that the collector currents of both dual and quad devices are matched to one another, even when the collector current exceeds several mA. Each npn collector has the possibility of two alternative contacts, for ease of interconnection. Figure 8

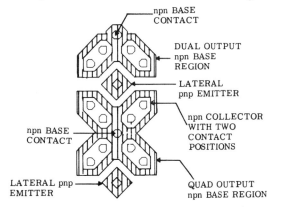

Figure 8. Slanted Symmetrical Dual and Quad Gates

shows a slanted symmetrical form of the same quad and dual output combination cell. This topography further reduces decoupling effects between the injector and the individual incremental npn transistors, and enables the npn base contact to better control the off-state of the gate under severe environmental conditions. The slanted topography also modifies the interconnection constraints when using single-layer metallizations.

Experimental Results

Figure 9 shows the npn collector current response tolerance of a combined dual/quad cell, compared to a conventional in-line topography quad output gate, fabricated on the same chip. The minimum response limit of the in-line conventional device corresponds to the output farthest from the injector, while the other extreme corresponds to the output nearest the injector.

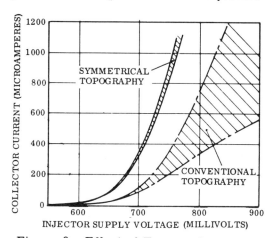

Figure 9. Effect of Topography on Collector Current Uniformity

Figure 10 shows the effective digital gain of a symmetrical quad output device as a function of the current in each incremental npn collector.

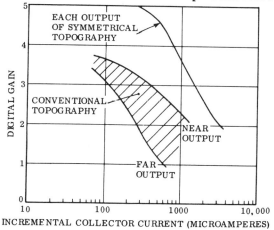

Figure 10. Quad Output Gate Gain Characteristics

9.1

Figure 10 also shows the comparable performance of the conventional in-line device. All symmetrical outputs are essentially equal to one another, while the conventional topography diverges at higher current levels.

Figure 11 shows a seven-stage ring oscillator using the symmetrical topography. Figure 12 shows a 260 logic gate code generator test array.

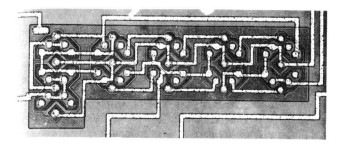

Figure 11. Seven Stage Ring Oscillator

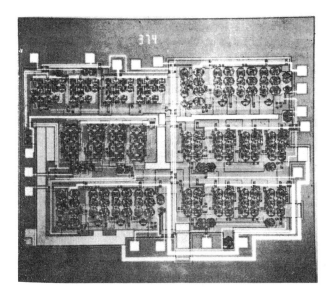

Figure 12. Code Generator Test Array

REFERENCES

(1) C.M. Hart and A. Slob, 1972 IEEE ISSCC Proceedings, pp. 92-93.

(2) H.H. Berger and S.K. Wiedmann, 1972 IEEE ISSCC Proceedings, pp. 90-91.

(3) H.H. Berger, IEEE JSSC, Vol. SC-9, No. 5, October 1974, p. 218.

(4) F.M. Klaassen, 1976 IEEE IEDM Technical Digest, pp. 299-303.

ACKNOWLEDGEMENTS

The device fabrication and valuable consultation were provided by B. Vanderleest, L. Cordes and P. Salvagni. Strong support was also received from D. Long, H. Frank, W. Kinney, and A. Flathers. H. Zimmer was responsible for most of the device layout work.

9.1

Part VII
Analog Integrated Circuit Process Compatible I²L

The almost direct compatibility with classical bipolar analog processes is one of the most important features of I²L. The ability to include digital logic on-chip with existing well-refined bipolar analog circuit designs immediately opens up a vast arena of applications for I²L. This is particularly true in view of the good noise immunity and reliability offered by I²L in those harsh environments which could best take advantage of a digital-analog circuit combination. Examples are the automotive industry and the telecommunications industry. Fortunately, these prime areas of application typically do not require high speed digital logic and, consequently, analog compatible I²L with its inherently longer propagation delays offers adequate speed performance.

The papers reprinted in this part represent means of achieving analog-compatible I²L without significant deviations from the classical bipolar analog processing approaches. This selection has been made because I expect that analog compatible I²L will be most widely applied by those laboratories which have already become well versed and well established in the analog circuit fabrication art. Consequently, these users of I²L are not likely to invest in wholly new approaches to analog processing in order to include I²L in their designs.

Paper VIII-1 by Saltich et al. presents the results of a comprehensive experimental investigation of the I²L performance which can be obtained in an analog process in which only the epitaxial layer thickness and doping are permitted to be altered. The results presented are in excellent agreement with the expected effects of epitaxial-layer thickness and doping upon the up-beta, fan-out capability, and propagation delay of I²L, as well as the breakdown voltage of normally downward operated devices.

Paper VII-2 presents one means of simultaneously achieving high voltage (60 V) analog devices and I²L which can be used for digital logic implementations. The process introduces a dual-emitter deposition and thereby attains differing integrated base dopings and punchthrough voltages for the analog and I²L portions of the chip. The drawbacks of the approach are

1) The low down-beta which resulted for the high voltage devices, and
2) the limited fan-out and speed capabilities which resulted for the I²L devices.

Paper VII-3, by Allstot et al. presents an alternative approach to the attainment of improved analog–digital performance using analog compatible I²L. These authors propose to selectively raise the effective doping level of the epitaxial layer in those portions of the chip where I²L is to be fabricated. The net effect is that the analog performance is left unaltered while the I²L dc up-beta and minimum propagation delay are improved. The increase in epitaxial layer doping accounts for the improved I²L performance by way of two principle mechanisms. 1) The increased effective emitter doping results in reduced hole injection into the epitaxial emitter. This reduces both the base current due to recombination and the stored charge in the emitter. 2) The net integrated base doping of the npn is reduced by way of compensation by the n-type phosphorous introduced by implantation into the epitaxial layer. Thus a higher up-beta results for a given base current drive. It should be noted that an epitaxial layer profile such as is shown in Fig. 4b can result in excessive charge storage in the valley between the implanted and buried n-type regions of the epitaxial layer. If such a valley actually exists it could be advantageously removed by way of a relatively low-doped up-diffusion of phosphorous from the n+ buried layer. The same mask could be used here as is used for the post–epi n-type implant.

Paper VII-4 by Halbo and Hansen provides a comparison of the competing techniques for the addition of I²L to an established analog process. These authors have carried out a rather detailed experimental study of the analog and digital performance attained in their analog process and they conclude that the approach proposed in paper VII-3 by Allstot et al. is a good choice. A technique known as poly-I²L has achieved excellent simultaneous analog and I²L performance. The technique is described in detail in [VII-5] of the bibliography and was not included here because of the unusual processing required to implement the structure. The interested reader is referred to paper V-1 where a comparison is made between the performance of poly-I²L and other analog compatible approaches to implementing I²L. For those applications requiring both high voltage and very high speed I²L, the extra effort involved in establishing the poly I²L process may prove worthwhile. However, the establishment of a manufacturing capability based upon a wholly new processing approach can be expensive in terms of the facilities, manpower, and man-years required to demonstrate a reproducible and reliable product. Thus the poly-I²L approach is not likely to be widely adopted. The bibliography for part VII contains additional papers on the topic of analog compatible I²L.

Processing Technology and AC/DC Characteristics of Linear Compatible I²L

JACK L. SALTICH, MEMBER, IEEE, WILLIAM L. GEORGE, MEMBER, IEEE, AND JOHN G. SODERBERG

Abstract—The processing, ac and dc characteristics of I²L structures integrated with common analog circuit elements are studied. Since the required breakdown voltage of the analog circuitry normally dictates the resistivity and thickness of the silicon epitaxial layer, we study the parametric performance of the I²L structure for common linear circuit voltages. Design criteria, processing, and device performance are presented for I²L structures built on several different types of material.

The I²L performance achieved in the linear compatible technology easily allowed a fan-out of four and gate propagation delay less than 50 ns with standard device breakdowns of 20 V; but fan-out is limited to three and gate delay to 100 ns for the process which attained 30-V breakdowns.

INTRODUCTION

SEVERAL articles have been written about the device physics [1] and applications [2] of integrated injection logic (I²L) structures in digital circuits. Little, however, has been said about I²L when used in a mixed mode with analog circuitry on the same silicon chip. Several aspects of I²L structures when they are used in a linear circuit compatible mode are examined. The I²L structure is treated, not as a new technology, but simply as another design tool. The intent is to gain a better appreciation for its usefulness and limitations. Primarily, the processing and ac/dc characteristics of linear compatible I²L structures are studied. Since the analog circuitry will dictate the material and processing specifications to be used, the I²L device is examined with this in mind using material specifications and design rules common to typical linear integrated circuits.

FABRICATION PROCEDURE

Fig. 1 shows a cross section of a typical three-collector I²L structure contained on the same silicon chip with a standard n-p-n transistor. Standard integrated-circuit processing is used throughout the fabrication sequence. The processing sequence is listed below.

1) Diffuse heavily doped n⁺ buried layer.
2) Deposit n-type epitaxial layer.
3) Diffuse p⁺ for junction isolation.
4) Diffuse deep heavy n⁺ to minimize extraneous base currents of inverted transistor (I²L device).
5) Diffuse p regions forming I²L injector bar, standard base of n-p-n's, emitter and collector of lateral p-n-p's, and resistors.

Manuscript received February 13, 1976; revised April 23, 1976.
The authors are with the Integrated Circuit Division, Motorola, Inc., Phoenix, AZ 85036.

6) Diffuse shallow n⁺ forming collectors of I²L device, emitters, and collector contacts of standard n-p-n's.
7) Open contact holes, deposit and delineate metal.

All structures were fabricated using the above processing sequence. Test structures were conservatively designed in that a 0.2-mil (5-μm) alignment tolerance was used. Key process parameters were perturbed to illustrate effects on several basic criteria of I²L performance, e.g., current gain of inverted transistor, gate delays, etc. Parameters of interest for the analog portion of the chip were determined.

DC CHARACTERISTICS

An important performance parameter for I²L devices is the upward gain (β_{up}) [3] of the inverted transistor. Several authors have discussed the minimum β_{up} requirement for the I²L device to function properly as

$$\beta_{up} \geqslant \text{total number of collectors.}$$

This is only a minimum requirement on β_{up}. To account for processing variations and for proper operation over temperature, a more conservative design criterion is

$$\beta_{up} \geqslant 2.5\times \text{total number of collectors.}$$

As discussed by Klassen [1] and more recently shown by Wulms [4], hole recombination is the main contribution to the base current for not-too-shallow inverted transistors built with a deep n⁺ completely surrounding the base region, as shown in Fig. 2. Using a device similar to the one shown in Fig. 2, Schmitz and Slob [5] demonstrated that recombination in the emitter (i.e., hole recombination) was dominant and they were also able to obtain the simple relationship

$$\beta_{up} = \beta_{down} \, A_E/A_B \qquad (1)$$

β_{down} = forward gain of n-p-n

A_E = area of n⁺ diffusion

A_B = area of p diffusion.

For (1) to hold, the "specific" emitter efficiencies [6] of the upward and downward operating transistors must be equal (i.e., the ideal components of the base current densities of the up and down devices at a given V_{BE} are equal).

The situation is more complex for a standard I²L structure built using an injector bar and a relatively thick n⁻ epitaxial layer. Fig. 3 shows a cross section of such an I²L structure identifying the various components of base current. The main

Reprinted from *IEEE J. Solid-State Circuits*, vol. SC-11, pp. 478–485, Aug. 1976.

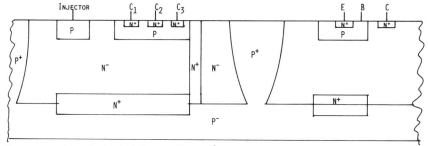

Fig. 1. Schematic cross section of a typical three-collector I²L structure and standard n-p-n device shown on the same silicon chip.

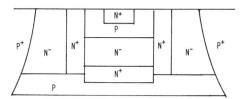

Fig. 2. Cross section of an n-p-n transistor which has a deep n⁺ diffusion completely surrounding the base.

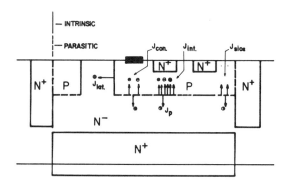

Fig. 3. Cross section of I²L structure showing various contributors of base current.

difference between the structure shown in Fig. 2 and a typical I²L structure shown in Fig. 3 is the additional base current J_{lat}, which is due to hole injection towards the injector. As shown by Berger [7] and Wulms [4], J_{lat} is the largest single contributor of base current for structures designed using n⁺ collars wherever possible and minimizing the amount of unused base area.

A suitable expression for monitoring the effects of processing and/or material perturbations on β_{up} can be obtained by altering (1) as follows.

$$\beta_{up}(\text{max}) = K\beta_{down}(\text{max}) \frac{(A_E)}{A_B} \frac{(\tilde{\beta}_{up})}{\tilde{\beta}_{down}} \qquad (2)$$

where $K \leqslant 1$ and is a parameter used to account for the excess base current due to J_{lat}. $\tilde{\beta}$ is a term discussed earlier [6] which is used to avoid normalization problems when comparing

structures fabricated using varying processing techniques. Specifically, $\tilde{\beta}$ is the reciprocal of the base substrate current density in $\mu A/mil^2$ when that junction is being utilized as an emitter at $T = 23.5°C$ with $V_f = 600$ mV; i.e., $\tilde{\beta} = 1/J_B$ where J_B is the ideal component of base current at 600 mV forward bias. For those who prefer to think in terms of saturation current densities or in terms of ϕ in $J_S = q\phi n_i^2 \exp(qV_f/kT)$, we offer Fig. 4 as a conversion means valid at $T = 23.5°C$.

The ratio $\tilde{\beta}_{up}/\tilde{\beta}_{down}$ reflects the ratio of hole current injected into the emitter of the upwardly operating transistor (J_P in Fig. 3) and the downwardly operating transistor, respectively. J_P (the hole current injected downward) can result from hole recombination in the n⁻ region, from hole recombination at the n⁻/n⁺ (buried-layer) interface, from hole recombination in the p-n junction space charge region, and/or from hole recombination in the n⁺ buried layer. $\tilde{\beta}_{up}/\tilde{\beta}_{down}$ is then the "specific" emitter efficiency ratio of the two devices and was found to be one for thin epi structures studied by Berger [7]. For the thicker epi structures considered for linear compatible applications, the emitter efficiency ratio is not one and becomes an important consideration for device design.

Fig. 5 shows typical β_{up} and β_{down} curves for triple-collector devices ($A_E/A_B = 0.36$) fabricated on low (0.5 $\Omega \cdot$ cm), intermediate (1 $\Omega \cdot$ cm), and high (2 $\Omega \cdot$ cm) resistivity n⁻ material having approximately the same epitaxial thickness ($\approx 8 \mu m$). The triple-collector device utilized, with pertinent dimensions labeled, is shown in Fig. 9(a). All devices shown in Fig. 5 were fabricated to have the same β_{down} (maximum); i.e., the same base charge under the emitter Q_B. This was verified by measuring I_C at $V_{BE} = 600$ mV and finding it to be within 5 percent on each of the three different device structures. The difference in low current gains for the various resistivity materials is attributed to the variance in J_{lat}. Since the back injected hole density varies as $1/n^-$ (epi doping density), J_{lat} is greater for 2 $\Omega \cdot$ cm than 0.5 $\Omega \cdot$ cm. Also, as pointed out by Klassen [1], because of the relatively low doping used in the epitaxial layers, high level effects occur at low values of injection currents in the lateral p-n-p transistor formed by injector (emitter)—epi (base)—p base (collector).

For the device pictured in Fig. 9(a), processed with injector diffusion depth of 2.5 μm, high level effects occur in the 15-25 μA region for an n⁻ region of 5×10^{15} cm⁻³. The effective area of the lateral transistor is taken as the diffusion

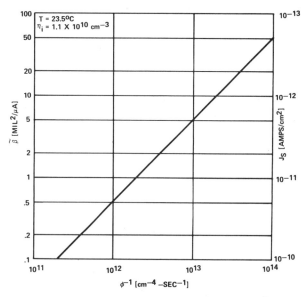

Fig. 4. Graph which converts specific emitter efficiency ($\tilde{\beta}$) to saturation current density (J_S) and ϕ, where $J_S = q\phi n_i^2 \exp(qV_f/kT)$.

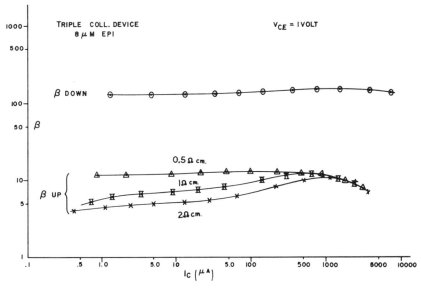

Fig. 5. Plots of β_{down} and β_{up} versus collector current for triple-collector devices on 8-μm thick 0.5 $\Omega \cdot$ cm, 1 $\Omega \cdot$ cm, and 2 $\Omega \cdot$ cm epi.

depth $\times$ width of the injector. Hence, the difference in β_{up} at low currents for the devices shown in Fig. 5 is attributed to the increase in J_{lat} as epi resistivity is increased. The similarity in the gains at higher currents implies that conductivity modulation of the epi has removed any differences in starting material; hence, J_{lat} and J_P are the same for all structures. All data presented in Fig. 5 and subsequent figures represent measurements taken on 10 devices from 3 different wafers. Further, since the area ratio is 0.36 while β_{up} (max)/β_{down} (max) is 0.09, the K and $\tilde{\beta}_{up}/\tilde{\beta}_{down}$ terms in (2) account for three-fourths of the total base current required for the up device, which is in agreement with data presented by Wulms [4]. The device design tradeoff illustrated here is that if high resistivity epi is utilized to ensure high lateral p-n-p gain in the

analog portion of a chip, the I^2L function on that chip will exhibit poor up-gain when operated at low currents.

In order to increase the up-gain of the I^2L device while still optimizing lateral β of the analog portion of the circuit, the distance from the injector bar to the p base can be increased. Fig. 6 shows β_{up} versus I_C for several injector bar to base spacings for a single collector device. The increase of J_{lat} and concomitant reduction of β_{up} as spacing is decreased is apparent. It should be pointed out that increased injector bar to base spacing will be effective only up to the point where the lateral gain of the p-n-p device formed by the injector bar, the epi layer, and the p base becomes low due to recombination in the n^- region. At this point, J_{lat} is determined by this recombination, not by collection by the grounded injector. However,

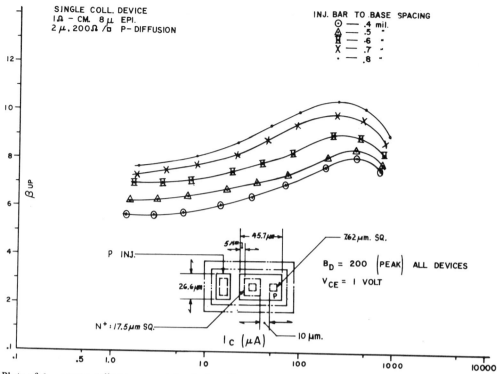

Fig. 6. Plots of β_{up} versus collector current for single-collector devices on 8-μm 1 $\Omega \cdot$ cm for various injector bar to p-base spacings.

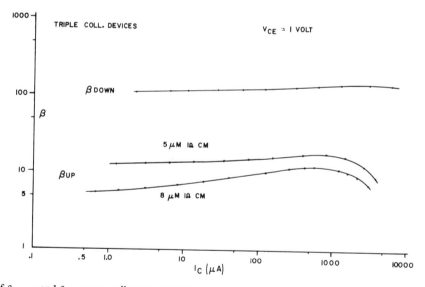

Fig. 7. Plots of β_{down} and β_{up} versus collector current for triple-collector devices on 1 $\Omega \cdot$ cm epi, 5-μm and 8-μm thick.

the injector current required to sustain operation is also excessive at this point so spacing is normally limited to distances less than 1 mil (25.4 μm). Also, as discussed by Klassen [1], reduced injection current which will occur as injector bar to base spacing is increased could be disadvantageous for certain applications. Minimum epi thickness and resistivity for any bipolar technology are determined by the required breakdown voltage of the device incorporated in that technology. The effects of epi thickness on I²L performance are shown in Figs.

7 and 8, which show β_{up} and β_{down} versus I_C for devices on various epi layers. Fig. 7 shows 1 $\Omega \cdot$ cm layers, 5 μm and 8 μm thick, while Fig. 8 shows 2 $\Omega \cdot$ cm layers, 8 μm and 12 μm thick. Typical BV_{CEO} values for the down transistors for each process are shown in Table I. The figures and table illustrate the increase of J_P with increased epi thickness and show that I²L performance is appreciably impaired when one is forced to use thick epi for high voltage analog circuitry.

Orientation of the injector with respect to the p base is an

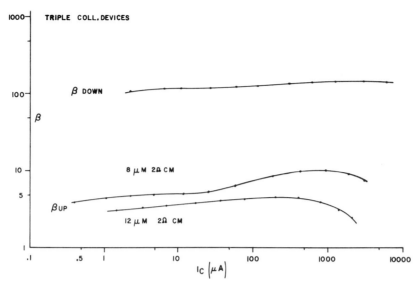

Fig. 8. Plots of β_{down} and β_{up} versus collector current for triple-collector devices on $2\,\Omega\cdot$ cm epi, 8-μm and 12-μm thick.

TABLE I
DATA IS FOR STRUCTURES WITH INJECTOR TO p BASE SPACING EQUAL TO
0.4 mil (10-μm), INJECTOR PERPENDICULAR TO p BASE, AND THE β_{down} TO β_{up}
RATIO IS GIVEN FOR THEIR PEAK VALUES

Material		β_{down}/β_{up}	BV_{CEO}
t	ρ		
5 μm	1 $\Omega\cdot$cm	8	8
8 μm	1 $\Omega\cdot$cm	11.5	16
8 μm	2 $\Omega\cdot$cm	13.6	20
12 μm	2 $\Omega\cdot$cm	30	30

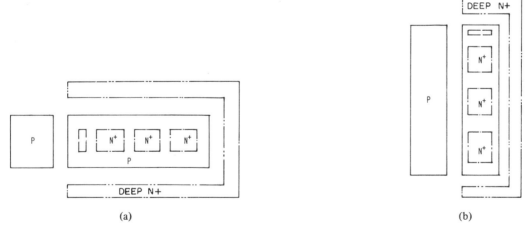

(a)   (b)

Fig. 9. (a) Schematic representation of I^2L structure which has injector
bar perpendicular to p base. (b) Schematic representation of I^2L
structure which has injector bar parallel to p base. Dimensions for
(a) and (b)—emitter size: 17.5 μm $\times$ 17.5 μm; emitter edge to base
edge: 5 μm; deep n$^+$ to base spacing: 7.5 μm; injector bar to base
spacing: 10 μm.

option which must be considered in design and layout of I^2L structures. Fig. 9(a) and (b) shows two obvious choices, wherein the injector is perpendicular [Fig. 9(a)] or parallel [Fig. 9(b)] to the p base. Fig. 10 shows a plot of β_{up} versus I_C for perpendicular and parallel structures. The lower β_{up} of the parallel structure is attributed to the higher J_{lat} component

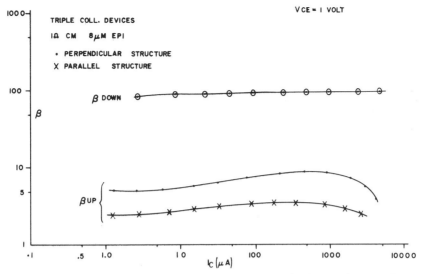

Fig. 10. Plots of β_{down} and β_{up} versus collector current for triple-collector devices on 1 Ω · cm 8-μm epi for different orientations of injector bar to p base.

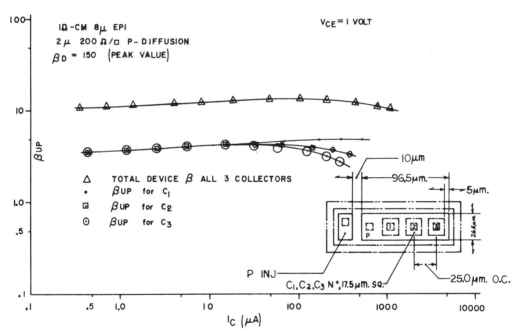

Fig. 11. Plots of β_{up} versus collector current for triple-collector devices on 1 Ω · cm 8-μm epi showing variation of β_{up} with respect to collector location.

which exists due to the greater emitting edge for hole injection. A possible shortcoming of a perpendicularly oriented structure is a debiasing effect of the emitter–base junction due to IR drop in the base. This could lead to a variation in β_{up} with the collector furthest from the injector exhibiting the lowest gain. Fig. 11 shows plots of β_{up} for the various collectors versus collector current. When the gain of a single collector is being measured, the other two are allowed to float and will therefore saturate. As may be seen from Fig. 11, debiasing is not a severe problem up to collector currents in the 100 μA range for the particular device characteristics noted.

The device structure utilized for these measurements is shown in the insert with pertinent dimensions indicated.

AC CHARACTERISTICS

As shown by Klassen [1], Berger [7], and Slob [5] the dynamic properties, specifically gate propagation delays, are a function of current level. It has been shown that space-charge layer capacitances determine the delay at lower currents and emitter stored charge at higher currents where the minimum delay occurs. Fig. 12 shows experimental data of gate delay (τ_{pd}) versus injector current obtained from test devices. A

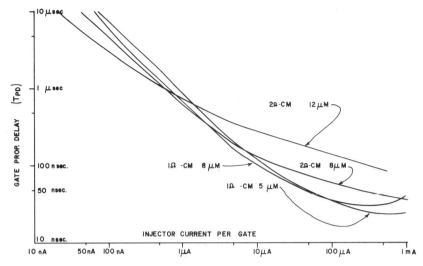

Fig. 12. Plots of gate propagation delay (τ_{pd}) versus injector current per gate for various materials.

Fig. 13. Photograph of ring oscillator used to obtain gate delay data.

photograph of the ring oscillator used to obtain the data is shown in Fig. 13. As may be seen from the curves, at low currents the gate delay is less for the higher resistivity, thicker epi due to lower capacitance. The order is reversed at high currents as expected due to the emitter stored charge. The data shows that high speed performance (<50 ns propagation delay) is achievable in linear compatible processes, but not without a substantial sacrifice in breakdown voltage. Fortunately, many applications require a low speed, low power logic integrated with analog function. For these applications, the higher resistivity material can furnish both reasonably high voltage and optimized gate delay for a given power level.

SUMMARY

DC and ac performance of I^2L devices built using processing compatible with standard linear integrated circuits has been presented to illustrate the compromises involved in the simultaneous fabrication of I^2L and analog functions on the same
monolithic chip. It was shown that fan-out is sacrificed as the required analog breakdown is increased due to increased hole injection into the n^- epitaxial layer. Further, it was shown that the minimum achievable gate delay is increased as the breakdown voltage is increased, but gate delay at very low power levels is in fact lower for high breakdown processing.

The I^2L performance achieved in the linear compatible technology easily allowed a fan-out of four and gate propagation delay less than 50 ns with standard device breakdowns of 20 V, but fan-out is practically limited to three and gate delay to 100 ns for the process which attained 30-V breakdowns.

REFERENCES

[1] F. M. Klassen, "Device physics of integrated injection logic," *IEEE Trans. Electron Devices*, vol. ED-22, pp. 145–152, Mar. 1975.
[2] C. M. Hart and A. Slob, "Integrated injection logic," *IEEE J. Solid-State Circuits*, vol. SC-7, pp. 346–351, 1972.
[3] C. M. Hart and A. Slob, "Integrated injection logic," *Philips Tech. Rev.*, vol. 33, pp. 76–85, 1975.

IEEE JOURNAL OF SOLID-STATE CIRCUITS, VOL. SC-11, NO. 4, AUGUST 1976

[4] H. E. J. Wulms, "Base current of I^2L transistors," in *ISSCC Dig. Tech. Papers*, 1976.
[5] A. Schmitz and A. Slob, "The effect of isolation regions on the current gain of inverse NPN–Transistors used in integrated injection logic," in *ISSCC Dig. Tech. Papers*, 1974.
[6] L. E. Clark, "On the measurement of the specific emitter efficiency factor in bipolar transistors," *Solid State Electronics*, vol. 15, pp. 1293–1294, Dec. 1972.
[7] H. H. Berger, "The injection model–A structure oriented model for merged transistor logic (MTL)," *IEEE J. Solid-State Circuits*, vol. SC-9, pp. 218–227, Oct. 1974.
[8] K. Hart and A. Slob, "Integrated injection logic–A new approach to LSI," *IEEE J. Solid-State Circuits*, vol. SC-7, pp. 346–351, Oct. 1972.

Linear Compatible I²L Technology with High Voltage Transistors

GÜNTHER BERGMANN

Abstract—A technology is proposed in which it is possible to realize both I²L circuits and linear transistors with V_{CBO} of 60 V. The essential step in such a technology is an additional n⁺-flat diffusion. The technological parameters are derived. From measurements on wafers processed in the outlined technology, we established functioning I²L elements and high voltage transistors.

INTRODUCTION

ONE OF THE most interesting technical aspects of integrated injection logic (I²L) is the possibility of realizing complex digital circuits and analog functions on the same (bipolar) chip. This allows the design of logic circuits with powerful driver stages which should lead to cost-effective "one chip" solutions.

I²L inverters are normally surrounded by a deep n⁺ ring to avoid lateral coupling. Thus, in the linear part of the chip downward operated n-p-n transistors have small collector spreading resistances and hence small saturation voltages. These analog transistors are capable of handling relatively large currents.

To attain high upward current gain in I²L circuits a low integrated base doping is necessary. This in turn means that breakdown voltages of the n-p-n transistors in the linear part of the chip are low because of punchthrough ($V_{CEO} \approx 15$ V).

The aim of this study was to develop a simple linear compatible I²L technology with a collector-base breakdown voltage of 60 V for the analog transistors in the downward mode.

TECHNOLOGICAL PARAMETERS

In the first part, the design procedure for a technology outlined above is given. Simple calculations, measurements, and [1] show that I²L combined with linear transistors ($V_{CBO} \approx$ 60 V) do not operate satisfactorily if the so-called "standard I²L technology" is used (processing sequence as in [1]). Because of the relative highly doped epitaxial layer (for well-performing I²L), punchthrough and avalanche multiplication are limiting factors for the blocking voltage of linear transistors.

We therefore suggest a modified processing using an additional n⁺-flat emitter diffusion for high voltage linear transistors (see Fig. 1). In principle, this is similar to the production of IC's with super gain transistors [2]. Here, however, the emitters of high gain transistors are diffused in two steps. This processing allows us to fabricate three types of linear transistors with the known tradeoff between breakdown voltage and current gain.

Epitaxial Doping (N_{epi}) and Base Diffusion

Breakdown voltages of 60 V require that the impurity concentration at the low doped side of planar p⁺n or n⁺p junctions must not exceed $9 \cdot 10^{15}$ cm⁻³ [3]. The base diffusion process, however, forms cylindrical and spherical curved boundaries which lead to a breakdown voltage which depends on base diffusion depth. Using graphs given in [4] and bearing in mind that the epitaxial doping should be as high as possible, we find a base–collector junction depth of $x_{jB} = 3.2$ μm and for the epitaxial layer an impurity concentration of $5 \cdot 10^{15}$ cm⁻³ ($1.1\ \Omega \cdot$ cm). In reality we should measure a higher breakdown voltage, because we have neglected the voltage drop in the space-charge layer penetrating into the base. At this point a safety margin will be useful and we therefore do not correct the results.

However, calculating the diffusion depth of the emitter of high voltage transistors ($\tilde{x}_{jE}$) we need a more realistic statement for base doping. A good approximation is a Gaussian profile, the diffusion parameter $D_p t_p$ of which can easily be determined if the surface concentration is known:

$$D_p t_p = \frac{x_{jB}^2}{4\ ln\ \dfrac{N_{AO}}{N_{epi}}} \approx 0.37\ \mu m^2. \tag{1}$$

N_{AO} is the surface concentration of acceptors. A value of $N_{AO} = 5 \cdot 10^{18}$ cm⁻³ is common in linear processing. The base doping per unit area (N_B) and the base sheet resistance (R_{SB}) are given by (2):

$$R_{SB} \approx 150\ \Omega/\square$$

$$N_B = N_{AO}\ (\pi\ D_p t_p)^{1/2} \approx 5.4 \cdot 10^{14}\ cm^{-2}. \tag{2}$$

Epitaxial Layer Thickness Under the Base ($x_{jC} - x_{jB}$)

If the depletion region of the reverse-biased collector-base junction contacts the buried layer (reachthrough condition), a further increase in reverse bias will push the depletion region mainly on the base side towards the emitter space-charge region [5]. To avoid this premature punchthrough,

Manuscript received March 9, 1977; revised June 1, 1977. This work has been supported under the Technological Program of the Federal Department of Research and Technology of the Federal Republic of Germany. The author alone is responsible for the contents.

The author is with the Research Laboratories, AEG-Telefunken, Ulm, Germany.

Reprinted from *IEEE J. Solid-State Circuits*, vol. SC-12, pp. 566–572, Oct. 1977.

300

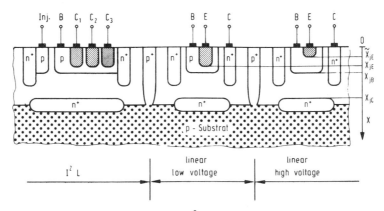

Fig. 1. Modified linear I^{2}L processing.

the widening of the collector depletion region must not be disturbed by the buried layer.

Calculating the necessary epitaxial layer thickness from abrupt p$^+$n junction theory will yield a higher value than we really need. This is due to the neglected voltage drop in the depleted base. Therefore (3) will imply a safety margin:

$$x_{jC} - x_{jB} = \left[\frac{2\epsilon_{si} V_{CBO}}{q N_{epi}} \right]^{1/2} \tag{3}$$

where ϵ_{si} is the permittivity of silicon and q is the elementary charge. With $V_{CBO} = 60$ V and $N_{epi} = 5 \cdot 10^{15}$ cm^{-3} results:

$$x_{jC} - x_{jB} \approx 4 \ \mu m. \tag{4}$$

The density per unit area of ionized impurity atoms $N^+_{D, epi}$ is given by:

$$N^+_{D, epi} = (x_{jC} - x_{jB}) N_{epi} = 1.97 \ 10^{12} \ cm^{-2}. \tag{5}$$

Flat Emitter Diffusion Depth ($\widetilde{x}_{jE}$) for High Voltage Transistors

In the foregoing chapters we have determined the maximum epitaxial doping, the minimum base diffusion depth, and the minimum epitaxial layer thickness under the base so that no avalanche breakdown will occur until 60 V are reached. We now have to derive the maximum emitter diffusion depth that punchthrough will not limit the breakdown capability of high voltage transistors.

As the sum of ionized doping atoms in the base and the epitaxial layer has to be zero (regardless of doping profile) and the density of ionized donors in the epitaxial layer is already known, we can write for the maximum diffusion depth of the flat emitter ($\widetilde{x}_{jE, max}$):

$$\int_{\widetilde{x}_{jE, max}}^{x_{jB}} \left[N_{AO} \exp \frac{-x^2}{4 D_p t_p} - N_{DO} \ erfc \frac{x}{2\sqrt{D_n t_n}} - N_{epi} \right]$$

$$dx = N_{epi} (x_{jC} - x_{jB})$$

$$[\ ] = N'_B \tag{6}$$

where we have assumed a complementary error function

profile for the n$^+$-emitter diffusion with N_{DO} as the surface concentration. We have neglected the thickness of the emitter space-charge layer, which means that devices satisfying (6) would punchthrough before 60 V are reached.

An approximate solution of (7) is given in the Appendix, which yields:

$$\widetilde{x}_{jE, max} \approx 2.21 \ \mu m. \tag{7}$$

As the integrated base doping [left-hand side of (6)] in a given process varies at least by a factor of 2 we have to solve (6) with the right-hand side multiplied by two.

This yields:

$$\widetilde{x}_{jE} \approx 1.9 \ \mu m. \tag{8}$$

With a reasonable surface concentration of $N_{DO} \approx 3 \cdot 10^{20}$ cm^{-3} we get for the diffusion parameter $D_n t_n$ of the flat emitter diffusion:

$$D_n t_n \approx 0.19 \ \mu m^2. \tag{9}$$

So far, avalanche multiplication has been neglected. This is not very serious if the transistors operate with constant emitter current (common base). Using the transistors with grounded emitter, one must take (10) into account:

$$V_{CEO} \approx \frac{V_{CBO}}{(B + 1)^{1/n}} \qquad n \approx 4. \tag{10}$$

n$^+$-Diffusion Depth for Low Voltage Transistors and I^{2}L Collectors (x_{jE})

In general, a thin base should be realized in order to obtain the necessary upward gain. "Standard technology" allows us to fabricate intrinsic base sheet resistances in the range of 10 kΩ/□ to 30 kΩ/□. This corresponds to an integrated base doping of (3 to 1) $\cdot 10^{12}$ cm^{-2}. Assuming the same surface concentration as with the n$^+$-flat diffusion, we have:

$$x_{jE} \approx 2.4 \ \mu m$$

and

$$D_n t_n \approx 0.22 \ \mu m^2. \tag{11}$$

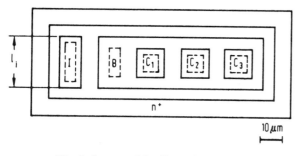

Fig. 2. Layout of 3-collector inverter cell.

Technology

The key parameters for a linear compatible I^2L technology with high voltage transistors have been derived. With the remaining parameters as standard values in linear bipolar processing we get the processing sequence listed below:

1) p substrate 5–10 $\Omega \cdot$ cm,
2) n^+-buried layer 14 $\Omega/\square$,
3) n^- epitaxy 1.1 $\Omega \cdot$ cm, 10 μm,
4) p^+ separation,
5) p base 150 $\Omega/\square$, 3.2 μm, $N_{AO} \approx 5 \cdot 10^{18}$ cm^{-3},
6) n^+ I^2L separation, 4 $\Omega/\square$, 5 μm,
7) n^+ I^2L collectors, 6 $\Omega/\square$, 2.4 μm,
8) n^+ flat 11 $\Omega/\square$, 1.9 μm.

In order to get very deep n^+ collars we can exchange step 6) with step 5).

Distance Between Base and Injector (W_B)

Strong interaction between the inverter cell and the appertaining injector leads to a restriction of the lateral transistor current constant I_{po} in relation to the vertical transistor current constant I_{no}. This relation is given by the bistability criterion derived in [6]. We find:

$$\beta_{up} \left(1 - \frac{I_{po}(W_B)}{I_{no}} \right) > 1 \qquad (12)$$

with

$$\frac{I_{po}}{I_{no}} = \underbrace{\frac{D_p}{D_n}}_{0.33} \underbrace{\frac{x_{jB} \, I_i}{A_C}}_{0.46} \frac{\int_{x_{jE}}^{x_{jB}} N'_B \, dx}{N_{epi} \, W_B} \qquad \int \% = 3 \cdot 10^{12} \text{ cm}^{-2} \qquad (13)$$

where

$D_{p(n)}$ is the diffusion constant of holes (electrons),
A_C is the n-p-n collector area (see Fig. 2), and
I_i is the injector length (see Fig. 2).

We obtain for a minimum upward gain $\beta_{up, min} = 2$ and the layout given in Fig. 2:

$$W_{B, min} = 1.8 \ \mu\text{m}. \qquad (14)$$

This means a minimum injector-base distance of 7.5 μm on mask, for lateral diffusion process.

MEASUREMENTS

From several wafers processed in the technology described above, the following data were obtained. The test chip contained linear transistors with deep and flat emitters and I^2L ring oscillators, delay-type flip-flops, and inverters with various numbers of collectors.

A. Linear Part

Linear Transistors with Deep Emitter Diffusion

These transistors exhibit practically the same parameters as transistors built in standard technology. The most important parameters are

$V_{CBO} = 36$ V $V_{CES} = 28$ V

$V_{CEO} = 16$ V $V_{EBO} = 7.8$ V

$\beta_{down, max} = 400 \, (I_C = 1 \text{ mA})$

$f_{T, max} = 400$ MHz $(I_C = 1 \text{ mA})$.

For punchthrough limited devices, the equation

$$V_{CBO} = V_{CES} + V_{EBO} \qquad (15)$$

holds [5]. It results from the above data that linear transistors with standard n^+ diffusion break down because of punchthrough.

Linear Transistors with Flat Emitter Diffusion

The data below have been measured:

$V_{CBO} = V_{CES} = 65$ V–70 V (70 V–75 V with field plate)

$V_{CEO} = 35$ V–40 V

$\beta_{down, max} = 15 \, (I_C = 1 \text{ mA})$

$f_{T, max} = 95$ MHz $(I_C = 1 \text{ mA})$.

From the comparison of transistors with different emitters, it is obvious that the flat emitter is not as deep as that given by (8). This means that f_T and β_{down} of the flat emitter transistor could be raised without violating the punchthrough condition. In devices where avalanche multiplication is the breakdown mechanism, V_{CES} equals V_{CBO} which supports the statement above.

Fig. 3 shows the output characteristics of a high voltage transistor (with field plate) in common-base mode. The rise in collector current is due to multiplication in the collector–base depletion layer.

B. I^2L Part

Most random logic can be implemented using gates with a fan-out of 3. We therefore restrict the measured curves to 3-collector inverters. The layout is shown in Fig. 2.

Static Performance of Lateral p-n-p

Fig. 4 shows the current gain of the lateral p-n-p transistor. Compared to standard I^2L, we have a high current gain. The

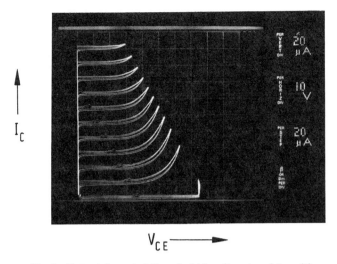

Fig. 3. Output characteristics of a high-voltage transistor with
field-plate (common base).

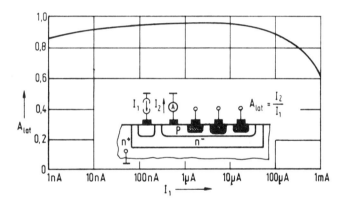

Fig. 4. Current gain of lateral p-n-p.

reason is the low epi-doping and the small intrinsic basewidth
[(14)]. Due to the small basewidth, the oxide covered area
between injector and base is relatively small. Surface recombination in this area therefore has only weak influence on
current gain at low current levels. The relatively high p doping
[(2)] also reduces the electron current density into the oxide-
covered injector surface (j_{nox}) and the contact-covered part
of the injector (j_{nc}) resulting in a high "injector" efficiency.

Static Performance of Vertical n-p-n

The upward current gain of the 3-collector inverter is shown
in Fig. 5 (graph A). In addition to the collector diffusion, the
collector C_2 has the n⁺-flat diffusion for high-voltage linear
transistors. In this way a very low effective base doping N_B' is
realized (punchthrough or high-gain transistor). In Fig. 5
(graph B) I_{C2} is plotted against I_B. I_{C2} is greater than I_{C1} by
a factor of 2. Thus, it can be stated that the effective base
doping (per unit area) under the high-gain collector is half of
the doping under "normal" collectors. This agrees with sheet
resistance measurements.

$$\frac{R_{S,\text{ normal}}}{R_{S,\text{ high-gain}}} = \frac{(20\text{–}30)\text{ k}\Omega/\square}{(40\text{–}80)\text{ k}\Omega/\square} \approx \frac{1}{2}.$$

The decrease in current gain at low current levels is small.
This can be explained with low surface recombination velocity
and high minority life times.

Measurements of the base current on structures with different numbers of collectors give the order of magnitude of
recombination current to the base contact in comparison to
the other recombination currents. According to the geometry
shown in Fig. 2, it holds roughly:

$$I_B \approx I_{nc} + (n+1)(I_{pv} + I_{nox}) \quad \text{(without injector!)} \quad (16)$$

where

I_B = base current,

I_{nc} = electron current to the base contact,

I_{pv} = hole current recombining the n⁻-epitaxial layer, at the
n⁻ n⁺ interface, in the n⁺-buried layer (n⁺ collar), or is
injected through the n⁺ layers,

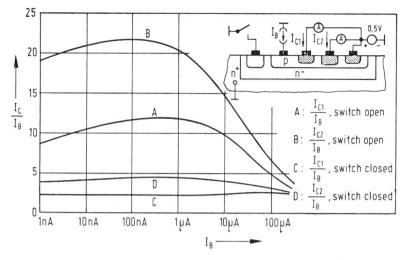

Fig. 5. Upward current gain of 3-collector inverter with C_2 as "super β collector."

n = the number of collectors per base,

I_{nox} = the electron current to the oxide covered base.

We find:

$$\frac{I_{nc}}{I_{pv} + I_{nox}} \approx 5 \cdots 12 \ (\text{at } \mu A \text{ current levels}). \tag{17}$$

It can be concluded from (17) that for this technological process, surface and hole recombination do not dominate.

For binary operation the effective current gain is important. β_{eff} is measured with the injector (Fig. 5, graphs C and D) shorted to the emitter. The small basewidth of the lateral transistor makes the back injected hole current density the largest part and in this case determines the base current. From [6] it results that

$$\beta_{eff} \approx \frac{1}{\dfrac{1}{\beta_{up}} + \dfrac{I_{po}}{I_{no}}} \xrightarrow{\beta_{up} \gg 1} \frac{I_{no}}{I_{po}}$$

$$= \text{constant} \ \frac{N_{epi} \ W_B}{I_i \ x_{jB} \displaystyle\int_{x_{jE}}^{x_{jB}} N'_B \, dx}. \tag{18}$$

If there is enough upward current gain the distance between base and injector determines the effective upward gain and makes β_{eff} = constant. This explains the flatness of curves C and D of Fig. 5.

Dynamic Performance

The delay-power curves have been measured on 11-stage ring oscillators with one collector per inverter. As Fig. 6 shows, a delay-power product of 0.15 pJ per gate is attained at low currents. A minimum delay of 35 ns is obtained for inverters with "normal" collector diffusion and 28.5 ns with high-gain collectors. This improvement agrees with measurements

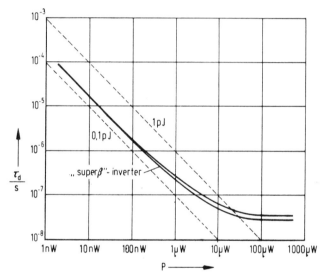

Fig. 6. Delay-power relation normalized for one inverter with one collector.

performed on wafers with an additional drive-in heat treatment [7].

CONCLUSION

In integrated circuits with less demand on minimum delay time, transistors of relative high blocking voltage (60 V) may be combined with I^2L circuits. The technology is not very different from standard technology used for linear circuits except for an additional n^+-flat diffusion. The I^2L part performs well, especially at low power levels. A delay-power product of 0.15 pJ per gate is reached. The minimum delay is 35 ns and 28 ns for inverters with high-gain collectors. The additional n^+-flat diffusion allows high current gain, which is important at low power and for minimum delay time. In the linear part there are three types of transistors differing mainly in gain and

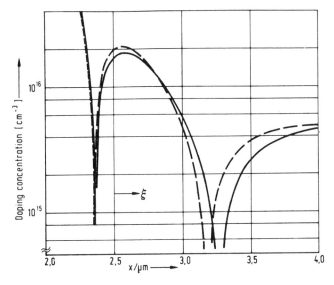

Fig. 7. Approximation of doping profile

$$—\quad N_{DO}\ \mathrm{erfc}\ \frac{x}{2\sqrt{D_n t_n}}\ -N_{AO}\exp\frac{-x^2}{4\,D_p t_p}+N_{\mathrm{epi}}$$

$$---\quad \frac{2\,N_{DO}\sqrt{D_n t_n}}{x_0\sqrt{\pi}}\ \exp\frac{-x_0^2}{4\,D_n t_n}\ \exp\frac{-2\xi}{4\,D_n t_n}$$

$$-\,N_{AO}\exp\frac{-x_0^2}{4\,D_p t_p}\ \exp\frac{-2\xi}{4\,D_p t_p}+N_{\mathrm{epi}}.$$

breakdown voltage. This technology may be further modified to produce even higher breakdown voltages and higher current gain for transistors with two n⁺ diffusions.

APPENDIX

To determine the emitter diffusion depth x_{jE} and $\widetilde{x}_{jE}$, respectively, an approximation method is proposed. First the complementary error function is approximated by a Gaussian function:

$$\mathrm{erfc}\left[\frac{x}{2\,(D_n t_n)^{1/2}}\right]\approx\frac{2\,(D_n t_n)^{1/2}}{x\,\pi^{1/2}}\ \exp\left[\frac{-x^2}{4\,D_n t_n}\right]$$

$$\cdot\, i\ \frac{x}{2\,(D_n t_n)^{1/2}}\gg 1 \tag{A1}$$

and with the new variable $\xi = x - x_0$ all Gauss functions become expanded. Fig. 7 shows that this leads to a reasonable accuracy.

Relation Between Doping Parameters $D_n t_n$ and Junction Depth x_{jE}

The junction depth is defined through:

$$N_{DO}\,\mathrm{erfc}\left[\frac{x_{jE}}{2\,(D_n t_n)^{1/2}}\right]-N_{AO}\exp\left[\frac{-x_j^2\,E}{4\,D_p t_p}\right]+N_{\mathrm{epi}}=0. \tag{A2}$$

Neglecting N_{epi} and with (A1) follows:

$$x_{jE}=\frac{x_0}{2}+\frac{\ln\left[\dfrac{N_{DO}}{N_{AO}}\ \dfrac{2\,(D_n t_n)^{1/2}}{x_0^{1/2}}\right]}{\dfrac{x_0}{2}\left[\dfrac{1}{D_n t_n}-\dfrac{1}{D_p t_p}\right]} \tag{A3}$$

with numerical values

$$x_0 = 2.4\ \mathrm{um}$$

$$D_p t_p = 0.371\ \mathrm{um^2}$$

$$N_{DO} = 3\cdot 10^{12}\ \mathrm{cm^{-3}}$$

$$N_{AO} = 5\cdot 10^{18}\ \mathrm{cm^{-3}}.$$

Equation (A3) may be approximated:

$$x_{jE}\approx x_0 + 13\left[\frac{D_n t_n}{\mathrm{\mu m^2}}-0.23\right]\mathrm{\mu m} \tag{A4}$$

(see Fig. 8).

Determination of Junction Depth x_{jE}

With the approximations given and using the abbreviations:

$$D_n t_n=\gamma=\left[\frac{x_{jE}-x_0}{13\ \mathrm{\mu m}}+0.23\right]\mathrm{\mu m^2}\,;\ \xi_{jB}=x_{jB}-x_0;$$

$$\cdot\,\xi_{jE}=x_{jE}-x_0$$

(6) leads to:

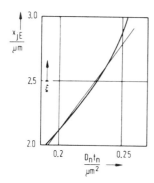

Fig. 8. Approximation of x_{jE} versus $D_n t_n$.

$$\xi_{jE} = x_{jC} - x_0$$

$$+ \frac{2N_{AO}}{N_{epi}} \frac{D_p t_p}{x_0} \exp\left(\frac{-x_0^2}{4 D_p t_p}\right) \left[\exp\left(\frac{-\xi_{jB} x_0}{2 D_p t_p}\right)\right.$$

$$\left. - \exp\left(\frac{-\xi_{jE} x_0}{2 D_p t_p}\right)\right] - \frac{4 N_{DO}}{N_{epi}} \frac{\gamma^{3/2}}{\pi^{1/2} x_0^2} \exp\left(\frac{-x_0^2}{4\gamma}\right)$$

$$\left[\exp\left(\frac{-\xi_{jB} x_0}{2\gamma}\right) - \exp\left(\frac{-\xi_{jE} x_0}{2\gamma}\right)\right]$$

which can be solved with a few iteration steps.

ACKNOWLEDGMENT

The author wishes to thank H. Schüssler for encouraging this work, H. Clauss for many helpful discussions, and K. Huwig for the fabrication of test wafers.

REFERENCES

[1] J. L. Saltich, W. L. George, and J. G. Soderberg, "Processing technology and AC/DC characteristics of linear compatible I²L," *IEEE J. Solid-State Circuits*, vol. SC-11, pp. 478–485, Aug. 1976.
[2] R. J. Widlar, "Super-gain transistors for IC's," *IEEE J. Solid-State Circuits*, vol. SC-4, pp. 249–251, Aug. 1969.
[3] S. M. Sze and G. Gibbons, "Avalanche breakdown voltages of abrupt and linearly graded p-n-junctions in Ge, Si, GaAs, and GaP," *Appl. Phys. Lett.*, vol. 8, no. 111, 1966.
[4] B. J. Baliga and S. K. Ghandi, "Analytical solutions for the breakdown voltage of abrupt cylindrical and spherical junctions," *Solid-State Electron.*, vol. 19, pp. 739–744, Sept. 1976.
[5] F. W. Hewlett, Jr., F. A. Lindholm, and A. J. Brodersen, "The effect of a buried layer on the collector breakdown voltages of bipolar junction transistors," *Solid-State Electron.*, vol. 16, pp. 453–457, 1973.
[6] F. M. Klaassen, "Device physics of integrated injection logic," *IEEE Trans. Electron Devices*, vol. ED-22, pp. 145–152, Mar. 1975.
[7] H. H. Berger, "The injection model a structure oriented model for merged transistor logic (MTL)," *IEEE J. Solid-State Circuits*, vol. SC-9, pp. 218–227, Oct. 1974.

A New High-Voltage Analog-Compatible I²L Process

DAVID J. ALLSTOT, STUDENT MEMBER, IEEE, SIK K. LUI, STUDENT MEMBER, IEEE, TOM S. T. WEI,
PAUL R. GRAY, SENIOR MEMBER, IEEE, AND ROBERT G. MEYER, SENIOR MEMBER, IEEE

Abstract—A new technique for realizing high-performance I²L circuits simultaneously with high-voltage analog circuits is described. The method is flexible and may be used with any standard linear bipolar process. Only one additional noncritical masking step and one phosphorous implant are required to form the I²L n-wells.

Experimental results are presented which show I²L betas of greater than eight per collector with the I²L BV_{CEO} exceeding 3 V. The measured minimum average propagation delay is 40 ns using a 14 μm thick, 5 $\Omega \cdot$ cm epitaxial layer, while the analog BV_{CEO} exceeds 50 V.

LIST OF SYMBOLS

A_B	I²L base region area.
A_C	I²L collector area.
B_{down}	Analog n-p-n forward (down) current gain.
$\beta_{\text{p-n-p}}$	Lateral p-n-p injector current gain.
β_{up}	I²L n-p-n reverse (upward) current gain.
D_n	Diffusivity of electrons.
F	Fan-out of I²L gate.
N_{epi}	Epitaxial doping concentration.
Q_B'	Intrinsic n-p-n base Gummel number.
Q_B	Extrinsic n-p-n base Gummel number.
Q_{imp}	n-well phosphorous implant dose.
s_p	Effective hole recombination velocity in epi.
t_{del}	Average I²L gate delay.
W_{epi}	Thickness of epi layer under base region.

I. INTRODUCTION AND OBJECTIVES

FOR large-scale integrated systems, it is often desirable to fabricate both analog and digital circuitry on the same chip using the same processing schedule. Analog compatibility was one of the main promises of I²L when it was introduced in 1972 [1]–[2]. This claim was based on the fact that I²L was a new circuit technique rather than a new process. Unfortunately, there are fundamental process tradeoffs between analog breakdown voltage and I²L performance which have impeded the development of bipolar analog/digital LSI circuits.

One solution to this problem is to juggle the epitaxial (epi) thickness and resistivity in an attempt to obtain satisfactory device characteristics [3]. This approach comprises both the analog and digital performance and, in addition, an extra masking step and deep n⁺ diffusion are usually required to form the I²L guard rings. This technique is not suitable

Manuscript received February 7, 1978; revised March 30, 1978. This research was supported by the Joint Services Electronics Program under Contract F44620-76-C-0100. D. J. Allstot was supported in part by an IBM Doctoral Fellowship. This paper was presented in part at the International Electron Devices Meeting, Washington, DC, December 1977.

The authors are with the Department of Electrical Engineering and Computer Sciences and the Electronics Research Laboratory, University of California, Berkeley, CA 94720.

where both high-voltage analog and high-speed I²L circuits are required.

A super-β process may also be used to gain analog compatibility [4]. This approach realizes excellent I²L dc performance, but only moderate ac performance is achieved due to excessive hole storage in the lightly doped epi. Control presents a problem since a small intrinsic base doping must be obtained in the presence of a high-resistivity epi region which is itself subject to large variations in doping.

Another method, poly I²L, uses a completely new process which has shown excellent I²L performance with moderately high analog breakdown voltages [5]. The main disadvantage of this approach is that it is so different from standard processes that it is difficult to incorporate into existing process schedules.

The goals of this work were to develop high-performance I²L on the same IC chip with high-voltage analog circuits while maintaining the process simplicity required for LSI capability. To achieve these goals, it was decided to modify a standard high-voltage linear bipolar process subject to the following assumptions: 1) a single epitaxial layer would be used with its parameters determined strictly by the analog breakdown voltage requirements; 2) any additional masking steps would be sufficiently noncritical so that the overall yield would not be significantly reduced, and 3) any additional doping steps would be performed by ion implantation to maintain controllability. Furthermore, it was required that the I²L performance be determined independently of variations in the epi layer thickness and starting resistivity. n-well I²L was conceived as a method for meeting these objectives.

II. PROCESS DESCRIPTION

A. Analog Processing Requirements

As mentioned above, the characteristics of the epitaxial layer were determined by the analog breakdown voltage requirements. A 5 $\Omega \cdot$ cm, 14 μm thick epi layer was chosen to give analog n-p-n down betas of about 200 with a BV_{CEO} of greater than 50 V as shown in Fig. 1. This analog performance is obtained independently of the additional processing steps required to form the I²L transistors.

B. Digital I²L Processing Requirements

The epi characteristics directly affect the I²L performance. The I²L up beta is given in terms of processing parameters as [6]

$$\beta_{\text{up}} = \left(\frac{A_C}{A_B}\right) \frac{1}{\left[1 + F\left(1 - \dfrac{A_C}{A_B}\right)\right] \dfrac{Q_B'}{Q_B} + \dfrac{(F+1) s_p Q_B'}{D_n N_{\text{epi}}}}. \quad (1)$$

Reprinted from *IEEE J. Solid-State Circuits*, vol. SC-13, pp. 479–482, Aug. 1978.

307

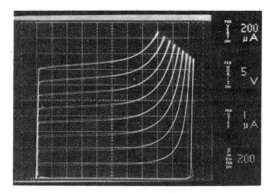

Fig. 1. Analog n-p-n transistor characteristics.

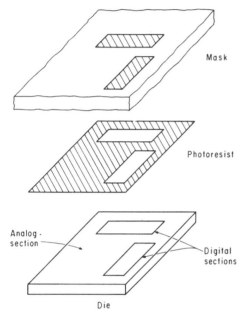

Fig. 2. Additional mask step permits n-well phosphorous implant only in I²L digital sections of the chip.

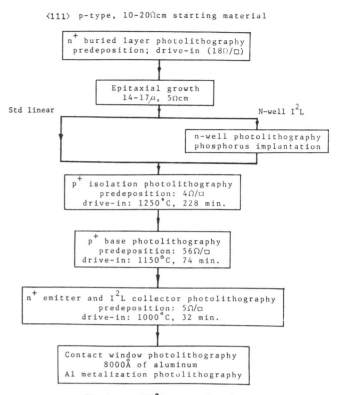

Fig. 3. n-well I²L process flowchart.

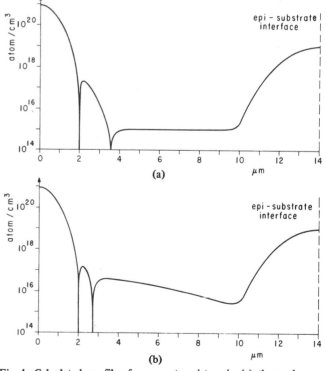

Fig. 4. Calculated profiles for n-p-n transistors in (a) the analog sections, and (b) the n-well digital I²L sections of the chip.

Hence, for high β_{up}, large epi concentration and a small intrinsic base Gummel number are required. Similarly, the I²L minority carrier storage delay is given in terms of processing parameters as

$$t_{del} = \left(\frac{A_B}{A_C}\right) \frac{(F+1)\,W_{epi}Q'_B}{D_n N_{epi}}. \qquad (2)$$

Again, small Q'_B and large N_{epi} are desirable. These requirements are opposite to those which achieve high analog breakdown voltage. Therefore, process modification is necessary to meet these objectives simultaneously, assuming that w_{epi} is fixed by analog breakdown requirements.

C. Process Modifications

In applications requiring combined analog/digital functions, it is usually possible to partition the chip into several separate analog and digital sections. This partitioning allows definition of a new masking step as shown in Fig. 2. This mask permits modification of the I²L epi regions, while the analog epi regions remain unchanged in order to preserve the desired analog parameters.

In order to increase N_{epi} and reduce Q'_B in the I²L sections, the new mask defines a photoresist pattern which permits phosphorous implantation only in the I²L regions. This masking step and implantation are performed after the epi growth, but before the isolation diffusion, as shown in the process flowchart of Fig. 3. During the subsequent high temperature cycles, the implanted phosphorous is driven into the I²L epi regions, forming an n-well. This n-well step improves the I²L performance in two ways: 1) the effective epi resistivity in the I²L region is decreased from 5 to about $0.2 \ \Omega \cdot$ cm, and 2) simultaneously, the intrinsic base Gummel number is reduced to about 1×10^{12} cm^{-2} due to base charge cancellation. Hence, this single processing step improves both the I²L ac and dc performance, while the n-p-n transistors in the analog regions are unaffected, thus preserving their high-voltage capability. Fig. 4 shows the calculated n-p-n profiles in both the analog and n-well regions.

Since the n-well is formed from the surface, variations in epi thickness have little effect on the I²L performance. In addition, the n-well resistivity (which is defined by ion implantation) is well controlled.

III. RESULTING PERFORMANCE

The performance of the n-well I²L devices was measured using the test chip shown in Fig. 5.

A. DC Performance

Fig. 6 shows the I²L betas for a four collector gate versus collector current for an implant dose of 2.34×10^{13} ions/cm². The dc up beta is greater than eight per collector for a device perpendicular to the injector, while the up beta remains greater than two for collector currents less than 200 μA. For these test devices, the lateral p-n-p mask-defined base width was 0.4 mils. In addition, a grounded p-ring surrounded the test devices to simulate injection losses under the shallow n$^+$ isolation rings to adjacent gates. Fig. 7 shows a typical set of I²L n-p-n common-emitter characteristics.

Table I gives the n-p-n up beta as a function of injector base width for an array of one-collector I²L gates, and also the lateral p-n-p injector beta versus $W_{p\text{-}n\text{-}p}$ for the same array of transistors.

B. AC Performance

The I²L ac performance was measured using a nine-stage, four collectors/gate ring oscillator with the results plotted in Fig. 8. The minimum average propagation delay is 40 ns at a gate current of 200 μA. The resulting power–delay product of 1.8 pJ could be improved by reducing the lateral p-n-p base-width which was 0.4 mils. The unused collectors were left floating during the measurement to simulate a worst case speed condition.

C. Comparison to Other Techniques

Table II compares the analog BV_{CBO} and digital ring oscillator performance parameters for the n-well process and the other three approaches mentioned earlier. It can be seen that only the n-well process combines high-voltage linear circuitry with high-speed I²L circuits.

D. Variations with n-Well Implant Dose

Since the n-well doping effectively determines the I²L performance, it is necessary to investigate parameter changes relative to phosphorous implant variations. Table III shows the I²L up beta versus n-well implant dose. It can be seen

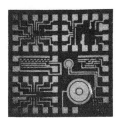

Fig. 5. Die photo of experimental test chip.

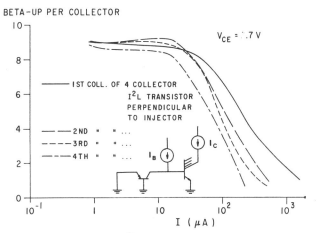

Fig. 6. Measured I²L β_{up} versus collector current.

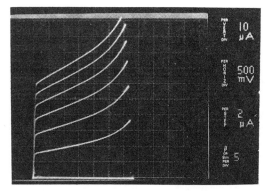

Fig. 7. I²L n-p-n characteristics for one collector of a four-collector transistor.

TABLE I
MEASURED β VARIATIONS WITH INJECTOR BASE WIDTH FOR ONE-COLLECTOR I²L GATES

$W_{p\text{-}n\text{-}p}$ (mils)	$\beta_{p\text{-}n\text{-}p}$	$\beta_{\mu p}$
0.4	0.28	20
0.5	0.24	22
0.6	0.20	23
0.7	0.16	24

that large variations in implant dose can be tolerated while still maintaining a beta of at least two per collector. Table III also shows the I²L breakdown voltage versus implant dose. Again, large changes in Q_{imp} can be tolerated with an I²L BV_{CEO} of at least 2 V.

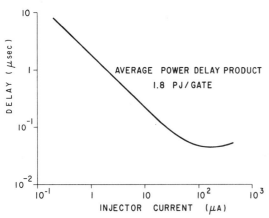

Fig. 8. Measured power–delay performance for a nine-stage ring oscillator with four collectors/gate.

TABLE II
COMPARISON FOR ANALOG AND RING OSCILLATOR PARAMETERS FOR DIFFERENT APPROACHES

Approach	BV_{CBO}	t_{min} (ns)	F (Ring Oscillator Fanout)
Epi Tradeoff [3] $2\ \Omega \cdot cm, 12\ \mu m$	70	100	1
Super-β [4]	70	35	1
Poly I^{2}L [5]	40	5	1
n-well I^{2}L	80	40	4

TABLE III
I^{2}L PARAMETERS VARIATIONS VERSUS n-WELL IMPLANT DOSE

Q_{imp} (ions/cm^2)	β_{up}	BV_{CEO} ($I_c = 10\ \mu A$)
0	0.3	7.5
7.81×10^{12}	3	4.2
2.34×10^{13}	7	2.8
3.91×10^{13}	6	1.5

IV. CONCLUSIONS

n-well I^{2}L achieves high-performance I^{2}L gates on the same chip with high breakdown voltage analog transistors. For the process described in this paper, I^{2}L betas of eight per collector were realized with propagation delays of 40 ns. These parameters were obtained simultaneously with analog transistors having a BV_{CBO} exceeding 80 V. The simplicity and flexibility of this process along with its complete analog/digital compatibility make it ideal for bipolar LSI system applications.

ACKNOWLEDGMENT

The measurement assistance of R. Kaneshiro is appreciated. Signetics, Inc. and Precision Monolithics, Inc. supplied the wafers. The authors also wish to acknowledge the contributions to this project of F. Ademic of Signetics, Inc.

REFERENCES

[1] H. H. Berger and S. K. Wiedmann, "Merged transistor logic—A low-cost bipolar logic concept," *IEEE J. Solid-State Circuits*,
[2] K. Hart and A. Slob, "Integrated injection logic: A new approach to LSI," *IEEE J. Solid-State Circuits*, vol. SC-7, pp. 346–351, Oct. 1972.
[3] J. Saltich, W. George, and J. Soderberg, "Processing technology and AC/DC characteristics of linear compatible I^{2}L," *IEEE J. Solid-State Circuits*, vol. SC-11, pp. 478–485, Aug. 1976.
[4] G. Bergmann, "Linear compatible I^{2}L technology with high voltage transistors," *IEEE J. Solid-State Circuits*, vol. SC-12, pp. 566–572, Oct. 1977.
[5] R. D. Davies and J. D. Meindl, "Poly I^{2}L—A high-speed linear-compatible structure," *IEEE J. Solid-State Circuits*, vol. SC-12, pp. 367–375, Aug. 1977.
[6] F. M. Klassen, "Device physics of integrated injection logic," *IEEE Trans. Electron Devices*, vol. ED-22, pp. 145–152, Mar. 1975.

I²L and High-Voltage Analog Circuitry on the Same Chip: A Comparison Between Various Combination Processes

LEIF HALBO AND TROND A. HANSEN

Abstract—Various simple processes are possible for obtaining a combination of I²L and high-voltage analog functions on the same IC chip. The simplest methods involve the introduction of one extra process step which affects only the I²L part, in addition to the analog process.

In this paper comparative experiments are presented for the I²L properties of: method *A*) a standard 25 V BV_{CE} analog process; method *B*) a modification of the same process with an extra N⁺ diffusion giving deeper I²L collectors; method *C*) a modification giving a more shallow I²L base; and methods *D*) two modifications involving a selective doping of the epi layer in the I²L part. Aside from the additional step in each method all process parameters, as well as the I²L gate geometry, are kept the same.

It is found that processes *D* give significantly higher effective gain for the n-p-n switching transistor than the other methods. The optimum speed is also higher for these processes, but the other methods have a lower power-delay product at low current level. The reasons for the differences are analyzed.

For one of the processes *D* the effect of a shallow versus deep N⁺ guard ring is discussed, and the sensitivity to variations in process parameters is commented on.

I. INTRODUCTION

FOR many purposes it is advantageous to combine logic and high-voltage ($BV_{CE} \sim$ 20–50 V) analog circuitry on one monolitic IC chip. Integrated injection logic (I²L) is a dense bipolar logic with great flexibility in power requirements, etc., and is particularly well suited for such a combination.

Among the many possible uses of such a combination are: A/D converters, logic and op amps for a standard ±15 V supply, sensors with logic for signal handling, logic and output driver-stages (for example, for audible telephone ringer signals), and automatic controls.

When a process is to be developed for combining I²L and high-voltage analog circuitry (hereafter referred to as a combination process), the properties of the analog part must be considered given, based on the optimization of the n-p-n transistor. This severely limits the performance of the I²L unless one accepts additional process steps and a more complex and costly process.

Manuscript received October 23, 1978; revised January 2, 1979. This work was supported by the Royal Norwegian Council for Scientific and Industrial Research. This paper is based in part on a paper presented at the Fourth European Solid-State Circuits Conference, Amsterdam, The Netherlands, September 18–21, 1978.

The authors are with the Central Institute for Industrial Research, Blindern, Oslo, Norway.

The I²L properties obtained in unmodified analog processes, corresponding to various breakdown voltages, were investigated by Saltich *et al.* [1]. For $BV_{CE} >$ 20 V they found poor I²L driving capability and fan-out limited to ≤3. The minimum delay for two-collector gates in a 30 V process was ≳100 ns/gate, which is very slow compared to optimized I²L.

The reasons for this poor I²L performance are that the high analog breakdown voltage requires 1) high active base integral doping in the n-p-n transistor (Gummel number G), 2) thick epitaxial layer with 3) low doping. These requirements cause in the I²L n-p-n switching transistor a low β_{up} and a high value of I_{po}/I_{no} [2]. Thus, a very low n-p-n effective up gain β_{eff} is obtained. Storage of much hole diffusion charge in the thick, lowly doped n-p-n emitter gives long delay times at high current levels.

An improved combination process, which can be used with existing high-voltage analog processes with a minimum of change, is highly desirable. Several principles for combination processes have been suggested. However, in most cases, few details have been given for the analog starting process, the I²L gate geometry used, and the electrical data obtained. Thus, it is not possible to make a direct comparison of the qualities of the different processes.

In this paper we wish to present and compare experimental results obtained for the I²L properties of various simple combination processes based on the same analog process. Each combination process is realized by introducing one extra mask and process step in addition to the analog process. The additional step is optimized with respect to the I²L properties but does not affect the analog part.

By using such a combination process one gets I²L with a shallow N⁺ guard ring. Better properties are obtained if one is willing to add one more masking step for a deep N⁺ diffusion. The merit of deep versus shallow N⁺ will be discussed for one of the processes.

II. SIMPLE COMBINATION PROCESSES

In all the methods to be compared the main purpose of the additional process step is to reduce the base Gummel number in the I²L n-p-n transistor. This is indicated schematically in Fig. 1. The cross section of an I²L gate produced by a standard analog process is shown on the left in *A*. The corresponding doping profiles are fully drawn in the figure to the right.

In (*B*) the N⁺ diffusion for the I²L collectors is made in a

Reprinted from *IEEE J. Solid-State Circuits*, vol. SC-14, pp. 666–671, Aug. 1979.

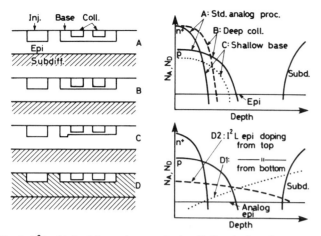

Fig. 1. I²L obtained by various methods: *A*) Standard analog process. *B*) Deep N⁺ diffusion for I²L collectors. *C*) Shallow p diffusion for I²L base. *D*) Enhancement of epi doping from below or above. Schematic cross sections are shown to the left and doping profiles to the right.

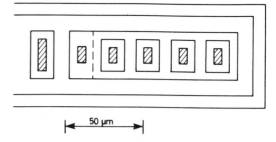

Fig. 2. Layout of four-collector I²L gate. In process *C* the base area to the right of the dashed line is lightly doped.

separate step [3], and these collectors are deeper than the analog emitter. The new N⁺ profile is dashed in the figure to the right. Thus, the active base thickness is reduced, as well as the active base integral doping.

In (*C*) a similar reduction in active base thickness is obtained by making the I²L active base in a separate process step of lighter doping and more shallow drive-in [4]. The corresponding doping profile is dotted.

Finally, in (*D*) a heavier doping is introduced through the whole depth of the epi layer in the I²L part of the chip, whereas the base and collector diffusions are the same as in the analog part. This doping may be introduced as an extra phosphorus buried layer which is diffused up through the epi layer, *D*1 [5], or it may be introduced after epi growth and diffused down, *D*2 [6].

The effect of these changes on the static I²L properties can be seen from the expression for β_{eff} [2]:

$$\beta_{\text{eff}} = [1/\beta_{\text{up}} + I_{po}/I_{no}]^{-1}.$$

Here

$$\beta_{\text{up}} = I_C/I_B, \quad I_C = I_{no} \exp(qV_{EB}/kT),$$

$$I_{no} = S_C q n_i^2 D_n/G, \quad \text{and}$$

$$I_{po} = S_{\text{inj}} q n_i^2 D_p/(N_{\text{epi}} w_{\text{p-n-p}}).$$

The symbols have their usual meaning [2].

By a reduction of the n-p-n base Gummel number $G \equiv \int N_B' \, dx$, I_{no} and β_{up} are increased in all processes *B*–*D*. For processes *D*, I_{po} is simultaneously reduced due to the higher epi doping. For processes *D*, I_B is also reduced, as will be shown later.

The big thickness of the epi underneath the base remains essentially unaltered despite the modifications. The stored charge here [2] remains large for *B* and *C*, but is reduced in *D* due to the higher doping.

Other methods for I²L/high-voltage analog combinations have been proposed [7]–[9]. However, they involve greater

modifications of standard processes and will not be further discussed here.

III. EXPERIMENTAL RESULTS

A. Process Details

The different processes *B*–*D* have been realized as modifications to our conventional 25 V BV_{CE} analog process. In order to get the most direct comparison between the methods, the same geometrical layout of the I²L gates is used in all cases, as shown in Fig. 2. For method *C* the base area to the right of the dashed line is lightly doped. Dynamic measurements are made on nine-stage ring oscillators with output buffer and coupling to the collector farthest from the injector. This gives the longest delay for that geometry and is a very conservative measure of the four-collector gate speed.

The processes are adjusted to give $BV_{CE} = 3$ V for the I²L gates to give some margin of safety in case of variations of processing parameters. The epi layers have $\rho = 2 \, \Omega \cdot$ cm $t = 12$ μm after growth, and the analog process gives $BV_{CE} \approx 30$ V, $\beta_{\text{n-p-n}} \approx 200$. I²L made in the unmodified analog process *A* is included in the following for comparison.

The combined processes are obtained in the following way. In process *B*, the deep collector process, an N⁺ predeposition of 5 $\Omega/\square$ (same as the analog emitter diffusion) is made for the I²L collectors and driven partly in. Then the analog emitter diffusion is predeposited and the drive-in is completed. In process *C*, the shallow base process, the ordinary base is first predeposited. The lightly doped base is implanted with a dose of 8×10^{14} cm⁻² and drive-in of both is done. Process *D*1, the selective epi doping from below, is made by implanting 5×10^{14} cm⁻² phosphorus into the substrate after drive-in of the regular arsenic buried layer. In process *D*2 a dose of 2×10^{13} cm⁻² phosphorus is implanted as the first step after epi growth. A deep N⁺ guard ring of 5 $\Omega/\square$ predeposition is used.

The process parameters for the I²L part are shown in Table I. The depths are measured by groove-and-stain and are not accurate. Also, the active base sheet resistivity R_p is only approximate.

B. Static Properties

Fig. 3 shows the measured β_{eff} versus I_C for processes *A*, *B*, *C*, and *D*2. *D*1 gave results very similar to *D*2 and is not shown in the figure.

It will be noted that the selective epi doping processes *D* give by far the highest β_{eff} at all current levels. At low currents

TABLE I
PROCESS PARAMETERS. W_b IS ACTIVE BASE THICKNESS, R_p IS ACTIVE
BASE SHEET RESISTIVITY

Parameter	A Std. analog	B Deep coll.	C Shallow base	D1 Epi up	D2 Epi down
ρ_{epi} (Ωcm) average	2.0	2.0	2.0	0.2	0.25
N_{epi} (x10^{15}cm^{-3}) average	2.5	2.5	2.5	40	25
W_{epi} (μm) net (under base)	4.5	4.5	4.5/4.7	4.9	4.9
R_B (Ω/□)	120	120	120/200	120	120
W_B (μm)	3.6	3.6	3.6/3.4	3.2	3.2
W_B' (μm) approx.	∿0.8	∿ 0.6	∿0.6	∿0.4	∿0.4
R_p (Ω/□) approx.	∿10k	∿ 100k	∿100k	∿40k	∿40k
BV_{CE}(V) I^{2}L	7.5	3	3	3	3

TABLE II
CURRENT MEASURED IN ONE- AND FOUR-COLLECTOR I^{2}L GATES,
AT $V_{BE} = 650$ mV. FOR THE FOUR-COLLECTOR GATES THE NEAREST
COLLECTOR IS USED. UNIT μA

Process	1-coll.gate			4-coll. gate		
	I_C	$I_B(V_{inj}=0)$	$I_B(I_{inj}=0)$	I_C	$I_B(V_{inj}=0)$	$I_B(I_{inj}=0)$
A	34	13.5	7.2	36	16.2	8.6
B	141	13.7	8.5	154	17.1	11.3
C	122	15.5	7.5	132	17.4	8.4
D1	120	2.6	2.5	137	4.9	4.9
D2	100	2.2	2.1	103	4.2	4.1

TABLE III
APPROXIMATE BASE CURRENT COMPONENTS IN FOUR-COLLECTOR GATES AT
$V_{BE} = 650$ mV CALCULATED FROM DATA OF TABLE II. UNIT μA

Process	I_{met}	I_B'	I_{rev}
A	6	2.5	7
B	6	5	6
C	7	2	9
D1	∿0.9	4	∿0.1
D2	∿0.7	4	∿0.1

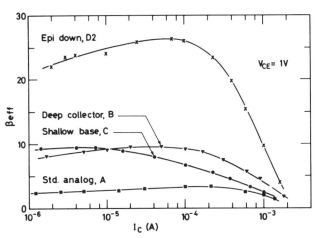

Fig. 3. Effective n-p-n gain versus collector current for four-collector gates for each process. The collector farthest from the base contact is used, the other collectors are floating.

processes B and C give nearly the same gain, but for B the gain starts dropping at a considerably lower current due to the higher base series resistance. Finally, the standard analog process A gives β_{eff} which is only slightly above 1. The common emitter gain of the p-n-p, β_{p-n-p}, is 4–5 for methods A–C, and ∼1.0 for $D1$ and $D2$.

To analyze the static behavior in detail, measurements on special test structures should be made. Here we shall limit ourselves to a comparison of data for one-collector gates and four-collector gates. Table II gives collector current, and base current with injector grounded or floating, at $V_{BE} = 650$ mV. For the four-collector gates the nearest collector is used to minimize effects of base series resistance.

The most important components of the n-p-n base current I_B are [10]–[12]

$$I_B = I_{rev} + I_{met} + I_{ox} + I_{bl} + I_{str} \qquad (1)$$

where I_{rev} represents reverse injection of holes to injector, and I_{met} and I_{ox} are electron recombination in the metal covered and oxide covered base, respectively. I_{bl} is hole recombination in the buried layer and the N$^+$ ring, and I_{str} is leakage current to the substrate.

Since the current densities are nearly independent of gate

geometry, I_{rev} and I_{met} are approximately the same for one- and four-collector gates. The remaining components are proportional to their respective areas. As a fair approximation we take the area ratio for four- and one-collector gates to be 2.5 for each of these current components. Also we neglect the difference in recombination in the predeposited and implanted parts of the base of method C. It is then possible to find approximate values of I_{met}, I_{rev}, and the sum of the remaining base current components $I_B' \equiv I_{ox} + I_{bl} + I_{str}$. The results are given in Table III.

The low collector current value of process A is related to the large Gummel number and is the reason for the much lower β_{eff} of A than of B and C. Processes A, B, and C have similar values of the base current components, as might be expected. Processes D have much lower base current than the other processes, with injector floating as well as grounded. Table III indicates the reason for this to be lower I_{rev} as well as lower I_{met}. The low I_{rev} is due to the high epi concentration. But the generally accepted expression for I_{met} [11], [12],

$$I_{met} = S_{met} \frac{qn_i^2 D_n}{\int N_B dx} \exp(qV_{BE}/kT),$$

does not predict any dependence on epi doping. The two most likely explanations for our data seem to be 1) the effective surface recombination velocity under the metal [13] is smaller for methods D than for the other methods, or 2) equation (1) is incomplete and additional recombination is of importance. This would make the magnitudes in Table III inaccurate. Detailed measurements on test structures [10]–[12] are in progress and will be discussed in a future paper.

To get sufficient driving capability and noise margin for I^{2}L it is desirable to have $\beta_{eff} \gtrsim 10$ for four-collector gates for the whole range of currents and temperatures of interest. At low

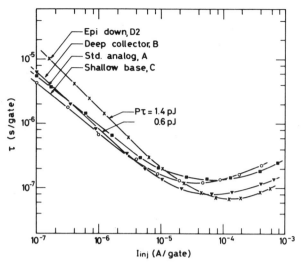

Fig. 4. Delay time versus injector current for four-collector gates for each process measured by nine-stage ring oscillators. The collector farthest from the injector drives the next stage.

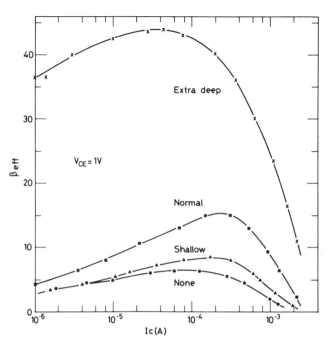

Fig. 5. Effective gain versus collector current for four-collector I^2L gates, process $D2$, with different depths of the N^+ guard ring.

temperatures β_{eff} is reduced [12]. Also, if a shallow N^+ guard ring is used, instead of the present deep N^+, β_{eff} is reduced by about a factor 2 (Section IV below). The data presented here show that the selective epi doping methods have static properties much superior to the other methods, giving flexibility in use of shallow/deep N^+ guard and use of geometrically unfavorable gates with several crossovers, etc.

C. Dynamic Properties

Fig. 4 shows four-collector gate delay time versus injector current for processes A, B, C, and $D2$. The data for method $D1$ are very similar to those for $D2$. It should be emphasized that four-collector gates of method A only operate marginally: from a number of wafers processed only a few ring oscillators worked at all. For all methods one-collector gates have approximately a factor 2 shorter delay at low currents and a factor 3 shorter at high currents.

Methods A, B, and C give low delay and are very similar at low currents, with a power-delay product at 1 μA/gate of ~ 0.6 pJ. Methods D have a power-delay product which is twice as high. The difference is caused by the increased charge storage in the n-p-n emitter-base depletion region for methods D, due to high epi doping [2].

At high currents methods D are best with a minimum four-collector gate delay $\lesssim 70$ ns/gate compared to 80 for B, 110 for C, and 140 for A. The superiority of methods D is due to less diffusion charge storage in the more highly doped epi layer [2]. The improvement is not as great as the epi concentration ratio alone would predict, because for a given injector current V_{BE} is higher for the methods with high epi doping.

The difference between methods A and B is due to the charge in the thicker active base of method A. The poor minimum delay of method C is due to the high base series resistance, which causes debiasing at lower currents for this method than for the other methods (cf. Fig. 3).

IV. ADDITIONAL PROPERTIES OF THE SELECTIVE EPI DOPING PROCESS $D2$

In view of the superior performance of the selective epi doping processes we shall present some additional results on method $D2$.

In some combined circuits parts of the analog circuitry require low collector series resistance and a deep N^+ diffusion. In that case the normal, deep I^2L guard ring is automatically available. Most often there is no such need in the analog part, and the deep N^+ process step is saved if the I^2L can do with only shallow N^+ guard.

To see the importance of deep versus shallow N^+ we have processed wafers with both types by method $D2$. (See [14] for analogous results for conventional I^2L process.) The use of no N^+ at all has been included for comparison, as well as an extra deep N^+ which makes certain that the concentration is high even where the guard ring hits the buried layer. The N^+ predeposition is in all cases 5 $\Omega/\square$; the depths at which the N^+ concentration is reduced to the implanted epi concentration are ~ 3.5 μm (shallow), ~ 7 μm (normal), and ~ 12 μm (extra deep).

The measured β_{eff} versus I_c in the four cases is shown in Fig. 5. (The gate geometry is slightly different from that used for Fig. 3, with a lower ratio of collector to base areas.) It will be seen that a shallow N^+ is only marginally better than none at all. This is because of the thick epi layer underneath the shallow N^+ diffusion which gives rise to a high base current due to hole recombination far away from the base. β_{eff} for normal, deep N^+ is approximately a factor 2 better.

The effect of the extra deep N^+ is dramatic, increasing β_{eff} by a factor 3 above that for the normal N^+ depth. The reasons for this are that the N^+ concentration is high all the way down

314

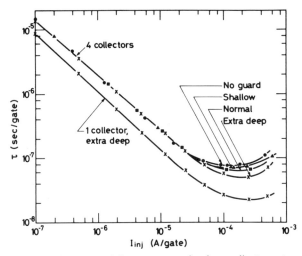

Fig. 6. Delay time versus injector current for four-collector gates, process $D2$, with different depths of the N^+ guard ring. Data for one-collector gates with extra deep N^+ are also included.

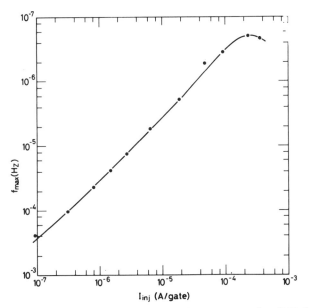

Fig. 7. Highest clock frequency versus injector current, for divide-by-two modules made by process $D2$.

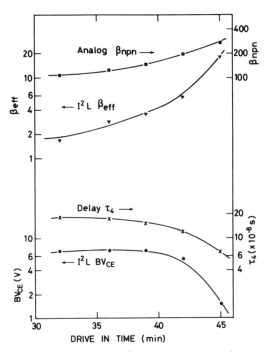

Fig. 8. Plot of basic analog and I^2L properties versus N^+ drive-in time, for process $D2$ with shallow N^+ guard ring. The top curve (scale to the right) shows analog β_{n-p-n}. The curves below show I^2L properties for four-collector gates: β_{eff} (scale to the left), τ (scale to the right), and BV_{CE} (scale to the left).

Finally, we wish to emphasize the sensitivity to variations in process parameters for all the combination processes discussed. As an illustration of this for process $D2$ various I^2L parameters, as well as analog β_{n-p-n}, were measured for various drive-in times for the shallow N^+ diffusion. (We could equally well have chosen to vary the diffusion temperature, or the base diffusion.) Fig. 8 shows the results. As the drive-in time is varied from 35 to 45 min the analog β_{n-p-n} increases by a factor ~ 2.5. The corresponding change in β_{eff} is a factor 10. The delay time is reduced by a factor ~ 2.5 and, equally significantly, BV_{CE} goes down from 7 to 1.5 V. Thus, process variations which give acceptable spread in analog parameters cause changes in the I^2L which are too big to be tolerated. The reason is that the I^2L active base is considerably thinner than the analog active base, and the *relative* change caused by a process variation is much greater in the I^2L part than in the analog part.

V. CONCLUSIONS

In this paper the I^2L properties of various combination processes have been compared. The processes are all based on the same standard analog process, and one additional step is introduced (or two, giving I^2L with deep N^+ guard ring).

Methods D, based on selective doping of the I^2L epi layer, give much better driving capability than the other methods. The electron recombination component of the base current appears to be smaller, giving a higher β_{up}. Also, the ratio I_{po}/I_{no} is lower due to higher epi doping, making β_{eff} much higher for these processes.

Methods D also give the shortest gate delay at high current levels, due to less hole storage in the more highly doped epi

into the buried layer, and out-diffusion causes the N^+ to touch the base area.

Fig. 6 shows gate delay versus injector current for the same cases of N^+ guard. At low currents there is no difference, but at high currents the delay is shorter for the deeper N^+. The difference in minimum delay for shallow and deep N^+ is ~ 10 percent.

The reason for the reduced delay with deeper N^+ is the reduction of hole charge in the epi underneath the N^+, as well as around the base area due to N^+ out-diffusion.

Fig. 7 shows for process $D2$ the highest clock frequency of D flip-flops in the divide-by-two mode versus injector current. By this process the maximum clock frequency is approximately 6 MHz, at a power of 0.15 mW/gate. This is considerably below the speed of optimized purely digital processes, but for many purposes it is very satisfactory.

layer. However, methods B and C, based on deep I^2L collectors and shallow I^2L base, respectively, have lower power-delay product than methods D, due to less charge in the emitter-base depletion region.

Comparing methods $D1$ and $D2$, with selective epi doping introduced from below and above, respectively, the electrical data are found to be very similar. One disadvantage of $D1$, however, is that it is sensitive to variations in the epi thickness [5]. The method of epi down-diffusion $D2$ is therefore to be preferred.

For that method it was shown that a deep N^+ guard ring gives approximately twice as high β_{eff} as a shallow one. However, the deep N^+ only gives a ~ 10 percent improvement in maximum speed.

Finally, it was demonstrated that the combination processes (represented by $D2$) are considerably more sensitive to variations in processing parameters than the standard analog process.

The "super-gain" transistors produced by the combination processes may also be used for analog circuitry. For processes B and C these have $\beta_{down} \sim 1000$ and $BV_{CE} \sim 8$ V, for processes D $\beta_{down} \sim 500$ and $BV_{CE} \sim 10$ V.

The common geometry used (cf. Fig. 2) is a compromise, and by using different geometries the results for each process can be somewhat improved.

ACKNOWLEDGMENT

We are grateful to ϕ. Engebretsen, D. J. Ruzicka, and P. R. Ulsnaes for growth of epi layers, H. Sandmo for ion-implantation, and H. Skarelven, E. Carlson, and H. Jakobsen for valuable discussions.

REFERENCES

[1] J. L. Saltich, W. L. George, and J. S. Soderberg, "Processing technology and AC/DC characteristics for linear compatible I^2L," *IEEE J. Solid-State Circuits*, vol. SC-11, pp. 478–485, Aug. 1975.

[2] F. M. Klaassen, "Device physics of integrated injection logic," *IEEE Trans. Electron. Devices*, vol. ED-22, pp. 145–152, Mar. 1975.

[3] G. Bergmann, "Linear compatible I^2L technology with high voltage transistors," *IEEE J. Solid-State Circuits*, vol. SC-12, pp. 566–572, Oct. 1977.

[4] L. Blossfeld, "I^2L und standard Bipolartechnik kombiniert: Ein neuer Prozess für digitale und analoge Schaltungen auf einum Chip," *Elektronik*, Heft 4, pp. 57–60, 1977.

[5] T. Watanabe, T. Okabe, and M. Nogaka, "Phosphorous buried emitter I^2L for high voltage operating circuits," *Jap. J. Appl. Phys.*, vol. 16, suppl. 16-1, pp. 143–146, 1976.

[6] D. J. Allstot *et al.*, "A new high-voltage analog-compatible I^2L process," *IEEE J. Solid-State Circuits*, vol. SC-13, pp. 479–483, Aug. 1978.

[7] R. D. Davies and J. D. Meindl, "Poly I^2L—A high-speed linear-compatible structure," *IEEE J. Solid-State Circuits*, vol. SC-12, pp. 367–375, Aug. 1977.

[8] T. Okabe, T. Watanabe, and M. Nagata, "A controller with high speed I^2L and high voltage analog circuits," in *1978 ISSCC Dig. Tech. Papers*, pp. 44–45.

[9] A. A. Yiannoulos, "Buried injector logic: Second generation I^2L performance," in *1978 ISSCC Dig. Tech. Papers*, pp. 12–13.

[10] H. E. Berger, "The injection model—A structure-oriented model for merged transistor logic (MTL)," *IEEE J. Solid-State Circuits*, vol. SC-9, pp. 218–227, Oct. 1974.

[11] H. E. Wulms, "Base current of I^2L transistors," *IEEE Solid-State Circuits*, vol. SC-12, pp. 143–150, Apr. 1977.

[12] W. H. Mattheus, R. P. Mertens, and J. D. Stulting, "Characteristics of I^2L at low current levels," *IEEE Trans. Electron. Devices*, vol. ED-24, pp. 1228–1233, Oct. 1977.

[13] E. L. Heaseli, "Recombination beneath ohmic contacts and adjacent oxide covered regions," *Solid-State Electron.*, vol. 22, pp. 89–93, Jan. 1979.

[14] A. Scmitz and A. Slob, "The effect of isolation regions on the current gain of inverse npn-transistors used in integrated injection logic (I^2L)," in *1974 IEDM Dig. Tech. Papers*, pp. 508–510.

Part VIII
Applications

The applications papers reprinted in this part have been selected on the basis of diversity. It is intended to show that I^2L covers a broad range of applications requirements covering a battery-operated watch, a unique timing circuit, a two-tone telephone dialing circuit, a controller for home appliances, a precision A/D converter, and mask programmable arrays. These papers are largely self-explanatory and there is little need for comment.

A unique feature introduced in paper VIII-1 by Tucci and Russell is a divide-by-two circuit which uses only four I^2L base regions. The authors avoid timing ambiguities in the circuit by introducing added delays by way of operating two of the four gates in the circuit with reduced current drive from the injector. The reduction in injector current drive is accomplished by selectively widening the injector pnp base widths. Use of this technique results in a substantial savings in chip area. The ability of I^2L to be stacked is also pointed out by these authors. Finally, it should be noted that the design was implemented in a standard TTL process. Described in paper VIII-2 by Müller is the applicability of I^2L in a timing circuit which contains some novel features. The technique of injection coupling is used to perform current ratioing in order to generate various levels of injector current on the chip. A second feature is the sensitivity of the timer to incident visible radiation which makes it possible to apply the timer in photographic applications. The design was implemented in a standard ECL process.

Paper VIII-3 by Janssen *et al*. presents an excellent example of the applicability of I^2L to a specialized problem, that of generating the dual tones for a frequency encoded telephone dialing system. A unique feature of the circuit is its ability to operate from a supply voltage of 1.3 V which is provided by the telephone line. Therefore, no additional power supply is required. The design encompasses I^2L digital, ECL digital and analog portions as well as an A/D converter implemented with I^2L techniques. The circiut was fabricated in a standard ECL process. In paper VIII-4, Bergman presents a second applications area (the home appliance) where the attributes of analog compatible I^2L permit a meaningful effort toward the reduction of the components required to implement increased system value with reduced system complexity. It is the impact of I^2L at the systems level that must be realized in order to appreciate the significant advantages gained from the use of analog compatible I^2L in a harsh, high power, electromechanical environment. The author has devised a ROM scheme in which he uses I^2L gates with 25 output collectors. With such a large fan-out, the effective up-betas are less than unity. However, since the gates do not perform a logic function but rather only need to permit the detection of an included or missing bit, satisfactory operation can be maintained by using the fan-out

25 gates to drive following gates which are operated at a reduced injector current drive level. Thus the low current out of the collectors of the fan-out 25 gates are clearly distinguished. The technique results in a highly efficient layout. A second notable feature of the design is the 4-bit A/D converter which is implemented by way of a 4-bit I^2L D/A converter and a comparator. The resulting layout is very compact. The chip was implemented in a standard, $1\,\Omega\cdot\text{cm}$, $7\,\mu$ thick epitaxial layer, analog bipolar process.

Although recent developments in MOS circuit techniques have initiated the implementation of certain analog circuit functions in MOS designs, the realm of general purpose, high precision analog circuits is still in the domain of the bipolar process. Paper VIII-5 by Brokaw provides an excellent example of a marrying of classical bipolar precision circuit techniques with the analog compatibility of I^2L. The author gives the details of his design which draws upon a strong past history of bipolar analog D/A converter designs. The result is a 10-bit D/A converter using analog techniques and a successive approximations register (SAR) implemented with I^2L. A unique feature of the circuit is the operation of the I^2L portion of the chip below ground potential. This technique avoids the need for voltage translation at the outputs of the SAR. The overall performance of the design is outstanding for a monolithic 10-bit A/D converter. Fabrication in a standard bipolar analog process results in an unusually low cost for such a precision device, and such low cost was made possible by the analog compatibility of I^2L.

The final paper (VIII-6) by Chan and Coussens describes the use of I^2L in a programmable gate array. The highly regular injector-gate layout arrangement of I^2L is ideally suited to the uncommitted gate array approach to semicustom LSI. Using a dual-level metalization for interconnections along with programmability at the metal, contact, and n^+ collector levels, the effective utilization of the gates in the array can approach 100 percent for regular logic and is on the order of 60 percent for random logic. The benefits in terms of time and design expense more than offset the expense due to a loss in effective packing density for low-volume, custom applications. The authors describe specific designs which have been successfully applied in semicustom applications involving I^2L digital logic, TTL, and analog circuits on the same chip. The overall turn-around time for such a logic array design is only a small fraction of the time required for a complete custom LSI design. Furthermore, the authors described a plan whereby the customer for the gate array can create his own chip interconnect layout. I expect that such uncommitted I^2L gate arrays will find even wider acceptance in the future, especially for the low-volume custom IC user. Other applications of I^2L are described in the Bibliography for Part VIII.

An I²L Watch Chip with Direct LED Drive

PATRICK A. TUCCI AND LEWIS K. RUSSELL

Abstract—A three function watch circuit using I²L technology has been fabricated on a chip measuring 86 mils × 96 mils. The circuit draws 7–10 μA in the run mode and has on-chip segment and digit drivers which are capable of sourcing 15 mA and sinking up to 70 mA, respectively. The low frequency (<1 kHz) transistors in this circuit operate with 5–10 nA base current. A unique four-base divide-by-two circuit, using current starving to implement delays, is the building block for the circuit and its small size (13 mil²) contributes to the small chip size. Segment and digit drivers which draw only 50 nA each in the run mode (no display) also contribute to the low chip current.

I. INTRODUCTION

CMOS technology, with its dense circuitry and low power dissipation, has dominated integrated-circuit designs for digital wristwatches. CMOS is well suited to liquid crystal displays, but is more troublesome when an LED display is desired. In the original CMOS watch designs, several chips were needed, one for the logic and one or more as LED drivers. At present, single-chip CMOS circuits which drive LED's are available; however large output MOS transistors are necessary. This results in a larger and more expensive chip.

The very dense, low power bipolar circuits which characterize I²L offer an attractive alternative to CMOS [1]–[3]. The ability to design output stages which easily sink or source large currents makes I²L especially desirable for use with LED displays.

An I²L three function watch chip has been fabricated. The chip draws 7–10 μA in the run mode (no display) and an average of 15 mA while the display is on. The entire watch system consists of the IC chip described here plus one external resistor, a trimmer capacitor, a quartz crystal, LED display elements, and a battery. The advantages of designing the watch chip with I²L technology and the operation of several of the key circuits which contribute to the small chip size (86 mils × 96 mils) and low current drain will be discussed.

II. CIRCUIT OPERATION

Fig. 1 shows a block diagram of the watch chip. The 32.768-kHz crystal oscillator signal is divided down to 8 Hz by twelve divided-by-two circuits. The 8-Hz signal is further divided to 1 Hz and fed into the seconds counter. The hours, minutes, and seconds counters are multiplexed and fed into a binary to seven segment decoder whose outputs drive the seven segment drivers. The digits are strobed at a 64-Hz rate and this signal, together with the display flags, controls which counter signals are passed through the multiplexer. By selecting one of the two switches, either hours and minutes or seconds can be displayed. The 8-Hz signal is also fed to the set logic and by de-

Manuscript received June 9, 1976; revised August 2, 1976.
The authors are with Signetics Corporation, Sunnyvale, CA 94806.

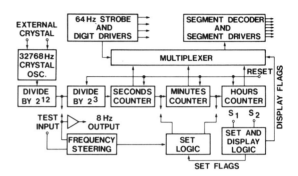

Fig. 1. LED watch chip block diagram.

pressing the two switches in proper sequence hours or minutes can be set at a 1-Hz rate. Upon completion of a set minutes operation, seconds are reset to zero. The set logic contains "lock out" circuits which prohibit the counters which are being set from interacting with other counters.

As mentioned previously, two desirable features of I²L for wristwatch chips are low power and small chip size. Low power operation is achieved by supplying all the n-p-n transistors operating below 1 kHz with only 5–10 nA of base current. n-p-n current gains per collector on a four collector device are still well above unity at 5 nA, thus making this low power operation possible. Above 1 kHz, rather than increasing the injection area of the lateral p-n-p's to provide more n-p-n base current, a higher current per unit area is supplied to the p-n-p emitters. This results in a smaller layout area despite a slightly more complicated current source. These higher frequency stages use 100 nA per transistor. Thus we have two distinct current supply lines, a low current supply line which feeds all the lateral p-n-p's which need low emitter current density, and a second supply line feeding the p-n-p's needing high emitter current density because of the higher frequency circuit operation. Both supply lines are controlled by rather standard current supply circuitry.

The small chip size is achieved as a result of the high overall packing density of I²L circuits (120 gates/mm²) and also through the use of a unique divide-by-two circuit which uses only four base regions.

Since bipolar oscillators and constant current supplies are adequately described elsewhere [4], [5], we will devote the remainder of this paper to a description of those areas of bipolar watch circuitry for which I²L offers some unique advantage.

III. DIVIDE-BY-TWO DESIGN

The highest gate density on the chip is 475 gates/mm² in the countdown chain from 32 kHz to 8 Hz. Fig. 2 shows a logic diagram and a circuit schematic of the four base divide-by-two

Reprinted from *IEEE J. Solid-State Circuits*, vol. SC-11, pp. 847–851, Dec. 1976.

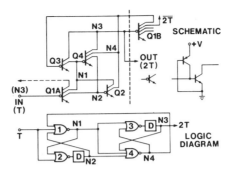

Fig. 2. Divide-by-two circuit.

TABLE I
LOGIC STATES OF DIVIDE-BY-TWO CIRCUIT

	NODES				
State	T	1	2	3	4
1	0	0	1	1	0
2	1	0,	0	1	0
3	0	1	0	0	0,
4	1	0	0	0	1,
1	0	0	1	1	0

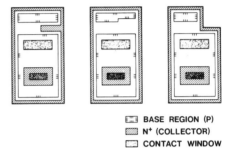

Fig. 3. Current starving methods for lateral p-n-p's.

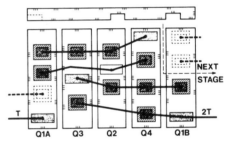

Fig. 4. Divide-by-two layout.

circuit which is the building block for the hours, minutes, and seconds counters as well as the divide chain. A reduction from six bases to four bases in the divider results in a 33 percent overall saving in area. This area reduction is significant since more than thirty-five divide-by-two circuits are incorporated in the chip. The key to the area reduction in this circuit is the ability to insert delays, which prevent two static hazards, without adding any additional chip area such as extra base regions. Table I shows the operation of the divide-by-two circuit. The static hazard occurs when the circuit switches from state 2 to state 3. The input T is applied to NOR's 1 and 2 at the same time. Since T changes from 1 to 0, and since all other inputs to the NOR's are 0, both nodes 1 and 2 will attempt to rise at the same time. Node 1 is allowed to rise first by slowing the rise of node 2. This is done by limiting the amount of charging current available to this node. A similar static hazard occurs when switching between states 3 and 4. Here node 1 is driving NOR's 3 and 4 at the same time and is changing from 1 to 0. The other inputs to the NOR's are 0 (nodes 2, 3, and 4), so that nodes 3 and 4 will attempt to rise at the same time. Here we allow node 4 to rise first by the same method.

In the schematic drawing of Fig. 2 note that transistors $Q1A$ and $Q1B$ both function in any given divide cell although the total function may be shared between adjacent cells. In the above discussion of the state table it was stated that nodes 2 and 3 are made to charge more slowly than nodes 1 and 4. This is indicated in the schematic by showing the lateral p-n-p's driving these nodes by solid circles on the bases of $Q2$ and $Q1B$ ($Q1A$). The solid circles represent p-n-p's with a smaller saturation current than normal p-n-p's. The faster nodes, 1 and 4, have lateral p-n-p's indicated by hollow circles associated with the bases of $Q3$ and $Q4$.

Fig. 3 shows three layout techniques available to limit the current to nodes 2 and 3. All these methods employ current "starving," that is each method limits the amount of current

injected into the node. Method (a) is the least desirable since its performance is alignment dependent. Method (b) limits the injected current directly by reducing the area over which hole injection takes place. However, by using a separate short source, as shown in Fig. 3(b), a metal interconnection is required between this source and the other sources. In single layer metal circuits, this eliminates the possibility of crossing the source to perform logic connection. Measurements on structures (a), (b), and (c) indicate rise times increase by factors of 1.36, 3.02, and 1.72, respectively, for the same supply voltage.

The alternative presented in Fig. 3(c) is the best choice to limit the current. A continuous source bar is used, which eliminates the need for metal connections, and current injected to the n-p-n is reduced by increasing the base width of the p-n-p. Fig. 4 shows a layout of a four base divide-by-two circuit. The rise time of node 2 can be expressed as

$$\Delta t = \Delta V_2 (C_2 / I_2)$$

where C_2 is the capacitance at node 2 and I_2 is the node 2

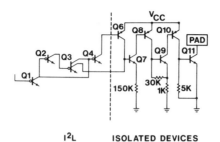

Fig. 5. Digit driver circuit.

charging current. Thus, not only must nodes 2 and 3 be starved of current, but for proper operation

$$C_2/I_2 > C_1/I_1$$

and

$$C_3/I_3 > C_4/I_4.$$

This relationship determines just how much current starving is required.

IV. DIGIT DRIVERS

All the I²L devices are minimum geometry, low current transistors to achieve low current drain and small chip size. In order to drive the LED segments, 10 mA peak current per segment or 2.5 mA average current is needed. To provide this current, several gain stages are needed in the drivers. The current drain problem is even more severe for the digit drivers which must sink a maximum of 70 mA. Several stages of isolated, down operated, n-p-n transistors are used to provide the required current gain. Fig. 5 shows a schematic of the digit driver. A low signal at the base of $Q1$ enables $Q11$ to sink current. Transistors $Q1$ through $Q4$ are I²L transistors and constantly drawing 5–10 nA per transistor. With a high signal at the base of $Q1$, transistors $Q6$ through $Q11$ are off, thus resulting in each digit driver drawing 50 nA in the off state. Transistor $Q1$ through $Q3$ ensure that any input signal less than two gate delays long will not result in the stage turning on. This same configuration is present at the input to the segment drivers and prevents "flashing" or the turning on of incorrect segments due to timing errors.

The required Beta for transistor $Q11$ to sink 70 mA is determined as follows:

$$\left(\frac{V_{be}(Q10)}{27\text{ K}} + \frac{V_{cc} - V_{ce\,sat}(Q8) - V_{be}(Q10)}{1\text{ K}}\right)\beta(Q9)\,\beta(Q11)$$
$$- \frac{V_{be}(Q11)}{5\text{ K}}\,\beta(Q11) \geqslant 70\text{ mA}.$$

Worst case assumptions:

$$\beta(Q9) = 2$$

$$V_{be}(Q10) = 0.8\text{ V} = V_{be}(Q11)$$

$$V_{cc} = 2.6\text{ V}$$

$$V_{ce\,sat}(Q8) = 0.2\text{ V}.$$

Thus,

$$\frac{0.8}{27\text{ K}} + \frac{2(2.6 - 0.2 - 0.8)}{1\text{ K}}\,\beta(Q11) - \frac{0.8}{5\text{ K}}\,\beta(Q11) \geqslant 70\text{ mA}$$

obtaining

$$\beta(Q11) \geqslant 23 \text{ at } I_c = 70\text{ mA}.$$

This is a simple requirement to meet and results in a layout consisting of minimum geometry p-n-p's and n-p-n's with the exception of the one output n-p-n transistor.

V. TIMING PROBLEMS

As mentioned above, timing is a problem with the watch chip. With only 5–10 nA per base the average delay per gate is 0.1 ms. With a 64-Hz strobe each digit and segment has a 4-ms wide pulse. Any overlapping of digit signals results in "ghosting" or signals appearing on more than one digit. To avoid this, blanking should be used on the digits; thus, for example, resulting in a 3.75-ms signal with 0.25 ms between signals. Also, to further ease the matching a divide-by-two not utilizing current starving should be used in the digit drive signal generation circuitry. To ensure that the segment and digit drive signal are matched, a variable length delay line can be incorporated in the digit drivers. This necessitates a re-masking to choose the proper delay.

The above problems can be minimized by "powering up" the circuit whenever a display is required. Since the average current during display is 15 mA, increasing the standby current from 7 to say 49 μA is not noticeable and the delay per gate is reduced by a factor of seven.

VI. THE LAYOUT

Fig. 6 shows a photomicrograph of the chip. Single level metal was used throughout. The very dense structure at the bottom is the divide chain. Above that is the logic for controlling the display as a function of the switches. Antibounce circuits are included in this section. In the chip center are the seconds and minutes counters. At the top center is the decoder, and to the right is the hours counter. The segment drivers are arranged in pairs along the left edge while the digit drivers are at the upper right edge. The oscillator is at the middle right with the current distribution circuitry below that. Eighteen bonding pads are needed for operation, while the remaining four are used in rapid testing of the circuit. Here we see a basic advantage of LED circuits that LCD circuits have heretofore not solved. The display can be multiplexed so that only seven segment pads and four digit pads are necessary.

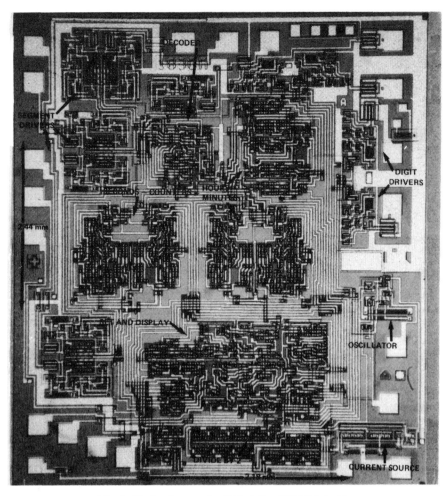

Fig. 6. Photomicrograph of 3-function LED watch chip.

With LCD the output would require at least 23 pads (with 23 drivers or latches), and a considerable amount of additional silicon area would be required.

VII. Operating Characteristics

Table II shows the basic operating conditions of the circuit. Two miniature $1\frac{1}{2}$ V cells are required to drive the LED display. These cells deliver 3.2 V when new and quickly fall to 3.0 V where the potential stabilizes over 95 percent of the cell life. The circuit will keep accurate time to a potential as low as 2.3 V. However, below 2.6 V the LED display is extremely dim. The chip has only one supply bonding pad to keep bonding requirements to a minimum. Since 3 V are available, it is used on chip in the oscillator circuit to make it more stable over the temperature range. The forward voltage of standard LED diodes plus the $V_{CE \, sat}$ voltage of the digit drivers and the V_{BE} of the segment drivers over temperature range also requires that a 3.0-V supply be used. For all these reasons a separate 1.5-V input was not used even though all the I²L circuitry requires only 0.7-V maximum. More complex I²L watch chips having more functionality can benefit further from a 3-V supply by "stacking" portions of I²L circuitry so that the same current is used over and over again at successively lower and lower voltages. Current "stacks" up to four deep are possible.

TABLE II
OPERATING CONDITIONS OF LED WATCH CHIP

RECOMMENDED OPERATING CONDITIONS

PARAMETER	LIMITS			UNIT
	MIN	TYP	MAX	
V_{CC} SUPPLY VOLTAGE	2.6	3.0	3.2	V
I_{JJ} INJECTOR CURRENT	5.0	7.0	10.0	μA
CRYSTAL FREQUENCY		32768		Hz
T_A OPERATING TEMPERATURE	−35		+70	°C

With the display off, the circuit draws an average of 7 μA and will operate correctly to below 5 μA over the temperature range. The injector current is controlled primarily by the value of the external resistor. With the typical current and an average of 30 displays/day, normal batteries will last over one year.

VIII. Processing

The watch chips were processed using an industry-wide process technology—Schottky T²L, to which two minor variations were added: a more highly doped buried n-plus region to provide better n-p-n emitter injection efficiency, and a shallow n diffusion which is driven more deeply into the base to increase base transport efficiency. The result of both changes is

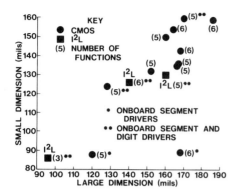

Fig. 7. Comparison of I²L and CMOS watch chip sizes.

forward current gains of from 200 to 250 and reverse current gains greater than 4 for a 1-of-4 collector over the collector current range of 10 nA to 100 μA. Measurements of base width show typical widths of 0.2 μm and resultant BV_{CEO} of >5.0 V.

The Schottky-like process was chosen because the thin epitaxy (3 μm) and shallow diffusion profiles permit more dense surface topologies. Indeed, standard Schottky T²L layout rules were used throughout. A second reason for choosing this process was the availability of instant factory production. The problems of bringing a completely new process into production are many.

IX. CONCLUSION

It has been demonstrated that I²L can match or exceed the performance of CMOS for watch circuits that drive LED displays. I²L can achieve equally low current drain, a smaller die size, and be processed on an existing high yielding bipolar line. The result is a chip that is very cost competitive. Fig. 7 shows a size comparison of this chip and two other I²L watch chips to a variety of CMOS chips with and without LED drive capability.

ACKNOWLEDGMENT

The authors wish to acknowledge the assistance of R. A. Blauschild who designed the linear circuit portions of the chip; P. Smith for contributions to solving some of the timing problems; and E. J. McCluskey who derived the logic for the four base divider.

REFERENCES

[1] K. Hart and A. Slob, "Integrated injection logic: A new approach to LSI," *IEEE J. Solid-State Circuits*, vol. SC-7, pp. 346–351, Oct. 1972.
[2] H. H. Berger and S. K. Wiedmann, "Merged transistor logic (MTL)—A low cost bipolar logic concept," *IEEE J. Solid-State Circuits*, vol. SC-7, pp. 340–346, Oct. 1972.
[3] N. C. deTroye, "Integrated injection logic—present and future," *IEEE J. Solid-State Circuits*, vol. SC-9, pp. 206–211, Oct. 1974.
[4] H. W. Rüegg and W. Thommen, "Bipolar micropower circuits for crystal-controlled timepieces," *IEEE J. Solid-State Circuits*, vol. SC-7, pp. 105–111, Apr. 1972.
[5] M. P. Forrer, "Survey of circuitry for wristwatches," *Proc. IEEE*, pp. 1047–1054, Sept. 1972.

I²L Timing Circuit for the 1 ms–10 s Range

RÜDIGER MÜLLER

Abstract—An I²L timing circuit without external components is presented, which makes use of some specific I²L properties—operation at low power levels, light sensitivity, variable delay, and long maximum delay times. The circuit comprises 45 gates on a chip area of 0.3 mm². It produces pulses from below 1 ms to more than 10 s which are inversely proportional to a single supply current. For this purpose, new methods for current splitting and amplification with I²L circuits are used. The temperature dependence of the output pulse width is better than 0.8 percent/K. If the circuit is irradiated by light, it produces pulses with a pulse width inversely proportional to the light intensity. For example, it can be used as an integrated exposure meter for all kinds of photographic applications.

I. INTRODUCTION

SOME OF THE I²L properties are quite outstanding and not commonly found with integrated logic circuits:

1) operation at low power levels, even with injection by incident light

2) wide supply current range at almost constant voltage swing, but varying delay times

3) maximum delay times well above 100 ms.

This paper describes an integrated circuit which makes use of these properties for the realization of a timing circuit without external components. In the triggered mode of operation, the pulse width of the single output pulses is in the range of 1 ms–10 s. These time periods can be used for all kinds of applications where, until now, IC's with external passive components were necessary. The total circuit comprises 45 gates on an area of 0.3 mm² and is thus ideally suited for the integration on LSI chips whenever there is a need for a monoflop function with long output pulse widths. For the realization, new current splitting and amplification principles for I²L circuits had to be found which gave a good tracking over four to five decades of supply current variation.

II. CIRCUIT DESCRIPTION

Fig. 1 shows the generalized block diagram of the circuit with an *N*-stage ring oscillator as the time base, a current amplifier, and an *M*-stage divider chain. The circuit is fed with a single supply current I_S which is split into three parts, I_{RO}, I_A, and I_D for these three blocks. A feedback loop couples back an internal output of the last divider to an internal input of the ring oscillator. In addition to the positive and negative supply lines, the circuit needs only two external connections, the trigger input *T* and the output *O*.

Manuscript received December 9, 1976; revised December 28, 1976. This paper was presented at the International Solid-State Circuits Conference, Philadelphia, PA, February 1977. This work was supported under the Technological Program of the Federal Department of Research and Technology of the FRG. The author alone is responsible for its contents.

The author is with the Research Laboratories, Siemens AG, Munich, Germany.

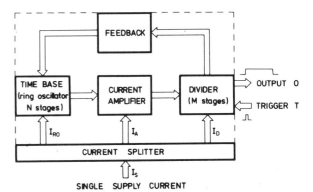

Fig. 1. Block diagram of the I²L timing circuit.

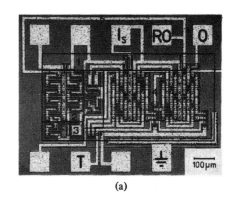

(a)

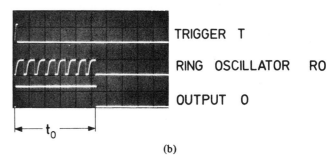

TRIGGER T

RING OSCILLATOR RO

OUTPUT O

(b)

Fig. 2. (a) Photomicrograph of the circuit with: (1): 2-stage current splitter, (2): 11-stage ring oscillator, (3): 2-stage current amplifier, (4): 4-stage binary divider, and (5): feedback loop. (b) Pulse diagram (schematic).

Fig. 2(a) gives a photomicrograph of the realized circuit with the current splitter 1, an 11-stage ring oscillator 2, a 2-stage current amplifier 3, a 4-stage binary divider 4, and the feedback loop 5. The four necessary external connections, namely, the supply current I_S, ground, trigger input *T*, and output *O*, are indicated. All other pads are only for testing purposes, as, for example, the one denoted *RO*, which gives the ring oscillator waveform. Fig. 2(b) shows the corresponding waveforms at the three pads *T*, *RO*, and *O*.

A trigger signal *T* presets the divider chain 4, which releases the ring oscillator 2 via the feedback loop 5. The ring oscillator

Reprinted from *IEEE J. Solid-State Circuits*, vol. SC-12, pp. 139–143, Apr. 1977.

drives a current amplifier 3, which runs at its input at about one third of the ring oscillator gate current, thus giving a minimum load effect. This small current is amplified by a gain of about 500 and is fed into a binary divider chain 4. For these dividers, the well-known 6-gate I^2L realization, as, e.g., in [1], was used. After 2^{M-1} periods, the output of the last divider switches to "low" and thus stops the ring oscillator via the feedback. This gives an output pulse width t_O of approximately

$$t_O = 2Nt_D \cdot 2^{M-1} \tag{1}$$

or, for the realized circuit with $N=11$ and $M=4$,

$$t_O = 176t_D \tag{2}$$

where t_D is the delay time for the ring oscillator gates. If the feedback loop 5 is left out, one gets a periodic output with a frequency

$$f_O = \frac{1}{2t_O}. \tag{3}$$

The three blocks 2, 3, and 4 are run at different current levels with a current ratio between ring oscillator and divider of approximately

$$i_{RO} : i_D = 1:90 \tag{4}$$

where i_{RO} and i_D denote the mean injector currents per gate. There are three reasons for this supply current splitting:

1) the additional delays of block 3 and 4 in comparison to 1 are kept low (less than 3 percent)

2) the noise immunity of the circuit is increased

3) even at low current levels, the output drive capability is sufficient.

The ratio in (4) can, of course, be adapted to any special need by a simple change in design. Because this mechanism of current splitting and amplification is very important for this type of circuit, it will be discussed in more detail. The new solutions which are used in this circuit can be applied to any I^2L circuit.

III. New Current-Splitting Technique

For current splitting with I^2L circuits, the use of CHIL gates [2] is proposed. CHIL gates (see Fig. 3) are very similar to I^2L gates, but have more than one p-region that is supplied by the same injector region. By grounding one or more of these regions, injection to the last p-region can be controlled. Letting them float, on the other hand, allows a current flow from the injector to the last p-region by the mechanism of current hogging [2].

The inherent current losses are discussed with the aid of Fig. 3. The current per gate i_E at the injecting emitter E is separated into a mostly vertical loss current i_{EV} and an active horizontal current i_{EH}. Grounding $I1$ and neglecting recombination in the active base region, this current i_{EH} is totally collected at $I1$ and we get a current loss factor A_s (which corresponds to the common base gain of the lateral p-n-p transistor) for single-sided injection:

$$A_s = \frac{-i_{I1}}{i_E} = \frac{i_{EH}}{i_{EH} + i_{EV}}. \tag{5}$$

Similarly, we get for the double sided injection at $I1$ and grounded E and $I2$ a loss factor

$$A_d = \frac{-(i_E + i_{I2})}{i_{I1}} = \frac{2i_{I1H}}{2i_{I1H} + i_{I1V}}. \tag{6}$$

For a constant voltage supply at E, floating $I1$, and grounded $I2$, one has to consider a superposition at the previous cases and gets the current-hogging loss factor for one intermediate p-region:

$$A_{ch1} = \frac{-i_{I2}}{i_E} = \frac{i_{I1H}}{i_{EH} + i_{EV} - i_{I1H}}. \tag{7}$$

We must take into account that i_E is now decreased by the back-injected current i_{I1H}. Looking at the ratio of the input currents, which have to be drawn from $I1$ and $I2$, respectively, for the two different cases of (5) and (7), one obtains

$$\frac{i_{I2} \text{ (grounded } I2, \text{ floating } I1)}{i_{I1} \text{ (grounded } I1)} = \frac{\frac{A_d}{2}(2i_{I1H} + i_{I1V})}{A_s(i_{EH} + i_V)} = \frac{A_d}{2} \tag{8}$$

which is somewhat higher than the loss factor A_{ch1}. For the technology considered in Section V, the mean values for A_s, A_d, and A_{ch1} were 0.62, 0.74, and 0.3, respectively. For this case, as a rough estimation one can simplify (5) to (7) into

$$A_s \approx A_d \approx 2A_{ch1} \approx A = 0.7. \tag{9}$$

With the knowledge of these terms, one can now calculate the ratio of a schematic current-splitter arrangement shown in Fig. 4.

On the left-hand side, there is a first chain of I^2L gates supplied with a constant voltage at a current level i_E per gate which is connected to the injector E of a CHIL gate 1. This gate supplies a second chain of I^2L gates 2 to L via its floating current-hogging input with a current i'_E per gate. For the approximation of grounded I^2L inputs (no back injection from gate 1 to L), one obtains for the current i'_E

$$i'_E = \frac{A_s i_E - i'_{EH}}{L} \approx \frac{Ai_E}{L+1}. \tag{10}$$

Since this injector has to feed L gates plus one back injection into the left-hand side I^2L injector, the right-hand side injector current $A \cdot i_E$ is divided into $L+1$ parts. By altering the

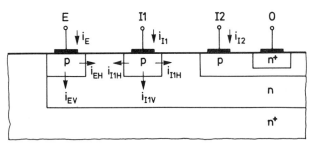

Fig. 3. Current distribution with a CHIL gate.

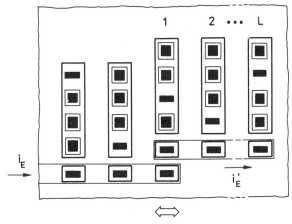

Fig. 4. Current splitting with a CHIL gate. Left-hand side: current per gate i_E. Right-hand side: current per gate $i'_E \approx i_E(A/L + 1)$. A: current loss factor.

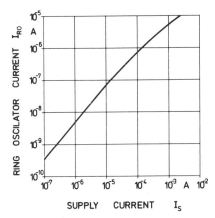

Fig. 5. Dependence of the ring oscillator current I_{RO} on the supply current I_S. $T = 25°C$.

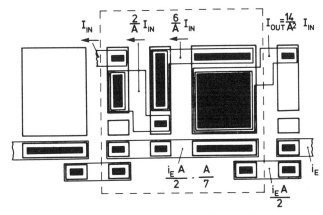

Fig. 6. Stage of a cascadable current amplifier. The approximate currents of the different gates are indicated.

overlap of E and $I1$ at the CHIL gate 1, one can easily change the splitting ratio, and by cascading this principle, one can cover several decades of current ratio. If one uses double-sided injection for the I²L gates or a CHIL gate with more than one current-hogging input, one has to take into account the other previously defined loss factors too.

These loss factors A are quite constant over a wide current range, and thus one can achieve an excellent tracking of the splitting ratio. This is shown in Fig. 5 for the two-stage current splitter of the timing circuit. The ring oscillator current I_{RO} depends linearly on the supply current I_S over more than three decades within ±20 percent. This corresponds to a splitting ratio of about 90 for the gate currents. If the loss factors of a certain technology are known, one can easily design a current splitter with better than 20 percent accuracy using the simple calculations demonstrated above.

IV. NEW CURRENT AMPLIFIER

For the signal transfer between a low-current and high-current level I²L gate, it is necessary to implement current amplifiers. A known principle of current amplification with I²L is, for example, the use of gates with increased injector length and collector area [3]. Because of the increased area

consumption, however, this principle is limited to rather low current gains, e.g., 10 to 20.

Fig. 6 shows an example of a current amplifier stage which has a gain of approximately 30 and can be cascaded directly. This amplifier also uses the current-hogging principle as a current-splitting technique. Here again the approximation for grounded gate inputs and constant injector voltages is used. The input CHIL gate has to amplify the current by a factor of $2/A$ according to (8). The second gate must have a gain of 3 because of the increased geometry of the output gate which, in its turn, draws the input current of the next stage. This input current is approximately $14/A^2$ times higher than I_{IN}, since one unit current i_E in the right-hand side injector is reduced by A, divided into two parts, once again reduced by A, and distributed on seven unit lengths. Assuming a loss factor A of 0.7, a minimum gain per gate of approximately 3 is necessary. By cascading these stages, one can easily cover several decades of current gain.

The circuit shown in Fig. 2(a) uses two similar stages, shown in block 3. The one on the lower left runs at the same level as the ring oscillator, and the one in the upper middle is connected to its own current splitter and drives the two divider inputs. With the simple model described above, a total current gain of 595 is calculated. Although these calculations assume zero back injection from the gates, constant voltage supply, and a mean value of 0.7 for the loss factor A, this is correct within ±20 percent to measured values of 500 to 700 for a supply current of 100 μA. The necessary minimum current gain per gate is again in the range of two to three. This rather low value assures proper operation at currents well below 1 nA per gate.

V. CIRCUIT PERFORMANCE

The following measurements were performed with test samples fabricated in a full bipolar process used for emitter-coupled logic. The thickness of the epitaxial layer was 2.7 μm at a resistivity of 0.8 $\Omega \cdot cm$. The sheet resistivity of the base diffusion was 300 Ω, and the I²L base regions were walled by a deep n⁺-collar. This technology yielded I²L gates with an upward current gain well above 3 for currents down to 100 pA and less.

The dependence of the output pulse width t_O on the supply current I_S is given in Fig. 7. The circuit can be operated over

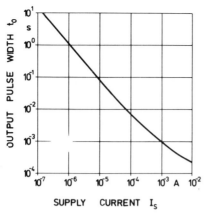

Fig. 7. Dependence of the measured output pulse width t_O on the supply current I_S. $T = 25°C$.

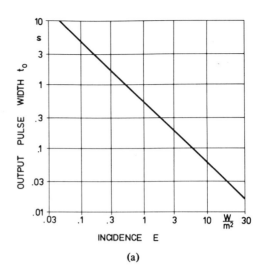

(a)

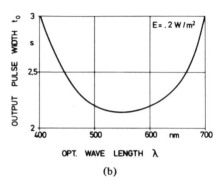

(b)

Fig. 9. Measured output pulse width t_O as a function of light incidence E at a wavelength $\lambda = 560$ nm (a) and as a function of the wavelength λ of the incidence light (b). $I_{RO} = 0, I_S = 1 \mu A, T = 25°C$.

more than five decades of supply current, and within ±20 percent, t_O is inversely proportional to I_S for more than three decades. The achievable maximum pulse widths are above 10 s, which corresponds to a ring oscillator period of more than 1 s. The saturation of the t_O versus I_S characteristic at high current levels is caused by high injection effects in the base region of the lateral p-n-p transistors of the current splitter. This can clearly be seen from the dependence of the ring oscillator current I_{RO} on I_S in Fig. 5. In the same way, the nonlinearity of t_O versus I_S for low supply currents is caused by the influence of recombination on the current gain of the lateral p-n-p transistor. The latter effect is also true for the t_D versus I_{RO} characteristic of single I^2L ring oscillators, whereas there the saturation of t_D at high currents is mainly caused by enhanced minority carrier storage in the emitter of the n-p-n transistor.

Another interesting characteristic is the temperature dependence to t_O. Fig. 8 shows the result for a constant supply current of $I_S = 100 \mu A$. For the full temperature range from 0 to 100°C, the temperature coefficient is less than 0.8 percent/K. This relatively small temperature coefficient is, of course, only valid for a constant current supply where t_O is mainly influenced by capacitance and current gain variations, but not that much by supply voltage drift. It can, however, be compensated for by a proper design of the current source.

I^2L circuits can not only be supplied with external currents, but also with minority carrier injection by incident light [4]. For this purpose, the ring oscillator supply was cut off the current splitter and the whole circuit was irradiated with light. Fig. 9(a) gives the result for the output pulse width t_O versus incidence E for a wavelength of 560 nm. The linearity is better than ±20 percent over more than three decades. Even though the ring oscillator was not especially designed for this purpose, e.g., the n$^+$-collar touched the base region at three sides, the circuit operates down to an incidence of less than 50 mW/m^2, which corresponds to about 10 lx the illuminance in a badly lit room.

Fig. 9(b) shows the dependence of the output pulse width t_O on the wavelength of the incident light. For a range of 450–660 nm, the pulse width variations are less than 10 percent. This range corresponds roughly to the visible spectrum. Thus, this circuit can be used as a simple integrated exposure control for photographic applications.

VI. CONCLUSIONS

The above-described circuit is the monolithic realization of a monoflop for long output pulse widths in the range of 1 ms to 10 s. It has an area consumption of 0.3 mm^2 and can thus be integrated on all kinds of bipolar analog and digital circuits. It can be used for the same purpose as a monoflop, e.g., the detection of short pulses and the generation of long delays. If

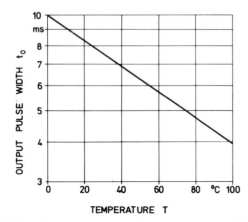

Fig. 8. Temperature dependence of the output pulse width t_O at a supply current $I_S = 100 \mu A$.

the circuit area is doubled, another seven divider stages can be added and output pulses in the range of 100 ms–15 min are produced. This opens the field for many timing applications where, until now, mechanical timers were in use. On the other hand, the circuit can also be applied to the control of a camera shutter if light is used for the power supply of the ring oscillator. All these applications are characteristics of the I^2L realization of such a circuit, and can probably not be achieved with any other type of logic.

ACKNOWLEDGMENT

The author wishes to thank K. Goser for stimulating this work and A. Kalb and F. Möllmer for support with the preparation of the samples.

REFERENCES

[1] R. L. Horton, "I^2L takes bipolar integration a significant step forward," *Electronics,* pp. 83–90, Feb. 6, 1975.
[2] R. Müller, "Current hogging injection logic–A new logic with high functional density," *IEEE J. Solid-State Circuits,* vol. SC-10, pp. 348–352, Oct. 1975.
[3] C. M. Hart, A. Slob, and H. E. J. Wulms, "Bipolar LSI takes a new direction with integrated injection logic," *Electronics*, pp. 111–118, Oct. 3, 1974.
[4] K. Hart and A. Slob, "Integrated injection logic: A new approach to LSI," *IEEE J. Solid-State Circuits*, vol. SC-7, pp. 346–351, Oct. 1972.

The TDA1077—An I²L Circuit for Two-Tone Telephone Dialing

DAAN J. G. JANSSEN, JEAN-CLAUDE KAIRE, AND PHILIPPE GUÉTIN

Abstract—The circuit-design aspects of an integrated circuit to perform two-tone telephone dialing are described. The circuit is believed to be unique in that it combines both the crystal-controlled frequency synthesizer and the output amplifier on the same chip. Moreover, no external power supplies are required; the circuit is powered by the telephone-line current. Designed to require a minimum number of external components, this LSI chip provides an economical and accurate two-tone dialing unit. A typical application circuit for existing telephone apparatus is shown and aspects of future development are discussed.

INTRODUCTION

CONVENTIONAL telephone apparatus uses rotary dials to produce a series of interrupting pulses in the line current. The number of these pulses corresponds to the number dialed. Push-button dialing units have been made to produce the pulses electronically. The series-pulse system is, however, both slow and liable to error. Interference on the lines may be seen as data by the exchange decoding circuits, resulting in an incorrect connection.

Frequency encoding of the dialed numbers allows faster dialing and gives a greater immunity to noise. The CCITT[1] has therefore recommended the use of a system in which each number is represented by a combination of two tones from a possible eight, see Fig. 1. Both tones representing a number are transmitted simultaneously, thus shortening the data transmission time. The tones have been carefully chosen to avoid problems caused by harmonics, while the use of two tones eliminates the possibility of line whistles causing dialing.

New decoding circuits are required in the exchange for the two-tone dialing system, but this can be done while retaining compatibility with existing series-pulse apparatus.

DESIGN OF THE INTEGRATED CIRCUIT

Two-tone dialing systems are already in existence, using *LC* and *RC* tone generators to obtain the required frequencies. These conventional oscillators suffer from long-term instability and the need for a number of accurate components. The TDA1077 overcomes these problems by the use of the principle of frequency synthesis within the LSI chip. All the components except the quartz crystal, a polarity guard, one resistor and two capacitors are contained in the integrated circuit. Fig. 2 shows the functional diagram of the TDA1077.

Manuscript received November 17, 1976.

D. J. G. Janssen is with N. V. Philips Gloeilampenfabrieken, Eindhoven, The Netherlands.

J.-C. Kaire and P. Guétin are with R. T. C. La Radiotechnique-Compelec, Caen, France.

[1]CCITT—the International Telephone and Telegraph Consultative Committee, Green Book VI-1, Recommendation Q23.

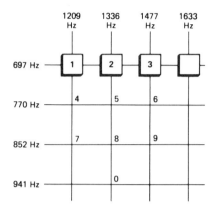

Fig. 1. Identification of the dialed numbers using two out of eight tones.

The choice of technology to produce the integrated circuit was influenced by the following factors: 1) low operating voltage; 2) low minimum current; 3) high maximum current; 4) implementation of both analog and digital elements; 5) compatibility with conventional fast logic elements.

Consideration of these points had led to an I²L design[2] with a small part in current mode logic for the high-frequency clock circuits, thus incorporating both fast logic and analog circuitry on one chip. The standard process for the ECL 10 000 family is used to achieve this.

LINE ADAPTOR

The dc voltage across the integrated circuit is regulated by the shunt amplifier $A1$ in Fig. 2. The line voltage is compared with a reference voltage via the low-pass filter formed by $R_3 C_2$ to provide the regulator with a low output impedance for dc without attenuating signals in the audio band of 300–3400 Hz. All the other circuits in the IC connected to the line present a high impedance to ac signals so that the ac input impedance of the IC is determined by resistors R_2 and R_4.

Fig. 3 shows the voltage across the IC. The dc component is about 3 V due to the action of the line adaptor. As the ac signal can be up to 3 V_{p-p}, all the circuitry must be designed for a minimum supply voltage of 1.3 V and must be unaffected by the presence of audio signals on the line. I²L technology is ideally suited to this application, providing low-voltage circuits driven by constant-current sources.

KEYBOARD OPERATION

The integrated circuit has four outputs corresponding to the lower tones and four inputs to select the upper tones. Depression of a key links an output to an input and selects two

[2]C. M. Hart and A. Slob, "Integrated injection logic: A new approach to LSI," *IEEE J. Solid-State Circuits*, vol. SC-7, p. 346, Oct. 1972.

Reprinted from *IEEE J. Solid-State Circuits*, vol. SC-12, pp. 238–242, June 1977.

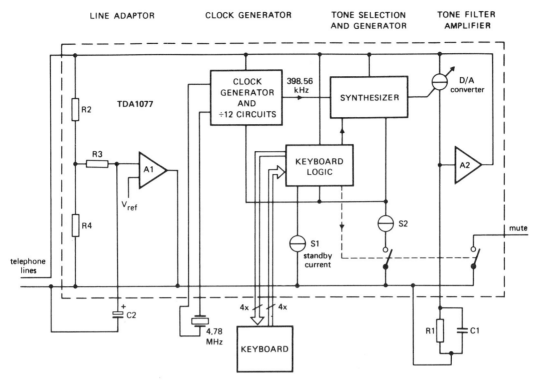

Fig. 2. Functional diagram of the TDA1077 and its external components.

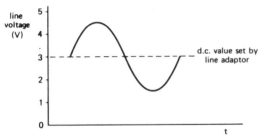

Fig. 3. The line voltage across the IC, after regulation by the line adaptor, showing the effect of dialing or audio signals.

tones, see Figs. 1 and 9. Unused tone combinations allow for future additions to the system.

FREQUENCY SYNTHESIZER

The synthesizer is implemented in I²L as a variable divider followed by a D/A converter. As each dialed number requires the simultaneous generation of two tones, the circuitry is duplicated with only small differences between the upper and lower tone circuits.

Ideally, the clock frequency should be chosen as the lowest common denominator of the eight required tones. This frequency (14×10^{13} Hz) is impractical. However, calculations have shown that close approximations (within 0.11 percent) to the required frequency can be achieved using a clock frequency of 199.28 kHz and integer divisors. As some of these divisors are odd numbers, the generated tones would possess unequal half-cycles and even harmonics. The half-cycles can be made symmetrical, and the even harmonics removed, by doubling the clock frequency and divisors. Table I shows the divisors, the resulting tones, and the errors.

TABLE I
GENERATION OF TONES FROM A 398.56-KHZ CLOCK

Tone required (Hz)	Dividing factor	Tone generated (Hz)	Absolute error (Hz)	Relative error %
697	572	696.78	− 0.22	− 0.03
770	518	769.42	− 0.58	− 0.08
852	478	851.62	− 0.38	− 0.04
941	424	940.00	− 1.00	− 0.11
1209	330	1207.76	− 1.24	− 0.10
1336	298	1337.45	+ 1.45	+ 0.11
1477	270	1476.15	− 0.85	− 0.06
1633	244	1633.44	+ 0.44	+ 0.03

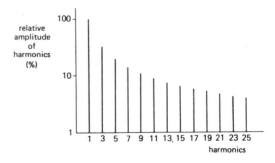

Fig. 4. Harmonic content of a symmetrical squarewave.

If a simple frequency divider is used, producing a squarewave, the output frequency spectrum contains a high percentage of odd harmonics, see Fig. 4. The higher harmonics (13th and above for the higher tones, 17th and above for the

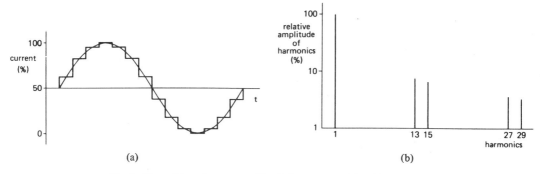

Fig. 5. Form (a) and spectrum (b) of the output of the D/A converter using seven current sources and 14 steps.

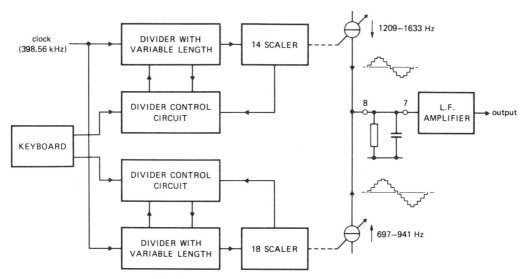

Fig. 6. Schematic diagram of the tone synthesis.

lower tones) are sufficiently attenuated (-36 dB) by the action of filter $R_1 C_1$ in Fig. 2.

To prevent generation of the harmonics up to and including the 11th for the higher tones, the output waveform is generated as a crude sine wave in a series of 14 steps, see Fig. 5. Seven current sources are used, providing a symmetrical approximation to the required tone. The frequency of the output is selected by the duration of the steps.

To provide this stepped output, the divisors for the higher tones in Table I must themselves be divided by 14; this results in noninteger divisors, which are not realizable in the physical circuits. Thus some of the steps must be one clock period longer so that the generated tone is of the correct frequency. For example, the 1209-Hz tone requires a division of the clock frequency by 330. The divisor now becomes $330/14 = 23\,4/7$. This means that each of the 14 steps should have a length of 23 4/7 clock periods. The problem is solved by giving 8 of the steps a length of 24 and the remaining 6 steps a length of 23, making a total of 330.

The lower tones are similarly produced, using nine current sources to produce a sinewave with 18 steps for each cycle of the generated tone.

Fig. 6 shows the total scheme of the synthesizer and D/A converter. The currents representing the lower and higher

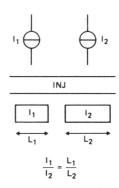

Fig. 7. Current sources use different collector widths to produce different currents in $I^2 L$ technology.

tones are generated in parallel and added at the input of the low-frequency amplifier. The current sources are switched on/off by the synthesizer logic.

The current sources are lateral p-n-p transistors of the same type as those used for the $I^2 L$ injectors, see Fig. 7. The value of the current is proportional to the width of the collector, as the current sources are mirrors of the special constant current source S_2 in Fig. 2. This has been designed to provide a constant current independent of the dc line voltage and the ac signals present on the line. Because of this construction, the

Fig. 8. Modes of connection for the two-tone dialing unit, serial connection (a), parallel connection (b).

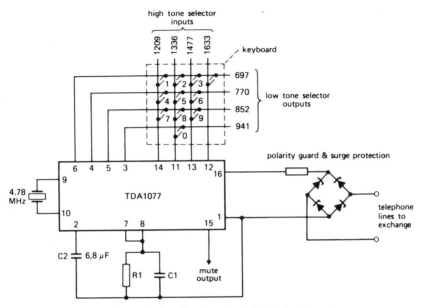

Fig. 9. Typical application circuit for the TDA1077.

circuits fulfill the requirement for operation at the minimum supply voltage of 1.3 V.

TIMING GENERATOR

The design of the frequency synthesizer has determined that the clock frequency must be 398.56 kHz, or a multiple thereof. To achieve the required long-term stability the timing generator is controlled by a quartz crystal, which only becomes an economic proposition at frequencies above about 4 MHz. Accordingly, a crystal with a nominal frequency of 4.78272 MHz has been chosen. A divide-by-12 circuit then produces the required 398.56 kHz.

MODE OF OPERATION

It is expected that many tone-dialing units will be produced as replacements for existing rotary dials. These units must therefore be suitable for series operation, as shown in Fig. 8. A great disadvantage of this mode is the requirement for a special contact short circuiting the dialing unit during standby. This contact must be a high-quality long-life low-resistance unit, which is relatively expensive. Moreover, this contact must be operated whenever any of the push-buttons are depressed, requiring a complicated and expensive mechanical link to the keyboard.

In the future, telephones are expected to operate in the parallel mode shown in Fig. 8. With the dialing unit in parallel

TABLE II
CHARACTERISTICS OF THE TDA1077

Parameter	Minimum	Maximum	Unit
Supply current "ON" (including output amplifier)	10	100	mA
Supply current "OFF"	3	100	mA
D.C. line voltage (I_{16} = 30 mA)		3	V
Generated frequency accuracy	- 0.5	+ 0.5	%
Nominal output, lower tones (adjustable)	- 11 to	- 7	dBm
Nominal output, higher tones (adjustable)	- 9 to	- 5	dBm
Pre-emphasis (high tones)	1	3	dB
Total distortion		- 23	dB

Note that the values for the nominal outputs are adjustable between the limits given by selection of the impedance of the output low-pass filter.

to the microphone and speaker electronics, the expensive short-circuiting contact can be replaced by an electronic inhibit control. The TDA1077 has been designed with parallel operation as a possibility, incorporating the following facilities.

1) A mute signal to inhibit the action of the microphone and receiver electronics during dialing and reduce current consumption. This has the added advantage of eliminating receiver noise due to dialing.

2) The dialing circuitry is inhibited while the keyboard is not in use, further reducing current consumption. Only a small standby current is then required to allow scanning of the keyboard.

APPLICATION CIRCUIT

Fig. 9 shows the completed circuit for a tone-dialing unit. The polarity guard and surge protection circuit are functions always required by all electronic circuitry in telephone apparatus. R_1 and C_1 form the low-pass filter at the output of the D/A converter. C_2 and an internal resistor form the low-pass filter for the line adaptor. Table II gives a summary of the characteristics of the TDA1077 integrated circuit.

CONCLUSIONS

The combination of both complex analog and digital circuits on a single LSI chip has led to the production of an economical two-tone generator that fully complies with the CCITT recommendations and satisfies most of the national European requirements. The TDA1077 provides a unique solution for the design of two-tone dialing apparatus: it is a complete system in one chip, working on a low voltage which permits the use of the maximum line length currently in use. The only critical external component required is the crystal, allowing simple production of two-tone dialing units with accurate tones.

ACKNOWLEDGMENT

The authors wish to thank G. C. Groenendaal and C. M. Hart of the Philips Research Laboratories, Eindhoven, for their cooperation in the development of the TDA1077.

A One-Chip I²L Controller for Appliances

G. BERGMANN

Abstract—An I²L LSI chip is described that can control the machine functions of home appliances. Using linear-compatible I²L, no additional peripheral IC's, such as drivers for triacs and displays, are needed. The program sequence is stored in a mask-programmable read-only memory. In this way, program changes are easy. For the ROM matrix and the A/D converter, new configurations have been developed.

I. INTRODUCTION

THE MAJORITY of home appliances have up to now been controlled by electromechanics. Conventional controllers are tried-and-true parts and can be manufactured cost effectively. However, they are not capable of extensions. This means that additional features, such as programmability, sensor control, safety functions, energy-saving programs, etc., cannot be realized cost effectively. Electronic controllers can satisfy these demands, but many problems have yet to be solved. The most difficult problems are:

1) power periphery;
2) safety insulation;
3) controller and supporting IC's.
4) sensors.

This "package of problems" is the reason why electronic controllers have not been in widespread use although they had been prognosticated years ago [1]. Programmable microwave ovens that require precise timing were the first appliances with an electronic controller produced in large volume [2]. It seems that for other home appliances (e.g., dishwashers, washing machines, etc.) these problems have still to be solved. In this paper we discuss the controller integrated circuit only, which in our case includes all supporting and peripheral functions. We start with some remarks on technology, discuss the situation of microcomputers in the field of home appliances, and describe an I²L LSI chip that performs all functions required to control, say, a dishwasher.

II. TECHNOLOGY

An electronic system that can replace the conventional mechanics requires approximately 1000 gate functions and slightly more than 2 kbit ROM memory if the architecture is dedicated to controller purposes.

All the requirements just mentioned can be satisfied both in MOS and bipolar technology. Thus the decision between tech-

Manuscript received October 16, 1978; revised December 18, 1978. This work was supported by the Technology Program of the Federal Ministry of Research and Technology of the Federal Republic of Germany. The author alone is responsible for the contents of this paper.
The author is with the AEG-Telefunken Research Laboratories, Ulm, Germany.

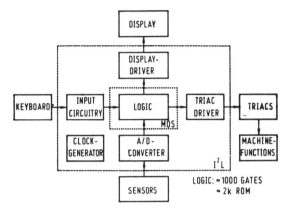

Fig. 1. MOS–I²L system partitioning.

nologies is only possible on system level. The controller circuit has to communicate with many elements that require relatively high current. Such elements are, for instance, displays, relays, thyristors, and triacs with actuating currents between 50 to 100 mA. In addition, some linear functions such as A/D conversions, amplifiers, reference sources, etc., should be available. Fig. 1 shows the system partitioning if an MOS controller is used (inner dashed lines) or if linear compatible I²L technology is chosen (outer dashed lines). With linear compatible I²L it is possible to integrate the logic functions with high packing density and the linear and driver functions on the same chip. Thus linear compatible I²L allows us to realize cost-effective "one-chip" systems in the field of home appliances.

The last several years have shown [3], [4] that by using sophisticated circuit concepts analog functions are also possible in MOS technology. Thus the partitioning of Fig. 1 may change slightly in the future. However, powerful driver stages cannot be realized cost effectively in MOS technology, since the chip area consumed by a MOS transistor is almost two orders of magnitude larger than that for its bipolar equivalent [5].

III. MICROPROCESSOR VERSUS CUSTOM DESIGN

In the discussion of electronic controllers for home appliances the microcomputer plays a major role. As long as the electronic systems are in the test phase, the microcomputer or the microcontroller [6] is an excellent tool for testing different program sequences. As soon as the "programming philosophy" is established, we do not need the free programmability of microcomputers and microcontrollers. Simple architectures will be possible and mask programmability will offer enough flexibility.

To make a detailed comparison between a microcomputer system and a custom design, a controller with a state-of-the-art general-purpose microcomputer and a system with our specially

Reprinted from *IEEE J. Solid-State Circuits*, vol. SC-14, pp. 569–573, June 1979.

TABLE I
MICROPROCESSOR VERSUS I²L LSI

MOS Microcomputer Controller	- 1 x 3870	single chip computer	40 pin	
		2 k bytes	ROM	
		64 bytes	RAM	
	- 4 x 7404	open collector driver		
	- 1 x 74C914	schmitt trigger		
	- 1 x 7400	nand gates		
	- 1 x 555	V/F converter		
	- 1 x 4006	18 bit memory		
	- 1 x 4009	CMOS-TTL-converter		
I²L - LSI Custom design	- 1 x LU329B	1000 gates	32 pin	
		1,5 k ROM		

designed I² L LSI circuit has been built. As Table I shows, the microcomputer concept requires 10 IC's for mainly driver and support functions. The custom-designed chip uses only one package.

This example shows that on a system level 1) the custom design leads to cost-effective solutions, since the costs for printed circuit boards, assembling, and testing are reduced to a minimum, and 2) the technology of the chip is strongly influenced by system considerations. Only with the optimal technology can minimum system configurations be realized.

IV. SYSTEM DESCRIPTION

In the following, an electronic system is described that can replace conventional mechanics in dishwashers and washing machines. The block diagram of the controller system is shown in Fig. 2. The purpose of the input/output section, shown on the left side of Fig. 2, is to receive and store the program selected by the operator, thereby blocking the input after one program is selected, and to present feedback to the operator about the chosen prorgram. The selected program may be indicated by LED's. After program selection, the controller has to activate the various machine functions, such as heating, pumps, valves, etc., successively. A straightforward solution to this problem uses a program-sequence counter that selects via a 1-out-of-n decoder a word of a ROM matrix for each program step. This ROM matrix contains all the information needed for internal organization and control of the output driver stages. In our particular case, our ROM word is 25 bits wide, 9 bits of the selected ROM word control, via logic and latches, and 9 output driver stages. Six bits of the ROM word are jump addresses to set the 6 bit program sequence counter. In this manner subroutines can be performed, or program parts can be omitted. Further, 4 bits are used to define time intervals. For this purpose a 15 bit counter is incremented by line frequency. Some outputs of the divider chain are coded and compared with ROM outputs; 3 bits of the ROM word are inputs for the data select block, which is essentially a decoder, which, using the information of the sensors, the chosen program, and the momentary program position, determines whether or not the program sequence counter has to be incremented. The remaining 3 bits control the program position LED's. Since we have approximately the same number of program inputs and program positions, multiplexing to reduce the pin count is possible. The system further contains a 4 bit A/D converter, and a burst frequency is available if firing transformers for triacs are used. Using directly driven triacs or op-

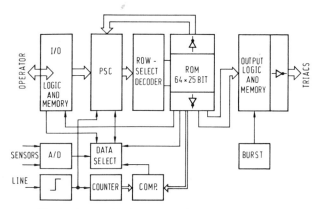

Fig. 2. System block diagram of complete controller.

tocouplers, the burst frequency can be switched off. For test purposes one can jump to certain ROM lines. These contain a special bit pattern that allows easy testing of the output latches, output drivers, time-interval counter, data select, etc.

V. SPECIAL I² L STRUCTURES

The construction of the ROM matrix and the 4 bit A/D converter in I² L technology are, in our opinion, the most interesting details of the hardware.

A. Design of the ROM Matrix

As mentioned in Section IV, the system uses a ROM matrix with 25 bit lines. In I²L technology only a limited number of collectors can be realized with one inverter (usually 4 to 5). Higher fan-out requires paralleling of inverters, which is not economic in chip area, since driver stages and diffused tunnels become necessary. A better way is to use read amplifiers. Such a read amplifier may be a normal I²L inverter with the p-n-p collector current reduced properly (see Fig. 3). The design of the ROM matrix and the read amplifiers is based on a worst case current gain of less than 1 in a 5-collector inverter. Therefore, in a 25-collector inverter, we can expect current gains of about 1/5. For proper operation, the p-n-p collector current of the read inverter must be reduced by a factor of 5, as compared to the p-n-p collector current of the ROM inverter. This reduction is achieved by increasing the p-n-p basewidth of the read inverter by a factor of 5. This method requires only slightly more chip area.

The photomicrograph in Fig. 4 shows details of parts of the read-only memory matrix (lower left), current amplifiers (center left), word-select decoder (lower right), and the driver stages for the word decoder (center right). As the photograph shows, the ROM matrix has maximum packing density with given layout rules.

Measured current-gain curves verify the considerations. Fig. 5 shows the current gain of a 25-collector inverter. It is shown that in the low-power region a current gain of 0.3 is attained. Because of lateral voltage drops in the base, we have an inhomogeneous current distribution leading to a current-gain enhancement at collectors near the base contact and a current-gain decrease for collectors far from the base contact. Up to a maximum gate current of 10 μA the current gain is sufficiently uniform for all the collectors. The upper curve of Fig. 5 shows

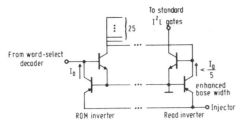

Fig. 3. Simplified schematic of ROM matrix with read amplifiers.

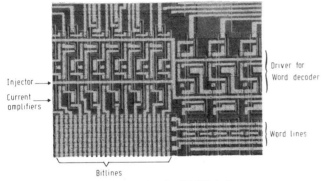

Fig. 4. Chip detail of ROM design.

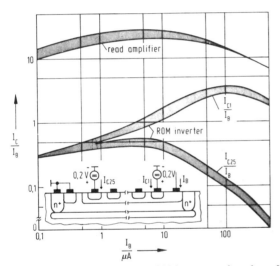

Fig. 5. Current gain of 25-collector ROM inverter and read amplifiers.

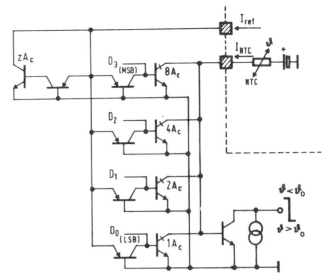

Fig. 6. Principle of A/D converter.

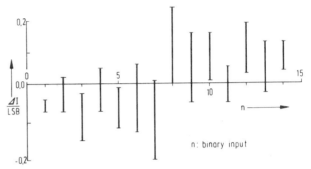

Fig. 7. Linearity of D/A converter.

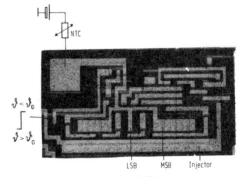

Fig. 8. Chip detail of D/A converter.

the current gain of the read inverter. With a gain greater than 10 it is possible to drive a following standard gate. The spread in the gain curves is from measurements on two different wafer lots.

B. A/D Converter

The A/D converter uses the principle of D/A conversion (current type) with comparator (see Fig. 6). The D/A converter consists of binary weighted current sinks that can be realized in I²L technology with little chip area. For the comparator, a downward operated n-p-n transistor is used. By using a negative-temperature-coefficient resistor (NTC) connected to a voltage source, a current, increasing with temperature, can be delivered to the current sinks. If the temperature of the NTC is high enough, the sink transistors will go out of saturation. Additional current will drive the n-p-n transistor into the on-condition. To compensate the spread in the resistance

of the NTC resistors, the A/D converter has a separate injector. Fig. 7 shows the linearity of the D/A converter. The small systematic errors result from the fact that the injector is not exactly voltage driven. This is necessary because of the "back injection" of switched-on inverters. To realize voltage control of the injector, a current-mirror technique is used. The current-mirror structure shown in Fig. 6 becomes evident when the combination of the lateral p-n-p transistor and the vertical upward-operated n-p-n transistor is considered as an n-p-n transistor with a current gain β_U^{comp} [7]. With a more sophisticated layout and larger dimensions to reduce etch tolerances, a linearity greatly in excess of ±0.25 LSB could be attained, but this is not necessary for appliances. Fig. 8 shows the chip

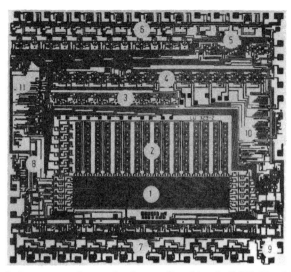

Fig. 9. Interconnection mask of controller chip. 1: ROM 64 × 25; 2: Row select; 3: Program-sequence counter; 4: Time-interval counter; 5: Input logic; 6: Input/output stages; 7: Triac drivers; 8: A/D converter; 9: Burst oscillator; 10: Time decoder; 11: Data select.

TABLE II
FEATURES OF CONTROLLER CHIP

buried layer resistinity	12 Ω/□		
Epi doping	$5 \cdot 10^{15}$ cm^{-3}	β_{down}	= 200 - 500
Epi thickness	7 μm	β_{eff}	= 3 - 7 (fan out = 3)
Base depth	2.4 μm	V_{CEO}	= 10 - 13 V
Base sheet resistinity	200 Ω/□	V_{CBO}	= 18 - 20 V
		$p \cdot \tau_0$	= 0.5...1 p J
		(fan out = 3, Gate current < 10 μA)	

TABLE III
PROCESSING TECHNOLOGY AND AC/DC CHARACTERISTICS OF THE CHOSEN LINEAR-COMPATIBLE I²L TECHNOLOGY

Supply voltage	5	V
Supply current	10	mA
Supply current at power failure	20	μA
Gate current	10	μA
Number of triac driver stages	9	
Triac driver capability	100	mA
I/O stages	6	
Display driver capability	50	mA
A/D converter	4	bit
Technology:	linear compatible I²L, 7 μm Epitaxy	
Chip area	19	mm²
Package	32 - pin DIP	

detail of the A/D converter. The least significant bit is defined by a minimum collector. The most significant bit consists of 8 such collectors. The injector rail shown on the bottom also makes connection to the n-p-n transistor with collector area zA_c, thus resulting in a very compact layout. The whole converter requires a chip area of only 0.1 mm².

VI. CHIP DESCRIPTION

Fig. 9 shows the topology of the controller IC. For the sake of clarity, only the aluminum mask is shown. Total chip area is 19 mm². The I²L part consumes 14 mm² and the linear part 3 mm². "Linear part" does not mean that in this part only linear functions are realized. In this part, linear functions are possible, since all the components of a standard buried-collector technology are available. Actually, simple current-limited amplifiers using n-p-n and p-n-p transistors are realized in the linear part.

Realizing current amplifiers of the desired capability in I²L technology [8] would lead to an unreasonably large chip area. The A/D converter, which uses I²L technology, and the burst oscillator, which also uses I²L gates, are the only linear functions on chip.

With more advanced layout rules in the I²L part, it should be possible to reduce the chip area. For the 1-out-of-64 decoder, another organization may lead to more compact structures. For the ROM matrix, the maximum density is reached because one bit is defined by the aluminum line and a diffused p-base perpendicular. Further blocks indicated in Fig. 9 are standard designs.

Technology is linear compatible I²L with 7 μm epitaxy thickness. The process sequence is similar to that given in [9]. Technological data and electrical data are listed in Table II. Since there is no critical timing in such a controller, the process does not need an extremely thin epitaxy for reduced hole storage under the I²L bases. Also, inhomogeneous current distribution in the 25-collector ROM inverters above 10 μA base

current does not allow high-speed operation. For test purposes, clocking up to 50 kHz is possible at 10 mA total current.

VII. CONCLUSION

A one-chip controller for home appliances has been realized. It has the data listed in Table III. For linear circuitry the supply voltage is 5 V. In normal operation the I²L part is fed with 10 mA injector current, resulting in a gate current of approximately 10 μA. During main failures only the program step counter and the program memory are fed with reduced injector current. This makes capacitive buffering possible. After a long line breakdown a restart is necessary because of the power on reset.

From the data on the driver stages, it is obvious that today linear compatible I²L is the only technology available that makes a one-chip system for appliances possible.

ACKNOWLEDGMENT

The author wishes to thank J. Dangel for managing this program and W. Barth, G. Forster, and R. Ring for their support in system development, circuit design, testing, layout, and simulations.

REFERENCES

[1] S. B. Sample et al., "An all-solid-state digital control system for appliances," IEEE Trans. Ind. Gen. Appl., vol. IGA-6, pp. 669–680, Nov./Dec. 1970.
[2] G. M. Walker, "LSI controls gaining in home appliances," Electron., vol. 14, pp. 91–99, 1977.
[3] D. A. Hodges, P. R. Gray, and R. W. Brodersen, "Potential of MOS technologies for analog integrated circuits," IEEE J. Solid-State Circuits, vol. SC-13, pp. 285–294, June 1978.
[4] Y. P. Tsividis, "Design considerations in single-channel MOS analog integrated circuits—A tutorial," IEEE J. Solid-State Circuits, vol. SC-13, pp. 383–391, June 1978.

IEEE JOURNAL OF SOLID-STATE CIRCUITS, VOL. SC-14, NO. 3, JUNE 1979

[5] E. Bächle et al., "Monolithic crosspoint arrays for private automatic branch exchanges (PABX)," *IEEE J. Solid-State Circuits*, vol. SC-12, pp. 407–415, Aug. 1977.

[6] A. Weissberger et al., "Processor family specializes in dedicated control," *Electron.*, vol. 8, pp. 84–89, July 1976.

[7] J. M. Herman et al., "Second generation I^{2}L/MTL: A 20 ns process/structure," *IEEE J. Solid-State Circuits*, vol. SC-12, pp. 93–101, Apr. 1977.

[8] O. Jakits, "Integrierte Injektionslogik, ein neuartiges Prinzip für Digitalschaltungen," *Valvo Berichte*, vol. 18, pp. 215–226, 1974.

[9] J. Saltich et al., "Processing technology and AC/DC characteristics of linear compatible I^{2}L," *IEEE J. Solid-State Circuits*, vol. SC-11, pp. 478–485, Aug. 1976.

A Monolithic 10-Bit A/D Using I²L and LWT Thin-Film Resistors

A. PAUL BROKAW, MEMBER, IEEE

Abstract—This paper describes the function, circuit details, and performance of a monolithic 10-bit A/D converter. The converter is a successive approximation type using linear compatible I²L for the SAR. The converter is completely self-contained, including both clock and voltage reference. Biasing is arranged to take advantage of naturally occurring interfaces in the circuitry, simplifying the overall circuit in comparison to discrete or hybrid approaches. The processing also includes on-chip thin-film resistors which are laser-wafer-trimmed (LWT) for overall accuracy and temperature stability. The finished circuits operate with no missing codes over the −55° to +125°C temperature range.

I. INTRODUCTION

THE functional requirement for analog-to-digital (A/D) conversion pervades much of electronics and most particularly the areas of measurement, instrumentation, and control. As the cost of digital complexity has fallen, applications have risen more than proportionally and many of the newer applications deal with analog signals. The decreasing cost of increasingly powerful digital integrated circuits has highlighted the relatively high cost of A/D conversion. Until quite recently most A/D converters were made in discrete, modular, or hybrid form. The structural complexity of these fabrication methods maintained a high lower limit to the cost of most converters.

Although many converters made good use of integrated circuits, the problem of efficiently combining digital and linear circuits on the same chip delayed many from starting monolithic A/D converter designs. Linear or analog circuits have traditionally been made using bipolar processes. The relatively large junction-isolated bipolar transistors used in linear circuits, such as current switching D/A converters (DAC), are poorly suited for the complex sequential logic required by most A/D conversion schemes. The smaller transistors used for bipolar logic circuits are poorly suited for making the linear circuits required for an A/D converter. Most of the successful monolithic A/D components to date have been based on MOS processes [1], [2]. These processes make possible compact logic arrays for A/D converters as well as high-performance analog switches. However, the performance of linear circuits, such as amplifiers, made with these processes is inferior to bipolar circuits. Nevertheless, some ingenious circuits have been devised to implement con-

Manuscript received May 1, 1978; revised June 9, 1978.
The author is with Analog Devices Semiconductor, Wilmington, MA 01817.

ventional A/D conversion methods, and some altogether new schemes have been built with MOS processes.

The advent of integrated injection logic (I²L) has made possible the integration of compact logic networks on chips made with a linear bipolar process [3], [4]. I²L geometries can be made to use a set of diffusions which are compatible with high-performance linear transistors. We have combined linear compatible I²L with laser-wafer-trimmed (LWT) thin-film on chip resistors to make a complete 10-bit successive approximation A/D converter in monolithic form.

II. FUNCTIONAL DESCRIPTION

The internal organization of the successive approximation converter is fairly conventional, as the block diagram of Fig. 1 shows. I²L is used to make up a 10-bit successive approximation register (SAR) with outputs to control a set of 3-state buffers and a current-output DAC. The output levels of this DAC are scaled by a buried Zener voltage reference. The output current of the DAC is directed into the analog input resistor, across which it develops a voltage. A latching comparator determines whether this voltage exceeds the applied analog input voltage and feeds this information back to the SAR.

In operation the control flip-flops of the SAR are reset by a blanking signal. As a result, all but the most significant bit (MSB) of the DAC are switched off. This MSB output current develops a voltage across the 5K analog input resistor. When the convert signal is given, the clock starts and the comparator output is subsequently latched in a state determined by its input signal. If the applied analog input voltage exceeds the voltage across the input resistor, the comparator will signal the SAR to retain the MSB. At the next clock edge the second bit, which is half the current of the MSB, will also be switched on. The sum of the MSB and bit 2 is then tested against the analog input voltage. If, for example, the sum exceeds the input signal, the comparator output will indicate to the SAR that bit 2 should be switched off. At the next clock edge bit 3 will be switched on and bit 2 will be switched off. Now the sum of the MSB and bit 3 will be tested against the analog input signal. At each clock edge the next binary weighted bit is switched on to form part of a linear sum of voltages across the input resistor. At the same time, the bit just tested is switched off if the comparator indicates that it caused the test sum to exceed the analog input voltage. By adjusting the test sum in this way to approximate the analog input voltage the SAR tests all 10 binary weighted bits of the

Reprinted from *IEEE J. Solid-State Circuits*, vol. SC-13, pp. 736–745, Dec. 1978.

338

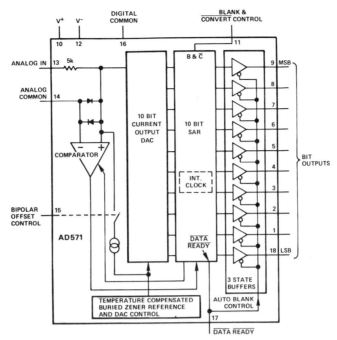

Fig. 1. Functional diagram of the monolithic converter.

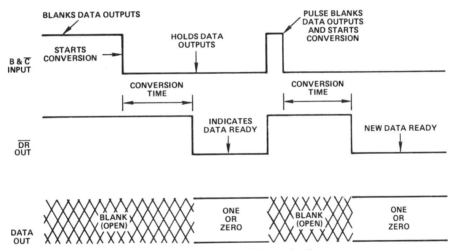

Fig. 2. Control and output signal format for the converter.

DAC. At the end of this sequence the test voltage across the input resistor will be within 1 least significant bit weight of the analog input voltage (assuming the input is within the conversion range). The on/off pattern of the bits of the DAC will reflect the parallel binary word corresponding to the analog input voltage. The SAR presents this pattern to the 3-state buffers and signals the end of the conversion process on the Data Ready output. This signal is internally coupled to the 3-state buffers, causing them to present the parallel binary word at the data outputs.

The control and output format of the converter is illustrated in Fig. 2. The Blank and Convert (B & $\overline{\text{C}}$) input is the single digital control for the converter. When B & $\overline{\text{C}}$ is high the SAR

is reset, the Data Ready ($\overline{\text{DR}}$) output is high, and the data outputs are blanked or open. Once the SAR is reset, driving the B & $\overline{\text{C}}$ low will cause a conversion to commence. The data outputs will remain blanked. At the end of the conversion sequence, as previously described, $\overline{\text{DR}}$ will switch low and the data output buffers will become active with the digital output. As shown in the figure, B & $\overline{\text{C}}$ can be driven with a narrow positive convert pulse, in which case the data will remain at the outputs between conversions. Alternatively, the B & $\overline{\text{C}}$ input can be returned to the high blank state between conversions, after the data have been read. This mode of operation permits several converters to be multiplexed simply by paralleling their data outputs. The converters are then all held in the

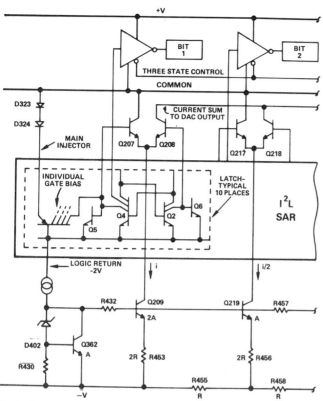

Fig. 3. Simplified schematic of the converter illustrating essential biasing arrangements.

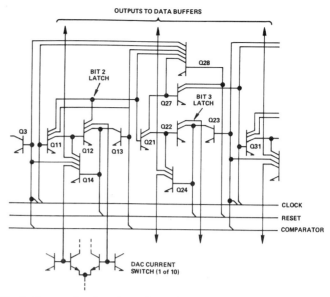

Fig. 4. Repeated subsection of the SAR showing extended control transistors.

blank mode, with the exception of the one selected for conversion. When its data have been collected, it is returned to the blank state and another converter is activated.

III. DESCRIPTION OF ESSENTIAL BIAS ARRANGEMENTS

The conventional arrangement for powering an I^2L array is to "ground" the common emitter diffusion and drive the injector positive with a current-limited source. Unfortunately, this sort of arrangement would require a level translator at each of the SAR outputs, to drive the current output DAC. Similar level translators in T^2L compatible monolithic DAC's take up substantial chip area [5].

To avoid the requirement for 10 level translators, the entire logic array is translated to a negative voltage. This voltage is selected to be directly compatible with the current switches of the DAC.

The bias voltage relationships between the I^2L and the rest of the A/D are illustrated in Fig. 3. In order to utilize currents already available from the voltage reference, and other circuits biased from the negative supply, the I^2L injector voltage is fixed and the common emitters are driven negative with a limited current. Each of the 10 differential n-p-n switches in the DAC is directly driven by a pair of outputs from the I^2L. Each stage of the SAR has an additional output which drives the input of the 3-state buffers. The voltage difference between the logic operating voltage and the buffer inputs is less than the I^2L inverter BV_{CES}, so that no level translator circuitry is required.

The buried Zener reference diode, $D402$, is referred to the negative power supply bus, along with the binary weighted current sources of the DAC.

IV. SUCCESSIVE APPROXIMATION REGISTER

A key section of the A/D converter which has been difficult to fabricate with a linear bipolar process is the SAR. Linear compatible I^2L makes possible the construction of a compact SAR on the same chip with the DAC and linear circuits making up the A/D converter.

A section of the circuit of the SAR is shown in Fig. 4. The register repeats modulo 2 so that it consists of five sections which are nearly identical, with slight differences in the first and last sections. The practice of using half-arrow emitters to indicate inverted-mode I^2L transistors has been adopted. Since all the emitters are joined by the I^2L structure, the individual connections are omitted.

The $Q12–Q14$ pair make up an R–S flip-flop which controls the DAC switch for the bit 2 current. During the blanking interval, in the converter control cycle, the bit 2 latch and all similar latches in the register are reset to their start of conversion state. The RESET line shown in Fig. 4 represents the base of an extended transistor. This transistor has multiple collectors which are switched on in unison to reset the SAR. One of these collectors turns off the base of $Q14$ to reset the bit 2 latch.

The CLOCK line is another extended transistor, similar to the reset transistor. At the beginning of the convert cycle this transistor is on so that it holds off the base of $Q11$, among others. At the next clock edge it goes off, allowing $Q11$ to set the bit 2 latch. This will cause the bit 2 current to be added to the linear sum which is tested against the analog input signal. At the next edge of the clock, one-half cycle later, $Q11$ will be switched off allowing $Q21$ to switch on and set the bit 3 latch, $Q22–Q24$.

At this time $Q13$ will be controlled by the extended com-

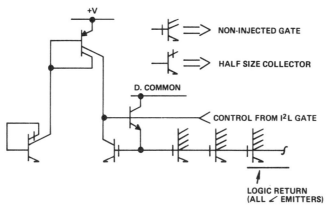

Fig. 5. Circuit diagram typifying the extended control transistor drives.

parator transistor. If the comparator is off, $Q13$ will reset the bit 2 latch; if not, the bit 2 latch will remain set. Shortly thereafter a signal will propagate through $Q21$, $Q27$, and $Q28$ which will block the comparator signal from $Q13$ during the remainder of the conversion.

The combined result of the actions just described is to add bit 3 to the DAC output test sum, to reset bit 2 if and only if the comparator transistor is off, and to block subsequent states of the comparator from affecting bit 2. Incidental to this process the $Q27$-$Q28$ latch is set which releases $Q31$ to the control of the clock. At the next edge of the clock, $Q31$ will set the bit 4 latch (not shown) and $Q23$ will be enabled briefly to possibly reset the bit 3 latch under comparator control.

The remaining bits of the DAC are tested and retained or reset similarly. One bit is tested at each edge of the clock so that during each full clock cycle 2 bits are tested. The use of modulo 2 circuitry results in economies in gate requirements which permit the complete SAR to be realized at an average complexity of only seven transistors per bit.

The two drive lines directed down from $Q12$ and $Q14$ in Fig. 4 control the bit 2 switch. To prevent interaction between the DAC switches and the SAR latches, the switches are driven by collectors rather than directly from the bases of the latch transistors. Current injected clamp diodes are used to establish the bias level of the "on" switch. These diodes are illustrated in Fig. 3. The structures labeled $Q5$ and $Q6$ appear to be unfinished in the drawing. In fact, they are injected I^2L gates without collectors. When they are released by the latch transistors they drive a DAC switch transistor to approximate the main injector voltage. These clamp diodes have the same "base current" as normal gates, so they can be readily driven off by the latch transistors.

Referring now to the complete schematic diagram, Fig. 10, the 10 I^2L latches can be seen to drive the 10 differential current switches of the DAC. Each of the drive lines uses an injected clamp diode, shown as a collectorless I^2L gate, to establish the positive drive level. The negative level is, of course, determined by the logic return voltage and the saturation voltage of the driving transistor.

The extended transistors shown in Fig. 4 are each made up of several multiple collector transistors located along the

I^2L array. These transistors are shielded from the I^2L injector so that they can be driven from a single base drive line. Fig. 5 illustrates how this drive is controlled. A small injected I^2L transistor has a half-sized collector tied back to its base to give it a controlled beta approaching 2. Its collector current will approximate twice the injected base current. This current is directed into the collector of a noninjected transistor, the base of which parallels the extended transistor. A normal mode n-p-n transistor drives the common base line until the dummy transistor absorbs the output of the current mirror. The extended transistor can be turned off by stealing the current mirror output with an oversized I^2L gate.

The circuit of Fig. 5 illustrates the drive scheme used for the clock transistor $Q136$ as shown in the complete schematic, Fig. 10. The reset transistor, $Q137$, has a similar arrangement with a level translator interposed between the current mirror and the buffer, to provide a ground-referenced logic-compatible input for the B & $\overline{C}$ input.

V. DIGITAL OUTPUT BUFFERS

Since the logic array is biased negatively, with respect to digital common, the latches can directly drive the 3-state buffers. In Fig. 6 the last stages of the SAR are shown driving their respective buffers. The $Q107$-$Q108$ latch, which is functionally analogous to $Q27$-$Q28$ in Fig. 4, acts as the converter status latch.

After bit 10 has been switched on and tested by the comparator, the next clock edge will momentarily enable $Q93$ which is then controlled by the comparator transistor (not shown) to reset the latch, should it be required. Subsequently, the $Q107$-$Q108$ latch will be set, inhibiting $Q93$ and indicating that the conversion is complete. One output of the status latch is used to stop the clock. Another output enables the controlled-beta transistor $Q109$. This transistor is buffered by $Q302$ to allow compliance over the full positive power-supply range. Current from $Q302$ drives a buffered current mirror composed of $Q305$ and $Q301$ to switch on $Q306$. This transistor provides the $\overline{DR}$ output signal. The current mirror also contains a resistor $R531$ and transistor $Q304$ which establish a bias voltage on the 3-state drive line, when the current mirror is driven by the status latch. This voltage activates a current

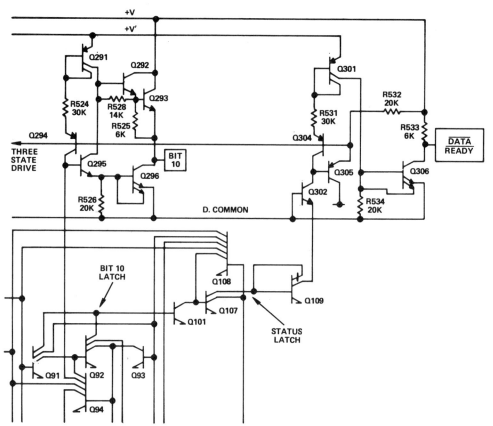

Fig. 6. Two types of digital output buffer with SAR interconnections.

mirror in all ten 3-state buffers through a similar resistor-transistor combination. The bit 10 buffer, shown in Fig. 6, is driven on by the 3-state drive voltage. Collector current from $Q294$ drives the base of $Q295$, while the mirror transistor $Q291$ supplies collector current to $Q295$. The transistors $Q292$, $Q293$, $Q295$, and $Q296$ make up a more or less conventional totem-pole logic output buffer. A collector of $Q94$, in the bit 10 latch, controls the state of this buffer when it is brought out of the blank mode. If $Q94$ is on (indicating that the weight of bit 10 should be included in the digital output) it will sink the collector current of $Q294$. As a result, $Q295$ and $Q296$ will remain off and the output of $Q291$ will turn on the Darlington output resulting in a bit 10 output of "one." If $Q94$ is off, $Q295$ will divert the current from $Q291$ to the base of $Q296$ resulting in a bit 10 output of "zero."

The other 9 data buffers are identical to the one shown in Fig. 6 and are similarly driven by their respective latches in the SAR.

VI. CURRENT OUTPUT DAC AND REFERENCE

The switches operated by the SAR steer currents generated by a binary weighting circuit, as shown in Fig. 3. This circuit is shown in more detail by Fig. 7. The binary weighting of the currents is established by an R–$2R$ ladder. The magnitude of the currents is established by a subsurface Zener-diode voltage reference and the currents are made available to the switches by 10 common-base n-p-n transistors.

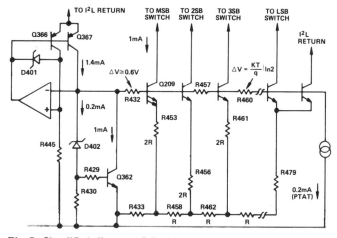

Fig. 7. Simplified diagram of the binary weighted current sources and voltage reference circuitry.

In order for the R–$2R$ ladder to produce binary weighted currents, each of the $2R$ branches must be terminated at the same voltage as the others. The 10 different binary weighted currents from the ladder would result in 10 different values for V_{BE} in the common base transistors if it were not for the fact that the MSB transistor has twice the emitter area of the second bit transistor. This device is oversized to accommodate the relatively high current through it. As a result, the first two devices operate at the same current density and have the same V_{BE}. The other eight transistors are all the same size as the bit 2 transistor and have each a different value of V_{BE}. Because the outputs of these transistors are in a descending binary weighting, the ratio of current density in any two adjacent transistors is 2 to 1. Therefore, the base-emitter voltages decrease by an amount $(kT/q)\ln 2$ from bit to bit. The emitter voltages are equalized by interposing an interbase voltage which is maintained equal to the ΔV_{BE} of $(kT/q)\ln 2$.

The interbase voltage is arranged by fixing the base voltage of the first two bits and attaching the remaining common-base transistors along a string of equal resistors [5], [6]. The resistor string is driven by a current which is proportional to absolute temperature and scaled to produce the proper interbase voltage.

This same current is used to create a voltage with a positive temperature coefficient to compensate the temperature coefficient of the Zener reference. The current is shown in Fig. 7 flowing through $R432$ as well as the interbase resistors. The voltage developed across $R432$ is proportional to absolute temperature (PTAT) and subtracts from the voltage at the top of $D402$. The magnitude of this PTAT voltage can be adjusted to compensate for the temperature coefficient of the Zener reference voltage.

The R-$2R$ ladder and $R432$, among others, are thin-film resistors on the monolithic chip. At the wafer probe stage the ladder resistors are laser trimmed to overcome resistor mismatches, similar to the trimming described by Holloway and Norton [5]. At the same time, $R432$ is adjusted to optimize the reference voltage temperature compensation.

Since it is the ladder voltage which determines the output current of the DAC, rather than the base drive voltage, additional compensation is required. Usual practice is to generate a stabilized, temperature-compensated, reference voltage and use a control loop with a reference or dummy transistor to adjust the voltage applied to the base and the ladder so that the ladder current will be proportional to the reference voltage. Where the reference voltage is not intended to appear as a feature of the device, or for some other internal purpose, the conventional scheme offers little return for its added complexity. Since it would be necessary to temperature compensate the Zener reference to produce a stabilized reference output, there is little added difficulty to directly compensate the voltage across the ladder.

Referring again to Fig. 7, current through the subsurface Zener diode $D402$ develops a voltage across $R430$ which turns on $Q362$. Additional current delivered to the anode of $D402$ will be diverted to $Q362$. The negative temperature coefficient of the V_{BE} of $Q362$ approximately compensates the temperature coefficient of $D402$.

The resulting stabilized voltage is used to control the current delivered to the anode of $D402$. A differential amplifier drives the p-n-p transistors $Q366$ and $Q367$. The current for these transistors is drawn from the I^2L pocket and powers the logic. When the voltage across $R455$ has been driven to equal the compensated Zener voltage, the current from $Q367$ will be proportional to the ratio of this voltage and $R455$.

This current divides into 3 components. The first is the

PTAT current activating the interbase resistors, the second is the Zener current, which develops a V_{BE} across $R430$, and the third is the current in $Q362$. The value of $R430$ is selected so that the Zener current complements the PTAT current. The sum of these currents is invariant with temperature, which leaves an approximately constant remainder for $Q362$. The value of $R445$ is selected so that this remainder current causes $Q362$ to operate at the same current density as $Q209$. As a result, the V_{BE} of $Q362$ compensates for the V_{BE} of $Q209$. The voltage across the ladder is just the actual Zener voltage minus the compensation voltage across $R432$.

If the ladder voltage is set to develop exactly the right currents in the ladder, there will be an error in the bit currents due to the base currents which escape from the signal path. This error is corrected by the inclusion of $R429$. The base current of $Q362$ develops a small voltage across $R429$ which increases the ladder voltage by an amount proportional to the base currents. The value of $R429$ is selected to compensate for the escaping base currents and for the voltage developed across $R432$ by base currents.

The differential amplifier which drives the Zener current loop has no input operating voltage when the Zener loop is off. To insure starting, $D401$ has been added.

VII. COMPARATOR

A simplified diagram of the comparator, and associated circuitry, is shown in Fig. 8. This comparator has a linear comparison mode and a latched output mode. It is switched between these states under control of the internal clock [7].

Fig. 8 shows the analog input resistor and the DAC output joined at the comparison node. Voltage at this node is compared to analog common by the differential amplifier $Q351$ and $Q352$. Any resulting difference current develops a differential signal across $R410$ and $R411$. When the comparison node has settled, after the DAC has been set to test a bit, the clock will switch $Q355$ off and $Q356$ on. This will divert the emitter current of $Q351$-$Q352$ to the inner emitters of $Q347$ and $Q348$. These transistors, along with their Darlington-connected drivers $Q345$ and $Q346$, make up a flip-flop circuit with $R410$ and $R411$. The differential signal, established by $Q351$ and $Q352$, prebiases the flip-flop so that it rapidly goes to the one of its stable states determined by the polarity of the differential input signal. This positive feedback converts the polarity signal into a standard level at the output of the flip-flop. This signal is buffered and level translated by $Z344$ and $Z343$ to another differential stage. This stage, composed of $Q343$ and $Q344$, drives a differential-to-single-ended converter which in turn drives $Q138$, the extended comparator transistor.

Approximately halfway through the next clock half-cycle, the clock will restore the comparator to its linear, unlatched mode. By this time the SAR will have responded to the comparator signal and then blocked further response during the current test. When the $Q355$-$Q356$ pair switches $i372$ back to the differential input transistors, $Q351$-$Q352$, the flip-flop is disabled. The outer emitters of $Q347$ and $Q348$ cause these transistors to act as cascodes conveying the differential stage currents to the two collector resistors, $R410$ and $R411$.

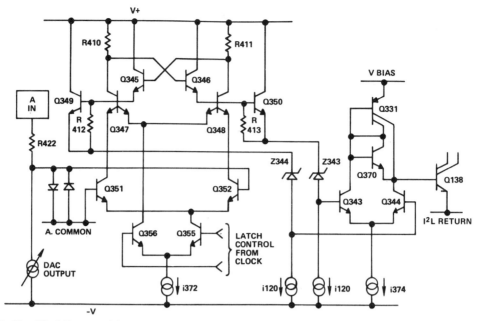

Fig. 8. Simplified diagram of the latching comparator showing its interconnections to input circuitry and the logic.

Near the end of each half-cycle of the main clock, the comparator is latched so that its output will remain stable while the next test is being set up. Positive feedback, also provided by the flip-flop, minimizes the settling time required for the comparator to accurately reach the standard output signal level.

Additional details of the comparator circuit, not shown by Fig. 8, should be self-explanatory as they appear on the main schematic diagram, Fig. 10.

VIII. BIPOLAR OFFSET CURRENT

The basic A/D converter using a negative current output DAC is capable of encoding positive input voltages only. However, a positive current injected into the comparison node will offset the input voltage range. To produce a symmetrical input voltage range, a positive current of half full scale is required. This current is developed by an extra MSB weight current in the DAC current sources. A precision current mirror, shown in Fig. 9, converts this output to a positive current at the comparison node. This mirror uses a matched pair of p-n-p transistors and emitter resistors to generate a pair of equal currents. One of these currents is measured against the dummy MSB, while the other drives the comparison node. A differential amplifier, consisting of $Q360$ and $Q361$, drives the bases of the p-n-p's to equalize the output of $Q359$ and the extra MSB current. The emitters of the differential amplifier connect to a control pin. Shorting this pin to common will disable the differential amplifier and cut off the bipolar offset current. This arrangement for generating and disabling the bipolar offset saves one of the two pins usually spent on the bipolar offset function.

The resistors used in the current mirror are the same as those in the R-$2R$ ladder. When the converter is at wafer probe, and after the ladder has been trimmed for linearity, the current

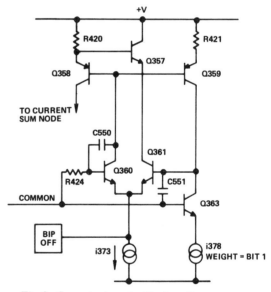

Fig. 9. Current mirror for bipolar offset generator.

mirror is trimmed to adjust the bipolar offset currents. This assures that, in the bipolar offset mode of operation, an analog input voltage of zero will result in an output code of 1000000000.

IX. COMPLETE CIRCUIT DIAGRAM

The circuit of the 10-bit converter is shown in its entirety by Fig. 10. Because of the high component density in this figure, most of the circuits are better illustrated by the other, simplified, diagrams. The complete schematic does illustrate how the individual circuits are interconnected and will be used to describe a few of the remaining subcircuits.

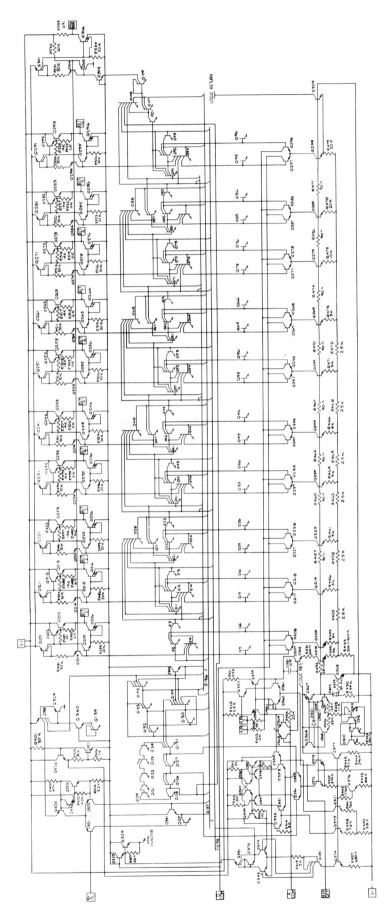

Fig. 10. Schematic diagram of the complete converter.

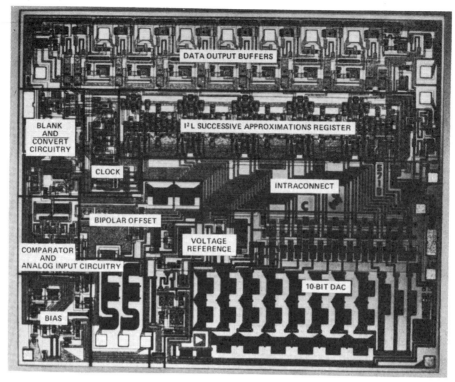

Fig. 11. Photomicrograph of the 120 × 151 mil² monolithic converter die.

The $\overline{DR}$ and bit-10 buffer of Fig. 6 are shown in the upper right portion of Fig. 10. To the left are nine more identical data output buffers and below the buffers is the I²L SAR. Notice the five repeating patterns marked by the loops typified by the outputs of $Q28$ in Fig. 4. Directly below the logic is the row of collectorless injected transistors used as combined driver-clamps. Finally, the bottom row of circuitry is the DAC current weighting circuits. These circuits are those shown in simplified form by Fig. 7.

To the left of the DAC is the voltage reference circuit with the amplifier shown in greater detail. A feature of this circuit is the PTAT current-generator of Fig. 7 which is implemented with a cross-coupled quad of transistors $Q310$–$Q313$. This circuit is activated by a resistor from the emitters of the differential amplifier in the Zener loop. The cross-coupled quad has the interesting property that its PTAT output is, to first order, independent of the activating current.

Just above the reference circuitry is the bipolar offset current mirror, and to its left is the comparator, as shown in Figs. 9 and 8, respectively. The clock circuit stretches out above both the comparator and offset circuit.

The left side of the clock is a ring oscillator made up of nine transistors. Two signal lines shown extending down from the ring control the comparator so that it compares and then latches once during each cycle of the oscillator. Since the SAR will advance with each clock edge, the output frequency of the oscillator is halved by a D-type flip-flop shown to the right of the oscillator. The output of this divider is buffered to drive $Q136$, an extended transistor.

At the upper left of Fig. 10 are several bias circuits and the B & $\overline{C}$ input. These circuits variously provide positive supply voltage for the comparator, control current for the clock buffer, emitter current for the B & $\overline{C}$ input pair, and the logic threshold voltage for the B & $\overline{C}$ input. The B & $\overline{C}$ input itself is a simple differential pair which drives the reset circuitry on or off. When the SAR has been reset and the reset is removed, the clock starts and the successive approximation sequence automatically begins.

X. FEATURES OF THE MONOLITHIC CHIP

The circuits described here have been implemented on a 120 × 151 mil² chip, a photomicrograph of which is shown in Fig. 11. The schematic diagram parallels the chip layout to a large extent. Across the top of the chip are seven of the ten data buffers using identical layouts. The MSB output is at the upper left and the ninth and tenth bit outputs are at the upper right of the chip, with the $\overline{DR}$ output buffer just below them. A single large pocket containing the I²L is just below the data buffers and is bracketed by them at the ends. The SAR is composed of the row of vertical gates, while the clock gates are arranged at right angles and to the left. Below the logic and interconnections are the DAC switch and current output transistors. The array of "sewer pipes" at the lower right is, of course, the R–$2R$ ladder. The ladder is composed of wide contact resistors with trim tabs shaped to provide wide trim range with high trim resolution.

To the left of the ladder is the voltage reference circuit including, at the bottom, the cross-coupled quad PTAT current generator. Further to the left are a pair of S-shaped input resistors. These two 10K resistors are normally bonded in parallel to make a 5K resistor for the 10-V input range. When separated, they permit the option of a 20-V (or ± 10-V) input range. These resistors have large trim tabs which are used to adjust the full-scale input voltage range at wafer probe.

In the lower left corner are the negative current bias circuits. Above these circuits is the comparator with the bipolar offset circuit to its right and the B & $\overline{\text{C}}$ input just above it.

XI. CONCLUSIONS

An I^2L successive approximation register has been integrated with the linear components of an A/D converter. The result is a 10-bit A/D converter with input ranges of 0 to +10 V, ±5 V, or 0 to +20 V, and ±10 V. The output is 10-bit positive true binary or offset binary and the conversion time is, typically, 25 μs.

The digital input and outputs meet all T^2L threshold requirements over the -55° to +125°C temperature range. The circuits powered by the positive supply are designed to operate from about 4 V up to 16 V. The logic input and outputs adapt their threshold and levels to be compatible with the logic family powered by the converter V^+ supply. Supply voltage sensitivity for the positive supply is typically less than one LSB change over the 4.5-V to 15-V range.

Circuits powered by the negative supply have more influence on the absolute accuracy of the converter. Nevertheless, the converter operates reliably from -12 to -15 V with less than one LSB change in full-scale sensitivity.

The device is trimmed at the wafer stage, resulting in a high yield to 10-bit accuracy in functional devices. The trimmed circuits are stable, so that functional 10-bit devices typically show no missing codes over the -55°to +125°C temperature range.

The linearity of full-scale temperature coefficient is better than 10 parts per million per degree Celsius (ppm/°C) and units have been tested showing overall full-scale input temperature coefficients of better than 10 ppm/°C. Wafer trimming of this temperature coefficient yields more than 50 percent to drifts less than 40 ppm/°C. Work now in progress on this trim method is expected to improve the yield of lower temperature coefficient devices.

The configuration of the circuit allows separation of analog circuits and signal returns from the power and digital common. The 3-state outputs together with the automatic control format permit multiplexing of several converters onto a common digital bus. These features, in conjunction with the accuracy and completeness of the converter function, make this device a flexible component for use in the design of both simple and complex systems. Its simplicity and monolithic construction promise to bring its cost more in line with the costs of available digital components.

ACKNOWLEDGMENT

This circuit is the result of a lot of caring work by many people at Analog Devices Semiconductor. The author wishes to give special thanks to B. Tsang, who devised the process, M. Libert, who made it all fit on the chip, M. Norton, who tamed the circuit with the laser, and P. Holloway, who suggested the right things to do in the comparator.

REFERENCES

[1] J. L. McCreary and P. R. Gray, "All-MOS charge redistribution analog-to-digital conversion techniques–Part I," *IEEE J. Solid-State Circuits*, vol. SC-10, pp. 371–378, Dec. 1975.

[2] R. E. Suarez, P. R. Gray, and D. A. Hodges, "All-MOS charge redistribution analog-to-digital conversion techniques-Part II," *IEEE J. Solid-State Circuits*, vol. SC-10, pp. 379–385, Dec. 1975.

[3] C. M. Hart and A. Slob, "Integrated injection logic–A new approach to LSI," in *Int. Solid-State Circuits Conf., Digest* (1972), pp. 92, 93, 219.

[4] N. C. de Troye, "Integrated injection logic–A new approach to LSI," in *Int. Solid-State Circuits Conf., Digest* (1974), pp. 12, 13, 214.

[5] P. Holoway and M. Norton, "A high yield, second generation 10-bit monolithic DAC," in *Int. Solid-State Circuits Conf., Digest* (1976), pp. 106, 107, 236.

[6] M. Shoji and V. R. Saari, "A monolithic 8-bit D/A converter with a new scheme for error compensation," *IEEE J. Solid-State Circuits*, vol. SC-10, pp. 499–501, Dec. 1975.

[7] R. A. Nordstrom, "High speed integrated A/D converter," in *Int. Solid-State Circuits Conf. Digest*, (1976), pp. 150, 151.

I2L LSI DESIGN WITH MASK PROGRAMMABLE ARRAYS

by

Louis Chan
Eugene Coussens
Exar Integrated Systems, Inc.
750 Palomar Avenue
Sunnyvale, California 94086

INTRODUCTION

The concept of semi-custom or *master-slice* approach to monolithic LSI design has been known since the early 1960's. In such an approach one uses a partially fabricated silicon wafer which is *customized* by the application of a special interconnection pattern. This technique greatly reduces the design and tooling cost and the prototype fabrication cycle associated with the conventional *full-custom* IC development cycle; and thus makes custom IC's economically feasible even at low production volumes.

Until recently, the application of semi-custom design technology to complex digital systems has been somewhat limited due to one key factor: to be economically feasible, a complex digital LSI chip must achieve a high functional density on the chip (i.e. high gate-count per unit chip area). Traditionally, this requirement is not compatible with the random interconnection concept which is key to the semi-custom or master slice design approach. This paper describes a *new* approach to the master-slice concept which overcomes this age-old problem. It achieves packing densities approaching those of full-custom digital LSI layout while still maintaining the low-cost and the quick turn-around attributes of semi-custom IC design. This is achieved by making use of unique layout and interconnection properties of I2L gates, and by extending the mask-programming to additional mask layers besides the metal interconnection.

FEATURES OF I2L TECHNOLOGY

Integrated Injection Logic (I2L) is one of the most significant recent advances in the area of monolithic LSI technology. Compared to other monolithic LSI technologies, I2L offers the following unique advantages:

High Packing Density
Bipolar Compatible Processing
Low Power and Low Voltage Operation
Low (power x delay) Product
Higher Speed than MOS

Performance Characteristic	Technology					
	I2L (N+ Isolated)	PMOS	NMOS (Si Gate)	CMOS	Schottky T2L	ECL
Speed (Fastest = 1)	3	6	5	4	2	1
Speed Power Product (Lowest = 1)	1	4	2	3	5	6
Linear/Digital Compatible	Yes	No	No	No	Yes	Yes
Functional Density (Highest = 1)	1	3	1	2	4	5

FIGURE 1: Comparison of Performance Features of Various Digital LSI Technologies

Figure 1 shows a comparative listing of some of the cost and performance advantages of I2L technology, in comparison with other monolithic LSI technologies. Figure 2 gives a comparison of the speed and power capabilities of various logic families, including I2L. Since I2L technology is a direct extension of the conventional bipolar IC technology, it readily lends itself to combining high-density digital functions on the same chip along with conventional Schottky-bipolar circuitry.

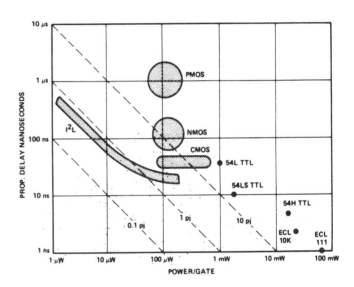

FIGURE 2: Comparison of Speed and Power Capabilities of Various Logic Families

The I2L logic technology is developed around the basic single-input, multiple-output inverter circuit shown in Figure 3. A recommended circuit symbol for this gate circuit is also defined in the figure. Most terminals of the I2L gate share the same semi-conductor region (for example, the collector of the PNP is the same as the base of the NPN; and the emitter of the NPN is the same as the base of the PNP). This leads to a very compact device structure, and results in very high packing density in monolithic device fabrication. Figure 4 illustrates the basic device structure and the cross-section for a bipolar-compatible I2L gate. Since the individual I2L gates do not require separate P-type isolation diffusions, they can be placed in a common N type tub. This feature greatly enhances the packing density on the chip since it eliminates the need for separate isolation pockets for individual gates. With conventional photo-masking and diffusion tolerances,

Reprinted with permission from *1977 WESCON Tech. Papers*, Sept. 1977, pp. 1–5.

gate densities of greater than 200 gates/mm^2 can be readily achieved in full custom layout. Using the semi-custom approach which is outlined in this paper, one can maintain a packing density of greater than 120 gates/mm^2 even with random metalization or inter-connection requirements. This offers at least a factor of four improvements over conventional bipolar mas-ter-slice technology and approximately a factor of two improvements over MOS master-slice approach in terms of gate-density and chip area utilization.

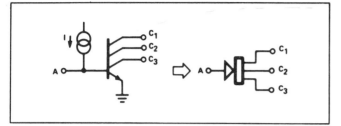

FIGURE 3: A Recommended Symbol for the Basic I^{2}L Gate

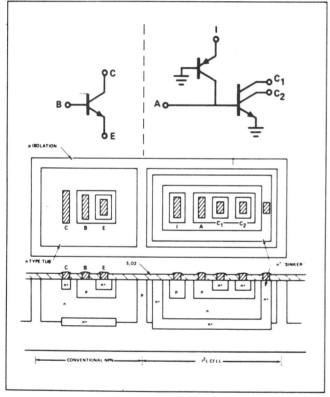

FIGURE 4: Basic Device Structure for Bipolar Compatible I^{2}L

DESIGNING WITH I^{2}L GATE ARRAYS

A number of I^{2}L gate arrays have been developed at Exar utilizing bipolar-compatible I^{2}L process tech-nology. The latest and the most complex among these gate arrays is the XR-800 chip whose layout is shown in Figure 5. This chip is intended for semi-custom IC designs involving complex digital systems and contains 864 multiple-output I^{2}L gates and 42 schottky-TTL input output buffers. The components contained in the XR-800 chip are listed in Table I.

TABLE I
LIST OF COMPONENTS ON THE XR-800 CHIP

Component Type	Quantities
Multiple Output I^{2}L Gates	864
Input/Output Buffers	42
Bipolar Transistors	
Schottky NPN	63
Pwr. NPN	4
Lateral PNP	21
Resistors	210
Cross-Unders	442
Bonding Pads	42
Chip Size	162 x 156 mils

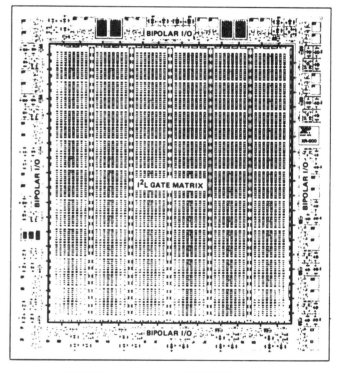

FIGURE 5: Basic Layout of XR-800 Gate Array

As indicated in Figure 5, the XR-800 chip is made up of two sections: (a) the I^{2}L gate matrix; and (b) the Schottky-bipolar input/output interface. The basic features of the XR-800 chip are outlined below:

a) The I^{2}L Gate Matrix

This section of the chip contains a total of 864 I^{2}L gates, arranged in 8 gate logic *cells*. There are a total of 108 such cells within the I^{2}L Gate Matrix section of XR-800. These are arranged in a matrix form, with six columns and 18 rows. Figure 6 shows a basic 8 gate cell section within the I^{2}L gate section, prior to customization. The basic 8 gate cells forming the I^{2}L gate matrix are made up of P-type injectors and gate *fingers* which serve as the base regions of the I^{2}L gates. The six dots on each gate area indicate the possible locations or *sites* for gate inputs or outputs. The particular use of these sites as an input or an output

11/4

is determined by two custom masks: an N-type collector diffusion mask which defines the locations of outputs, and a custom contact mask which opens the appropriate input and output contacts. Finally, a third custom mask is applied to form the metal interconnections between the gates, as shown in the sample layout example of Figure 7. In the case of a complex digital system, multi-layer metallization is used with a standard *via* mask to provide interconnection between the two metal layers. The use of multi-layer metal interconnection greatly enhances the gate utilization and the layout density. In this manner, approximately 75% gate utilization can be obtained with random logic. In the case of organized or repetitive logic such as counter-chains, gate utilization approaches 100%.

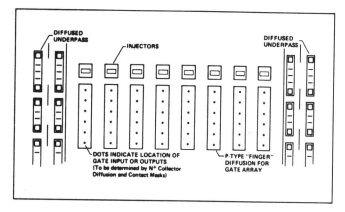

FIGURE 6: Basic 8-Gate Cell Layout Before Customization

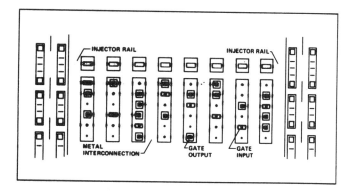

FIGURE 7: Sample Layout of 8-Gate Cell After Customizing it with N+ Collector Diffusion, Contact Mask & Metal Interconnection Pattern

Figures 8 and 9 show the typical operating characteristics of the I^2L gates within the gate matrix. As indicated in Figure 8, the average power-delay product for a four-output gate is approximately 0.5pJ at low currents; and the typical propagation delay, t_{pd}, at high currents is 40 nano-seconds.

Figure 9 shows the toggle frequency of D-type flip flops utilizing the basic gate structure shown in Figures 6 and 7. As indicated in the figure, toggle rates of 5 MHz are obtained at injector current levels of approximately 100μA per gate.

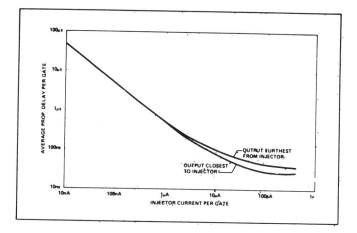

FIGURE 8: Propagation Delay Characteristics of I^2L Gates as a Function of Injector Current

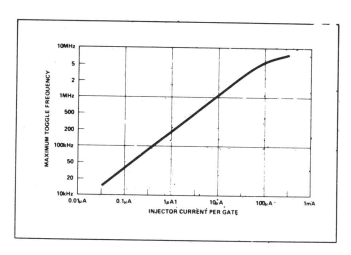

FIGURE 9: Maximum Toggle Rate of D-type Flip-Flop as a Function of Injector Current

b) Schottky Bipolar I/O Section

The I/O sections are located along the periphery of the XR-800 chip. In addition to the basic interface circuitry, this section of the chip also contains four high current transistors, each capable of handling currents in excesss of 100mA. Figure 10 shows the basic component locations for a typical input/output interface cell. Each cell can be used as either an input or an output interface. The I/O interface section is customized only by a single metal interconnection pattern. Figure 11 shows a typical layout example and the equivalent circuit of a Schottky-TTL input interface stage.

11/4

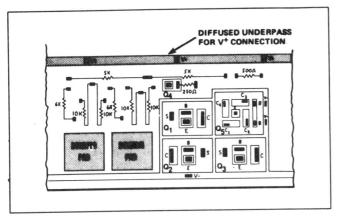

FIGURE 10: Component Layout Within the Schottky-Bipolar Input/output Interface Cell

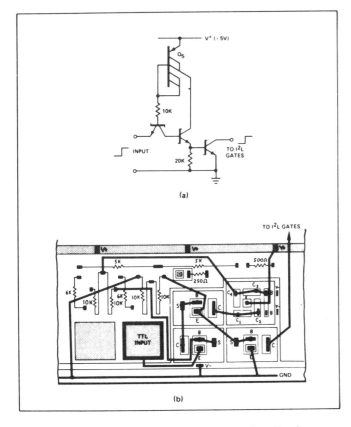

FIGURE 11: Typical TTL-Type Input Interface Circuit a) Equivalent Circuit; b) Recommended Layout in I/O Interface Cell

SEMI-CUSTOM DESIGN CYCLE

Figure 12 gives the basic steps associated with a typical semi-custom IC development cycle using a complex I^2L gate array, such as the XR-800 chip. Starting with the customers logic diagram, the first step is to review the logic diagram, and convert it into I^2L gates. At this stage a computer simulation of the logic diagram may also be performed, if deemed necessary.

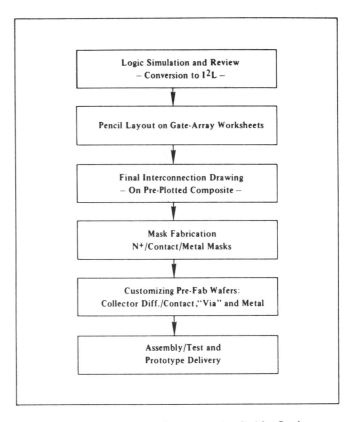

FIGURE 12: Sequence of Steps Associated with a Semi-Custom LSI Development Cycle

The second step is to form a pencil layout on a gate-array worksheet. This pencil layout is done on a blank worksheet containing an array of gates such as those shown in Figure 6; where the gate *input* and *output* locations are shown as dots. During the layout a symbol *X* or *O* is placed over the appropriate dot on the gate outline to indicate the location of an input or output connection, respectively. The gate interconnections are shown as single pencil lines. Next, this layout is transferred to a 254 X scale grid mylar which has a preplotted accurate composite of the chip layout. The complete set of custom tooling necessary can then be obtained from this final composite in a single digitizing step, and subsequent pattern generation. During the digitizing step, the interconnection lines serve as the centerline of the metal interconnection traces to be generated.

Figures 13 and 14 show a simple layout example for a 1-of-8 decoder circuit: first the logic diagram is drawn in terms of the I^2L gates as shown in Figure 13. Then, the appropriate *target dots* on the worksheet are interconnected with pencil lines, and identified as inputs and outputs, as indicated in Figure 14. It should be noted that the X and O symbols correspond to a set of pre-programmed mask cuts. Thus, the entire step of mask generation can be obtained in a single digitizing step, from a pencil layout such as that of Figure 14, drawn on an accurate grid background.

11/4

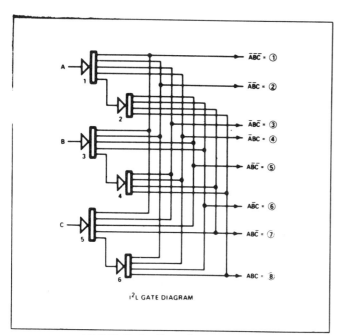

FIGURE 13: Design Example:
1-of-8 Decoder I²L Logic Diagram

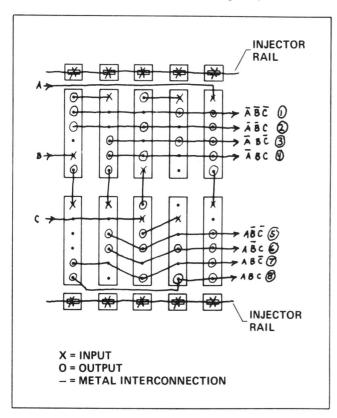

X = INPUT
O = OUTPUT
— = METAL INTERCONNECTION

FIGURE 14: Layout Example:
1-of-8 Decoder on I²L Gate Array

With reference to the flow chart of Figure 12, once the custom collector-diffusion, contact and metal masks are generated, pre-fabricated I²L wafers containing the P-type base diffusion and the gate *fingers* (see Figure 6) are then customized into completed monolithic LSI chips. These chips are then electrically tested, scribed and packaged to form the completed monolithic IC.

Figure 15 shows the photo-micrograph of a complex LSI system, utilizing over 600 gates, fabricated using the XR-800 I²L gate array. Typical development cycle containing all the steps outlined in the flow-chart of Figure 12 takes 12 to 18 weeks, depending on circuit complexity.

Presently, a new computer program is under development which will enable one to do computerized metal routing, to enable one to proceed directly from logic-simulation to artwork generation. It is anticipated that such a system would reduce the over-all development cycle to less than 10 weeks, from the start of logic conversion to the delivery of the monolithic LSI prototype.

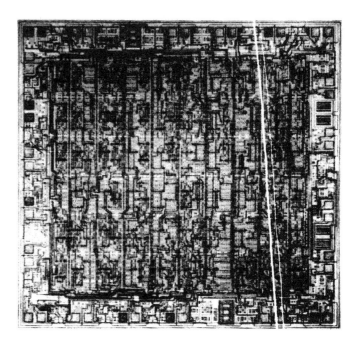

FIGURE 15: Photo-micrograph of a Complex LSI
System Built on XR-800 I²L Gate Array

CONCLUSION

The unique structure and layout characteristics of I²L gates make them ideally suited for semi-custom design using prefabricated gate arrays which can be *customized* by application of custom single or multi-layer interconnection patterns. In most cases, design and layout efficiency can be greatly enhanced by further programming the gate arrays with selected custom diffusion masks, in addition to the basic interconnection patterns. The use of multiple-mask programming and automated layout techniques allow random interconnection of logic cells without impairing the high packing density of I²L gates. Using the design technique LSI systems approaching 1,000 gate complexity can be integrated in monolithic form at a fraction of the development cost and the design turn-around associated with conventional full-custom designs.

11/41

352

Part IX
I²L Memory Techniques

The I²L concept grew out of efforts to improve upon the size of bipolar static memory cells in the late 1960's and early 1970's. Since that time little effort has been applied toward further improvements in I²L-like memory techniques. In this part the early memory cell design efforts of Wiedmann and Berger are reprinted along with a recent paper describing a 4 K-bit static RAM which uses an I²L memory cell and a final paper which introduces a new approach to a static memory cell design.

The now familiar technique of operating a bipolar transistor in its inverse or upward mode was introduced by Wiedmann and Berger in paper IX-1 in which they described a new small-size, low-power bipolar memory cell. This early cell used an upward npn as the switch in a cross-coupled cell with lateral pnp's as loads and a downward npn as an emitter–follower read and write device. However, in this early design, the load pnp's were not merged with the switch npn's but were located in a separately isolated n-type island and merged with the downward npn's. This early design established some of the fundamental concepts which were later to be applied in I²L in general. The performance of the memory cell design was good but the cell size of 14 mils² was very large by modern-day standards.

Paper IX-2 is a follow-up to paper IX-1. Here Berger *et al.* describe modifications to the original memory cell design which result in improved writing speeds and a smaller cell size. The modification places a (parasitic) resistance in series with the collector of the read–write downward npn. Consequently, since the npn is merged with the load pnp, the pnp is automatically turned on harder when the npn saturates. This results in a current redistribution along the (constant voltage) power supply which connects to the emitters of all load pnp's of a given row. Thus the cell is automatically powered-up during the write operation and shorter write times are achieved. It should be noted that the labels (a) and (b) for the write curves of Fig. 4 are reversed. The cell exhibited good read delays, but the 30-ns write delay was considered somewhat long in comparison to typical static bipolar memory cell designs. The new design reduced the cell area to 9 square mils.

In paper IX-3 Wiedmann and Berger introduced a further refinement of their memory cell design. Here they have merged the load pnp's and the switch npn's. This paper appeared almost simultaneously with the introduction of the I²L/MTL concepts at the 1972 ISSCC. The merging of the load pnp into the npn in the memory cell is exactly analogous to the merged pnp injector of the now familiar I²L structure.

The schematic representation of the new cell design is almost unchanged from that of paper IX-1. The difference is that now the bases of the pnp loads are connected to the upward emitters of the switch npn's. The upward and downward npn's now share the same p-type base islands, which also serve as the collectors of the pnp loads. The area of the new cell has been reduced to 4 square mils and the read and write performance are virtually the same as for the original design of paper IX-1.

Bibliography paper [IX-4] describes processing modifications which reduce the down-betas of the emitter-follower npn coupling devices, and consequently a larger effective write current is realized within the cell. The result is a reduced write time. The interested reader is referred to that paper for the details.

All of the above mentioned publications have centered their discussions upon the actual cell operation and none have described a complete memory design using the I²L cell. Paper IX-4 by Kawarada *et al.* presents a complete 4 K-bit memory design, including the addressing and read and write circuits, which incorporates the npn-coupled I²L cell of Berger and Wiedmann. These authors have applied the I²L memory cell technique in a high performance, oxide-isolated bipolar process which results in impressive memory performance. Most notable is the combination of read and write times (on the order of 20 ns) and the total power dissipation of less than 350 mW. The authors describe a new decoding technique which is fast and dissipates very low power. The decoder design contributes substantially to the overall low power dissipation of the complete memory design. The appearance of this complete 4 K-bit memory design with its excellent speed and power performance clearly establishes the I²L memory cell as an important factor in future large high-performance memory designs.

In paper IX-5 Wiedmann introduced his injection-coupled memory cell in which merged lateral pnp's are employed for the read and write operations rather than the downward emitter follower npn's of the earlier designs. The injection coupling resulted in improved write times in comparison to the earlier cell designs. However, the read times of the cell are limited by the transit times of the lateral pnp's, and therefore the design may be restricted from use in very high speed applications.

The authors of paper IX-4 and [IX-4] of the Bibliography have specifically stated their preferences for the npn coupled version of the I²L memory cell because of the trade-offs between speed and cell layout considerations. Nonetheless, the injection-coupled cell has been designed into a commercially available 4 K-bit RAM from Texas Instruments, the 54S400.

Bibliography paper [IX-5] proposed a modification to Wiedmann's design which eliminated one load pnp and one read/write coupling pnp. Consequently, the remaining two pnp's serve simultaneously as load and coupling devices. Although operation of a 4 × 4 array has been demonstrated, no complete large scale memory design has been announced using this modification.

I²L techniques have also been used to build dynamic memories in a bipolar technology. Bibliography papers [IX-6] and [IX-7] describe such 4-K-bit and 16-K-bit designs. The speed performance attained by this approach is not impressive, and, historically speaking, those applications where bipolar technology has been required have also benefitted from a static memory mode of operation. The dynamic I²L memory technique is more in competition with the MOS technologies than with the high performance bipolar memory approaches. Consequently, I do not expect the technique to be vigorously pursued.

A new I²L-like memory cell has been recently introduced by Hewlett in paper IX-6. The author's collector-coupled static RAM cell is analogous to the Berger and Wiedmann npn-coupled I²L cell. However, the new cell uses pnm devices in place of the npn switches and emitter followers of the earlier design. The loads of the cell are formed by npn current sources which are analogous to the pnp loads of the earlier

cell design of Berger and Weidmann. A distinguishing feature of the new cell is that the read/write Schottky collectors cannot operate as emitter followers as in the npn-coupled version. Consequently, the name collector-coupled is used. This new cell design exhibits impressive size as a result of the vertical stacked nature of the load and switch devices. The speed and power performance which could be achieved with this new design were not reported.

Historically, bipolar memory techniques have provided the very high speed memories used in mainframe computer applications. The ability to fabricate very large digital logic systems on a single silicon chip places great economic pressure upon semiconductor technology to increase the storage capacity of such memories without undue loss in speed performance. Yet, simultaneously, power dissipation must be maintained at a level which can be accomodated by inexpensive packaging techniques. The I²L technique holds the potential to provide the means of meeting these ambitious goals.

Small-Size Low-Power Bipolar Memory Cell

SIEGFRIED K. WIEDMANN AND HORST H. BERGER

Abstract—A dc-stable random-access memory cell employing n-p-n and p-n-p transistors has been designed in a concurrent circuit-layout approach. Test chips with 2×3 arrays have been processed in a standard bipolar technology using present manufacturing tolerances. Due to the merging of devices, the area required for a cell is only 14 mil². Furthermore, the cells have been operated at an extremely low dc standby power of less than 0.1 μW/cell. In spite of this low standby power, an array access time of 10 ns has been measured on a simulated 512-bit array in a pulsed power mode.

Manuscript received March 10, 1971.
The authors are with the IBM Laboratories, Boeblingen, Germany.

I. INTRODUCTION

MAIN criteria in appraising monolithic memories are bit density, power dissipation, and performance.

Low power dissipation and high-speed performance have traditionally been incompatible. The superiority of the bipolar transistor technology for high-performance applications is unquestioned, but its potential for storage chips with high bit density and low power dissipation has been doubted in comparison with IGFET technology [1]. This belief is related to the experience that usual bipolar

Reprinted from *IEEE J. Solid-State Circuits*, vol. SC-6, pp. 283–288, Oct. 1971.

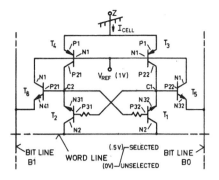

Fig. 1.   Circuit schematic of memory cell.

circuitry needs a relatively large silicon area for the device isolation and for the high ohmic load resistors required particularly for low power consumption. In spite of this problem, some attractive bipolar memories have already been proposed [2]–[8].

In the following, a novel dc-stable bipolar flip-flop memory cell is described that simultaneously solves the problem of both the power dissipation and the storage density on the chip [8]. This is achieved by extensively merging devices in a combined circuit-layout design, which employs lateral p-n-p and inversely operated n-p-n transistors. It will be shown that the p-n-p load devices not only contribute to the small cell size but also enable operation of the cell in the submicrowatt power range. Furthermore, the use of inverse n-p-n transistors substantially simplifies the cell structure. Results obtained from 2 × 3 array chips processed in a conventional bipolar transistor technology fully verify the features of the novel cell, which are

1) extremely low dc standby power;
2) small size;
3) fast access time.

II. Basic Memory-Cell Structure and Operation

A. Cell Circuit

The electrical circuit schematic of the novel memory cell is shown in Fig. 1, as it finally emerged from the combined circuit-layout design. In Fig. 2, the cell arrangement in an array is depicted.

The flip-flop transistors T_1 and T_2 are preferably fabricated as inversely operated common-collector n-p-n transistors. In this case, the usual emitters N_{31} and N_{32} actually work as collectors. As will be shown later, such an approach offers decisive advantages in the layouts of the cell itself and the memory array. The normal n-p-n transistors T_5 and T_6 provide the decoupling from the bit lines $B0$ and $B1$.

Instead of ohmic resistors, p-n-p transistors T_3 and T_4 in common-base configuration have been employed as load devices. This measure is the key for the extremely low dc power achievable, and it also contributes to the small cell size. The low power feature will be ascertained by the following considerations. A flip-flop circuit loses

its bistability when the loop gain drops below unity. Assuming that both flip-flop transistors conduct equal currents at the verge of bistability, and that the transistor output resistance is much larger than its input resistance, the following approximate condition for a loop gain larger than unity is valid

$$\frac{\beta}{1 + r_{e0}/r_c} > 1 \tag{1}$$

where

β small-signal current gain of flip-flop transistors in common-emitter configuration;
r_{e0} differential input resistance;
r_c differential load resistance.

From this equation, the theoretical minimum current of a flip-flop memory cell can be derived by considering mainly the current dependencies of β and r_{e0}.

The differential input resistance r_{e0} may be expressed by

$$r_{e0} \approx (1 + \beta) \cdot \lambda \cdot v_T / I_E \tag{2}$$

where

$\lambda = 1 \cdots 2;$

$v_T = k \cdot T / q = 26$ mV at 300°K;

I_E emitter current.

Two approximations are of special practical interest. In cases where $\beta \gg 1$, it follows from (1) and (2) that

$$I_E > (\lambda \cdot v_T / r_c) = I_{E\,\text{min}} \tag{3}$$

assures stability. Since the minimal cell current $I_{z\,\text{min}} = 2I_{E\,\text{min}}$ (both transistors drawing equal currents), we arrive at

$$I_{z\,\text{min}} \approx \frac{2\lambda \cdot v_T}{r_c} \approx \frac{50\ \mu\text{A}}{r_c / k\Omega}\bigg|_{\lambda=1}. \tag{4}$$

It is the load resistance r_c that determines the theoretical stability limit in this case.[1] Hence, we may call it the r_c-limited case.

However, in the cell circuit of Fig. 1, the p-n-p load transistor represents a much larger load resistance r_c than input resistance r_{e0} of the n-p-n flip-flop transistor. Therefore, (1) is reduced to the simple condition

$$\beta > 1. \tag{5}$$

In this β-limited case, the minimum cell current is determined by that current at which the current gain β_I of the inversely operated transistors T_1 and T_2 has dropped to unity. This is typically at a few nanoamperes. Of course, the current I_{cell} supplied to the cell has to be somewhat larger due to the common-base current gain α (p-n-p) < 1.

---

[1] For noise immunity reasons, the practical minimum cell current has to be approximately 5–10 times larger to assure a sufficient voltage difference between the two collector nodes.

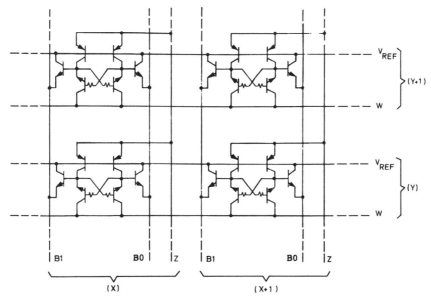

Fig. 2. Word-organized array of memory cells.

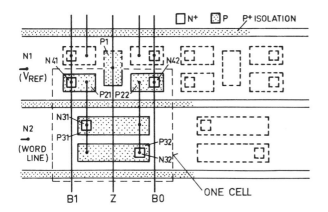

Fig. 3. Principal layout of memory cell (Fig. 1).

B. Principal Layout

The principal layout in Fig. 3 shows how the devices are arranged to achieve a small-size structure. Since the flip-flop transistors T_1 and T_2 in Fig. 1 are inversely operated, a common n bed N_2 can be used for all those transistors of a common word. As this n pocket is, in addition, utilized as a word line, an n$^+$ buried layer is preferably applied to achieve lower series resistances. The n$^+$ layer also enhances the inverse current gain of T_1 and T_2. The diffused p and n regions P_{31} and N_{31} as well as P_{32} and N_{32} of T_1 and T_2, respectively, are cross connected to provide the cross coupling of the flip-flop transistors. The p regions P_{31} and P_{32} have been prolonged so that the metal line Z can cross the devices. The resulting resistance appears in the cross-coupling path of T_1 and T_2 in Fig. 1.

A second n stripe N_1 provides the bases of the lateral p-n-p load transistors of two adjacent word rows. In order to reduce series resistances of the N_1 pockets, additional metal lines running in parallel with the bit lines and interconnecting these N_1 stripes can be inserted (not shown in the layout of Fig. 3). A common emitter P_1 is

used for the collectors P_{21} and P_{22} of two cells. The n-p-n decoupling transistor T_5 can be merged with the N_1 base and the P_{22} collector of the p-n-p load transistor T_3. Accordingly, this applies to transistor T_6. Therefore, only the additional n$^+$-diffused areas N_{42} and N_{41} are necessary to implement these transistors. The n$^+$ emitters are tied to the bit lines $B0$ and $B1$. Thus, in total, the layout yields a truly integrated circuit with no need for double-layer metalization or area-consuming crossunders. Of course, the series resistance of the n-pocket lines have to be considered in the array design, depending on operating conditions.

C. Operation

In the word-organized array of Fig. 2, the power lines Z have been chosen to run parallel to the bit lines. This leads to an optimum layout in single-layer metalization, as has been shown in Fig. 2, but the Z lines can be also laid parallel to the word lines. The currents for all cells of a common Z line are supplied by a common current source, and the voltage V_{ref} for the common-base load transistors has to be chosen equal or larger than the word-line voltage. Adequate current sharing is provided because of the excellent base–emitter voltage tracking of the p-n-p devices, as will be demonstrated later by the experimental results.

When a cell is selected we raise the corresponding word-line voltage so that the bit-line potentials are determined by the potentials of the cell on the selected word line. Then reading is performed by simply sensing the potential difference on the corresponding bit-line pair. Since the bit-line transistors operate as emitter–followers, a multiple of the cell current is available to charge up the bit-line capacitances. This results in a fast READ operation even at relatively low cell currents, which is one of the outstanding features of this novel memory cell.

For writing, the word-line voltage is raised as for a

READ operation and the corresponding bit line is held at a slightly lower potential (typically 100–300 mV below word-line voltage). For example, if T_1 in Fig. 1 is conducting, the bit line $B1$ of transistor T_6 is held on this fixed potential causing T_6 to conduct. Thus, transistor T_1 is switched off via the base of T_6, and T_2 can turn on. The peak current in bit line $B1$ is considerably larger than the current to be pulled off the base of T_1, due to the current gain of T_6. However, the average WRITE current is much smaller than its peak value, since the memory cycle time is much larger than this period of WRITE current flow. Obviously, this current can be reduced by reducing the effective current gain of the bit-line transistor at least at higher currents. Introduction of a collector series resistance to obtain saturation at higher currents is also possible—however, at the expense of some additional cell area. Another measure would be the insertion of special WRITE switch transistors; such devices can be integrated with minor area sacrifice. In any case, the influence of the n-bed series resistances on the WRITE current flow also has to be taken into account.

It should be mentioned that the cell switching time is mainly determined by the time required to charge up the capacitance at node C_1 (Fig. 1) by the p-n-p collector current. As soon as transistor T_2 turns on, the current in bit line $B1$ is switched off.

D. Array Power Modes

The p-n-p transistor load offers additional significant benefits. The current of the p-n-p transistors—and thus the cell current—can be controlled over a few orders of magnitude by small voltage changes across the emitter-base junction. Furthermore, different from ohmic load flip-flops, there is no discharge path through the load for the capacitances of the cross-coupled transistors. This permits complete turnoff of the cell current supply for a certain period of time that depends mainly on the leakage currents. These features can be utilized for various array powering modes.

A straightforward mode is to operate the memory cells at a constant cell current throughout standby and addressing. In this case, the switching speed of the p-n-p transistor has obviously no impact on the memory performance.

Usually, a good tradeoff between power dissipation and performance of a memory system can be achieved by a pulsed power operation of the memory cell. This means that relatively few memory cells of the selected chip are powered up during addressing in order to increase their READ/WRITE speed. In this power mode, it is conceivable not only to boost addressed cells, but also to turn off unselected cells during the address period. Such an operation may offer advantages for some applications, e.g., to simplify the selection scheme.

The choice of a specific power mode heavily depends on the memory system objectives and process technology. Therefore, general guidelines cannot be given.

III. EXPERIMENTS

A. Actual Layout

The actual layout of the cell for a certain technology depends on many parameters: layout rules; desired power/performance range and operation mode of the cell; basic device parameters given by the technology (particularly parasitic effects); and finally parameters such as size, shape and organization of the array, chip size, and peripheral circuits. Hence, based on the principal layout scheme of Fig. 3, many somewhat different layout schemes can be devised, each with its special advantages.

The experimental cell designs have been primarily intended for very low power applications with cell standby currents in the order of 1 μA. A test chip with fully wired 2×3 arrays, single cells, and single devices has been designed to be processed with a conventional technology (no gold doping). Fig. 4 shows the actual layout of this approach; the subcollector areas are not shown in the drawing for the sake of clarity. The cell size is only 13.7 mils^2 in a conventional 6-μ epitaxial layer process with a minimum metal linewidth of 0.4 mil and a minimum spacing of 0.2 mil on mask level. A photomicrograph of a test chip section is depicted in Fig. 5 showing a cell array, where a 2-word $\times$ 3-bit matrix has been wired.

B. Device Measurements

As pointed out in Section II-C, a uniform current sharing of the p-n-p load transistors connected to a common supply is desired for the memory-cell array. There was no suitable chip metalization pattern for measuring this tracking parameter on chip level. As a substitute, the p-n-p load devices from eight randomly picked chips of the same wafer have been analyzed. Although this is a rather pessimistic selection, the total deviation of the individual collector currents at a fixed base–emitter voltage has been less than ± 20 percent in the current range of $I_c = 1 \cdots 100$ μA. This includes the variation between the four collectors of a particular device.

Fig. 6 shows the common-base current gain of the four-collector p-n-p transistor versus the total collector current. With rather conservative emitter–collector distances of approximately 6 μ (9 μ on mask level) an alpha of 0.75 has been obtained in a current range between 1 and 100 μA. This means that 75 percent of the current supplied to the cell reaches the cross-coupled flip-flop transistors, so that only 25 percent of the cell current is not utilized. Because of the large basewidth the cutoff frequency is 3 MHz at 100-μA emitter current. This latter value can be substantially improved by decreasing the basewidth in order to achieve a better performance in a pulsed power operation.

The inverse current gain[2] of the n-p-n flip-flop tran-

---

[2] For comparison, the forward current gain of these devices is about 50 at 100-μA emitter current.

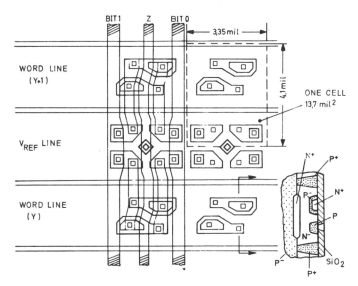

Fig. 4. Actual layout of memory cell.

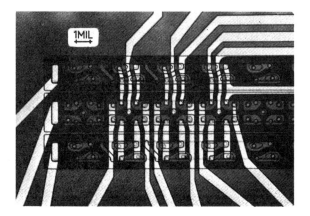

Fig. 5. Chip microphotograph of memory-cell array (2 × 3 cells are wired).

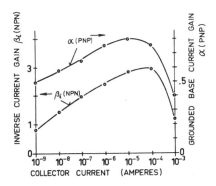

Fig. 6. Grounded-base current gain α_{p-n-p} of four-collector p-n-p transistor and grounded-emitter-current gain β_I of inverse n-p-n transistor.

sistor is also depicted in Fig. 6. It remains well above unity down to currents in the order of 10 nA. Since the current gain α (p-n-p) of the load devices also drops little, the cells retain their information at these extremely small dc currents. This has been verified by measurements: the cells proved to be stable at currents of 10–50 nA, corresponding to a power dissipation of 0.02–0.1 μW. Similar to the dc gain, the cutoff frequency $f_{T \text{ inv}}$ in the

inverse mode is also much smaller than in normal operation ($f_{T \text{ inv}} \approx 15$ MHz at 100 μA). As in the case of the dc gain, this is not essential for the cell operation.

Because of the highly integrated cell structure one has to pay attention to parasitic transistors, especially as no gold doping may be employed. Gold doping would deteriorate both the lateral p-n-p and the inverse n-p-n transistor. If the lateral p-n-p transistor is kept out of deep saturation there is only a very small parasitic current to the p⁺ isolation walls and substrate, which does not harm the cell operation.

The inverse n-p-n transistors require more attention. Fig. 7 depicts a schematic cross section showing the two cross-coupled flip-flop transistors of one cell and the devices of an adjacent cell. Here, transistor T_1 has been assumed conducting. Since it is inversely operated, the p-n junction of the p base and the n epitaxy is heavily forward biased. Hence, the p base can also act as an emitter and inject holes into the n region, where they can be partially collected by the other p regions. The numbers at the arrows in Fig. 7 indicate the measured currents. 20 percent of the total base current I_B has been found to flow into the substrate, mainly via the p⁺ isolation walls (not drawn in the figure). Another 20 percent reaches the base of the other cell transistor T_2, but only 0.2 percent is collected by the p region (base) of a transistor belonging to the adjacent cell.

The effect of the substrate current is a slight reduction of the effective inverse current gain of the flip-flop transistor. The current injected into the base of T_2 has to be taken over by the collector of T_1 via the cross connection, thus requiring a minimum inverse current gain β_1 somewhat larger than unity to assure the cell bistability. Finally, the current injected into an adjacent cell might cause this to switch, if it is operated at a much lower current level (pulsed power operation). To reduce this coupling, e.g., an n⁺ stripe can be laid between the devices to enhance the minority carrier recombination. This has been done in some parts of the cell array layout in Fig. 5. A decrease of the parasitic current by a factor of three has been observed, but even without this measure it is sufficiently small. In total, the parasitic transistors do not impose real problems, but have to be considered in the design.

C. Cell Performance

The measured READ and WRITE delay times have been plotted in Fig. 8 versus the constant cell current I_{cell} (no pulse powering). In these measurements a capacitive bit-line load corresponding to 16 cells has been provided in order to simulate a 16 word × 32 bit array. The READ delay time in Fig. 8 has been defined as the time period between the beginning of the word select pulse and the appearance of a 100-mV differential signal on the bit line pair.

According to Fig. 8, the cell exhibits a good READ performance as expected from the emitter–follower opera-

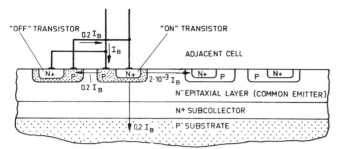

Fig. 7. Schematical structure of inverse n-p-n flip-flop transistors, showing parasitic current flow.

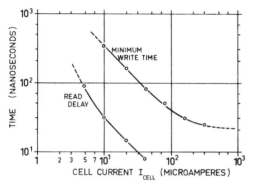

Fig. 8. READ delay and minimum WRITE time versus constant cell current I_{cell}.

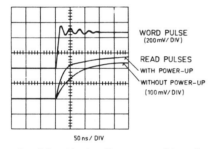

Fig. 9. READ signal for 10-μA cell current with and without powering-up to 250 μA.

tion of the bit line devices. The WRITE delay time, however, is considerably longer. This is not so critical in many applications; on the contrary, it offers the advantage of an excellent cell stability.

At low currents, a powering up of the cell during addressing significantly decreases the delay times. As an example, the oscillogram of Fig. 9 demonstrates how the READ speed is improved by pulsing the cell current from a 10-μA standby current to 250 μA synchronously with the word-line selection pulse. A 100-mV output signal is obtained after 10 ns, as compared to 30 ns without power-up. The WRITE delay time has been reduced from 400 to 80 ns at the same powering conditions.

IV. CONCLUSIONS

The novel dc-stable flip-flop memory cell investigated and described in this paper is characterized by a small-size structure and concurrently by an extremely low power dissipation. The mergence of devices, the replacement of ohmic resistors with active devices, and the uti-

lization of isolation pockets for interconnections have led to the highly integrated cell structure. In particular, inversely operated n-p-n flip-flop transistors and lateral multicollector p-n-p load transistors are employed.

The memory cells have been successfully operated in the submicrowatt power range due to the p-n-p load devices. These load transistors also permit a variety of pulsed power operation modes to provide a wide range of power/performance tradeoffs. Remarkable in this context is the excellent READ performance even at a low cell power.

The feasibility of the novel approach has been fully verified by 2 × 3 array test chips processed in a conventional 6-μ epilayer bipolar process. With conservative dimensions (e.g., 0.4-mil minimum metal linewidth on mask level) the cell needs only 14 mil². At a total standby power of 10 mW, an array access time of 10 ns and a WRITE time of 80 ns has been achieved for a simulated 16 × 32 bit array.

From these characteristics (summarized below) it is concluded that monolithic READ/WRITE memories can be built in *bipolar* transistor technology with much higher density and much smaller power dissipation than expected so far. The memory cell characteristics are as follows.

1) Lateral p-n-p transistors as current–source load devices.

2) Inversely operated common-collector n-p-n transistors.

3) Cell size—14 mil² (6-μ epitaxial, 0.4-mil metal lines).

4) Standby power dissipation < 0.1 μW.

5) Access time 10 ns (array only) and write time 80 ns for 512-bit array and power-up of 0.5 mW per cell.

ACKNOWLEDGMENT

The authors wish to thank the members of the Applied Physics Department at the IBM Laboratories, Boeblingen, Germany, for their excellent support.

REFERENCES

[1] L. L. Vadasz, A. S. Grove, T. A. Rowe, and G. E. Moore, "Silicon-gate technology," *IEEE Spectrum*, vol. 6, Oct. 1969, pp. 28–35.
[2] D. A. Hodges *et al.*, "Low-power bipolar transistor memory cells," *IEEE J. Solid-State Circuits*, vol. SC-4, Oct. 1969, pp. 280–284.
[3] W. Jutzi and C. Schuenemann, "Ein Symmertisches Bistabiles Thyristor Flip-Flop," in *Mikroelektronik*, vol. 3. München-Wien, Germany: Oldenburg, 1969, pp. 277–294.
[4] S. Waaben and H. A. Waggener, "100-ns electronically variable semiconductor memory using two diodes per memory cell," *IEEE J. Solid-State Circuits*, vol. SC-5, Oct. 1970, pp. 192–196.
[5] J. Mar, "Two-terminal transistor memory cell using breakdown," *ISSCC Digest Tech. Papers*, pp. 10–11, 1971.
[6] K. Jannigudin *et al.*, "A switched collector impedance memory," *ISSCC Digest Tech. Papers*, pp. 14–15, 1971.
[7] P. T. Panousis, "A trim memory employing both n-p-n and high-gain unijunction transistors," *ISSCC Digest Tech. Papers*, pp. 16–17, 1971.
[8] S. K. Wiedmann and H. H. Berger, "Small-size low-power bipolar memory cell," *ISSCC Digest Tech. Papers*, pp. 18–19, 1971.

Write-Current Control and Self-Powering in a Low-Power Memory Cell

HORST H. BERGER, ROBERT SCHNADT, AND
SIEGFRIED K. WIEDMANN

Abstract—A modification of a previously published dc-stable all-transistor memory cell is described that reduces the write current required for high speed writing. Moreover, it introduces a self-powering mechanism that improves the writing speed up to a factor of 10 at small cell standby currents in the order of 1 μA. In addition cell area has been reduced by 40 percent to 9 mil² by use of a shallower structure and tightened design rules.

In the October 1971 issue of this JOURNAL a novel bipolar memory cell was described[1] that offers fast access and small size at a submicrowatt power dissipation. It was mentioned in that paper that the introduction of a collector series resistor R_{cs} in the bit-line transistors T_5, T_6 of this cell (Fig. 1) would allow better control of the write current. This is important for high writing speeds ($\lesssim$60 ns) for which the cell is operated at higher current. The collector series resistor then limits the write current as it allows the transistors T_5 or T_6 to saturate.

In the following a realization of the collector series resistor in a modified cell layout is described. Results from measurements verify the write current control and demonstrate an interesting feature of this cell structure, the "self-powering" in an array that improves the writing speed up to a factor of 10. In addition, the shallower structure and tightened layout rules reduced the cell size (9 mil² versus 14 mil² of the original design).[1]

Fig. 2 depicts the new cell layout in its principal structure and microphotographs out of an experimental 4 × 4 array. In contrast to stripe N_2 where a continuous buried n⁺ layer is provided (not shown in figure), stripe N_1 carries only islands of n⁺ buried layer beneath the emitters of the lateral p-n-p transistors. The reference voltage V_{REF} is now supplied via metal lines connected to the N_1 stripes via small n⁺ contact diffusions N_c and running parallel to the other metal lines. As can be seen from the upper part of Fig. 3(a), the relatively high ohmic epitaxial layer now gives rise to the wanted series resistor between N_c and the collector of the bit-line transistor T_6 or T_5. But such a series resistor exists also in the baselead of the lateral p-n-p transistor T_3, T_4. A rough equivalent circuit of the T_4, T_6 (or T_3, T_5) section of the cell valid for the write operation is shown in the inset of the diagram in Fig. 3(b). With the layout Fig. 2 and the vertical dimensions and resistivity depicted in the cross section of Fig. 3(a), the resistor values were measured as

$$R_A \approx 250 \ \Omega, \qquad R_B \approx 180 \ \Omega, \qquad R_C \approx 250 \ \Omega.$$

The diagram Fig. 3(b) shows that the write current, measured as a function of cell current, saturates at about 2 mA. This agrees with the measured resistance values.

Manuscript received September 22, 1972.
The authors are with the IBM Laboratories, Boeblingen, Germany.
[1] S. K. Wiedmann and H. H. Berger, "Small-size low-power bipolar memory cell," *IEEE J. Solid-State Circuits*, vol. SC-6, pp. 283–288, Oct. 1971.

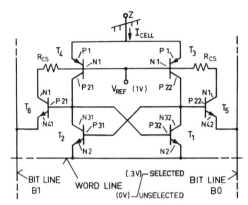

Fig. 1. Introduction of collector series resistors R_{cs} into the all-transistor cell of footnote 1.

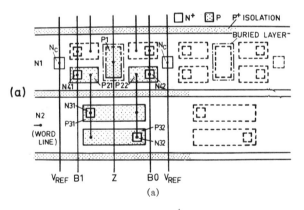

(a)

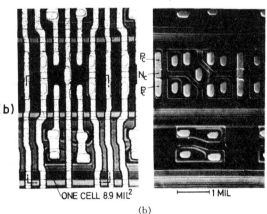

(b)

Fig. 2. (a) Principal layout of the cell with resistors R_{cs} (Fig. 1). (b) Photomicrograph out of a 4 × 4 array of this cell with and without aluminum connections. Regions P_c were introduced to suppress parasitic injection coupling between adjacent cells. Measurements indicated that they are not necessary.

Reprinted from *IEEE J. Solid-State Circuits*, vol. SC-8, pp. 232–233, June 1973.

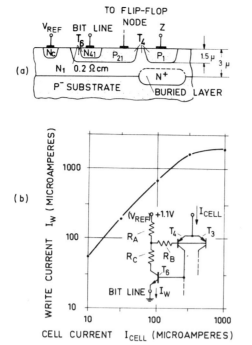

Fig. 3. (a) Schematical cross section of the device region T_4/T_6 having a buried layer only under the emitter region P_1. Thus epitaxial series resistances become effective in the collector of T_6 and in the base of T_4. (b) Equivalent circuit of the region shown in (a) and measured write current versus cell current.

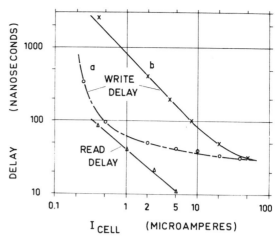

Fig. 4. Read and write delays versus quiescent cell current. Write delay curve (a) for constant current supply and (b) for constant voltage supply.

Fig. 4 shows read and write delays versus cell current. The different write delay curves a and b are due to different power supply conditions.

Curve a is valid for a constant current individually supplied to the cell. However, in a large array with a large number of cells supplied in parallel by a constant current, the power supply for the individual cell being written appears nearly as a constant voltage (current can be withdrawn from other cells). This condition was simulated by a capacitor at Z (Fig. 1). With this capacitor, the much better performance according to curve b was measured. This is due to an internal powering (self-powering) of the cell. It is clear from the inset of Fig. 3(b) that the initial write current I_w will cause a voltage drop at resistor R_A, so that the base potential of T_4, T_3 moves down. This, with constant supply voltage, causes the cell current to increase and so does the write current. Thus an internal feedback mechanism turns on until the saturation of T_6 limits the currents. This explains why with curve b the write speed limit of ≈ 30 ns is reached at much smaller quiescent cell current. In an actual array, the current withdrawal from the other cells is harmless as these would keep their information even under total power off for much longer times than the write time.[1]

The read performance is not noticeably affected by the self-powering because of the much smaller read time period. The read delay was measured as in footnote[1] (100-mV output signal) but with smaller load capacitance (≈ 6 pF) simulating the load of 32 of such smaller cells on a column of 32×32-bit array.

ACKNOWLEDGMENT

The authors wish to thank P. Gansauge, K. Kroell, and F. Seidenschwann for their excellent work in developing the process.

Superintegrated memory shares functions on diffused islands

Device, made by standard process, achieves small size by injecting minority carriers into inversely operated flip-flop transistors, which replace usual resistive load

by Siegfried K. Wiedmann and Horst H. Berger,
IBM World Trade Corp., Boeblingen, West Germany.

☐ A novel bipolar static memory device has almost the packing density of dynamic MOS storage devices. Further, it dissipates little power, and it is economical because it can be made by conventional processing.

Individual cells can be read in less than 10 nanoseconds and written in less than 40 ns. In a 2,000-bit array on a 150-mil square chip, taking into account the additional delay of peripheral circuits, these times would be under 60 ns and 150 ns respectively. The key to the device's small size is a direct injection of minority carriers into inversely operated flip-flop transistors, which are used instead of the conventional resistive load.

The bipolar device, diagramed in Fig. 1, and shown in a photomicrograph in Fig. 2, occupies an area of only about 4 square mils per device, including isolation. Two memory devices appear in the photo, but only one of them is wired. This photo clearly demonstrates the reasons for the extremely small size of this static memory cell; the structure is substantially determined by the size of the contact holes—there are only six and a half holes per cell. Furthermore, the device uses no ohmic load resistors and needs no internal isolation. Isolation is required only between rows in an array, not between devices in a row.

As shown in Fig. 1, a standard n+ buried layer is diffused into the p_ substrate, the n epitaxial layer is deposited, and the p and n regions are diffused into the n layer. Metalization layers connect p_2 to n_2, n_1 to p_3, and p_1, n_3, and n_4 to pads for external connections or to adjacent portions of an integrated circuit. This structure forms a transistor at n_1p_2n and n_2p_3n. There are also lateral grounded-base pnp transistors at p_1np_2 and p_1np_3.

When current is applied to the center p region (p_1), the latter injects holes into the n region. A substantial number of these holes is collected by the adjacent p regions, p_2 and p_3. Because of the symmetrical structure, both p regions collect equal currents, I_p. These currents—unless withdrawn through the metal lines—forward-bias the base-collector junctions p_2n and p_3n, thus turning on the corresponding transistor n_1p_2n or n_2p_3n in its inverse mode.

Device is flip-flop

Once the right-hand transistor is on, it draws the base current I_p away from the p_2 region of the left-hand transistor through the metallic connection to the n^+_2 region, provided that the inverse current gain is greater than 1. Of course, the other state with the left-hand transistor on and the right-hand transistor off is also possible. Thus, the structure is a flip-flop. The outer regions n_3 and n_4 couple the flip-flop to the read-write lines in an array organization. This coupling is discussed later in connection with the equivalent circuit.

The structure's bistability depends on the saturation of the "on" transistor, a condition in which the collector-to-emitter voltage is small enough to keep the other transistor off. As the "on" transistor receives equal cur-

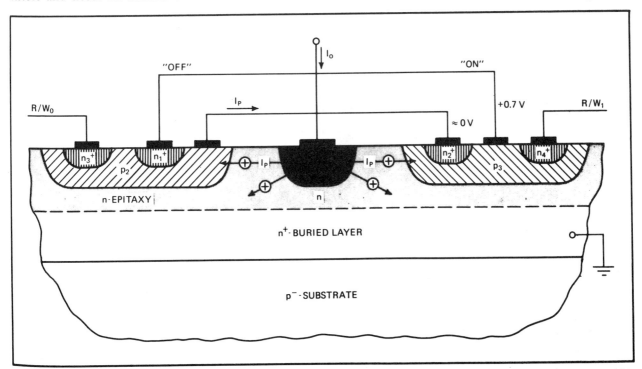

1. Compact memory cell. Standard fabrication techniques are used in the production of this bipolar transistor structure. It stores one bit in only 4 square mils. Key feature is the lateral pnp transistors sharing the region p_1, which serve in lieu of load resistors.

Reprinted with permission from *Electronics*, February 14, 1972, pp. 83-86. Copyright © McGraw-Hill, Inc. 1972. All rights reserved.

rents at its base p_3 (or p_2) and its n^+_2 (n^+_1) region, an inverse current gain larger than unity is sufficient to obtain saturation. The necessary inverse current gain can be attained by conventional processes, since the emitter efficiency depends not only on the doping ratio, but also on the ratio of diffusion length to base width.

Measuring inverse gain

An inverse current gain (β_{inv}) larger than unity is not a very stringent condition. Besides, β_{inv} decreases only slowly as I_o decreases, assuring bistability even with extremely low currents. Its value at various current levels was determined experimentally on devices with special metalization patterns that permitted the component currents to be measured separately; these patterns disrupt the flip-flop cross connections. The current I_p received at the base of one inverse npn transistor (region p_2 in Fig. 1), when divided by half of the supply current

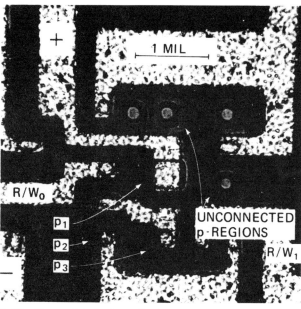

2. Why it's small. In the two cells shown here, the contact holes are the limiting factor in small size. Also no external isolation is needed.

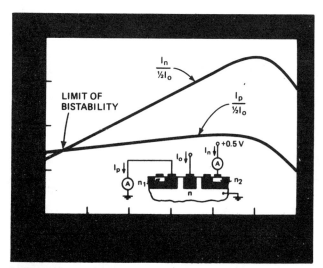

3. Bistability conditions. As long as the I_n curve lies above the I_p curve, the compact memory cell is bistable, even at very low current levels. Ordinarily it would operate in the microampere range.

I_o, indicates the grounded-base current gain α_{pnp} of the lateral pnp transistor.

This gain is nearly constant for values of I_o up to about 10 microamperes and decreases for larger currents. Likewise, the collector current I_n of the other inverse npn transistor (region n^+_2), also divided by half of the device supply current, represents the product of the pnp transistor's alpha and the npn transistor's inverse beta; it rises to a substantial peak at about 100 μA.

The ratio of these two quantities is the inverse current gain:

$$\beta_{inv} = (\alpha_{pnp}\beta_{npn})/(\text{pnp current gain}) = I_n/I_p$$

Bistability is assured as long as this ratio is greater than 1—that is, as long as the I_n-curve in Fig. 3 runs above the I_p-curve.

The plot in Fig. 3 shows that bistability is maintained down to a cell current of about 3 nanoamperes, corresponding to a power dissipation of about 3 nanowatts. In tests, the memory device has been safely operated with a supply current of as little as 10 nA.

This low current level was tried on test devices made by a process not optimized for this purpose. These devices had an inverse current gain of approximately 2; a larger gain is possible with a proper adjustment of the process, thus probably shifting the bistability limit even into the picoampere range.

Equivalent circuit

An equivalent circuit for the superintegrated memory device, shown in Fig. 4, resembles that of a low-power small memory cell described at the 1971 International Solid State Circuits Conference in Philadelphia.[2] It is distinguished from these earlier circuits only by an additional short-circuit connection indicated by a heavy

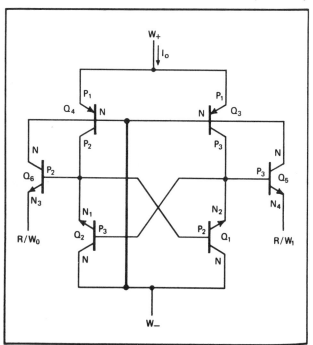

4. Equivalent circuit. Labels correlate this circuit to the structure in Fig. 1. Its distinguishing features are the pnp transistors as current sources and the sharing of single diffusions as regions of different transistors. The short circuit between the current-source bases and the W_- reference point is an important feature of this design.

Electronics/February 14, 1972

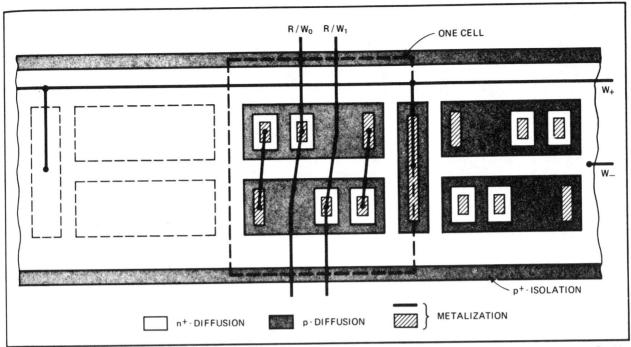

5. Word-organized array. A single n-stripe embeds all cells in a common word-line pair. Pairs of cells share a single p-type emitter. Double-rail read-out lines lie perpendicular to the common n-stripe, interconnecting cells in adjacent n stripes.

line in Fig. 4, between the common n-base of pnp load transistors Q_3 and Q_4 and the common n-collector region of the inversely operated npn flip-flop transistors Q_1 and Q_2. This connection corresponds to the use of a common n-layer to accommodate all the elements of the superintegrated memory device. The device can also be derived formally by superintegrating a double silicon-controlled rectifier cell,[3] but it is not operated in SCR mode.

The labeling of the p and n zones of the six transistors in the equivalent circuit shows how these elements correspond to the p and n regions in the principal structure of Fig. 1. Thus the emitter p_1 is common to both pnp load transistors Q_3 and Q_4, while the collector p_3 of pnp transistor Q_3 is physically identical with the bases of the inverse transistor Q_2 and of the decoupling transistor Q_5. Likewise, the p region p_2 serves for the transistors Q_4, Q_1, and Q_6 respectively. This extensive merging of separate transistors saves interconnection lines and contact holes, which contributes significantly to the small size attained.

This structure can be laid out in a word-organized array, as shown in Fig. 5. In this layout, all the memory cells belonging to a common word line pair (W_+ and W_-) are embedded in a common isolated n-stripe. The cell structure is essentially the same as shown by the principal structure in Fig. 1, except that a single p_1 emitter serves two memory cells.

The W_- line is simply the common n-stripe between the isolation walls, whereas the W_+ line is a metal strip deposited in a second metalization step; it connects all p emitters of one word. If the series resistance of the W_- line is too high, another metal line can be added parallel to it. The read-write transistors are connected to a read-write metal line pair R/W_0 and R/W_1, perpendicular to the n-stripes.

With contact holes 0.1 mil wide, this layout requires

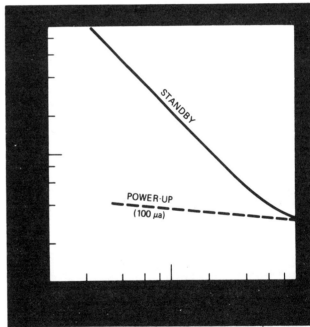

6. Faster writing. Although the compact memory cells' writing time is short, it can be reduced even more without significantly increasing power dissipation by increasing current just before writing.

only about 4 square mils per bit of storage, so that 2,000 bits should fit on a chip about 150 mils square. An oxide isolation would further cut down the size by a factor of about two, permitting 4,000 bits per chip.[4]

Reading and writing

To read a word from this array, the W_+ line serving all devices in a word row is raised by about 0.5 volt. This raises the potential of one line in each read-write line pair—the line that is connected to the "off" side of the corresponding device on the selected word line.

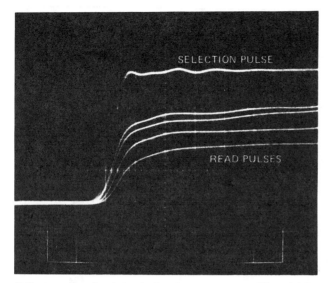

7. Fast reading. Read signals (four lower traces) are differential signals that show less than 10 ns delay even at supply currents as low as 3 microamperes. The four traces are for 100, 30, 10 and 3 µA respectively; the top trace is the 0.4-V selection pulse. Scales are 0.1 V per vertical division and 10 ns per horizontal division.

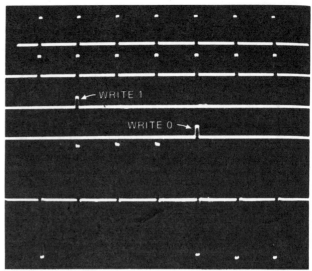

8. Data retention. Memory cell can retain information for quite a long time after current is shut off—here 700 µs. From top, traces are 0.5-V selection pulses, 100 µA power pulses, write 1 and write 0 signals, and read signals of about 0.3 V. Positive pulses on read line are 1s, negative pulses are 0s. Time scale is 500 µs per division.

Thus, the sign of the potential difference on each read-write line pair denotes the information stored in the corresponding cell of that row.

To write a bit in a cell—that is, to change the state of the device—the proper read-write line is held down. This draws away the base current of the corresponding transistor in the flip-flop, if it happens to be on, thus switching it off. The potential of the other flip-flop node then increases as the current of the pnp transistor is no longer diverted from this point, and the other transistor turns on. The length of time for this charging action determines the minimum write time; it is, of course, longer for smaller device currents, as shown in Fig. 6.

In the low-current range of the device, where the node capacitances are substantially current-independent, the product of device supply current I_o and the minimum writing time is approximately constant. The graph shows, for example, that the write time for a stand-by current of 20 µA is about 100 ns. Although this time is not unreasonably long, it can be considerably reduced by momentarily increasing the supply current from its standby level.

Bilevel operation is easy

For example, increasing I_o to 100 µA simultaneously with writing reduces the write time from 100 ns to about 40 ns— as compared to a write time of about 30 ns for a steady supply current of 100 µA, which would increase considerably the circuit's power dissipation. Such a bilevel operation is easy with this device, because the emitter-base junction of the pnp transistor provides a very low external impedance.

As the emitter-follower configuration of the read-write transistors suggests, reading is extremely fast (see Fig. 7). In addition, speed is enhanced because the base-collector junction of this transistor is forward biased in standby, so that the transistor that delivers the read current is already on before the word selection pulse arrives. The oscillograms in Fig. 7 were taken with a simu-

lated read-line load corresponding to an array of 2,000 to 4,000 bits.

Overcoming drawbacks

In the superintegrated structure, parasitic transistors are present, and their influence must be considered in the operation of an array. For example, in Fig. 5, a parasitic transistor is formed where the underlying n-stripe lies between P_2 and P_3. The effects are essentially the same as in the low-power small memory cell, described last year at ISSCC. These parasitic effects are not serious, since they can be kept under control by proper design.

But inverse transistor action of the read transistors can be troublesome. In an actual array, the read transistors of non-addressed memory cells draw an inverse current from the read-write line if they are on. This parasitic current decreases the net sense current from the addressed cell.

However, this decrease does not present a severe problem, because of the option to power up the addressed cell during the read or write operation. In fact, the non-selected cells can be switched off during a read operation, because the device can retain the stored information in its internal capacitances.

The oscillogram in Fig. 8 demonstrates this data retention capability. After each write or read operation, the supply current has been completely turned off for about 700 microseconds without destroying the information. Even much longer retention times of about 10 milliseconds have been measured—a much longer time than would be needed in any practical application. □

REFERENCES
1. S.K. Wiedmann and H.H. Berger, "Superintegrated Bipolar Memory Device for High-density, Low-power Storage," Proceedings, IEEE Electron Devices Meeting, 1971.
2. S.K. Wiedmann and H.H. Berger, "Small Size Low-Power Bipolar Memory Cell," International Solid State Circuits Conference, IEEE Journal of Solid State Circuits, Oct. 1971, p. 283.
3. W. Jutzi and C. Schuenemann, "Ein Symmetrisches Bistabiles Thyristor Flip-flop," Mikroelektronik, vol. 3, 1969, p. 277.
4. Doug Peltzer and Bill Herndon, "Isolation method shrinks bipolar cells for fast, dense memory," Electronics, March 1, 1971, p. 52.

A 4K-bit Static I²L Memory

KUNIYASU KAWARADA, MASAO SUZUKI, TOSHIO HAYASHI, KAZUHIRO TOYADA, AND CHIKAI OHNO

Abstract—A 4096-bit ECL random-access memory using high-density I²L memory cell has been developed. Novel ECL circuit techniques and I²L flip-flop memory cells are introduced for realizing high-speed performance, low-power operation, and small chip size. It operates typically under 20-ns access time and 300 mW of power dissipation, realizing 1.46 pJ/bit of access time and power-per-bit product, a figure of merit of memory devices. The memory cell and chip size of 1122 μm^2 (33 μm × 34 μm) and 9.9 mm^2 (3 mm × 3.3 mm), respectively, are achieved with V-groove isolated bipolar process technology. The memory is organized into 4096 words × 1 bit, and is packaged into 18-pin DIP and also 18-pad leadless chip carrier package.

Development results have shown that the n-p̄-n-coupled superintegrated I²L flip-flop memory cell is very promising for high-speed and low-power static RAM's above 4K-bit/chip area.

I. INTRODUCTION

CAPACITY and operating speed of semiconductor memories have been greatly progressed with steadily improving process technology. 7.5-ns [1] access time and 64K-bit/chip [2] in capacity have been achieved with bipolar and MOS technologies, respectively.

Large-scale integration was enabled mainly by reduction of device size and operation energy of circuit elements.

However, since an improvement of speed performances is generally inconsistent with a requirement of power reduction, it is a challenge to realize a memory that satisfies simultaneously three important features of memory devices, i.e., 1) high-speed, 2) low power, and 3) large capacity. Recent developments of static RAM in 4K-bit region attempt to realize such characteristic-balanced memories. High-performance 4K static RAM's using HMOS [3], CMOS [4], and bipolar [5]–[7] technologies have been reported in these two years. Besides these devices, I²L memories have been anticipated because of their high speed, high density, and low-power capabilities. Although the first proposal of I²L memory cell was on the static (flip-flop) cell, a dynamic memory cell of injection principle was adopted in the first I²L memory developed for commercial application performing 4K-bit and recently 16K-bit integration per chip [8], [9]. As for the static I²L memories, 1K-bit chip for checking feasibility has been reported [10], and an anouncement of 4K-bit chip had been made without a detailed description of device structure, circuit configuration, or characteristics.

The authors observed that the static I²L memory would be a promising device for buffer memory, for writable control storage, and even for main frame memory of small/middle-

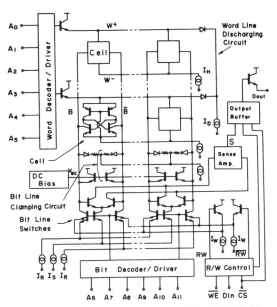

Fig. 1. Main circuit block diagram of 4K × 1 RAM chip.

scale computer systems. The first target of development was set to realize a 4K-bit static RAM which operates under 30-ns access time and 350-mW power dissipation.

The characteristics of experimental devices are as follows: 1) address access time (t_{ACC}): 20 ns (typ.); 2) total power dissipation: 300 mW/chip (typ.); 3) write pulsewidth (t_{WW}): 22 ns (typ.); 4) chip size: 9.9 mm^2 (3.0 mm × 3.3 mm); and 5) cell size: 1122 μm^2 (33 μm × 34 μm).

These were performed by a combination of novel ECL circuit techniques applied outside the memory cell array matrix especially in address decoder circuits, superintegrated Wiedmann–Berger type I²L memory cell and the high-speed bipolar process technologies including a passive isolation with V-groove and a shallow diffusion process with doped polysilicon.

The results have shown its propriety as a high-performance static memory and also a potential of expansion to 16K-bit static RAM.

II. CIRCUIT DESIGN

A. General Description

In order to obtain a high-speed access maintaining low-power and high-density capabilities, the complete ECL circuit systems and I²L memory cell array matrix were combined. The main circuit block diagram organized as 4096 words by 1 bit is represented in Fig. 1. A memory cell is selected by raising one of the upper word lines (W^+) through the word decoder and

Manuscript received September 28, 1978; revised December 8, 1978.

K. Kawarada, M. Suzuki, and T. Hayashi are with the Musashino Electrical Communication Laboratory, Nippon Telegraph and Telephone Public Corporation, Musashino-shi, Tokyo 180, Japan.

K. Toyada and C. Ohno are with Fujitsu Limited, Kawasaki, Japan.

Reprinted from *IEEE Trans. Electron Devices*, vol. ED-26, pp. 886–892, June 1979.

TABLE I
POWER DISTRIBUTION IN THE MAIN CIRCUIT BLOCKS

Circuits	Power (mW)	Percentage (%)
Word Selection Ckt.	105.0	34.7
Bit Selection Ckt.	39.8	13.2
Memory Cell Array	41.8	13.8
Read Write Control Ckt.	61.9	20.5
Sense Amp. Ckt.	21.8	7.2
Reference Voltage Source etc.	32.2	10.6
Total	302.5	100.0

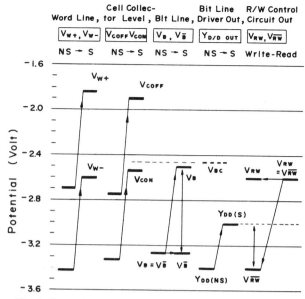

Fig. 2. Potential level diagram of the internal circuit nodes.

the driver circuit, and by switching the bit-line switches so as to cause the read/write current to flow out from the selected cell. Since the n-p-n-coupled cell has a threshold characteristics in altering the stored data, the write current greater than the write threshold value (I_{wth}) is required in write operation mode. In the read mode, the data are read at the read current (I_R) which is smaller than I_{wth}. Therefore, two pairs of current source for I_R and I_w are independently provided.

Potential difference of selected bit-line pair is detected by the emitter coupled transistor pair consisting a differential presense amplifier and is transfered to common-sense amplifier and output buffer. The bit-line clamping circuit operates so as to prevent the released bit lines from floating and not so as to go up to the ground potential by sinking a small current through the clamping transistor pair. By this circuit, the potential of nonselected bit lines are clamped at the low level decided by the bit-line clamping dc bias (V_{BC}), resulting in fast cycle time in bit-line accessing mode. Moreover, the clamping transistor acts as the write current supplier taking the cell transistors place just after the memory data are changed until the write-enable pulse is removed.

The word-line discharging circuit decreases the word-line fall time. It is to be noticed that by using a base–collector diode in this discharging circuit, discharging speed can be improved because the time period in which the discharging circuit effectively operates is increased by using the slow-recovery C–B diodes. In case of the base–emitter diode, the effective discharging period is only from the beginning of the fall of word-line potential to the cross point of rising and falling potential curves, and after that, the fall time will be slowed. By using this discharging circuit, the cycle time in the word-access mode can be improved.

Besides these circuit considerations, the decoder circuit system was also greatly improved as described in the later section. Although the principle of decoding circuit is similar to the one adopted in the ultra-high-speed 7.5-ns ECL-1K-RAM which the authors had developed and reported [2], the total power was made considerably smaller than in the 1K-bit device.

Table I shows the power distribution in the main circuit blocks, in which the total power dissipation was designed to be about 300 mW. The power in decoding system is about 145 mW which is 48 percent of the total power. Memory-cell

array matrix consumes only 42 mW (14 percent) as the result of introducing an I²L memory cell with low-power standby characteristics.

Fig. 2 is the potential level diagram of the important circuit nodes in the memory. As shown from Fig. 2, the selected word-line level is about -1.8 V, and the voltage swing is about 900 mV. Bit-line clamping bias V_{BC} is set to about -2.5 V, resulting in the -3.3-V clamped level. The voltage swing of the bit decoder/driver is 400 mV, and the selected level is -3.0 V. The read/write control circuit generates -2.6 and -3.4 V on its outputs depending on write data in the write mode, and -2.6 V in the read mode.

B. Memory Cell

The superintegrated all-transistor memory cells using an injection principle have been proposed by Wiedmann and Berger [10], [11]. As is well known, these I²L memory cells have the very attractive feature that they make very compact cells in contrast with the conventional bipolar memory cells using resistors for the load impedance of the flip-flop transistors. Besides, since the flip-flop can operate over a wide current range owing to the behavior of p-n-p load transistors as the current source, it is possible to hold the data in the very-low-current region. Fig. 3 shows an example of memory holding capability of the I²L memory cell. I_i, I_{BR}, and I_{BL} represent the injection current, bit-line current of right- and left-hand side, respectively, flowing into the I²L unit cell of n-p-n-coupled type as shown in Fig. 3(b). As far as the cell operates as a flip-flop, current unbalance occurs between two bit lines. In this case, I_{BR} is several orders greater than I_{BL} which corresponds to the reverse saturation current of the p-n junction. The difference of bit-line current becomes small with the decrease of injector current and voltage applied to the cell (injector voltage, V_i). Above the 0.5-V region of V_i, the internal state of the cell can be alterable, whereas the cell is fixed to its proper state below 0.5 V of V_i. The critical injecter current is as small as 6 nA, which corresponds

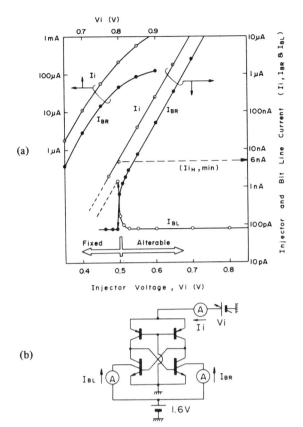

Fig. 3. Memory holding characteristics. (a) Experimental results in n-p-n-coupled I^2L unit cell. (b) Measurement circuit.

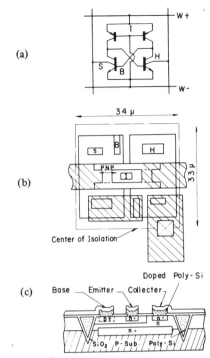

Fig. 4. Concepts of I^2L memory cell. (a) Simplified circuit expression. (b) Cell pattern layout. (c) Vertical structure of typical n-p-n transistor.

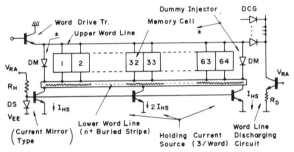

Fig. 5. Cell array structure in the word direction.

to the minimum holding current (I_{iH}, min) of alterable data. If one tries to obtain this small holding current characteristic using a conventional memory cell with resistance load, a very high resistance of the order of 50 MΩ will be required without enlarging the cell area. But, it is very difficult to make such a high-resistance load into a reasonable size, comparable to the merged p-n-p-transistor load of I^2L memory cell.

Here, it must be mentioned that there are two types of I^2L-memory cell depending on types of coupling transistor with bit lines, and that the n-p-n-coupled type has been adopted in this 4K RAM rather than the p-n-p-coupled type because it has a good compatibility with the peripheral read/write ECL circuit. Since n-p-n coupling transistors operate in normal direction, while the n-p-n flip-flop transistors operate in an inverse mode, enough read current and high reading speed can be obtained. However, the rewriting speed is slower than that of the p-n-p-coupled type. The authors selected the cell type by considering the tradeoffs between reading and rewriting speed, cell size, and simplicity of cell structure.

An electrical structure and an unique symmetric pattern layout of memory cell are shown in Fig. 4(a) and (b), respectively. Injector (I) of p-n-p emitter is located in the center and is connected to the upper word line (W^+) of the first metal layer. The n⁺ buried layer is used for the lower word line (W^-).

Since the cell circuit of Fig. 4(a) is expressed in I^2L-type circuit, it is drawn as if the cell were connected to the bit line by one of the collectors of the multicollector flip-flop tran-

sistor. However, this collector actually operates as the emitter in a normal n-p-n-transistor mode performing fast read/write operations. A very small cell size, as small as 1122 μm^2 (33 μm × 34 μm) is achieved. Fig. 4(c) shows a vertical structure of the typical circuit transistor using V-groove isolation which is also applied in the memory cell.

C. Cell-Array Construction

Besides the memory cell itself, the total area of cell array can also be reduced by using the structural property of I^2L. That is, since the emitters of I^2L flip-flop transistors, which must be connected to the lower word line, are composed of n⁺ buried stripe for the lower word line without using a metal line. By using this structure, considerable area for metal wiring and contact hole to n⁺ layer can be saved. However, the series resistance of n⁺ buried stripe causes a nonuniformity in injector current resulting in cell-position dependency of holding and write-threshold characteristics. In this device, holding current sources were distributed into three locations as shown in Fig. 5. It is also to be noticed that the current mirror-type circuit without emitter resistance for current

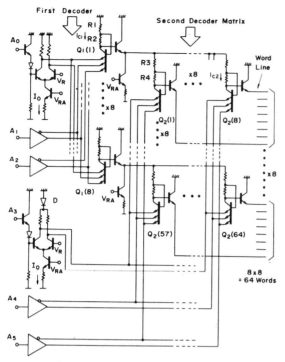

Fig. 6. New decoding circuit system.

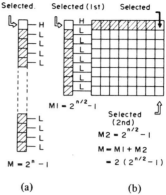

Fig. 7. Figure for comparison of two decoding circuit systems concerning on-power dissipation. (a) Original decoding circuit. (b) New decoding circuit system.

limiting is used in order to solve the problem of reduced margin for memory holding characteristics. This was caused by lowered standby level of the lower word-line potential as low as −3.4 V (see Fig. 2), owing to the matrix-type decoder system.

Although the cell can hold data with very small current, as low as an order of 10 nA, the average holding current was set to be about 1.7 μA/cell considering the speed performances and operating margins.

Two diodes provided to both ends of the word line are dummy injectors. Without these dummy injectors, the write threshold current in the cells located at the end of the word line increases. With dummy injectors, it is possible to suppress the increase of the write threshold current by effectively equalizing the writing characteristics of the end cells to those of the internal cells in the same word line.

D. New Decoder Circuit

In order to reduce the total power dissipation, it is necessary to reduce the power in the address decoding system as well as in the cell-array matrix.

A new decoding system with greatly improved speed and power product will be described in this section. High-performance decoder has been already proposed and adopted in the high-speed 1K-bit RAM which the authors had developed. It has achieved, for example, 2.5 ns of decoding speed and 152 mW of total decoder power in a five-address decoding system. The speed–power product per gate in this decoder system is 10.3 pJ/gate. A new decoder circuit represented in Fig. 6 was developed on the basis of above decoder circuit. The figure shows the word decoding system to select one out of 64 word lines. Six address inputs are divided into two groups (A_0–A_2 and A_3–A_5). The first address group is de-

coded by the "first decoder" in the ordinary way of the original decoder. Decoded signals are transferred into the second decoder matrix which contains 8 × 8 multiemitter decoding transistors. The complement outputs of the second address group generated by the address buffers and current switches are connected to the emitters of the multiemitter transistors in the second decoder matrix. Only one out of eight horizontal lines driven by the emitter follower transistors in the first decoder circuit is raised to the high level. On the other hand, only one out of eight groups containing eight multiemitter transistors vertically arranged is selected in the second decoder matrix. Then, only one multiemitter transistor where both select conditions of the first and the second decoder circuit are satisfied is selected generating about −1.8 V ($2V_{BE}$) for the word-line potential level. The new decoding system has a performance of 4.8 ns of decoding speed, 105 mW of total power, and 7.2 pJ/gate of speed–power product per gate as an example of 1 out of 64-words decoder system. Although the decoding delay is somewhat increased, considerable reduction of power was achieved in spite of the increased decoder scale. The reason of improved power efficiency will be explained as follows.

In the original decoder system without the second decoder matrix, the total current of decoder system (I_{D1}), except current in level shift circuits of address inputs, is given by the following expression:

$$I_{D1} = I_C (2^n - 1) \tag{1}$$

where I_C is a collector current required for logic swing of the multiemitter decoder output and n is a number of address inputs.

While in the new decoder system, the total current (I_{D2}) is given as

$$I_{D2} = (I_{C1} + I_{C2}) \cdot (2^{n/2} - 1) \tag{2}$$

where I_{C1}, I_{C2} are collector currents of the multiemitter decoder of the first and the second decoder, respectively.

Equations (1) and (2) are explained as follows using Fig. 7. In the figure, a unit box means a multiemitter decoding transistor. The hatched box means on-state transistor while the white one means off-state.

In the original decoding system, the collector current must

flow in collector circuits of all transistors except one to be selected in order to generate the low level for nonselected word lines. The number of on-state decoding transistors (M) is given by ($2^n - 1$).

In the new decoding system, the number of on-state transistors in the first decoder ($M1$) is given by ($2^{n/2} - 1$). Since these on-state transistors generate low-level lines, the transistors the collector circuits of which are connected to these low-level lines are all cut off in the second decoder matrix. Therefore, the number of on-transistors in the second decoder matrix ($M2$) is also given by ($2^{n/2} - 1$) as shown in Fig. 7(b).

A somewhat rough assumption that I_C, I_{C1}, and I_{C2} are the same value reduces the ratio of I_{D1} to I_{D2} into the following equation:

$$I_{D2}/I_{D1} = 2/(2^{n/2} + 1). \qquad (3)$$

In case of $n = 6$, the current ratio is 0.22. It means that the new decoding system can reduce the total decoding power by an amount of 78 percent as compared with the original decoding system. Besides, since the current ratio of (3) becomes smaller with an increase of n, it may be said that the new decoding system is effective in large-scale memories.

A similar decoding circuit is used in a bit-decorder system wherein the logic level is shifted by the amount of V_{BE} on an average. Since the required voltage swing to drive the bit-line switches is less than one for word-line driving, the total decoder power is reduced to about 39.8 mW which is 62 percent smaller than the word decoder power.

III. FABRICATION PROCESSES

In order to obtain high-speed characteristics and to integrate a large number of elements into the small chip area, a passive isolation process with V-groove (IOP: *I*solation by *O*xide and *P*olysilicon), a shallow emitter diffusion process with doped polysilicon (DOPOS: *D*oped *Po*ly*s*ilicon) [13], and a fine Al-wiring process with 7-μm pitch were used in this device. The structural concepts are given in Fig. 4(c). Fig. 8 is a microphotograph of the chip. By using the above technologies and the superintegrated I^2L memory cell array, the chip size was reduced to 9.9 mm² which is probably the smallest chip in 4K static RAM's previously reported. Microphotographs of the cell array are shown in Fig. 9(a) and (b), corresponding to the two-level metallization and without metallization, respectively. In Fig. 9(a), the upper word line is seen as the horizontal first-layer metallized stripe and the bit-line pair is seen as the vertical second-layer metallized stripes.

The memory chip which is called ECL-1544 was mounted into the conventional 18-pin dual-in-line package and also small, leadless 18-pad chip-carrier package. The chip-carrier-type device was aimed to mount on the mother board on which 8 chip carries can be mounted. Fig. 10 shows two types of packaged memory. One mother board which has 40 pins and contains 8 memory chips operates as the 4K-byte memory unit with a capability of high-density packing for the memory system. The size of the chip-carrier and the mother board

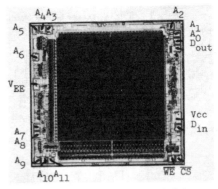

Fig. 8. Microphotograph of chip. Chip size is 3.0 mm × 3.3 mm.

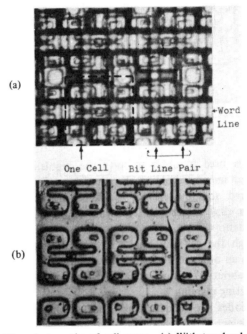

Fig. 9. Microphotographs of cell array. (a) With two-level metallization. (b) After metallization is removed.

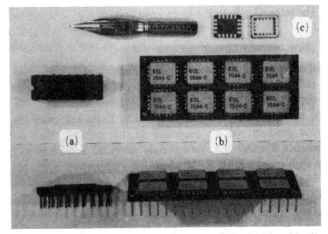

Fig. 10. Package outlines. (a) Standard 18-pin DIP. (b) 18-pad leadless chip carriers on ceramic mother board. 4K-byte memory unit. (c) Chip carrier package.

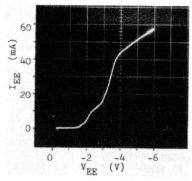

Fig. 11. I_{EE} versus V_{EE} characteristics on curve tracer.

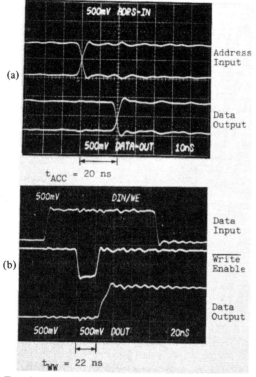

Fig. 12. Transient waveforms of read/write operation. (a) Read mode. $t_{ACC} = 20$ ns. (b) Write mode at minimum write pulsewidth. $t_{WW} = 22$ ns.

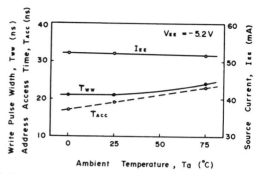

Fig. 13. Temperature dependency of source current, access time, and minimum write pulsewidth.

TABLE II
ESTIMATED DELAY-TIME DISTRIBUTION IN WORD ACCESSED READ MODE

Circuit Blocks	Signal Path	Delay Time
Word Decoder/Driver	Add → W+	4.8 ns
Memory Cell	W+ → B,B̄	5.9 ns
Pre-Sense Amp.	B,B̄ → S	2.6 ns
Output Buffer	S → Dout	2.4 ns
Total (Access Time)	Add → Dout	15.7 ns

The temperature dependencies of source current and the read and write speeds are shown in Fig. 13. By designing fully temperature-compensated circuits, the source current is made to be almost constant over the temperature range from 0°C to 75°C. Access time increases linearly from 17 to 23 ns over the above temperature range. And, the write-enable pulsewidth required for writing also increases from 22 to 26 ns.

Table II shows the estimated delay-time distribution of access time. Delay in memory cell amounts to 38 percent of access time and delay in decoder/driver is about 31 percent in this device.

In evaluating the total performance of this device, an access-time and power-per-bit product figure of merit of 1.46 pJ/bit has been achieved. This value means that it was improved by about four times comparing with 6.09 pJ/bit in the 7.5-ns-832-mW-1K-bit RAM of the authors' previous work.

V. SUMMARY

The design and characteristics of a 4K-bit I²L static RAM have been described. It has been shown that a combination of n-p-n-coupled, superintegrated I²L memory-cell array and the high-speed ECL circuits is one of the superior approaches for realizing high-speed, low-power, and also large-capacity memories. Besides the small-chip and memory-cell size, the low-power operation achieved in this device suggests a potential of a 16K-bit static RAM which achieves 30-ns access, 500-mW power within a 4.8-mm² chip. It will be possible to use the device developed in this work for various applications such as

are 7.13 mm × 8.75 mm and 50.8 mm × 20.0 mm, respectively. The leads of the mother board are formed in the same pitch as the standard DIP. This high-packing structure was made possible by a decreased power of the device.

IV. DEVICE CHARACTERISTICS

In this section the characteristics of the device are described. First, the low-power operation is shown in Fig. 11 which is an I_{EE}-V_{EE} characteristic. The source current is about 53 mA at −5.2 V of source voltage, a little less power (276 mW) than the design target as shown in Table I. Fig. 12(a) and (b) shows the waveforms in read and write operations, respectively.

It is seen that the device operates typically with 20 ns of address access time and that the data can be rewritten with a write pulse wider than 22 ns. The read and write currents are designed to be 0.2 and 3 mA, respectively.

large buffer memory systems, writable control storages, and also main memory systems of small/medium scale computers. Finally, the device characteristics and the features are summarized as follows:

memory organization:	4096 words by 1 bit
input/output interfaces:	ECL compatible
chip size:	9.9 mm^2 (3.0 mm $\times$ 3.3 mm)
memory cell size:	1122 μm^2 (33 μm $\times$ 34 μm)
cell type:	n-p-n coupled, I^{2}L flip-flop
access time:	20 ns (typ.)
write pulsewidth:	22 ns (typ.)
operating power:	300 mW (typ.)
figure of merit:	1.46 pJ/bit (typ.)
package:	18-pin DIP and 18-pad chip carrier on mother board.

ACKNOWLEDGMENT

The authors wish to thank M. Watanabe, H. Mukai, T. Sudo, and K. Kataoka of N.T.T. and also J. Mogi, Y. Kondo, and S. Asuma of Fujitsu Ltd. for their helpful discussions and encouragements.

REFERENCES

[1] A. Yoshimura, M. Hirai, T. Asaoka, and H. Toyoda, "A 64Kbit MOS RAM," in *ISSCC Dig. Tech. Papers*, pp. 148–149, Feb. 1978.

[2] K. Kawarada, M. Suzuki, H. Mukai, K. Toyoda, and Y. Kondo, "A fast 7.5ns access 1K-bit RAM for cache-memory systems," in *IEEE J. Solid-State Circuits*, vol. SC-10, pp. 206–211, 1975.

[3] R. Pashley, W. Owen, K. Kokkonen, R. Jecmen, A. Ebel, N. Ahlguist, and P. Schoen, "A high performance 4K static RAM fabricated with an advanced MOS technology," in *ISSCC Dig. Tech. Papers*, pp. 22–23, Feb. 1977.

[4] T. Masuhara, O. Minato, T. Sasaki, Y. Sakai, M. Kubo, and T. Yosui, "A high speed low-power Hi-CMOS 4K static RAM," in *ISSCC Dig. Tech. Papers*, pp. 110–111, Feb. 1977.

[5] W. Herndon, W. Ho, and R. Ramirez, "A 4096 $\times$ 1 static bipolar RAM," in *ISSCC Dig. Tech. Papers*, pp. 68–69, Feb. 1977.

[6] A. Hotta, Y. Kaot, K. Yamaguchi, N. Homma, and M. Inadachi, "A high-speed, low-power 4096 $\times$ 1 bit bipolar RAM," in *ISSCC Dig. Tech. Papers*, pp. 98–99, Feb. 1978.

[7] K. Okada, K. Aomura, J. Nokubo, and H. Shiba, "A 4K static bipolar TTL RAM," in *ISSCC Dig. Tech. Papers*, pp. 100–101, Feb. 1978.

[8] W. B. Sander, J. M. Early, and T. A. Longo, "A 4096 $\times$ 1 (I^{3}L) bipolar RAM," in *ISSCC Dig. Tech. Papers*, pp. 182–183, Feb. 1976.

[9] P. M. Quinn, J. M. Early, W. B. Sander, and T. A. Longo, "A 16K $\times$ 1 I^{3}L dynamic RAM," in *ISSCC Dig. Tech Papers*, pp. 154–155, Feb. 1978.

[10] S. Kato, K. Murakami, M. Ueda, Y. Horida, and T. Nakano, "A high speed I^{2}L 1K static RAM with 20 ns access time," in *Dig. Tech. Papers 10th Conf. on Solid State Devices*, pp. 25–26, Aug. 1978.

[11] S. K. Wiedmann and H. H. Berger, "Super-integrated bipolar memory shares functions on diffused islands," *Electron.*, pp. 83–86, Feb. 14, 1972.

[12] S. K. Wiedmann, "Injection-coupled memory: A high-density static bipolar memory," *IEEE J. Solid-State Circuits*, vol. SC-8, pp. 332–337, 1973.

[13] M. Takagi, K. Nakayama, C. Terada, and M. Ueoka, "Improvement of shallow base transistor technology by using a doped polysilicon diffusion source," *J. Jap. Soc. Appl. Phys.*, vol. 42, p. 101, 1972.

Injection-Coupled Memory: A High-Density Static Bipolar Memory

SIEGFRIED K. WIEDMANN

Abstract—The design of a new static bipolar memory comparable with dynamic FET storages in density, but superior in performance and power dissipation is discussed. The concept of direct minority carrier injection is utilized for both the cell current supply and the coupling to the read/write lines. This has led to an extremely high degree of device integration resulting in a cell size of 3.1 mil² using a standard buried layer process with 5-μ line dimensions and single layer metallization. Investigations on exploratory chips containing small arrays have fully verified the feasibility. The cells have been operated at an extremely small dc standby power of below 100 nW. For a 4K b chip of about 160 × 150 mil², an access time around 50 ns can be projected from the measurements simulating a 64 × 64 bit array. An extrapolation of the memory cell layout with oxide isolation and self-aligned N⁺ contacts has resulted in a 1.1-mil² cell with 5-μ line dimensions.

Manuscript received April 18, 1973; revised June 1, 1973.
The author is with the IBM Laboratory, Boeblingen, Germany.

I. INTRODUCTION

FOR the past few years, attractive integrated circuit design concepts have been developed to increase the density of bipolar memory arrays and to decrease their power dissipation—in short, to make them competitive with FET's in cost, while retaining their speed advantages (e.g., see [1]–[9]). At the same time new technologies have been introduced that significantly reduce the silicon area necessary for device isolation [10]–[13], thus enhancing the density advantages obtained from the novel integrated-circuit approaches.

This paper describes a new static bipolar flip-flop memory [14] for main memory applications that is comparable with dynamic FET storages in density, but that is superior in performance and power dissipation. It uti-

Reprinted from *IEEE J. Solid-State Circuits*, vol. SC-8, pp. 332–337, Oct. 1973.

lizes the principle of direct minority carrier injection not only for the current supply as known from the super integrated memory cell, described earlier [8], but also for the coupling to the read/write lines. With this novel memory approach an extremely high degree of device integration is achieved, resulting in a cell size of only 3 mil² in a standard bipolar technology with 5-μ line dimensions. The number of metal contacts has been reduced to 5½ per cell. An unconventional array addressing scheme minimizes the number of array selection and data lines, so that only 1½ metal lines in single layer metallization are necessary for connecting a cell to the array matrix.

In the following sections the fundamental cell structure and its equivalent circuit are explained, and the operation principle in an array organization is discussed. Experimental results are presented, verifying the feasibility of the new approach. These results have been obtained from small arrays on exploratory chips fabricated in a standard buried layer process. Finally, some projections on the potential of the novel memory concept are made, e.g., by applying an oxide isolation technology.

II. BASIC MEMORY CELL STRUCTURE AND EQUIVALENT CIRCUIT

Fig. 1 shows the electrical equivalent circuit of the injection-coupled storage cell. Both the load and addressing transistors are complementary to the cross-coupled flip-flop transistors. The p-n-p load devices (T_3, T_4) allow the cell to operate at an extremely low dc standby power. The p-n-p bit-line transistors (T_5, T_6) provide a very simple coupling means. They are operated in normal or inverse mode depending on whether a write or read operation is performed. This circuit diagram looks complex compared to the schematical cross section of one cell shown in Fig. 2, but the schematic cell structure illustrates the reasons for the small size. All elements are placed in one common N pocket, and since only active devices are used, the cell size is essentially determined by the contact hole and metal line dimensions. As demonstrated later by the array layout, there are only 5½ contact holes and 1½ array metal lines for one cell, because some elements are shared among adjacent cells.

The cross-coupled n-p-n transistors T_1 and T_2 are carried out as upside down operated transistors with the common N_1 plane acting as an emitter. Their base current supply[1] results from minority carriers that are injected from the center P region into the N region and essentially collected by the adjacent P base regions P_1 and P_2. Due to the symmetrical structure, both currents are about equal. If the current gain of the upside down

---

[1] Note that the base current supply of T_1 (or T_2, respectively) corresponds to the collector current of T_2 (or T_1, respectively).

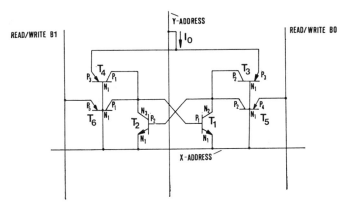

Fig. 1. Equivalent circuit of injection-coupled cell.

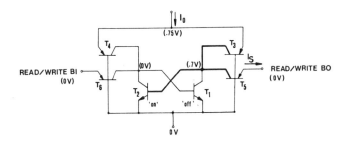

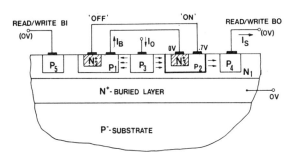

Fig. 2. Schematical cross section showing read operation.

operated n-p-n transistors is just larger than 1, a bistable operation is achieved. With present devices, this condition can be fulfilled over a very large current range with a lower limit in the order of nanoamperes and an upper limit in the order of milliamperes. As a result, this structure represents a flip-flop with controllable constant current load devices.

In the equivalent circuit, the p-n-p transistors T_3 and T_4 stand for these load devices. Their common bases are connected with the common emitters of the n-p-n transistors (because of the common N region) and their collectors are tied with the bases of the corresponding n-p-n transistors.

To extend this flip-flop device to a memory cell, some coupling means to the read/write data lines are needed. This is accomplished by just adding the two outer P regions P_4 and P_5. Assuming that the right-hand transistor in the cross section is "on," its forward biased base–emitter junction also injects carriers into the adjacent

N region. These carriers are partially collected by the closely located P region P_4. The resulting current I_s, which is dependent on the lateral current gains of the two injecting devices, can be sensed, and thus the state of the flip-flop can be detected. In the equivalent circuit, this transistor action is represented by the p-n-p transistors T_5 and T_6, respectively. With the chosen symbols they are inversely operated during sensing.

Fig. 3 illustrates how to change the state of the memory cell or—in other words, how to write it. Let us assume the left-hand n-p-n transistor in the cross section is off and shall be turned on. This is done by switching off the cell current supply to the center P region and by applying a write current pulse I_w to the left P region P_5 of read/write line B1. This causes an injection current that turns the left n-p-n transistor on, which then discharges the base–emitter junction of the right-hand n-p-n transistor. Now the write current I_w is switched off, and the cell current supply is switched on again. It should be mentioned that a relatively long delay time between these switching operations can be tolerated, since the state of the cell is maintained by the charges of the depletion layer capacitances for a rather long time, when the cell is switched off from power.

Briefly summarized, the operation principle can be characterized the following way. For reading, the current supplied to the cell is routed to the proper read/write line by means of double injection via an intermediate station. This intermediate station acts as a directional switch that is controlled by the state of the flip-flop. For writing, the current supplied to the bit line causes an injection current from the bit line P region to the P base of the flip-flop transistor, turning it on.

III. Array Operation

After having described the basic structure and operation of a single memory cell, its implementation and operation in an array organization is discussed. Fig. 4 shows how the memory array is in principle laid out on a chip. Since all cell components can be accommodated in a single N bed, all the memory cells of one X-address line are placed in a single N stripe that automatically serves as crossunder for the Y address and read/write lines. A common P emitter P_3 connected to the Y_1-address line is used for two adjacent cells. The read/write line P regions P_4 and P_5 are also shared among two adjacent cells of different Y-addresses Y_1 and Y_2. By this measure, only $1\frac{1}{2}$ metal lines per cell for the array wiring are necessary. This is a significant factor for the small cell size.

Fig. 5 elucidates the read operation of a selected cell. In standby, all cells are fed via the Y-address lines from a dc current supply. The excellent tracking of the emitter–base voltages of the p-n-p transistors provide adequate current sharing among the cells on Y lines. For reading cell 21, the X_1-line potential is slightly lowered and a current pulse is applied to the selected

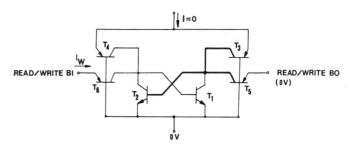

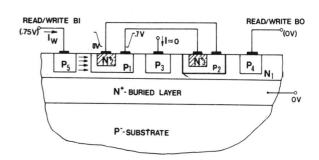

Fig. 3. Schematical cross section showing write operation.

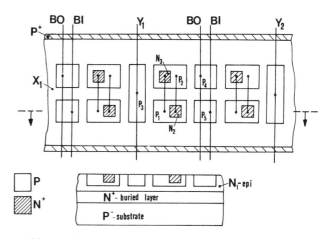

Fig. 4. Fundamental layout of injection-coupled cell.

Y_1 line only. This means that only cell 11 and cell 21 are supplied with a cell current. If the upper flip-flop transistor with base P_2 is conducting, it causes an injection current I_s in bit line B0. Hence, the state of the cell can be detected by sensing the current I_s. Note, that there is no sense current from any other cell connected to the same bit-line pair, since all these cells are cutoff from power. As mentioned before, their information is retained in the cell capacitances for a relatively long time.

Fig. 6 illustrates the write operation. For writing a "1" in cell 21, again a negative pulse is applied to the X_1 line. But opposite to the read operation, the current in the Y_1 line of the selected cell is switched off. A current pulse is applied to the corresponding read/write line B1. The lower bit-line emitter P_5 feeds an injection current into the bases P_1 and P_6 of the lower n-p-n transistors of cell 21 and 31, respectively. This causes

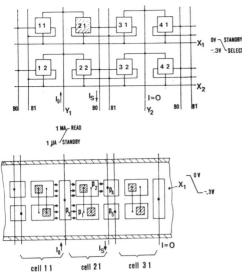

Fig. 5.   Read operation in array.

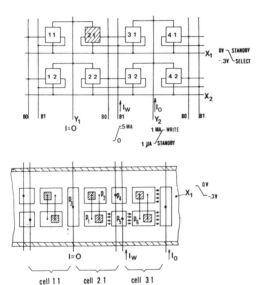

Fig. 6.   Write operation in array.

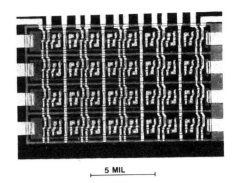

Fig. 7.   Chip photomicrograph of 4 × 8 array.

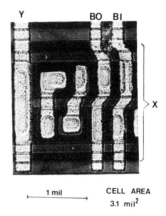

Fig. 8.   Chip photomicrograph of single cell.

the n-p-n transistor (base P_1) of the selected cell to be turned on, while the n-p-n transistor (base P_6) of the unaddressed cell 31 is prevented from switching by applying a sufficiently large cell current through the Y_2 line.

IV. EXPERIMENTAL RESULTS

After these theoretical discussions experimental results obtained from exploratory chips are presented. The chips have been fabricated in a standard buried layer process with a 3-μ epitaxial layer and 5-μ minimum line dimensions. Fig. 7 shows a chip photomicrograph of a 4 × 8 bit array, and in Fig. 8 an enlarged chip photomicrograph of one cell is depicted. The topology corresponds very closely to the fundamental layout of Fig. 4.

These memory cells have been safely operated at a dc standby power below 100 nW. The cell current deviation between the cells on a common supply line is less than ±8 percent within a current range of 100 nA to 1 mA.

In Figs. 9 and 10 the most relevant current gains of the cell transistors have been plotted. Because of the extensive component merging it is necessary to clearly define the measurement conditions. Therefore, diagrammatic top views of the structures have been added, which show the boundary conditions of the adjacent transistor regions. The common-base current gain α_1 (Fig. 9) of the four-collector p-n-p load transistor is better than 0.7 in a fairly large emitter current range between 300 nA and 1 mA. This means that 70 percent of the current supply to the cell reaches the cross-coupled flip-flop transistors, so that only 30 percent of the cell current is not utilized. The current gain β_I (Fig. 9) of the upside down operated n-p-n transistor stays well above unity down to currents of a few nanoamperes.

Fig. 10 shows the current gains of the coupling transistor for both the bit-line P region acting as emitter (write operation) and as collector (read operation). Because of the interdependence of this p-n-p transistor with the upside down operated n-p-n transistor, there is a relationship between α (p-n-p) and the effective β_I (n-p-n). In essence, β_I (n-p-n) is reduced if α (p-n-p) is made large. Thus, the emitter–collector distance of the p-n-p transistor has to be properly chosen, so that the best tradeoff between β_I (n-p-n)—determining the bistability—and α (p-n-p)—affecting the read/write performance—is obtained.

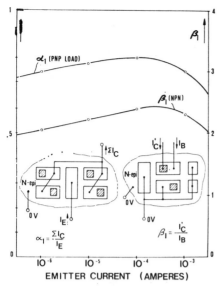

Fig. 9. Current gains of p-n-p load and n-p-n flip-flop transistors.

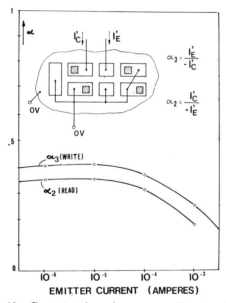

Fig. 10. Current gains of p-n-p coupling transistor.

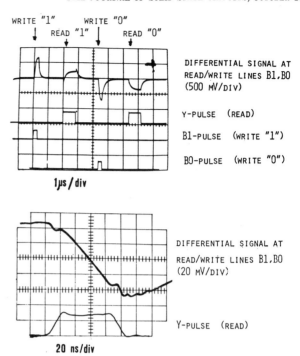

Fig. 11. Oscillograms of read/write operation.

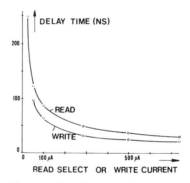

Fig. 12. Read/write performance.

The following two figures refer to ac measurements. In Fig. 11(a) an oscillogram of the read/write operations is shown. Writing a "1," a current pulse is applied to the B1 read/write line, whereas the Y-address line of the current is unpowered. The 700-mV differential signal at the read/write lines originates from the forward biased emitter–base junction of the read/write line transistor. In the next cycle, a current pulse is applied to the Y-address line for a read operation. This results in a positive read signal at the read/write lines, which have been loaded with a capacitance corresponding to 64 cells. In the following write "0" operation a current pulse is applied to the B0 read/write line. During the next Y-address current pulse, a negative differential signal appears at the read/write lines corresponding to a "0." The lower oscillogram [Fig. 11(b)] shows the Y-address and read signals at a higher speed.

In Fig. 12 the read delay time as a function of the read select current at the Y address line and the minimum write time as a function of the write current applied to the read/write line are plotted. The read delay is dependent on the transit time of the p-n-p bit line and load transistors, whereas the write delay is determined by the time constants of the upside down operated n-p-n and the p-n-p bit-line transistors.

V. EXTRAPOLATIONS OF PRESENT APPROACH

The previous results are based on a standard buried layer process using isolation diffusion. In this section, some potential extrapolations of the present approach are pointed out. Fig. 13 shows a schematical array configuration, where the whole memory array can be implemented in a single N plane, so that no isolation walls are necessary at all. The cell area is reduced by about 15 percent compared to the present approach with the same photo groundrules. However, in this case two layers of metallization must be used for crossing the word address and data lines. Furthermore, it is not

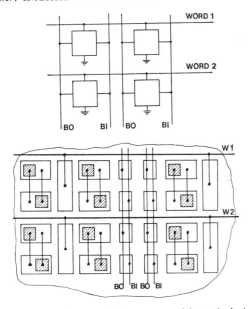

Fig. 13. Injection-coupled memory without isolation.

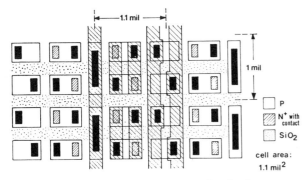

Fig. 14. Array layout in advanced technology.

possible to share the emitter regions of both the p-n-p load and p-n-p bit-line transistors between adjacent cells. As a result, a tradeoff between a simpler silicon structure and a more complex wiring system is offered.

Fig. 14 demonstrates that the cell size can be significantly reduced by taking advantage of some technological improvements. This layout study, which assumes the same dimensional groundrules as the present approach, is based on a technology using oxide isolation and self-aligned N⁺-contacts. The cell area is only 1.1 mil² compared to 3.1 mil² with the present approach.

VI. Conclusions

By applying direct carrier injection for both the current supply and the coupling to the read/write lines, a static flip-flop memory of very high density and extremely low power is achieved. Due to this concept, all memory cell components can be accommodated in a single N bed and can be extensively merged with one another so that only $5\frac{1}{2}$ contacts and $1\frac{1}{2}$ array metal lines are required for one cell. This is the key for the small cell size of only 3.1 mil² in a conventional bipolar process with 3-μ epitaxy and 5-μ line dimensions. Despite the very low dc standby power of less than 100 nW/b a good read/write performance is obtained, since the memory cell can be powered up during addressing by orders of magnitude. Thus, for a 4K b chip of 150 × 160 mil² an access time of about 50 ns can be projected.

By taking advantage of oxide isolation and self-aligned N⁺ contacts, the cell size can be further reduced to about 1 mil² assuming the same layout groundrules. This means that an 16K b chip of about 175 × 175 mil² can be realized.

References

[1] D. J. Lynes and D. A. Hodges, "Memory using diode-coupled bipolar transistor cells," *IEEE J. Solid-State Circuits,* vol. SC-5, pp. 186–191, Oct. 1970.
[2] J. Mar, "A two-terminal transistor memory cell using breakdown," *IEEE J. Solid-State Circuits,* vol. SC-6, pp. 280–283, Oct. 1971.
[3] S. K. Wiedmann and H. H. Berger, "Small-size low-power bipolar memory cell," *IEEE J. Solid-State Circuits,* vol. SC-6, pp. 283–288, Oct. 1971.
[4] K. Taniguchi, A. Hotta, and I. Imaizumi, "Switched collector impedance memory," *IEEE J. Solid-State Circuits,* vol. SC-6, pp. 289–296, Oct. 1971.
[5] H. H. Henn, "Bipolar dynamic memory cell," *IEEE J. Solid-State Circuits,* vol. SC-6, pp. 297–300, Oct. 1971.
[6] P. T. Panousis, "A TRIM-memory employing both n-p-n and p-n-p high-gain unijunction transistors," in *ISSCC Dig. Tech. Papers,* pp. 16–17, Feb. 1971.
[7] W. Jutzi and C. H. Schuenemann, "Cross-coupled thyristor storage cell," *IBM J. Res. Develop.,* vol. 16, pp. 35–44, Jan. 1972.
[8] S. K. Wiedmann and H. H. Berger, "Super-integrated bipolar memory shares functions on diffused islands," *Electronics,* pp. 83–86, Feb. 14, 1972.
[9] W. D. Baker, W. H. Herndon, T. A. Longo, and D. L. Peltzer, "Oxide isolation brings high density to production bipolar memories," *Electronics,* vol. 46, pp. 65–70, Mar. 29, 1973.
[10] B. T. Murphy, V. J. Glinski, P. A. Gary, and R. A. Pedersen, "Collector diffusion isolated integrated circuits," *Proc. IEEE,* vol. 57, pp. 1523–1527, Sept. 1969.
[11] J. A. Appels, E. Kooi, M. M. Paffen, J. J. Schatorje, and W. H. Verkuylon, "Local oxidation of silicon and its application in semiconductor device technology," *Philips Res. Rep.,* vol. 25, pp. 113–132, 1970.
[12] D. Peltzer and B. Herndon, "Isolation method shrinks bipolar cells for fast, dense memories," *Electronics,* pp. 52–55, Mar. 1, 1971.
[13] M. B. Vora, "A self-isolation scheme for integrated circuits," *IBM J. Res. Develop.,* vol. 15, pp. 430–435, Nov. 1971.
[14] S. K. Wiedmann, "High-density static bipolar memory," in *ISSCC Dig. Tech. Papers,* pp. 56–57, Feb. 1973.

The Collector-Coupled Static RAM Cell

FRANK W. HEWLETT, JR., MEMBER, IEEE

Abstract—The collector-coupled static RAM cell uses a Schottky collector transistor switch with merged vertical n-p-n load. The cell is constructed with two dual Schottky collector transistors and one merged dual collector n-p-n transistor. It has been fabricated in an infant oxide isolated bipolar technology and bistability has been demonstrated over four orders of magnitude in cell current (10 nA $< I_{CELL} <$ 100μA). The approach taken here of stacking active load and switch elements provides static bit densities comparable to MOS memory and superior to other known bipolar approaches.

INTRODUCTION

THE collector-coupled static RAM cell [1] uses the Schottky collector transistor switch with merged n-p-n load [2] to obtain bit densities comparable to MOS memory. As compared to the injection-coupled cell [3] used in the 54S400,[1] the collector-coupled cell is higher in performance and 18 percent smaller in size for the same design rules (4.08 mil^2 versus 4.96 mil^2). In this paper, the cell and its operation are described. The Schottky collector transistor switch is described in a companion paper [2].

THE COLLECTOR-COUPLED CELL

The collector-coupled cell consists of two dual Schottky collector or *PNM* (M = metal) transistors [T1 and T2 in Fig. 1(a)] and a merged dual collector n-p-n load transistor (T3). The upper word line (W_U) contacts the n-p-n base/*PNM* emitter. The lower word line (W_L) contacts the upward-operated n-p-n emitter. One collector of each dual collector *PNM* drives the adjacent *PNM* base crosscoupling the latch. The second collector couples the cell to the bit lines, b0 and b1 [Fig. 1(a)]. The cell topography and cross section through T2 are shown in Fig. 1(b) and (c). The cell is an upward-operated dual collector n-p-n transistor with two Schottky (*PNM* collector) and one ohmic (*PNM* base) contact per collector.

The photomicrograph of a test structure (Fig. 2) fabricated in an oxide-isolated bipolar technology (see [2] for details) corresponds to Fig. 1(b) and (c). The structure contains a dual collector *PNM* transistor (top) with each collector available for beta measurement, and a cross-coupled latch with bit line collectors available (bottom). The cell area, which includes overhead for n-p-n emitter and base contact, is 4.08 mil^2 (5 μm metal lines and spaces).

Latch stability has been demonstrated over four orders of magnitude of cell current (10 nA $< I_{CELL} <$ 100 μA). The *PNM* beta per collector must be greater than 1 for stable op-

Manuscript received April 11, 1979; revised June 19, 1979.
The author is with Texas Instruments, Inc., Dallas, TX 75265.
[1] The 54S400 is Texas Instruments 4K clocked static RAM.

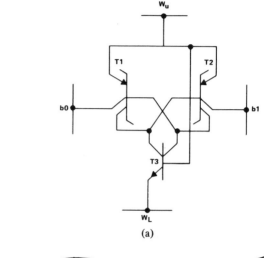

(a)

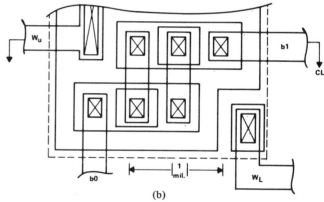

(b)

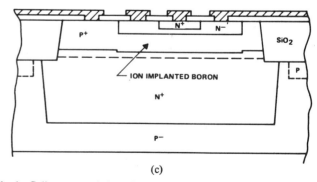

(c)

Fig. 1. Collector-coupled static RAM cell. (a) Schematic. (b) Topography. (c) Cross section.

eration. The beta measurement configuration for the dual collector structure is defined in [2]. The two collectors are tied in parallel for this measurement. β_{PNM} falloff causes cell instability at both low and high values of cell current. Schottky collector area (3.80 $\times$ 5.0 μm) could be doubled with no in-

Reprinted from *IEEE J. Solid-State Circuits*, vol. SC-14, pp. 865–867, Oct. 1979.

380

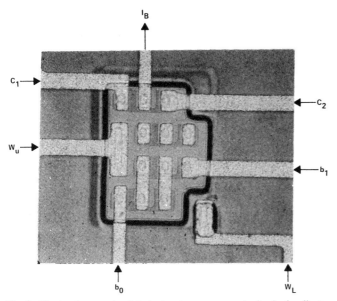

Fig. 2. Photomicrograph of test structure composed of a dual collector *PNM* (top) and a static RAM cell (bottom).

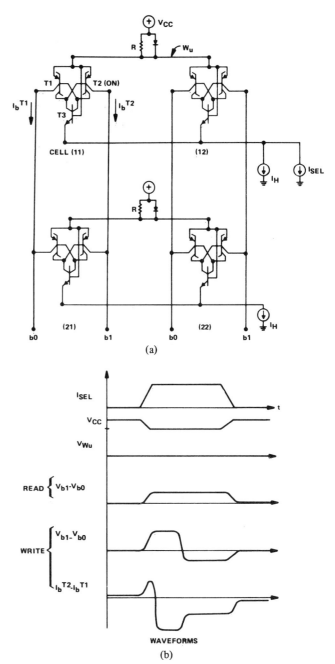

Fig. 3. (a) 2×2 array which demonstrates collector-coupled cell read and write operations. (b) Corresponding waveforms.

crease in cell size by reducing the *PNM* collector to base separation (Schottky to diffused p+) to 2.54 μm from the present 3.80 μm. The larger collector area would approximately double cell operating range on the high current end. Mask registration tolerance would be improved by ion implanting the p+. Presently available walled structures which permit the Schottky to overlap oxide would provide dramatic reduction in cell size and improvement in current gain.

Cell current withdrawn via the lower word line (W_L) is equal to the sum of the two n-p-n collector currents plus n-p-n base current. At the n-p-n beta of 4, 20 percent of the cell current is n-p-n base current and approximately 40 percent flows in each n-p-n collector. Slightly less current flows in the n-p-n collector merged with the "on" *PNM* than in that of the "off" *PNM* due to its deeper saturation. In the case of $T2$ "on," n-p-n collector currents flow from the base of $T2$ and collector of $T2$ tied to the base of $T1$. Current supplied to the sense line from the upper word line (W_U) is β_{PNM} multiplied by the base current of $T2$. At a *PNM* beta of 3, current supplied to the sense line is greater than the cell current.

In contrast, the injection-coupled cell [3] sense line current (~20 percent of cell current in 54S400) is equal to the cell current diminished by the product of two lateral p-n-p alphas. Thus, the collector-coupled cell can be more efficient in supplying current to the sense lines than the injection-coupled cell. Access time below 50 ns is projected for a 4K static RAM using the collector-coupled cell based on 54S400 experience and the relative cell efficiencies.

CELL OPERATION

The array and waveforms of Fig. 3 are used to describe cell read/write operation. Initially, all cells are in standby mode with balanced bit line potentials. The upper word line potential is 1.5 V above bit line potential to ensure that all *PNM* transistors are in the active mode ($VEC^{PNM} = 1.5$ V). The holding current/bit is on the order of nanoamperes.

To read cell (11), select current (I_{SEL} in Fig. 3) is withdrawn from its lower word line. The upper word line potential, which is clamped at a forward diode voltage above the lower word line by the n-p-n emitter base diode, falls to a forward diode voltage (V_D) below that of standby. Current sourced from the bit (11) charges $b1$ positive ($T2$ on) with respect to $b0$. The bit lines coupled to cell (11) have been selected via Y-address circuitry and may be sensed differentially. The small bit line Schottky collectors determine the low sense line capacitance. All *PNM* transistors are active during the read operation. Read access time is limited by vertical n-p-n transit time plus vertical *PNM* transit time. The *PNM* is an internal circuit element requiring low values of sustain voltage (about 1.5 V) which permit narrow base width and low transit time.

To write into cell (11), the cell is selected (I_{SEL} is flowing) and bit line potential $b1$ is raised, causing the collector of $T2$ coupled to $b1$ to saturate. Current sourced from $T2$ of cell (11) in the selected row assists the potential rise. Base drive is robbed from the second collector of $T2$, permitting turn-on base current to flow from the base of $T1$ into the merged collector of $T3$. The low inverse alpha [2] of the PNM transistor ($T2$) provides very effective current robbing. $T1$ turns on and cell (11) changes state. As voltage on the PNM collector of $T2$ making Schottky contact to the n-p-n collector is raised, current begins to flow into the bit, as indicated by the waveform of $I_b^{T2} - I_b^{T1}$ in Fig. 3(b). The n-p-n is pulled out of saturation and $T2$ is turned off. $T1$ has ~300 mV (V_{on} of PNM) forward bias on its emitter base junction and will turn on before $T2$, allowing immediate lowering of bit line potential $b1$ to its standby state. Writing in this manner is fully static as only $T2$ of cell (11) is allowed to saturate. The upper word line of cell (21) which is in standby remains above the $b1$ potential by an amount which ensures that $T2$ of cell (21) remains active.

Operating at low levels, n-p-n base and emitter power distribution can be accomplished in p+ and n+ diffusions, requiring one level of metal only. However, practical implementation of large memory arrays would require shunting diffused resistance with a second level of metal.

SUMMARY

The collector-coupled static RAM cell employs a vertical PNM switch and merged vertical n-p-n load to obtain bit densities comparable to MOS memory. The cell has been fabricated and stability has been demonstrated over four orders of magnitude of cell current. The approach of stacking switch and load elements has been taken in MOS static memory using polysilicon load resistors to obtain high density, but is unprecedented in static bipolar memory. Stacking active load and switch elements is unique in static memory applications.

ACKNOWLEDGMENT

The author thanks D. Falkner for stimulating discussion and layout support.

REFERENCES

[1] F. W. Hewlett, Jr., U.S. Patent 4 104 732, Aug. 1, 1978.
[2] ——, "A compact efficient Schottky collector transistor switch," this issue, pp. 801–806.
[3] S. K. Wiedmann, "Injection-coupled memory—A high density static bipolar memory," *IEEE J. Solid-State Circuits*, vol. SC-8, pp. 332–337, Oct. 1973.

Part X
Reliability and Radiation Hardness

The reliability and radiation hardness of I^2L are only rarely mentioned in the bulk of the literature directed at the analysis, development, and application of the I^2L technique. This may result in part from the long-established reliability of bipolar processes in general and certainly the application which requires a consideration of radiation hardness is the exception in the general integrated circuit marketplace.

When alternative approaches are considered for LSI or VLSI in those important applications areas where reliability and radiation hardness must be weighed heavily, then I^2L emerges as an excellent choice. Examples are military, space, communications systems, and the telephone system. These applications areas represent situations where failures cannot be tolerated for reasons of maintaining operability of the systems which employ the LSI or VLSI circuit. Other areas of applications are the automobile, the home appliance, and industrial controls. For reasons of economy, these applications also cannot tolerate frequent failures or unpredictable lifetimes of their LSI or VLSI components.

Paper X-1 by Hewlett and Pedersen presents an impressive testimonial to the reliability of I^2L in the Bell System. In addition to enjoying the immediate advantage of the long-established reliability of bipolar technology, I^2L benefits from its very low voltage operation, less than 1 V.

Paper X-2 by Raymond and Pease presents a detailed study of the susceptibility of I^2L to neutron displacement damage, long-term ionization effects, and transient photoresponse. Each of these radiation mechanisms give rise to failures in semiconductor devices in general, and I^2L is no exception. These authors discuss the trade-offs which can reduce the susceptibility of I^2L to such radiation. The penalty paid is usually speed performance or processing complexity. However, the general trend is that the highest performing I^2L will exhibit the best inherent radiation hardness. Consequently, radiation hardness may well be attained with I^2L without a greatly deliberate effort. Three specific I^2L implementations are considered by Raymond and Pease. Their experimental results and theoretical discussions lead them to some conclusions regarding these three I^2L types as well as I^2L in general. My interpretation of the results presented in Figs. 8–10 is that the up-diffused approach shows good radiation hardness. This observation, when coupled with my observations with regard to the prospects for a high performance I^2L technology (in Part V), suggests to me that the upward bipolar technology represents an excellent overall choice for an LSI and VLSI technology of the future. The authors conclude with a comparison of various technologies ranging from TTL to CMOS/SOS. In this comparison which includes performance as well as radiation hardness, I^2L is revealed as a good choice for a radiation hardened LSI technology.

Paper X-3 by Bahraman et al. presents a theoretical and experimental study of the effects of neutron radiation upon I^2L. The authors found that the theoretical predictions agreed quite well with experimental results. The general conclusion which can be drawn is that one should minimize the volumes of those regions of the gate where excessive recombination might cause degradation of the gate's performance. Total dose (gamma radiation) and transient photoionizing radiation effects were also investigated experimentally and the critical irradiation levels determined. In the case of the transient upset experiments, the authors found that the hardness of the I^2L circuit could be a function of geometric layout and relative physical sizes of the I^2L devices. Once again these authors' results indicate that the proper direction to be taken for improved radiation hardness is in sympathy with the direction to be taken to achieve higher performance I^2L in general.

The final paper (X-4) by Donovan et al. makes a one-to-one comparison between CMOS/SOS and I^2L from the point of view of the need for a standard, commercially produced VLSI technology which is radiation hard. The motivation for such a comparison lies in the need for the military to meet their requirements for radiation hard VLSI without the confrontation of an intolerably expensive custom VLSI technology. The authors conclude that I^2L now holds the promise of being the commercial technology for VLSI which will most likely meet military environmental specifications.

THE RELIABILITY OF INTEGRATED INJECTION
LOGIC CIRCUITS FOR THE BELL SYSTEM

by

F. W. Hewlett, Jr. and R. A. Pedersen
Bell Telephone Laboratories, Incorporated
Allentown, Pennsylvania 18103

Abstract

The reliability of Integrated Injection Logic (I^2L) or Merged Transistor Logic (MTL) circuits fabricated in a standard bipolar technology with Ti-Pt-Au interconnection is reported. The study is based on accelerated stress aging and actual field results.

Experiments are described which demonstrate that I^2L circuit failure in humid ambients due to Au electrolysis will not occur because of low voltage operation. Failure rates less than 10 FITs for an LSI part (.001% failure per 1000 device hours) under normal stress over a 40 year life are predicted for the main population by accelerated bias temperature and bias humidity stress. Well behaved current gain (βu) under bias temperature step stress indicates that βu degradation will not be a significant failure mechanism.

At this writing, more than 60 million device hours have been accumulated for LSI chips in specific applications with no reported chip failures. This field result firmly supports accelerated stress reliability predictions.

I. Introduction

This paper reports on the evaluated reliability of Integrated Injection Logic[1] (I^2L) or Merged Transistor Logic[2] (MTL) circuits fabricated in a standard bipolar technology with Ti-Pt-Au interconnection (Beam Lead Sealed Junction or BLSJ Technology[3]). Experiments are described in which I^2L circuits are subjected to corrosive medium, bias temperature, and bias humidity stresses. Field results in specific applications are discussed.

I^2L is a bipolar circuit technique which may be fabricated using standard bipolar technology. A schematic of an I^2L logic unit (with FO=4) is shown in Figure 1, and the corresponding topography and cross section in Figure 2. An active pnp load injects base drive into the bases of the npn switching transistors which are operated inversely and direct coupled to obtain logical functions. The logic swing and power supply voltage are equal to a forward diode voltage (<1.0v). Each output is constrained to tie to only one input and must be capable of sinking current supplied to that node. Therefore, for identical units, the current gain of each output (βu) must be ≥ 1.0.

Low voltage operation is a novel feature of the I^2L circuit technique which contributes to excellent reliability. Independent electrolysis tests with metal "comb" patterns indicate a threshold for Au electrolysis occurring at ~1.0v in salt water for the BLSJ system. I^2L operating voltages are well below this threshold. In addition, low voltage on metal lines and high surface concentrations on all surfaces (see Figure 2) makes the I^2L unit less sensitive to surface inversion than most other bipolar and MOS configurations.

The unit may be fabricated with three selective diffusions into n/n+ material. The complete process with contact window and metalization operations requires five masks. Two additional diffusion steps, buried layer and isolation, are required if other bipolar circuit forms, e.g., T^2L, are desired on the same chip (a seven mask process). These processes are referred to as the nonisolated and isolated processes, respectively.

Both nonisolated and isolated I^2L circuit forms have been fabricated in the BLSJ technology. A nonisolated circuit form requiring no on-chip voltage greater than 1.0 volt is the vehicle used to demonstrate I^2L BLSJ circuit immunity to Au electrolysis. An isolated custom LSI part has been subjected to bias temperature and bias humidity accelerated stress. Failure rates less than 10 FITs under normal stress over a 40 year life are anticipated based on these results.

Finally, step stress aging of the I^2L transistor indicates current gain stability under the specified conditions.

At this writing, more than 60 million device hours have been accumulated in the field with no reported chip failures.

II. Devices and Stress Conditions

A nonisolated gated inverter chain (Figure 3) which requires no on-chip voltage above 1.0v has been mounted on a TO-5 header with no moisture protection and operated in salt water. Au wire bonds were used for this test device instead of beam leads. The circuit continued to operate when immersed in Pur-A-Gold 70GV, a high speed neutral type electroplating formulation. The output device driving an external resistive load tied to a variable voltage supply is shown in the segment of inverter chain schematic, Figure 4. The potential of node A monitored by an oscilloscope is equal to the variable supply voltage for half the period of oscillation. The potential on node B is held at V_{SAT} (saturation voltage <0.1v). In this configuration, a voltage greater than the Au electrolysis threshold voltage may be applied between nodes A and B. These results are reported in Section III a.

Another device, a 250 gate, T^2L compatible, I^2L random-logic chip for a telephone system application (Figure 5) requires device isolation and a 5.0v supply for the T^2L-compatible buffers. This chip has been packaged in a 24-pin ceramic DIP (Figure 6) with flow coat (RTV) for moisture protection and subjected to bias temperature (100 units/20mW/300°C) and bias-humidity (74 units/24mW/85°C/85% RH + HCl dip before stress) stresses. The inputs were tied alternately to 0v and 4.5v to assist electrolysis failures which could occur in the T^2L buffer sections (see Figure 5) during bias humidity stress. Device failures as functions of time for each of the samples are contained in Section III b and c.

The LSI chip contains a single logic unit located in the upper right hand corner with accessible input and output (Figure 7). Twenty-five units have been mounted on TO-5 headers and subjected to bias temperature step stress. The stress conditions were 3.0v reverse bias on the collector and emitter junctions with temperature varying from 150°C to 325°C in 25°C increments, one week for each increment. The current gain

Reprinted from *Proc. IEEE 14th Annual Reliability Phys. Symp.*, Apr. 1976, pp. 5–10.

384

was measured at each interval using the circuit config-uration in Figure 8. The purpose of this step stress acceleration was to determine current gain stability in time. These results are contained in Section III d.

Section III e reports currently available field results.

III. Results

(a) Electrolysis

Operation of the ring oscillator chip in salt water is demonstrated in Figure 9. Salt water is placed on the chip surface which is kept wet by the water bub-bler (foreground). The waveform is displayed on the oscilloscope and supply voltage (650mV) on the digital multimeter in the background. The variable supply volt-age is set at 0.7 volts. The frequency of operation is much lower for a wet chip than a dry one because of parasitic capacitances introduced between lines by the water. Thus, a frequency monitor determines moisture presence. Figure 10 is a photomicrograph of this chip which shows the presence of moist salt crystals. Two devices have successfully operated in this ambient for more than 1000 hours each. One unit experienced a package failure after approximately six weeks; a header lead post disintegrated. The second inverter chain failed after two and one-half months. The precise cause of failure was not determinable since the chip was coat-ed with various deposits and/or organic growths and could not be cleaned.

A voltage was applied to the external resistor of a third inverter chain which resulted in a potential difference between nodes A and B (see Figures 4, 11, 12 and 13) greater than the threshold for Au electrolysis in salt water. In less than one minute, the output waveform dropped to V_{SAT} indicating a short circuit be-tween nodes A and B.

A scanning electron micrograph 500X, Figure 11, shows a dendritic growth which occurred at the point where the lines are most closely spaced (12μm). The Au wire from the bonding post may be seen in the fore-ground. An SEM close-up (5000X) is pictured in Figure 12. Au has been transported from the anode, node A, to the cathode, node B, and piled up in fern-like deposits which build back towards the anode. The X-ray image, Figure 13, positively identifies the dendrite as gold.

A fourth unit was successfully operated in Pur-A-Gold 70GV, a neutral type gold plating formulation for more than one hour. The experiment was terminated at this time without failure. At this writing, twenty units are being placed in a well controlled chlorine gas ambient for analysis.

(b) Bias Temperature

Cumulative failures at each test point for the isolated I^2L BLSJ circuit form (Figure 4) are given in Table 1. For a log normal failure distribution (Figure 14) these data indicate a 600,000 hour median life and a 3.99 standard deviation. The failure rate calculation as outlined by Peck and Zierdt[4] using a conservative activation energy of 1.02 ev predicts a failure rate of <1.0 FIT for this mechanism at 60°C operation.

Table 1

Bias Temperature Stress (100 Units)

Time (hours)	Cumulative Failures
8	0
48	0
283	2
1000	8
2000	8
3000	8
4000	8
5000	9

(c) Bias Humidity

Table 2 contains the cumulative failures at each test point for bias-humidity stress of the same 250-gate circuit. For the log normal distribution (Figure 15), the median life is 100,000 hours and the standard devi-ation is 2.3. Using the electrolysis model[5] and a 10°C rise in junction temperature above ambient, the failure rate for the typical U.S. condition[5] (25°C/50% RH) is <10 FITs over a 40 year life. For a severe U.S. condi-tion,[5] a summer night in Baton Rouge, La., the predicted maximum failure rate is ∿50 FITs over a 40 year life.

Table 2

Bias Humidity Stress (74 Units)

Time (hours)	Cumulative Failures
7	0
80	0
300	0
500	1
1000	1
2000	5
3000	5
4000	6
5000	6
6000	11
7000	11
8000	11

(d) Current Gain

The twenty-five (25) I^2L units subjected to bias temperature step stress showed slight gain degradation with a maximum of 21%. Average current gain (βu) ver-sus temperature is contained in Table 3. One unit failed catastrophically at the 300°C test point. Ex-amination revealed severe mechanical damage (cracked chip) apparently present from the outset which caused premature failure in this unit (#5). These data indi-cate that an initial gain specification 10% greater than than the end of life requirement (40 years which equivalently occurs between the 250°C and 275°C step stress data points for a 1.02ev activation energy) is conservative in providing adequate gain during life.

Table 3

Average Current Gain at Each Temperature
25 Units

Temperature (C)	Average Current Gain (βu) @ $I_{BX}=10\mu a$ $V_{CE}=.5v$
Initially	2.40
150	2.45
175	2.40
200	2.40
225	2.34
250	2.35
275	2.30
300	2.27
325	2.19

Average % Change = -8 3/4%
Worst Case % Change = -21%
Unit #12

(e) Field Results

Two different systems have been in field trial for over 6 months. The first of these has 2 beam leaded LSI I^2L chips packaged in a single 24 pin ceramic DIP with RTV encapsulation. The system operates on customer premises and devices have purposely been put in service in unfavorable environments. As of March 1, 1976, 4.7 million device hours have been accumulated with no device failures.

A second system, utilizing one I^2L chip design, has accumulated 8.3 million device hours in field trial in a central office environment with no device failures. Product shipments are now underway and more than 60 million device hours have been accumulated with no device failures reported.

In all cases, no burn-ins or humidity screens have been employed on the encapsulated chips prior to service. The composite of all data at this time would indicate an average failure rate over early life less than 17 failures/10^9 device hours.

IV. Conclusions

Successful Operation of a nonisolated I^2L BLSJ circuit form in salt water and a neutral type gold plating solution has been demonstrated. This result suggests that failure due to Au electrolysis will not occur in such circuits because of the low voltage operation.

Failure rate calculations based on bias temperature stress of a T^2L compatible I^2L BLSJ chip predict a conservative failure rate <1 FIT at 60°C due to temperature-bias induced mechanisms. Failure rate calculations based on bias humidity stress of the same circuit predict a failure rate <10 FITs for typical U.S. conditions and ∿50 FITs maximum for a severe case when operating 10°C above ambient.

Finally, I^2L current gain stability under bias temperature step stress aging indicates current gain degradation will not be a significant failure mechanism.

At this time, 60 million device hours have been accumulated in the field with no reported chip failures. This result firmly supports accelerated stress reliability predictions.

Acknowledgments

The authors thank B. R. Jones and C. H. Zierdt, Jr. for informative discussions; R. A. Darnall for supplying bias-temperature, bias-humidity, and step stress data; and J. B. Bindell and B. J. Snyder for the scanning electron micrograph work.

References

1. K. Hart and A. Slob, "Integrated Injection Logic: A New Approach to LSI," IEEE J. Solid-State Circuits, Vol. SC-7, pp. 346-351, October 1972.

2. H. H. Berger and S. K. Wiedmann, "Merged-Transistor Logic (MTL) - A Low-Cost Bipolar Logic Concept," IEEE J. Solid-State Circuits, Vol. SC-7, pp. 340-346, October 1972.

3. M. P. Lepselter, "Beam-Lead Sealed-Junction Technology," Bell Laboratories Record, pp. 299-303, October - November 1966.

4. D. S. Peck and C. H. Zierdt, Jr., "The Reliability of Semiconductor Devices in The Bell System," Proceedings of the IEEE, Vol. 62, p. 185, February 1974.

5. D. S. Peck and C. H. Zierdt, "Temperature-Humidity Acceleration of Metal Electrolysis Failure in Semiconductor Devices," Eleventh Annual IEEE Reliability Physics Symp., Las Vegas, Nevada, April 1973, pp. 146-152.

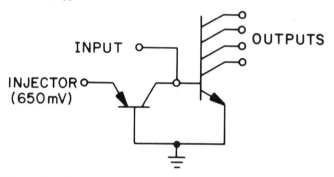

Figure 1. Integrated Injection Logic Unit

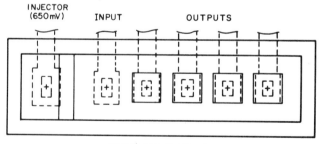

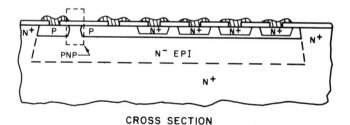

Figure 2. Logic Unit Topography and Cross Section

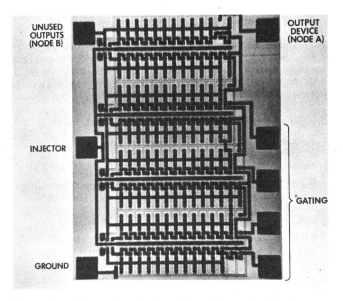

Figure 3. Photomicrograph of Gated Inverted Chain

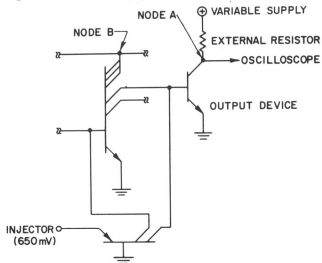

Figure 4. Segment of Inverter Chain

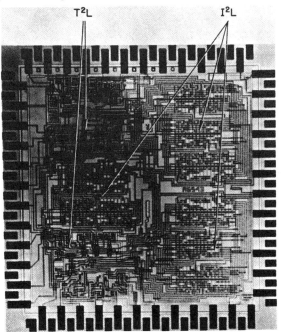

Figure 5. Photomicrograph of Small Telephone System IC

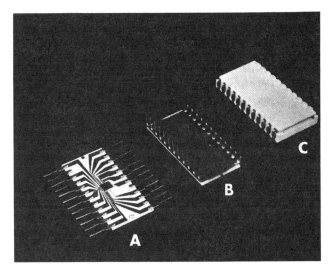

Figure 6. 24 Pin Ceramic DIP

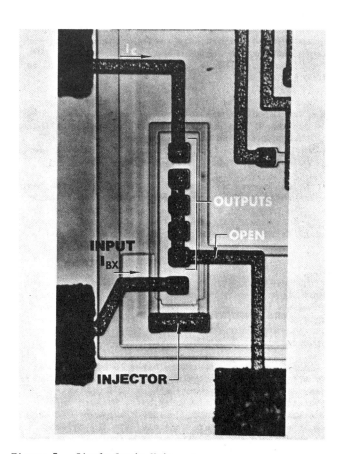

Figure 7. Single Logic Unit

387

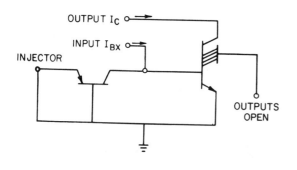

$$\beta_u \equiv \frac{I_C}{I_{BX}} \geq 1.0$$

Figure 8. Logic Unit Configured for Gain Measurement (Worst Case)

Figure 11. Scanning Electron Micrograph of Dendritic Growth (500X)

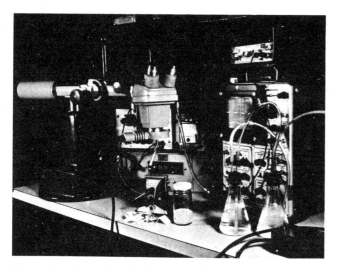

Figure 9. Corrosive Medium Test Setup

Figure 12. Scanning Electron Micrograph of Dendritic Growth (5000X)

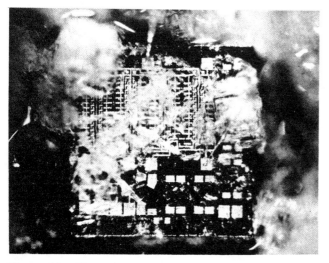

Figure 10. Photomicrograph of Gated Inverter Chain Showing Moist Salt Crystals

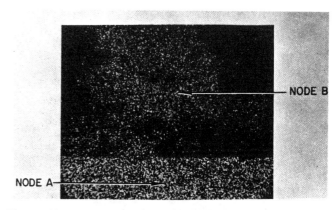

Figure 13. Gold X-ray Image (5000X)

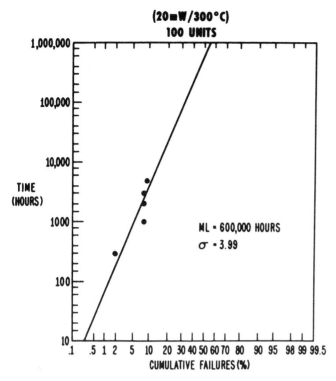

Figure 14. Cumulative Failure Distribution Bias Temperature Stress

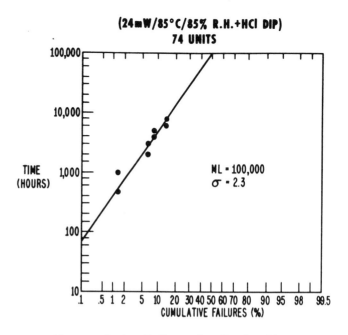

Figure 15. Cumulative Failure Distribution Bias Humidity Stress

A COMPARATIVE EVALUATION OF INTEGRATED INJECTION LOGIC*

J. P. Raymond
Mission Research Corporation
La Jolla, California 92037

R. L. Pease**
Naval Weapons Support Center
Crane, Indiana

Summary

Radiation effects on integrated injection logic arrays are presented in terms of available data on "conventional" structures and new test data on advanced structures. The advanced structures were developed for improved electrical performance, independent of radiation hardness. These results are used as a basis of reviewing the considerations in hardened I^2L development as an LSI technology in comparison to other contemporary LSI technologies.

Introduction

Radiation effects studies have been performed on a wide variety of I^2L test structures and arrays. Initial studies were performed on devices designed to allow evaluation of electrical performance capabilities and limitations. Study of radiation effects on these initial or "conventional" I^2L structures suggested the principal failure mechanisms in neutron-induced permanent damage, long-term ionization effects and transient photoresponse. We have reviewed these failure mechanisms in terms of trade-offs of electrical performance and radiation hardness. In most cases, however, a trade-off is involved.

Experimental results are presented on three major variations of the conventional I^2L structures: up-diffused, ion-implanted and substrate-fed. Each of these advanced structures represents development motivated primarily for improved electrical performance, but also represents an additional perspective on hardening trade-offs. Based on these experimental results, a subjective comparison is suggested for radiation effects on I^2L and other LSI technologies.

I^2L Radiation Hardening Trade-offs

The conventional I^2L structure is that formed in an n-epitaxial layer on an n^+ substrate, with n^+ diffused collars around the p-diffusions, and n^+ diffusions for the output regions. Extensive radiation effects studies have been performed on test structures and arrays of conventional I^2L.[1-4] Observed failure levels from neutron induced displacement damage range from less than 10^{13} n/cm² at low bias currents, to $6-8 \times 10^{13}$ n/cm² at optimum bias current levels. Observed failure levels from long-term ionization effects vary substantially between arrays. At the lower limit, failure has been observed at total dose exposures of 3×10^4 rads(Si) at low bias currents in contrast to the best results which showed failure levels of greater than 6×10^6 rads(Si) at optimum bias current. Observed pulsed ionizing radiation induced logic upset levels also vary substantially. The lower limit is a wide-pulse upset level of 2×10^7 rads(Si)/s on a complex array[4] with the upper limit of $10^9 - 10^{10}$ rads(Si)/s for narrow-pulse exposure of flip-flop test cells.[2,3]

Experimental and analytical studies on conventional I^2L have lead to the identification of the critical failure mechanisms and suggestions for radiation hardening. In our study, we have reviewed these results in terms of potential trade-offs between electrical performance and radiation hardness, and have determined the radiation susceptibility of advanced I^2L structures developed primarily for improved electrical performance.

Permanent damage effects in I^2L structures resulting from neutron displacement damage and long-term ionization are reflected principally in the degradation of the cell output gain and the transistor gain defining the efficiency of the injector as a current source. The output cell gain is defined as that of the common-emitter gain of the multicollector npn transistor from the substrate up to the output collectors (defined as up-gain or β_u). This up-gain essentially defines the critical fan-out capability of the I^2L logic cell. The inverse (or down-gain) of the I^2L npn transistor is necessary to maintain low output "on" voltages and to eliminate current-hogging. Previous experimental studies on conventional I^2L and our results on advanced structures have not indicated cell failure from the degradation of the down-gain and therefore results of npn gain degradation are presented only in terms of the up-gain or fan-out. The efficiency of the injector as a current source is a critical and sensitive I^2L parameter and is defined as the common-base current gain of the pnp (injector-npn-emitter-npn-base) transistor. Gain degradation of the pnp transistor reduces the effective bias current of the npn transistor switch and may be compounded by lower npn current gain at the lower effective bias level.

The radiation hardness of any semiconductor microcircuit is determined by both the available design margin in the critical circuit parameters and their rate of radiation-induced damage (or damage constant). The logic cell fan-out (or up-gain) design margin is a critical parameter in I^2L array neutron and long-term ionization radiation hardness. The fan-out is a function of both the geometry and doping profile of the npn transistor. Fan-out design margin per collector of an inverter can be increased by restricting the number of collectors in a logic cell, minimizing the distance of any of the collectors from the injector region, and maximizing the ratio of collector areas to the emitter area of the npn transistor. Each of these geometric adjustments, however, must be traded off against cell density. Restricting the number of collectors in the cell will require a greater number of logic gates to perform the same overall function. Reducing the distance from the collectors to the injector will tend to complicate the metallization pattern, increasing the spacing between logic cells and increasing the size of the overall array. In a minimum geometry logic cell, the ratio of collector areas to the emitter area is generally defined by the minimum spacing and alignment tolerances. However, the base area of the transistor can be increased to allow for a metallization cross-over. Elimination of these cross-overs will complicate the metallization pattern and will increase the overall size of the array.

---

* Research sponsored by the Defense Nuclear Agency and the Navy Strategic System Project Office.

** Mr. Pease is currently with the BDM Corporation, Albuquerque, New Mexico

Reprinted from *IEEE Trans. Nucl. Sci.*, vol. NS-24, pp. 2327-2335, Dec. 1977.

Gains of the I^2L logic cell can also be increased by minimizing unwanted carrier injection at the sidewalls of the p-regions. This injection is typically reduced by an n^+ collar around the periphery of the cell diffused with the n^+ collector regions. Gain can be further increased by driving the n^+ collar all the way down to the substrate or by eliminating the collar and restricting carrier injection with a side-wall oxide isolation region. The disadvantage of these isolation techniques is that the cell geometry for the deep n^+ collars and oxide isolation both require additional processing steps.

The doping profile of the npn transistor is critical in obtaining high logic cell fan-out. The fan-out of an unirradiated cell is generally limited by the emitter efficiency, the effective base width, electron injection to the base contact and the current injected laterally to the injector. Emitter efficiency of the transistor can be improved by minimizing the epitaxial thickness to minimize hole injection to the substrate. Because of the base doping profile in the conventional I^2L structure there is a built-in electric field that retards electron flow from the emitter to the collector. Reducing, or reversing this built-in electric field will increase fan-out but requires more sophisticated processing techniques. Electron injection in the extrinsic base region can be reduced by increasing the doping level, but the associated increase in the intrinsic base region will reduce the emitter efficiency. Exclusive increase of the doping level in the extrinsic base region and not the intrinsic base region increases the complexity of the fabrication process.

Output breakdown voltage requirements are modest compared to other LSI technologies but must be greater than 5 volts for an output TTL interface or 2 volts for internal functions. Process modifications such as increasing the doping level of the p-base or n^+ collars to increase fan-out design margin will also reduce the breakdown voltage. Similarly, decreasing the epitaxial thickness and npn base width is a trade-off against high breakdown voltages.

Increasing the design margin for the injector efficiency in the logic cell is important, but not as critical as that for cell fan-out. In the conventional I^2L structure, the current gain of the lateral pnp transistor can be improved by decreasing the epitaxial width and increasing the depth of the diffused p-regions. As reflected in the improvement in the npn emitter efficiency, a narrow epitaxial region reduces hole injection to the substrate and improves gain. This requirement, however, places tighter requirements on process control. Increasing the depth of the p-regions increases the effective face area of the lateral pnp base region, but since the p-diffusion is also the base of the npn transistor, a deep region makes it more difficult to get narrow npn base widths. The effective injector efficiency in an I^2L array may also be limited by resistive drops in the injector rails, particularly at high injector bias currents. Limiting the maximum length of the injector rails will require additional complexity in the metallization routing and an overall increase in the size of the semiconductor chip.

In addition to increasing the design margin of critical parameters it is desireable to decrease the radiation damage constants. To reduce the effects of neutron displacement damage, dependence of the cell parameters on minority carrier lifetime must be minimized.

For neutron displacement damage effects, reductions in the gain damage constants can be achieved by reducing the effective volume of semiconductor regions active in carrier recombination. Thus, reducing or reversing the built-in npn transistor base field would decrease the effective base width, as would the decrease in epitaxial width. For the lateral pnp transistor of conventional I^2L, hardening would be realized by reducing the width of the base region or implementing an aiding built-in electric field to reduce the effective base width. For a uniformly-doped base region, however, decreasing the lateral pnp base width will also decrease the output fan-out. Considerations for the npn transistor in reducing the damage factor are all consistent with those presented in increasing the design margin and with the same trade-offs. Increasing emphasis, however, would be in decreasing the effective base width and minimizing the volume of the extrinsic base region.

The susceptibility to long-term ionization effects can be reduced by increasing the surface dopant concentrations and incorporating processing techniques which minimize the alkali impurities in the oxide and the time-temperature stress at the semiconductor-oxide interface during processing. In order to substantially increase the p surface doping for a fixed deposition concentration, a shallower p-drive is required. This, however, will result in a steeper base doping profile and thus a larger base retarding electric field. Also, unless the epitaxial layer is very thin, it would mean a large n-region under the base diffusion which would degrade the injector efficiency and the up-gain. Increasing the overall base doping concentration in order to increase surface doping will result in lower npn emitter efficiency. A second base deposition and shallow drive could be used to increase the dopant concentration only in the extrinsic base region, but with an increase in processing complexity.

Hardening to long-term ionization effects by process modifications affecting the oxide-silicon interface is an excellent example of decreasing the damage constant without affecting the initial design margins. These hardening techniques have been extensively developed for MOS microcircuit elements.

Failure mechanisms in transient logic upset resulting from I^2L photoresponse have not been clearly identified. It appears that two mechanisms may be involved: turn-on of the "off" npn transistor by resistive voltage drops of the radiation-induced photocurrent, and an effective increase in operating current by the npn emitter-base junction photocurrent which increases the total current to the point where the npn transistor gain decreases and cell fanouts are no longer sufficient. In the first case, the effect may be reduced by minimizing the area of the npn emitter-base junction, increasing the doping concentration of the epitaxial region and/or decreasing the epitaxial thickness. The trade-offs in terms of the epitaxial region parameters have been discussed previously, and the emitter-base junction area is generally held to a minimum in order to reduce the emitter junction depletion capacitance and improve the cell speed-power product. In the second case, the effect may be minimized by increasing the operating range of the logic cells to higher injector bias currents, especially for the collectors farthest from the injector. In general, the high current gain can be increased by going to larger geometries to reduce parasitic voltage drops. Larger npn transistor geometries, however, will increase the emitter junction photocurrent and may be counterproductive to hardening.

The I^2L hardening trade-offs suggested by our study are summarized in Table 1 in terms of the identified geometric and processing parameters.

DESIGN PARAMETER	TRADEOFF
A. NEUTRON DISPLACEMENT DAMAGE	
1. OPTIMIZE npn COLLECTOR LAYOUT	DECREASE IN CELL PACKING DENSITY, INCREASED LAYOUT COMPLEXITY, AND INCREASED CHIP SIZE.
2. INCREASE npn COLLECTOR-EMITTER AREA RATIO	DECREASED BREAKDOWN VOLTAGES, INCREASED CHIP AREA, AND INCREASED EXTRINSIC BASE RESISTANCE.
3. MINIMUM pnp BASE WIDTH	INCREASE IN PROCESS CONTROL AND DECREASE IN FAN-OUT.
4. MINIMUM n-EPITAXIAL THICKNESS	INCREASED PROCESS CONTROL AND DECREASED BREAKDOWN VOLTAGES.
5. DEEP n^+ COLLARS	ADDITIONAL PROCESSING COMPLEXITY AND DECREASED BREAKDOWN VOLTAGE.
6. OXIDE ISOLATION COLLARS	INCREASED PROCESS COMPLEXITY
7. INCREASED n-EPITAXIAL DOPING	DECREASE IN SPEED-POWER PRODUCT AND DECREASED INJECTOR EFFICIENCY.
B. LONG-TERM IONIZATION EFFECTS	
1. MINIMUM pnp BASE WIDTH	INCREASE IN PROCESS CONTROL, DECREASE IN FAN-OUT.
2. MINIMUM npn SURFACE AREA	DECREASED BREAKDOWN VOLTAGES, INCREASED CHIP AREA, AND INCREASED EXTRINSIC BASE RESISTANCE.
3. OPTIMIZE OXIDE HARDNESS	INCREASE PROCESS CONTROL.
4. MAXIMUM p-SURFACE DOPING BY:	
- SHALLOW DRIVE-IN	DECREASED INJECTOR EFFICIENCY AND DECREASED FAN-OUT.
- INCREASED p-DOPING	DECREASE IN FAN-OUT.
5. MINIMUM npn EMITTER JUNCTION SURFACE	INCREASE IN PROCESS CONTROL FOR MINIMUM CELL GEOMETRIES.
C. TRANSIENT PHOTORESPONSE	
1. MINIMIZE n-EPITAXIAL THICKNESS	INCREASED PROCESS CONTROL, AND DECREASED BREAKDOWN VOLTAGES.
2. INCREASE n-EPITAXIAL DOPING	DECREASE IN SPEED-POWER PRODUCT AND DECREASED INJECTOR EFFICIENCY.
3. OPTIMIZE LAYOUT FOR HIGH BIAS CURRENT OPERATION	DECREASED CELL DENSITY, INCREASED CHIP SIZE.

Table 1: Summary of radiation hardening trade-offs for conventional I^2L LSI.

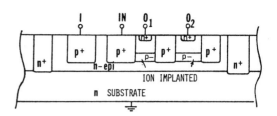

Figure 1: Cross section of Texas Instrument Ion Implanted I^2L Inverter Cell.[5]

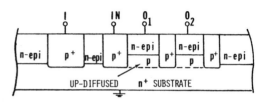

Figure 2: Cross section of Hughes Up-diffused I^2L Inverter Cell.[6]

Advanced I^2L Radiation Effects

A substantial goal of I^2L development has been to improve its electrical switching response. In our study three types of advanced I^2L arrays, each developed for improved electrical performance without regard to radiation hardness, were obtained for radiation effects characterization and analysis. These were samples of Texas Instruments second-generation I^2L which uses ion implantation extensively to optimize the doping profile (which we will refer to as T.I. ion implanted), Hughes Semiconductor I^2L which uses ion implantation, dopant up-diffusion, and Schottky diode outputs (which we will refer to as Hughes up-diffused), and Harris Semiconductor substrate-fed-logic (SFL) in which the lateral pnp structure of conventional I^2L is replaced by a completely vertical structure (which we will refer to as Harris SFL). Samples of each of these advanced I^2L technologies were obtained by NWSC (Crane) with the cooperation of the manufacturer for radiation effects characterization. The NWSC (Crane) study included the characterization of neutron displacement damage effects, long-term ionization effects and transient photoresponse as well as the analysis of data with regard to failure mechanisms. We present these results as specific examples of trade-offs in I^2L electrical performance and radiation hardness as well as indicative of that to be expected in the development of the technology.

Texas Instruments Ion Implanted I^2L

The extensive use of ion implantation in I^2L is employed by several semiconductor manufacturers including Fairchild in their Isoplanar Integrated Injection Logic, I^3L, and the Schottky collector I^2L from Hughes Semiconductor and Bell Telephone Laboratories. The Texas Instruments process is unique, however, in that it represents a second generation development of an I^2L/LSI production process.

The structure of the T.I. ion implanted I^2L cell is shown in Figure 1 for a two-output inverter cell.[5]

The intrinsic npn base regions are formed by a boron implant into a thin n-epitaxial region. Deep p^+ diffusions form the extrinsic npn base regions as well as the lateral pnp emitter and collector. The n^+ collars are diffused through the epitaxial layer and shallow n^+ implants are used to increase the surface doping level of the n-epitaxial collector regions. Although developed for improved electrical performance, the T.I. structure represents several of the features considered for improved radiation hardness. The retarding base electrical field of the npn transistor has been eliminated and the relatively greater doping of the extrinsic base region over that of the intrinsic base region increases cell fan-out and reduces the effects of base resistance in limiting operation at high bias currents. The high p-dopant surface concentration should also minimize long-term ionization effects.

Hughes Semiconductor Up-Diffused I^2L

Development of I^2L by Hughes Semiconductor has been directed to obtaining maximum performance of the structure with process optimization. A cross-section of the Hughes Semiconductor I^2L structure is shown in Figure 2.[6] In this process, a boron implant on an n^+ substrate is partially up-diffused through the n-epitaxial region as the epitaxial region is grown. This up-diffused region forms the intrinsic npn base regions. The extrinsic npn base regions and injectors are formed by a deep p^+ diffusion. The inverter outputs are realized by Schottky contacts made to the n-epitaxial collector regions. The major differences between this up-diffused process and the ion implanted process are the doping profile of the intrinsic npn base region, and the Schottky collector outputs. With the up-diffused process, the built-in base electric field aids carrier transport from emitter to collector just as in normal application of a planar transistor. The up-gain of the up-diffused structure is very high (typically on the order of 100). It would be expected that the increase in design margin would result in improved hardness, and that the transistor base doping profile would decrease sensitivity to long-term ionization radiation effects.

Harris Substrate Fed Logic

Substrate Fed Logic (SFL) was first introduced by Plessey in 1974 and represents a substantial departure from the conventional I^2L form.[7] In SFL, a p^+ substrate is used as the injector region. This is a completely vertical structure and the injector supplies carriers uniformly across the semiconductor chip. The form of SFL developed by Harris Semiconductor is shown in cross-section in Figure 3.[8] The structure is formed by growing an n-epitaxial layer on a p^+ substrate, followed by a p-epitaxial growth on the n-epitaxial layer. The surface of the lightly doped p-epitaxial layer is covered with a shallow p^+ diffusion so that contact may be made to the npn base regions (inverter inputs). A deep n^+ diffusion through the p-epitaxial layer provides contact to the n-epitaxial region for the inverter ground, and a final n^+ diffusion forms the npn collectors.

Unlike conventional I^2L, the injector is a vertical pnp transistor consisting of a heavily doped emitter, a moderately doped base (2-3 μm wide), and a lightly doped collector. The gain of the vertical pnp transistor is much better than that of the lateral pnp in conventional I^2L which can result in substantial improvement in injector efficiency if a major portion of the chip is active.

The npn transistors of SFL consist of a moderately doped emitter (n-epi), a lightly doped base (p-epi) with no retarding electric field in the intrinsic region, and a heavily doped collector. Because the npn base width is determined by the collector diffusion depth and the p-epitaxial thickness, very tight control must be maintained on the p-epitaxial thickness and resistivity to obtain uniform up-gain across a wafer. The neutron hardness of this structure should be better than that of conventional I^2L since the npn emitter efficiency can be reasonably high (the ratio of emitter to base doping is typically greater than 20), because there is no retarding electric field in the npn base, and since lateral injection from the extrinsic base region is reduced by the deep n^+ diffusion which defines the cell. Also, the pnp transistor has very high initial current gain because the base region is narrower than in conventionaal I^2L. A disadvantage of large SFL arrays is that it is difficult to design to a fan-out per collector of one as in conventional I^2L since the bias current of a SFL cell is proportional to its base area. Thus, the amount of current that an output collector must sink is a function of the ratio of the base area driving the collector to the base area of the collector being driven. For the Harris MSI circuits characterized in this study, the maximum base area ratio, or the worst-case fan-out per collector was equal to four.

The long-term ionization hardness of SFL should be excellent since the entire p-surface is heavily doped **and the** pnp transistor active emitter-base junction is not exposed to a silicon-silicon-dioxide interface.

Photoresponse effects in SFL may differ from those in conventional I^2L. In conventional I^2L the major photocurrent is that of the npn emitter junction which is in the same direction as the effective bias current. In SFL, however, the npn emitter photocurrent is reduced because of the decreased volume of the emitter region. The major photocurrent in the SFL structure is that of the pnp emitter (injector) junction which may work to decrease the logic upset level of the SFL array.

Characterization of Radiation Effects on Advanced I^2L Structures

The test structures and circuits representative of the three advanced I^2L technologies characterized in the NWSC (Crane) study[9] are presented in Table 2 along with the number of samples exposed to each radiation environment.

All of the structures listed in Table 2 are non-isolated with open collector I^2L outputs. The Harris SFL samples were from the first diffusion run using MSI level development chips. The T.I. ion implanted samples were test chips of the SBP 9900 16-bit microprocessor micro instruction set ROM. The ring oscillators and inverters were accessed by a special metallization mask interconnecting elements of the ROM. The Hughes up-diffused samples were from an early diffusion run of an I^2L development chip.

Experimental Results - Neutron Displacement Damage

Neutron/gamma exposures were performed passively on the test samples using the White Sands Missile Range Fast Burst Reactor. Electrical performance of the samples was determined for all critical d-c and switching parameters. The critical parameters for I^2L operation emphasized were the d-c fan-out per collector and the injector efficiency. Although a precise measurement of fan-out requires a determination of the ratio of output sink current to the short circuit input sink current with each measurement at constant bias voltage; a reasonable estimate of fan-out per collector is obtained by direct measurement of the npn transistor gain (β_u) on a curve tracer. For these devices β_u was within 10-20% of the fan-out for output collector currents of less than 100 μA for each collector. Above 100 μA the

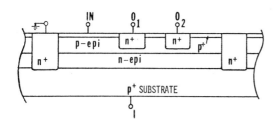

Figure 3: Cross section of Harris Substrate Fed Logic Inverter Cell.[7]

I^2L STRUCTURE	TEST DEVICE DESCRIPTION	NUMBER OF SAMPLES		
		NEUTRON	TOTAL DOSE	DOSE RATE
T. I. ION IMPLANTED	1. FOUR COLLECTOR, 5 STAGE RING OSCILLATOR; 4 COLLECTOR INVERTER.	3	3	0
	2. MICROINSTRUCTION SET ROM.	2	2	2
HUGHES UP-DIFFUSED	1. SINGLE COLLECTOR INVERTER; THREE-OUTPUT, TWO-INPUT INVERTER.	2	2	0
	2. SINGLE COLLECTOR, 15-STAGE RING OSCILLATORS.	2	2	0
	3. 10-STAGE DIVIDE-BY-TWO FREQUENCY DIVIDER.	2	2	2
HARRIS SUBSTRATE FED LOGIC	1. 1 K ROM	3	3	3
	2. 4 COLLECTOR, 7-STAGE RING OSCILLATOR WITH 2-STAGE OUTPUT BUFFER; SINGLE COLLECTOR INVERTER.	4	5	0
	3. 32 BIT SERIAL SHIFT REGISTER; 10 COLLECTOR INVERTER; SINGLE-COLLECTOR, 7-STAGE RING OSCILLATOR WITH 4-STAGE OUTPUT BUFFER.	4	4	2

Table 2: Summary of advanced I^2L test structures.

departure was more significant. The pnp common base current gain, α, is a direct measure of the injector efficiency. The results of the average β_u as a function of I_C for the three advanced I^2L structures are shown in Figure 4. In this summary, data are presented only for the initial gain and the degraded gain after exposure to 10^{14} n/cm^2 (1 MeV equiv.). Data on T.I. conventional I^2L is shown for comparison. All of the data in Figure 4 is taken from single collector inverters except for the T.I. ion implanted samples. In that case, the gain shown is that for the collector nearest the base current source on the four collector inverter. All β_u gain measurements were made at a d-c collector-emitter voltage bias of 0.5 volts.

In Figure 5, the results of α as a function of d-c injector current, I_I, are shown before irradiation and after exposure to 10^{14} n/cm^2 (1 MeV equiv.). The measurement was straightforward for the T.I. and Hughes samples. The nature of the SFL structure, however, prohibits a direct measurement of the cell current gain. The data shown in Figure 5 for the Harris samples was obtained by using the inverter cell input as the pnp emitter. The current gain determined is the "inverse" α and was assumed to be representative of the "normal" α or injector efficiency.

Other critical performance parameters of I^2L are the electrical switching response and the minimum operating injector bias current (I_{TH}). Measured values on ring oscillators of initial performance and after exposure to 10^{14} n/cm^2 are presented in Table 3. The post-irradiation switching speeds shown in Table 3 were measured at the bias current required for minimum delay in the unirradiated device (I_{min}).

For other samples, the T.I. ROM was severely degraded at 10^{14} n/cm^2 and failed to operate at 3×10^{14} n/cm^2. The Harris shift register and ROM showed significant degradation at 3×10^{13} n/cm^2 and 3 of the 4 shift registers and all 3 ROM's failed completely at 10^{14} n/cm^2.

Experimental Results - Long-Term Ionization Effects

The long-term ionization exposures were performed using the Indiana State University cobalt-60 source. All devices were irradiated under bias with injectors and inputs grounded and +0.7 volts on the outputs. The pre-irradiation and 10^6 rad(Si) average β_u results are shown in Figure 6 for the same device types used for the neutron irradiations. The average α curves before irradiation and after 10^6 rad(Si) are given in

I^2L STRUCTURE	t_{pd} (min) $\phi = 0$	$t_{pd}(I = I_{min})$ $\phi = 10^{14}$ n/cm^2	I_{TH} $\phi = 10^{14}$ n/cm^2
HUGHES UP-DIFFUSED	4.6ns	3.0ns	11.2 μA/STAGE
T.I. ION-IMPLANTED	9.0ns	8.0ns	44 μA/STAGE
HARRIS SFL	14ns	98ns	*
T.I. CONVENTIONAL	25ns	DID NOT OPERATE	

* I_{TH} TOTAL INJECTOR CURRENT WAS 4mA, THRESHOLD CURRENT PER STAGE COULD NOT BE DETERMINED.

Table 3: Summary of neutron damage effects on ring oscillator parameters.

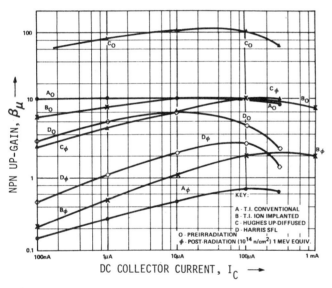

Figure 4: Neutron induced degradation of NPN up-gain for conventional I^2L and three forms of advanced I^2L.

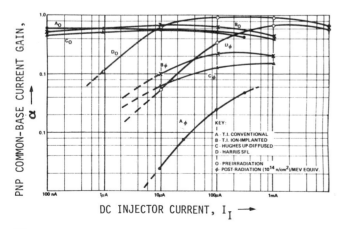

Figure 5: Neutron-induced degradation in pnp gain for conventional I^2L and three forms of advanced I^2L.

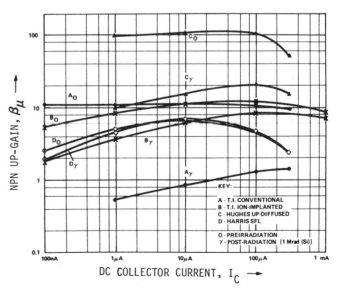

Figure 6: Total-dose-induced degradation of npn up-gain for conventional I^2L and three forms of advanced I^2L.

Figure 7, again showing inverse α for the Harris SFL devices. The long-term ionization tests on the ring oscillators showed essentially no change for the Harris SFL and T.I. ion implanted structures. The Hughes up-diffused ring oscillators showed an increase in propagation delay from 4.3 ns pre-irradiation to 8.0 ns after 10^6 rad(Si) for an injector current per stage of 1 mA. At an injector current per/stage of 100 µA, the increase in propagation delay was from 14 ns before radiation to 150 ns at 10^6 rad(Si). The total dose tests on the T.I. ROM and Harris ROM and shift register showed no measurable change in operating characteristics at 10^6 rad(Si).

Experimental Results - Transient Photoresponse

Photoresponse tests were performed on the T.I. ion implanted ROM, the Harris SFL shift register and the Hughes up-diffused 10 stage divide by two frequency divider. The tests were conducted on the White Sands Missile Range LINAC using a radiation pulse width of 100 ns. The total injector current was varied over the device operating range to determine the effect on the dose rate upset level.

The threshold dose rate upset level ($\dot{\gamma}_{TH}$) on the two up-diffused dividers was 2-3 x 10^9 rad(Si)/sec over the usable range of operating currents and occurred preferentially for the transition from output high to output low.

The Harris 32 bit serial shift register showed a definite linear dependence of $\dot{\gamma}_{TH}$ on injector current

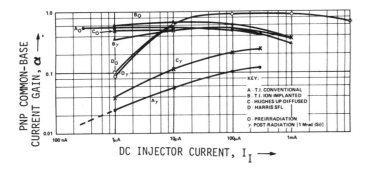

Figure 7: Total-dose-induced degradation in pnp gain for conventional I^2L and three forms of advanced I^2L.

with results ranging from 1 x 10^8 rad(Si)/sec at I_I(total) = 23 mA to 7.5 x 10^8 rad(Si) at I_I(total) = 1mA.

The threshold dose rate upset on the T.I. ion implanted ROM was more difficult to determine since a permanent change of state does not occur at the outputs. Therefore, $\dot{\gamma}_{TH}$ was loosely defined as the dose rate to cause a transient change in the output voltage equal to one-half the output voltage swing. With this criteria, $\dot{\gamma}_{TH}$ was approximately 7-9 x 10^9 rad(Si)/sec over the useful operating current range and showed no clear injector current dependence.

I^2L Radiation Effects Summary

Results on the experimental characterization of radiation effects on the advanced I^2L structures have been presented to illustrate possible variations with modifications in the conventional I^2L structure. Our estimates of the critical levels of neutron, total ionizing dose, and pulsed ionizing exposure are presented in Figures 8, 9 and 10 for conventional I^2L and the advanced I^2L structures. Figures 8 and 9 present the neutron fluence and total ionizing dose levels at which moderate degradation would be observed, the levels at which array failure may be expected at limiting

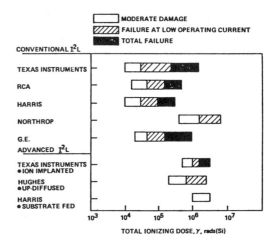

Figure 9: Summary of long-term ionization effects on Integrated Injection Logic.

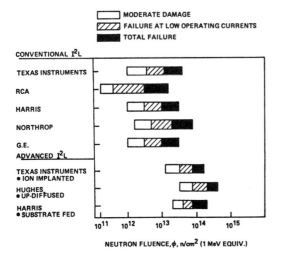

Figure 8: Summary of neutron damage effects on Integrated Injection Logic.

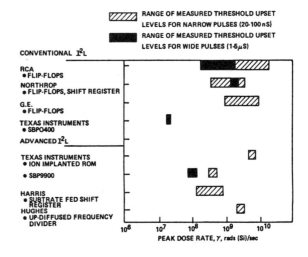

Figure 10: Summary of Integrated Injection Logic transient photoresponse.

operating conditions, and the levels at which complete failure of the array can be expected. As shown, the advanced structures are substantially less sensitive to neutron displacement damage effects than those observed for conventional I^{2}L. The relatively tight spread of the range shown for the advanced structures must be interpreted in terms of the relatively few samples characterized. The advanced structures also show less sensitivity to long-term ionization effects in comparison to effects observed on most of the conventional structures. Results on the Northrop conventional I^{2}L structures are substantially better than the results reported on other conventional I^{2}L structures. Data on the T.I. ion implanted structure shows a substantial improvement over the T.I. conventional structure, but probably shows greater susceptibility than either the Northrop conventional I^{2}L or the Hughes or Harris advanced structures.

The summary of critical logic upset levels for pulsed ionization exposures are presented in Figure 10 as a function of the radiation pulse width. Based on limited data it appears that the photoresponse of the T.I. and Hughes advanced structures is comparable to that observed on conventional I^{2}L test structures and is substantially greater than that observed of the T.I. SBP0400 microprocessor. The range of threshold upset level presented in Figure 10 includes the observed dependence on injector bias current.

LSI Performance Considerations

At this point we consider I^{2}L as an LSI technology in comparison with other contemporary LSI technologies. A wide variety of electrical performance parameters as well as radiation susceptibility must be considered. Results of this subjective comparison are summarized in Figure 11.

Cell density is a major LSI parameter as a critical determinant in the overall chip area for a given complex function. The qualitative ranking shown in Figure 11 is based on both calculated areas for basic logic functions using the same mask layout rules,[10] and the relative maximum complexity for arrays of similar logic function (e.g., random-access memories).[11] Interestingly, each of these criteria lead to the same ranking despite major variations in the nature of the

logic cells, physical limitations on the fabrication of large arrays, and constraints of maximum array size due to power dissipation.

Maximum cell density and array complexity are realized by n-MOS/LSI followed closely by I^{2}L and then by CMOS/SOS. Each of these technologies are comparable in LSI cell density and the relative densities in specific arrays could vary significantly depending on the layout optimization for the specific logic function. Following these in cell density are the Schottky-clamped TTL and junction-isolated CMOS. The density of S/C TTL is limited by the area required for the diffused resistors and the maximum array complexity is limited by power dissipation. The cell density limits in junction-isolated CMOS are due to required guard rings or closed geometry to prevent unwanted surface inversions under the field oxide and metallization routing limitations. The development of reduced geometry silicon-gate CMOS will, in our opinion, increase the cell density past that of S/C TTL, but not to that of the high-density technologies. The cell geometry of ECL is large because of the area required for the diffused resistors, but a more important consideration is power dissipation which limits the maximum array complexity.

Electrical switching speed is a critical performance parameter for LSI arrays. Increasing data processing and control requirements seem to continuously demand greater array speeds. Among LSI technologies, switching speed is a function of the array complexity, specific electrical bias or cell circuit design and the output load requirements. In complex arrays, the switching speed is determined principally by internal gate delays. These gate delays are a decreasing function of increasing electrical bias for I^{2}L and CMOS arrays. Gate delays in n-MOS, S/C TTL and ECL are determined by the cell circuit design which can be varied between products to trade-off switching speed against power dissipation (e.g., low-power, standard, and high-speed TTL families). In smaller logic arrays the output switching time can become a substantial fraction of the overall switching response. This is particularly critical in switching capacitive loads with limited output drive.

Maximum electrical switching response of LSI technologies is obtained for ECL, typically in relatively small arrays, and for CMOS/SOS in relatively large arrays. The electrical switching time of CMOS in small arrays is limited by output drive. This is particularly critical for CMOS/SOS because of its higher intrinsic speed and lower output drive. Following these high speed technologies closely is S/C TTL with a substantial decrease to n-MOS, I^{2}L and CMOS which have comparably slower switching responses.[11] The relative switching speed of I^{2}L and n-MOS is based on performance of the Texas Instruments TMS9900 and SBP9900 microprocessors.[12] In this case the architecture and levels of integration are comparable and maximum clock rates are close. Switching speed limitations of junction-isolated CMOS will be relieved with smaller device geometries and higher levels of array integration as in advanced silicon-gate arrays. Switching responses obtained are faster than n-MOS or conventional I^{2}L, but not up to the speed of S/C TTL.

Power dissipation is a critical parameter in LSI because of system importance and limitations in chip heat sink capability. Because of the variations in nature between the LSI technologies, static power dissipation is considered separately from dynamic power dissipation. For S/C TTL, ECL, n-MOS and I^{2}L the total power is determined principally by static dissipation with a relatively small increase as the maximum frequency of operation is approached. For CMOS and CMOS/SOS, however, the principal power dissipation

	S/C TTL	ECL	I^{2}L	n MOS	CMOS	CMOS/SOS
CELL DENSITY	0	-	++	++	0	+
SWITCHING SPEED	+	++	0	0	-	++
STATIC POWER DISSIPATION	-	--	+	-	++	++
DYNAMIC POWER DISSIPATION	+	+	++	+	0	+
SPEED-POWER PRODUCT	0	0	++	+	0	++
OUTPUT DRIVE CAPABILITY	+	+	0	0	-	--
NOISE IMMUNITY	+	0	--	0	++	++
TEMPERATURE RANGE	+	+	+	-	0	-
NEUTRON DAMAGE	0	++	-	+	+	++
LONG-TERM IONIZATION DAMAGE	+	+·+	+	--	--	--
TRANSIENT LOGIC UPSET LEVEL	0	0	+	0	+	++

++ SUPERIOR, + GOOD, 0 AVERAGE, - BELOW AVERAGE, -- WEAK

Figure 11: Subjective comparison of LSI technologies.

occurs during the switching transient. The static power is very low and in most applications the total power is determined primarily from the dynamic component. The static power dissipation of all other LSI technologies is determined by trade-off with switching response by cell design or external bias. By design, the static power dissipation is generally lowest for n-MOS, increased for S/C TTL and is greatest for ECL.[11] In each case, the switching response also decreases with increasing static power dissipation. I^2L is a unique LSI technology in that the power dissipation can be adjusted by the external bias with a direct trade-off in switching response. Static power can be reduced to approach that of CMOS, but with substantially slower switching response.

In terms of dynamic power dissipation only, the CMOS technologies are at a substantial disadvantage. For relatively small arrays and with limited output drive, the dynamic power dissipation at the output interfaces can dominate the dynamic power of the array. CMOS/SOS arrays have the advantage of reduced internal capacitance and a higher level of integration, but generally have reduced output drive capability which limits the overall improvement in dynamic power dissipation over that of bulk CMOS.

Because of the apparent trade-off between power dissipation and switching speed, the speed-power product can be used as a measure for the non-CMOS LSI technologies. For I^2L at low-moderate bias currents, the switching response time is inversely proportional to the power dissipation. The speed-power product is a constant even under varying bias conditions, with a value on the order of 1 pJ per logic gate in complex arrays.[13] The speed-power product of the fixed-bias non-CMOS technologies is a single value, which is on the order of 10 pJ for n-MOS, 20-60 pJ for S/C TTL and 50 pJ for ECL.[12]

The speed-power product of CMOS is a function of operating frequency because substantial dissipation occurs only during the switching transient. To eliminate the frequency dependence, the energy of a single switching transient can be used as a measure. To measure the technology rather than the output load, the energy switched in the output load should be subtracted. The energy in the switching transient is defined as the product of the dynamic power dissipation times the switching time. For the relatively small-scale arrays of junction-isolated CMOS, the switching energy per gate is on the order of 500 pJ for a supply voltage of 10 volts. Thus, at low frequencies, it compares very favorably to the other technologies but loses its advantage at moderate to high operating frequencies. We could not find data on the internal gate switching energy for complex CMOS/SOS arrays, but it is expected that the reduction in internal capacitance could reduce the switching energy by a factor of 2-4. The major advantage in CMOS/SOS in this case is the ability to operate at higher clock frequencies than junction-isolated CMOS.

Output drive capability of the LSI technologies was compared basically by the individual transistor elements. On this basis, the output transconductance of bipolar transistor elements is substantially greater than that of MOS transistor elements.[14] The output drive of I^2L must be derated from that of the other bipolar technologies because of the limited gain of the inverted output transistor. The output drive capability of the MOS transistor elements is measured by the channel mobility and so CMOS/SOS must be derated from junction-isolated CMOS and n-MOS.

Noise immunity is a critical parameter of LSI technology but very difficult to completely assess outside the requirements of a specific system. Three ways of

evaluating potential noise sensitivities are through the d-c input/output transfer function, power supply variation tolerance, and transient noise energy required to produce a logic error. In terms of d-c noise voltage margin the CMOS technologies have the best with a worst-case noise margin. For commercial CMOS with a minimum supply voltage of 5 volts, the minimum noise margin is 2.2 volts. The worst-case noise margin for S/C TTL, and n-MOS with TTL interfaces, is approximately 1.2 volts. ECL noise margin is on the order of 500 mV.[11] I^2L comes up last in this measure with a worst-case d-c noise margin on the order of 40-100 mV assuming a direct input to the I^2L network.[15] In terms of sensitivity to power supply variations both I^2L and CMOS can be operated over a wide range of bias current/voltage assuming no induced errors from the variations in switching time. In this case I^2L has an advantage since the total time-dependent power supply current can be regulated more smoothly than that for CMOS with current surges during the switching transients. Power supply regulation is significantly more critical for the S/C TTL and n-MOS technologies and is very critical for ECL operation operating at high data rates.

Consideration of the noise energy required for logic error[16] leads to essentially the same qualitative ranking of technologies as the d-c noise margin. The required energy is on the order of that required for a electrical switching transient and is of the same order as the speed-power product. Calculated noise energies ranged from approximately 1 nJ for junction-isolated CMOS and TTL to approximately 1 pJ for I^2L. I^2L arrays will probably have to include TTL-compatible interfaces to improve the worst-case noise margin with a penalty in overall array size and power dissipation.

The final LSI electrical parameter considered was the recommended operating temperature range. Certainly all the LSI technologies considered can be designed for operating over the full military range of -55 to +125°C. The qualitative ratings shown in Figure 11 are based on an interpretation of the measure of difficulty as reflected in commercial product specifications including the Texas Instruments n-MOS/I^2L microprocessors and TTL product, RCA junction-isolated and CMOS/SOS products, and a wide variety of n-MOS and ECL products.[11] We concluded that the greatest measure of difficulty in wide temperature range was in the n-MOS and commercial CMOS/SOS technologies with decreasing difficulty for S/C TTL, ECL and I^2L. It also seemed that low temperature operation was the greatest challenge for the bipolar technologies because of the decrease in transistor gain, and high temperature operation was most difficult for the MOS technologies because of the decrease in carrier mobility.

Neutron displacement damage effects (in the absence of any ionizing radiation) are minimum in CMOS/SOS arrays and are of minor consideration in junction-isolated CMOS and n-MOS arrays. In the bipolar technologies, displacement damage effects are minimum in ECL arrays and are of comparable hardness to CMOS/SOS arrays. Damage susceptibility of Schottky-clamped TTL arrays is generally somewhat less than that of CMOS or n-MOS arrays. Conventional I^2L is clearly the most sensitive of the LSI technologies to neutron displacement damage. Results on the advanced devices, however, suggests that the hardness can be improved to come close to that of S/C TTL.

The relative advantages of the LSI technologies reverse in consideration of long-term ionization effects. In this case the bipolar technologies have the advantage with ECL as the least sensitive and S/C TTL and I^2L as comparable. The long-term ionizing radiation susceptibility of the MOS technologies varies greatly with design margins allowed for threshold voltage shifts and the degree of control used in processing to produce a hardened oxide. Junction-isolated CMOS arrays have been developed to hardness levels better than those of some conventional I^{2}L arrays, and comparable to advanced I^{2}L structures. Principally as commercial products, however, the long-term ionization sensitivity of junction-isolated CMOS is substantially greater with even greater sensitivity observed in commercial CMOS/SOS and n-MOS arrays.

Transient logic upset effects due to transient ionizing radiation are minimum in LSI arrays in CMOS/SOS technology. In this case, the nature of the logic cell is relatively insensitive to the junction photocurrents, and the photocurrents themselves are minimized by the minimum volume of active semiconductor material. Junction-isolated CMOS is also relatively insensitive to the junction photocurrents, but the logic upset levels are reduced by the increase in junction photocurrents. Radiation-induced latch-up is also a possibility in junction-isolated CMOS although special processing techniques can be used to eliminate the effect. The logic upset levels observed on I^{2}L are much better than those observed on junction-isolated CMOS. Radiation-induced latch-up has not been observed on any I^{2}L array, but is a potential consideration particularly on arrays with high-voltage signal interfaces or combined analog and digital functions on the same chip. The transient logic upset levels of n-MOS, ECL and S/C TTL are all comparable with specific failure levels determined by individual circuit function and internal design margins, and are all substantially less than that of I^{2}L logic cells but are comparable to the failure levels observed in I^{2}L/LSI arrays.

In conclusion, we have presented a wide range of considerations on the I^{2}L technology in comparison to other LSI technologies, and in terms of the design trade-offs in conventional I^{2}L design and have presented data on radiation effects on advanced I^{2}L technologies representative of the development of the technology to improved electrical performance. We do not suggest conclusions on the present or eventual radiation hardness of I^{2}L/LSI but have attempted to illustrate some of the critical factors which must be included in either the application of commercial I^{2}L or to its development as a hardened LSI technology.

References

1. Pease, R.L., K.F., Galloway and R. A. Stehlin, "Radiation Damage to Integrated Injection Logic Cells", IEEE Trans. on Nucl. Sci., NS-22, No. 6, December 1976.

2. Raymond, J.P., T.Y. Wong and K.K. Schuegraf, "Radiation Effects on Bipolar Integrated Injection Logic", IEEE Trans. on Nucl. Sci., NS-22, No. 6, p. 2605-2610; December 1975.

3. Long, D.M., et. al., "Radiation Effects Modeling and Experimental Data on I^{2}L Devices", IEEE Trans. on Nucl. Sci., NS-23, No. 6, December 1976.

4. Measel, P.R., et. al., "Development of a Hard Microcontroller", IEEE Trans. on Nucl. Sci., NS-23, No. 6, December 1976.

5. Herman, J.M., et. al., "Second Generation I^{2}L/MTL: A 20 ns Process/Structure", IEEE Journal of Solid State Circuits, p. 93-101; April 1977.

6. Roesner, B.B., and D.J. McGreivy, "A New High Speed I^{2}L Structure", IEEE Journal of Solid State Circuits, p. 114-118; April 1977.

7. Blatt, V., et. al., "Substrate Fed Logic - An Improved Form of Injection Logic", IEEE Electron Devices Meeting, Digest of Technical Papers, p. 511-514; December 1974.

8. Sanders, T.J., et. al., "The Effects of Neutron and Gamma Radiation on I^{2}L", 1976 GOMAC Digest of Papers, p. 166-169; November 1976.

9. Pease, R.L., and J. P. Raymond, "Technology Assessment and Radiation Effects Characterization of Integrated Logic", DNA Final Report to be published.

10. Horton, R.L., J. Englade, and G. McGee, "I^{2}L Takes Bipolar Integration a Significnat Step Forward", Electronics, Vol. 48, p. 83-90; February 1975.

11. Standard product catalogs of Intel, Motorola, Texas Instruments and RCA, 1976.

12. Texas Instruments product specifications on the TMS 9900 and SBP9000 and private communication with the staff of Texas Instruments.

13. Torrero, E.A., "The Multifacets of I^{2}L", IEEE Spectrum, Vol. 14, No. 6, pp. 28-37; June 1977.

14. Verhofstadt, P.W.J., "Evaluation of Technology Options for LSI Processing Elements", Proceedings of the IEEE, Vol. 64, No. 6, pp. 842-851; June 1977.

15. Klaassen, F.M., "Device Physics of Integrated Injection Logic", IEEE Trans. on Electron Devices, Vol. ED-22, No. 3, p. 145-152; March 1975.

16. Motorola Application Note, "Noise Immunity Comparison of CMOS versus Popular Bipolar Logic Families".

RADIATION-HARDENED PERFORMANCE-OPTIMIZED I²L LSI

A. Bahraman, S. Chang, D. Romeo, K. Schuegraf and T. Wong

Northrop Research and Technology Center
3401 West Broadway, Hawthorne, California 90250

Abstract

Experimental data and theoretical calculations are presented on the effects of neutron irradiation on I²L circuits. It is shown that neutron-induced degradation of I²L gate performance can be theoretically predicted with reasonable accuracy. Operation of custom designed I²L 32-bit serial shift registers to a neutron fluence level of $1 \times 10^{14} \text{n/cm}^2$ is demonstrated. Shift register data are also given from total dose gamma and transient upset radiation experiments with thresholds exceeding $3 \times 10^6 \text{rads(Si)}$ and $2 \times 10^9 \text{rads(Si)/s}$, respectively.

Introduction

Integrated Injection Logic (I²L) has been established as a high density, low cost LSI technology primarily for low-power, medium speed applications. Radiation performance data on I²L circuits have been rather limited to date, and little has been done to provide an analytical description of neutron effects on I²L gate performance. Initial radiation data revealed rather low neutron[1,2] and total dose[3] failure thresholds, but significantly improved results were reported recently.[4,5] This paper presents an analysis of the I²L gate electrical characteristics and performance degradation in high energy neutron radiation environments. Experimental data are also presented for various I²L devices which show good agreement with theoretical calculations over a wide range of neutron fluences. Using optimized designs, we have achieved a minimum delay of 6 ns for standard I²L inverters and have demonstrated operation of I²L-32bit serial shift registers up to a fluence of $1 \times 10^{14} \text{n/cm}^2$. This is the highest neutron failure threshold reported to date for I²L circuits. The 32-bit shift register used in this work consisted of 224 multicollector gates.

The design and processing of the devices used in this work did not include any special steps for hardening against total dose γ radiation or γ̇ transient upset. The shift register performance data after irradiation to about $3 \times 10^6 \text{rads(Si)}$ γ dose and up to $5 \times 10^9 \text{rads(Si)/s}$ γ̇ are also discussed.

Device Analysis

The basic I²L cell consists of an npn transistor and a lateral pnp current source. Fig. 1 shows the cell geometry and the current components in the transistors.[6,7] A computer program was formulated that calculates the above current components, the I²L switching response, and the gate delay in terms of layout geometries and processing data such as base and collector diffusion profiles, epitaxial doping and width, minority-carrier lifetimes and diffusion lengths, etc. From these theoretical results, appropriate steps have been identified and subsequently verified experimentally for minimizing the I²L gate delay and increasing the neutron radiation failure threshold of I²L circuits.

The parameters that determine device performance and radiation tolerance are briefly discussed below.

The npn transistor collector current is given by

$$I_C = I_{CO} \exp(q V_B/kT); \quad I_{CO} = \frac{q n_i^2 S_C D_e}{\int_o^{W_N} N_B(x) \, dx} \tag{1}$$

where S_C is the collector area, D_e is the electron diffusion constant, $N_B(x)$ is the base net impurity concentration per unit volume, W_N is the basewidth, n_i is the intrinsic carrier concentration, and V_B is the base-emitter voltage.

The primary base current component of the npn transistor is hole injection into the emitter and is briefly discussed below. The other current components shown in Fig. 1 are calculated in our computer model but not further discussed here.

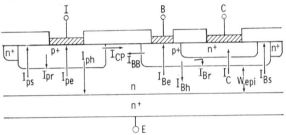

Fig. 1. Basic I²L cell and current components. The arrows indicate the direction of minority carrier injection.

A rather simple model can be developed for the hole current of the standard I²L cell by considering minority carrier storage in the n and n+ regions of the emitter. For $W_{epi} \ll L_h$, where L_h is the hole diffusion length in the epitaxial layer, the recombination occurs in the substrate. The parameter W_{epi} is defined in Fig. 1. Since the epitaxial layer donor concentration is much less than the substrate impurity concentration, the charge stored in the epitaxial layer is much larger than the charge stored in the substrate. The base current supplies the stored charge in the epitaxial layer and the recombination loss in the substrate and at the n-n+ interface. Hence, reducing W_{epi} will reduce the stored charge and the base current. The small charge stored in the substrate and its limited spatial extent suggest modeling the n-n+ interface as a recombination plane with an appropriate surface recombination velocity. This approximation leads to the result[8]

$$I_{BhO} = \frac{q D_h n_i^2}{N_{epi} L_h} \frac{\sinh(W_{epi}/L_h) + \alpha \cosh(W_{epi}/L_h)}{\cosh(W_{epi}/L_h) + \alpha \sinh(W_{epi}/L_h)} S_E$$

$$I_{Bh} = I_{BhO} \exp(q V_B/kT) \tag{2}$$

The parameter α is the normalized recombination velocity, D_h is the hole diffusion constant, and S_E is the emitter area. The base current is thus dependent on the value of α and the recombination lifetime, τ_h, in the epitaxial layer. The critical parameters that affect

Reprinted from *IEEE Trans. Nucl. Sci.*, vol. NS-24, pp. 2321-2326, Dec. 1977.

the npn gain are the basewidth, the base junction depth, the base impurity surface concentration, the epitaxial donor concentration, and the width of the n-region under the p-diffusion, W_{epi}.

The lateral pnp collector current is given by [6]

$$I_{CP} = I_{PO} \exp(q V_{EB}/kT); \quad I_{PO} = \frac{q n_i^2 D_h L_I X_B F_G}{N_{epi} L_h \sinh \frac{W_p}{L_h}} \quad (3)$$

where D_h is the hole diffusion constant, N_{epi} is the epitaxial layer donor concentration, W_p is the pnp base-width, X_B is the p-diffusion depth, L_I is the injector length, and F_G is a correction factor which takes into account the two-dimensional geometry of the pnp base region. [6] F_G is about unity for the devices used in this study.

The pnp base current components are similar to the npn base current components, with appropriate substitutions for geometries, etc.

The minimum logic gate pair delay, $2 t_d$, is calculated by solving for the transient response of series connected gates in a chain of I²L inverters and is given by [7]

$$\frac{2 t_d}{\overline{\tau}_s} = \ln\left[\frac{1 + 2 t_d/\overline{\tau}_s}{1 - 1/\overline{\beta}}\right] \quad (4)$$

where

$$\overline{\tau}_s = \tau_s / (1 + I_{PO}/I_{BO}); \quad \overline{\beta} = \beta / (1 + I_{PO}/I_{BO})$$

The parameter $\overline{\beta}$ is the npn common emitter gain measured with the pnp emitter grounded to the npn emitter. (The maximum fanout permissible per gate is $\overline{\beta}$.) I_{BO} is given in terms of the npn base current,

$$I_B = I_{BO} \exp(q V_B/kT)$$

and τ_s is the emitter storage time. Most of the contribution to I_B is from the hole injection current given by Eq. (2).

The above calculations indicate that the delay-time is minimized by maximizing β, $\overline{\beta}$ and I_{CO}/I_{PO}. These results can also be concluded from qualitative considerations: Each transistor, T_n, must sink the injector current and base charge of the next stage, T_{n+1}. A large $\overline{\beta}$ and ratio of I_{CO}/I_{PO} will simply guarantee that the maximum T_n collector current will be much larger than the T_{n+1} base input current during a transient excursion. In addition, reducing the charge stored in the base of T_{n+1} will also speed up the turn-off process. Hence, making W_{epi} smaller will reduce the stored charge and the propagation delay. This also results in a smaller I_B and therefore contributes to a larger $\overline{\beta}$.

Neutron Irradiation Effects

Neutron-induced degradation in I²L performance is primarily attributed to the increase in npn and pnp base currents due to increased hole injection into the epitaxial layer and the substrate and increased recombination in the emitter-base space charge regions. In addition, the pnp collector current will decrease substantially when the hole diffusion length becomes comparable to the pnp basewidth at high fluence levels. These effects result in higher power consumption and eventual logic circuit failure when the effective gain, $\overline{\beta}$, per collector falls to unity.

Neutron-radiation induced degradation in L_h can cause a large increase in I_{BO} and a decrease in I_{PO} (see Eqs. (2) and (3)), thus resulting in a smaller $\overline{\beta}$. It can be shown that large values of the ratio I_{PO}/I_{BO} and gain β are needed in order to make $\overline{\beta}$ insensitive to degradations in τ_h and L_h. A large I_{PO}/I_{BO} ratio is equivalent to having a large pnp (common-base) current gain, α_F. Therefore, radiation hardened I²L requires both high gain npn and pnp transistors.

In order to evaluate neutron irradiation effects, a computer program was used for parametric calculation of the terminal currents and the emitter storage time. The minority-carrier lifetime and mobility were varied using known neutron damage coefficients for silicon. In this work, experimental data[9] were used to calculate lifetime as a function of injection level. [10] The low-level damage constant, K_{low}, was chosen from published data. [9, 10, 11] Best agreement with the experimental data was obtained with the value of $K_{low} = 2.5 \times 10^5$ ns/cm², which is the value assumed by Ref. (10). The pre-irradiation value of α in Eq. (2) was in the range 0.1 - 0.15, in good agreement with other published data. [6] (α is a function of substrate and epitaxial layer lifetimes and donor concentrations.) For the calculations, the initial lifetimes in the epitaxial layer and the substrate were chosen 0.45 μs and 0.15 μs, based on transient MOS C-V measurements and other published data. [12]

Experimental Data and Comparison with Theory (Neutron Irradiation)

In order to experimentally verify our theoretical calculations and analysis, several neutron irradiation tests were conducted on various I²L devices from different wafer lots having different values of W_{epi} (see Fig. 1) and diffusion depths. Thus, with devices having the same base and collector diffusions and geometries but different W_{epi} parameters, it was possible to evaluate the dependence of neutron hardness on W_{epi}. On the other hand, with devices which had the same processing parameters but different npn basewidths, it was possible to determine the effect of npn β on radiation hardness.

The devices were single and multicollector I²L cells, ring oscillators, and 32-bit shift registers. I-V terminal characteristics were measured for the npn and pnp transistors at each fluence level. In addition, power-frequency data were recorded for the ring oscillators and the shift registers. A pseudo-random sequence input word of 63 bits in length was used for testing the shift-registers. The neutron source was Northrop's TRIGA reactor, and lead shielding was used in radiation tests to minimize the γ-dose. (The accumulated dose was below 10^4 rads(Si).)

Fig. 2 shows measured and calculated emitter-base I-V data for a typical device before and after irradiation. As noted in Fig. 2, neutron-induced degradation is more severe at low than at high currents, resulting in a change in the slope of I_B-V_B curves. In addition, devices with large W_{epi} degraded more and showed a larger change in I_B-V_B slope as compared to devices with small W_{epi}. This behavior was explained by taking into account the injection-level dependence of lifetime in the epi region and lifetime degradation in the emitter-base junction. Neutron-induced lifetime degradation is most severe at very low injection levels. However, as the injection level increases, lifetime degradation decreases, thus resulting in a smaller increase in hole current. The slope of the I-V plot would therefore change, showing a larger increase in current and power dissipation at low voltages and much less increase at higher voltages.

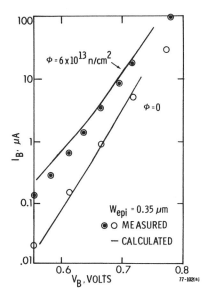

Fig. 2. I_B - V_B data for npn transistor.

The npn collector current at a fixed base voltage showed very little degradation with neutron fluence for all the inverter types studied in this work. This is in agreement with theoretical expectations and confirms our original assumption that the increase in base current is the primary neutron irradiation-induced degradation, as discussed in the previous paragraph.

Fig. 3 shows a plot of normalized npn gain as a function of W_{epi} at a neutron fluence of 6×10^{13} n/cm^2. As expected, gain degradation is more severe for devices with larger W_{epi}.

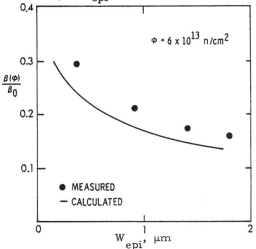

Fig. 3. Fraction of initial gain at 6×10^{13} n/cm^2, plotted as a function of W_{epi}.

The variation of npn gain β and effective gain $\bar{\beta}$ with neutron fluence is given in Fig. 4 for a single-collector inverter from an optimized wafer lot. As indicated, very good agreement is obtained between measured and calculated data. At 1×10^{14} n/cm^2, $\bar{\beta}$ is about 6. Therefore, using a safety factor of 2, a maximum fanout of 3 is allowable for operation to 1×10^{14} n/cm^2. That is, circuits composed of 3-collector gates would operate up to 1×10^{14}/cm^2 with $\bar{\beta} \simeq 2$ per collector at 1×10^{14} n/cm^2. This was demonstrated by the shift register data, to be discussed later in this section.

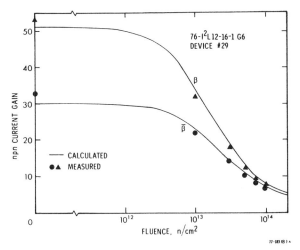

Fig. 4. Variation of npn gain with neutron fluence.

Degradation of gain for a 3-collector inverter is shown in Fig. 5. This device was from a wafer lot that showed failure in the range 3×10^{13} to 6×10^{13} n/cm^2. At 6×10^{13} n/cm^2, the gain of the first collector at a base current of 100 μA was degraded by a factor of 4, whereas the gain degradation for the third collector is by a factor of 7. Due to the lateral base voltage drop, the third collector operates at a lower injection level then the first. It was shown earlier that neutron-induced degradation is more severe at low injection levels. Consequently, the third collector would experience more gain degradation, as observed above.

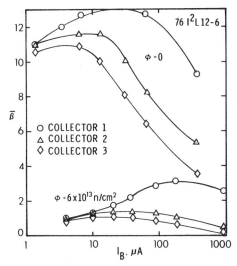

Fig. 5. Measured variation of npn effective gain with base current for a 3-collector inverter

Fig. 6 shows a plot of the measured and calculated pnp collector current before and after neutron irradiation. High-level injection effects are taken into account in the calculation. Both drift and diffusion current components were considered in the solution of the continuity equation. Good agreement is obtained between the measured and calculated data over most of the current range. At low currents, the calculated degradation in current is larger than observed experimentally. Again, degradation is more severe at low injection levels, in agreement with the injection-level dependence of lifetime damage constant.

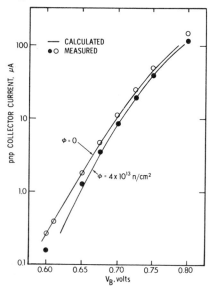

Fig. 6. Pnp collector-base I-V characteristics before and after neutron irradiation.

From the measurement of maximum oscillation frequency of ring oscillator devices, a minimum delay of 6 ns per gate was deduced for optimized single-collector devices. Also, it was noted experimentally that the minimum delay time, t_d, varies as $1/\sqrt{\overline{\beta}}$ for devices with different $\overline{\beta}$ values. This is expected theoretically for large values of $\overline{\beta}$. The minimum delay per gate for the 32-bit shift register was about 10 ns.

At high current levels, the minimum delay is affected by two opposing radiation-induced changes. The degradation in lifetime with neutron fluence reduces the emitter storage time which tends to lower the minimum delay. On the other hand, a decrease in β has the effect of increasing the minimum delay. Consequently, the minimum delay remains fairly insensitive to neutron irradiation. Our calculations show that initially the minimum delay decreases slowly as the neutron fluence increases. However, at high fluence levels when the failure threshold is being approached ($\overline{\beta}$ nearing 1), the delay time will increase rapidly with neutron fluence. This has been verified experimentally by the ring oscillator and shift register data described below.

The effect of neutron irradiation on the shift register performance is shown in Fig. 7. (The register bias current supplied power to 224 gates.) Several important changes in the shift register data are noted: 1) At low to medium currents, the maximum operating clock frequency decreases as neutron fluence, ϕ, increases. Equivalently, for operation at a specified frequency, more injector current is required as ϕ increases.

2) At high current levels, the maximum clock fequency shows a slight increase with increasing ϕ, except at 1×10^{14}n/cm^2. 3) The shift register operating current range shrinks as ϕ increases. The last effect occurs mostly at low currents. At the highest fluence level, the shift register ceases operation at high currents as well.

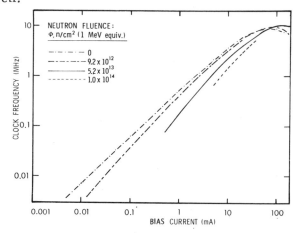

Fig. 7. 32-bit shift register clock frequency-bias current characteristics.

The above results are in agreement with theoretical expectations and other I²L inverter and ring oscillator data. At any neutron fluence level, the shift register will operate over the injector current range where the condition $\overline{\beta} > 1$ is satisfied for each collector. Because degradation is more severe at low injection levels, a lower neutron failure threshold is reached at low currents than at high currents. This causes the contraction in operating current range observed above. At low currents, the gate delay is associated with the time period needed to charge the npn input capacitance to, say, 0.6V. Since I_B increases with fluence, the input current required to achieve the same base voltage and gate delay likewise increases. For operation at high currents, the failure threshold is controlled by the gain of the remote collector, e.g., the 3rd collector in a 3-collector gate. Compared to the first collector, the remote collector has a lower $\overline{\beta}$ and experiences more $\overline{\beta}$ degradation at high fluences. This causes a contraction in operating current range at high currents and a reduction in maximum operating frequency, as observed for the shift register.

Total Dose Effects

Several experiments were conducted to determine the effects of γ-radiation and short transient photoionizing radiation pulses on various I²L circuits including shift registers. Northrop's Co⁶⁰ source and the Febetron flash x-ray were used in these tests. Two types of device structures were available on chip for the total dose experiments. Type I did not have any gap between the n+ collar and the p+ base diffusion, as shown in Fig. 1. Type II devices had a 10 μm gap between the n+ collar and the p+ diffusion. Only single-collector inverters and ring oscillators were available in Type II.

High energy ionizing radiation causes an increase in the npn and pnp base currents. The increase is appreciable at low currents, resulting in the degradation of $\overline{\beta}$ at low injection levels. Consequently, the operating current range contracts. Table I shows comparative data on 7.5 μm-minimum-linewidth single-collector ring oscillators with and without a 10 μm base-n+ collar gap. After a radiation dose of 2.7 Mrads(Si), the device without the gap operates over the current range of 0.3 μA-7 μA per gate. For the other device, the current range is 3 μA-7 μA per gate. Both devices operated down to 16 nA before irradiation. Clearly, the device with a 10 μm base-collar gap has degraded more severely. Both devices showed only small changes in electrical characteristics at medium and high current levels after a total dose of 2.7 Mrads(Si).

TABLE I.

RING OSCILLATOR PERFORMANCE DATA AT 2.7 MRADS(Si), 7.5 μm MINIMUM GEOMETRY

DEVICE	POWER-DELAY PRODUCT	MINIMUM DELAY/GATE	OPERATING CURRENT RANGE
TYPE I	2.7 pJ	9 ns	0.3 μA - 7 mA
TYPE II	1.8 pJ	10 ns	3 μA - 7 mA

The relative degradation of the two devices and the increase in base current at low injection levels indicate that the degradation in device characteristics is primarily due to increased carrier recombination at the surface. The inverter with the 10-μm gap has a wider emitter-base junction width at the surface and a larger low-concentration epitaxial surface compared to the inverter without the gap, and is therefore more susceptible to radiation-induced degradation.

Fig. 8 shows the shift register data before irradiation and after a total dose of 2.7 Mrads(Si). (Shift registers did not have the base-collar gap.) The shift register operated to a minimum bias current of 20 nA/gate and 0.7 μA/gate before and after irradiation, respectively. The maximum clock frequency was 10 MHz and did not change after irradiation.

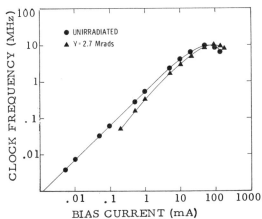

Fig. 8. 32-bit shift register frequency-bias current characteristics before and after γ-irradiation

The I^2L cell surface recombination current (depletion region and bulk) is much less than the hole injection current into the n-n+ region at medium and high injection levels. Consequently, very large changes in the surface recombination velocity are necessary in order to make these currents comparable and cause

device failure. Therefore, I^2L circuits should be very hard to total dose ionizing radiation at medium and high injection levels, as demonstrated above with 32-bit shift registers.

Determination of Transient Upset Levels
for I^2L Flip Flops

In order to experimentally determine the transient upset levels for non-hardened I^2L flip flops, the 32-bit serial shift register (i.e., a series connection of 32 D-type flip flops) was used. Samples within 1/2-inch round 40 lead gold-plated Kovar flat packages were irradiated using the Febetron 705, 2 MeV flash x-ray source. A pulse generator operated in "single pulse" mode was used to drive a large geometry npn clock buffer transistor fabricated on the I^2L chip. This device exhibits the same characteristics as npn transistors within I^2L gates with the exception of much higher upward current gain due to a more favorable collector/emitter area ratio and the absence of a pnp injector region. A similar large geometry npn is included as a buffer at the first shift register bit. Data bits were entered into the shift register by means of a manually operated switch.

During transient irradiation, both the data and clock inputs were grounded through series resistors. A single output from register bit number 32 was used to monitor the status of the data after the transient. This open collector output was connected to a pull-up resistor to + 0.5V. During the experiment all inputs and outputs were shielded, and the bias current supply to the I^2L register was decoupled at the flat package pin with RF type capacitors. The procedure used during this testing was to shift in the test word, using the manual controls as described. Input and clock were then grounded, and the register was irradiated. The data bits were subsequently shifted out. Pre- and post-irradiation data were compared to determine the upset of any flip flops in the shift register. The samples tested were exposed to seven irradiation levels between 1×10^7 and 5×10^9 rads(Si)/s. The injection current bias level was set to 50 mA total, corresponding to approximately 200 μA per gate. Table II contains a summary of the experimental results obtained on a typical sample.

TABLE II.

SUMMARY OF TRANSIENT PHOTOCURRENT EFFECTS ON I^2L 32-BIT SHIFT REGISTER

PEAK DOSE RATE (Rads(Si)/s)	EFFECTS ON SHIFT REGISTER DATA PATTERN
5×10^8	Bit 1 forced 1 to 0, bits 2 - 32 unchanged
1×10^9	Bit 1 forced 1 to 0, bits 2 - 32 shifted 1 bit
2×10^9	Bit 1 forced 1 to 0, bits 2 - 32 shifted 1 bit
5×10^9	Bits 2 - 12 and bits 23 - 32 remain at 1, bit 1 and bits 13 - 22 forced to 1

The results clearly show that several effects exist at various peak dose rates. The first critical photocurrent level is between 2×10^8 and 5×10^8 rads(Si)/s. In each case, it was found that the flip-flop connected to the input buffer was forced from a "one" state to a "zero" state due to the primary photocurrent generated within the large emitter-base volume of the npn buffer transistor. It is this current that was "beta multiplied" by the buffer transistor that caused the change in state of the first flip-flop, while each of the other flip-flops retained its original state.

A similar result was observed at a level of 1×10^9 rads(Si)/s. In this case the data in each of the bits 2-32 were shifted 1 bit position in the proper direction (i.e., bits advanced in the same direction as if a single clock pulse were applied.) This result is entirely analogous to the previous case and the difference is merely quantitative. One npn base from each of the 32 flip flops is connected to the common metallization bus line which is tied to the collector of an npn clock buffer transistor. Hence it is required that 32 times more "beta-multipled" current be generated in order to observe the effect as compared to the previous case. Therefore, these experimental results are believed to be consistent with measured and computed values of "beta multiplied" I^2L npn buffer photocurrents. As such, this experiment does not indicate the inherent upset levels of I^2L flip flops.

In fact, the unhardened I^2L flip-flop transient upset level appears to be between 2×10^9 and 5×10^9 rads(Si)/s, and can be explained by analyzing the photocurrents generated within the flip-flop. The basic cross-coupled latch configuration appears to be the hardest portion of the flip-flop, and it is upset at these levels only due to the response of photocurrents generated within the steering logic. Specifically, the latch will not be upset unless an input tends to "steal" base current away from the particular cross-coupled gate that is in saturation. This happens by means of photocurrent generated in the emitter-base region of a small-geometry 3-collector npn transistor within the steering logic. The fact that this transient occurs simultaneously with the clock-line transient described previously permits only those stages initially in a logic "zero" state to be forced to a logic "one" state. In effect, the measured transient upset level is merely the result of transient photocurrents in the flip-flop steering logic, and not the inherent upset level of the cross-coupled latch.

Summary

Theoretical calculations and experimental data presented here indicate that the performance characteristics of unirradiated and neutron-irradiated I^2L gates and logic circuits can be estimated with good accuracy. It is shown that high levels of neutron radiation hardness are attainable with I^2L gates having high-gain npn and pnp transistors, built on thin epitaxial structures. These steps also minimize the I^2L gate propagation delay. I^2L 32-bit serial shift registers (224 gates), fabricated according to the above guidelines, showed neutron failure thresholds exceeding 1×10^{14} n/cm^2 and average delays of 10 ns/gate.

The effects of γ-radiation on I^2L circuit performance were also investigated. It is shown that better total dose hardness is achieved by layouts using coincident base and collar masks. No device failure was observed at 2.7×10^6 rads(Si). Furthermore, it was shown that I^2L gates within a serial shift register are capable of operation down to bias currents comparable to those for CMOS devices (e.g., $\sim 1\,\mu A$/gate) after exposure to an ionizing dose of 2.7×10^6 rads(Si). It is expected that properly designed I^2L circuits would show total dose failure thresholds exceeding 10^7 rads(Si) when biased in the minimum-delay region of operation.

Although no special steps were undertaken to harden the devices used in this study against ionizing radiation pulse transient upset, the 32-bit shift registers showed upset thresholds above 2×10^9 rads(Si)/s. Special attention must be paid to the design of input buffer transistors to safeguard against premature upsets. It is anticipated upset levels above 10^{10} rads(Si)/s can be realized by eliminating the base series resistance effects in multi-collector gates and large buffer transistors.

Acknowledgment

The authors would like to thank D. N. Pocock, J. R. Srour and O. L. Curtis, Jr., for helpful discussions. Assistance by D. N. Pocock in transient upset measurements is greatly appreciated.

References

1. J. P. Raymond, T. Y. Wong, and K. K. Schuegraf, IEEE Trans. Nucl. Sci. 22, 2605 (1975).

2. D. Long, C. Repper, L. Ragonese, and N. Yang, presented at the 1976 Radiation Effects Conference.

3. R. Pease, K. Galloway, R. Stehlin, IEEE Trans. Nucl. Sci. 22, 2600 (1975).

4. A. Bahraman and K. K. Schuegraf, presented at the 1976 GOMAC.

5. T. Sanders, M. Weiant, N. Van Vono, and B. Doyle, presented at the 1976 GOMAC.

6. R. Dutton and R. Whittier, IEEE Trans. Electron Devices ED-16, 458(1959). Also see: K. VenKateswaren and D. Roulston, Solid State Electron. 15, 311 (1972).

7. S. Chou, Solid-State Electronics 14, 811 (1971).

8. F. M. Klaassen, IEEE Trans. Electron Devices ED-22, 145 (1975).

9. O. L. Curtis, Jr., and C. A. Germano, IEEE Trans. Nucl. Sci. NS-14, 68, (1976).

10. B. Gregory and C. Gwyn, IEEE Trans. Nucl. Sci. 17, 325 (1970).

11. J. R. Srour, IEEE Trans. Nucl. Sci. NS-20, 190 (1973).

12. P. A. Iles and S. I. Soclof, presented at the 11th IEEE Photovoltaic Spec. Conf., Scottsdale, Az., 1975.

RADIATION HARDENED LSI FOR THE 1980'S: CMOS/SOS VS. I^{2}L

R. P. Donovan
M. Simons
R. M. Burger
Research Triangle Institute
P. O. Box 12194
Research Triangle Park, North Carolina 27709

Introduction

The selection of semiconductor hardware best suited for a given electronic system function is becoming more difficult as the number and the performance capability of the available semiconductor technologies increase. For the designer of radiation-hardened electronics the choice is further complicated by the operating environment. Tradeoffs between performance in these adverse environments and cost and availability of the components add to the complexity of the decision.

To assist designers of radiation-hardened electronic systems in making these decisions the Research Triangle Institute, under AF Avionics Laboratory support, completed a 1976 state-of-the-art review of eight candidate semiconductor technologies for present and future military missions.[1] The electronic capability needed for these hypothetical missions was assumed to require chips of LSI complexity. The expected performance of chips from each technology was assessed with respect to an operating environment consisting of neutrons, total gamma dose and gamma dose rate. Each of these environments was considered independently.

Of the eight technologies evaluated [four bipolar (T^{2}L, ST^{2}L, ECL, I^{2}L) and four MOS (bulk PMOS, bulk CMOS, PMOS/SOS, AND CMOS/SOS)], I^{2}L and CMOS/SOS emerged as high-risk, less developed technologies but the two technologies with potentially the greatest payoff for radiation-hardened electronics.

CMOS is the preferred MOS technology because of its low standby power requirements and its high noise immunity. The SOS construction reduces the photocurrents generated by a transient radiation pulse and increases the circuit speed and packing density. The total dose susceptibility of CMOS/SOS, initially a serious shortcoming, is now reported to be on the order of 5×10^5 to 10^6 rads (Si).

I^{2}L is the leading bipolar candidate for LSI in the 1980's because its packing density and speed-power product are superior to those of the other bipolar technologies. That this circuit technique uses no resistors and can be fabricated as a self-isolating structure enhances its ability to maintain performance in a radiation environment.

While the RTI study[1] was very broad, this paper represents an extension and amplification of just this one conclusion--the anticipated role of I^{2}L and CMOS/SOS in future radiation-hardened applications. Performance differences aside from radiation hardness were assumed to be second order. Clearly applications exist in which a unique performance feature of one technology (such as the low standby power of CMOS/SOS) would make it the only acceptable choice. Such special situations are ignored in this paper and the two technologies are assumed to be equally qualified for the non-radiation related specifications of military electronic systems.

Background

The explosive growth and impact of semiconductor integrated circuit technology, already phenomenal by any standards, continues unabated. At the processing level this growth can be measured in terms of the component packing density, as illustrated in Figure 1. The data points in this plot are drawn according to the bottom abscissae and the left hand ordinate. The top abscissae is an approximation and is used to deduce the second curve and its scale (the right hand ordinate). For example, in 1970, the state-of-the-art IC contained about 2,000 components and was about 20 mm^2 in area. The area per component was about 10^4 µm^2.

Figure 1 shows that the number of components/chip has been doubling every year since the development of integrated circuits in 1958. Most of this growth is attributable to increases in component density but a part is also contributed by a growth in chip area (about a four-fold increase every five years).

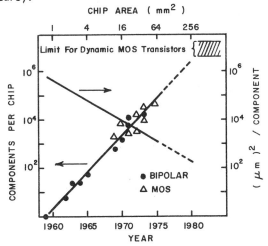

Figure 1. History of IC component packing density [adapted from Ref. 2].

Figure 1 also suggests that the number of components/chip have at least an order of magnitude growth remaining before encountering fundamental material limitations set by such phenomena as oxide or junction breakdowns, punchthrough or power dissipation. By extrapolation of the previous growth these limits are expected to be reached in the early 1980's; so it is these chip sizes (≥ 300 mm^2) and number of components (10^6-10^7) that are implied in

Reprinted from *IEEE Trans. Nucl. Sci.*, vol. NS-24, pp. 2336-2340, Dec. 1977.

the term, LSI for the 1980's. The decade of the 1980's will be the VLSI decade.

Electronic functional capability tracks component density closely, as would be expected, and, hence, also has been doubling every year as illustrated by the RAM data given in Figure 2.

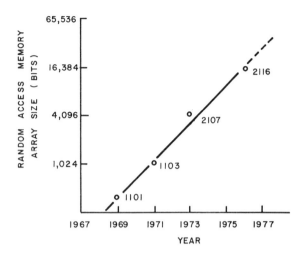

Figure 2. RAM Capacity.[3]

Implications

The questions now raised are:

1) What electronic functions will be the VLSI chips of the 1980's be performing?

2) What are the implications of this continuing growth in technology and electronic capability for military hardware procurement and system design?

The limiting factor in the advance of semiconductor hardware is not one of how many components can be squeezed onto a chip but rather how complex or large an electronic array can be profitably manufactured and used. The processing technology needed to achieve the packing densities forecast for the VLSI of the 1980's seem well within grasp. Such developments as X-ray and electron beam photolithography[4], improved crystal growth, and advanced processing methods are easily-visualized, incremental advances that will lead to increased component density and chip sizes. The more demanding question now is how to best use this predicted processing capability. Continued growth in semiconductor functional capability, as forecast in Figure 1, depends upon identifying the right applications for VLSI technology. No specification as to the nature of the next chip function/application breakthrough will be made here; question No.1 will not be answered. The specific form or function that will characterize the VLSI of the 1980's is less certain than the fact that it will be developed and represent an advance beyond contemporary LSI. Certain properties can be assumed:

1) VLSI in the 1980's will include universality and versatility, like today's microprocessors.

2) It will be made in large numbers.

3) It will open up new horizons in electronic applications and lead society into dependence on electronic information, communication, and control systems.

This background and forecast leads to the conclusion that at the VLSI level of the 1980's the traditional custom-chip approach to radiation-hardened system design and hardware procurement will have become much more expensive and consequently less popular.

In the past designers of radiation-hardened electronic systems established an acceptable radiation performance level for all hardware making up the system. Frequently the radiation specifications, as well as other specifications, led to the need for a custom circuit, employing custom technology such as thin film resistors, dielectric isolation, and photocurrent compensating elements. The justification for this apporach is clear and simple--if an electronic system won't remain functional in its operating environment, it's pointless to build it.

By and large this approach succeeded for the procurement of the SSI/MSI electronic systems of Minuteman and Poseidon and is being followed for the MX, Trident and other systems now in design and development. Costs, admittedly, are large (an order of magnitude higher than comparable commercial units). What is worse, reliability and availability of these custom parts are becoming difficult to guarantee because the key to profitable semiconductor manufacturing is, as always, the identification of products which can be built and sold in huge volumes.[5] Huge volumes mean perhaps a million units/ month for a market of long duration. The largest procurement of radiation-hardened chips on record is miniscule in comparison. Such limited production runs will become even more difficult to justify in the context of 1980-decade VLSI. Even now semiconductor technology has pushed the interface between the producers and the users well beyond the subsystem hardware level. With microprocessors as a standard "component" in the conventional sense, the job of the user is now primarily one of preparing software programs to interact with the microprocessor in order to carry out a desired function. Computer architects, system designers and software engineers themselves now work at the semiconductor manufacturer's plant in the design and development of today's microprocessors. This "component" represents considerably more design time and talent than the predecessor SSI/MSI components since the total development costs include supporting software, user's manuals, programming instructions and the like. The more complex VLSI of the 1980's will intensify these trends so that the total cost of developing a new "component" will expand even more. Building a large number of custom "components" under VLSI rules is therefore an unlikely operating mode for semiconductor manufacturers. Indeed it is only the programmability of contemporary microprocessors, enabling them to perform useful functions over a sufficiently wide spectrum of applications, that creates sufficient demand for them. Without such versatility the demand would not support enough production volume to justify even the 1977 LSI.[5]

The conclusion is that the cost squeeze that contemporary custom IC procurement entails will continue to pinch more and more until it becomes intolerable.

Recommended Response

Will the 1980-decade radiation-hardened electronics therefore be limited to today's SSI/MSI/LSI designs and will designers of these systems have to write off the system advantages of commercial 1980-decade VLSI? Not necessarily, although this option exists and may sometimes be the preferred course of action. A more flexible approach to the procurement of radiation-hardened electronics will make available more of the state-of-the-art. What is recommended here is the strategy of adopting the commercial market technology as much as possible before customizing for radiation-hardening. Such an approach is not novel but the emphasis on it is. In the outlook recommended this philosophy becomes the cornerstone of hardware procurement. The designer incorporates redundancy, fault tolerance, anything he can think of before specifying custom VLSI. Custom VLSI becomes a last resort for the 1980's. Departures from it are the exception. The designer uses the volume technology until he can justify abandoning the state-of-the-art and settling for custom SSI/MSI/rudimentary LSI.

The distinction between CMOS/SOS circuits and I^2L serves to illustrate the differences between the traditional approach and the 1980 approach recommended here. This choice of examples is illustrative primarily and, while the properties ascribed to each of these technologies do correspond as closely as possible to reality, the main point is not to choose between these two technologies but to choose between the two general approaches to technology selection that they represent. Technological breakthroughs and surprises will continue to occur and alter the present perception of these two technologies. Even if the specific recommendations were to change by 180°, the general considerations presented here are still valid. They are independent of the specific examples. CMOS/SOS is at present a low volume, custom technology just recently designed into a major military system. Federal support of the development of CMOS/SOS as a radiation-hardened technology capable of meeting most military/space requirements extends back over at least 10 years. The radiation performance of the present state-of-the-art is very impressive (Table 1). However, commercial market penetration has so far been limited essentially to custom applications—the major market for CMOS/SOS continues to be the military. Hence, this technology is a prime example of the traditional approach to radiation-hardened electronics.

I^2L, on the other hand, is quite the reverse. The initial interest in I^2L stemmed from purely commercial, high volume applications; commercial microprocessors using I^2L are now in the market. The driving force behind I^2L is the commercial/consumer market and its potential for the huge volume required to sustain 1980-decade VLSI. The future of I^2L is independent of military support.

How about the radiation performance of I^2L? How does it compare? The summarizing results in Table 1 present a discouraging picture. The data contained in Table 1 represent the 1976 status and show that I^2L chips are vulnerable to all radiation environments. Simple scanning of these tests results could easily convince the user of radiation-hardened electronics that I^2L is not what he wants.

Such a conclusion would be hasty, however. What is presented in Table 1 are test results on first generation I^2L—the initial chips manufactured with this circuit design. What is of more importance and of more promise is the performance of second and later generations of I^2L. Table 2 is a conservative forecast of I^2L radiation performance in the 1980's—conservative because many of these goals have already been met (although not all simultaneously by a single design or structure). The projected values for I^2L neutron and total dose hardness are comparable to the present capability of other bipolar technologies (TTL, STTL, ECL). These projections are based on the I^2L trend toward modified and higher performance transistor designs which also have an improved tolerance to both neutron and surface effects.[1] Although various process controls (such as minimum metallization thickness, nonplastic packages, various acceptance tests and screens) would have to be followed or incorporated in a

TABLE 1. BEST PUBLISHED PERFORMANCE FOR CMOS/SOS AND I^2L

	CMOS/SOS	I^2L
Packing Density (gates/mm^2)	200 - 300	150 - 300
Propagation Delay (ns)	4 - 20	7 - 50
Speed-Power Product (pJ)	0.5 - 30	0.2 - 2.0
Guaranteed Noise Margin (V)	3.5 - 4.5	<0.1
Technology Maturity (arbitrary scale, 1 (lowest) to 10)	5	3
Neutron Hardness (n/cm^2)	$>10^{15}$ - 10^{16}	$1-5 \times 10^{13}$
Total Dose Hardness (rads(Si))	5×10^5 - 10^6	10^5 - 10^6
Dose Rate Hardness (rads(Si)/sec)	10^{10} - 10^{11}	10^9 - 10^{10}

TABLE 2.   PROJECTED RADIATION TOLERANCES OF LSI IN THE 1980'S

	CMOS/SOS	I^2L
Neutron Hardness (n/cm^2)	$>10^{15} - 10^{16}$	$10^{14} - 10^{15}$
Total Dose Hardness (rads(Si))	$10^6 - 10^7$	$10^6 - 10^7$
Dose Rate Hardness (rads(Si)/sec)	$5 \times 10^{10} - 1 \times 10^{11}$	$1-5 \times 10^{10}$

commercial product line to insure device hardness (as well as reliability), such modifications would be relatively minor and would not disturb compatibility with the commercial line.

Table 2 also reflects a modest improvement in hardness capability of CMOS/SOS devices in the 1980's in the area of total dose hardness where it is assumed that improvement in the quality and hardness of thermal oxides will continue.

The significant point above is that the I^2L radiation hardness levels are forecast for the commercial (or nearly commercial) product line-- not a custom, radiation-hardened line. These levels of radiation hardness are likely to come into existence because of the demands of the commercial market and the attempts of manufacturers to meet those needs. The improved radiation performance accrues as a bonus upon which military electronics can capitalize. The situation whereby a commercial product line meets the radiation requirements of many military systems does not seem far fetched in view of these prognostications.

Indeed it is this property of I^2L that justifies this renewed commitment to a volume technology. The structural features of I^2L that seem most desirable for the commercial market often coincide with those required for improved radiation hardness as summarized in Table 3. Not all of these features are common to all second generation I^2L and not all these features are beneficial in a radiation environment. Above all, the listings in Table 3 are neither final nor complete; they are illustrative only. For example:

1) the small volume and shallow junctions that raise transistor switching speed also increase neutron hardness[1] (this relationship holds for all bipolar transistors, not just I^2L transistors).

2) the higher operating current densities that improve circuit speed also increase total dose hardness.

3) the higher emitter doping that increases the up-beta of the n-p-n stage also raises the neutron and total dose thresholds of the n-p-n section.

4) the use of ion implantation to selectively increase the doping of the parasitic base region that minimizes the lateral voltage drops along the base also reduces photocurrent-induced voltage drops.

This duality of advantages wherein performance improvements also mean improvement in radiation

hardness has generally been true of bipolar processing.[1] With I^2L circuit technology other advantages exist:

1) thin film technology is not required for depositing resistors (I^2L requires no resistors).

2) dielectric isolation is unnecessary (the circuit/structure operates in a self-isolating mode--like enhancement-mode MOS).

3) the small area of the base-collector junctions (with respect to other bipolar technologies) reduces the susceptibility of I^2L designs to base-collector junction photocurrents, normally the major source of photocurrent for other bipolar circuit technologies. In I^2L other photocurrent sources will probably limit circuit operation in γ environments.

I^2L technology is undergoing a period of intensive development.[6] New construction techniques and designs abound, as researchers seek to achieve even faster speeds and larger packing densities. Already these second generation structures have delivered some of the improved radiation performance promised in Table 2. The outlook for a relatively radiation hard technology has never been better.

CMOS/SOS itself is not out of the competition as a volume technology. Touted from its inception as a candidate for low cost microcircuit production ("SOS will rule the world"--J. Scott, RCA), CMOS/ SOS continues to slowly advance into more applications and to find more markets. That CMOS/ SOS will not become a first line commercial VLSI technology in the 1980's is by no means established. This development would also benefit radiation-hard electronics, since CMOS/SOS is a proven radiation-hard technology (Table 1). One uncertainty in the benefits resulting from this development, however is the possibility that a commercial CMOS/SOS process may not retain the total dose hardness characteristic of the custom CMOS/SOS developed for military applications. Oxide hardening has been primarily a military problem and would be of little interest commercially unless the properties of the hardened oxide can be shown to be superior in commercial service as well. Historically the duality of advantages previously cited for bipolar development has not occurred for MOS. The techniques for preparing oxides that exhibit the best radiation hardness to total dose have been developed by researchers in the radiation effects community rather than those working in the commercial market. And so, while it is tempting to argue that the competition of I^2L vs. CMOS/SOS means no loser for

TABLE 3. IMPACT OF I^2L STRUCTURAL/DESIGN FEATURES UPON RADIATION HARDNESS

Features	Commercial Consequence	Radiation Hardness Consequence
First Generation I^2L		
No resistors	High packing density	Higher $\dot{\gamma}$ threshold (because of reduced p-n junction area)
Self-isolation	" " "	" " " " "
Collector area <emitter area	" " "	Higher $\dot{\gamma}$ threshold
Lateral p-n-p	High (but low α)	Lower n, γ thresholds
Inverted n-p-n	High (but low β)	Lower n threshold
Retarded base impurity gradient, low base doping (n-p-n)	Low gain, Low f_T	Lower n threshold
Second Generation I^2L		
Up-diffused, ion implanted n-p-n	Higher gain, speed	Higher n, γ thresholds
Double base doping	Reduced lateral voltage drop	Higher n, γ, $\dot{\gamma}$ thresholds
Double diffused p-n-p	Higher gain p-n-p	Higher $\dot{\gamma}$ thresholds
Substrate injection	Higher gain p-n-p	Lower $\dot{\gamma}$ threshold (?)
Sidewall oxide isolation	Higher packing density	Lower γ threshold (?)

n = neutron; γ = total gamma dose; $\dot{\gamma}$ = gamma dose rate; (?) = speculative

the military so long as there is a winner between the two in the commercial market, this happy conclusion is probably a deceptive oversimplification. Any commercial line is unlikely to qualify for military operations without some customizing. The I^2L line, if it matures into a 1980-decade VLSI line, now holds the promise of being that commercial line requiring the least customizing to meet military environmental specifications.

Conclusions

This discussion has emphasized the commercial potential of I^2L and the limited commercial success of CMOS/SOS, because this is the way it looks now. Technology changes rapidly and dramatically, however.

So the message is not I^2L over CMOS/SOS (we could be as comfortable the other way around) but a high volume base over a low volume custom base--an obvious enough conclusion but one that tends to get buried in the search for high performance military hardware. With volume comes reliability and low cost. This has always been true. At the complexity levels forecast for the VLSI of the 1980's, the low volume, radiation-hardened, custom circuit may become extinct.

References

1. "Integrated Circuits for Radiation Hardened Systems: A State-of-the-Art Review," AFAL-TR-76-194, Research Triangle Institute, Research Triangle Park, N.C., January 1977.

2. B. Hoeneissen and C. A. Mead, "Fundamental Limitations in Microelectronics I. MOS Technology," Solid State Electronics 15, July 1972, pp. 819-829.

3. J. E. Coe and W. G. Oldham, "Enter the 16,384-bit RAM," Electronics, February 19, 1976, pp. 116-121.

4. Special Issue of "Pattern Generation and Microlithography," IEEE Trans. Electron Dev., ED-22, No. 7, July 1975.

5. G. E. Moore, "Microprocessors and Integrated Electronic Technology," Proc. IEEE 64, June 1976, pp. 837-841.

6. "Special Issue on Integrated Injection Logic," IEEE J. Solid State Circuits, Vol. SC-12, April 1977.

Acknowledgement

It is a pleasure to thank Dr. Hans J. Hennecke of the Air Forces Avionics Laboratory for his review and critique of various versions of this paper.

Bibliography

PART I: CONVENTIONAL I²L

1. C. G. THORNTON AND N. C. DE TROYE, "FOREWORD, SPECIAL ISSUE ON INTEGRATED INJECTION LOGIC," IEEE J. SOLID-STATE CIRCUITS, VOL. SC-12, NO. 2, APRIL 1977, PP. 91-92.

2. C. M. HART AND A. SLOB, "INTEGRATED INJECTION LOGIC-A NEW APPROACH TO LSI," 1972 ISSCC DIGEST TECH PAPERS, PP. 92-93 AND 219.

3. N. C. DE TROYE, "INTEGRATED INJECTION LOGIC-A NEW APPROACH TO LSI," 1974 ISSCC DIGEST TECH PAPERS, PP. 12-13 AND 214.

4. C. M. HART, A. SLOB AND H. E. J. WULMS, " BIPOLAR LSI TAKES A NEW DIRECTION WITH INTEGRATED INJECTION LOGIC," ELECTRONICS MAGAZINE, OCT. 3, 1974, PP. 111-118.

5. N. C. DE TROYE, "INTEGRATED INJECTION LOGIC-PRESENT AND FUTURE," IEEE J. SOLID-STATE CIRCUITS, VOL. SC-9, NO. 5, OCT. 1974, PP. 206-211.

6. H. H. BERGER AND S. K. WIEDMANN, "MERGED TRANSISTOR LOGIC-A LOW-COST BIPOLAR LOGIC CONCEPT," 1972 ISSCC DIGEST TECH PAPERS, PP. 90-91 AND 219.

7. H. H. BERGER AND S. K. WIEDMANN, "THE BIPOLAR LSI BREAKTHROUGH, PART 1: RETHINKING THE PROBLEM," ELECTRONICS MAGAZINE, SEPT. 4, 1975, PP. 89-95.

8. P. W. J. VERHOFSTADT, "EVALUATION OF TECHNOLOGY OPTIONS FOR LSI PROCESSING ELEMENTS," PROC. IEEE, VOL. 64, NO. 6, JUNE 1976, PP. 842-851.

9. E. A. TORRERO, P. GARY, P. VERHOFSTADT, E. SACK, W. RAY, AND D. KLEITMAN, "THE MULTIFACETS OF I²L," IEEE SPECTRUM, JUNE 1977, PP. 29-36.

10. L. ALTMAN, "THE NEW LSI," ELECTRONICS MAGAZINE, JULY 10, 1975, PP. 81-92.

11. J. L. STONE, "I²L: A COMPREHENSIVE REVIEW OF TECHNIQUES AND TECHNOLOGY," SOLID STATE TECHNOLOGY, JUNE 1977, PP. 42-48.

PART II: INJECTION COUPLED LOGIC

1. H. LEHNING, "CURRENT HOGGING LOGIC-A NEW LOGIC FOR LSI WITH NOISE IMMUNITY," 1974 ISSCC DIGEST TECH PAPERS, PP. 18-19 AND 216.

2. R. MULLER, "CURRENT HOGGING INJECTION LOGIC: NEW FUNCTIONALLY INTEGRATED CIRCUITS," 1975 ISSCC DIGEST TECH PAPERS, PP. 174-175.

3. A. W. WIEDER, W. L. ENGL AND H. LEHNING, "TWO-DIMENSIONAL ANALYSIS AND DESIGN PROCEDURE FOR CURRENT-HOGGING LOGIC," 1975 ISSCC DIGEST TECH PAPERS, PP. 170-171 AND 228.

4. W. KIM, P. K. SEEGEBRECHT AND W. L. ENGL, "(MI)²L: MULTIINPUT-MULTIOUTPUT INTEGRATED INJECTION LOGIC," IEEE J. SOLID-STATE CIRCUITS, VOL. SC-14, NO. 5, OCT. 1979, PP. 807-811.

5. P. K. SEEGEBRECHT AND W. KIM, "A NEW STRUCTURE FOR VLSI BIPOLAR TECHNOLOGY," 1979 IEDM DIGEST TECH. PAPERS, PP. 184-187.

PART III: SECOND GENERATION I²L: STRUCTURES AND FABRICATION TECHNIQUES

1. R. A. ALLEN AND K. K. SCHUEGRAF, "OXIDE-ISOLATED INTEGRATED INJECTION LOGIC," 1974 ISSCC DIGEST TECH PAPERS, PP. 16-17.

2. Y. TOKUMARU, S. SHINOZAKI, M. NAKAI, S. ITO AND Y. NISHI, "I²L WITH SELF-ALIGNED DOUBLE-DIFFUSION INJECTOR," 1976 ISSCC DIGEST TECH PAPERS, PP. 100-101.

3. T. NAKANO, Y. HORIBA, A. YASUOKA, O. TOMISAWA, K. MURAKAMI, AND S. KATO, "VERTICAL INJECTION LOGIC," 1975 IEDM DIGEST OF TECH PAPERS, PP. 555-558.

4. O. TOMISAWA, Y. HORIBA, S. KATO, K. MURAKAMI, A. YASUOKA AND T. NAKANO, "VERTICAL INJECTION LOGIC," IEEE J. SOLID-STATE CIRCUITS, VOL. SC-11, NO. 5, OCT, 1976, PP. 637-643.

5. V. BLATT, L. W. KENNEDY, P. S. WALSH AND R. C. A. ASHFORD, "SUBSTRATE FED LOGIC-AN IMPROVED FORM OF INJECTION LOGIC," 1974 IEDM DIGEST TECH PAPERS, PP. 511-514.

6. V. BLATT, P. S. WALSH AND L. W. KENNEDY, "SUBSTRATE FED LOGIC," IEEE J. SOLID-STATE CIRCUITS, VOL. SC-10, NO. 5, OCT. 1975, PP. 336-342.

7. H. H. BERGER AND S. K. WIEDMANN, "SCHOTTKY TRANSISTOR LOGIC," 1975 ISSCC DIGEST TECH. PAPERS, PP. 172-173.

8. H. H. BERGER AND S. K. WIEDMANN, "THE BIPOLAR LSI BREAKTHROUGH, PART 2: EXTENDING THE LIMITS," ELECTRONICS MAGAZINE, OCT. 2, 1975, PP. 99-103.

9. J. M. HERMAN, III, "HIGH PERFORMANCE OUTPUT SCHOTTKY I²L/MTL," 1977 IEDM DIGEST TECH. PAPERS, PP. 262-265.

10. J. MIDDLEHOEK AND A. KOOY, "POLYCRYSTALLINE SILICON AS A DIFFUSION SOURCE AND INTERCONNECT LAYER IN I²L REALIZATIONS," IEEE J. SOLID-STATE CIRCUITS, VOL. SC-12, NO. 2, APRIL 1977, PP. 135-138.

11. H. MIKOSHIBA, "I²L WITH POLYSILICON DIODE CONTACT," IEEE J. SOLID-STATE CIRCUITS, VOL. SC-13, NO. 4, AUG. 1978, PP. 483-489.

12. J. W. HANSON, J. N. FORDEMWALT AND R. J. HUBER, "FABRICATION AND PERFORMANCE OF ION IMPLANTED I²L DEVICES," 1975 IEDM DIGEST TECH PAPERS, PP. 281-283.

13. J. C. PLUNKETT, J. L. STONE AND A. HYSLOP, "INVERSE CURRENT GAIN IMPROVEMENT OF BIPOLAR TRANSISTORS BY DOUBLE-BASE DIFFUSION," IEEE TRANS. ELECT. DEVICES, VOL. ED-24, NO. 10, OCT. 1977, PP. 1269-1270.

PART IV: I²L DEVICE PHYSICS, MODELS, AND LSI SIMULATION

1. H. H. BERGER, "DESIGN CONSIDERATIONS FOR MERGED TRANSISTOR LOGIC (INTEGRATED INJECTION LOGIC CIRCUITS)," 1974 ISSCC DIGEST TECH. PAPERS, PP. 14-15 AND 215.

2. R C. JAEGER, "AN EVALUATION OF INJECTION MODELING," 1976 ISSCC DIGEST TECH. PAPERS, PP. 96-97 AND 236.

3. A. SCHMITZ AND A. SLOB, "THE EFFECT OF ISOLATION REGIONS ON THE CURRENT GAIN OF INVERSE NPN-TRANSISTORS USED IN INTEGRATED INJECTION LOGIC (I²L)," 1974 IEDM DIGEST TECH. PAPERS, PP. 508-510.

4. H. E. J. WULMS, "BASE CURRENTS OF I²L TRANSISTORS," 1976 ISSCC DIGEST TECH. PAPERS, PP. 92-93.

5. W. MATTHEUS, R. MERTENS, AND J. STULTING, "BASE CURRENT OF I²L GATES AT LOW CURRENT LEVELS," 1976 IEDM DIGEST TECH. PAPERS, P. 316.

6. F. MOLLMER AND R. MULLER, "A SIMPLE MODEL FOR THE DETERMINATION OF I²L BASE CURRENT COMPONENTS," IEEE J. SOLID-STATE CIRCUITS, VOL. SC-13, NO. 6, DEC. 1978, PP. 899-905.

7. M. H. ELSAID, D. J. ROULSTON, AND L. A. K. WATT, "VERTICAL CURRENT COMPONENTS IN INTEGRATED INJECTION LOGIC," IEEE TRANS. ELECTRON DEVICES, VOL. ED-24, NO. 6, JUNE 1977, PP. 643-647.

8. T. POOTER, "BASE CURRENT AND DOMINANT TIME CONSTANT OF AN $N^+N^-PN^+$ TRANSISTOR OPERATING IN THE UPWARD MODE," SOLID-STATE ELECTRONICS, VOL. 22, 1979, PP. 311-325.

9. E. L. HEASELL, "RECOMBINATION BENEATH OHMIC CONTACTS AND ADJACENT OXIDE COVERED REGIONS," SOLID-STATE ELECTRONICS, VOL. 22, NO. 1, JAN. 1979, PP. 89-93.

10. D. J. ROULSTON AND M. H. ELSAID, "CORNER CURRENTS IN P^+-N-N^+ DIODES WITH N^+ ISOLATION DIFFUSIONS," IEEE TRANS. ELECTRON DEVICES, VOL. ED-25, NO. 11, NOV. 1978, PP.1327-1328.

11. M. H. ELSAID AND D. J. ROULSTON, "A METHOD FOR THE CHARACTERIZATION OF P^+-N-N^+ DIODES USING DC MEASUREMENTS," IEEE TRANS. ELECTRON DEVICES, VOL. ED-25, NO. 12, DEC. 1978, PP. 1365-1368.

12. S. Y. YU AND G. THOMAS, "THE EFFECT OF CURRENT SUPPRESSION IN THE PN^-N^+ DIODE OF INTEGRATED INJECTION LOGIC," SOLID-STATE ELECTRONICS, VOL. 20, NO .1, JAN. 1977, PP. 19-25.

13. R. D. DAVIES, D. B. ESTREICH, J. D. MEINDL, AND R. W. DUTTON, "I²L DC FUNCTIONAL REQUIREMENTS," IEEE J. SOLID-STATE CIRCUITS, VOL. SC-12, NO. 2, APRIL 1977, PP. 208-210.

14. S. A. EVANS, J. M. HERMAN, III, AND B. J. SLOAN, "ON THE ELECTRICAL PROPERTIES OF THE I²L N-P-N TRANSISTOR," IEEE TRANS. ELECTRON DEVICES, VOL. ED-23, NO. 10, OCT, 1976, PP. 1192-1194.

15. S. S. ROFAIL, M. I. ELMASRY, AND E. L. HEASELL, "FUNCTIONAL MODELING OF INTEGRATED INJECTION LOGIC-DC ANALYSIS," IEEE TRANS. ELECTRON DEVICES, VOL. ED-24, NO. 3, MARCH 1977, PP. 234-241.

16. C. S. DEN BRINKER AND A. N. MORGAN, "THE EFFECT OF SERIES RESISTANCE AND DISTRIBUTED PARASITIC DIODE ACTION ON MULTICOLLECTOR I^2L STRUCTURES," PROC. FIRST EUROPEAN SOLID-STATE CIRCUITS CONF. (ESSCIRC), SEPT. 1975, PP. 18-19.

17. F. M. KLAASSEN, "PHYSICS OF AND MODELS FOR I^2L," 1976 IEDM DIGEST TECH. PAPERS, PP. 299-303.

18. F. M. KLAASSEN, "SWITCHING SPEED OF FAST MODES OF INTEGRATED INJECTION LOGIC," 1975 IEDM DIGEST TECH. PAPERS, LATE NEWS, P. 13.

19. T. POOTER, "ELECTRICAL PARAMETRERS, STATIC AND DYNAMIC RESPONSE OF I^2L," IEEE J. SOLID-STATE CIRCUITS, VOL. SC-12, NO. 5, OCT. 1977, PP. 440-449.

20. T. E. HENDRICKSON AND J. S. T. HUANG, "A STORED CHARGE MODEL FOR ESTIMATING I^2L GATE DELAY," IEEE J. SOLID-STATE CIRCUITS, VOL. SC-12, NO. 2, APRIL 1977, PP.171-176.

21. J. LOHSTROH, "DYNAMIC BEHAVIOR OF ACTIVE CHARGE IN I^2L TRANSISTORS CALCULATED WITH LUMPED TRANSISTOR MODELS," IEEE J. SOLID-STATE CIRCUITS, VOL. SC-12, NO. 2, APRIL 1977, PP. 176-184.

22. W. H. MATTHEUS, "MODELING THE DYNAMIC BEHAVIOR OF THE I^2L INVERTER," 1977 ISSCC DIGEST TECH. PAPERS, PP. 44-45.

23. M. H. ELSAID, D. J. ROULSTON, AND L. A. K. WATT, "CURRENT AND BASE TRANSIT-TIME RELATIONS IN NORMAL AND INVERTED (IIL) BIPOLAR TRANSISTORS," IEEE J. SOLID-STATE CIRCUITS, VOL. SC-12, NO. 3, JUNE 1977, PP. 761-763.

24. S. C. RUSTAGI, S. K. CHATTOPADHYAYA, D. J. ROULSTON, M. S. ELGWAILY, AND M. H. ELSAID, "COMMENTS ON "CURRENT AND BASE TRANSIT-TIME RELATIONS IN NORMAL AND INVERTED (IIL) BIPOLAR TRANSISTORS," IEEE TRANS. ELECTRON DEVICES, VOL. ED-25, NO. 9, SEPT. 1978, P. 1172.

25. S. S. ROFAIL, M. I. ELMASRY, AND E. L. HEASELL, "FUNCTIONAL MODELING OF INTEGRATED INJECTION LOGIC-TRANSIENT ANALYSIS," IEEE TRANS. ELECTRON DEVICES, VOL. ED-25, NO. 9, SEPT. 1978, PP. 1120-1125.

26. S. S. ROFAIL AND M. I. ELMASRY, "THE EFFECT OF COLLECTOR LOCATION ON B_U OF I^2L STRUCTURES," IEEE TRANS. ELECTRON DEVICES, VOL. ED-24, NO. 3, MARCH 1977, PP.289-291.

27. B. COOK, "ANALYZE I^2L ACCURATELY," ELECTRONIC DESIGN, VOL. 13, JUNE 21, 1977, PP. 90-92.

28. F. W. HEWLETT, JR., "A MODEL FOR THE DESIGN OF THE INTEGRATED INJECTION LOGIC UNIT," 1974 IEDM DIGEST TECH. PAPERS, LATE NEWS, P.10.

29. F. W. HEWLETT, JR., "I^2L CURRENT GAIN DESIGN," IEEE J. SOLID-STATE CIRCUITS, VOL. SC-12, NO. 2, APRIL 1977, PP. 206-208.

30. A. BHATTACHARYYA AND D. P. GAFFNEY, "BASE RESISTANCE, PARASITIC DIODE SHUNTING AND HIGH-LEVEL PNP INJECTION EFFECTS ON I^2L PERFORMANCE," 1976 IEDM DIGEST TECH. PAPERS, LATE NEWS, PP. 11-12.

31. D. P. GAFFNEY AND A. BHATTACHARYYA, "MODELING DEVICE AND LAYOUT EFFECTS OF PERFORMANCE DRIVEN I^2L," IEEE J. SOLID-STATE CIRCUITS, VOL. SC-12, NO. 2, APRIL 1977, PP. 155-162.

32. S. SHINOZAKI, T. IIZUKA, F. MASUOKA, K. SHINADA, AND J. I. MIYAMOTO, "ROLE OF THE EXTERNAL N-P-N BASE REGION ON THE SWITCHING SPEED OF INTEGRATED INJECTION LOGIC (I^2L)," IEEE J. SOLID-STATE CIRCUITS, VOL. SC-12, NO. 2, APRIL 1977, PP. 185-191.

33. S. SHINOZAKI, K. SHINADA, AND J. I. MIYAMOTO, "EFFECTS OF GATE GEOMETRY ON PROPAGATION DELAY OF INTEGRATED INJECTION LOGIC (I^2L)," IEEE J. SOLID-STATE CIRCUITS, VOL. SC-13, NO. 2, APRIL 1978, PP. 225-230.

34. T. IIZUKA, "EFFECTS OF OXIDE ISOLATION ON PROPAGATION DELAY IN INTEGRATED INJECTION LOGIC (I^2L)," IEEE J. SOLID-STATE CIRCUITS, VOL. SC-12, NO. 5, OCT. 1977, PP. 547-552.

35. G. PERLEGOS AND S. P. CHAN, "MODELING AND OPTIMIZATION OF THE OXIDE ISOLATED SUBSTRATE FED I^2L STRUCTURE," IEEE J. SOLID-STATE CIRCUITS, VOL. SC-13, NO. 4, AUG. 1978, PP. 491-499.

36. J. L. DUNKLEY, S. D. KANG, AND P. A. NYGAARD, "MODULAR BIPOLAR ANALYSIS," 1976 IEDM DIGEST TECH. PAPERS, PP. 312-315.

37. J. SMITH, "PROCESS-RELATED MODELING AND CHARACTERIZATION OF INTEGRATED INJECTION LOGIC," WESCON PAPER 11-1, SEPT. 1977.

38. S. A. EVANS, "AN ANALYTIC MODEL FOR THE DESIGN AND OPTIMIZATION OF ION-IMPLANTED I^2L DEVICES," IEEE J. SOLID-STATE CIRCUITS, VOL. SC-12, NO. 2, APRIL 1977, PP. 191-198.

39. D. B. ESTREICH, R. W. DUTTON, AND B. W. WONG, "AN INTEGRATED INJECTION LOGIC (I^2L) MACROMODEL INCLUDING LATERAL AND CURRENT REDISTRIBUTION EFFECTS," IEEE J. SOLID-STATE CIRCUITS, VOL. SC-11, NO. 5, OCT. 1976, PP. 648-657.

40. D. B. ESTREICH AND R. W. DUTTON, "MODELING OF I^2L PERFORMANCE AND OPERATIONAL LIMITS," 1977 ISSCC DIGEST TECH. PAPERS, PP. 46-47.

41. D. B. ESTREICH AND R. W. DUTTON, "MODELING INTEGRATED INJECTION LOGIC (I^2L) PERFORMANCE AND OPERATIONAL LIMITS," IEEE J. SOLID-STATE CIRCUITS, VOL. SC-12, NO. 5, OCT. 1977, PP. 450-456.

42. D. B. ESTREICH AND R. W. DUTTON, "AN INTEGRATED INJECTION LOGIC (I^2L) MACROMODEL," WESCON PAPER 11-2, SEPT. 1977.

43. G. R. BOYLE, "SIMULATION OF INTEGRATED INJECTION LOGIC," PH. D. DISSERTATION, UNIVERSITY OF CALIFORNIA, BERKELEY, 1978.

44. A. F. LACHNER, "AN INTEGRATED INJECTION LOGIC (I^2L) MODEL FOR COMPUTER-AIDED DESIGN," M. S. THESIS, UNIVERSITY OF CALIFORNIA, BERKELEY, 1978.

45. D. C. DENING, L. J. RAGONESE AND S. C. Y. LEE, "INTEGRATED INJECTION LOGIC WITH EXTENDED TEMPERATURE RANGE CAPABILITY," 1979 IEDM DIGEST TECH. PAPERS, PP. 192-195.

PART V: HIGH-PEFORMANCE I^2L STRUCTURES

1. F. M. KLAASSEN, "DESIGN AND PERFORMANCE OF MICRON-SIZE DEVICES," SOLID-STATE ELECTRONICS, VOL. 21, NO. 3, MARCH 1978, PP. 565-571.

2. F. M. KLAASSEN, "SOME CONSIDERATIONS ON HIGH-SPEED INJECTION LOGIC," IEEE J. SOLID-STATE CIRCUITS, SC-12, NO. 2, APRIL 1979, PP. 150-154.

3. J. LOHSTROH, "PERFORMANCE COMPARISONS OF ISL AND I^2L," 1979 ISSCC DIGEST TECH. PAPERS, PP. 48-49.

4. F. HENNIG, H. K. HINGARH, D. O'BRIEN, AND P. W. J. VERHOFSTADT, "ISOPLANAR INTEGRATED INJECTION LOGIC: A HIGH-PERFORMANCE BIPOLAR TECHNOLOGY," IEEE J. SOLID-STATE CIRCUITS, VOL. SC-12, NO. 2, APRIL 1977, PP. 101-109.

5. B. COOK, S. H. MCNALLY, A. SAN, "I^2L II," 1975 IEDM DIGEST TECH. PAPERS, PP. 284-287.

6. D. J. MCREIVY AND B. B. ROESNER, "UP-DIFFUSED I^2L, A HIGH SPEED BIPOLAR LSI PROCESS," 1976 IEDM DIGEST TECH. PAPERS, PP. 308-311.

7. A. BAHRAMAN AND S. CHANG, "DESIGN TRADE-OFFS IN SCHOTTKY-BASE I^2L – AN ADVANCED BIPOLAR TECHNOLOGY," 1978 IEDM DIGEST TECH. PAPERS, PP. 205-208.

8. S. A. EVANS, J. L. BARTELT, AND B. J. SLOAN, "HIGH SPEED I^2L FABRICATED WITH ELECTRON-BEAM LITHOGRAPHY AND ION IMPLANTATION," 1977 IEDM DIGEST TECH. PAPERS, PP. 266-270.

9. S. A. EVANS, J. L. BARTELT, AND B. J. SLOAN, "FABRICATION OF INTEGRATED INJECTION LOGIC WITH ELECTRON-BEAM LITHOGRAPHY AND ION IMPLANTATION," IEEE TRANS. ELECTRON DEVICES, VOL. ED-25, NO. 4, APRIL 1978, PP. 402-407.

10. F. W. HEWLETT, JR., "A COMPACT EFFICIENT SCHOTTKY COLLECTOR TRANSISTOR SWITCH," IEEE J. SOLID-STATE CIRCUITS, VOL. SC-14, NO. 5, OCT. 1979, PP 801-806.

11. D. D. TANG, T. H. NING, S. K. WIEDMANN, R. D. ISAAC, G. C. FETH AND H. N. YU, "SUB-NANOSECOND SELF-ALIGNED I^2L/MTL CIRCUITS," 1979 IEDM DIGEST TECH. PAPERS, PP. 201-204.

12. S. A. EVANS, S. A. MORRIS, J. ENGLADE, C. R. FULLER AND L. A. ARLEDGE, "A 1 UM BIPOLAR VLSI TECHNOLOGY," 1979 IEDM DIGEST TECH. PAPERS, PP. 196-200.

13. K. KANZAKI, M. TAGUCHI, G. SASAKI, A. FURUKAWA AND K. AOKI, "A NEW SUPER HIGH SPEED ECL COMPATIBLE TECHNOLOGY," 1979 IEDM DIGEST TECH. PAPERS, PP. 328-331.

PART VI: NOVEL I^2L TECHNIQUES: LOGIC, CIRCUITS, AND LAYOUTS

1. T. T. DAO, L. K. RUSSELL AND D. R. PREEDY, "MULTILEVEL I^2L WITH THRESHOLD GATES," 1977 ISSCC DIGEST TECH. PAPERS, PP. 110-111 AND 243.

2. M. I. ELMASRY, "FOLDED-COLLECTOR INTEGRATED INJECTION LOGIC," IEEE J. SOLID-STATE CIRCUITS, VOL. SC-11, NO. 5, OCT. 1976, PP. 644-647.

3. M. I. ELMASRY AND E. L. HEASELL, "INTERDIGITATED I^2L STRUCTURES," IEEE J. SOLID-STATE CIRCUITS, VOL. SC-13, NO. 6, DEC. 1978, PP. 917-921.

4. U. ABLASSMEIER, "COMPARISON OF VARIOUS BINARY DIVIDERS IN I^2L AND CHIL TECHNOLOGY," IEEE J. SOLID-STATE CIRCUITS, VOL. SC- 14, NO. 3, JUNE 1979, PP. 657-660.

5. T. IIZUKA, "FREQUENCY DIVIDERS BY SCHOTTKY COUPLED I^2L GATES," IEEE J. SOLID-STATE CIRCUITS, VOL. SC-12, NO. 5, OCT. 1977, PP. 530-532.

Part VII: Analog Integrated Circuit Process Compatible I^2L

1. H. H. FLOCKE, "I^2L DESIGN IN A STANDARD BIPOLAR PROCESS," IEEE J. SOLID-STATE CIRCUITS, VOL. SC-13, NO. 6, DEC. 1978, PP.914-917.

2. D. J. ALLSTOT, T. S. T. WEI, S. K. LUI, P. R. GRAY, AND R. G. MEYER," A HIGH-VOLTAGE ANALOG-COMPATIBLE I^2L PROCESS," 1977 IEDM DIGEST TECH. PAPERS, PP. 175-177.

3. M. I. ELMASRY, M. H. ELSAID, D. J. ROULSTON, AND S. S. ROFAIL, "INTEGRATED INJECTION LOGIC FOR A LINEAR/DIGITAL LSI ENVIRONMENT," IEEE TRANS. ELECTRON DEVICES, VOL. ED-25, NO. 3, MARCH 1978, PP. 351-357.

4. R. D. DAVIES AND J. D. MEINDL, "POLY I^2L - A HIGH-SPEED LINEAR-COMPATIBLE STRUCTURE," 1977 ISSCC DIGEST TECH. PAPERS, PP. 218-219 AND 254.

5. R. D. DAVIES AND J. D. MEINDL, "POLY I^2L - A HIGH-SPEED LINEAR-COMPATIBLE STRUCTURE," IEEE J. SOLID-STATE CIRCUITS, VOL. SC-12, NO. 4, AUG. 1977, PP. 367-375.

6. R. D. DAVIES AND J. D. MEINDL, "DEVICE CHARACTERISTICS FOR POLY I^2L," 1977 IEDM DIGEST TECH. PAPERS, PP. 170-174.

7. T. OKABE, T. WATANABE AND M. NAGATA, "A CONTROLLER WITH HIGH-SPEED I^2L AND HIGH-VOLTAGE ANALOG CIRCUITS," 1978 ISSCC DIGEST TECH. PAPERS, PP. 44-45 AND 264.

8. O. OZAWA, S. KAMEYAMA AND Y. SASAKI, "A HIGH SPEED I^2L COMPATIBLE WITH HIGH VOLTAGE ANALOG DEVICES," 1979 IEDM DIGEST TECH. PAPERS, PP. 188-191.

9. W. A. VINCENT AND T. A. DEMASSA, "THE EFFECT OF DOWNWARD GAIN ON THE MAXIMUM TOGGLE FREQUENCY OF I^2L, LINEAR COMPATIBLE FLIP-FLOPS," IEEE J. SOLID-STATE CIRCUITS, VOL. SC-14, NO. 5, OCT. 1979, PP 896-898.

Part VIII: Applications

1. P. A. TUCCI AND L. K. RUSSELL, "AN I^2L WATCH CHIP WITH DIRECT LED DRIVE," 1976 ISSCC DIGEST TECH. PAPERS, PP.66-67 AND 233.

2. Y. HORIBA, T. NOGUCHI, AND K. KIJIMA, "A VERTICAL INJECTION LOGIC WATCH IC WITH CMOS EQUIVALENT CURRENT DRAIN," IEEE J. SOLID-STATE CIRCUITS, VOL. SC-12, NO. 6, DEC. 1977, PP. 690-692.

3. F. W. HEWLETT, JR., AND W. D. RYDEN, "THE SCHOTTKY I^2L TECHNOLOGY AND ITS APPLICATION IN A 24X9 SEQUENTIAL ACCESS MEMORY," 1976 IEDM DIGEST TECH. PAPERS, PP. 304-307.

4. F. W. HEWLETT, JR., AND W. D. RYDEN, "THE SCHOTTKY I^2L TECHNOLOGY AND ITS APPLICATION IN A 24X9 SEQUENTIAL ACCESS MEMORY," IEEE J. SOLID-STATE CIRCUITS, VOL. SC-12, NO. 2, APRIL 1977, PP. 119-123.

5. R. E. CRIPPEN, D. O'BRIEN, K. RALLAPALLI, AND P. W. J. VERHOFSTADT, "MICROPROGRAM SEQUENCER UTILIZING I^3L TECHNOLOGY," 1976 ISSCC DIGEST TECH. PAPERS, PP. 98-99.

6. R. E. CRIPPEN, D. O'BRIEN, K. RALLAPALLI, AND P. W. J. VERHOFSTADT, "HIGH-PERFORMANCE INTEGRATED INJECTION LOGIC: A MICROPROGRAM SEQUENCER BUILT WITH I^3L," IEEE J. SOLID-STATE CIRCUITS, VOL. SC-11, NO. 5, OCT. 1976, PP. 662-668.

7. C. ERICKSON, H. K. HINGARH, R. MOECKEL, AND D. WILNAI, "A 16-BIT MONOLITHIC I^3L PROCESSOR," 1977 ISSCC DIGEST TECH. PAPERS, PP. 140-141 AND 247.

8. R. MULLER, "I^2L TIMING CIRCUIT WITHOUT EXTERNAL COMPONENTS," 1977 ISSCC DIGEST TECH. PAPERS, PP. 112-113 AND 244.

9. A. CENSE AND J. VAN STRAATEN, "A VERTICAL SYNCHRONIZING CIRCUIT FOR TV RECEIVERS USING INTEGRATED INJECTION LOGIC TECHNIQUES," 1975 ISSCC DIGEST TECH. PAPERS, PP. 184-185.

10. R. B. JARRETT AND W. D. PACE, "A MONOLITHIC SPEED-CONTROL MICRO-SYSTEM FOR AUTOMOTIVE APPLICATIONS," 1978 ISSCC DIGEST TECH. PAPERS, PP. 46-47 AND 265.

11. A. P. BROKAW, "A MONOLITHIC 10-BIT A/D USING I^2L AND LWT THIN-FILM RESISTORS," 1978 ISSCC DIGEST TECH. PAPERS, PP. 140-141.

12. R. A. BLAUSCHILD, P. A. TUCCI, H. T. RUSSELL JR., D. M. PRUINTON, AND E. N. MURTHI, "A SINGLE-CHIP I^2L PCM CODEC," IEEE J. SOLID-STATE CIRCUITS, VOL. SC-14, NO. 1, FEB. 1979, PP. 59-64.

13. J. L. HENRY AND B. A. WOOLEY, "AN INTEGRATED PCM ENCODER USING INTERPOLATION," 1978 ISSCC DIGEST TECH. PAPERS, PP. 184-185 AND 277.

14. M. USAMI, Y. HATTA AND M. TANAKA, "A 5000-GATE I^2L MASTERSLICE LSI," 1979 ISSCC DIGEST TECH. PAPERS, PP. 58-59 AND 278.

15. S. H. NUSSBAUM, "CURRENT SOURCE FOR I^2L SAVES ENERGY," ELECTRONICS MAGAZINE, AUG. 16, 1979, P. 115.

Part IX: I^2L Memory Techniques

1. S. K. WIEDMANN AND H. H. BERGER, "SMALL-SIZE LOW-POWER BIPOLAR MEMORY CELL," 1971 ISSCC DIGEST TECH. PAPERS, PP. 18-19.

2. S. K. WIEDMANN AND H. H. BERGER, "A NEW STATIC SHIFT REGISTER WITH DYNAMIC TRANSFER," SOLID-STATE ELECTRONICS, VOL. 16, 1973, PP. 1007-1010.

3. S. K. WIEDMANN, "HIGH-DENSITY STATIC BIPOLAR MEMORY," 1973 ISSCC DIGEST TECH PAPERS, PP. 56-57.

4. S. KATO, K. MURAKAMI, M. UEDA, Y. HORIBA AND T. NAKANO, "A NEW I^2L MEMORY CELL-DOUBLE DIFFUSED BASE STRUCTURE-," 1978 IEDM DIGEST TECH. PAPERS, PP. 213-216.

5. R. A. HEALD, "A FOUR-DEVICE BIPOLAR MEMORY CELL," 1978 ISSCC DIGEST TECH. PAPERS, PP. 102-103.

6. W. B. SANDER AND J. M. EARLY, "A 4096 X 1 (I^3L) BIPOLAR DYNAMIC RAM," 1976 ISSCC DIGEST TECH. PAPERS, PP. 182-183.

7. P. M. QUINN, J. M. EARLY, W. B. SANDER, AND T. A. LONGO, "A 16K X 1 I^3L DYNAMIC RAM," 1978 ISSCC DIGEST TECH. PAPERS, PP. 154-155.

8. F. HEWLETT, JR., "A SCHOTTKY COLLECTOR TRANSISTOR SWITCH WITH MERGED VERTICAL NPN LOAD," ABSTRACTS, 1979 DEVICE RESEARCH CONF., BOULDER, COLO.

Part X: Reliability and Radiation Hardness

1. R. L. PEASE, K. F. GALLOWAY, AND R. A. STEHLIN, "GAMMA RADIATION EFFECTS ON INTEGRATED INJECTION LOGIC CELLS," IEEE TRANS. ELECTRON DEVICES, VOL. ED-22, NO. 6, JUNE 1975, PP. 348-351.

2. D. M. LONG, C. J. REPPER, L. J. RAGONESE, AND N. T. YANG, "RADIATION EFFECTS MODELING AND EXPERIMENTAL DATA ON I^2L DEVICES," IEEE TRANS. NUCLEAR SCI., VOL. NS-23, NO. 6, DEC. 1976, PP. 1697-1702.

3. R. L. PEASE, K. F. GALLOWAY, AND R. A. STEHLIN, "RADIATION DAMAGE TO INTEGRATED INJECTION LOGIC CELLS," IEEE TRANS. NUCLEAR SCI., VOL. NS-22, NO. 6, DEC. 1975, PP. 2600-2604.

4. J. P. RAYMOND, T. Y. WONG, AND K. K. SCHUEGRAF, "RADIATION EFFECTS ON BIPOLAR INTEGRATED INJECTION LOGIC," IEEE TRANS. NUCLEAR SCI., VOL. NS-22, NO. 6, DEC. 1975, PP. 2605-2610.

Author Index

A

Argraz-Guerena, J., 254
Allstot, D. J., 307

B

Bahraman, A., 258, 399
Berger, H. H., 21, 88, 120, 127, 142, 219, 355, 361, 363
Bergmann, G., 300, 333
Blackstone, S. C., 101, 158, 239
Blatt, V., 186
Boyle, G. R., 199
Brokaw, A. P., 338
Burger, R. M., 405

C

Chan, L., 348
Chan, S-P., 265
Chang, S., 399
Chang, S. Y. S., 258
Coussens, E., 348

D

Dao, T. T., 270
Davies, R. D., 208
De Smet, L., 172
Donovan, R. P., 405

E

Engl, W. L., 50
Englade, J., 28
Evans, S. A., 67, 230

F

Friedman, N., 58, 280

G

George, W. L., 292
Gray, P. R., 307
Guétin, P., 328

H

Halbo, L., 311
Hansen, T. A., 311
Hart, C. M., 11
Hart, K., 5
Hayashi, T., 367
Heimeier, H. H., 142
Helwig, K., 219
Herman, J. M., III, 67
Hewlett, F. W., Jr., 82, 380, 384
Holmes, F. E., 280
Horton, R. L., 28

I

Ito, S., 75

J

Jaeger, R. C., 137
Janssen, D. J. G., 328

K

Kaire, J-C., 328
Kaneko, K., 283
Kawarada, K., 367
Kerns, D. V., Jr., 180
Kirschner, N., 164
Klaassen, F. M., 112

L

Lehning, H., 39, 50
Lohstroh, J., 170
Lui, S. K., 307

M

Mattheus, W. H., 152, 172
McGee, G., 28
McGreivy, D. J., 249
Meindl, J. D., 208
Mertens, R. P., 101, 152, 158, 172, 239
Meyer, R. G., 307
Mulder, C., 242
Müller, R., 45, 323

N

Nagata, M., 283
Nakai, M., 75
Nishi, Y., 75

O

Ohno, C., 367
Okabe, T., 283

P

Panousis, P. T., 254
Pease, R. L., 390
Pedersen, R. A., 384
Perlegos, G., 265
Pritchett, R. L., 254

R

Ragonese, L. J., 286
Raymond, J. P., 390
Roesner, B. B., 249
Romeo, D. E., 258, 399
Russell, L. K., 318

S

Salama, C. A. T., 58, 280
Saltich, J. L., 292
Schnadt, R., 361
Schuegraf, K. K., 258, 399
Shinozaki, S., 75
Simons, M., 405
Sloan, B. J., Jr., 67
Slob, A., 5, 11
Soderberg, J. G., 292
Stulting, J. D., 152
Sumerling, G. W., 96, 186
Suzuki, M., 367

Subject Index

Editor's Biography

James E. Smith received the B.S.E.E. degree summa cum laude from Christian Brothers College, Memphis, TN, in 1969, and the M.S.E. and Ph.D. degrees in electrical engineering from the University of Florida, Gainesville, in 1971 and 1974, respectively.

During 1969 he was employed by the James K. Dobbs Medical Research Institute of the University of Tennessee where he was engaged in cardiovascular research. In 1974 he joined the integrated circuit design group of Tektronix Laboratories, Beaverton, OR. While at Tektronix he was involved in the design of charge coupled devices (CCD's) for analog applications, the design and development of magnetically sensitive carrier domain devices (CDD's), characterization and modeling of integrated injection logic, and the development of device and process characterization techniques. During 1977 he was a Visiting Professor in the Department of Electrical Engineering and Computer Science of the University of California, Berkely, where he taught graduate coursework in bipolar digital LSI circuit design. In 1977 he joined the Technology Development Center of Burroughs Corporation, San Diego, CA, as a Staff Engineer where he established an automated device characterization laboratory. He is presently the head of the Device Physics, Modeling and Characterization Department at the Burroughs Technology Development Center.

Dr. Smith was the recipient of the IEEE Second Student Prize for 1969-1970 for work connected with his cardiovascular research.